MIND ASSOCIATION OCCASIONAL SERIES

KNOWING OUR OWN MINDS

MIND ASSOCIATION OCCASIONAL SERIES

This series consists of occasional volumes of original papers on predefined themes. The Mind Association nominates an editor or editors for each collection, and may co-operate with other bodies in promoting conferences or other scholarly activities in connection with the preparation of particular volumes.

Publications Officer: M. A. Stewart
Secretary: C. Macdonald

Also published in the series

Perspectives on Thomas Hobbes
Edited by G. A. J. Rogers and A. Ryan

Reality, Representation, and Projection
Edited by J. Haldane and C. Wright

Machines and Thought
The Legacy of Alan Turing
Edited by P. J. R. Millican and A. Clark

Connectionism, Concepts, and Folk Psychology
The Legacy of Alan Turing, Volume II
Edited by A. Clark and P. J. R. Millican

Appearance versus Reality
New Essays on the Philosophy of F. H. Bradley
Edited by Guy Stock

Knowing Our Own Minds

Edited by

CRISPIN WRIGHT
BARRY C. SMITH
and
CYNTHIA MACDONALD

CLARENDON PRESS · OXFORD
1998

Oxford University Press, Great Clarendon Street, Oxford OX2 6DP
Oxford New York
Athens Auckland Bangkok Bogota Bombay Buenos Aires
Calcutta Cape Town Dar es Salaam Delhi Florence Hong Kong Istanbul
Karachi Kuala Lumpur Madras Madrid Melbourne Mexico City
Nairobi Paris Singapore Taipei Tokyo Toronto Warsaw
and associated companies in
Berlin Ibadan

Oxford is a registered trade mark of Oxford University Press

Published in the United States
by Oxford University Press Inc., New York

British Library Cataloguing in Publication Data
Data available

Library of Congress Cataloging-in-Publication Data
Knowing our own minds / edited by Barry C. Smith, Crispin Wright, and
Cynthia Macdonald.
(Mind Association occasional series)
"This anthology is based on a conference on self-knowledge held at
the University of St. Andrews in August, 1995"—Pref.
Includes bibliographical references and index.
1. Self-knowledge, Theory of. 2. Philosophy of mind. I. Smith,
Barry C. II. Wright, Crispin, 1942- . III. Macdonald, Cynthia,
1951- . IV. Series.
BD450.K629 1998 128—dc21 98–17368
ISBN 0–19–823667–0

1 3 5 7 9 10 8 6 4 2

Typeset by Graphicraft Typesetters Ltd, Hong Kong
Printed in Great Britain
on acid-free paper by
Biddles Ltd, Guildford and King's Lynn

PREFACE AND ACKNOWLEDGEMENTS

This anthology is based on a conference on self-knowledge held at the University of St Andrews in August 1995. The relatively large number of speakers from North America necessitated an ambitious budget, and we are pleased to record our gratitude to our sponsors—the J. N. N. Wright Trust, the Scots Philosophical Club, the Royal Society of Edinburgh, *Analysis*, the University of St Andrews, and, chief of all, the Mind Association—for enabling this ambition to be realized. While the conference was a particularly successful one, the publication of this volume now provides tangible justification of their generosity.

Of the fifteen papers to follow, all but Paul Boghossian's contribution[1] are here published for the first time. Each of the others is a descendant of a presentation at the conference save that co-authored by Brian McLaughlin and Michael Tye, who were in attendance and wrote their paper specially for this volume. We thank all of our fellow authors for their hard work both for the conference and since, their patience with the regrettably usual pattern of receding deadlines, and for their excellent respective contributions to a collection which will surely provide a focal point for some time to come for work on this cluster of fundamental issues.

CRISPIN WRIGHT
BARRY C. SMITH
CYNTHIA MACDONALD

June 1997

[1] Originally published in *Proceedings of the Aristotelian Society*, 97 (1997), 161–75. It presents the main line of argument that Boghossian gave in chairing the concluding plenary session of the conference.

CONTENTS

Contents

LIST OF CONTRIBUTORS

AKEEL BILGRAMI is Johnsonian Professor of Philosophy, Columbia University, New York, New York, USA.

PAUL BOGHOSSIAN is Professor of Philosophy, New York University, New York, New York, USA.

TYLER BURGE is Professor of Philosophy, University of California at Los Angeles, Los Angeles, California, USA.

MARTIN DAVIES is Wilde Reader in Mental Philosophy and Professor of Philosophy at the University of Oxford and a Fellow of Corpus Christi College, Oxford, England.

JIM EDWARDS is Senior Lecturer in Philosophy, University of Glasgow, Glasgow, Scotland.

ELIZABETH FRICKER is Fellow of Magdalen College, Oxford, England.

JAMES HIGGINBOTHAM is Professor of General Linguistics, University of Oxford, Oxford, England.

CYNTHIA MACDONALD is Professor of Philosophy, University of Canterbury at Christchurch, Christchurch, New Zealand.

JOHN MCDOWELL is University Professor of Philosophy, University of Pittsburgh, Pittsburgh, Pennsylvania, USA.

MICHAEL MARTIN is Lecturer in Philosophy, University College London, London, England.

BRIAN MCLAUGHLIN is Professor of Philosophy, Rutgers University, New Brunswick, New Jersey, USA.

CHRISTOPHER PEACOCKE is Waynflete Professor of Philosophy, Magdalen College, Oxford, England.

DIANA RAFFMAN is Associate Professor of Philosophy, Ohio State University, Columbus, Ohio, USA.

BARRY SMITH is Lecturer in Philosophy, Birkbeck College, London University, London, England.

MICHAEL TYE is Professor of Philosophy, Temple University, Philadelphia, Pennsylvania, USA.

CRISPIN WRIGHT is Professor of Logic and Metaphysics and Bishop Wardlaw Professor at the University of St Andrews, St Andrews, Scotland.

Introduction

I THE BASIC PROBLEM

The temple of the Delphic oracle carried the legend, γνωθι σαυτον, 'know thyself'. If our powers of self-knowledge are as ordinarily conceived, then nothing is easier. Each of us effortlessly knows an enormous amount about those of our attributes which go with our rationality, sentience, and affective susceptibilities: our beliefs, hopes, desires, and fears, whether we have a headache or an itchy toe, whether we are elated or depressed, whom we love or hate, what attracts or repels us. We are unhesitatingly sure about the normal run of our intentional states, both content-bearing (states that p) and object-directed (thinking of x, minding about y), our sensations, and our emotions. Having great sweeps of such knowledge is the normal condition of a mature human being. True, it is also normal to know at least some other folk very well. However, knowledge of the sensations, emotions, and intentional states of others demands reliance upon independently articulable grounds—considerations concerning their sayings and deeds and context. By contrast, self-knowledge is characteristically immediate, at least in basic cases (though self-interpretation has its place).

This immediacy would already be enough to raise a philosophical issue. For, of course, the mere fact that an attribute belongs *to* a particular subject will not in general enable her to know of it differently from the way anyone else can know of it. If someone wants to know their height, or location, or precise date of birth, they must carry out exactly the same kind of investigation as anyone else. So why, when the case is that of (some) psychological attributes, is the situation any different? But there is more. Not merely is it not necessary in general, in order for them to count as knowledge, that one's opinions concerning one's own psychological attributes be grounded in evidence. Typically, they are received as authoritative just in virtue of their being held. Not only do you know *differently* from others what you think, hope, and feel; you are also (defeasibly) regarded as knowing *best*. If you take it that you exemplify a certain mental attribute, then, *ceteris paribus*, that is an authoritative indication that you do. Indeed, the converse also obtains: mental attributes are characteristically *salient* to the subject—if you hope that *p*, or are frightened of *x*, or have toothache, then it is to be expected that you will know it.

These three features of the epistemology of self-knowledge—*immediacy, authority,* and *salience*—combine to set a certain explanatory problem to which the first six chapters in this collection react, in their various ways. Crispin Wright is concerned with the issue in the context of the philosophy of mind of the later Wittgenstein. He provides detailed stage-setting for the explanatory problem, and argues that the Cartesian conception of the mind—the acceptance of mental states as composing an inner realm, directly knowable only by their subject—is best viewed as a product of an attempt to solve the problem by means of a broadly observational conception of self-knowledge. He contends that it is a major achievement of Wittgenstein's later philosophy to expose the essential inadequacy of the Cartesian response, by considerations prior to and independent of its culmination in aporia, in the sceptical problem of other minds. However, the primary focus of Wright's paper is the elusiveness of any constructive alternative in Wittgenstein's work. The 'expressive' concept of first-person psychological claims which some early commentary found in the *Philosophical Investigations* is explored, and, after some refurbishment, is shown to be useless for the purpose. Rather, Wright suggests, we should regard Wittgenstein's attitude here as of a piece with his general admonitions against projects of philosophical explanation. He concludes on a note of qualified dissatisfaction with this response.

Wright's chapter (1) is, in part, a continuation of an earlier exchange with John McDowell,[1] and McDowell here responds again (Ch. 2). He is dissatisfied with Wright's contention that the captivating power of the Cartesian conception may be traced to the apparent explanation it offers of the various points of asymmetry between self-knowledge and knowledge of others, arguing that it is a point of contrast between self-knowledge and genuinely perceptual knowledge—a point which the Cartesian conception simply ignores—that the former is *groundless* in a way in which the latter is not. The proper explanation of the attractiveness of Cartesianism is, in McDowell's view, different, having to do

---

[1] See their respective contributions, 'Wittgenstein's Later Philosophy of Mind: Sensation, Privacy and Intention' and 'Intentionality and Interiority in Wittgenstein', in K. Puhl (ed.), *Meaning Scepticism* (Berlin and New York: de Gruyter, 1991), 126–47, 148–69.

with the distinctively seductive shape that the Myth of the Given takes in reflection about the inner.[2]

The other principal point of difference between Wright and McDowell is this. In Wright's treatment, Wittgenstein, although he offers no constructive philosophical explanation of the distinctive differences between self-knowledge and knowledge of others, nevertheless makes a positive contribution: the thesis that demand for explanation is inappropriate—something which Wright allows may be defensible, but, if so, on grounds that Wittgenstein himself never fully provided. McDowell responds that since the attraction of Cartesianism was not that of an explanation, its demise need not be seen as generating an explanatory vacuum; nor does he see Wittgenstein as recommending the positive thesis that the attempt to provide an explanation here would be inappropriate. For McDowell is not satisfied that it emerges sufficiently clearly from Wright's account what exactly the demand for explanation is supposed to come to.

Christopher Peacocke's careful, fine-grained contribution (Ch. 3) focuses on the case of conscious occurrent attitudes, and brings to bear the kind of apparatus of concept individuation via possession conditions which he pioneered in *A Study of Concepts*.[3] One effect of the view which Wright (*pace* McDowell) finds in Wittgenstein would be that the superiority of a thinker's views concerning her own mental attributes would be a *constitutive principle*—a primitive constraint on what anyone should take it to be correct to think about those attributes—rather than a reflection of any genuinely cognitive advantage. It is very natural to think that if both perceptual and inferential accounts of the cognitive mechanics of self-knowledge are rejected, this broad kind of 'default' view remains the only option. An important contention of Peacocke's discussion is that this is a false trichotomy. The core of his proposal is an account of the possession conditions of the concept of belief in particular which explains how, contrary to the kind of view which Wright elicits from Wittgenstein (and the 'no reasons' account of Sydney Shoemaker[4]), a conscious belief can *give reason for* the corresponding second-order judgement without it being the case either that the latter should be regarded as justified by inference or that it is justified by introspection. In Peacocke's view, we need, and can provide for, a rational basis for the self-ascription of psychological states which is neither inferential nor observational, yet which allows such

---

[2] This idea is further elaborated in McDowell's 'One Strand in the Private Language Argument', *Grazer Philosophische Studien*, 33/4 (1989), 287–303.

[3] Christopher Peacocke, *A Study of Concepts* (Cambridge, Mass.: MIT Press, 1992).

[4] See Sydney Shoemaker, 'Special Access Lies Down with Theory-Theory', *Behavioral and Brain Sciences*, 16 (1993), 78–9.

ascriptions to be answerable to—to 'track'—independently character-izable first-order states. Peacocke proceeds to elaborate this account of conscious attitudes in such a way that, as he observes, it clashes with a number of recently advocated theses about consciousness: for instance, that the consciousness of a mental state can be explained in terms of a tendency of states of that kind to generate self-ascriptions, that a purely reliabilist account of second-order beliefs can explain their status as know-ledge, and that the consciousness of occurrent propositional attitudes consists in their extensive inferential integration.

Michael Martin's response (Ch. 4) focuses on the core of Peacocke's account. He brings forward examples of self-ascriptions which are based on conscious episodes but are nevertheless not authoritative, thereby suggesting that Peacocke's treatment stands in need of some limiting principle to characterize just which kinds of conscious thought can pro-vide a rational basis for authoritative self-ascription. Martin suggests that one such class of cases is where knowledge of one's belief issues from one's apparent knowledge of how matters stand in the world. The question therefore arises as to how apparent knowledge of how the world is can provide a reason for the self-ascription of a belief; and Martin argues that the possession-conditions account, unsupplemented, is not sufficient to answer this question.

A contention *ob iter* of Wright's discussion is that the drawbacks of Cartesianism afflict any broadly observational model of self-knowledge. Cynthia Macdonald (Ch. 5) disagrees, defending a qualified observa-tional model which centres on two features of ordinarily observable characteristics that help to explain a subject's direct awareness of them: that they are basic—one does not have to know of any underlying fact in virtue of which they apply when they do—and that it is generally necessary and sufficient for the application of such a characteristic that it seem to a normal observer in normal circumstances that it does apply. Macdonald argues that analogues of these features apply in certain cases of authoritative self-knowledge, specifically—taking perhaps the most apparently unpromising case—in the '*cogito*-type' cases (like 'I am currently thinking that philosophy is difficult') highlighted in Tyler Burge's writings.

Macdonald defends her view by responding to two well-known mis-givings about modelling self-knowledge on observation: first, that there is a telling structural disanalogy, since observation normally involves three components, namely, the item perceived, an intermediary, non-conceptual sensation state, and a judgement grounded in that sensation state, whereas self-knowledge of an intentional state seemingly involves analogues of the first and third components only, namely, a first-order (content-bearing) state and the second-order state which it validates; and second that, whereas the relations between a perceptual state and the item perceived are causal and contingent, those between first- and corresponding second-order intentional states are in general non-contingent, and so not (merely) causal. Each of these concerns, she contends, can be met.

The trichotomy—observation, inference, groundlessness—which has tended to structure so much work on these issues was remarked upon above. But of course no one could coherently suppose that self-knowledge was *in general* inferential; that idea would be viciously regressive, since before she can take on board any inference-based claim about her own psychological states, a thinker must first recognize that she believes the premisses from which that conclusion may be inferred.[5] So in the basic case the trichotomy must reduce to a dichotomy between two kinds of account, one positing some form of direct cognitive access to their own mental states which subjects enjoy uniquely and which ordinary epistemic practice reflects and is vindicated by, the other viewing the authority accorded to self-ascriptions not as reflecting a commonly known, prior fact of special access, but as being, rather, partly determinative of the identity of the states in question, so that the self-ascription of a particular mental state would be a criterion, in something like the popular Wittgensteinian sense, of the subject's being in that state. Elizabeth Fricker's contribution (Ch. 6) examines this dichotomy—special access accounts versus constitutive accounts—and concludes that, unqualified, it is a false one. First, not just Cartesianism, but a number of quite different kinds of account of the nature of mental states and of our self-knowledge of them, come under the special access heading. One such group comprises functionalist accounts—special access theories which involve non-Cartesian conceptions of the individuation conditions of mental states, and need make no play with any form of 'inner perception'. Fricker is thus in substantial (though not terminological) agreement with both Macdonald and Peacocke in holding that a number of possibilities come under the heading of special access accounts which are not discredited by the demise of Cartesianism. Second, there is in any case, she argues, theoretical space between the poles—room for intermediate theories according to which 'grammar' and empirical regularities collaborate inextricably to hold our actual mental state concepts together, and play a joint role in explaining the reliability of our basic (non-inferential) self-ascriptions of mental states. Finally, Fricker contends that there is no coherent account of mental concepts which allows the

---

[5] Cf. Paul Boghossian, 'Content and Self-Knowledge', *Philosophical Topics*, 17 (1989), 5–26, at 8–10.

authority of self-ascriptions to be *wholly* 'grammatical'—wholly a constitutive matter. Rather, all viable concepts of mental states which may competently be non-inferentially self-ascribed must be multi-criterial concepts.

II THE PLACE OF SELF-KNOWLEDGE: RATIONALITY AND AGENCY

Chapters 1–6 are all broadly concerned with issues to do with the explanation of certain distinctive features of self-knowledge. A closely related but distinct set of concerns has to do with the conceptual liaisons of self-knowledge, with the role of our knowledge of our own psychological states in our functioning as rational agents. It is these latter concerns which, though their arguments also bear on the explanatory issues, are central to the contributions of Akeel Bilgrami and Tyler Burge.

Bilgrami (Ch. 7) champions a distinctive and original form of the constitutive view. Specifically, he argues, in a fashion acknowledgedly inspired by Strawson's famous line of reasoning in 'Freedom and Resentment',[6] that self-knowledge is implicated in free, responsible agency in a way which requires the following strong biconditional thesis: wherever responsible agency is operative in thought or action, then the subject has an intentional state that P if and only if she believes that she has it. We are thus committed to treating a subject's self-conception as accurate, and her mental states as essentially salient to her, just by and to the extent that we regard her as a fully responsible agent. It follows, Bilgrami argues, that the connection between first- and second-order attitudes cannot be, in however extended a sense, a causal one. If it were causal, then it might, in a particular case, break down. There would then be a mismatch between such a subject's self-conception and her actual first-order intentional states. But we would never be prepared to countenance such a mismatch: rather, to the extent that we take ourselves to understand a subject's self-ascriptions, we take it that they are expressions of responsible agency, and are thus committed, if Bilgrami's argument is correct, to regarding her first-order states as being in accord with them.

The primary focus of Tyler Burge's chapter (8) is on certain infrequently explored aspects of the role played in thought and action by possession of the concept expressed by the first-person pronoun—the concept of *oneself*. Burge argues that only one who possesses that concept is in a position fully to articulate certain fundamental, a priori aspects

---

[6] P. F. Strawson, 'Freedom and Resentment', *Proceedings of the British Academy*, 48 (1962), 1–25.

of the concept of reason. A theoretical reasoner recognizes commitments flowing from, and warrants for, particular thoughts. A practical reasoner recognizes how particular sets of attitudes rationalize, require, or clash with particular courses of action. These are forms of rational evaluation. But it is only in cases where the thoughts and attitudes considered come marked as *one's own*—indexed by the first-personal concept, as it were —that such rational evaluation can connect immediately with an implementation—with, say, revising one's thoughts, or selecting one choice of action among alternatives. If a subject scrutinizes a set of attitudes and finds them rationally wanting, that is so far nothing to her—unless they come flagged to her as her own. It is the first-person concept which, by simultaneously designating the agent of appraisal and flagging the attitudes and thoughts appraised, makes the appraisal immediately relevant to changing or maintaining those attitudes.

This line of argument is developed in the first half of Burge's chapter. Though Burge does not himself take it in this direction, it might encourage a version of the constitutive view, since it implicates both authority and salience in a subject's capacity for effective self-criticism as a thinker and agent, and it is arguably a commitment merely of regarding someone as a person that she be deemed an effective self-critic. In the second, more speculative part of his chapter Burge sketches a view of the asymmetries between first- and third-personal knowledge of mental states in which a basic role is played by a non-empirically warranted sensitivity to the difference between commitments that are one's own and commitments that are not, and canvasses a line of argument therefrom that non-empirically warranted knowledge of other minds is possible via non-empirically warranted understanding of speech. These intriguing suggestions are directions for further work.

III SELF-KNOWLEDGE AND EXTERNALISM

The sense that the ordinary conception of self-knowledge makes a philosophical problem out of it has intensified recently with the realization of the apparent tension between immediacy, authority, and salience, on the one hand and, on the other, certain widely accepted arguments that psychological content is *externally*—socially and environmentally— determined. If the contents of our attitudes characteristically depend on relations in which we stand to others in our speech community and to objects and kinds in the material world, then what states of mind we are in at any given point is going to be a function of prevailing empirical circumstance of a kind to which, in our ordinarily effortless and groundless self-ascriptions, we pay absolutely no attention. Is there here a compelling case for revision of the ordinary conception—should our customary treatment of self-knowledge claims be modified to accommodate externalism? Or should their authority somehow be regarded as extending over the various external conditions of content? Or is there perhaps no genuine tension: can a compatibilist position be made out according to which an ignorance of the external factors that condition mental content can be reconciled with our possession of non-empirical knowledge of the contents of our thoughts?

Paul Boghossian (Ch. 9) advances the case that the tension is genuine: that if the ordinary conception of self-knowledge is retained alongside an externalist conception of mental content, it must follow that certain propositions can be known immediately, without empirical investigation, which everyone agrees can be known only on the basis of empirical investigation. His argument is of the same general type as that offered by Michael McKinsey in his 'Anti-Individualism and Privileged Access', but is distinctive in its focus on the 'empty case'—the case in which a thinker gives expression to what he takes to be a genuine thought concerning a natural kind where there is in fact no relevant natural kind, so that the putative natural kind term in the expression of this thought is actually devoid of reference. In such a case, on an externalist conception of the meaning of natural kind terms, a thinker *delusively* takes himself to have a thought of a certain kind. And such a delusion is not consistent with first-person authority over the nature of one's thought as traditionally conceived.

Brian McLaughlin and Michael Tye reject that conclusion. Their chapter (10) is concerned with versions of content externalism which may be supported by Twin Earth thought experiments alone. They review in detail a leading line of argument for incompatibilism contained in the literature: that, like Boghossian's, which seeks to develop the thought that combination of the traditional conception of self-knowledge with content externalism leads to paradoxical over-extension in the domain of what can be known non-empirically. They argue in detail that this line of argument does not succeed.

Martin Davies's chapter (11) notes an analogy between the latter form of the problem posed by externalism and the structurally parallel problem posed by certain substantive philosophical theses about the requirements for being a thinking being at all, specifically certain requirements on internal cognitive architecture. In both cases an argument is presented of the following form (MC):

1. I have mental property M.
2. If I have mental property M, then I meet condition C.
∴ 3. I meet condition C.

Self-knowledge as traditionally conceived allows a subject to have non-empirical knowledge of appropriate instances of premiss (1); and content externalism, or the considerations which Davies adverts to concerning thinking and its internal cognitive requirements, may be thought respectively to provide a priori support for appropriate instances of premiss (2). Granted only that what is entailed by non-empirically known premisses may itself be non-empirically known, it would follow that the appropriate instances of (3) may also be known non-empirically. And this seems quite wrong for the instances in question. For in the case of externalism, the conclusion will say something about the world outside the subject's head; and in the case of many philosophical theses about the requirements of thought, the conclusion will say something about the unobserved cognitive architecture within his head.

McLaughlin and Tye contend in effect that there are no genuinely problematical instances of the argument form (MC). Davies is unconvinced. He therefore proposes, as an insurance, to invoke principles limiting the transfer of epistemic warrant across known entailments. He notes the precedent of such a limitative principle canvassed in Crispin Wright's 'Facts and Certainty',[7] though some modification is called for to motivate the specific kind of principle needed in the present context. Just how the principle might have to be improved in the face of certain apparent counter-examples is left for further work.

Diana Raffman (Ch. 12) contends that Davies misdiagnoses the trouble with the architecturalist and externalist arguments that are his targets. Whether or not there are independent grounds for principles limiting the transfer of epistemic warrant across known entailments, the primary problem with the two types of argument, in her view, is, rather, that they equivocate. In each case, if premiss (1), that I have mental property M, expresses something about which the subject is non-empirically authoritative, then, Raffman contends, it should be viewed as empty of substantive empirical content; whereas if the second premiss expresses something knowable a priori, then since its consequent involves substantive empirical content, so must the antecedent. In brief: if both premisses, (1) and (2), express something knowable non-empirically, it must follow that there is an ambiguity in what is expressed by 'I have

---

[7] Crispin Wright, 'Facts and Certainty', *Proceedings of the British Academy*, 71 (1985), 429–72.

mental property M', and hence that the *modus ponens* step is flawed by equivocation.

In the last chapter in this group, Jim Edwards (Ch. 13) argues that externalism may issue in a hitherto unnoticed, rather subtler form of compromise of the first-personal transparency of mental contents. This argument depends on two collateral assumptions: John McDowell's contention, developed in his *Mind and World*,[8] that experience is passively structured by concepts, and the so-called Simple Theory of Colour, supported by writers such as John Campbell,[9] according to which those properties which actually are the semantic values of colour concepts are just as they appear to be to normal observers under standard conditions. Edwards develops an example to suggest that it must nevertheless be an epistemic possibility that the semantic values of such concepts, in so far as they are externally determined, are not such properties—not the properties which the Simple Theory takes them to be. If such a possibility were to obtain, there would be a mismatch between the properties which colour concepts present as their semantic values and their actual, externally determined semantic values; and such a mismatch, he crucially contends, would induce incoherence into colour concepts of such a sort that they would be unfitted passively to structure colour experience. Since the difference between this situation and that which the Simple Theory supposes actually to obtain, wherein the semantic values of colour concepts are just as it requires them to be, cannot be salient to a subject just on the basis of the quality of her experience, it follows that it is not transparent to a subject whether her colour experiences are indeed conceptually structured, *à la* McDowell, by concepts answering to the Simple Theory of colour, or accordingly what content is carried by such experience.

IV   KNOWING WHAT ONE MEANS

The chapters mentioned so far are all concerned with our knowledge of our own psychological states. But conscious knowledge of some of the properties of one's own language—for instance, of what particular expressions mean, where their use would be deviant, under what circumstances it would be appropriate to utter them, and the like—is both commonplace and typically arrived at without reflection on evidence,

[8] John McDowell, *Mind and World* (Cambridge, Mass.: Harvard University Press, 1994).
[9] See John Campbell, 'A Simple View of Colour', in J. Haldane and C. Wright (eds.), *Reality: Representation and Projection* (New York: Oxford University Press, 1993), 257–68.

and thus presents a special case of the issues concerning immediacy, authority, and salience.

This facet of self-knowledge is explored in the contributions by Barry Smith and James Higginbotham. Smith (Ch. 14) argues that any attempt to ground our knowledge of our own minds on knowledge of what we mean when we speak our minds—as in Davidson's famous discussions[10]—must either lead to circularity or leave a lacuna in the explanation. Closing the lacuna will demand an independent account of our first-person knowledge of meaning. Smith proceeds to consider the form which a full explanation of linguistic understanding would take, drawing on first-personal, third-personal, and subpersonal elements of linguistic knowledge, and argues that all these elements must be harnessed to explicate what is made available and expressed by instances of disquotational knowledge, typified by the knowledge that 'Snow is white' means that snow is white. Such expressions, he contends, do express substantial knowledge of what we mean just when they are the upshot of facts about our internal linguistic systems and about the effects these systems have upon our conscious experience of speech and our communicative dealing with others. Thus there is a genuine species of immediate, substantial knowledge of one's own meanings which may be expressed by disquotation, but the authority attaching to whose expression is not (merely) an artefact of disquotation.

Higginbotham (Ch. 15) disagrees, arguing that nothing more than thinly conceived disquotational knowledge is needed to account for first-personal knowledge of one's meanings. However, he distinguishes the kind of authority that attaches to disquotational claims from that which attaches to our intuitive judgements about what we mean. The latter may fall short of genuine knowledge while still involving *entitlement* and a presumption of correctness. Higginbotham assesses each of these species of authority in turn, with respect to both the discussion in Smith's paper and some wider issues, and defends the view that neither is threatened by externalism.

[10] See Donald Davidson, 'First Person Authority', *Dialectica*, 38 (1984), 101–12, and 'Knowing One's Own Mind', *Proceedings and Addresses of the American Philosophical Association*, 60 (1987), 441–58.

I

Self-Knowledge: The Wittgensteinian Legacy

CRISPIN WRIGHT

It is only in fairly recent philosophy that psychological self-knowledge has come to be seen as problematical; once upon a time the hardest philosophical difficulties all seemed to attend our knowledge of others. But as philosophers have canvassed various models of the mental that would make knowledge of other minds less intractable, so it has become unobvious how to accommodate what once seemed evident and straightforward—the wide and seemingly immediate cognitive dominion of minds over themselves.

My programme in this chapter involves characterizing this dominion with some care. We need to be as clear as possible why one form of traditional thinking on the matter has seemed so attractive—even unavoidable—and what a satisfactory account of the issues in this region has to accomplish. However, my underlying and primary concern is with the later Wittgenstein's contribution to the question. Ultimately I think we are provided with a most vivid illustration—and can perhaps gain an insight into the intended force—of something which I do not think has so far been very well understood: the *anti-explanatory* motif that runs through the pronouncements on philosophical method occurring in the *Philosophical Investigations*.

I

People can be variously deluded about themselves: self-deceived about their motives, for instance, or overly sanguine, or pessimistic, about their strengths of character and frailties. But it is none the less a truism that for the most part we know ourselves best—better than we know others and better than they know us.

In one kind of case, the explanation of this would seem straightforward. It is (merely) that our own presence is, for each of us, a constant factor in the kind of situation, usually but not always social, in which the evidence emerges which bears on various of our psychological characteristics. No one else is so constantly around us. So no one else observes as much of us or is as much observed by us. Selves have the best evidence about themselves.

Evidently, however, this form of explanation of the truth in the truism can run only in cases where one's own and another's knowledge of oneself must draw on the same kind of evidence. So it is restricted, it would seem, to broadly dispositional characteristics like honesty, patience, courage, and conceit—cases where there is no essential self/other asymmetry in the means of knowledge. And this is not, of course, the most salient type of case. In the most salient type of case, we do not merely know ourselves best, but also *differently* from the way in which we know others and they know us. The distinction is complicated, admittedly, by the fact that many apparently dispositional psychological characteristics are distinctively manifested not by raw behaviour, as it were, but by psychological performance in respects that may themselves exhibit self/other epistemological asymmetries. Conceit, for instance, will be, *inter alia*, a disposition to form certain kinds of belief. It remains that the type of case that sets our problem is that which gives rise to the phenomenon of *avowal*—the phenomenon of authoritative, non-inferential self-ascription. The basic philosophical problem of self-knowledge is to explain this phenomenon—to locate, characterize, and account for the advantage which selves seemingly possess in the making of such claims about themselves.

The project will be conditioned by whatever more precise characterization we offer of the target phenomenon. It seems safe to suppose that we must begin by distinguishing two broad classes of avowal. The first group—what I will call 'phenomenal avowals'—comprise examples like 'I have a headache', 'My feet are sore', 'I'm tired', 'I feel elated', 'My vision is blurred', 'My ears are ringing', 'I feel sick', and so on. Such examples exhibit each of the following three marks.

First, they are *groundless*. The demand that somebody produce reasons or corroborating evidence for such a claim about themselves—'How can you tell?'—is always inappropriate. There is nothing they might reasonably be expected to be able to say. In that sense, there is nothing upon which such claims are based.

Second, they are *strongly authoritative*. If somebody understands such a claim, and is disposed sincerely to make it about themselves, that is a guarantee of the truth of what they say. A doubt about such a claim has to be a doubt about the sincerity or the understanding of the one making it. Since we standardly credit any interlocutor, in the absence of evidence to the contrary, with sincerity and understanding, it follows that a subject's actually making such a claim about themselves is a criterion for the correctness of the corresponding third-personal claim made by someone else: my avowal that I'm in pain must be accepted by others, on penalty of incompetence, as a ground for the belief that I am.

Finally, phenomenal avowals exhibit a kind of *transparency*. Where P is an avowal of the type concerned, there is typically something absurd about a profession of the form, 'I don't know whether P'—don't know whether I have a headache, for instance, or whether my feet are sore. Not always: there are contexts in which I might be uncertain of a precondition—for instance, whether I have feet. But in the normal run of cases, the subject's ignorance of the truth or falsity of an avowal of this kind is not, it seems, an option.

None of the examples listed is an avowal of a *content-bearing* state. It is the hallmark of the second main group of avowals—what I shall call 'attitudinal avowals'—that the psychological characteristics, processes, and states which they concern are partially individuated by the propositional content, or intentional direction, which informs them—for instance, 'I believe that term ends on the 27th', 'I hope that noise stops soon', 'I think that professional philosophers are some of the most fortunate people on earth', 'I am frightened of that dog', 'I am thinking of my mother'. In order to see what is distinctive about an author's relation to avowals of this kind, we need first to take account of the fact that such claims can also be made as part of a process of *self-interpretation* —in the kind of context where we say that we have *learned* about our attitudes by finding that certain events cause us pleasure, for instance, or discomfort. Consider the following passage from Jane Austen's *Emma*:

Emma's eyes were instantly withdrawn; and she sat silently meditating in a fixed attitude, for a few minutes. A few minutes were sufficient for making her acquainted with her own heart. A mind like hers, once opening to suspicion, made rapid progress. She touched—she admitted—she acknowledged the whole truth. Why was it so much the worse that Harriet should be in love with Mr. Knightley than with Mr. Churchill? Why was the evil so dreadfully increased by Harriet's having some hope of return? It darted through her, with the speed of an arrow, that Mr. Knightley must marry no-one but herself.[1]

Here Emma has just been told of the love of her protégée, Harriet, for her—Emma's—bachelor brother-in-law, a decade older than Emma, a

---

[1] Jane Austen, *Emma*; Penguin Books edn. (London, 1987), 398. I borrow this nice example from Julia Tanney's 'A Constructivist Picture of Self-Knowledge', *Philosophy*, 71 (1996), 405–22.

frequent guest of her father's, and hitherto a stable, somewhat avuncular part of the background to her life. She has entertained no thought of him as a possible husband. But now she realizes that she strongly desires that he marry no one but her, and she arrives at this discovery by way of surprise at the strength and colour of her reaction to Harriet's declaration, and by way of a few minutes' reflection on that reaction. She is, precisely, not moved to the realization immediately; it dawns on her as something she first suspects and *then* recognizes as true. It *explains* her reaction to Harriet.

In such self-interpretative cases, none of the three features we noted of phenomenal avowals is present. There is no Groundlessness: the subject's view is one for which it is perfectly in order to request an account of the justifying grounds. There is no Strong Authority: mere sincerity and understanding will be no guarantee whatever of truth—it is for Jane Austen to stipulate, as it were, that Emma's self-discovery is the genuine article, but in any real context such a conclusion could be seriously mistaken. Finally, there is no Transparency: within a context of self-interpretation, it is in no way incongruous if the subject professes ignorance of particular aspects of her intentional psychology. But what it is vital to note for our present purpose is that such self-interpretative cases, although common, cannot be the *basic* case. For the body of data on which self-interpretation may draw is not restricted to recollected behaviour and items falling within the subject-matter of phenomenal avowals. When Emma interprets her reaction to Harriet's declaration as evidence that she herself loves Knightley, there is an avowable ground —something like 'I am disconcerted by her love for that man and, more so, by the thought that it might be returned'—which is a *datum for*, rather than a *product of*, self-interpretation. Self-interpretation, that is to say, will typically draw on non-inferential knowledge of a basic range of attitudes and intentionally characterized responses. These will not be distinguished, I think, from non-basic, interpretative cases by any generic features of their content; rather, they will reflect matters which, for the particular subject in the particular context, happen to require no interpretation to be known about—matters which are precisely *avowable*. It is these basic examples which comprise the attitudinal avowals.

Such avowals will have the same immediacy as phenomenal avowals, and will exhibit both groundlessness and transparency—groundlessness rather trivially, in so far as, any interpretational basis having been excluded, there will naturally be nothing a subject can say to justify such a self-ascription; transparency in the sense that, except where the matter is one of interpretation, we think a subject ought to know without further ado what she believes, or desires, etc., so that any profession of ignorance or uncertainty, unless coupled with a readiness to allow that the matter is not basic but calls for (self-) interpretation, will seem perplexing. However, attitudinal avowals do not exhibit the strong authority of phenomenal avowals: to the extent that there is space for relevant forms of self-deception or confusion, sincerity-cum-understanding is no longer a guarantee of the truth of even basic self-ascriptions of intentional states. Any avowal may be discounted if accepting it would get in the way of making best sense of the subject's behaviour. But with attitudinal avowals, it is admissible to look for explanations of a subject's willingness to assert a bogus avowal other than those provided by misunderstanding, insincerity, or misinterpretation. This is the space occupied by the ordinary notion of self-deception; but the more general idea is just that we can be caused to hold mistaken higher-order beliefs in ways—wishful thinking, for instance—which do not go through misguided self-interpretative inference.

It is striking that attitudinal avowals would appear to exhibit a form of weak authority nevertheless: that is, they provide criterial—empirically assumptionless—justification for the corresponding third-person claims. Since it cannot be attributed, as with phenomenal avowals, to the fact of sincerity-cum-understanding guaranteeing truth, what does this weak authority consist in? It might be suggested that it is nothing other than the presumptive acceptability of testimony generally. And certainly that proposal would be enough to set our problem: for the presumptive acceptability of *original* testimony—testimony for which the source is not itself testimony—extends no further than to subject-matters which an informant is deemed competent to know about. So the question would recur: how is it possible for subjects to know about their intentional states in ways that involve no consideration of the evidence on which a third party must rely? Actually, however, I think the suggestion is wrong. What distinguishes the presumptive acceptability of attitudinal avowals from anything characteristic of testimony generally is that the authority which attaches to them is, in a certain sense, *inalienable*. There is no such thing as showing oneself chronically unreliable in relation to the distinctive subject-matter of attitudinal avowals. I may have such poor colour vision that you rightly come to distrust my testimony on matters of colour. I may, unwittingly, have a very bad memory, and, learning of this, you may rightly come to a state of wholesale suspicion about my testimony on matters of personal recall. But no corresponding wholesale suspicion concerning my attitudinal avowals is possible. You may not suppose me sincere and comprehending, yet chronically unreliable, about what I hope, believe, fear, and intend. Wholesale suspicion about my attitudinal avowals—where it is not a doubt about sincerity or understanding—jars with conceiving of me as an intentional subject at all.

II

Both groups of avowals exhibit a further feature which it is worth attending to briefly.[2] In a famous passage in the *Blue Book*, Wittgenstein writes as follows

There are two different cases in the use of the word 'I' (or 'my') which I might call the 'use as object' and 'the use as subject'. Examples of the first kind of use are these: 'my arm is broken', 'I have grown six inches', 'I have a bump on my forehead', 'the wind blows my hair about'. Examples of the second kind are: 'I see so-and-so', 'I hear so-and-so', 'I try to lift my arm', 'I think it will rain', 'I have toothache'. One can point to the difference between these two categories by saying: the cases of the first category involve the recognition of a particular person, and there is in these cases the possibility of an error or as I should rather put it: The possibility of an error has been provided for . . . [but] it is as impossible that in making the statement 'I have toothache', I should have mistaken another person for myself, as it is to moan with pain by mistake, having mistaken someone else for me.[3]

The characteristic to which Wittgenstein here calls attention is often called 'immunity to error through misidentification'.[4] In a large class of cases, when someone makes a subject–predicate claim, they may mistake or misidentify the subject in a way for which, it appears, there is no provision in the case of an avowal. If I see someone running along the beach, and, taking it to be my colleague NN, say, 'NN will catch up with us in a minute', I may be mistaken in ways which correspond either to the subject identified or to the predication I make: it may be that the character approaching us is not NN at all, and it may be that he will turn away before he reaches us. But if I avow my indifference to a forthcoming ballot, for instance, then there is a provision for correction only for my predication—I can't be mistaken about whom I'm making that predication of.

Shoemaker writes that the absence of the possibility of misidentification 'is one of the main sources of the mistaken opinion that one cannot be an object to oneself, which in turn is a source of the view

---

[2] I am indebted in this section to many discussions, years ago, with Andy Hamilton.

[3] Ludwig Wittgenstein, *The Blue and Brown Books* (Oxford: Blackwell, 1964), 66–7.

[4] The term is originally Shoemaker's, I believe. It is taken up by Gareth Evans in *The Varieties of Reference* (Oxford: Oxford University Press, 1982); see esp. ch. 7, sect. 2.

that "I" does not refer'.[5] The line of thought he has in mind runs from the impossibility of *misidentifying* myself to the conclusion that, in reflection about myself, there is no identification of *any* object, that such reflection is not object-directed at all, and that 'I' accordingly has no referential function.

Wittgenstein may, indeed, have been inclined to such an idea—the passage which I quoted continues: 'To say, "I have pain" is no more a statement *about* a particular person than moaning is.'[6] But whether he was so inclined or not, it is simply a mistake to suppose that where there is no fallible identification, there is no reference either. It will be clear what's wrong with this idea once we have a better characterization of what immunity to error through misidentification (IEM) consists in. And we shall also thereby learn why, in the present context, the phenomenon need not be of primary concern.

The key point is that IEM is not a characteristic which a statement has simply in virtue of its subject-matter. It depends upon the kind of ground which a speaker has for it. Specifically, the ground has to be such that in the event that the statement in question is somehow defeated, it cannot survive as a ground for the corresponding existential generalization. Consider again the case of the figure on the beach, and suppose that, having asserted 'NN will catch up with us soon', I turn to see NN standing just a little in front of me. In that case, my original thought is defeated; but the basis for it survives as a ground for the claim, 'Someone will catch up with us soon'. Or suppose I catch sight of my reflection passing a shop window, and I say to myself, 'My hair is blowing in the wind'. If it becomes apparent that the reflection I saw was not mine but someone else's, the basis for my claim will still remain as a ground for the existential generalization, 'Someone's hair was blowing in the wind'. A claim, made on a certain kind of ground, involves immunity to error through misidentification just when its defeat is *not* consistent with retention of grounds for existential generalization in this kind of way.

Now, avowals do characteristically so behave. If an avowal of mine is somehow defeated, there is no question of my original entitlement surviving, without my gathering additional information, in such a way that I may justifiably claim that someone—though not me—exhibits the property which I avowed. However, two points are evident in the light of the characterization just offered. First, the idea that Wittgenstein's 'as subject' uses of 'I' are somehow shown to be non-referential by their

---

[5] See his 'Self-Reference and Self-Awareness', *Journal of Philosophy*, 65 (1968), 568 ff.

[6] Wittgenstein, *Blue and Brown Books*, 67.

having IEM should have been strangled at birth by the reflection that a similar immunity is characteristic of many *demonstrative* claims, in which case there is of course no question but that reference to an object is involved. If I see an object hurtling towards us and say, 'That thing is approaching very fast', there is no way in which that claim can be defeated; yet my original grounds for it survive as grounds for the claim, 'Something is approaching very fast'. Second, it is clear that many *non-psychological* claims about the self can exhibit the same feature. Consider, for instance, my assertion 'My hair is blowing in the wind' when based not on a shop-window reflection but on certain characteristic feelings of the scalp and face and my auditory sensations. Or consider 'The bedclothes have fallen off my leg', uttered by an unwitting recent amputee. In neither case is there the possibility of a justified fall-back to an appropriate existential generalization if the claim is defeated. Immunity to error through misidentification is not a distinctive characteristic of *psychological* self-ascriptions or, more specifically, of avowals.

When I said a moment ago that a better characterization of IEM would teach us why this feature need not be of special concern to us in the present context, I was not merely anticipating this point. That the phenomenon extends to examples like those just given will seem to be quite consistent with its still betokening something essential about avowals once the plausible thought occurs that the *source* of IEM in non-psychological first-personal claims is always their being based on avowable psychological matters (for instance, my sensations of scalp and face and the rushing in my ears, or the amputee's sensations as of a draught around his foot). The IEM of non-psychological self-ascriptions, when they have it, is presumably to be viewed as an inheritance from their basis in an underlying possible avowal. It is not the fact that IEM is not the exclusive property of psychological claims which entitles us to bracket the phenomenon in the present context, but rather the reflection that avowals' exhibition of it is a *derived* feature, as it were —effectively a consequence of respects in which we have already noted their distinction from third-personal psychological claims. Specifically it is a consequence of their being groundless while the corresponding third-personal claims demand evidential support. For if an avowal, 'I am ϕ', did not exhibit IEM, then its defeat would be consistent with the subject's retention of an entitlement to the corresponding existential generalization—'Someone (else) is ϕ'—which could then be asserted *groundlessly*. But to suppose that such a claim could be both admissible and groundless would clash with the original asymmetry. Claims about the psychological states of others are acceptable only when grounded, one way or another; that goes both for particular such claims and for generalizations of them as well.

III

It is natural to wonder what, if any, independent, general characterization may be possible of the psychological distinction marked by the contrast between phenomenal—and attitudinal—avowals, as outlined. Here I can only observe that neither of two initially suggestive proposals seems to be quite right. Familiarly, the *Investigations* repeatedly counsels against construing understanding, hoping, fearing, intending, etc. as mental *states* or *processes*. Wittgenstein's idea was not, of course, that there are no such things, strictly, as mental processes, or the states that would constitute their end-points, so to speak, but only that understanding, etc. will be misunderstood if assimilated to them. So the suggestion invites consideration that the distinction he is making, between mental events and processes strictly so termed—turns in consciousness, if you like—and other psychological states, corresponds nicely to that between phenomenal and attitudinal avowals: that phenomenal avowals register states or processes of mind which Wittgenstein would be content to describe as such, whereas attitudinal avowals mark cases where danger lurks in that description.[7] The exegetical question is worth marking, but I shall not pursue it here.[8] Suffice it to say that some things which are surely 'turns in consciousness' in anyone's book—for instance, a lover's face passing before your mind's eye, or the thought occurring to you that you should have phoned home twenty minutes ago, or being startled by an opponent's outburst at the umpire—such cases are, unlike any of our prototypes of the phenomenal-avowable, also *contentful*; moreover, the proper description of such an episode is, at least in some cases, something about which a subject might just conceivably be self-deceived.

Another mark of many phenomenal-avowable states—and certainly of each example I cited originally—is that, at least as we ordinarily suppose,

[7] See e.g. Ludwig Wittgenstein, *Philosophical Investigations*, trans. G. E. M. Anscombe (Oxford: Blackwell, 1953), §§34, 146, 152, 154, 205, 303, 330–2, 427, 577, 673; also part II, §vi, p. 181, and §xi, pp. 217–18. The distinction is prominent in the *Remarks on the Philosophy of Psychology* (trans. G. E. M. Anscombe (Oxford: Blackwell, 1980)) as well, where Wittgenstein uses the terminology of *dispositions* versus *states of consciousness*; see e.g. vol. ii, §§45, 48, 57, and 178.

[8] No speedy resolution is to be expected, for Wittgenstein was content to gesture at his distinction quite loosely—perhaps believing that it is vague, that the concept of a 'mental process' is a family resemblance concept, or whatever.

creatures may be subject to them while *having no concept of them*: a dog can be tired, or afraid, or have an itch, without having any concept of those states. But this distinction too seems not to coincide quite cleanly with that between the phenomenal- and the attitudinal-avowable. Some phenomenal-avowable conditions do appear to require the subject to have a concept of them. I doubt, for instance, that a dog can have *Auld Lang Syne* run through its head, although that is presumably a process amenable to strongly authoritative avowal by a suitably endowed subject—though I suppose it depends on what you regard as required by an understanding of 'I am imagining a rendition of *Auld Lang Syne*'. Conversely, we tend quite freely to ascribe attitudinal states to (sufficiently intelligent, adaptable) creatures—primates and dogs, for instance —who presumably have no concept of such states.

In any case, we have sufficient of a focus for our central question. The cardinal problem of self-knowledge is that of explaining *why* avowals display the marks they do—what it is about their subject-matter, and the subject's relationship to it, which explains and justifies our accrediting her sincere pronouncements about it with each of Groundlessness, Strong Authority, and Transparency in the case of phenomenal avowals, and with Groundlessness, Weak Authority, and Transparency in the case of attitudinal avowals. How is it possible for subjects to know these matters non-inferentially? How is it (often) impossible for them *not* to know such matters? And what is the source of the special authority carried by their verdicts?

IV

There is a line of response to these questions that comes so naturally as to seem almost irresistible—indeed, it may even seem to ordinary thought to amount merely to a characterization of the essence of mind. According to it, the explanation of the special marks of avowals is that they are the product of the subject's exploitation of what is generally recognized to be a position of (something like) *observational privilege*. As an analogy, imagine somebody looking into a kaleidoscope and reporting on what he sees. No one else can look in, of course, at least while he is taking his turn. If we assume our hero to be perceptually competent, and appropriately attentive, his claims about the patterns of shape and colour within will exhibit analogues of each of the marks of phenomenal avowals:

(i)   The demand that he produces reasons or corroborating evidence for his claims will be misplaced—the most he will be able to say is that he is the only one in a position to see, and that is how things strike him;

(ii)   Granted his proper perceptual functioning, it will be sufficient for the truth of his claims that he understands them and is sincere in making them; so for anyone who understands the situation, our hero's merely making such a claim will constitute a sufficient, though defeasible, reason for accepting its truth; and

(iii) Where P is any claim about the patterns of shape and colour visible within, there will be no provision—bearing in mind our hero's assumed perceptual competence and attentiveness—for his intelligibly professing ignorance whether or not P.

The analogy isn't perfect by any means. In order to construct it, we have had to assume normal perceptual functioning and full attentiveness on the part of our observer. And no such assumption conditions our reception of other's avowals. But once into one's stride with this type of thinking, this difference will not seem bothersome. The line will be that in the *inner* observational realm, in contrast to the outer, there is simply no room for analogues of misperception or of oversight or occlusion—for the objects and features there are necessarily salient to the observing subject. Or, at least, they are so in the case where they are objects and features recordable by phenomenal avowals. In the case of the subject-matter of attitudinal avowals, by contrast, space for an analogue of misperception can and should be found—that will be what explains the failure of strong authority in those cases. In brief, this—Cartesian—response to the problem of avowals has it that the truth-values of such utterances are non-inferentially known to the utterer via her immediate awareness of events and states in a special theatre, the theatre of her consciousness, of which others can have at best only indirect inferential knowledge. In the case of phenomenal avowals, this immediate awareness is, in addition, infallible and all-seeing; in the case of basic attitudinal avowals, it is merely very, very reliable.

So presented, the Cartesian picture—of the transparency of one's own mind and, by inevitable contrast, the opacity of others'—emerges as the product of a self-conscious attempt at philosophical explanation. This may seem congenial to John McDowell's claim that 'We need to be seduced into philosophy before it can seem natural to suppose that another person's mind is hidden from us'.[9] McDowell recoils from the idea that anything like the Cartesian picture might be part of ordinary unphilosophical thought. But I think he is wrong about this, the theoretical

[9] John McDowell, 'Intentionality and Interiority in Wittgenstein', in K. Puhl (ed.), *Meaning Scepticism* (Berlin: de Gruyter, 1991), 148–69, at 149.

setting I have given to the picture notwithstanding. To be sure, it is unclear what should count as a 'seduction into philosophy'. But if every mani- festation of the Cartesian picture is to rate as the product of such a seduction, then the seductive reach of philosophy is flatteringly wide. I do not imagine, of course, that people typically self-consciously fol- low through the train of thought I outlined. But we ought not to baulk at the notion that no intellectual routine characteristically pursued by those in its grip should capture exactly the best reconstruction of why an idea appeals. The privacy of the inner world is a recurrent idea in literature.[10] It is arguably a presupposition of the whole idea of the continuation of one's consciousness after death. The thought of the undetectable inverted colour spectrum is something which can engage quite young children without too much difficulty. And in each of these cases, what comes naturally is essentially nothing other than the notion of a kind of privileged observation of one's own mind, which works, in the ways we have reviewed, to explain the first-third-person asym- metries in ordinary psychological discourse.

The privileged observation explanation is unquestionably a neat one. What it *does* need philosophy to teach is its utter hopelessness. One very important realization to that end is that nothing short of full-blown Cartesianism can explain the asymmetries in *anything like the same way*— there can be no scaled-down observational model of self-knowledge which preserves the advantages of the Cartesian account while avoiding its un- affordable costs. The problem is that the kind of authority I have over the avowable aspects of my mental life is not transferable to others: there is no contingency—or, none of which we have any remotely satis- factory concept[11]—whose suspension would put other ordinary people in a position to avow away on my behalf, as it were. So the concep- tion of avowals as reports of inner observation is saddled with the idea that the observations in question are ones which *necessarily* only the subject can carry out. And once that conception is in place, others' means of access to the states of affairs which their subject (putatively) observes is bound to seem essentially second-rate by comparison, and to be open to just the kinds of sceptical harassment which generate the traditional problem of other minds—the unaffordable cost referred to.

---

[10] It is, in a sense, the entire subject-matter of George Eliot's novella, *The Lifted Veil*.
[11] In particular, I do not think that we have any satisfactory concept of what it would be to be in touch with others' mental states *telepathically*. I do not mean, of course, to rule it out that someone might prove, by dint of *his own* occurrent suspicions and afflictions, to be a reliable guide to the states of mind of another. But that possibility falls conspicu- ously short of the idea that a subject might share direct witness of another's mental states.

V

If this is right, then a deconstruction of the privileged observation solution to the problem of self-knowledge is the indispensable prerequisite for an overall satisfactory philosophy of mind. It seems to me that it was Wittgenstein who first accomplished such a deconstruction, and I shall here try briefly to defend a certain conception of the way the deconstruction goes. In essentials, what he does is to mount a two-pronged attack on the Cartesian picture, with the two prongs corresponding to the distinction between the two main kinds of avowals. It is the so-called private language argument—the batch of considerations that surface in §§243 to the early 300s in the *Investigations*—which targets the idea of phenomenal avowals as inner observation reports, while the corresponding conception of attitudinal avowals is challenged by the various phenomenological and other considerations which Wittgenstein marshals in the, as we may call them, 'not a mental process' passages recurrent throughout the text.[12]

We need some preliminaries about *Investigations* §258, the famous passage in which Wittgenstein suggests that the 'private linguist' lacks the resources to draw a distinction which is essential if the 'reports' that he logs in his diary are to have a truth-evaluable content: the distinction, namely, between what seems right to him and what is really right. It seems clear that such a distinction is called for if these 'reports' are to have anything of the objectivity implicit in the very idea of an observational report, the objectivity implicit in the idea of successful representation of some self-standing aspect of reality. But it is not obvious that such a distinction is in good standing only if it can be drawn *operationally*—only if, that is, the diarist has the resources for making principled, presumably retrospective, judgements about occasions when he has been ignorant or mistaken. It ought to be enough if what constitutes the fact of the correctness of a report and what constitutes the diarist's impression of its correctness are not all the same thing, so to speak, even if no one can ever be in the position of ascertaining the one without the other.

Some commentators have taken it that Wittgenstein has missed this: that his objection here is implicitly verificationist—implicitly demands *contrastive uses* for locutions corresponding to the two halves of the distinction, and thus in effect begs the question against the idea that a subject might be *infallibly* aware of aspects of her inner life which are nevertheless constitutively independent of that awareness in the

---

[12] See n. 7.

manner which the seems right/is right distinction, properly understood, demands. This accusation seems to me mistaken. Any idea that the private diarist's jottings might be subject to a non-operational, but still valid, seems right/is right distinction comes into collision with an important aspect of Wittgenstein's discussion of the notion of intention. Broadly: the fact of an aspect of the diarist's inner world being as one of his reports states it to be demands, if it is to be constitutively independent of his impression of the fact, the existence of facts about what is required by the *semantics of the private language* which are likewise constitutively independent of his impressions of facts about them. Since the semantics of the private language are to be constituted in certain original intentions of the diarist, the upshot is that a similar constitutive independence is required between facts concerning what really complies with the diarist's original semantic intentions and his own subsequent impression of those facts, even under best conditions—conditions of the utmost lucidity, perfect recall, etc. But that is a sustainable demand only if the content of an intention is objectionably *platonized*, in a fashion which, after Wittgenstein's discussions (especially in *Investigations* §§600 ff.), we should know better than to do.

That, of course, is merely to sketch a line of interpretation which I have pursued before, but have no space to elaborate here.[13] But the sketch should be enough to set the stage for three objections which John McDowell has lodged,[14] to which I now turn.

VI

The first objection is a perfectly natural one. Is there not a prior, rather obvious doubt about the whole idea that the semantics of a private language could be constituted in certain original intentions of its practitioner? We should ask, McDowell says,

how an intention could be constitutive of a concept, as opposed to annexing an independently constituted concept to a word as what it is to express. The private linguist's semantical intention is supposed to be inwardly expressible by something like 'Let me call this kind of thing "S" in future'. But for this story even to seem to make sense, the classificatory concepts supposedly expressed, with the help of an inward focusing of the attention, by 'this kind of thing' would need to be at the linguist's disposal already; it cannot be something he equips himself with by such a performance. If a new classificatory concept can

[13] See Crispin Wright, 'Wittgenstein's Later Philosophy of Mind: Sensation, Privacy and Intention', in Puhl (ed.), *Meaning Scepticism*, 126–47.
[14] McDowell, 'Intentionality and Interiority in Wittgenstein'.

be set up by focusing on an instance, that is only thanks to the prior availability of a concept that makes the right focus possible, in the presence of the instance, by fixing what kind of classification is in question.[15]

McDowell's suggestion is that my putative difficulty with the idea of a report's complying with the semantics of the private language is a distraction: that the place at which the real difficulty is to be found is in the idea that the diarist could intentionally constitute a semantics for his language in the first place. For how exactly is the private ostensive definition supposed to work? If focusing the attention has to be mediated by concepts—surely one of the prime intended morals of Wittgenstein's discussion of ostensive definition—then a private ostensive definition could take place only in a context akin to the Augustinian setting introduced right at the start of the *Investigations*, wherein the trainee is assumed already to be a *thinker*—already to be master of a range of concepts of which, as a result of ostensive training, he will for the first time acquire means of expression. That won't do.

There is no doubt about the Wittgensteinian resonances of this line of thought. But McDowell doesn't see that there is nothing in it to disturb the essentials of the Cartesian view. The reason is that the self-directive role which Wittgenstein gives to his diarist in §258 is actually quite inessential to the putative upshot—the operation of a private language. We are not, after all—or had better not be—tempted to say that a similar difficulty must afflict normal, public ostensive teaching. We don't think that a child must somehow already be equipped with concepts of colour if he is to benefit from a normal ostensive training in the use of colour words—that, indeed, is the point of the *Investigations* contrast between ostensive definition proper and what Wittgenstein calls ostensive *teaching*.[16] But if that is right, there is in general no barrier to the idea that something conceptless—a colour-sensitive machine, say—might serve to do the teaching in place of a normally colour-concepted adult. Better, there ought to be no difficulty in the idea that a blind man, taking himself to have some form of prosthetic indication of variations in colour, might successfully introduce a normally sighted child to a range of colour concepts which he himself lacked. But *that is* essentially the model that Cartesianism, in so far as it figures in ordinary thought, offers of the teaching of sensation concepts. According to that model, I am screened from the inner goings-on when my child exhibits pain behaviour. But I take it that the behaviour gives me a kind of prosthesis—that it betokens inner phenomenal saliences which I can accordingly train him to vocalize, and thereby to conceptualize.

---

[15] Ibid. 164–5.   [16] Wittgenstein, *Philosophical Investigations*, §6.

In short, the diarist/private linguist doesn't have to be an autodidact. So no essential difficulty with the Cartesian conception of sensation language is disclosed by drawing out problems inherent in the idea of such autodidacticism. At some point, the Cartesian should say, a subject's competence in the linguistic routines in which, in both the inner and the outer cases, he is trained, will amount to the possession of concepts. And the identity of the concepts then possessed will supervene on the linguistic intentions of the subject: on the patterns of use which he will be willing to uphold. So there is no alternative but that a discussion of the idea of a subject's unwitting and undetectable departure from a prior intention must take centre stage if Wittgenstein's deconstruction is to succeed.

VII

McDowell's second objection is that the interpretation I offer winds up saddling Wittgenstein with the denial of certain platitudes. My claim was that we should elicit from Wittgenstein's discussion of intention and cognate concepts the moral that, as I put it in the discussion to which McDowell is responding, 'there is nothing for an intention, conceived as determining subsequent conformity and non-conformity to it autonomously and independently of its author's judgements on the matter, to *be*'.[17] McDowell glosses this as 'there is nothing but platonistic mythology in the idea that an intention determines what counts as conformity to it independently of its author's judgements'. He continues:

So [Wright's] thesis is that what the private linguist needs in his semantical intentions is something that cannot be true of any intentions at all, on pain of platonism.

But suppose I form the intention to type a period. If that's my intention, it is settled that only my typing a period will count as executing it. Of course I am capable of forming that intention only because I am party to the practices that are constitutive of the relevant concepts. But if that is indeed the intention which—thus empowered—I form, nothing more than the intention itself is needed to determine what counts as conformity to it. Certainly it needs no help from my subsequent judgements. (Suppose I forget what a period is.) So there is something for my intention to type a period, conceived as determining what counts as conformity to it autonomously and independently of my judgements on the matter, to be: namely, precisely, my intention to type a period. An intention to type a period is exactly something that must be conceived in that way. This is commonsense, not platonism.[18]

[17] Wright, 'Wittgenstein's Later Philosophy of Mind', 146.
[18] McDowell, 'Intentionality and Interiority in Wittgenstein', 163–4.

This response is indeed commonsensical, but it completely misses the point. Of course, if I form the intention that P, what will comply with it is only and exactly the bringing it about that P; and it will typically be a matter independent of my subsequent judgements whether or not just that has been effected. The role of subsequent judgement is indeed not to mediate somehow in the connection between the content of an intention and its execution—granted, that idea jars with the very idea of an intention having a determinate content—but rather to enter into the determination of *what* the content of an anterior intention is to be understood as having been. If I form the intention to type a period, then, sure, only typing a period will do. The anti-platonist point is rather that there is nothing for my intention's having had *just that content* to consist in, if the fact has to be constitutively independent of anything which I may subsequently have to say about compliance or non-compliance with the intention, or about what its content was.

The platonist mythology is a mythology of such constitutive independence. And it is exactly what the private linguist needs if the required seems right/is right distinction is to exist in the kind of way we are currently considering. Against this platonism I want to set what I take to be an idea of Wittgensteinian authorship, although it is of course very familiar from the writings of Davidson: that the content of a subject's intentional states is not something which may merely be *accessed*, as it were indirectly, by interpretative methods—rather as, on a platonistic philosophy of mathematics, a good proof is merely a means of *access* to a mathematical truth—but is something which is intrinsically sensitive to the deliverances of best interpretative methodology. That is a methodology which in principle must include within its conspectus the whole sweep of a subject's sayings and doings, including future ones, without bound.

VIII

The foregoing concerns the first prong of Wittgenstein's deconstruction of the Cartesian view—the anti-private language argument. The second prong, according to my reading, concerns certain special difficulties in the idea that attitudinal avowals describe introspectable mental occurrences. The suggestion of mine to which McDowell principally takes exception here is that one such special difficulty concerns the answerability of ascriptions of intentional states, like expectation, hope, and belief, to aspects of a subject's outward performance that may simply *not be available* at the time of avowal. If an expectation, say, were a determinate, dated occurrence before the mind's eye, then in any particular case it would either have taken place or not, irrespective of how I subsequently went on to behave. So we ought to be guilty of a kind of conceptual solecism if we hold claims about expectation to be answerable to subsequent sayings and doings in a fashion broadly akin to the way in which the ascription of dispositional states is so answerable. Yet that is exactly what we actually do.

The point was meant to be, then, that the conception of attitude avowals as reports of inner observation enforces a view of their subject-matter which is at odds with another, fundamental feature of their grammar—their 'disposition-like theoreticity'.[19]

McDowell—this is his third objection—thinks this is wrong, both in substance and as a reading of Wittgenstein. There cannot, he contends, be a difficulty of this kind if there are examples of unquestioned phenomena of consciousness which nevertheless bear the same kind of internal connections to the outer. Yet there surely are. The coming of a picture before the mind is an episode in consciousness if anything is; yet the relation between the picture and the real scene it pictures, if there is one, is presumably comparable in relevant respects to that between an expectation and its fulfilment. So intentional states can indeed be mental occurrences—indeed, we noted this earlier. And equally, non-intentional occurrences—including the proto-example of pain itself—are in a similar case: if a pain isn't an inner scenario, then nothing is—yet the ascription of pain is, likewise, answerable in complex but constitutive ways to the subject's outward performance.

McDowell lodges this objection in the context of a reading which has me attempting a rigorous and exhaustive division between strict phenomena of consciousness—Rylean 'twinges and stabs'—which, McDowell thinks I think, involve no intentionality, and whose occurrence is independent of the conceptual resources of the subject, and intentional states and processes which are never, properly speaking, occurrent phenomena of consciousness. That is a misreading, and the second prong does not require any such clean distinction. All that is required is that there be a difficulty along the indicated lines for at least one wide class of avowals. Still, the objection remains: isn't any such difficulty defused by the perfectly valid observation that items which certainly ought to be counted as mental *occurrences* do, after all, sustain internal relations to the outer?

[19] This idea is elaborated a little in my 'Wittgenstein's Rule-Following Considerations and the Central Project of Theoretical Linguistics', in Alexander George (ed.), *Reflections on Chomsky* (Oxford: Blackwell, 1989), 233–64, at 237 ff.

I don't think so. For one thing, remember that the dialectical setting is one in which even the claim of twinges and stabs to count as pure occurrences before an inner eye is under question. Conceived as by the Cartesian, a pain and the behaviour which expresses it are *quite distinct existences*, the one visible only to the subject, the other in public view. There *is* an incongruity, on that conception, in the conceptual linkage between the two which conditions ordinary psychological discourse. It is an instance of a more general incongruity which the sceptic quite rightly—when mentality is conceived as on the Cartesian view—finds in our empirically ungrounded reliance upon what is outer as a guide to subjects' mental lives.

The real counter to McDowell's objection, however, comes with a second consideration. When an image, or picture, comes before my mind, it presumably cannot constitute a more explicit or substantial presence than the coming of a real physical picture before my physical eye. And when the latter happens, it is of course consistent with my being in full command of all manifest features of the object that I remain ignorant precisely of its intentionality—of what it is a picture of. I want to say that, analogously, in the sense in which an image or mental picture can come before the mind, its intentionality cannot. Wittgenstein himself is making this point when he asks, 'What makes my image of him into an image of *him*?'[20] and answers, having said that 'the same question applies to the expression "I see him now vividly before me" as to the image', 'Nothing in it or simultaneous with it'. But this aspect—the intentional content—of expectation, belief, and their kin still falls firmly within the province of the non-inferential authority which we accord to attitudinal avowals. And it remains that the model of inner observation is bankrupt to explain the fact.

McDowell writes:

Wright's reading actually puts it in doubt whether anything could be an occurrent phenomenon of consciousness. . . . The kinds of connection that raise the problem for intentional states are, as I said, connections involving the 'normative' notion of accord. But such connections are a species of a wider genus, that of internal relations. If Wright's a priori argument worked, it would have to be because nothing introspectable could sustain internal relations to anything outer.[21]

I have already said that I think there *is* a doubt whether occurrences in a Cartesian theatre of consciousness could sustain the kind of conceptual connections with outward performance which sensations, as we

---

[20] Wittgenstein, *Philosophical Investigations*, pt. II, §iii.
[21] McDowell, 'Intentionality and Interiority in Wittgenstein', 152.

actually conceive of them, do sustain. But this ought to be consistent
with the ordinary idea that a pain, say, is an item for introspection. It
is a misunderstanding of the argument if it seems that, were it successful,
nothing introspectable could sustain internal relations to anything
outer. It all depends on the character and source of the internal relations in question. Both a sunburned arm, if I may borrow Davidson's
example, and a triangle can be presented as ordinary objects of observation, and each sustains, *qua* presented under those particular respective
concepts, certain internal relations: the sunburned arm to the causes
of its being in that condition, and the triangle to, for instance, other
particular triangles. And the point is simply that while identification of
the triangle as such can proceed in innocence of its internal relations
of the latter kind—maybe the subject has no knowledge of the other
triangles at all—recognition of the sunburned arm as just that cannot
proceed in like innocence, but demands knowledge that its actual causation is as is appropriate to that mode of presentation of it. The general
form of the point that I take Wittgenstein to be making in the second
prong of his attack is that the internal relations to the outer which are
constituted in the intentionality of psychological items, of whatever sort,
are all of the latter, sunburn-style kind. Hence there is indeed a standing
puzzle in the idea that an appropriate characterization of them, incor-
porating such intentionality, is somehow vouchsafed to their subject by
something akin to pure observation, *a fortiori* in the idea that it is the
privileged character of this observation which underlies first-personal
authority about such states. This thought, it seems to me, continues to
be impressive.

   Interpreting Wittgenstein on these issues is a subtle and difficult matter, and not just because of the subtlety and difficulty of his thinking.
McDowell's own positive reading[22] involves construal of the target of
the anti-private language argument as a version of the Myth of the Given,
transposed to the inner sphere; and he holds that the correct interpretation of the 'not a mental process' passages should still be consistent with the capacity of items such as meanings, intentions, and their
kin to 'come before the mind', as he likes to say.[23] I must defer further
consideration of his proposals. Here, I merely want to say at least a
minimum to explain my continuing conviction that the reading of

---

[22] See his 'One Strand in the Private Language Argument', *Grazer Philosophische Studien*,
33/4 (1989), 287–303. This paper should now be taken in the context of the more
general ideas about the interface between thought and the external world presented
in McDowell's John Locke lectures, *Mind and World* (Cambridge, Mass.: Harvard
University Press, 1994).
[23] McDowell, 'Intentionality and Interiority in Wittgenstein', 158.

Wittgenstein I have defended should lead one to recognize deep incoherences in the Cartesian response to our problem—incoherences that
are prior to its inordinate sceptical costs. And if what I said earlier is
right—namely, that there is no alternative for one disposed to pursue
the privileged observation route than to see the privilege as *necessarily*
the exclusive property of the observing subject—then the incoherence
of the Cartesian response is the incoherence of *any* broadly observational model of a subject's relation to their ordinary psychological states.
That's the lesson I want to carry forward.

IX

There is a proposal about our problem that for a time was widely accepted
as Wittgenstein's own. In *Investigations* §308 he writes:

How does the philosophical problem about mental processes and states and
about behaviourism arise?—The first step is the one that altogether escapes notice.
We talk of processes and states and leave their nature undecided. Sometime
perhaps we shall know more about them—we think. But that is just what commits us to a particular way of looking at the matter.

And a little earlier (§304) he urged that we need to 'make a radical
break with the idea that language always functions in one way, always
serves the same purpose: to convey thoughts—which may be about houses,
pains, good and evil, or anything else you please'. These sections
advance the diagnosis that our difficulties in this neighbourhood are generated by 'the grammar which tries to force itself on us here' (§304). They
go, Wittgenstein suggests, with a conception of avowals as *reports* and
the associated conception of a self-standing subject-matter which they
serve to report. We take it that there are mental states and processes
going on anyway, as it were—the 'first step' that escapes notice—and that
each person's avowals serve to report on such states and processes as
pertain to her. The immediate effect is to set up a dilemma. How, in the
most general terms, should we think of the states of affairs which confer
truth on these 'reports'? There is the Cartesian—events-in-an-arena-
accessible-only-to-the-subject—option; this does a neat job of explaining
the distinctive marks of avowals, at least at a casual muster, but it relies
on an 'analogy which . . . falls to pieces' (§308)—the analogy between
avowals and observation reports made from a privileged position. But
the only other option seems to be to 'go public': to opt for a view
which identifies the truth-conferring states of affairs with items which
are somehow wholly manifest and available to public view—an option
which Wittgenstein expects, writing when he did, will naturally take a

behaviourist shape, so that 'now it looks as if we had denied mental processes'. Of course, a philosopher who takes this option—whether in behaviourist or other form—will want to resist the suggestion that she is *denying* anything—according to *her* recommended understanding of 'mental process', just as Berkeley resisted the suggestion that he was denying the existence of matter. But the manifest problem is to reconcile any such conception of the truth-conditions of avowals with their distinctive marks: for as soon as you go public, it becomes obscure what advantage selves can enjoy over others.

This line of difficulty may seem to point to an obvious conclusion. Conceiving of avowals as reports of states and processes which are going on anyway appears to enforce a disjunction: *either* accept the Cartesian view, which cannot accommodate ordinary knowledge of others, *or* accept some form of externalization—perhaps behaviourist, nowadays more likely physicalist—which cannot sustain the special place of self-knowledge. So we should reject the parent assumption. And one tradition of commentary, encouraged especially by *Investigations* §244,[24] interprets Wittgenstein as doing this in a very radical way: as denying that avowals are so much as *assertions*—that they make statements, true or false—proposing to view them rather as *expressions* of the relevant aspects of the subject's psychology.[25]

Expression? To give expression to an aspect of one's psychology just means, presumably, to give it display, in the way in which wincing and a sharp intake of breath may display a stab of pain, or a smile may display that one is pleased, or a clenching of the teeth that one is angry. Propositional attitudes too can be open to natural expression of this kind: a prisoner's rattling the bars of his cell is a natural expression of a desire to get out. (It is not a way of acting on that desire, of course—it is not rationalized by it.) Wittgenstein's famous suggestion in §244 is that we should see the avowal of pain as an acquired form of pain behaviour—something one learns to use to supplant or augment the natural expression of pain and which, the *expressivist* tradition of commentary suggests, is no more a *statement*—something with a truth-evaluable content—than are such natural forms of expression.

The immediate question is how well an expressivist treatment of avowals can handle their distinctive marks. And the answer appears to

<hr />

[24] But see also *Remarks on the Philosophy of Psychology*, vol. i, §§450, 501, 593, 599, and 832.
[25] The sometime popularity of this interpretation is traceable to its being advanced by several of the first reviewers: P. F. Strawson, for instance, in his critical study of the *Investigations* in Mind, 53 (1954), 70–99; and Norman Malcolm in his 'Wittgenstein's *Philosophical Investigations*', *Philosophical Review*, 53 (1954), 530–59.

be: not badly at all. For instance, if the avowal 'I'm in pain' is not a statement, true or false, then naturally it is inappropriate to ask its author for grounds for it (Groundlessness), and naturally there is no question of her ignorance of its truth-value (Transparency). And if, when uttered with proper comprehension, it is to be compared to an episode of pain behaviour, then only its being a piece of dissimulation—not sincere—can stand in the way of a conclusion that the subject really is in pain (Strong Authority). (And of course it will provide a criterion for the subject's being in pain in just the way that ordinary pain behaviour does.)

Nevertheless, the expressivist proposal has come to be viewed more or less universally as a non-starter, for reasons preponderantly to do with the perceived impossibility of making coherent philosophy of language out of it. The claim that the avowal 'I am in pain' serves to make no statement, true or false, has to be reconciled with a whole host of linguistic phenomena whose natural explanation would exploit the opposed idea that it is, just as it seems, the affirmation of a truth-evaluable content. Here are four of the snags:

(i)   What has the expressivist proposal to say about transformations of tense—'I was in pain' and 'I will be in pain'? If either is a genuine assertion, doesn't there have to be such a thing as an author's making the *same* assertion at a time when doing so would demand its present-tense transform? If, on the other hand, they are regarded likewise merely as expressions, *what* do they serve to express? (Doesn't an expression have to take place at the same time as what it expresses?)

(ii) How is the proposal to construe a locution like 'He knows that I am in pain'? If there is a use of the words 'I am in pain' so embedded, which I can use to express the content of someone else's possible knowledge, why may I not *assert* that very same content by the use of the same words?

(iii) There are genuine—for instance, quantified—statements which stand in logical relations to 'I am in pain'. It entails, for instance, 'Someone is in pain'. How can a genuine statement be entailed by a mere expression?

(iv) 'I am in pain' embeds like any normal assertoric content in logical constructions such as negation and the conditional. 'It's not the case that I am in pain' and 'If I am in pain, I'd better take an aspirin' are syntactically perfectly acceptable constructions. But how can a mere expression, contrast: assertion, be *denied*? And doesn't the antecedent of a conditional have to be understood as the hypothesis that *something is the case*?

This kind of point—I shall dub the whole gamut 'the Geach point'[26] —has often been used as a counter to various forms of expressivism, notably in ethics, and much ingenuity has been expended (squandered?) by philosophers of expressivist inclination in the attempt to meet it. But in the present case I don't think it ought to have been influential at all. In the ethical case, the expressivist thesis is, crudely, that there are *no* real moral states of affairs; so the occurrence of what are apparently truth-evaluable contents couched in distinctively moral vocabulary has to be some kind of illusion. In that case the Geach point represents a very serious challenge, since it seems to show that everyday moral thought, in exploiting perfectly standard syntactic resources like those afforded by ordinary sentential logic, requires, to the contrary, that truth-evaluable moral contents exist. By contrast, it is no part of the present, allegedly Wittgensteinian expressivist proposal that there is no such thing as a statement of ordinary psychological fact. No one is questioning that '*He* is in pain' is an assertion. The expressivist thesis distinctively concerns *avowals*.

How does that difference help? Well, it is clear that we have to draw a distinction in any case between the question whether an indicative sentence is associated with a truth-evaluable content and the question whether its characteristic use is actually *assertoric*. For the two notions routinely come apart in the case of standard performatives like 'I promise to be on time', 'With this ring, I thee wed', 'I name this ship . . .', and so on. Each of these locutions embeds in all the ways the gen-eralized Geach point focuses on; and none of them is standardly used, in the atomic case, as an assertion. We should conclude that what the Geach point signals is merely the presence of truth-evaluable content. It is powerless to determine that the standard use of a locution is to *assert* such a content. And now the expressivist thesis about avowals can be merely that the typical use of such sentences is as expressions rather than assertions. There need be no suggestion that one *cannot* make assertions about one's own psychology. But the suggestion—now initially rather exciting—will be that the appearance of the *epistemic* superior-ity of the self which avowals convey is an illusion created by attempting to find a home for features of such utterances which they carry *qua* expressions in the context of the mistaken assumption that they are ordinary assertions. When selves *do* make strict assertions about their own psychology, the story should continue, any epistemic advantages

---

[26] After P. T. Geach's emphasis of such difficulties for moral expressivism, Austin's performatory account of knowledge, etc. See his 'Assertion', *Philosophical Review*, 74 (1965), 449–65.

they enjoy are confined to those of superiority of evidence which I noted briefly at the beginning.

That, it seems to me, is, in outline, how the best expressivist proposal should go. Now to its real problems. Perhaps the most immediate awkwardness, if a general account of avowals is to be based upon the §244 idea, is that, even in the case of sensations, the range of cases where there are indeed *natural*, non-linguistic forms of expression—cases like pains, itches, and tickles—is very restricted: contrast, for instance, the sensation of coolness in one foot, or the smell of vanilla. In the latter kind of case, the suggested model of the acquisition of competence in the avowal simply won't grip, and the theorist will have to try to live with the idea of a range of sensations whose *only* expression consists in their avowal. The same is evidently true in Spades of psychological items other than sensations. This threatens a worrying dilution of the key notion of *expression*.

That's a worry that might, I suppose, be worked on. But the next one seems decisive. Suppose a highly trained secret agent under torture resolutely gives no ordinary behavioural sign of pain. However, his torturers are men of discernment, with subtle instruments, who know full well of his agony, none the less: they know the characteristic signs —patterns on the electroencephalograph, raised heart rate, activation of reflexes in the eye, changes in surface skin chemistry, etc. If the suggestion really is to be that the superiority of the first-person viewpoint is *wholly* an artefact of a grammatical misunderstanding—the misconstrual of expressions as assertions—then, any *knowledge*, strictly so conceived, which the victim has of his own pain has to originate in the same way as that of his tormentors. But by hypothesis he isn't expressing pain behaviourally. And the signs that leave them in no doubt are things which, in his agony, he may not be attending to, or which, like the print-out on the electroencephalograph, he may not be able to see, or interpret if he could see. So in such a case, when it comes down to knowledge, it looks as though the expressivist account must represent the victim as actually *at a disadvantage*. That's evident nonsense.

In general, merely to conceive of avowals as expressive does not, when it goes in tandem with an acceptance of the reality of the states of affairs which they express, provide any way of deflecting the question: how, broadly speaking, should we conceive of the kind of state of affairs which is apt to confer truth on psychological ascriptions, and in what sort of epistemological relationship do their subjects themselves in general stand to such states of affairs? If this relationship is in any way more than evidentially privileged, we have our original problem back. If it isn't, we seem to get absurdities like that just illustrated.

A different way of seeing the unplayability of the expressivist position is to reflect that the content of an avowal is always available to figure just in a subject's thoughts, without public expression. You may sit reading and think to yourself, 'My headache has gone', without giving any outward sign at all. And anyone versed in ordinary psychology will accept that *if* you have that thought, not by way of merely entertaining it, but as something you endorse, then you will be right (Authority); that there is no way that your headache could have passed unless you are willing to endorse such a thought (Transparency); and that your willingness to endorse it will not be the product of inference or independently formulable grounds (Groundlessness). Thus analogues of each of the marks of avowals that pose our problem engage the corresponding unarticulated thoughts. It must follow that the correct explanation of the possession of them by avowals cannot have anything to do with illocutionary distinctions.

We should conclude that the expressivist proposal flies rather further than is usually thought. But it is a dead duck all the same.

X

For sure, the textual evidence for attributing the expressivist view to Wittgenstein was always pretty exiguous. *Investigations* §244 in particular should be contrasted with the much more cautionary and nuanced remarks elsewhere.[27] Such apparent equivocations, of course, are fuel for the common complaint that while Wittgenstein has suggestive criticisms to offer of certain tendencies in the philosophy of mind, he left any intended positive contribution shrouded in fog. What exactly— or even roughly—is Wittgenstein saying about avowals, if he is not proposing the expressivist view? How exactly does he propose we should liberate our thinking from Cartesian tendencies? What did he think we should put in their place?

Well actually, I don't think it is all that difficult to glean what his positive recommendation is, at least in general outline. The difficulty is, rather, to live with it. The first essential in interpreting him here is to give due prominence to the *Investigations'* explicit conception of the genesis of philosophical problems and of proper philosophical method. Wittgenstein wrote, recall, that

[27] e.g. *Investigations*, pt. II, §ix: 'a cry, which cannot be called a description, which is more primitive than any description, for all that serves as a description of the inner life. A cry is not a description. But there are transitions. And the words "I am afraid" may approximate more, or less, to being a cry. They may come quite close to this and also be *far* removed from it.'

we may not advance any kind of theory. There must not be anything hypothetical in our considerations. We must do away with all *explanation*, and description alone must take its place. . . . [Philosophical problems] are solved, rather, by looking into the workings of our language, and that in such a way as to make us recognize those workings: *in despite of* an urge to misunderstand them. . . . Philosophy is a battle against the bewitchment of our intelligence by means of language.[28]

And, very famously: 'Our mistake is to look for an explanation where we ought to look at what happens as a "proto-phenomenon". That is, where we ought to have said: *this language-game is played*'.[29]

The bearing of these strategic remarks is immediate if we reflect that our whole problem is constituted by a demand for explanation. We are asking: what is the *explanation* of the characteristic marks of avowals? And we easily accept a refinement of the question along the lines: what is it about the subject-matter of avowals, and about their authors' relation to it, which explains the possession by these utterances of their characteristic effortless, non-inferential authority? Cartesianism takes the question head on, giving the obvious, but impossible, answer. And the expressivist proposal, radical though it is in its questioning of the assumption that the authority of an avowal is the authority of a claim to truth, is not so radical as to raise a question about the validity of the *entire explanatory project*. But Wittgenstein, seemingly, means to do just that. Against the craving for explanation, he seemingly wants to set a conception of the 'autonomy of grammar'.[30] The features of avowals which set our problem—the features which seem to betray something remarkable about self-knowledge—do so only if we suppose that they are in some way *consequential* upon something deeper: for instance, the nature of their subject-matter and of their author's relationship to it. But what imposes that way of looking at the matter? Why shouldn't psychological discourse's exhibition of these features be regarded as primitively constitutive of its being *psychological*, so that the first-third-person asymmetries that pose our question belong primitively to the 'grammar' of the language-game of ordinary psychology, in Wittgenstein's special sense—'grammar' which 'is not accountable to any reality' and whose rules 'cannot be justified by showing that their application makes a representation agree with reality'?[31]

---

[28] Ibid. §109.
[29] Ibid. §654. It doesn't matter that this is said in the context of discussion of a different issue (recollection of the content of a prior intention).
[30] As Baker and Hacker style it.
[31] Wittgenstein, *Philosophische Grammatik*, ed. R. Rhees, tr. A. Kenny (Oxford: Blackwell, 1974), sect. X, §§133 and 134.

What did Wittgenstein suppose entitled him to this? In his later work, as everyone knows, he radically rethought his early conception of the relation between language and reality. It is to this readjustment, I suggest, that we must look if we are to understand the doctrine of the 'autonomy of grammar'. As I read the early 300s, the obstacle which Wittgenstein sees as lying in the way of our philosophical understanding of 'mental processes and states' is not the assumption of the truth-evaluability of avowals, as the expressivist interpretation has it, but rather a general picture of the working of *truth-evaluable* language. Wittgenstein means to reject a certain picture of what truth-evaluability involves: the picture gestured at in §304, that our statements always serve 'the same purpose: to convey thoughts—which may be about houses, pains, good and evil, or anything else you please'. This picture involves thinking of assertions as expressing propositions which are laid over against reality in the manner of the *Tractatus*, so that there have to be self-standing states of affairs to correspond to avowals, when they are true, and it has therefore to be possible to raise general questions about the nature of these self-standing states of affairs, and the nature of the subject's knowledge of them. And then, when we are mindful of the distinctive marks of avowals, it appears that the states, and the mode of knowledge, must be something rather out of the ordinary—the relevant states of affairs have to be conceived as somehow especially transparent to the subject, or, at the least, as working on her by some form of curiously reliable 'blindsight'—whose curious reliability, moreover, would have to be common knowledge if the authority credited to avowals is to be explained. Wittgenstein's diagnosis is that the 'philosophical problem about mental processes and states and about behaviourism' arises because we insist on interpreting the truth-evaluability of avowals—the source of the linguistic features on which the Geach point fastens—as imposing a conception of their being true, when they are, in terms which have to raise these constitutive questions about nature and access. But these are the very questions, Wittgenstein is saying, which we must free ourselves from the temptation to raise; they are the questions which lead to the fast track into the fly-bottle.

Of course, the conception of truth and truth-makers which, in Wittgenstein's diagnosis, is here at the root of our difficulty is the core of the outlook which Hilary Putnam has called 'metaphysical realism'. Perhaps the single most significant departure effected in Wittgenstein's later philosophy is his coming to believe that we have to stop thinking about the relationship between language and reality, and about the truth-predicate, in that kind of way.

XI

Wittgenstein's stance deserves a much finer-grained depiction than I can attempt here. If we abstract from the globally anti-explanatory background mantra, the cash value of the proposal, just for the issue of self-knowledge, involves a generalization to all avowable subject-matter, phenomenal and attitudinal, of a view which might be characterized like this:

the authority standardly granted to a subject's own beliefs, or expressed avowals, about his intentional states is a *constitutive principle*: something which is not a consequence of the nature of those states, and an associated epistemologically privileged relation in which the subject stands to them, but enters primitively into the conditions of identification of what a subject believes, hopes and intends.[32]

I'll call this general viewpoint the 'Default View'. According to the Default View, it is just primitively constitutive of the acceptability of psychological claims that, save in cases whose justification would involve active self-interpretation, a subject's opinions about herself are default-authoritative and default-limitative: unless you can show how to make better sense of her by overriding or going beyond it, her active self-conception, as manifest in what she is willing to avow, must be deferred to. The truth-conditions of psychological ascriptions are primitively conditioned by this constraint. In particular, it is simply basic to the competent ascription of the attitudes that, in the absence of good reason to the contrary, one must accord correctness to what a subject is willing to avow, and limit one's ascriptions to her to those she is willing to avow.

It would be a great achievement of Wittgenstein's discussion if it made it possible to understand how the Default View need not be merely an unphilosophical turning of the back. But it is anything but clear, actually, how a repudiation of the metaphysical realist picture of truth could just by itself directly enjoin this conception. Moreover, it is very difficult to rest easy with the general anti-explanatory mantra. For it is seemingly in tension with a diagnostic thought which is very important to Wittgenstein himself: that philosophical problems characteristically arise because we are encouraged by surface-grammatical analogies to form expectations about an area of discourse which are appropriate only for a particularly salient surface-grammatical analogue of it. That is *exactly* Wittgenstein's diagnosis in the present case: the target analogy is that between the use of avowals and ordinary reports of observation.

---

[32] Wright, 'Wittgenstein's Later Philosophy of Mind', 142.

So then that diagnosis itself requires that the explanatory questions which we are required *not* to press in the case of avowals are, by contrast, perfectly properly raised, and answerable, in the case of ordinary reports of observation. There cannot, accordingly, just be a blanket prohibition against explanatory questions of that kind. Put that simple thought alongside the plausible claim that there are perfectly legitimate modes of *conceptual* explanation—informal mathematics, in particular, is full of them—and it appears that it cannot in general be merely a confusion to seek to explain features of the practice of a discourse a priori by reference to our concepts of the kind of subject-matter it has and of the epistemic capacities of speakers. Thus the insistence that these questions are misplaced in the target case of psychological self-ascriptions begins to seem merely dogmatic.

Is there any way this impression of dogmatism might be dispelled? In the analogy of the kaleidoscope, our conception is that of a range of independent features and events—evolving patterns of shape and colour—to which the privileged observer is sensitive—responsive—by dint of his situation and his possession of certain germane cognitive capacities, notably vision. There is a story to be told about the kind of things on display and how things of that kind can elicit a response from someone with a suitable cognitive endowment. Now one way to try to exculpate the Default View from the charge of dogmatism, it seems to me, is to seek a framework which places controls on the relevant idea of *responsiveness*.[33] One form of control might be elicited from pursuing certain recently much discussed issues to do with judgement dependence and the *Euthyphro contrast*: we may pursue the details of the relations, in different regions of thought, between best opinion and truth, attempting thereby to arrive at a conception of what it is for them to relate too closely, so to speak, for their congruence to count as a *success in tracking*. Another control might emerge from consideration of the question of how wide the potential *explanatory range* has to be of a certain type of state of affairs if we are to think of our judgements about it as genuinely responsive to its subject-matter at all (*Width of Cosmological Role*).[34] We can seek a framework of such controls and try to show that first-person psychological discourse emerges on the wrong side of the tracks, so to speak, under the application of such controls. Then, if its apparent urgency does indeed derive from a tacit assumption of the *responsiveness* of selves to their own psychological states, the

[33] I suppose this is a programme of what McDowell has disparagingly called 'constructive philosophy'.

[34] Both these ideas are explored in my *Truth and Objectivity* (Cambridge, Mass.: Harvard University Press, 1994).

general explanatory question about self-knowledge, which official Witt-gensteinian philosophical method would have us ignore, can emerge as something which we can understand *why* we ought not to ask.

By contrast, lacking such a framework, and the right kind of upshot within it concerning psychological discourse, it is hard to see how the Default View can come to much more than a take-it-or-leave-it recom-mendation: a mere invitation to *choose* to treat as primitive something which we have run into trouble trying to explain, and to do so just on that account. Wittgenstein notoriously came to view philosophical problems as akin to a kind of self-inflicted intellectual *disease*; they would thus contrast starkly with *mathematical* problems as traditionally viewed (not by Wittgenstein, of course)—a kind of sublime, objective puzzle whose force can be felt by any rational intellect. If philosophical problems are justly deflated in Wittgenstein's way, then a kind of 'Here: think of matters this way, and you'll feel better' remedy might be the best we can do. But the prospect immensely disappoints. For most of us, after all, the attraction of philosophy is all about gaining understanding. Except in cases where one can *explain* a priori why the demand for under-standing is inappropriate, it is apt to seem like a mere abrogation of the subject to be told one mustn't make it at all.

XII

We owe to Wittgenstein the insight that we are making an assumption in regarding it as a deficiency of understanding to lack a satisfactory explanation of the distinctive marks of avowals. The assumption is, roughly, that those distinctive marks must be *consequential*: that they must either derive from the nature of the subject-matter—something which therefore drives our discourse about it into the relevant characteristic turns—or else they must derive from some unobvious feature of the semantics of first-person psychological discourse (its being, for in-stance, expressive rather than assertoric). So, according to the assump-tion, there must be an explanation which we have yet to assemble and get into focus.

There is a frontal collision between this way of thinking and the con-ception of the nature of legitimate philosophical enquiry seemingly quite explicit in Wittgenstein's later official methodological pronouncements. According to Wittgenstein, the limit of our philosophical ambition should be to recognize the assumptions we are making in falling into philo-sophical difficulty, and to see our way clear to accepting, by whatever means, that nothing forces us to make them. It is, for Wittgenstein, the very craving for legitimizing explanations of features of our talk about mind, or rules, or mathematics that leads us into hopeless puzzles about the status—the epistemology and ontology—of those discourses. Philosophical treatment is wanted not to solve these puzzles but to undermine them—to assuage the original craving that leads to the construction of the bogus models and interpretations by which we attempt to make sense of what we do, but which are the source of all our difficulties, and yet whose want is felt as a lack of understanding. The problem of self-knowledge is a signal example. It can have—I believe Wittgenstein thought—no solution of the kind we seek; for that very conception of a solution implicitly presupposes that there must be a something-in-virtue-of-which the distinctive marks of avowals are sustained. But those marks are part of 'grammar', and grammar is not sustained by anything. We should just say 'This language-game is played.'

The generalization of this position—the execration of all philosophical explanation—seems to me vulnerable to a version of what one might call 'the paradox of postmodernism'. The paradox is that while, like all 'deflationists', Wittgenstein needs to impress us of the illegitimacy of more traditional aspirations, *argument* for that is hard to foresee if it is not of the very coin which he is declaring to be counterfeit. For what is needed here is precisely a *philosophical explanation*. Sure, what belongs to 'grammar', in Wittgenstein's special sense of that term, requires no explanation. *Of course*; that's a matter of definition. But even a sympathetic reading of him will find a frustrating inattention to the question of when something may legitimately be taken to be part of 'grammar'. It may be a crucial first step to recognize that the problem of self-knowledge is occasioned by an assumption of explicability—an assumption that may be discarded with a clear conscience if the special position of subjects in determining what is true of their psychology is indeed 'grammatical'. But, one wants to say, what shows that? Once one recognizes the Default View as a possibility, the immediate instinct is to ask: what might *justify* the idea that it is the whole truth? That is the instinct to attempt to understand when and why it is a good move to dismiss the attempt to understand. To succumb is to re-enter the space of explanatory philosophy. To resist is to have no reason for the Default View.

To feel this dissatisfaction is not to have a reason to deny the insight that in a wide class of cases philosophical perplexity does indeed take the form of a casting about for what strike us as satisfying explanations of features of our language, and of failing to find any that do not generate singularities of one sort or another. (Just briefly to mention a second prominently Wittgensteinian example: how are we to make sense of the intelligibility of the distinction between whether a statement is really true and whether anybody ever takes it to be true unless the rule incorporated in its truth-condition may be thought of as issuing its verdict autonomously and independently of any human judgement? So isn't the very idea of unratified truth an implicit commitment to 'rules-as-rails' platonism?!) But to accept Wittgenstein's insight, that some of the hardest-seeming philosophical problems take this form, is not a commitment to an explanation-proscribing view of philosophy. Even if it is misguided to persist in assuming that there must be *something* that can satisfactorily take up the explanatory slack left by the demise of platonism, or Cartesianism, it may yet be possible to explain why such an assumption need not be true in particular cases. It does not seem merely confused to seek, in particular, to characterize with some care the conception we have of the kinds of ways the marks of avowals might in principle be explained. It is even foreseeable that such a characterization might lead to a clear-headed realization that nothing could fulfil it. *That* would be the discovery that, in this area, 'gives philosophy peace' (§133).

2

Response to Crispin Wright

JOHN MCDOWELL

I

We are prone to be gripped by a 'Cartesian' conception of our relation to our own inner lives. On Wright's account, this derives from the fact that a 'Cartesian' picture of the mental gives the appearance of meeting a certain pressing explanatory need. This supposed need is for an explanation of the asymmetry, or asymmetries, between our epistemic relations to our own inner lives and our epistemic relations to the lives of others. According to Wright, Wittgenstein's *negative* achievement is to provide a 'deconstruction' of this supposed captivating power of a 'Cartesian' conception. (Wright thinks that we can at least dimly glimpse a *positive* achievement in Wittgenstein too. I shall come to that in section III below.) Wright finds in Wittgenstein a complex two-pronged line of argument, whose point is supposed to be that a 'Cartesian' conception does not, after all, meet this explanatory need. In Wright's view, showing this is 'the indispensable prerequisite for an overall satisfactory philosophy of mind' (p. 25). He evidently thinks that the negative achievement he thus credits to Wittgenstein is an important execution of a difficult task.

I think this note of importance and difficulty is misplaced. It would be a disappointment if, in the relevant texts, Wittgenstein were doing no more than showing us that a 'Cartesian' conception does not explain what Wright thinks it purports to explain. It would be mysterious why *this* task should seem to need such a complex and subtle dialectical engagement with the frame of mind that Wittgenstein considers. Wright says it takes philosophy to teach the hopelessness of a 'Cartesian' picture of the mental as he conceives it, considered as a response to the supposed explanatory requirement that organizes his picture of what is required in the philosophy of mind. Maybe so; but it does not need as much philosophy as Wittgenstein evidently thinks it worth devoting to his target. A few sentences would be enough for the task that Wright depicts as so difficult.

This may be obscured by a way in which Wright sometimes presents the feature of our knowledge of our own inner lives that we are supposed to find puzzling. In the places I mean, he describes the supposedly puzzling feature as a matter of *non-inferential* authority. But his own detail shows that this wording fails to capture the fundamental point. When Wright rehearses the marks of avowals, it becomes clear that the fundamental point is that our authority in our avowals is not just non-inferential but, in a certain sense, *baseless*. As he says, ' "How can you tell?"—is always inappropriate'; and 'there is nothing upon which such claims are based' (p. 14).[1] Now Wright takes it that the essence of the 'Cartesian' conception attacked by Wittgenstein is the idea that the authority of avowals can be understood on the model of observational authority. And the authority of observations is indeed *non-inferential*. But it is precisely *not* baseless. The question 'How can you tell?' is precisely *not* excluded as inappropriate. Wright says of his hero, alone in looking into his kaleidoscope, that 'the most he will be able to say is that he is the only one in a position to see, and that is how things strike him'. But if he can say that much, he can say *too* much for the supposed explanation of the epistemic asymmetry even to *seem* to be any good. No doubt his hero is not open to requests for 'reasons or corroborating evidence' for his claims about the patterns of shape and colour in the kaleidoscope. That is just to say that the knowledge he expresses in those claims, observational as it is, is non-inferential. But he does not reject the question 'How can you tell?' He accepts it and answers it when he says, perfectly properly, that he is in a position to see.

Suppose someone claims to have a philosophical problem that finds expression in asking: 'How is it possible that our knowledge of our own inner lives is baseless?' I am going to urge (section III below) that such a form of words fails to present us with any determinate philosophical difficulty; but for now the mere claim to have a difficulty that can be expressed like this will serve my purpose. If someone claims to have such a difficulty, it is *obviously* unhelpful to respond by giving a picture that merely leaves the baselessness out. But that is what the observational picture does. Given Wright's construal of why we are gripped by a 'Cartesian' picture of the mental, the immediate problem with it is not the point he first mentions, that we have to go quickly past the

---

[1] This wording occurs when Wright is spelling out the marks of phenomenal avowals. But the point carries over to attitudinal avowals.

need for some assumptions about 'normal perceptual functioning and full attentiveness' (p. 23). The immediate trouble is that on a not very searching inspection, the picture as Wright takes it stands revealed as simply not responding to the supposed problem that is supposed to be what motivates it. If it were true that the attraction of an observational model for self-knowledge derived from our taking ourselves to be faced with the explanatory requirement that figures in Wright's account, we would not even need to start counting the model's 'unaffordable costs'. Only by an easily exposed sleight of hand—the slide between 'non-inferential' and 'groundless'—can an observational model be made to give so much as an appearance of doing the advertised explanatory job.

Of course, I am not disputing that a conception that perhaps deserves to be called 'Cartesian' can captivate us, and that it takes a great deal of philosophical work to loosen its grip. As Wright mentions, I have offered a different picture of Wittgenstein's target in the texts that are under dispute between us. I shall not go into more detail about this now than Wright does, except for one correction, which will allow me to gesture at the possibility of a different account of what makes it difficult and important to exorcize what Wittgenstein seeks to exorcize. Wright finds in Wittgenstein a two-pronged argument: the private language argument, strictly so called, to deal with phenomenal avowals, and a second prong to deal with attitudinal avowals. From his quick sketch of my alternative reading, one might gather that I invoke the Myth of the Given only as the target of the private language argument, narrowly construed. That would imply that I offer some simply different story about what figures in Wright's reading as the second prong of the two-pronged argument. But any such impression would be wrong. I invoke the Myth of the Given in presenting a picture of the deep source of the *whole* syndrome that Wittgenstein attacks: not just the misconception of sensations, but also the tendency to have one's mind boggle over avowals whose conceptual apparatus involves intentionality. I depict the syndrome as the result of an intelligibly felt need to make a certain move in the battle between realism and idealism; the conception of the inner that Wittgenstein attacks seems obligatory if we are to resist an intelligibly unpalatable appearance of idealism.

Now I have been urging that Wright's account of what gives Wittgenstein's target its grip on us leaves it a hard question why dislodging that conception should require the dialectical subtlety and complexity that Wittgenstein evidently thinks are called for. I need not go into detail in order to suggest that my alternative stands at least a chance of doing better on that score. On my account, the conception that Wittgenstein attacks presents the inner world as a good battlefield on which to resist

the insidious encroachments of idealism. It is still true on my reading
that a victim of the conception under attack will naturally fall into seeing the epistemology of self-knowledge in observational terms. But, on
my reading, that is not the fundamental point about the syndrome.[2] My
alternative account of the motivation for the syndrome, and thus of the
syndrome itself, promises to make the syndrome's capacity to grip us
more satisfactorily intelligible than would be possible on the basis of the
unimpressive claim of an observational model to address the explanatory question that Wright thinks Wittgenstein's target conception aims
to respond to.

II

Wright's reading of the private language argument has at its core something along these lines. Given that the private diarist of *Investigations*
§258 cannot operationally equip himself with a 'seems right'/'is right'
distinction for his diary entries, the distinction would have to be put
in place by a semantic intention, supposedly formed when the diarist
gives himself his private ostensive definition. And according to Wright,
the demand this places on the intention can seem sustainable 'only if
the content of an intention is objectionably *platonized*' (p. 26).

Now there seem to be some cross-purposes in Wright's response to
the first of the three objections of mine that he considers. What risks
going missing is that I can sum up how I take the argument around
Investigations §258 to work in words that are, from one point of view,
almost vanishingly different from those words of Wright's. According
to me, the demand placed on the private linguist's supposed semantic
intention by the requirement that it provide for the 'seems right'/'is right'
distinction can seem sustainable only if the content of *that supposed
intention* is objectionably platonized. That is, I agree with Wright that
Wittgenstein unmasks *these supposed semantic intentions* as platonistic mythology. When I urge that he is simply applying considerations
from his discussion, much earlier in the book, of ostensive definition in
general, my point is not to deny that Wittgenstein's attack on the semantic intentions supposedly formed in private ostensive definitions can be
put in terms of an objectionable platonism, but to object to Wright's thought
that unmasking the private linguist's supposed intentions as platonistic

[2] See my 'Intentionality and Interiority in Wittgenstein', in K. Puhl (ed.), *Meaning
Scepticism* (Berlin: de Gruyter, 1991), 168–9: 'Within this alternative, it looks like a
mistake to be too concerned with the observational model as such; that model is merely
a natural form for the epistemology of self-knowledge to take if the framework is in
place, and it is the framework that is the real villain of the piece.'

mythology figures as the conclusion of an *a fortiori* argument, from the premiss that, on pain of objectionable platonizing, *no* intention can draw the distinction between conformity and non-conformity 'autonomously and independently of its author's judgements on the matter' (p. 28). If we see the discussion of private ostensive definition in the context of the discussion of ostensive definition in general, we can see a way to take Wittgenstein as unmasking the private linguist's supposed semantic intentions *in particular* as platonistic mythology—so that there is no need for Wright's *a fortiori* argument.[3] Supposing I can earn the right to an accusation of objectionable platonizing in this different way, the argument that these supposed intentions cannot carry the weight of the 'seems right'/'is right' distinction can proceed, according to my reading, just as Wright says it does. Wright and I differ over the pretext for the right to bring the accusation of platonism, but for the way the argument itself works, that difference is irrelevant.

So I am puzzled by Wright's claim that the private language argument as I see it would be telling only if the private linguist had to be an autodidact, in a way in which he does not have to be one. I cannot see that an argument that exploits my way of unmasking the private linguist's supposed semantic intentions as platonistic mythology is any worse off on this score than an argument that exploits Wright's way. No doubt the private language picture can incorporate other people, encouraging and discouraging vocalizations in something like the way that figures in a schematic common-sense picture of language acquisition in general. But if we are to conceive the result as the formation of semantic intentions that are determinative of *private* meanings, the idea has to be that the trainee does the essential thing—focusing his attention on the relevant inner item—for himself (cf. *Investigations* §210). At the crucial point in the story he *does* have to be, in a certain sense, an autodidact. The essential step in the formation of private understandings would have to be private ostensive definitions. It makes no difference if the words that are supposed to acquire the private meanings are public words, so that other people select the occasions for the private ostensive definitions (cf. *Investigations* §273). My claim can be put like this: by simply applying considerations from the discussion of ostensive definition in general, we can see that it can seem to make sense that private ostensive definitions (whether or not their occasions are determined by others) might set up semantic intentions—intentions capable of providing for a 'seems right'/'is right' distinction—only if the

---

[3] See my 'Intentionality and Interiority in Wittgenstein', 165, first whole paragraph (which Wright does not quote).

supposed intentions are objectionably platonized. This shows that if we set out to talk of semantic intentions determined by private ostensive definitions, we are only under the illusion of expressing an idea. The conclusion emerges pretty much as it does in Wright's reading; the point is just that there is no need for the general thesis about intentions that figures in Wright's *a fortiori* argument.

The second of my objections to which Wright offers a response is my objection to the premiss of his *a fortiori* argument: the general thesis about intentions, that 'there is nothing for an intention, conceived as determining subsequent conformity and non-conformity to it autonomously and independently of its author's judgements on the matter, to *be*' (p. 28). Wright quotes part of my attack on this, and says 'it completely misses the point'. But who is missing whose point? Wright goes on to say again the very thing whose clash with common sense I meant to be bringing out.

I was not accusing Wright of thinking, with obvious absurdity, that an intention can have a content that is somehow already determinate, but *still* need subsequent judgements on the part of its author—over and above already having its content—to help it out in determining whether some performance is in conformity to it. I was registering, and objecting to, something he does think (he says it again here): that the author's subsequent judgements 'enter into the determination of *what* the content of an anterior intention is to be understood as having been'. This undermines the idea that an intention can *have* a determinate content in advance of its author's judgement as to whether some performance is in conformity to it. Wright says: 'Of course, if I form the intention that P, what will comply with it is only and exactly the bringing it about that P; and it will typically be a matter independent of my subsequent judgements whether or not just that has been effected' (p. 29). Certainly it will typically be a matter independent of my subsequent judgements whether or not what I have done is bringing it about that P. But on Wright's picture, it will *not* be a matter independent of my subsequent judgements whether or not the intention I formed *was* the intention that P. So we still seem to be stuck with needing to think along these lines: whether or not my subsequent performance (suppose, by all means, that —independently of any judgements of mine—it *is* bringing it about that P) is an execution of my intention awaits my verdict on the performance, since only then is the intention's content determined; only then is it determined whether or not the intention was the intention to bring it about that P. It is as if we have to wait and see whether what we find ourselves to have done strikes us as an execution of our intention before it can be determinate what our intention was.

If using accusations of platonism to clear away illusions of talking sense is to stand any chance of being a way to express a *Wittgensteinian* line of thought, the platonism we claim to uncover should exemplify the characteristic hysteria of philosophers, and the alternative in which we take refuge should be a bit of obvious sanity. But surely nobody but a philosopher would entertain the thesis that we have to wait and see whether what we find ourselves to have done strikes us as an execution of our intention before it can be determinate what our intention is.

This thesis about intention is a counterpart to a kindred thesis about meaning, which Wright attributes to Wittgenstein elsewhere.[4] The thesis about meaning is that, similarly on pain of platonism, we have to renounce the idea that the meaning of, say, the principle of a numerical series 'determines the steps in advance' (cf. *Investigations* §190), in such a way that the correctness of a certain move at a certain point in the series is independent of judgements ratifying it as correct, made by people who understand the principle of the series. In this latter case, Wright enthusiastically traces out, on Wittgenstein's behalf, a visibly philosophical consequence of the supposedly compulsory renunciation, applied to meaning and understanding in general: that, supposedly on pain of platonism, we have to give up an idea that has all the appearance of being a bit of plain common sense—the idea of things being thus and so anyway, independently of ratification by judgements on the matter made by people who possess the relevant concepts.

In these parallel stretches of dialectic, about intention and about meaning, avoiding platonism is supposed to require of us, according to Wittgenstein as Wright reads him, substantive and—one might naturally think—distinctly unprepossessing theses of a discernibly philosophical kind, certainly not theses that 'it would never be possible to debate . . . because everyone would agree to them' (*Investigations* §128). The characteristic nuttiness of philosophers—their willingness to say anything if an argument seems to compel it—is on the side of these exchanges that Wright takes to be Wittgenstein's side, and that egregiously fails to fit Wittgenstein's own pronouncements about the kind of thing he does in philosophy.

How embarrassing this ought to be for Wright depends in part, I suppose, on the prospects for the idea that we can credit Wittgenstein with offering, or at least making available to us, positive philosophical theses, as it were in spite of himself. This idea would lead us to discount remarks such as the one I have just quoted, perhaps as versions of a

---

[4] See e.g. Crispin Wright, *Wittgenstein on the Foundations of Mathematics* (London: Duckworth, 1980), ch. 11.

'globally anti-explanatory background mantra' (p. 41) that disfigures
or obscures the philosophical achievements we can nevertheless dimly
glimpse in Wittgenstein. I shall come to these issues in due course
(section III below). But whatever we conclude about them, surely we
should try to respect Wittgenstein's own self-conception at least to this
extent: that we not cast him as just another thesis-mongering philosopher unless we cannot avoid it. Of course, I cannot here give a complete alternative to Wright's reading of how platonistic mythology figures
in Wittgenstein. But I can gesture in that direction as follows: I think
we can *always* frame threats of platonistic mythology, as they figure in
Wittgenstein's landscape, on the pattern of *Investigations* §195. The
following is not a Wittgensteinian exchange, though on Wright's reading it ought to be: 'An intention determines what counts as conformity
to it autonomously and independently of any subsequent judgements
of its author'—'Platonism! Anathema!' The following is: 'An intention
in some sense determines, in a *queer* way, what counts as conformity
to it autonomously and independently of any subsequent judgements
of its author.'—'But of course it does, "in *some* sense"! Really the only
thing wrong with what you say is the expression "in a queer way".'

In Wright's third response to me, I think he contrives that the objection I was making goes missing, rather than getting answered. Of course
I was not trying to *defend* the model of inner observation. I was objecting to a thesis Wright attributed to Wittgenstein that was not formulated
in those terms; it was formulated in terms of 'phenomena of consciousness' or 'occurrences in consciousness'. Wright found in Wittgenstein a
principle to this effect: nothing that is 'a matter purely of the occurrence
of certain events in consciousness' could stand to extra-mental circumstances in the relations that are constitutive of the topics of intentionality-
involving avowals—relations we can summarily capture in terms of
accord.[5] This was how Wittgenstein was supposed to show that it is
a mistake to assimilate attitudinal avowals to phenomenal avowals—

---

[5] See Crispin Wright, 'Wittgenstein's Later Philosophy of Mind: Sensation, Privacy
and Intention', in Puhl (ed.), *Meaning Scepticism*, 130: 'But the more fundamental point
is that the details of the phenomena of consciousness which may be associated with understanding, expecting, intending, hoping, etc., are neither in general called upon, nor able,
to sustain the kinds of internal connection with aspects of a subject's subsequent doings
and reactions which mental states of this kind essentially sustain. To take a very familiar
instance: if coming to understand "in a flash" the rule governing a decimal expansion
were a matter purely of the occurrence of certain events in consciousness, then it would
be a point of contingency that people who so come to understand something are able
subsequently to deliver appropriate kinds of performance. But this is not a contingency.'
(Incidentally, the relevant internal connections are not just with the subject's subsequent
doings and reactions; in the case of, say, expectation, the occurrence of a loud bang
might fill the relevant role.)

phenomenal avowals, that is, on a supposedly neutral conception, not phenomenal avowals construed, dubiously, on an observational model. That it is a mistake to construe phenomenal avowals on an observational model was supposedly shown separately, in the other prong of the two-pronged argument. Against this, I protested that what it is about the relevant relations that generates the kind of difficulty Wittgenstein is concerned with is not, specifically, that they can be summarily captured with the notion of accord, but, more generally, that they are *internal* relations. So the putatively Wittgensteinian principle would have to be seen as an application of a more general principle, to this effect: nothing that is 'a matter purely of the occurrence of certain events in consciousness' could stand in internal relations to extra-mental circumstances. And that, I insisted, could not be a Wittgensteinian principle, since it would saddle Wittgenstein with the intolerable consequence that, say, episodes of *pain* cannot be 'a matter purely of the occurrence of certain events in consciousness'.

Wright's first response to this is to remark that my protest cannot help someone who wants to explain the authority of avowals in terms of the picture of an inner eye. Certainly; it was not meant to. The point was that, in order to accommodate the avowability of sensations satisfactorily, we need to be able to make sense of something that is *both* 'a matter purely of the occurrence of certain events in consciousness' *and* internally connected to things not in consciousness; and if we can make sense of that combination, the argument Wright finds in Wittgenstein, against assimilating attitudinal avowals to phenomenal avowals, cannot work. Alternatively (contraposing): if it did work, we would be left without a satisfactory way to accommodate sensations.

Wright's second response is similarly directed against someone who doubts the bankruptcy of the model of inner observation. As I have insisted, I was not defending that model. I was expressing a doubt about the way in which Wright, on Wittgenstein's behalf, suggests that the notion of something that is 'a matter purely of the occurrence of certain events in consciousness' would have to function. I do not dispute that considerations about internal relations put paid to the idea that first-person authority is underwritten by a special observational access to its topic. What I dispute is Wright's suggestion that an argument with that shape works only for attitudinal avowals, showing that their subject-matter is not to be assimilated to matters 'purely of the occurrence of certain events in consciousness', and leaving such matters in need of separate treatment.

This second response of Wright's turns on the following remark: 'I want to say that . . . in the sense in which an image or mental picture can come before the mind, its intentionality cannot' (p. 31). This strikes me as back to front. The truth is more like this: the *only* thing that comes before the mind, when (as we say) an image does, is its intentionality—the image's content, what it is that is pictured. It is *my wife's face* that comes before my mind when I imagine my wife's face. Nothing else does, at least nothing that is relevant to the fact that I am imagining my wife's face; certainly not some inner analogue of, say, a photograph, with properties describable independently of any content it can be seen as carrying.[6] Wright's wish to say the different thing he wants to say seems to me to call for diagnosis. It looks like reflecting a version of the very principle I protested against: that what *can* come before the mind (be 'a matter purely of the occurrence of certain events in consciousness') *cannot* be such that the very idea of it is—like the intentionality of visualizing—internally connected with extra-mental circumstances.

I agree, of course, that an argument aimed at showing that 'occurrences in a Cartesian theatre of consciousness' cannot sustain internal relations with outer circumstances 'ought to be consistent with the ordinary idea that a pain, say, is an item for introspection'. My point was that the argument *as Wright gave it* flouted that reasonable expectation, just because it implied a principle to the effect that nothing that is 'a matter purely of the occurrence of certain events in consciousness' can sustain such internal relations. And I do not think this is just a point about some perhaps incautious *wording* on Wright's part (the wording I have repeatedly cited). The problem is deeply connected with the way Wright sees the considerations about intentionality as separable—a different prong—from the considerations about the avowability of sensations. I do not dispute that 'the internal relations to the outer which are constituted in the intentionality of psychological items . . . are all of the . . . sunburn-style kind'. What I dispute is the suggestion that this is special to the topics of attitudinal avowals, and not equally true of the topics of phenomenal avowals, so that phenomenal avowals need a quite different treatment.

An implication of this suggestion might be put in the following way (adapting Wright's image). The idea might be that episodes of feeling pain, say, have two aspects: first, the internal connectedness to the normal expression of pain that is embodied in the very idea of feeling pain (this would be parallel to how the idea that someone's arm is sunburned

---

[6] When Wittgenstein says 'Nothing in [the image]', in the passage Wright cites (*Investigations*, pt. II, sect. iii), he means: nothing of that sort. (He is talking about imagining a person, not about imagining an image of a person—which can also happen, as when I visualize the portrait of President Clinton in the hall of University College, Oxford.)

is internally connected to the idea of the sun); and, second, another aspect not constituted by outward-looking internal relations (this would be parallel to the skin's being reddened, blistered, and so forth). And then the idea would be that it is only in this latter aspect that episodes of pain can be items for consciousness—matters 'purely of the occurrence of certain events in consciousness'. This double-aspect conception of, say, episodes of pain, separating their foothold in consciousness (conceived to suit the phrase 'items for consciousness') from their internal connectedness to normal expressions of pain, strikes me as misguided. It purports to yield a picture of what it is for pain to be an item for consciousness, available for avowal; but what it provides would serve at most as a picture of what it is, minimally, for someone (or just something) to feel pain (which is not the same as pain's being available for avowal). If Wright thinks along these lines, it raises a question about whether he is really entitled to disown, as he does, the vestigially Rylean position I found in him.[7]

III

A way to put the point I made in section I above would be to say this: if, with Wright, we suppose that 'the basic philosophical problem of self-knowledge' or 'the cardinal problem of self-knowledge' (p. 22) is constituted by a need to explain epistemic asymmetries between self-knowledge and knowledge of others, then we are left without a satisfying understanding of why the conception of the mental that Wittgenstein undermines is as gripping as it is. On Wright's picture, being captivated by the picture of the mental that he thinks is Wittgenstein's target looks like a rather superficial mistake. But the grip of Wittgenstein's target conception is surely deeper than that. So we should query the credentials of the 'cardinal problem'.

I do think Wright is unsatisfactorily casual when he sets about putting the supposed 'cardinal problem' in place. 'How is it possible that . . . ?'—a form Wright uses—is indeed a good way to express philosophical difficulties of a familiar kind, and some such difficulties may be worth tackling. Whether that is so depends on the specifics of the case. If a question of that shape is to express a determinate philosophical difficulty, it must be asked from a frame of mind in which there is at least a risk of its looking as though whatever the question is asked about is *not* possible. So one's first move, if someone tries to interest

---

[7] The first whole paragraph on p. 131 of his 'Wittgenstein's Later Philosophy of Mind' certainly seems to me to encourage the vestigially Rylean reading.

one in a 'How is it possible?' question, should be to ask: why exactly
does it look to you, and why should it look to me, as if such-and-such
a thing (e.g. baseless authority about oneself) is *not* possible? If the
response to this follow-up question discloses a frame of mind that can
intelligibly and interestingly captivate one, then the question poses a
worthwhile task for philosophy. For contrast, consider a crude version
of a kind of problem that bothered some ancient Greeks (though I need
not claim historical accuracy here). The question is: 'How are false statements possible?' What makes it look as if false statements might not be
possible is a conception according to which meaningfulness in general,
including the meaningfulness of statements, is a matter of a relation—
something along the lines of the name-bearer relation—to something
actual. Such a difficulty in making room for falsehood does not (at least,
not any longer) pose a worthwhile task for philosophy.

Now, as I said, Wright sometimes frames his 'cardinal problem' in
'How is it possible?' questions: for example, 'How is it possible for
subjects to know these matters [the circumstances they can avow] non-
inferentially?' (p. 22). As I have urged, instead of 'non-inferentially', we
ought—by Wright's own lights—to have 'baselessly'. But what exactly
is the difficulty that is supposed to be put before us in these terms? What
exactly is supposed to make it look as if it might *not* be possible for
subjects to know these matters baselessly? Wright simply does not address such questions. Suppose someone said this: baseless self-knowledge
looks as if it ought to be impossible, because it would have to be non-
inferential, and only observational knowledge can be non-inferential,
whereas avowable self-knowledge is not observational. Anyone who
thought along those lines would certainly be in a bind about baseless
self-knowledge; it would seem to him to have contradictory requirements.
Modelling self-knowledge on observation would plainly be of no help
with this bind; offering an observational model would involve blankly
denying part of what would be generating this person's problem. But,
more to the present point, whether the difficulty expressed by the 'How
is it possible?' question, if it is equipped with a background like this,
is one that deserves our attention (as the one about falsehoods does
not) depends on whether we can see how it would be possible to be
gripped by the thought that only observational knowledge can be non-
inferential, so that we would face a real task in trying to dislodge it.
Maybe it would be possible to depict the thought that only observational knowledge can be non-inferential as intelligibly captivating. (I doubt
it.) But Wright makes no moves of the requisite sort, in this or any
similar framework.

Let me try a different tack. In connection with the 'anti-explanatory mantra', Wright suggests that Wittgenstein's diagnostic thought—that philosophical anxieties arise when we are deceived by grammatical analogies—puts pressure on (what Wright sees as) the prohibition of explanatory questions. According to Wright, Wittgenstein's diagnosis, in the case of the supposed problems about self-knowledge, is that we are taken in by surface-grammatical similarities between avowals and reports of observation, and 'that diagnosis itself requires that the explanatory questions which we are required *not* to press in the case of avowals are, by contrast, perfectly properly raised, and answerable, in the case of ordinary reports of observation' (p. 42). Wright thinks that the assimilation of avowals to reports of observation is, according to Wittgenstein, the root of the trouble, and I have been objecting to that. But, even letting that pass, what *same* explanatory questions are these, exactly, that are all right in the case of ordinary reports of observation but, mysteriously, prohibited in the case of avowals? I cannot see how to work out the suggestion; it seems to me altogether too glib.

Wright thinks he has put before us a real philosophical problem: a need to explain the epistemic asymmetries between avowals and knowledge of others. The 'Cartesian' conception is supposed to be a tempting response to this problem, one that it takes a laborious 'deconstruction' to reveal as unacceptable. Once things are seen like that, it is irresistible to look for a different solution, a different 'positive contribution', from Wittgenstein himself. How could clearing away that one response somehow clear away the problem itself? And now of course it seems only natural to go on as Wright does, and contemplate crediting Wittgenstein with at least pointing towards a positive contribution in spite of himself: 'It would be a great achievement of Wittgenstein's discussion if it made it possible to understand how the Default View need not be merely an unphilosophical turning of the back' (p. 41)—although to get this supposed potential contribution properly into view, we would have to see the Default View as opening into things Wittgenstein does not go in for, such as the *Euthyphro* contrast, Wide Cosmological Role, and the like. Discussing self-knowledge in connection with such topics would be engaging in an investigation from whose results, Wright suggests, we might hope to derive a warranted prohibition on *some* explanatory questions, as opposed to intoning an unsupported mantra. But I have been urging that this whole train of thought starts from an illusion. We really have *not* been told what this pressing problem is—what worthwhile puzzlement we are supposed to have about self-knowledge, which is still with us after the observational model has been discarded.

Wright says: 'For most of us, after all, the attraction of philosophy is all about gaining understanding' (p. 43). Well, of course; how could it not be a fine thing to aspire to understanding? But if someone merely points to a phenomenon and demands that it be 'explained', it is a legitimate preliminary to ask what purpose exactly the requested explanation is to serve. Otherwise we simply do not know what we are being asked for. What puzzlement is to be alleviated? Not, presumably, in our case, a puzzlement about causes (which might be met by an explanation of one sort); but then what? If no answer is forthcoming, it is legitimate—not a betrayal of some intellectual obligation—to shrug one's shoulders and move on to some more worthwhile investigation. It would be silly to construe such a gesture, in a dialectical context like this, as implicitly propounding a positive thesis—a Default View—whose content is that 'the demand for understanding is inappropriate'. Failing some response to such questions as 'Why exactly should we find it puzzling that avowals differ from reports about others in the ways they do? Why might it look as if these differences could not be as they are?', no determinate demand for understanding has been made; there is nothing to be the topic of such a thesis. Wright does not bother to supply an answer to such questions; he seems not to acknowledge that there could be any point in pressing them. He reads into Wittgenstein a rejection of a demand for understanding, but he does not bother to respond to scepticism about whether the words he takes to express the supposedly rejected demand actually express any determinate demand at all.

This converges with my point in section I above: the idea of the standing problem—the supposed problem that Wright too easily pronounces 'basic' and 'cardinal'—presupposes what I have urged is an unconvincing account of why we find an observational model of self-knowledge seductive. As Wright presents it, the 'Cartesian' conception is a transparent failure to respond to something whose status as a good question has not been vindicated, or even addressed. As before, of course I am not suggesting that the target of Wittgenstein's negative move is anything but gripping. So I think we need a *different* answer to the question 'Why is the conception of the mental that Wittgenstein attacks so gripping? And how can we dislodge the grip?' That composite question, indeed, has a better claim to capture 'the cardinal problem of self-knowledge'. Wright's demand for an explanation of epistemic asymmetries yields no satisfactory answer to *this* question; that was my point in section I above. To revert at this point to the sketch I gave there of what I have elsewhere suggested: in order to account for the captivatingness of Wittgenstein's target conception, we need to uncover and exorcize a felt need to make out that the inner world is a good place for a stand against the encroachments of a pernicious idealism. And now there is no difficulty about the thought that doing that—satisfactorily responding to what really is 'the cardinal problem'—would *leave nothing needing to be said* to alleviate anxieties about asymmetry. Such anxieties are themselves part of the package that, in this prospect, would have been 'deconstructed'. If we get Wittgenstein's target straight, we need not follow Wright in his seemingly inexorable progression into the supposed 'positive contribution' and its suppression by the 'anti-explanatory mantra'.

I have urged that the conception of the mental that Wittgenstein attacks has a power to captivate that goes much deeper than the feeble claim of an observational model of self-knowledge to yield an explanation of epistemic asymmetries. I need not be concerned to claim, as against what Wright insists, that the conception of the mental is anything but widely found tempting. It is true that children are often struck by the inverted spectrum idea. I can happily acknowledge that when that happens, they are being sucked into at least the fringes of the field of force that attracts us to a 'Cartesian' conception of the mental. The relevant influences are complex, and being subject to them is not just a matter of academic philosophy. When Wright mentions children and the inverted spectrum idea, he is responding to a remark of mine against a suggestion I thought I found in Wright's earlier paper, to the effect that the very idea of the *inner world* is inextricably bound up with the tendentious philosophical idea of 'introspection' as inner *observation*. As I pointed out, this does not fit Wittgenstein, in view of passages such as *Investigations* §423, where he is plainly not hostile to the idea of the inner world. As far as I can see, Wright is still making this false suggestion here, when he says, as if it illustrated how pervasive the 'Cartesian' conception is, that 'the privacy of the inner world is a recurrent idea in literature' (p. 24).

When Wright credits Wittgenstein with the Default View, he is taking it that Wittgenstein's main contribution to philosophical reflection about self-knowledge is an explicit refusal to engage in the activity within which Wright places the 'Cartesian' conception: the activity of explaining the distinctive marks of avowals. Wright concedes that such a move might not be 'unphilosophical', but only if supplemented by something Wittgenstein does not offer: a substantive argument to show that we ought not to seek an explanation to replace the one Wright thinks the 'Cartesian' conception constitutes. I have urged, against this, that Wright has given us no determinate explanatory problem for the 'Cartesian' conception to be seen as a response to, no determinate philosophical activity for Wittgenstein to be understood, in the texts in which Wright finds the Default View, as refusing to engage in. Wittgenstein engages in plenty of philosophy about self-knowledge, but this is not the context in which to understand it.

Of course, it is true that the posture of refusing to play other people's philosophical games is characteristically Wittgensteinian, and it understandably infuriates people who think we ought to be playing those games. What I have been urging is that the particular case of that kind of infuriation to which Wright gives expression is not well placed. Wright is bothered about what he sees as an explicit refusal on Wittgenstein's part to play a certain philosophical game; but he has not presented us, or (so to speak) Wittgenstein, with a sufficient account of what the game is supposed to be to give content to a gesture of refusing to play it.

I do not dispute, however, that a gesture of that kind is typical of Wittgenstein. I shall end with the point that it is not new with him.

Wittgenstein is not the first philosopher to believe in a kind of philosophical advance in which it becomes clear that the moves and counter-moves, felt as dischargings of intellectual obligations, that drove philosophy before the advance were strictly empty, so that in principle the whole 'debate' —which was only the appearance of a debate—can now be cleared away. Here is Kant, talking about how the 'debate' between dogmatists and sceptics looks after he has made his move:

There is properly speaking no polemic in the field of pure reason. Both parties beat the air, and wrestle with their own shadows, since they go beyond the limits of nature, where there is nothing that they can seize and hold with their dogmatic grasp. Fight as they may, the shadows which they cleave asunder grow together again forthwith, like the heroes of Valhalla, to disport themselves anew in the bloodless contests.[8]

I think that this conception of philosophical advance *is* new with Kant; before Kant the posture was that one set one's predecessors straight, not that one revealed that they had been engaged in no more than shadowboxing. Of course, and unsurprisingly, in Kant the idea does not yet have its full-fledged Wittgensteinian form. For Kant, what constitutes the advance is itself a patently philosophical move. We do not find in Kant the special twist we find in Wittgenstein, that the apparent need to make such moves—even in order to reveal that previous apparent moves were only shadow-boxing—ushers itself off the stage. But even that is not unprecedented. Let me end with this thought: consider how comic it could easily seem to label Hegel 'a philosophical quietist'. But in the only sense in which the label fits Wittgenstein, it also fits at least the young Hegel. If this thought could be made to stick, it might discourage the idea that 'quietism' is a matter of making things easy for oneself in philosophical reflection.

---

[8] Kant, *Critique of Pure Reason*, A756/B784.

3

Conscious Attitudes, Attention, and Self-Knowledge

CHRISTOPHER PEACOCKE

———•———

What is involved in the consciousness of a conscious, 'occurrent' propositional attitude, such as a thought, a sudden conjecture, or a conscious decision? And what is the relation of such consciousness to attention? I hope the intrinsic interest of these questions provides sufficient motivation to allow me to start by addressing them. We will not have a full understanding either of consciousness in general or of attention in general until we have answers to these questions. I think there are constitutive features of these states which can be identified by broadly philosophical investigation, and in the early part of this chapter I will try to do some of that identification.

Beyond the intrinsic interest of the topic, the nature of such conscious attitudes is highly pertinent to a philosophical account of psychological self-knowledge. So I will also say something about the significance of the constitutive features of these conscious attitudes for a philosophical account of how it can be that a thinker has a distinctive kind of knowledge of some of his mental states. The general challenge in this area is to find anything intermediate between the unexceptionable but uninformative, on the one hand, and the absolutely unbelievable on the other.[1]

[1] In addition to the presentation at the 1995 St Andrews conference on self-knowledge, versions of this material were given in lectures in Oxford in 1994, in a talk to a conference on consciousness and attention organized by the Institute for Advanced Studies at London University in 1995, and to seminars and a colloquium at New York University and the Graduate Center, CUNY, in spring of 1996. I am particularly grateful to Michael Martin for his detailed, sympathetic, and very helpful comments delivered at the St Andrews meeting. In particular, he raised the question which opens section IV below. My thanks also to Paul Boghossian, Tyler Burge, Tony Atkinson, John Campbell, Martin Davies, John McDowell, Thomas Nagel, Stephen Schiffer, Barry Smith, Michael Tye, and Crispin Wright for observations that have influenced the present version. The later stages of preparation of this paper were carried out with the support of a Leverhulme Research Professorship, which I very gratefully acknowledge.

I   CONSCIOUS ATTITUDES AND THE OCCUPATION OF ATTENTION

Perceptual experiences and sensations, on the one hand, and so-called occurrent conscious propositional attitudes, on the other, differ in many respects. But there is one property they share. They both contribute to what, subjectively, it is like for the person who enjoys them. A person may try to recall who was Prime Minister of Czechoslovakia when the Soviet Union invaded. It then occurs to this person that Dubček was the Prime Minister. Its so occurring to him contributes to the specification of what it's like for the person then. It would be subjectively different for the person if it were to occur to him (falsely) that it was Husak; and subjectively different again if nothing comes to mind about who was Prime Minister. This example is a case of memory, but the point is in no way restricted to memory. The same is true of ordinary thinking in general, as when it suddenly strikes you that you have left the kitchen tap (faucet) running. In that case, your thought is not a conclusion inferred by you from other premisses; but reasoned conclusions may be conscious in this familiar sense too. When, on an appointing committee, you conclude in thought 'On balance, Smith would be the best person', your so concluding can be a partial specification of what it's like for you then. On the general point that occurrent conscious propositional attitudes are often subjective states, I am in agreement with such writers as Flanagan (1992: 214) and Goldman (1993: sect. 8). It is important to note, though, that acceptance of this point does not require any internalist theory of conceptual content. I would want to defend the view that the intentional contents which, in each of these examples, contribute to the specification of what it's like for the thinker are composed of concepts which are in part externally individuated.[2] I will return to this issue.

When a thought occurs to you, or you make a conscious judgement, your attention is engaged. Your attention will often be shifted from whatever external events may have been the object of your attention at the time. The engagement of your attention in conscious thought is by no means confined to those moments at which thoughts occur to you or you make a judgement. Any one of the following can occupy your attention:

the very activity of trying to find a proof of a particular proposition
trying to reach a conclusion on the basis of conflicting evidence
trying to remember something
trying to find evidence for a particular hypothesis.

[2] Here I differ from Goldman.

Ryle, whose late writings on thinking do not contain the slightest hint of behaviourism, once considered an example involving a blindfolded chess-player. Ryle noted that 'when, after struggling to remember the positions of the pieces, the chess-player does remember, then his seeing them in his mind's eye, if he does do this, is not something by means of which he gets himself to remember. It is the goal, not a vehicle, of his struggle to remember' (1971: 398). Ryle is emphasizing that the occurrence of a memory image cannot be identified with, or taken as the vehicle of, the thinking that led to the image. My present point is that this thinking—what Ryle calls 'the struggle to remember'—is itself occupying the player's attention prior to any success he may have in that project.

If we are to describe correctly the relation between conscious thought and attention, we must respect the distinction between the *object* of attention and what is *occupying* attention. In a normal case of perceptual attention to some physical object, feature, or event, there is something to which the subject is attending. The object of attention is perceived; it causally affects the subject. No doubt we may want to say that there is, or can be, some sort of object of attention in a pure case of perceptual hallucination. But such cases are plausibly understood as parasitic on the central case of genuine perception. In the case of pure hallucination, it is for the subject as if there were a genuine object of attention.

In conscious thought, by contrast, there is no object of attention (nor is it as if there is). The notion of an object of attention which is inapplicable in conscious thought is that of an *experienced* object, event, or state of affairs. In mental states other than those of conscious thought, a genuine object of one's attention might be a material object, or a continuing event, or the continuing or changing features of an object or event, or an object's changing relations to other objects or events. Having a sensation is also an experience. A pain, for instance, can equally be an object of attention. But thinking is not experiencing. There are objects of thought, but an object of thought is not thereby an experienced object, and is not an object of attention in the sense in question.

All the same, in conscious thought, your attention is still *occupied*—as it is also occupied in the perceptual cases and in cases of imagination. It would be a crude *non sequitur* to move from the true point that there is no object of attention in conscious thought to the false conclusion that conscious thought does not involve attention. I will attempt some further analysis of the notion of the occupation of attention a few paragraphs hence.

It has to be said that those who have recognized the involvement of attention in conscious thought have not always been helpful to its best elaboration. It is a great virtue of William James's justly famous discussion of thought and attention that he recognizes a general category of what he calls 'intellectual attention'. But the effect is somewhat spoiled by his distinguishing the intellectual variety of attention by its alleged distinctive objects, which he says are 'Ideal or represented objects'.[3] It emerges from his other discussions that by 'Ideal object' he means a certain kind of concept. But genuine objects of attention are, in the central cases, experienced objects. Correlatively, in central cases genuine objects of attention are also such that their continuing and changing properties at the time of the state involving attention causally contribute to the way that object is given in the conscious state. Neither of the objects James proposes as objects of intellectual attention, concepts of a certain kind or the objects thought about (the 'represented objects'), need stand in that sort of relation to conscious thought. I suspect that it is not an accident that those, like James, who have supposed that there are objects of intellectual attention have also been drawn to perceptual models of knowledge of one's own mental states. It was James who wrote, in making the transition from the volume of the *Principles of Psychology* containing his famous chapters on the stream of thought, attention, and memory, to the volume dealing with perception, 'After inner perception, outer perception!' (1983: 651, the first sentence of vol. ii).

To believe in a single, general kind of attention which is occupied both in cases of perceptual attention and in cases of conscious thought is not to be committed to a perceptual model of thought, or to a perceptual model of our knowledge of it. In addition to the applicability to both perceptual attention and conscious thought of a pre-theoretical ordinary notion of there being something it's like for their subject, there are also some explanatory consequences of the hypothesis that there is a single, general kind of attention of which perceptual and sensational attention and conscious thought and imagination are all subspecies. It is a familiar truth about attention that any one of these kinds of attention can interrupt any one of the others. Perceptual attention can be interrupted by conscious thought; conscious thought can be interrupted by external events which capture the thinker's attention; either of these two subspecies of the occupation of attention can be interrupted by imagination; and so on. What we have here is not merely some family resemblance between varieties of conscious states, but apparently some form of competition for the exclusive use of a limited single faculty of attention. The familiar facts about attention are explained if there is a single, suitably high-level resource, drawn upon by either perception,

[3] Second paragraph of the section 'The Varieties of Attention' in the chapter 'Attention' in James 1983, vol. i.

conscious thought, or imagination, a resource with access to some of its own recent states and to memory representations generated by its own previous states. I do not say that it is absolutely impossible to explain any one of these facts in some other way. I conjecture, though, that other explanations will be *ad hoc*, and unable to explain the full range of familiar facts. For instance, one might try to explain the facts about the interruption of the occupation of attention in thought by perceived events as follows. One might say that there are two radically different kinds of attention, drawing on quite different resources, but that there is some separate explanation altogether of why a normal thinker is subject to severe limitations in his ability to be in both kinds of state in parallel. There is, though, a real danger that any such theory will need to postulate some additional system which favours now one of the two alleged attentional systems, now the other, but cannot favour both. This additional system would appear to have just the features of the limited high-level resource to which this account was proposed as an alternative.

I now attempt some further analysis of the occupation of attention by conscious thought. When you have a thought, it does not normally come neat, unconnected with other thoughts and contents. Rather, in having a particular thought, you often appreciate certain of its relations to other thoughts and contents. You have a thought, and you may be aware that its content is a consequence, perhaps gratifying, perhaps alarming, of a conclusion you have just reached; or you may be aware that its content is evidence for some hypothesis that you have formulated; or indeed that it is a counter-example to the hypothesis. Now when you think a particular thought, there is of course no intention in advance to think that particular thought. But there can be an intention to think a thought which stands in a certain relation to other thoughts or contents. It is thought carried out in accordance with such an intention that is directed, as opposed to idle, thought.

The relation that one intends one's subsequent thoughts to bear to one's earlier thoughts may be that of logical consequence, or that of being evidence for the earlier thought, or that of being an amusing observation about some event, or the like, if one is engaged in writing an after-dinner speech. As always, there is a distinction between the intended and the actual relation a later thought bears to earlier thoughts. On a particular occasion, there may in fact be no intended relation, but an actual thought appreciated as bearing certain relations to others may none the less occur to the thinker. Or there may be an intended relation, but one may be distracted from one's goal in thought by the occurrence of a thought bearing a relation different from the intended relation; or, as in the case of the uninspired drafter of the after-dinner speech, nothing bearing the intended relation may come to mind.

It is worth reflecting further on the striking fact about attention and consciousness that your attention can be occupied by your trying to do something in thought. Your state is subjectively different in the case in which you are trying, in thought, to achieve a particular kind of result from that in which you are casually drifting in thought. This can be so even if the same sequence of thoughts occur to you in the each of the two cases. Though striking, the point seems to be a special case of a more general phenomenon. In general, a subject's trying to do something (and what it is he is trying to do) contributes to what it is like for the subject. It does so in a way which goes beyond any occupation of attention by external events, sensations, or thoughts. The phenomenon can be illustrated, beyond the realm of conscious thought, in the first instance by some perceptual cases.

Consider an example in which doing something is occupying your attention. Your attention might be occupied by driving down a narrow street without scraping the cars parked on each side, or by getting the cursor from the top left-hand corner to the bottom right-hand corner of your computer screen, or by getting someone with whom your are in conversation to decide to take a certain course of action without pressurizing them. Your attention being occupied in such actions cannot be identified with your attending to the events in the external world which they involve. In the example of driving down the narrow street, you could attend to exactly the same external movements and objects without being the driver at all. Similarly, in the example of moving the cursor, your pattern of attention to motions and symbols on the screen could be exactly the same as when someone else is operating the mouse which controls the cursor. Nor can the action occupying your attention be identified with attention to some further external events or perceptual states. In the driving example, it does not consist in your attending to the movements of the steering-wheel, or to sensations of pressure on the wheels and pedals. The experienced driver will not be attending to such things when his attention is occupied with the action of driving down the narrow street. Nor, again, is the object of your attention any event of trying (whatever that might mean).

So it seems that the occupation of your attention by your doing something always goes beyond mere perceptual attention to particular events or objects. It follows that there could not be events or objects your mere perceptual attention to which constitutes the occupation of your attention by your doing something. There could not be, because trying, in thought or action, to achieve a certain goal is a subspecies of consciousness in its own right, and, when present, is additional to perceptual attention and the occupation of attention by occurrent thoughts. To make this point is not to deny that attention is a perceptual phenomenon in at least one important respect. Attention is a perceptual phenomenon at least in the sense that a full specification of what it is like for a perceiver must include a statement of which of the perceived objects, events, properties, or relations he is attending to in having that experience. The present point is just that a specification of whether the subject's attention is occupied in trying to do something must also be included in an account of what it is like for him.

Corresponding to this relation between attention and action are certain divisions between imaginative possibilities. You can imagine seeing your hands and arms making certain movements in front of you, from your standpoint in the imagined world as the owner of the hands and arms. That is one thing, but it is another visually to imagine moving your hands and arms to make those motions. In characterizing imaginings, we can distinguish between what is suppositionally imagined to hold in the imagined world and what it is imagined to be like for the subject in the imagined world. When you imagine seeing a suitcase with a cat wholly obscured behind it, you suppositionally imagine (S-imagine) that there is a cat behind the suitcase. Suppositionally imagining that there is a cat behind the suitcase is to be distinguished from imagining what it would be like for someone in the imagined world— that is, imagining from the inside the subjective state of the person seeing the suitcase in the imagined world.[4] Now the distinctive contribution made to imagination by imagining doing something seems to fall on the side of what it is like subjectively for the person in the imagined world, rather than merely on the side of what is suppositionally imagined. This is just what one would expect in advance, given the general principle that to non-suppositionally imagine something is to imagine being in a subjective state of a certain kind, and given that doing something contributes to the specification of a subjective state. The point that imagining doing something falls on the non-suppositional side also receives some confirmation when one reflects on the different requirements for suppositionally imagining that one is doing something, as opposed to imagining (not merely suppositionally) doing it. To imagine non-suppositionally doing something requires that one know how do it. For this kind of imagining, only someone who knows how to play the 'Appassionata' Sonata can imagine, from the inside, playing it. This last species of imagining is distinct from imagining moving one's hands

[4] For further discussion of the distinction see Peacocke 1985.

on the keyboard in any old fashion and hearing the sounds of the
'Appassionata' come out. Merely to suppositionally imagine that one is
playing that sonata does not require any knowledge of how to play it.

There is disagreement within psychology about the subpersonal mechanisms underlying perceptual attention at the personal level. There would,
though, be less disagreement on the proposition that perceptual attention serves a function of selection. It selects particular objects or events,
or particular properties and relations of objects and events, in such a
way as to improve the perceiver's informational state concerning the
selected items. The details of the nature of the improvement are a matter for empirical investigation. The improvement might be a matter of
more detailed, and new, kinds of informational content; or it might
be a matter of the speed with which states of given informational content are attained. Whether this capacity for improved informational
states for selected items is used effectively or wisely is another matter.
Attention is a resource which may be drawn upon whatever the subject's purposes.

If what I have said about the occupation of attention by conscious
thought is along the right lines, then the occupation of attention at least
in directed thought also performs a function of selection. One can expect
that the parallel will not be precise, just because of the difference noted
between the presence of objects of attention in the perceptual and sensational cases and their absence in the case of conscious thought. None
the less, when a thinker is engaged in directed thinking, he is in effect
selecting a certain kind of path through the space of possible thoughts
—thought contents—available to him. There is not selection for particular thoughts, of course: that would involve the rejected view that there
are intentions to think certain particular thoughts. But there is selection
of a certain kind of thought, given by the content of the thinker's aim
in thought. Without such selection, human thought would be chaotic,
at the mercy of associational connections not necessarily at all pertinent
to the thinker's current goals. And as in the perceptual case, this capacity may be used wisely and effectively, or not.

Our ordinary, everyday notion of a conscious attitude does not apply
only to occurrent attitudes. Each one of us has myriad conscious beliefs, intentions, desires, hopes, fears, suspicions, and the rest, and obviously these cannot all be contributing to what it's like for each one of us
at any given time. Often when we talk of a conscious attitude we are
concerned with an underlying state, capable of producing manifestations in conscious occurrences which do contribute to a specification of
what it's like for the subject. In the case of a conscious belief that p, some
of these manifestations in consciousness—judgements and propositional

impressions that *p*—may be prompted by an explicit question of whether or not it's the case that *p*. Much else may also trigger such a conscious state. It may be triggered by reflection on related subject-matters, on other things learned in the same circumstances, or indeed on virtually anything that associative memory may link to the belief that *p*. In the case of belief, we will also want to distinguish what is already believed from beliefs formed when the issue arises. Length of time to conscious retrieval, and difficulty of retrieval or formation, which will itself be relative to the thinker's current intellectual and perceptual context, make these partially dispositional notions of a conscious but non-occurrent propositional attitude essentially a matter of degree along many dimensions.

II · CONSCIOUSLY BASED SELF-ASCRIPTIONS

Conscious thoughts and occurrent attitudes can, like other conscious mental events, give the thinker reasons for action and judgement. They do so also in the special case in which they give the thinker a reason for self-ascribing an attitude to the content which occurs to the thinker, provided our thinker is conceptually equipped to make the self-ascription. On the position I am developing, we can, for instance, take at face value the statement that someone's reason for self-ascribing the belief that Dubček was Prime Minister of Czechoslovakia when the Soviet Union invaded is his just then judging that Dubček was Prime Minister at the time of the invasion. To spell it out in more detail, we can distinguish three stages a thinker may pass through when asked 'Whom do you believe was Prime Minister there when the Soviet Union invaded?' First, after reflection, he may have

(1) an apparent propositional memory that Dubček was Prime Minister then. Since he is, we may suppose, taking memory in these circumstances, and for this sort of subject-matter, at face value, he moves to endorse the content of the apparent memory, and makes

(2) a judgement that Dubček was Prime Minister then.

This judgement makes it rational for him to make

(3) a self-ascription of the belief that Dubček was Prime Minister then.

To say that (2) is the thinker's reason for making the judgement in (3) is not to say that he infers the self-ascription from a premise that he has made such a first-order judgement. A mental event can be a thinker's reason for doing something (including the special case in which what is done is making a judgement), without the case being one of inference. An experience of pain can be a thinker's reason for judging that he is in pain. To try to construe this as a case of judgement reached by inference would make it impossible to give an epistemology of the self-ascription of sensations. (Am I supposed to rationally reach the conclusion that I am in pain from the premiss that I am in pain?) The pain case shows too that the model need not be that of perception, either. The conscious pain itself, and not some alleged perception of it, is reason-giving.

Let us call an ascription of an attitude with a certain content, by a subject to himself, made for the reason that he has an occurrent conscious attitude of a certain kind, with that same content, a 'consciously based self-ascription'. In the example as imagined, the self-ascription of the belief that Dubček was Prime Minister when the Soviet Union invaded is a consciously based self-ascription.[5] This characterization of a consciously based self-ascription also includes cases in which the self-ascription is made on the basis of the conscious occurrence of a mental event of the very kind ascribed, as when you judge 'It has just occurred to me that p' because indeed it has just occurred to you that p. Reaching a self-ascription of a belief by basing it upon a conscious state is of course only one of several means, each of them special to self-ascription, by which a thinker may knowledgeably come to self-ascribe a belief. It is a very important point that some knowledgeable self-ascriptions are not based on any intermediate conscious state at all.[6] I return to those cases and their significance in section V below. My task in this section and the next is just to try to understand the consciously based self-ascriptions better.

The description of a self-ascription made on a particular occasion as consciously based should not be regarded as in competition with the description of it as reached by Evans's (1982) procedure. In employing Evans's procedure, 'I get myself in a position to answer the question whether I believe that p by putting into operation whatever procedure

---

[5] I should also emphasize that the procedure discussed in the example given here is considered as a procedure for reaching beliefs, where belief is understood as a form of acceptance. We do, as Michael Martin emphasized to me, sometimes use 'belief' for a feeling of conviction; the above procedure is not meant to apply to those interesting cases, which need a different treatment.

[6] The case in which there is no intermediate conscious state is considered also in Peacocke 1996: 121. There are other kinds of cases as well. The self-ascription may, for instance, be contextually self-verifying—the case which Tyler Burge (1988, 1996) has investigated in detail.

I have for answering the question whether *p*' (1982: 225). Searching your memory to see if you have any information about who was Prime Minister when the Soviet Union invaded is precisely one of the methods you have for answering the first-order question of who was Prime Minister then. Coming to self-ascribe a belief on the basis of the deliverances of stored information is a special case of use of Evans's procedure, rather than any kind of rival to it.

The idea of consciously based self-ascriptions is sometimes regarded with great suspicion. In fact, in respect of the rational sensitivities required for consciously based self-ascription to proceed properly, these ascriptions are importantly similar to other, very different cases. Consider for a moment beliefs which are reached by inference. When a belief is reached by inference from certain premisses, the contents of some of the thinker's states are taken by the thinker to support the inferred conclusion, and they do so in the case of valid inference. Now the thinker who successfully reaches new beliefs by inference has to be sensitive not only to the contents of his initial beliefs. He has also to be sensitive to the fact that his initial states are *beliefs*. He will not be forming beliefs by inference from the contents of his desires, hopes, or daydreams.

Another pertinent case is that of beliefs reached by endorsing the content of one of the thinker's perceptual experiences. Here too the thinker makes a transition—and this time not an inferential transition —from one state with a certain content to a belief with an overlapping, or an appropriately related, content (depending on your views about the nature of perceptual content). Again, the sensitivity does not involve merely some grasp of relations of content between the two states involved in the transition. The thinker is also sensitive to which kind of initial state it is that has the content. He will not be prepared to take the content of imaginings, for instance, at face value in the same way.

In cases of consciously based self-ascription of attitudes and experiences, a thinker similarly makes a transition not only from the content of some initial state, but also because the initial state is of a certain kind. There is, though, a difference from the cases of inference and perception mentioned in the last paragraph. In the case of consciously based self-ascription, the distinction between those events which are occurrent attitudes of the right kind to sustain the resulting judgement and those which are not is a distinction which is (partially at least) conceptualized by the thinker. The self-ascriber thinks of his state as belief, or as experience of a certain kind, or whatever it may be. He also thinks of himself as the state's subject. Possession of these important conceptual capacities does, of course, go far beyond the ability to make judgements rationally in response to one's own conscious states.

Taking short cuts in reaching knowledgeable judgements, without making explicit in conscious thought all the intermediate steps, is a ubiquitous phenomenon in human thought. Judgements in which a thinker self-ascribes a particular attitude with a particular content are no exception. For instance, many a thinker, when asked our earlier question about the Prime Minister of Czechoslovakia, will move straight from the apparent memory (1), in a context in which the deliverances of memory are taken at face value, to the self-ascription in (3). Such short cuts are permissible, and can still result in knowledgeable judgements, provided they are taken only in circumstances in which the thinker could take the longer route, with each transition in the longer route made for the right sort of reasons. This is not to make a concession to a purely reliabilist theory of knowledge. A pure reliabilism would not require the possibility of taking the longer route with full rationalization at each step.

It is worth noting a certain phenomenon when a short cut is taken. We can continue with the example of the short cut in the Dubček example. For the thinker who takes this short cut, the conscious apparent memory (1) is certainly causally and rationally influential in producing his self-ascription of the belief that Dubček was Prime Minister at the time. However, even in a context in which memory is taken at face value, an apparent propositional memory that Dubček was Prime Minister then is *not* a reason for self-ascribing the belief the Dubček was Prime Minister then. This may be puzzling: what is going on here?

What we have here can be called 'a failure of pseudo-transitivity'. The apparent memory gives a reason for judging that Dubček was Prime Minister then; the occurrence of such a judgement gives a reason for self-ascribing the belief that he was; but the apparent memory does not give a reason for the self-ascription. More generally: from

(4)   A conscious event of φ-ing gives a thinker reason to J that p,

taken together with

(5)   A conscious event of J-ing that p gives a thinker a reason to H that p,

it does not follow that

(6)   A conscious event of φ-ing gives a thinker a reason to H that p.

The Dubček example is an illustration of (6) not following from (4) and (5).

I call this a failure only of 'pseudo-transitivity', because what is rationalized in (4) is not literally the same as what does the rationalizing in (5). What is rationalized in (4) is the action-type of J-ing that *p*. What does the rationalizing in (5) is the occurrence of an actual event of J-ing that *p*. This indeed is the key to why pseudo-transitivity should fail. There must actually be an event of J-ing that *p* for the thinker to be given a reason to H that *p*. (4) does not itself ensure that there is such an event, even if there is a conscious event of ϕ-ing. The thinker may not act on the reason which is given by the event of ϕ-ing. We should, indeed, positively expect pseudo-transitivity to fail when what gives the reason is the occurrence of a conscious event of a certain kind.

By contrast, when the rationalizing is done just by a relation between contents, transitivity must hold when it is conclusive reasons which are in question. From the premisses that

    (7)   *p* gives a conclusive reason for accepting *q*

and

    (8)   *q* gives a conclusive reason for accepting *r*

it does follow that

    (9)   *p* gives a conclusive reason for accepting *r*.

The conclusiveness of the reason stated in (8) does not require anyone to be in any particular state of consciously accepting that *q*. The relation of conclusive support holds between the contents themselves, independently of any psychological relations any particular thinker bears to them. What, then, would be a general characterization of the cases in which pseudo-transitivity fails? It fails in instances where the content of the rationalized judgement (or other attitude) mentioned in the second premiss is fixed at least in part by the nature of the psychological state which does the rationalizing, and not just by the content of that state. In a case of pure logical inference, it would be fixed just by the content of that state, and transitivity would not fail.

Am I cheating by trading on the fact that I have chosen a relation of conclusive support to illustrate cases in which transitivity does hold? No cheating is occurring here. This is shown by the fact that even in cases where the reasons are conclusive, as long as the rationalizing of the content of the final judgement (or other attitude) is done by the nature of the rationalizing psychological state, and not just its content, pseudo-transitivity still fails. Thus we have both

    (10)   An experience of pain gives a thinker a reason to judge that he is in pain

and

> (11)   A judgement that he is in pain gives a thinker reason to self-ascribe the belief that he is in pain.

It still does not follow, however, that

> (12)   An experience of pain gives a thinker reason to self-ascribe the belief that he is in pain.

III   STEERING BETWEEN INTERNAL INTROSPECTIONISM AND A 'NO REASONS' ACCOUNT

The position on consciously based self-ascription which I have sketched so far occupies an intermediate stance between two more extreme positions, elements of which can be found in some recent discussions. One of these more extreme positions can be called the 'no reasons' account of self-ascription of attitudes. At the other extreme is a form of internalist introspection. Those who have leant towards these positions may not have intended them to apply to consciously based self-ascriptions. I think it will provide us with a better understanding of such self-ascriptions if we consider how neither extreme can be applicable to them.

The spirit of the 'no reasons' account can be introduced by quoting a paragraph from Shoemaker. Shoemaker is discussing the self-ascription of belief, and he writes:

Compare another sort of case in which mental states 'automatically' give rise to other mental states—that in which a set of beliefs, B, give rise to a further belief, C, whose content is an obvious consequence (deductive or inductive) of their contents. No doubt there is a microstory (as yet unknown) about how this takes place. But one sort of microstory seems out of the question. It would be wrong-headed to suppose that having identified the underlying mechanisms or structures in which the possession of the various beliefs (and the various concepts they involve) is implemented, one must postulate *additional* mechanisms, completely independent of these, to explain how it is that B gives rise to C. Given a neural or other subpersonal mechanism, nothing could justify regarding that mechanism as an implementation of a given belief if the nature of the mechanism is not such that the microstory of its existence and operation involves an implementation of the inferential role of that belief (and so involves relations to a larger system). It is equally wrong, I think, to suppose that having identified the underlying mechanisms in which beliefs, thoughts, sensations, and so on, are implemented, and those in which the possession of concepts of these is implemented, one must postulate yet other mechanisms, independent of these, that explain how it is that these states give rise to introspective beliefs about themselves. (Shoemaker 1993: 78–9)

It should be uncontroversial that it is an error to postulate mechanisms 'completely independent of' the mechanisms linking the subpersonal realizing states. Such complete independence would lead to familiar problems about overdetermination. But complete independence is not the issue I want to focus on. I want to consider the position of someone who says that there never is a personal-level, causal, reason-giving explanation of why a thinker has the belief that he has a certain belief, in normal cases. There is, according to this 'no reasons' position, a genuine explanation at the subpersonal level, but that is not at the personal, reason-giving level. It is written into the functional role of the concept of belief, according to this position, that normally when someone has a first-order belief, he is willing to self-ascribe that first-order belief (if he has the concepts of himself and of belief, and if he considers the question). This, according to the 'no reasons' position I am considering, is a definitional remark. It is like the remark that valves allow only a one-way flow. It should not be confused with a causal explanation.

The epistemology which naturally accompanies the 'no reasons' theory is that of reliabilism. The reliabilist epistemology in this area is summarized by Shoemaker:

Our minds are so constituted, or our brains are so wired, that, for a wide range of mental states, one's being in a certain mental state produces in one, under certain conditions, the belief that one is in that mental state. This is what our own introspective access to our own mental states consists in. . . . The beliefs thus produced will count as knowledge, not because of the quantity or quality of evidence on which they are based (for they are based on no evidence), but because of the reliability of the mechanism by which they are produced. (1994: 268)

Reliabilism in this area may be elaborated in various different ways. Shoemaker's own view is that 'believing that one believes that P can be just believing that P plus having a certain level of rationality, intelligence and so on' (1994: 289). On that version of the approach, it would, as Shoemaker immediately notes, be wrong to regard the second-order belief as caused by the first-order belief. But equally, someone who holds that the first-order belief causes the second-order self-ascription, in ordinary cases, could endorse the reliabilist epistemology. What will be common to all variants of the 'no reasons' theory is the claim that there are no reasons in the offing of the sort which would be required for the second-order beliefs to be knowledge on any more reason-based approach to epistemology.

The 'no reasons' theory, then, is one of the two extreme positions I want to identify.[7] The other extreme position is occupied by the internalist introspectionist, exemplified by Alvin Goldman in some of his recent writings (1993). The internalist introspectionist holds not only that conscious attitudes are subjective states, such that there is something it is like to have them. He believes further in an internalist theory of content. The internalist introspectionist holds that there is some level of intentional content of which we have knowledge, which is not individuated by anything outside the thinker's head, neither his perceptual nor his social environment. For this internalist introspectionist, any externally individuated features of a state—any such feature of its content or of its role—are not available in consciousness itself.

It seems to me that each of these two extreme positions is correct in the criticisms available to it of the position at the other extreme, and that each of them is wrong in its own positive account. Suppose it consciously occurs to someone that that liquid (presented in perception) is water. The content here has many externalist features, even for someone who does not endorse Evans's (1982) and McDowell's (1984) 'object-dependent' view of senses. The content of the perceptual demonstrative involves the liquid being presented as occupying a certain region of space relative to the thinker, and such contents can be elucidated only in externalist ways (Peacocke 1993). The concept 'water' is itself the topic of some of the most famous externalist discussions (e.g. Putnam 1975b). When it occurs to you that the liquid is water, or you hear someone else asserting that it is so, it seems that these very externally individuated conceptual contents enter the content of your consciousness. We do not have a full description of your subjective state if we omit what you are thinking or what you hear the other person as saying.

Actually, infidelity to the phenomenology would be the least of it. It would be an epistemological disaster to suppose that, in having a conscious belief, or in understanding someone else's utterance, we are aware only of something weaker than an externally individuated intentional content. For it is a datum that we do know the full, ordinary, externally individuated intentional content of our own thoughts, and of other

---

[7] I have drawn elements of the 'no reasons' theory from Shoemaker's writings, but I should note explicitly that I have not found an endorsement of it by him in so many words. I should also note, without developing the point, that if introspection involves the occupation of attention, and the treatment of the occupation of attention in section I above is roughly correct, then it is less tempting to elucidate introspection simply in terms of the production, in some specified way, of a certain kind of *belief* (as one of the sentences quoted from Shoemaker in the preceding paragraph suggests it can be).

people's utterances, without reliance on inferences from, or presuppositions about, something weaker, which is all, in some alleged stricter sense, we would be aware of on the internalist introspectionist's view. How this ordinary non-inferential awareness and knowledge of one's own thoughts, and of the meaning of others' utterances, is possible at all would remain a mystery on the internalist introspectionist's view.

The problem would not be confined to knowledge of the content of one's own thoughts, and of the meaning of others' utterances. Let us take it as granted that the content of non-occurrent beliefs, desires, and intentions is externally individuated, and likewise for the representational content of perceptual states. To deny then that conscious occurrent attitudes have an externally individuated content would lead to trouble on the following three fronts.

(a) It is a truism that conscious thinking can lead rationally to the formation of beliefs which constitute knowledge. How could such belief formation have the status of knowledge if the content of the formed belief is externally individuated, but that of the rational thinking leading to it is not? The belief formed would require that the thinker stand in certain environmental relations which, on the internalist introspectionist's account, are not ensured by the contents of the conscious thoughts which rationally produce the belief.[8]

(b) Conscious thought can provide the rational explanation of an action under one of its environmental descriptions, such as reaching in one direction rather than another. Yet it seems that an action, under the given environmental, relational description, cannot be rationalized by conscious thoughts which are not relationally individuated. There would be a gap between the content of the thoughts and the pertinent relational property of the action which is, to all appearances, the property explained by the thought.

(c) If the content of perceptual experiences is, at least in part, externally individuated, then conscious judgements made rational by perceptual experience would involve a massive loss of information and specificity if the content of the conscious judgement were not externally individuated. I see no reason in principle why this information must be thrown away in rational thought. As a fully rational intermediary between perception on the one side and belief, desire, intention, and action on the other, it seems that conscious thought must retain the externalist character of what rationalizes it, and what in turn it rationalizes.

---

[8] This argument has certain affinities to that given in Peacocke 1994, in support of the conclusion that if a subpersonal psychology is to be capable of explaining externally individuated propositional attitudes, the explanatory states introduced by the psychology must also be externally individuated.

It would be possible to continue in this vein, but the general problems which are emerging are enough to motivate a question: why should anyone feel forced into a position in which they deny that conscious, occurrent states with externally individuated contents can give reasons for thought and action, including, among others, knowledgeable self-ascriptions?

There seem to be three reasons influencing those who make the denial. The first is the idea that the nature of knowledgeable self-ascription of intentional states is inconsistent with externalism about content. This was certainly influencing Goldman, who supports his view by observing that 'Cognizers seem able to discern their mental contents—what they believe, plan or desire to do—without consulting their environment' (1993: 25). Like many others, I hold that cognizers are indeed able to do this, but that this truth is consistent with externalism about content. Burge (1988) and Davidson (1987) were pioneers in addressing the question of how the reconciliation is to be effected. I discuss the correct way of effecting the general reconciliation elsewhere (Peacocke 1996), and to keep this chapter within tolerable bounds, must simply refer the reader to those several discussions.

A second factor influencing those who reject the conception I have been outlining is reflection on particular examples. Even an objector who believes in the consistency of externalism with a range of authoritative intentional self-knowledge may still have a more specific concern. He may worry that it is subjectively exactly the same for someone on Earth who has the occurrent thought that water is wet as it is for his twin on Twin Earth who has the occurrent thought that twater is wet. A natural way of elaborating this second source of concern runs as follows. When John thinks that water is wet, and Twin John thinks that twater is wet, they are thinking of different liquids in exactly the same way—only their contexts differ.[9] According to this second objection, the subjective character of the occurrent thought that water is wet is fully captured by this way—'W' we can call it—in which water is thought of, together with the way—<is wet>, let us say—in which the property of being wet is thought of. These ways, the objection continues, are common to the thought that water is wet and the thought that twater is wet. So according to this objector,

John thinks that water is wet

will receive some analysis with the initial structure

Thinks (John, water, W^<is wet>)

---

[9] Their thoughts are *relationally similar* in the sense discussed in Peacocke 1996: 150–1.

while

Twin John thinks that twater is wet

receives some analysis with the initial structure

Thinks (Twin John, twater, W^<is wet>).

Our objector's point can then be formulated concisely: it is that only the third term of this relation contributes to the subjective character of the occurrent thought.

The objector who presses this point need not be disagreeing with the main thrust of the argument I have been presenting. The objector can agree that the fact that it occurs to a thinker that water is wet can contribute to fixing what it is like for him then. He is just offering a particular view of the way in which the first-order content of this occurrent thought is to be analysed. Equally, this objector can be hospitable to the idea that a self-ascription of an attitude can be rationally based on a subjective state or event with a certain content.

Suppose we were to grant that there is some component of intentional content which cannot vary between Earthly and Twin Earthly counterparts, and that only that component contributes constitutively to the specification of subjective phenomenology. (I am not sure it is right to grant this, but let us do so for the sake of argument.) Granting that by no means implies that all subjective similarities involving intentional content are internally individuated. Suppose John has the perceptual-demonstrative thought, of a liquid he sees in a glass, that that liquid is drinkable; and that Twin John equally has the perceptual-demonstrative thought, of a liquid *he* sees in a glass, that that liquid is drinkable. We can fill out the example so that the liquids are thought of in the same perceptual-demonstrative way, in the objector's use of this term. This way must involve the liquid's being presented as in a certain direction and distance from the subject. It is overwhelmingly plausible that this way can be individuated only in external terms. One who has a perception, or thought, whose content includes it stands in certain complex, potentially explanatory relations to a place a certain distance and direction from him (Peacocke 1993). But this perceptual-demonstrative way certainly contributes to what it is like for one who has the occurrent thought 'That liquid is drinkable'. I would also say the same of the perception itself, which makes available the perceptual-demonstrative way of thinking of that liquid in the subject's vicinity. The perception has an externally individuated content, and contributes to the nature of the thinker's subjective state. Both the occurrent thought and the perception can provide reasons for the thinker to make knowledgeable self-ascriptions of attitudes with externally individuated intentional contents. The upshot is that insisting that there are no subjective differences between an Earthly person and his Twin Earth replica by no means eliminates the phenomenon of conscious states with externally individuated attitudes giving reasons for knowledgeable self-ascription of those very states.

There is also a third influence, of a rather different kind, upon those who think that conscious events with externally individuated contents cannot give reasons for thought and action. The factor is well identified —though not, I hasten to add, endorsed—in Paul Boghossian's discussion of a paradox. He writes: 'We sometimes know our thoughts directly, without the benefit of inference from other beliefs. . . . This implies that we know our thoughts either on the basis of some form of inner observation, or on the basis of nothing' (1989: 5). Later he continues: 'Ordinarily, to know some contingent proposition you need either to make some observation, or to perform some inference based on observation. In this sense, we may say that ordinary empirical knowledge is always a *cognitive achievement* and its epistemology always *substantial*' (1989: 17). Similarly, Crispin Wright suggests that if we are to have 'a substantial epistemology of intentional states', 'then it seems that the only relevant possibilities—since one does not know a priori of one's own beliefs, desires, etc.—are observation and inference' (1989: 631).

Now if the categories by observation, or by inference, or by nothing are exhaustive, then one can see how pressure against the position I have been advocating increases. As Boghossian says, observation of a coin cannot tell us about its relational properties, such as its place of minting. Yet it is apparently relational properties of a mental state that we know in knowing its content. Nor are conscious attitudes known only by inference. If those three categories were exhaustive, we would already be moving on to the freeway which leads to the conclusion that psychological self-ascriptions are judgement-dependent. But the three categories are not exhaustive. Consider your knowledge of some feature of the content of your current visual perception. You do not observe your perceptual states; nor do you know about them only by inference; and there is certainly a good case to be made that many, if not all, of the contents featuring in perceptual experience are in part externally individuated. There is no evident obstacle to holding that a perceptual experience's having a certain content makes reasonable, for one conceptually equipped to think it, the first-person judgement that he is having an experience with a certain content. The reasonableness of such a judgement does not at all rely upon some level of internalist content which the experience has, and for which the transition to a judgement about the experience is unproblematic. On the contrary, for perceptual experience we seem to have externalism about representational content all the way down. I would make corresponding points for self-ascriptions of thoughts with particular contents, when they are consciously based.

On the other hand, the internalist introspectionist is right at least to the extent that he emphasizes the subjective aspect of conscious attitudes, their ability to contribute to a specification of what it is like for the thinker. Such conscious states can give reasons, and there is equally no evident reason to deny that, for a conceptually equipped thinker, they give reasons for a self-ascription of the attitudes that they are, with the contents they have. If one state gives a thinker's reason for a second state, they must be distinct states, and the reason-giving character of this explanation places it at the personal, not the subpersonal level. These points rule out the 'no reasons' theory.

If each of the extreme views' criticisms of the other is sound, as I suggest, then indeed neither of the extreme views can be correct. We need to recognize conscious propositional attitudes as a non-perceptual, non-sensational category of subjective, conscious states in their own right, with their externally individuated contents contributing ineliminably to the particular conscious states they are.

We have discussed the reasons which appear to, but do not in fact, support internalist introspectionism; but what of the considerations which lead to the 'no reasons' view? Of course, the spurious trilemma 'by observation, by inference, or by nothing' could be influential here too. But Shoemaker also offered some more specific analogies with other kinds of case.

The parallel with logical inference mentioned in the quoted paragraph from Shoemaker actually seems to me to count against, rather than in favour of, a 'no reasons' theory. Consider a belief with a content containing a logical constant, where the belief is reached by inference from another conscious belief. Suppose the logical transition in question is one the willingness to make which, without further inference, is partially constitutive of grasp of the logical concept in question. Acceptance of the premiss of this transition does give the thinker a *reason* for acceptance of the conclusion, and, in standard cases, the premiss will be the thinker's reason for accepting the conclusion. Like any other statement about reasons, this is a statement about the personal, not the subpersonal, level. In fact, the proper way of individuating the logical concept in the content would itself make reference to, or at least entail, that acceptance of certain contents containing it is, in certain very central cases, the thinker's reason for accepting the corresponding conclusions. The crucial point is this: the fact that certain transitions are involved

in the very identity of a concept is entirely consistent with the fact that
entering the second state of the transition is done for the reason that
the thinker is in the first state in the transition. The consistency of this
combination is a commitment of anyone who holds the plausible view
that concepts are individuated in part by what are good reasons for
making judgements involving them, or by which contents involving them
give good reasons for judging other contents.

An ordinary thinker's mastery of the concept of belief can then
equally include as one component his willingness to self-ascribe the belief
that p when he makes a conscious judgement that p (for the reason that
he has made the judgement, and in circumstances in which the question
arises). Such a component of ordinary mastery adverts to an explanation of the self-ascription which is neither wholly subpersonal, nor definitional in a way which excludes reason-involving explanation of one state
by another. Nor, as I emphasized, does recognition of such explanations
involve a reversion to perceptual models of self-knowledge. Once such
explanations are acknowledged, we would also expect the short-cut
mechanisms mentioned in section II to come into play: states which would
lead to a judgement that p can come to produce a self-ascription of the
belief that p without proceeding through the middle stage of the first-
order judgement.

The intermediate position I have been advocating for the case of consciously based self-ascriptions would actually be in agreement with
Shoemaker when he writes that second-order belief about one's own
beliefs 'supervenes on the first-order state plus human intelligence, rationality, and conceptual capacity' (1993: 79). The truth of this supervenience claim cannot be used to decide the issue between a 'no reasons'
theory and the intermediate position. Suppose it is indeed so that having
the concept of belief involves taking certain conscious judgements as
reasons for self-ascribing the corresponding belief, and that first-order
beliefs produce such reason-giving conscious judgements. Then failure
of the supervenience claim which Shoemaker makes would be as impossible on the intermediate view as it is on the 'no reasons' view.
The intermediate view will hold that the first-order beliefs produced
judgements which, in someone with minimal rationality and suitable
conceptual capacity, will rationalize the self-ascription of the first-order
state. Correlatively, the holding of the supervenience claim cannot be
used as evidence for the view that second-order beliefs about one's own
first-order beliefs are not distinct existences from the first-order beliefs
they are about.

Neat and simple as this exposition of the intermediate position
for consciously based self-ascriptions may sound, I think it would be

oversimple unless we draw a further important distinction. Within the class of conscious states, we can distinguish a proper subclass of states each member of which has the following property: it is either individuated in terms of what are good (non-instrumental) reasons for being in the state, or its individuation has consequences for what are good (non-instrumental) reasons for being in the state. A paradigm example of a state in this proper subclass is that of having a belief with a given content. This is a state which is either individuated by what are good reasons for being in it, or its individuation has consequences for what are good reasons for being in the state. Paradigm examples of states outside the proper subclass are those of having an experience with a given representational content, and the state of having a certain kind of sensation. These are states which are outside the immediate control of reason.

This classification is a classification of states themselves, rather than anything to do with the aetiology of a thinker's coming to be in one of the states on a particular occasion. There may be no good reasons at all producing the paranoid's belief that others are out to get him. But the individuation of the belief does have consequences for what would be good (non-instrumental) reasons for being in that belief state. States in our distinguished class are not necessarily responsive to reason, but they are respon*sible* to reason. I call states in the distinguished class 'reason-led' states. (An acknowledged leader may be disobeyed, but it is disobedience which is in question, rather than a weaker relation of not doing what fulfilment of the content of the command would require.) There is some rough overlap between the class of states which are not reason-led and that of those which are exercises of a faculty of receptivity, rather than of spontaneity, in the sense used by Kant and revived by McDowell (1994). Some overlap is to be expected, since states in which one receives information about the world by perceptual contact are not ones the thinker is in because he has certain reasons.[10]

To be in a reason-led state is to be committed to something: to a certain content's being the case, or to one's doing something, or to something's being good in a certain respect (in the case of reason-led desires). Because of this element of commitment, there is always the possibility of a thinker raising a practical question of whether he should be in a given reason-led state—whether he should believe that p, or form a

---

[10] The coincidence of the classifications is not exact, though. For instance, states of visual imagination are not states of receptivity in the Kantian sense. But I also do not think (though this might take some argument) that they are individuated by, or that their individuation has consequences for, what are good, non-instrumental reasons for being in them.

certain intention.[11] To enter one of these states is an action, which may be undertaken rationally or irrationally, and the general apparatus of action explanation is applicable to it.

With all this in mind, let us go back to the case of a person who self-ascribes the belief that Dubček was the Czech Prime Minister at the time of the Soviet Union's invasion, and does so because he has a conscious propositional memory which represents Dubček as having that office then. The self-ascription of the belief on this basis goes beyond a mere report of oneself as having an apparent memory with that content. One makes the self-ascription in part because one is *endorsing* the content of the apparent memory. The self-ascription of the belief would, after all, not be correct if one were suspending judgement on the content of the apparent memory. So when a self-ascription of a reason-led state is made on the basis of the occurrence of a conscious state in this way, it is not a *mere* report of that state. It involves the same kind of endorsement and commitment as would be made in entering the first-order, reason-led state itself. This is a major difference from consciously based self-ascriptions of experiences, sensations, or mental images. The distinction can give one some limited sympathy with those who say that self-ascriptions of belief and certain other states are not just descriptions of mental states. To say that the self-ascriptions are not consciously based at all, however, would overstep the limits of legitimate sympathy.

IV   TRACKING PROPERTIES, THE NATURE OF A MENTAL STATE, AND CONCEPT POSSESSION

For any concept, it is always illuminating to try to answer this question: why does it have to be as it is if proper applications of the concept are to track instances of the property picked out by the concept?[12] In the case of an observational concept, we have at least the rudiments of an answer to this question. The possession condition for the concept would mention the role of a particular kind of perceptual experience in possessing the concept. We would begin to answer the question, as applied to a perceptual concept, by explaining how ordinary perceptual experience involves a sensitivity of the perceiver to instantiation of the property picked out by the concept. It is clear, in outline at least, how other theories of the concept of belief would aim to answer the same question as posed for the concept of belief. A 'no reasons' theorist

[11] Cf. Moran 1988.
[12] On the distinction between properties and concepts, see Putnam 1975*a* and Wiggins 1984.

would speak simply of a reliable sensitivity of a thinker's self-ascriptions of beliefs to instances of the property of believing the relevant contents, a sensitivity built into the account he would offer of possession of the concept of belief. Equally, a theorist such as Wright (1989), who treats the correctness of belief ascriptions as constitutively partially dependent upon a subject's willingness to self-ascribe them, will also have his own answer to the question. For such a judgement-dependent theorist, the correctness of an ordinary self-ascription of a belief will not be independent of the thinker's willingness to make the self-ascription. This is a very different explanation of how the offered account of mastery connects with the truth of the self-ascriptions of belief. It may not be plausible; but at least it addresses the question. I, however, have rejected the pure 'no reasons' view, and I have not endorsed any judgement-dependent theory. So how do *I* answer the question of why the concept of belief has to be as it is if its proper applications are to track instances of the property it picks out?

There are at least two sub-questions to be distinguished here.

Sub-question (a): what account, if any, is available in the present framework of the nature of the first-order property of believing a given intentional content, the property whose instances in the thinker are to be tracked by properly made self-ascriptions? Subject to some further elaborations below, I would answer this first sub-question by drawing on the material in *A Study of Concepts* (Peacocke 1992). The nature of the property of believing that p, for a given content p, is fixed by the possession conditions for the various concepts which comprise the content p, together with their mode of composition. Each such possession condition for a concept contributes, at a point determined by the mode of composition, a requirement on a state's being a belief with a content containing that concept. The totality of such requirements fixes the condition for a state to be a belief with the given content p. This condition fixes a property whose instances may or may not be tracked.

The condition is fixed in a quite specific way, but there is no plausibility that this way—which involves a detailed statement of the possession conditions for the concepts involved—is a route employed at the personal level when a subject knowledgeably self-ascribes a belief. Ordinary thinkers need not have any personal-level conscious knowledge of the possession conditions of the concepts they employ. So this response to the first sub-question takes us only as far as a fixing of the property about which the opening question of this section can be raised. It is not an answer to that question, for it does not explain how any tracking takes place. It merely specifies the property which might be tracked.

Sub-question (b): how do the points in the preceding sections of this chapter, about the nature of conscious, occurrent propositional attitudes, and their availability as reasons in their own right, contribute to answering the question of how properly made self-applications of the concept of belief track instances of the property of believing a given content? If they are irrelevant to answering the question, should they not be omitted from an account of ordinary mastery of the concept of belief? If they are relevant, how do they contribute to tracking the property?

To address the cluster of issues in sub-question (b), I suggest that we need to step back a little and consider the nature of belief. If we were asked about the nature of belief, we would very plausibly include the following principles:

(i)   To make a judgement is the fundamental way to form a belief (or to endorse it when it is being reassessed). Judgement is a conscious rational activity, done for reasons, where these reasons are answerable to a fundamental goal of judgement: that it aims at truth.[13]

(ii) Beliefs store the contents of judgements previously made as correct contents, and these stored contents can be accessed so as to result in a conscious, subjective state of the thinker which represents the stored content as true. (The contents will often need to be adjusted as the spatio-temporal location of the thinker varies. This is why a cognitive dynamics, in Kaplan's sense (1989), is essential in the description of the mental life of any creature with beliefs.)

(iii) Beliefs equally aim at the truth, rather than being a mere record of what was once judged. Hence their contents are always potentially open to revision by later judgements, perceptions, memories, and reconsiderations of reasoning and evidence.

There is a vast amount more to be said about the nature of belief and judgement, but it seems that features (i)–(iii) of belief are core characteristics which will be retained in any more extensive elaboration.

Now we can bring this to bear on our second set of sub-questions, (b) above. I claim that our distinctive ways of coming to knowledgeably self-ascribe beliefs are correct methods in part because of the nature of belief given in characteristics (i)–(iii). It is important for this claim

[13] My own view is that judgements are in fact *actions*, a species of mental action. Judgements are made for reasons. Perhaps (though even this is debatable) they are not intentional under any description. I do not regard that as sufficient for them not to be actions. Forming an intention to do something seems equally to me to be an action (and can also be done for reasons). But in the sense in which judgements are not intentional under some description, forming an intention is not intentional under some description either.

that these characteristics do not themselves mention knowledgeable self-ascription. It also matters for the claim that these are a priori characteristics of belief. They are not a posteriori in the way in which, as a true principle about its nature, the statement 'Water is H_2O' is a posteriori.

Consider the procedure of making a self-ascription of a belief that p for the reason that one has just consciously judged that p. By characteristic (i) of belief, the first-order judgement will, when all is working properly, be an initiation (or continuation) of a belief that p. So the self-ascription will be correct.

Consider also the case in which someone has a propositional memory representation of its being the case that p, is taking this representation at face value, and rationally moves, directly or indirectly, from this particular memory to the self-ascription of the belief that p. Again, when all is working properly, the memory representation will be a manifestation of an underlying stored belief that p, the kind of representation which, according to characteristic (ii), stored beliefs will generate. So the self-ascription will be correct. Equally, when there is new evidence which means that the memory must be re-evaluated, characteristic (iii) of beliefs explains why a rational self-ascription cannot just consist in re-endorsement of the stored information (or misinformation).

In summary, when all is working properly, knowledgeable self-ascriptions track the property of belief for this reason: the very means by which they are reached are ones whose availability involves the thinker's having the relevant belief. When all is working properly, these means would not be available were he not to have the relevant first-order belief.

On this approach, representations in conscious thought of contents as true can be produced by underlying beliefs, can contribute to what it's like subjectively for the thinker, and can give reasons for self-ascriptions of a kind involved in ordinary mastery of the concept of belief. All of this is consistent with knowledgeable self-ascriptions tracking the instantiation of the property of belief in the appropriate content. The position I have been developing seems to me to endorse all those propositions simultaneously.

It is worth noting the special link—whose existence one would well expect in advance—between the means for coming to make knowledgeable self-ascriptions and the first person. A conscious memory representation, and equally a conscious judgement, can give a reason for making a self-ascription (or indeed for doing anything else) only to the person who has that memory, or who is making that judgement. So these rational means are restricted to *self*-ascriptions of beliefs and other mental states and events. Certainly, a premiss that someone else has a certain memory, or is making a judgement, can give a thinker reason to ascribe beliefs to someone else. But I have emphasized that consciously based self-ascription is not a case of inference, and *a fortiori* not a case of moving inferentially from premisses about one's own mental states to a conclusion. The mental event itself, rather than some premiss about the event, is the thinker's reason for making the judgement.

I said that for some ways of coming to make knowledgeable self-ascriptions, the nature of belief and judgement is part of the explanation of their correctness. It is not the full explanation, and my exposition was peppered with occurrences of the qualifying phrase 'when all is working properly'. Someone can make a judgement, and for good reasons, but it not have the effects that judgements normally do—in particular, it may not result in a stored belief which has the proper influence on other judgements and on action. A combination of prejudice and self-deception, amongst many other possibilities, can produce this state of affairs. Someone may judge that undergraduate degrees from countries other than her own are of an equal standard to her own, and excellent reasons may be operative in her assertions to that effect. All the same, it may be quite clear, in decisions she makes on hiring, or in making recommendations, that she does not really have this belief at all. So the ways of coming to make self-ascriptions which I have been discussing are by no means infallible. In so far as they are authoritative, in a wide range of ordinary cases, they are so only because those cases are not like the self-ascription of the belief about degree standards. It is an important question for further work exactly what further restrictions ensure an authoritative self-ascription. I do not think, though, that acknowledgement of this situation reinstates anything like a perceptual model of self-knowledge. Nothing here supports the conception of a distinction between mental states and our perceptions, or experiences, of them. Our recently imagined subject is mistaken about whether she has the belief that degrees from other countries are of equal value with those from her own; but not every case of error is a case of perceptual error.

A second question meriting further investigation is how far the model developed in this section is generalizable to knowledge of other mental states. What I have done in the case of belief is to argue that the explanation of the correctness of certain distinctive ways of coming to knowledgeable self-ascriptions is in part the essential nature of the mental state ascribed. Can we do this for other mental states too? Certainly it seems at first blush as if the approach can be developed *pari passu* for self-ascriptions of intention. This is partly because decision stands to intention and the self-ascription of intention somewhat as judgement stands to belief and the self-ascription of belief. If the approach can be developed for other mental states and their self-ascription too, we have the promise that the connection we noted in the case of belief between the nature of the mental state, reasons for knowledgeable self-ascription, and the first person may generalize to other mental states. It may be another general connection between the mental and first-person thought.

V REPERCUSSIONS: CONSCIOUSNESS, KNOWLEDGE, AND RATIONALITY

I turn now to consider some consequences of this account of conscious occurrent attitudes and consciously based self-ascription, and some questions and challenges they raise.

(a) It is worth reflecting further on what is involved in the consciousness of those conscious mental events which are capable of contributing to the rational explanation of self-ascriptions. If the conscious nature of the mental event is partially explanatory of the self-ascription, this consciousness cannot *consist* in the event's availability to belief or to verbal report. Similarly, if the conscious nature of the mental event is partially explanatory of some other non-verbal action or behaviour, this consciousness cannot consist in its disposition to produce such behaviour.

There are occasions on which a person expresses a first-order belief, or indeed makes a self-ascription of a belief, and in which this is not consciously based in the way I have been discussing. Most of us, when it becomes conversationally appropriate to say 'I know my name is NN', or 'I know my address is such-and-such', have no need to wait upon its surfacing in consciousness what our names and addresses are. We make these utterances intentionally and knowledgeably, but not because it has just occurred to us that our names and addresses are such-and-such. If we were to analyse the consciousness of an occurrent thought in terms of its availability to immediate first-person belief or report, we would be failing to distinguish the genuinely consciously based self-ascriptions from these latter cases—from which they are distinct. We would also undermine the possibility of explaining certain examples of self-ascription in part by reference to a conscious event. On the theory I am currently rejecting, the consciousness of a mental event would consist in its disposition to produce self-ascriptions in thought or language. A disposition cannot be the cause of its manifestations.

How, then, do the conscious mental events which can support consciously based self-ascriptions stand in relation to the well-known and, in my judgement, valuable distinction drawn by Block (1993, 1995a) between 'phenomenal' consciousness and 'access' consciousness? Phenomenal consciousness ('P-consciousness') has been characterized as experience in general, understood in Block's writings so widely as to include occurrent thoughts. Block characterizes a state as access-conscious ('A-conscious') 'if, in virtue of one's having the state, a representation of its content is (1) inferentially promiscuous (Stich 1978), that is, poised for use as a premise in reasoning, (2) poised for rational control of action, and (3) poised for rational control of speech' (Block 1995a: 231). When someone knows what he is thinking because he has just consciously thought it, his first-order thinking is access-conscious *because* it is phenomenally conscious, in Block's broad sense. For conscious mental events of a sort which support consciously based self-ascriptions, their access consciousness is not independent of their phenomenal consciousness.

In one of his papers, Block writes: 'I don't know whether there are any actual cases of A-consciousness without P-consciousness, but I hope I have illustrated their conceptual possibility' (1995a: 233). Elsewhere he notes that, 'If indeed there can be P without A, but not A without P, this would be a remarkable result that would need explanation' (1995b: 272). Other writers have also placed some weight on the alleged non-existence of cases of access consciousness without phenomenal consciousness.[14] But consider knowledgeable self-ascriptions like 'I know that my name is Christopher Peacocke', where there is no intermediate conscious state rationally producing the utterance (or the judgement). These seem to me to be straightforwardly cases in which the knowledge or belief is access-conscious without being phenomenally conscious. In accordance with Block's definition, the representation of the content of the knowledge or belief is inferentially promiscuous, and can certainly be poised for rational control of action and speech. (It is actually controlling it when I say 'I know my name is Christopher Peacocke'.)

On the view I am proposing, then, there is more than one sort of availability for verbal report, and we should distinguish between the case in which there is an intermediate conscious event playing a role in the explanation of the verbal report and the case in which there is not. It should be noted that we do in fact still call a belief conscious if its content is expressed, or even reported, without the occurrence of any

[14] e.g. Dennett (1995), Morton (1995).

intermediate occurrent conscious state. This is one strand in our ordinary notion of a conscious state. Whether its presence is fundamental, or owed rather to its connection with another element which is fundamental, is a further question, to which I turn almost immediately.

(b) Cases of knowledgeable self-ascription not based on any intermediate conscious state raise many questions. One of the most pressing is the support they may seem to give to the 'no reasons' view of section III above. For the 'no reasons' theorist may counter-attack the arguments developed above in two ways. First, the 'no reasons' theorist may say that a reliability account of a thinker's knowledge of his own attitudes is the only epistemology which can properly accommodate those knowledgeable cases where there is no intermediate conscious state. Second, the 'no reasons' theorist may even say that the correctness of his account is not confined to no-intermediate-conscious-state ('NICS') examples. It can be extended to cases where there is an intermediate conscious state, since a conscious judgement that *p* is precisely something which is reliably correlated with a thinker's believing that *p* (certainly, he may say, sufficiently reliably to ground attributions of knowledge).

We need, then, to address two clusters of questions:

(i) Are reliability accounts the only epistemological accounts which can explain why second-order beliefs in NICS examples amount to knowledge?
(ii) Is the class of NICS examples philosophically more fundamental than the class of intermediate-conscious-state examples? Or vice versa? Or is neither more fundamental than the other?

There are general reasons for thinking that there must be some alternative to a reliabilist treatment of NICS self-ascriptions. For the objections to pure reliabilism—its omission of any rationality or entitlement requirement—are well known, and have not, so it seems to me, been overcome.[15] It would be very puzzling if reliabilism were right about just one kind of psychological self-ascription, but wrong everywhere else. In fact, it seems to me that there is an alternative account which treats NICS self-ascriptions as knowledge, but which is not a purely reliabilist account. This alternative account says that an NICS self-ascription of (say) a belief that *p* is knowledge only if it is made in circumstances in which the thinker is also willing to make the first-order judgement that *p*. We can call the requirement appealed to in this alternative account

---

[15] See e.g. Bonjour 1985: 37–57.

'the requirement of first-order ratifiability'.[16] There is considerable plausibility in the claim that it is the holding of first-order ratifiability which makes an NICS second-order self-ascription of belief a case of knowledge (makes the ascriber entitled to his second-order judgement, if you will). Suppose a thinker were to make an NICS self-ascription of a belief, but that first-order ratifiability failed—when he reflects on it, the thinker is not prepared to make the first-order judgement that *p*. In these circumstances, the second-order judgement would, other things equal, be unstable. The second-order judgement would in those circumstances normally be withdrawn. If it were the case that our subject had been told that his NICS self-ascriptions were a way of tapping his unconscious beliefs, perhaps the second-order self-ascription would not be withdrawn. That would clearly be a case of inferential knowledge, though, very different from the normal case in which NICS self-ascriptions constitute non-inferential self-knowledge.

A requirement of first-order ratifiability can also help to explain the evident rationality of the Evans procedure for self-ascription. Necessarily, someone self-ascribing a belief by Evans's procedure meets the condition that he self-ascribes the belief that *p* in circumstances in which he is also willing to make the first-order judgement that *p*.

If first-order ratifiability is the correct explanation of how NICS self-ascriptions can constitute knowledge, then in order of philosophical explanation—as opposed to frequency of examples—the intermediate-conscious-state cases are philosophically more fundamental than their NICS counterparts. If first-order ratifiability is required for these cases to be knowledge, as I am inclined to believe, then NICS cases count as knowledge (when they do) because of the relation in which they stand to conscious first-order attitudes, and to the rational basis those conscious first-order attitudes provide for self-ascribing attitudes. On this approach, then, the existence of NICS self-ascriptions which constitute knowledge can be squarely acknowledged without embracing a purely reliabilist epistemology.[17]

---

[16] One may want to strengthen the requirement somewhat, so that it does not merely talk of 'the circumstances' in which one would be willing to make the corresponding first-order judgement. A plausible stronger requirement is that the mechanism which produces the second-order judgement in the NICS case must persist because it has the property of first-order ratifiability.

[17] The points of this section also tell against the view that a full account of how self-ascriptions of belief are knowledge is given as follows: whenever a sentence *s* is stored in someone's 'belief-box', the sentence *I believe that s* is also stored in his belief-box. Some such subpersonal mechanism may—perhaps must—exist. But some additional account has to be given if we are to explain why the belief realized by storing the sentence *I believe that s* in the belief-box is knowledge.

(c) The present approach must incline one to scepticism about the view that the consciousness of an occurrent propositional attitude consists in its massive inferential integration. Let us fix on one reading of an example of Dennett's, that of the father who is self-deceived in his belief that his son is a good painter (1978: ch. 3). This belief may well not be strongly inferentially integrated. All the evidence which, in the case of anyone else, would convince the father that some third person is not a good painter is ineffective in the case of his son's painting. The belief that his son is a good painter is conscious all the same, and such thoughts as 'My son is a good painter' may pass through his mind as an objection when he hears someone assert 'None of the good painters have living parents'.

The conscious belief will be inferentially integrated in a somewhat weaker sense. The father will respond to evidence offered that his belief is false by trying to undermine or discount the evidence. But that weaker sort of integration can also be present when there is no conscious belief. The mother who does not know whether her soldier-son has survived a battle may have no conscious opinion on the matter, but may still try to undermine or discount any evidence that he has not. (This could be caused by a desire that he be alive.) This falls short of amounting to a conscious belief that her son is alive, a belief which she may sincerely deny she has. If one consciously accepts that p, there will indeed normally be extensive inferential integration of the belief that p with one's other conscious attitudes, practical reasoning, and emotions. It seems to me that this is a normal—though as the examples show, not an invariable—consequence of the consciousness of a belief that p. It is not what its conscious status consists in. The mother's unconscious belief that her son is alive may have as extensive ramifications for her other attitudes and her reaction to apparent counter-evidence as does the father's conscious belief that his son is a good painter. If this is possible, then the consciousness of an attitude cannot be elucidated in terms of extent of influence. This point also seems to count against approaches to consciousness in terms of 'cerebral celebrity', as Dennett felicitously calls it (1993: 929–31). It looks as if the father's conscious belief and the mother's unconscious belief may be on a par in respect of cerebral celebrity.

A different manœuvre might be attempted. For instance, it is also true in the imagined examples that the father, unlike the mother, is under a rational obligation to explain away the contrary evidence, to show it is not contrary, or to change his views, whereas the mother is under no such rational obligation. This too, though, seems to me to be a consequence of the conscious status of the father's belief. A conscious state or event with content imposes rational requirements on a thinker, for it gives reasons for thinking or doing. If it gives reason for accepting something the thinker also has other reasons for rejecting, the thinker is under a rational obligation to revise his beliefs.

In the basic, personal-level case in which something is done for a reason, whether it be in thought or in bodily action, the reason-giving state must be either conscious or be capable of becoming conscious for the thinker. A reason-giving state need not be actually conscious. If you decide to fly to Paris, you may call one airline rather than another. There need not be any conscious state, one contributing to what it's like for you, just before or after your decision, which is the reason-giving state which rationally explains your calling that airline. But if this was a minimally rational action, your reason could become conscious if the question arose. In a case in which no reason becomes conscious when the question arises, and the thinker consequently cannot explain why he chose to call that airline, we have a much-diminished sense of the rationality of the action. The requirement that the reason could become conscious is reminiscent of a Kantian position: 'It must be *possible* for the "I think" to accompany all my representations; for otherwise . . . the representation . . . would be nothing to me' (1929: B131, my emphasis). The requirement that the reason-giving state is one which is, or could become, conscious is intimately related to our conception of an agent as someone with a point of view, one whose rational actions make sense to the subject himself (and not just to other experts) given that point of view. For an alleged reason-giving state which could not even become conscious, this condition would not be met. Any action produced by it would not make sense even to the subject himself.

There is more than one way to regard this principle linking conscious states and reasons. One approach regards this connection as part of a positive elucidation of consciousness in terms which do not, according to this first approach, presuppose consciousness. I do not find this first approach plausible. It certainly does not promise any explication of the important distinction between what is actually conscious and what is only potentially so. The approach would also apparently rule out the existence of more primitive creatures who enjoy what are, in some general but univocal sense, conscious states, but to which the full apparatus of reason-based explanation is inapplicable. A more plausible approach does not aim to treat the connection as contributing to some kind of reduction of consciousness, but rather sees it as linking reason-involving explanation with some general notion of consciousness which has a life outside the principle. This second approach allows for the possibility of the existence of conscious states prior to that of reason-based explanation. In any case, whatever the correct attitude to the connection, its mere existence would suffice to explain why rational subjects must be capable of enjoying conscious states.

REFERENCES

Block, N. (1993), review of D. Dennett, *Consciousness Explained*, *Journal of Philosophy*, 90: 181–93.

—— (1995*a*), 'On a Confusion about a Function of Consciousness', *Behavioral and Brain Sciences*, 18: 227–47.

—— (1995*b*), 'How Many Concepts of Consciousness?', *Behavioral and Brain Sciences*, 18: 272–87.

Boghossian, P. (1989), 'Content and Self-Knowledge', *Philosophical Topics*, 17: 5–26.

Bonjour, L. (1985), *The Structure of Empirical Knowledge* (Cambridge, Mass.: Harvard University Press).

Burge, T. (1988), 'Individualism and Self-Knowledge', *Journal of Philosophy*, 85: 649–63.

—— (1996), 'Our Entitlement to Self-Knowledge', *Proceedings of the Aristotelian Society*, 96: 91–116.

Davidson, D. (1987), 'Knowing One's Own Mind', *Proceedings and Addresses of the American Philosophical Association*, 60: 441–58.

Dennett, D. (1978), *Brainstorms* (Vermont: Bradford Books).

—— (1993), 'The Message is: There is no *Medium*', *Philosophy and Phenomenological Research*, 53: 919–31.

—— (1995), 'The Path not Taken', *Behavioral and Brain Sciences*, 18: 252–3.

Evans, G. (1982), *The Varieties of Reference* (Oxford: Clarendon Press).

Flanagan, O. (1992), *Consciousness Regained* (Cambridge, Mass.: MIT Press).

Goldman, A. (1993), 'The Psychology of Folk Psychology', *Behavioral and Brain Sciences*, 16: 15–28.

James, W. (1983), *The Principles of Psychology* (Cambridge, Mass.: Harvard University Press).

Kant, I. (1929), *Critique of Pure Reason*, trans. N. Kemp Smith (London: Macmillan).

Kaplan, D. (1989), 'Demonstratives', in J. Almog, J. Perry, and H. Wettstein (eds.), *Themes from Kaplan* (New York: Oxford University Press), 481–563.

McDowell, J. (1984), '*De Re* Senses', *Philosophical Quarterly*, 34: 283–94.

—— (1994), *Mind and World* (Cambridge, Mass.: Harvard University Press).

Moran, R. (1988), 'Making up your Mind: Self-Interpretation and Self-Constitution', *Ratio*, NS 1: 135–51.

Morton, A. (1995), 'Phenomenal and Attentional Consciousness may be Inextricable', *Behavioral and Brain Sciences*, 18: 263–4.

Peacocke, C. (1985), 'Imagination, Possibility and Experience', in J. Foster and H. Robinson (eds.), *Essays on Berkeley* (Oxford: Oxford University Press), 19–35.

—— (1992), *A Study of Concepts* (Cambridge, Mass.: MIT Press).

—— (1993), 'Externalist Explanation', *Proceedings of the Aristotelian Society*, 93: 203–30.

—— (1994), 'Content, Computation and Externalism', *Mind and Language*, 9: 303–35.

—— (1996), 'Entitlement, Self-Knowledge and Conceptual Redeployment', *Proceedings of the Aristotelian Society*, 96: 117–58.

Putnam, H. (1975a), 'On Properties', in *Mathematics, Matter and Method* (Cambridge: Cambridge University Press), 305–22.

—— (1975b), 'The Meaning of "Meaning"', in *Mind, Language and Reality* (Cambridge: Cambridge University Press), 215–71.

Ryle, G. (1971), 'A Puzzling Element in the Notion of Thinking', in *Collected Papers*, ii: *Collected Essays 1929–1968* (London: Hutchinson), 391–406.

Shoemaker, S. (1993), 'Special Access Lies Down with Theory-Theory', *Behavioral and Brain Sciences*, 16: 78–9.

—— (1994), 'Self-Knowledge and "Inner Sense"', *Philosophy and Phenomenological Research*, 54: 249–314.

Stich, S. (1978), 'Beliefs and Sub-Doxastic States', *Philosophy of Science*, 45: 499–58.

Wiggins, D. (1984), 'The Sense and Reference of Predicates: A Running Repair to Frege's Doctrine and a Plea for the Copula', in C. Wright (ed.), *Frege: Tradition and Influence* (Oxford: Blackwell), 126–43.

Wright, C. (1989), 'Wittgenstein's Later Philosophy of Mind: Sensations, Privacy and Intention', *Journal of Philosophy*, 76: 622–34.

4

An Eye Directed Outward

M. G. F. MARTIN

———•———

Staring at the lavender bush at the end of my street, I am conscious of the bush and its bedraggled shape—I not only experience the bush, I believe it to be there; in addition, I am aware that I am conscious of the bush and its appearance. We have here awareness of the world; conscious experience and thought; self-knowledge and, seemingly, self-awareness. In being aware of the world, I am aware of my own awareness of it. How are these things linked?

One approach to these questions shies away from all talk of content of consciousness for fear of reintroducing the supposedly ridiculous 'theatre of the mind' model of self-awareness. As a consequence, such discussions tend to contrast qualia and phenomenal states of mind with states which have a representational content, and suppose that there can be little in common between phenomenal states on the one hand and propositional attitudes on the other. Against this background, one cannot but feel sympathy with Richard Rorty's complaint that 'The attempt to hitch pains and beliefs together seems ad hoc—they don't seem to have anything in common except our refusal to call them "physical".'[1] And it is no surprise that theorists of consciousness, in the light of an assumption that the phenomenal lacks any representational content and has no intrinsic structure, have sought to define consciousness principally in terms of accessibility to thought, as with 'higher-order thought' theories of consciousness, defended by Sydney Shoemaker and David Rosenthal, amongst others.[2]

It seems to me that such theories are far removed from phenomenology—perhaps; here I speak only for myself, but I have at least the suspicion that the inner lives of others are as complex, troubling, and difficult to articulate as my own. It is no surprise that one may end up

[1] Rorty 1979: 22.   [2] See in particular Shoemaker 1994; Rosenthal 1990.

with the feeling that the *explananda* have been lost in the construction
of the theory, when confronted with most discussions of the phenomenal and consciousness. The great strength of Christopher Peacocke's
discussion of attention and consciousness is that we are kept firmly in
mind of what the life of the mind is really like.

This project seems laudable and highly engaging. It is germane to link
the problem of self-knowledge to consciousness, and plausible that, in
resisting an observational model of such self-knowledge, we should not
go as far as to deny that we have reasons for our authoritative self-
ascriptions of conscious states. In directing our attention to the links
between consciousness and attention, Peacocke forces us to recognize
quite how rich and structured consciousness is, given our quotidian
conception of it. Nevertheless, I shall argue that there is a persisting
puzzle as to how directing our attention out at the world gives us
knowledge of our own minds which Peacocke's account in the end does
nothing to solve.

First I have some comments to add to Peacocke's discussion of attention and consciousness, before turning to the question of how consciousness and self-knowledge are linked. Peacocke claims that resistance
to his account of self-ascription may be rooted in an acceptance of
what he calls 'the spurious trilemma "by observation, by inference, or
by nothing"' (p. 82). I shall suggest that the puzzlement may come from
a much simpler source.

                                    I

The first question I want to raise concerns the distinction Peacocke draws
between objects of attention and occupying attention. He suggests on
page 65 that there are no objects of attention for thought. In saying
this, it is clear that he uses the phrase 'object of attention' as a term of
art. For in ordinary English the phrase 'object of thought' has various
acceptable applications. When I think that five is not the largest prime
number, it is perfectly intelligible to say that the proposition that five
is not the largest prime number is the object of my thought, or that
five is the object of my thought, or even that the property of being the
largest prime number is the object of my thought. Now, since consciously
thinking the thought that five is not the largest prime number is a mode
of attending to what is thought, there is no more impropriety in ordinary usage to talk of any of these as an object of attention.

Clearly what Peacocke has in mind is some property of attention
which thoughts will fail to have, and which is particularly associated

with sensory states—perceptual experiences and sensation. But, one may wonder whether his distinction cuts the nature of attention at an obvious place, and whether it is a confusion concerning that distinction that lies behind William James's attitude towards inner sense and attention to thought.

One contrast that we could appeal to harks back to the discarded image of the theatre of the mind, but not, I suggest, in an objectionable manner. There is a sense in which we might talk of the objects of perception being present to the mind or given to a perceiver when she is conscious of them. Likewise, we may think of the objects of imagination, as when I visualize a pink elephant, or listen with my mind's ear to the Dies Irae, as being present to the mind, although we cannot think of presence to the mind as genuinely relational in these cases or for those of hallucination, unless we make the unfortunate move of endorsing some representative account of these states. This picture does not have the same application within the realm of 'pure thought'. It is one of the great liberations from empiricism offered to us at the end of the nineteenth century that conscious thought does not always require the presence of an object (or of some surrogate for that object) to the mind in order for one's thoughts to be about the object in question: I can have five as an object of thought without having to suppose that the number five, or some symbol for it, or some other surrogate for it, is present to me as if in sensory contact with it, or imagined sensory contact with it.

So, one might suggest, the term of art 'object of attention' is intended to apply to those objects which are present to the mind. Since conscious thoughts can (although they need not) lack objects given in this manner, conscious thought does not require an object of attention. Yet, this is not the contrast that Peacocke intends. For him, objects of attention belong solely to cases of experience, where that includes perceptual experiences and sensations, but excludes sensory imagination. So all thought will lack objects of attention, although they will occupy it.

This division has much grounding in empirical research. If we look to the psychological literature on attention, we find a notable division between research on attentional mechanisms in perception and that on attentional mechanisms associated with thought, such as those employed in scheduling and planning action.[3] Various distinctions salient within this literature have proper application only within one field or the other —the contrast between voluntary and involuntary attention has a very

[3] For the former cf. Shallice and Burgess 1993; for the latter cf. Treisman and Gelade 1980.

different content depending on whether one is talking about perceptual attentional mechanisms or not.

However, Peacocke's intention seems to be to find a distinction which has some phenomenological grounding, and will have application, as he might put it, at the personal level, rather than just within a theory of subpersonal mechanisms of attention. Is there a way of justifying the distinction that Peacocke draws by drawing solely on such phenomenological considerations?

One suggestion, which would seem to cut in a different position from that of the presence of objects to the mind, is the contrast between examples of conscious states for which there is a significant contrast between the foreground of consciousness, or the focus of attention, and the background, that which is there to be attended to but which is not focused upon.[4] When you stare at the projected image on the screen, you focus on only a small part of the display (in fact you focus on much less at a moment than is phenomenologically apparent). Nevertheless, it is not for you as if nothing but what you focus on is present to your mind— quite the reverse; for it seems to you as if you are aware of a much greater extent of the world which could also command your attention and which is already such that how it is would determine what your focused experience would be like were you to attend. For such states, sticking at the level of phenomenology, what things are like for one outstrips what one focuses one's attention on, and hence there is the appearance of a stuff of consciousness upon which the attention can act. We must be careful here—the claim is made purely at the level of phenomena. No claim is being made about what one genuinely is aware of, or possesses perceptual information about: readers of Dennett's *Consciousness Explained* will recall experiments which cast a sceptical light on any such reading of the phenomenology.[5] Nor should we over-read this phenomenology as committing us to the image of attention as inner spotlight; but if we wish to reject that model of perceptual attention, we should not forget the phenomenology which makes it tempting.

Now this contrast between a foreground of consciousness and a background does not have the same application in the case of thoughts. When I think of how to construct a schedule for next term's tutorials, it is not as if there is some aspect of what I am thinking of, there already before the mind but unattended to, which I could reveal further by shifting my attention. While in the case of sensory experience we feel inclined to make a distinction between those aspects of a conscious experience which are the focus of attention and those which are not, one's thoughts

---

[4] Naomi Eilan suggested this way of putting the point to me.

[5] Dennett 1991: 344–56; for the original research see McConkie 1979; see also Grimes 1996; and the introduction to Akins 1996.

are conscious only inasmuch as they are a matter of attention in the first place.[6] If we adopt this view, then we can see Peacocke's talk of a thought's occupying the attention as indicating that conscious thoughts are determinations of the attention, rather than something independent of one's attention to which one then applies this faculty.

Many mental images—perhaps all—fall on the thought side of this contrast and not the sensory. This claim seems to lie behind Sartre's inexact and hyperbolic claim that 'In a word, the object of perception overflows consciousness constantly; the object of the image is never more than the consciousness one has; it is limited by that consciousness: nothing can be learned from an image that is not already known.'[7]

Taken literally, the claim cannot be correct: long-suffering sophomores often employ imagery to determine the answer to the question, 'Do frogs have lips?' or to work out which among a selection of shapes are congruent. But the idea lying behind it has great appeal: how the world seems to one in perceptual experience is that there is more to discover through attending to what has been presented; what is there for one in imagination, as in thought, already occupies one's attention: there is not more to be discovered.

We sometimes talk of being preoccupied by some matter, meaning that it takes up our attention in such a way that the latter cannot be drawn to some new subject-matter. Talk of thoughts occupying the attention might then be read as ambiguous between supposing that the subject-matter of the thoughts takes up one's attention and supposing that the very acts of thinking themselves do. I take it that Peacocke has in mind only the former. If we conceive of conscious thoughts as determinations of attention, this will make clear that the former idea alone is in play.

I should mention briefly two corollaries of this discussion. First, there is more of a gap between James's inclination to an observational model of the contents of the mind and the quasi-perceptual terms in which he discusses attentive thought. The latter might arise first from an empiricist approach to thought which takes sensory or quasi-sensory states, such as images, as the basic unit of all cognitive activity.[8] As we have

---

[6] This is not to say that there is no distinction between foreground and background of the mind for thoughts, just that it is a different one. We may talk of some thought or emotion being in the background of one's mind, but such talk relates more to issues to do with scheduling of plans, and ways of avoiding focusing on certain issues, than with the subject-matter of the thought being somehow arrayed before the mind's eye.

[7] Sartre 1991: 12.

[8] James is certainly not an uncritical assimilator of this sort; imagery may play a central role in the stream of thought, but the contents of the mind are not reducible simply to imagery: see e.g. the discussion in James 1983: 251–62, and the criticisms of Hume and Berkeley's views of imagery, ibid. 691–5.

already noted, thinking in terms of imagery may justify talk of something being before the mind in a way which does not commit one yet to thinking of that on the model of causal encounter with an object. Whatever one thinks of that, one should not lose sight of the gap between thinking of the object of a thought as being offered in quasi-sensory contact and one's awareness of the thought itself as being a form of quasi-sensory contact with it. Second, Peacocke does an admirable job in laying to rest the kind of scepticism that psychologists such as Alan Allport have evinced concerning the coherence and unity of our concepts of consciousness and attention.[9] But that need not touch their scepticism concerning the unity of the actual mechanisms of attention: consciousness and attention appear to us to be a unity, and that appearance needs explanation; an actual unity underlying them would be only one potential such explanation.

II

The states of mind we have been concerned with make up aspects of the stream of consciousness, or of phenomenal consciousness as that term has recently been used. How should the nature and structure of such consciousness bear on self-knowledge? The latter part of Peacocke's essay can be seen as offering a partial answer to this question. He claims that there is a way of self-ascribing mental states which is 'consciously based' (pp. 71–2) among which are included self-ascriptions of beliefs. In the account he develops, conscious thoughts, as determinations of the attention, are to stand as reasons for such self-ascriptions. This distances Peacocke from any view of self-ascription which denies that there can be a substantive epistemology of self-knowledge. At the same time, however, he is keen to stress that he does not wish to embrace an observational model of self-knowledge, on which conscious thoughts are the objects of conscious awareness. The middle way is intended to avoid these two extremes by attention to the conditions under which a subject can genuinely be said to possess the concept of belief.

It is tempting to see Peacocke's account as offering a solution to the problems of self-knowledge by meshing the account of the structure of phenomenal consciousness with the account of the concept of belief and the nature of self-ascription. What I shall suggest is that, instead, the account only shows us where the fundamental problems are located.

---

[9] See e.g. Allport 1988, 1993.

Even if we do not have a solution to difficult problems, it is no small effort to have located what is really problematic.

We can see Peacocke's concentration on the link between attention and consciousness, and the apparent unity to our notion of attention, as offering a partial answer to Rortian scepticism about the mental. Experiential states give us a conscious awareness of their objects, and conscious thoughts as occupying or being determinants of consciousness put us in mind of what they are about. We can give content to the idea of these forming a unified stream of consciousness without having to appeal at this stage to any idea of accessibility to further thought about their occurrence. So we do not have to appeal at this stage to the materials used by a higher-order thought theory of consciousness in order to explain why the various elements of phenomenal consciousness belong together. This sets the stage for an account of self-ascription which allows conscious thought to have an explanatory role in an account of self-ascription, rather than self-ascription playing an explanatory role in an account of conscious thought.

Peacocke's general approach to the theory of concepts predisposes him to the idea that the conditions for possessing the concept of belief should not presuppose a grasp of that concept. He proposes that conscious states, and conscious beliefs in particular, are to act as reasons for self-ascriptions. Hence, having a conscious belief cannot depend on one being able to self-ascribe such a belief, on his view, without that violating a circularity constraint on a theory of concepts. Peacocke is thus committed to rejecting higher-order thought theories of consciousness, where the self-ascriptions are explanatory of consciousness, even if he grants that there is a close parallel between conscious states and thoughts about them.[10]

Peacocke hopes to hold on to what he takes to be an insight in observational models of self-knowledge—as he says, 'the internalist introspectionist is right at least to the extent that he emphasizes the subjective aspect of conscious attitudes, their ability to contribute to a specification of what it is like for the thinker. Such conscious states can give reasons . . .' (p. 83)—by exploiting the gap between conscious thought and self-ascription. What I shall focus on here is the question how Peacocke can defuse the problems that motivate a 'no reasons' view of self-ascription without introducing some form of inner observation.

Peacocke himself focuses on difficulties for particular versions of the observational model of self-knowledge, views which posit introspection

---

[10] Here I assume that Peacocke is continuing aspects of the approach in an earlier work (Peacocke 1992), in which see the general condition against circularity, pp. 9, 33–6, and on the concept of belief in particular, pp. 151–5.

of states of mind with intentional contents that are not externally individuated. For our purposes we need to look to more general reasons
for adopting or resisting a 'no reasons' view of self-knowledge.

First, I want to take up a slightly different perspective on why one
might wish to resist a 'no reasons' view of authoritative self-ascription.
From its title, one might suppose that such a view need consist in no
more than the negative thesis that certain self-ascriptions of one's first-
order states require one to have no reason for the self-ascription. This
epistemological claim would be quite consistent with the metaphysical
view that the two states of mind are entirely distinct. But, typically, views
which deny that there is a substantive epistemology of self-knowledge
defuse the problems which such an epistemology would set out to solve
by appealing to a metaphysics of mind. Such 'no reasons' views look
to replace an epistemological connection between distinct states with a
constitutive connection between lower-order and higher-order states.

The weakest form of constitutive view claims that a rational thinker
cannot form first-order beliefs without being such as to form in general the correct second-order beliefs; and that this is so simply in virtue
of the nature of rational belief, so there is no room for a further account
of how any of those second-order beliefs relate to the first-order beliefs
that they are about. For Peacocke, even this constitutive claim is too
strong: he suggests that a conscious thinker should be able to form beliefs
and reason even if he lacks the concept of belief, and hence lacks a capacity for self-ascription. But if it is too strong for Peacocke, it also seems
too weak to answer all of the questions that force on one a constitutive
form of the 'no reasons' view.[11] If we are told simply of a general constraint—that on the whole one must have correct higher-order beliefs
to have lower-order beliefs—this tells us nothing about the relation
between any particular higher-order belief and its subject-matter, the
corresponding lower-order belief.[12]

A stronger form of constitutive view supposes that for a significant
range of higher-order states there is a constitutive link between each
of these states and their corresponding lower-order states. There is a
wide variety of such accounts, some taking the lower-order state to be

[11] I assume that we require a stricter condition on first-person authority than that
indicated by Davidson 1987/1994: 45–6. Such a stricter condition would seem to be
assumed by Peacocke also; otherwise the problem which his possession condition for
belief is intended to solve would not arise.

[12] Peacocke notes that this form of constitutive account may favour a reliabilist epistemology (p. 77), but in fact on this weak form of the constitutive view, it is not even
clear that certain central forms of reliabilism—in particular, process reliabilism—will
have any purchase: for none of the relevant higher-order beliefs will have any reliable
process as its origin.

fundamental, others taking the higher-order state to be fundamental.[13] On any such view, the higher-order state and the lower-order state will not be distinct existences, something Peacocke takes his own positive view to be committed to.

However, there does seem to be prima-facie reason to prefer an account in which the paired states are distinct. We are familiar with the occurrence of beliefs which the subject comes to acknowledge only by an indirect route, through observation of his own behaviour or the testimony of others. In such cases, the higher-order belief that the subject acquires may lack the authority of the central cases of self-ascription that is the target of explanation. For example, one might mistakenly take on trust the authority of some expert that one has a certain belief and that this explains part of one's behaviour: if the belief in question would be distasteful to one, there need be no form of identification with, or commitment to, the belief in forming the higher-order belief. It seems conceivable that in such a situation one forms the higher-order belief mistakenly: the expert is wrong, and the corresponding lower-order belief is simply absent. In such a situation, the higher-order belief must be distinct from the lower-order one, since the one is present without the other. Likewise, it is conceivable that the lower-order belief should be present without a corresponding higher-order one.[14] So in these cases at least, the higher- and lower-order beliefs are distinct; and, we may suppose, are distinct even if they do occur together, since they need not do so. Now, there is no general constraint on which propositions may be believed unconsciously, so for a large range of self-ascriptions where one is authoritative it is possible that someone should have a pair of beliefs with the same contents and not be authoritative. In addition, it seems plausible that we individuate beliefs by reference to their contents, so we will have belief pairs of the same fundamental type some of which must be distinct.[15] While it is not inconsistent to suppose that

[13] Cf. Heal 1994, which supposes that the higher-order belief is partly constituted by having the lower-order belief, and Wright 1989, which suggests, but not does not explicitly endorse, a view on which the higher-order states determine the lower-order ones.

[14] Note that the authority in question is over whether one has the belief or not: a constitutive account would seem to be able to explain why, when one forms the belief that one has a certain belief, that belief is correct. That alone would not explain why, when one forms the belief that one lacks a certain belief, that denial would itself also be correct.

[15] One should contrast the problem raised here with that typically made in reference to the theory of avowals that some critics find in Wittgenstein's later philosophy. According to that view, there is a crucial metaphysical difference between first-person ascriptions of mental states, 'I believe that *p*', and second- or third-person ascriptions, 'You/she believe/s that *p*'. Whether or not such a contrast is objectionable, there is an arguable difference in content between the two types of ascription; the point in the text here is

some pair instances of a belief type are constitutively tied and other pair instances are distinct, since prima facie we are dealing with instances of the very same category, it is surely preferable to suppose that the conditions for the occurrence of such states of mind are the same, and hence that the relevant differences between them must rather be epistemological rather than metaphysical. It is not the mode of existence of the beliefs that explains authority, but rather the manner in which one has come to acquire the higher-order belief.

This would imply that the problem of delimiting the range of mental states about which one is authoritative is a problem within epistemology. It is tempting to see Peacocke's discussion of consciously based self-ascriptions as giving us at least a significant subset of these mental states.[16] So for these states, the guarantee will be given in epistemological terms concerning the link between conscious thought and our abilities to self-ascribe.

Of course, we should not suppose that 'no reasons' views are simply blind to the prima-facie support for an epistemological account of authority. They reject that motivation because they suppose that there are insuperable problems for any epistemological account. The question is whether Peacocke's positive account lays to rest all of these problems.

There are a number of overlapping worries which one may have with a reason-based or observational model of self-knowledge. One that looms large follows from the assumption that if a subject is infallible or near-infallible about her conscious states, and these states are relatively transparent to her, then there will be a near-perfect match between her beliefs about this subject-matter and the subject-matter itself. If the two sets of beliefs are genuinely distinct, then it is at least logically possible that the one set should occur without the other. Since this is apparently not a real possibility, we have to attribute to the subject a near-miraculous power of observation or theorizing in forming beliefs about her own beliefs. On the other hand, if we suppose that the two beliefs are constitutively linked, and hence not distinct, it will be no surprise that the higher-order beliefs will be matched by the lower-order beliefs.

Peacocke aims to solve this problem by appeal to the possession conditions for the concept of belief (p. 87). If we look back to his earlier

that there is not even this kind of difference in content, despite the need to claim that there is a difference in metaphysical status.

[16] On pp. 91–2, Peacocke admits conscious mental states about which we are authoritative but for which our self-ascriptions are not consciously based in his sense. So Peacocke is keen to admit a plurality of sources for authority which will have to be related to the concept of belief; cf. also pp. 89–90.

A Study of Concepts, we find the following account of the possession conditions for the concept of belief:

Possession Condition for the Concept of Belief A relational concept R is the concept of belief only if

(F) the thinker finds the first-person content that he stands in R to p primitively compelling whenever he has the conscious belief that p, and he finds it compelling because he has that conscious belief; and

(T) in judging a thought of the third person form aRp, the thinker thereby incurs a commitment to a's being in a state that has the same content-dependent role in making a intelligible as the role of his own state of standing in R to p making him intelligible, were he to be in that state.[17]

For our purposes here, clause (F) is the relevant one. If this is the right possession condition for the concept of belief, it will follow that a condition of possessing the concept is: (i) when not distracted, one has higher-order beliefs corresponding to the conscious beliefs one has (and hence to avoid infinite regress, one has some non-conscious higher-order beliefs); (ii) these beliefs are correct. On this condition there is no simple necessary link between two beliefs, but rather a necessary connection between two beliefs and the concept exploited in one of them: one would not be in possession of the relevant concept, were one not to form the one belief in the presence of the other. As Peacocke points out, just such necessary links hold in other cases where we are dealing solely with first-order judgements, and so give us no special reason to think that in this case the one belief must be constitutive of the other.[18]

But Peacocke is at least as interested in the epistemic aspects of self-ascription and its pragmatic consequences, and here too problems have been posited for observational models, and have been assumed to apply to any reason-based view. As Peacocke notes, for states he calls 'reason-led', the commitments associated with the self-ascription closely parallel those of the state self-ascribed, and it has been thought that this creates problems for any observational model of the way in which we self-ascribe.

The worry could be put crudely like this: take a subject's conscious belief about the world. If the subject is rational, she will be in that world-directed state because she has evidence relating to how the world is —we can take evidence here in a broad sense to include not just

---

[17] Peacocke 1992: 163–4.
[18] Peacocke is here applying to the case of belief a strategy that Gareth Evans advocated for the connection between experience and judgement about it (and denied applied to the case of self-ascription of belief); see Evans 1982: 229.

inferential reasons but also grounding in sensory states. How, then, are we to model the kind of evidence or grounds the subject has for a higher-order state about that first-order state? In consciously thinking the thought, the subject's attention is directed at its subject-matter. So could the evidence that the subject has for consciously believing that also be evidence for her higher-order thought that she has that belief? If we suppose so, we face two problems. The less important one is that, if such evidence grounds the self-ascription in just the same manner that it grounds the lower-order thought, then the self-ascription will be justified only to the same degree that the lower-order thought is. This would be to forego claiming any epistemic overtones to authority: for one's conscious beliefs can be badly grounded, so, consequently, the self-ascriptions would be equally badly grounded.

The more important worry here concerns the sense in which such evidence could even *be* evidence for a self-ascription. For why should the evidence that the subject has about how the world is have any bearing on what beliefs a particular person has? The kind of evidence that grounds our beliefs about the world would seem in general not to be relevant to the question of what beliefs we ourselves have. This motivates the thought that there must be some evidence which distinctively relates to which beliefs one has and which is proprietary to self-ascription. But then one is faced with the question of what evidence that could be, and whether the self-ascriptions that result would have the properties that our self-ascriptions actually do have. What could such evidence be? Perhaps some inner subjective feeling? Once we find something which is distinctive of the state of mind rather than what the state is about, we dissociate the self-ascription from the evidential base that the lower-order state has. In that case, we would have no expectation that the self-ascription should carry over the commitments of the lower-order state; yet, as Peacocke emphasizes, for self-ascriptions of belief (and perhaps other states such as intentions), that is just not so.

In short, the question is, given that the self-ascription is made for a reason, what kind of evidence can there be for this self-ascription? If there cannot be evidence for the self-ascription, in what sense is the ascription made for a reason. But Peacocke would reject this worry as simply being in the grip of the 'spurious trilemma that influences the "no reasons" view' (p. 93). Peacocke does think that a rational transition is made when one self-ascribes a belief, but he does not claim that there is any evidence which one would use to ground one's making this rational transition.[19]

---

[19] See pp. 71–6.

The foundations for this are laid earlier in the paper when he observes that 'the thinker who successfully reaches new beliefs by inference has to be sensitive not only to the content of his initial beliefs. He has also to be sensitive to the fact that his initial states are *beliefs*. . . . [in the perceptual case] the thinker makes a transition—and this time not an inferential transition—from one state with a certain content to a belief with an overlapping, or an appropriately related, content' (p. 73). In the case of inference or perceptual judgement, a rational transition in belief turns on the propositional content of a state, which is what a subject will often take as evidence, and on the kind of state which has that propositional content. The suggestion for the case of self-ascription is therefore that there is another kind of rational transition in the offing as well: that from consciously believing that *p* to believing that one believes that *p*. The content of the first-order conscious state does not provide evidence for the higher-order belief in the manner in which beliefs can offer inferential support to other beliefs, but it does stand in a reason-giving relation all the same: self-ascription is just one more of the kinds of primitive rationally compelling transitions among mental states which thinkers make. In effect, the suggestion here is that anyone who denies that such a transition is either primitive or rational is simply in the grip of the spurious trilemma.

Is this sufficient to allay all worries that a reason-based view needs to supply evidence to ground self-ascription, but that no such evidence is to hand? I suspect that some such worries remain. There is certainly a nice point of dialectic here: it is not enough for a critic of reason-based views to point to some feature distinctive of self-ascription, given that a reason-based view of Peacocke's ilk claims that this kind of rational transition is not to be reduced to any other form of reason-based transition which will lack such a feature. Nevertheless, I think that the point can be pursued somewhat further.

One might imagine a doubter complaining, 'Our problem was to explain how a certain central class of self-ascriptions is such that a subject who self-ascribes in that way is authoritative in his judgement. You, Peacocke, suggest that it is in the nature of the concept of belief, that no one will possess that concept unless they self-ascribe beliefs in the authoritative manner. Of course, we all accept that, for this is our problem for which we require a solution.' In part, Peacocke has an answer to this question which is just implicit in the thesis that self-ascription is one of the primitive rationally compelling transitions among one's beliefs. If we have specified correctly the possession conditions for the concept of belief, then a unique semantic value for that concept should be determined: namely, the relation of believing, and given the nature of that relation, we have as a consequence the various properties of self-ascription which we all agree hold of judgements containing that concept. At a general level, then, there is an account of how the possession conditions of the concept match up with the truth of appropriate judgements containing that concept.

However, the difficult question here is whether there needs to be any further explanation or justification besides the general form of one offered here. In the case of logical concepts, one might think that there really is no more to be said at this juncture,[20] while in the case of perceptual judgements there does seem to be more to say. For example, take the case of an observational concept of the colour red. A subject who takes his experience at face value will be disposed to judge that there is something red before him when he has a visual experience as of something red being before him. In this case, too, we can ask the question why a subject should be such that he makes judgements about red things in this way; and an answer is just to point out that the possession conditions for the observational concept of red will include a clause to the effect that a subject will find it primitively compelling to judge that something is red when he has an experience as of something red. We can then raise the further question of why one's concept of red should be this way. A general answer which parallels the answer given above for self-ascription, and one which could be given for logical concepts, is to appeal to the role of perception as a source of information about the world. Certain properties in the world are such that we can have experiences of them, and the means by which we come to have those experiences lead us to track the properties in question when we form judgements on the basis of those experiences. That would be to suggest that there are certain transitions among one's mental states which preserve or aim at truth, and when we make judgements in accord with these kinds of transition, we succeed in acquiring truths. Given that in making judgements and forming beliefs we aim at truth, we have reason to possess such concepts.

But we can say things which are more specific and more substantial about particular cases of experience and observational concepts. These specific stories, indicating things about the various modes of perception, lend content to the more general and formal account according to which having perceptual experience is such that one can form true judgements by making judgements on the basis of it. For the observational concept of red, we can add various claims about the conditions under which one can tell the colour of something, the ways in which

---

[20] Cf. here Peacocke 1987.

one can experience differently surface colours from film colours, and so on. Furthermore, these specific instances help give content to the general explanation because, for the case of perceptual concepts, we can tell that the particular cases of application are examples not only where the property corresponding to the concept is present, but that these are the sorts of cases which we can recognize as being cases in which we would take ourselves to be aware of the property.

Should we think of the case of the concept of belief, and our self-ascriptions of conscious belief, along the lines of logical concepts, or should we think of it as more akin to the case of observational concepts and perceptual judgements? One reason to think that it will be more like the case of perceptual judgement would be that we are dealing with cases in which we have specific instances of belief and self-ascriptions of those instances. So it does seem appropriate to ask how a subject might track in particular cases instances of believing.

In section III of his paper, Peacocke takes up this challenge, and aims to show how, by appeal to the nature of belief, we can see that the various procedures he discusses and the possession conditions of the concept of belief lead to correct judgements about what one believes. Now my lingering worries concern whether those kinds of specific explanation give us the same handle on the general account as the corresponding specific explanations of perceptual judgement do for the examples of observational concepts. But to make good these doubts, I think we first need to look at what Peacocke has to say about the role of self-ascription in endorsing one's first-order beliefs, and to question the range of consciously based self-ascriptions.

III

Peacocke suggests that in the case of self-ascription on the basis of apparent memory, 'The self-ascription of the belief on this basis goes beyond a mere report of oneself as having an apparent memory with that content. One makes the self-ascription in part because one is *endorsing* the content of the apparent memory. . . . when a self-ascription of a reason-led state is made on the basis of the occurrence of a conscious state in this way, it is not a *mere* report of that state. It involves the same kind of endorsement and commitment as would be made in entering the first-order, reason-led state itself' (p. 86).

What is the force of this suggestion? We might distinguish at least two situations here: one in which I ask myself the question, who was

Prime Minister in the Prague Spring, and, on recalling Dubček, take myself to have an answer to that question. In this case, I have engaged in an enquiry about the world, and as a result make a judgement about the world and also about my own state of mind, that I believe that Dubček was Prime Minister in the Prague Spring. In the other case, I may have some seeming memory of Dubček as Prime Minister in the Prague Spring, but I may hesitate in taking this at face value. Peacocke's point is that I cannot move from this to the self-ascription of belief that Dubček was Prime Minister without thereby accepting the commitments of the belief self-ascribed.[21]

I want to contrast what Peacocke has to say here, which lays stress on the role of self-ascription, with a suggestion drawn from Evans, but which has its roots in Wittgenstein. Evans claims: 'The crucial point is . . . : in making a self-ascription of belief, one's eyes are, so to speak, or occasionally literally, directed outwards—upon the world.'[22] This is to claim that the commitments associated with a second-order enquiry are explained through its dependence on some first-order enquiry: it is because one engages in the first-order enquiry that with the answer to the second-order enquiry one ends up with the commitments associated with the answer to the first-order one.

Peacocke's own interpretation of Evans on this point (pp. 72–3) suggests a model on which the procedure engaged in is one which leads to the formation of a first-order belief, and that this is what explains the truth of the self-ascription made at that time. But the underlying picture that Evans appeals to need not be interpreted in this manner. It needs no more than the idea that it is through our attention to the world outside us, the world as it is for us, that we come to make judgements about our own beliefs. This observation will equally apply to beliefs already held, which will govern the result of the first-order enquiry, to conscious thoughts and to the procedure that Peacocke attributes to Evans.

Now the further suggestion that Peacocke makes, that self-ascriptions based on 'intermediate conscious states' will endorse the commitments of the ascribed state, does not seem to me to be invariably correct. To see this, we should first consider Peacocke's example of a subject who lacks full rational integration of his beliefs. In the example he discusses drawn from Dennett, the father has the conscious thought that his son is a fine painter, even though he has by no means sufficient evidence for this conviction. As Peacocke points out, this belief will be no more rationally integrated with the subject's other beliefs than an irrational

---

[21] In his 1996: 119–21, Peacocke marks this distinction between types of case explicitly.
[22] Evans 1982: 225.

and unconscious belief may be in another person. It cannot then be that the essence of conscious thought is for it to be rationally integrated.

Now for the mildly self-deceiving father, it would seem possible that engaging in the first-order enquiry, in certain circumstances, would lead to the judgement that his son is not a fine painter, or that there are no longer any fine painters alive. For the father's evidence to this effect does not positively support his belief. Nevertheless, when engaged in the second-order enquiry, the father may well come to realize that he does have the conviction that his son is a great painter. In some cases it may well be that the father thereby takes over the commitments of this conviction when he recognizes it through his self-scrutiny; but it is also quite possible that the father should be led to a sense of a lack of inner integrity, feeling forced to distance himself from what he recognizes is one of his own strongly held convictions.

In fact, this case is complicated, and many different dimensions of irrationality are involved: the father believes something on insufficient evidence, even by his own lights; he has motives for believing this other than an aim to discover the truth; he is also motivated to discount evidence which weighs against the belief. I suggest that we can find examples of lack of higher-order commitment which do not present as many layers of irrationality as the over-proud father.[23]

On occasion, particularly when engaged in abstract enquiry much removed from direct practical interest, one may discern neither proof nor disproof for a proposition that one is interested in. For instance, one may be considering various theorems of set theory, or certain difficult philosophical claims. On reflection, however, one may come to realize that, despite lack of firm proof or disproof one way or the other, one does actually have a strong conviction that one of the propositions in question is true. In this case, one's conviction may certainly guide behaviour when selecting research methods, areas of interest, and so on—much of this guidance may not seem fully explicit. In at least some of these cases, self-conscious reflection on one's conviction may lead one to distance oneself from that commitment, and this may be reflected in one's discussion of it with others—one won't put forward the proposition in as unquestionable a manner as one might otherwise.[24]

---

[23] That there are such cases was pressed on me forcefully by my colleague Marcus Giaquinto, someone too careful in his own thought to be an exemplar of them.

[24] This is certainly a matter of higher- versus lower-order convictions—there is no reason to suppose that it can be modelled simply on one dimension of subjective degrees of belief; evidence may be such that the subject has no reason to have a degree of belief much different from 0.5, and yet act unselfconsciously with conviction that the proposition must be so.

It seems to me rather unclear what a subject's rational obligations are in such cases. And these cases pose problems for an account of belief and self-ascription which are not defused simply by claiming that the title of 'belief' for them is really just honorific. On the contrary, these seem to be cases for which the much-derided Humean model of belief offers a better fit. We would not be overstating the case, when we insist that it really cannot be the case that all belief is like this, to deny the fact that at least some examples are. The guidance that one has as to whether one believes something in these cases does indeed go via some subjective feeling of conviction. If we merely follow the Evans proced-ure, we can determine no answer to the question of what we believe; but our independent awareness of a conviction gives an answer to the second-order enquiry. Furthermore, just as was suggested in our earlier discussion of evidence for self-ascription, where we have a self-ascription which is distinctively second-order, identification with (and commitment to) the self-ascribed belief is possible, but is not necessary.[25]

This modification has further repercussions for the account. Some of our self-ascriptions of belief lack authority. Earlier I suggested that we can see Peacocke's account as implicitly offering to delimit in part the range of such beliefs about which we have authority: namely, those which we can ascribe on the basis of conscious thoughts.[26] But we can now see that this is too broad a basis for authoritative self-ascription. For the Humean beliefs give us examples of consciously based self-ascription where error is conceivable. A too familiar phenomenon in philosoph-ical enquiry is the realization that the proposition that one felt that one had a real conviction was so, turns out to be not the proposition that one identified initially, but really another proposition, which is a close cousin. Here the kind of subjective feeling which is taken as a guide to conviction is mistakenly associated with the wrong content (note that both contents can be before the mind), while the kind of dis-tancing that can be present in such self-ascription rules out the further response that the commitments undertaken in such self-ascription will guarantee that the subject does, after all, have the belief self-ascribed.

If we consider the range of self-ascriptions which are in some sense based on conscious states, so as to include these Humean self-ascriptions,

---

[25] Peacocke's (1996) suggestion to the contrary turns on features of what one is com-mitted to in *saying* that one believes something; of course, the commitments of what one can say need not have consequences for an account of the commitments involved in believing that one believes something.

[26] As noted above, Peacocke thinks that the range of beliefs about which we have authority is in fact broader than this, since there are authoritative self-ascriptions not made on the basis of any phenomenal conscious state.

then we cannot really suppose that a subject is authoritative across the range, since it is quite possible that some of these judgements are false, and there is no reason to believe that for the class as a whole there should be a guarantee of reliability. This does not impugn the possession condition cited above, of course; but that in itself gives no comfort, since the condition guarantees the truth of the self-ascription simply because the antecedent of the condition limits itself to cases in which one does consciously believe the proposition in question.

Of course, I don't mean to suggest that this kind of *outré* example shows that we don't have authority in self-ascription, any more than Peacocke takes the example of bad faith on page 90 to undermine authority. What these examples show is that the task of delimiting the range of beliefs about which we have authority is more difficult than a focus on self-deception and unconscious belief might have suggested.

This is the other moral that we could draw from Evans's approach. When the subject has her eyes directed outwards, they are directed on the world, as it is for her. Now, we should not assume that all of a subject's conscious states form part of the world as it is for her, not even all of her conscious beliefs. So, we might say, what we expect is that a subject should at least have authority with respect to those mental states which comprise in part her point of view on the world. Peacocke himself endorses a close link here between consciousness and the subjective point of view when he claims that 'The requirement that the reason-giving state is one which is, or could become, conscious is intimately related to our conception of an agent as someone with a point of view, one whose rational actions make sense to the subject himself . . . given that point of view' (p. 96).

In fact, the contrast here between self-ascription based on conscious beliefs which comprise a subject's point of view and self-ascription based on Humean cases parallels the horns of the dilemma raised earlier concerning evidence for self-ascription. In the former case, we focus on examples in which the subject's attention is directed out at the world, out at how the subject takes the world to be, and the self-ascription which results carries over the commitments of the state ascribed. In the latter kind of case, we can indeed discern a distinctive kind of evidence for the presence of a mental state, a feeling of conviction, and, as one might anticipate in this kind of case, lack of identification with the belief seems conceivable. What is inconceivable is that all self-ascription should be like the latter case; if it is in the former kind of case that we possess the interesting properties of authority, it is that which we have to explain.

We can restate the puzzle which motivated the 'no reasons' view thus: in relation to cases where the subject is self-ascribing beliefs which form part of how the world is for her, which mirror her point of view on the world, the subject is aware of aspects of the world, and her attention is drawn out into the world. Yet, by directing her eyes outward, so to speak, she gains knowledge of her own mind. Why should this be so?[27]

IV

I can hardly claim that the notions invoked here to state the puzzle are themselves clear, or without need of further elucidation and explanation. Talk of a subject's point of view and of how the world is for a subject are slippery indeed; but it seems to me wrong to think that one can dissolve the problem simply by refusing to make sense of these things. So they will do for the moment as a way of pressing home the worry that I have about Peacocke's account.

He suggests that correctness of self-ascription can be explained in terms of various aspects of the nature of belief and of the concept of belief: our beliefs may be 'capable of producing manifestations in conscious occurrences' (p. 70); those conscious occurrences can act as (non-inferential) reasons for a thinker in making a self-ascription of belief. As I have just argued, and as Peacocke himself notes anyway in relation to the example of bad faith on page 90, the actual explanation here needs to be more complicated. We need to specify additional conditions, or to look to a narrower range of conscious states in order to explain the correctness. But I think we can bring out what seems still to be lacking in this explanation without having to add such complications.

In the case of perceptual judgements, what helps us grasp the fact that, in applying the concept in the situation specified by possession conditions, the subject does what she has reason to do is that for specific examples we have an independent handle on the fact that the subject is aware of an instance of the property, and so has some grasp herself that this is the kind of situation in which her judgement would be appropriate. One might think that in the case of self-ascription, a similar move would be made: the specific instances would be ones in which the subject is *aware* of the belief in question, and that is why it seems appropriate to her to make the judgement that she does.

Two things might encourage, or mislead, one into supposing that this is what Peacocke has in mind. In the original possession conditions quoted above, the relevant case of belief in which the subject self-ascribes is

[27] Cf. Evans 1982: 231.

one in which she has a conscious belief; in the passage just quoted, Peacocke talks of the conscious state being 'a manifestation' of the belief ascribed. But our discussion of attention, and of the Humean cases, should show that this could not be the right interpretation. When someone consciously thinks something, it occupies her attention, in Peacocke's phrase, which I suggested earlier is to say that it is a determination of attention: the subject's attention is directed to the subject-matter of the thought, not to the having of the thought itself. That is to say, in such cases the subject's attention is directed out at the world, not in any way within herself. So the talk of manifestation here should not be loaded with any cognitive or epistemological connotations: the conscious thought is a manifestation simply in the sense that the breaking of a glass is a manifestation of its fragility.

One might be justified in taking the conscious thought to count as a case of the subject being aware of her own thought as such, if one thought that consciousness presupposed self-consciousness. In that case, one could claim that all states of conscious awareness were primarily cases of self-awareness, as well as an awareness of other things. This is one way in which we can interpret Kant's talk of all representations being determinations of inner sense.[28] It is far from clear to me that in taking all such conscious states to be states of self-awareness one is thereby adopting an observational model of self-knowledge. So for this approach we would have the beginnings of an answer to why the subject should have the concept of belief she does based on a form of awareness which is not observational, clearly not inferential, and yet not nothing either.

Would this approach be consistent with Peacocke's account? There are reasons to think not. First, Peacocke wants to hold on to the possibility of creatures who are conscious without being self-conscious (p. 96). Presumably such creatures will lack self-awareness of their conscious states.[29] The suggestion in the previous paragraph would then have to be relativized to creatures like us, sophisticated enough to have the concepts of belief and the first person. Now we can ask what difference there needs to be between a creature who is conscious but lacks self-awareness and someone just like us, who has self-awareness

---

[28] See e.g. Kant 1929: A98, A210 (B255).

[29] Could one claim that one can have a non-conceptual form of self-awareness without any psychological concepts or concept of the self, just as some philosophers claim that there are non-conceptual states of awareness in perception of the world around us? The difficulty with this suggestion is that in the case of sensory perception we have some handle on states of mind distinct from their objects which may be ascribed a non-conceptual content—if we avoid an observational model of inner sense, there would be no appropriate non-conceptual states distinct from their object to support the claim that there was a form of self-awareness here without self-conscious judgement.

and the concepts of belief and the first person. It is unclear whether Peacocke is offering us anything more than would be given by the possession conditions for these concepts, which indicate situations which, seemingly, could occur were we otherwise to lack self-awareness. But the suggestion of the previous paragraph is really that self-awareness has to be appealed to in order to explain why these possession conditions are indeed the right ones, the ones which reveal why conscious states are reasons for our self-ascriptions, and that is something that Peacocke would be committed to denying.

Peacocke would not, of course, be the only person inclined to reject that assumption. That view threatens to land us with an account on which we take the notion of self-awareness as primitive and one for which we can give no further account. But it is in rejecting this position, while still attempting to avoid the 'no reasons' view, that I think we find a lingering puzzle. The puzzle was to explain why in attending to the world I should be given reason to self-ascribe my state of mind. The 'no reason' view attempts to dissolve this puzzle by denying that I am given any such reason or that I need it. I side with Peacocke in finding such a dissolution unsatisfactory. However, I am not sure that I have a grasp on how he can give us an account of what it is for my conscious state, which is an attending to some aspect of the world, to be a reason for my self-ascription which does not presuppose that such states of mind are simply cases of self-awareness.[30]

REFERENCES

Akins, Kathleen (1996) (ed.), *Introduction to Perception* (Oxford: Clarendon Press), 3–17.

Allport, Alan (1988), 'What Concept of Consciousness?', in A. Marcel and E. Bisiach (eds.), *Consciousness and Contemporary Science* (Oxford: Clarendon Press).

—— (1993), 'Attention and Control: Have We Been Asking the Wrong Questions? A Critical Review of Twenty-five Years', in D. E. Meyer and S. Kornblum (eds.), *Attention and Performance*, xiv (Cambridge, Mass.: MIT Press), 183–218.

Davidson, D. (1987/1994), 'Knowing One's Own Mind', *Proceedings and Addresses of the American Philosophical Association*, 60: 441–58; repr. in Q. Cassam (ed.), *Self-Knowledge* (Oxford: Oxford University Press), 43–64.

[30] I am grateful to Tim Crane, Christopher Peacocke, Diana Raffman, Mark Sainsbury, and Julia Tanney for comments on an earlier version of this chapter; and to Naomi Eilan, Marcus Giaquinto, and Jerry Valberg for stimulating discussion of this topic. The essay was written while on a leave funded by the British Academy Research Leave Scheme.

Dennett, D. C. (1991), *Consciousness Explained* (New York: Little, Brown).

Evans, G. (1982), *The Varieties of Reference*, ed. J. McDowell (Oxford: Clarendon Press).

Grimes, John (1996), 'Failure to Detect Changes in Scenes across Saccades', in Akins (1996), 89–110.

Heal, Jane (1994), 'Wittgenstein and Moore's Paradox', *Mind*, 103: 5–24.

James, William (1983), *The Principles of Psychology* (Cambridge, Mass.: Harvard University Press); orig. pub. in 2 vols. by Henry Holt in 1890.

Kant, Immanuel (1929), *The Critique of Pure Reason*, trans. Norman Kemp Smith (London: Macmillan).

McConkie, G. W. (1979), 'On the Role of and Control of Eye Movements in Reading', in P. Kolers, M. Wrolstad, and H. Bouma (eds.), *Processing of Visible Language*, i (New York: Plenum Press), 37–48.

Peacocke, C. A. B. (1987), 'Understanding Logical Concepts: A Realist's Account', *Proceedings of the British Academy*, 73: 153–99.

—— (1992), *A Study of Concepts* (Cambridge, Mass.: MIT Press).

—— (1996), 'Entitlement, Self-Knowledge and Conceptual Redeployment', *Proceedings of the Aristotelian Society*, 96: 117–58.

Rorty, R. (1979), *Philosophy and the Mirror of Nature* (Oxford: Blackwell).

Rosenthal, D. M. (1990), *A Theory of Consciousness*, report no. 40/1990, Centre for Interdisciplinary Research [ZiF], Research Group on Mind and Brain, University of Bielefeld.

Sartre, Jean-Paul (1991), *The Psychology of the Imagination* (New York: Citadel).

Shallice, Tim, and Burgess, Paul (1993), 'Control of Action and Thought Selection', in A. Baddeley and L. Weiskrantz (eds.), *Attention: Selection, Awareness and Control* (Oxford: Clarendon Press), 171–87.

Shoemaker, Sydney (1994), 'Self-Knowledge and "Inner Sense"', *Philosophy and Phenomenological Research*, 64: 249–314.

Treisman, A., and Gelade, G. (1980), 'A Feature-Integration Theory of Attention', *Cognitive Psychology*, 12: 97–136.

Wright, Crispin (1989), 'Wittgenstein's Rule-Following Considerations and the Central Problem of Linguistics', in A. George (ed.), *Reflections on Chomsky* (Oxford: Blackwell), 233–64.

5

Externalism and Authoritative
Self-Knowledge

CYNTHIA MACDONALD

Externalism in the philosophy of mind has been thought by many to pose a serious threat to the claim that subjects are in general authoritative with regard to certain of their own intentional states.[1] In a series of papers, Tyler Burge (1985a, 1985b, 1988, 1996) has argued that the distinctive entitlement or right that subjects have to self-knowledge in certain cases is compatible with externalism, since that entitlement is environmentally neutral, neutral with respect to the issue of the individuation dependence of subjects' intentional states on factors beyond their bodies. His reason is that whereas externalism—the view that certain intentional states of persons are individuation-dependent on objects and/or phenomena external to their bodies—is a metaphysical thesis, authoritative self-knowledge is an epistemological matter. This being so, there is no reason to suppose that the two need conflict with one another.

I agree, but do not think that Burge's account of the nature and source of a subject's distinctive entitlement to self-knowledge establishes it. Burge claims that certain forms of self-knowledge (such as the *cogito* cases, which involve thoughts of the form *I am thinking that I am thinking that p*, for some propositional content *p*) are contextually self-verifying. That is, a subject's thinking such thoughts makes those thoughts true. But this does not, he thinks, in itself account for the peculiarly authoritative position that the subject has with regard to knowing what contentful thoughts she is thinking.[2] He acknowledges, that is, that a substantial epistemology is needed to account for first-person authority, even in cases

---

[1] See e.g. Burge 1985a, 1985b, 1988; Davidson 1988; Heil 1988, 1992; and Boghossian 1989.

[2] This point is especially clear in Burge 1996. The account given here is based on this source.

like the *cogito* ones, where one is presently consciously thinking about
a thought while thinking it, and where the first-order thought is a constituent of the second-order, or reflective, thought. His view is that such
an epistemology can account for the peculiar entitlement that one has to
knowledge of one's own intentional states, without being justificatory
—without consisting of reasons or other factors that a subject is able
explicitly to bring to bear on it. The distinctive entitlement is explicable
simply in terms of a subject's being in a favoured position with regard
to her own intentional states. The question is: what is the nature of this
favoured position, and what is the source of the authoritative status it
confers on subjects' self-knowledge?

Burge's claim is that the source of a person's distinctive entitlement
or right to self-knowledge lies, first, in the role that first-person thoughts
or judgements play in critical thinking, and second, in the non-causal,
constitutive, relation that holds between reflective thoughts and their
subject-matter, or contents. Subjects reason critically, or reflectively, and
in order to do so, they must be capable of thinking first-person thoughts
knowledgeably. Since this is necessary for critical thinking, and subjects
do reason critically, they must be entitled to, and must possess, knowledge of their own intentional states. What explains the *distinctiveness*
of this entitlement is the fact that, in cases of self-knowledge, one is the
sole subject of both one's first-order and one's second-order states. This
gives the subject a single perspective on her own states, which forges a
rational connection between reflective thoughts and the subject-matter
of those thoughts. Since this is one perspective, *what* one is thinking
and *what* is being thought about cannot regularly come apart; unlike
cases of third-person knowledge of a subject's contentful states, there
is no 'space' within which to distinguish the perspective of the thinker
from the perspective of what is being thought about.

This single perspective affords an explanation of a subject's distinctive entitlement to self-knowledge only against the background of the
role which first-person thoughts or beliefs play in critical thinking.
This is so, not in the sense that one must be reasoning critically when
one thinks first-person thoughts, but in the sense that one must have
the capacity to think critically in order to be *entitled* to think these
thoughts. One cannot reason critically unless one not only has reasons
for one's beliefs but recognizes these *as* reasons. One uses one's knowledge of what counts as good reasons for thinking that p to 'guide' one's
first-order reasoning, *as* reasons for thinking that p.[3] Critical reasoning
requires that one be capable of evaluating one's first-order thoughts and

---

[3] This is Burge's (1996) terminology.

beliefs in the light of the norms that govern reasoning. One is incapable of doing this unless one is able not only to think about one's thoughts, but also to know what thoughts one thinks. So such reasoning requires self-knowledge.

However, one can agree with Burge that first-person thoughts play a distinctive role in critical reasoning, and that subjects could only engage in such reasoning if they were in general entitled to knowledge with regard to at least certain of their own intentional states, without accepting his explanation for this entitlement. Christopher Peacocke (1996) has argued that it is one thing to hold that a subject must be entitled to first-person knowledge of her own intentional states if she is to be capable of reasoning critically, another to hold that the *source* of such entitlement lies in the role that such knowledge plays in critical reasoning. His objection is that one can reason critically without making use of self-ascriptions, and so without thinking knowledgeably about one's thoughts. Furthermore, there seem to be cases of reflective thinking which involve self-ascriptions but are not *truth*-seeking, and so do not count as cases of critical reasoning: as cases of evaluating, justifying, criticizing and amending one's first-order beliefs or thoughts. In day-dreaming, for example, one may think reflectively while suspending judgement on the truth of one's thoughts. This does not show that Burge's claim that one's ability to reason critically requires that one be entitled to knowledgeable self-ascriptions is false. But it does strongly suggest that the role that they play in critical thinking is not part of the source of subjects' entitlement to self-knowledge.

Moran's (1994) distinction between theoretical-descriptive and prescriptive bases for psychological ascriptions brings this out nicely. He invites us to consider a person who, in the process of wondering about her current intentional states, asks herself the question, 'What do I think about X?'. This question can be interpreted in two ways: (a) as a theoretical-cum-descriptive one about an attitude antecedently held, or (b) as a prescriptive one about what the subject *ought* to believe about X. Normally, these two ways of interpreting such a question interact with one another. However, Moran argues that they are distinct, and that it may be possible to detach one from the other. His point (or one of them) is that reflective thinking is not (or not always) exclusively of the prescriptive form, where the question of rational interpretation, of having reasons by which to criticize, evaluate, and amend one's thoughts or beliefs, enters into the very process of first-order belief formation and 'guides' one's own first-order reasoning. There are descriptive elements in such reasoning, even where there are also prescriptive ones. Day-dreaming may be a case of this kind.

If this is right, then Burge's claims about the role of first-person judge-ments/thoughts in critical reasoning do not establish that this is the source of subjects' entitlement to self-knowledge. It is plausible that there is a more primitive form of critical reasoning which does not require knowledgeable self-ascription (Peacocke 1996), and it is plausible that self-ascription plays a *descriptive* role in reflective thinking that either does not involve critical thinking or, if it does, does so in addition to the prescriptive role. Further, it may be that the descriptive, and not the prescriptive, role is the source of our entitlement to self-knowledge.

The aim of this chapter is to explore and defend this latter claim further by developing a quasi-observational account of authoritative self-knowledge.[4] I want to explore this not only because Burge's claims leave room for the development of such an account, but also because his explanation for our entitlement to self-knowledge does not clearly suffice to explain why authoritative self-knowledge is compatible with externalism.

Burge notes that there is an asymmetry between first- and third-person knowledge of a subject's intentional states, in that, in the former, but not the latter, a single perspective is involved, and that this single per-spective forges a rational, non-contingent connection between reflective thought and thought reviewed.[5] Suppose that there is this asymmetry. Then the question arises as to why we should think that this, and the rational connection it forges, confers authority on the subject and not on others. *What* is it about the perspectives possibly 'coming apart' that makes others *less* authoritative than me about the contents of my intentional states, about *what* is known? Why is it not the case that others, in having another perspective on my states, are better placed

---

[4] It is *quasi*-observational for two reasons. The first is that there is a clear disana-logy between the observational model upon which the account is based and cases of authoritative self-knowledge with regard to the position of the subject. The second is that authoritative self-knowledge involves both causal and rationalistic elements.

[5] It is unclear why it should be assumed that this is generally the case, or that it must be so: if I can take a different perspective on other subjects, or on what is visually pres-ent before me, or, as in my own reasoning, on the soundness of that reasoning, it seems possible that my perspective as thinker might 'come apart', even regularly, from my per-spective as subject of what is thought about. It seems that for Burge this possibility is ruled out by the fact that, in the *cogito* cases, the first-order states are not only thought while being thought about, but are literally constituents of the second-order, reflective thoughts. The result is that there are not here two thoughts, whose relations to one another might be such that a subject's perspective on one might differ from her perspective on the other. However, this construal of the *cogito* cases is not the only possible one, as discussion of objections to the observational model in section II makes clear; nor are the *cogito* cases the only ones concerning which the question of authoritative self-knowledge arises, as Burge (1996) expressly concedes.

than me to know what I am currently thinking? It is not obvious that different perspectives must be less authoritative. This would seem to be particularly true if externalism is true. So, unless these questions can be given satisfactory answers, the difficulty in seeing how authoritative self-knowledge is compatible with externalism remains.

Burge (1985b, 1988) thinks that it is the *immediacy* of the relation between subject and content that this unified perspective confers that makes for one's authority with regard to one's own intentional states. Indeed, it is generally thought that a person's authority with regard to the contents of certain of her intentional states (e.g. the *cogito*-like ones) consists at least in part in the *direct accessibility* to subjects of their own states, in the sense that knowledge of those states is typically not based on evidence.[6] This in turn is thought to make for an asymmetry between first- and third-person knowledge of subjects' intentional states, since the latter is typically based on evidence. This asymmetry poses two prima-facie problems for externalism.

The first, which is not the primary concern here, is how to reconcile such non-evidence-based knowledge with the externalist view that the contents of certain intentional states are individuation-dependent on factors beyond person's bodies. The problem is that externalism seems to require what self-knowledge evidently rules out, namely, that knowledge of one's own intentional states be based on empirical evidence. The second problem, which is the primary concern here, is not how first-person *knowledge* can be seen to be compatible with externalism, but how *authoritative* knowledge can be reconciled with that position. The problem is that beliefs that are not based on evidence are not generally thought to be more reliable than ones that are. However, first-person authority seems to ground such authority precisely in the fact that it is not based on evidence.

So it is the peculiar epistemic *directness*, or immediacy, of the relation between a person and the contents of her own intentional states when she thinks about them, which Burge and others emphasize as crucial to the authoritative status of self-knowledge, that seems to pose problems for externalism. Why? If, for instance, first-person knowledge

---

[6] See Burge 1979, 1985a, 1985b; Davidson 1987; Heil 1988; and Wright 1989. Some, like Wright, emphasize the non-evidence-based character of such knowledge, whereas others, like Heil, emphasize the fact that such knowledge is not empirically evidence-based. Alston (1971) gives an illuminating account of the different senses that might attach to the notion of direct access. He argues that the notion of directness that is relevant to self-knowledge is epistemic, not causal, and is explicable in terms of being non-evidence-based, where this is distinct from being non-inferential. Heil (1992) endorses this view.

were like one's non-evidence-based knowledge of certain empirical facts external to one's body—say, knowledge that the table before one is white—then there would be no special problem for externalism to explain. For knowledge of this kind does not confer upon a subject an epistemic advantage over others. What makes the authoritative status of self-knowledge peculiar to it is that one's *right* or *entitlement* to it is *independent* of knowledge of the factors that individuate intentional content. This conflicts with the belief, which externalism apparently fosters, that others who have access to such factors are equally, and perhaps better, placed to know what the contents of a subject's intentional states are than the subject. That subjects should actually be *better* placed seems to be inexplicable on an externalist account.

Burge's account of our distinctive entitlement to self-knowledge does not resolve this apparent conflict. In his view, a subject's distinctive entitlement to self-knowledge has its source in the role such knowledge plays in critical reasoning and in the distinctive constitutive (non-causal) relation that holds between a subject's reflective thoughts and their subject-matter. This, he holds, is independent of knowledge of factors that individuate intentional content. But then a subject's entitlement to self-knowledge seems to conflict with the intuition that others who know more than the subject about the environmental factors that help to individuate intentional content are better placed to know whether, for example, in the presence of water, the thoughts she is thinking are indeed *water* thoughts. How is it that a subject's relation to the contents of her first-order states is such that an expert's better knowledge of certain contents does not compromise that subject's authority with respect to knowing that those states have those contents?

My claim is that careful development of a quasi-observational model can shed light on, and help to give an illuminating answer to, this question. At the same time, it can provide an account of the source of subjects' entitlement to self-knowledge that does not conflict with the role that first-person thoughts or judgements play in critical reasoning. This claim will be defended in two stages. First, I shall develop an account of a subject's direct epistemic access to the contents of her first-order intentional states that is broadly speaking observational in trading on important affinities between this access and subjects' epistemic access to certain observational properties of objects. This account explains the *source* of subjects' entitlement to self-knowledge, but not the *distinctiveness* of that entitlement. So, second, I shall mount an argument for first-person authority which exploits these affinities plus the further fact that subjects are the sole subjects of their own intentional states. It is this latter feature of self-knowledge that makes subjects' entitlement to self-knowledge *distinctive*, and so explains the asymmetry between first- and third-person knowledge of subjects' intentional states.

The plausibility of the resulting position depends crucially on how the model of observational properties upon which it is based is developed, and in this connection two objections to the position need to be addressed. The first is that, whereas the relation between observational properties and perceptual states of subjects is a causal one, the relation between first- and second-order intentional states in cases of authoritative self-knowledge is not. If so, then *no* observational model is appropriate for deployment in an account of authoritative self-knowledge. The second is that, whereas there are three items involved in observational models—observational property, perceptual experience, and conceptual states, such as beliefs, which those experiences ground —there are only two items involved in cases of self-knowledge—first-order intentional state and second-order reflective state. This makes for a structural disanalogy, so to speak, between the two types of case, which threatens the applicability of any observational model to cases of self-knowledge.

The final section of this chapter addresses these objections, first by discussing the issue of the types of cases of self-knowledge to which the observational model is best construed as being applicable, and second by sketching two different ways in which the model might be developed so as to preserve structural similarity. Neither of these ways is entirely unproblematic; but then the aim is not so much to defend one particular way of developing the observational model as to defeat one line of objection to its applicability to cases of self-knowledge.

Thus, the aim is to develop in these two stages an account of first-person authority for a certain class of intentional states, the *cogito*-like ones, that is capable of explaining why such authoritative self-knowledge is peculiarly authoritative, and why this is compatible with externalism. This is clearly a restricted class of states, but it is the focus of much of the recent discussion of authoritative self-knowledge, and it is arguably the most important class, since states like these are the most obvious cases of such knowledge. Moreover, the account is capable of being generalized to other cases of self-knowledge.[7] For the sake of simplicity, the discussion will be restricted to thoughts whose specifications invoke terms for natural kinds, a class of thoughts concerning which many consider externalism to be most plausible.

---

[7] For example, to the kinds of cases that Peacocke (1996) discusses: cases where a subject is presented with a perceptual experience which is a memory, and self-ascribes a belief that *p* on the basis of the fact that memory represents (or misrepresents) it to her as being the case that *p*.

I STAGE ONE: THE OBSERVATIONAL ANALOGY AND THE
      ARGUMENT FOR FIRST-PERSON AUTHORITY

Consider a situation in which a subject, who knows nothing about chemistry and Twin Earth, believes that she is currently thinking that water
is transparent. Her justification for this seems weaker than that of another
individual who, knowing about chemistry and Twin Earth, knows that
the water content in question relates to H_2O, and that the subject has
not (unbeknownst to her) been transported to Twin Earth. This seems
to be a case where externalism conflicts with authoritative self-knowledge,
intuitively understood. Burge's response to this apparent conflict is to say
that not all cases of epistemic right or entitlement involve justification
by reasons that subjects are capable of employing explicitly, and that
cases of authoritative self-knowledge count as among these. The question, then, is where best to locate the source of such distinctive entitlement. The view that I shall defend is that authoritative self-knowledge
consists in a combination of two factors. One is the *epistemic directness*
of subjects' access to the contents of their first-order intentional states
in such cases; the other is the fact that in these cases subjects are the
only ones to whom these states are directly presented. The former can
be developed by giving an account of direct epistemic access which is
based on an observational model. The latter introduces the idea of a
single subject and perspective that figures centrally in Burge's account
of the *distinctive* entitlement which subjects have to knowledge of their
own intentional states. On the whole, I shall concentrate on the former
in the remaining parts of this chapter, since this is where I think that
the source of subjects' entitlement to self-knowledge lies. However, the
latter is necessary to forging a rational connection between reflective
thought and thought reviewed, which is also required for authoritative
self-knowledge (Burge 1996).

   Let us turn, then, to the notion of direct epistemic access. Descartes
held that we know some of our intentional states, namely, those that
we are consciously undergoing while we are thinking about them, in
an epistemically direct and authoritative way.[8] His paradigm for this

---

[8] See his *Meditations*, especially Meditation II: 'Finally, I am the same who feels, that
is to say, who perceives certain things, as by the organs of sense, since in truth I see
light, I hear noise, I feel heat. But it will be said that these phenomena are false and
that I am dreaming. Let it be so; still it is at least quite certain that it seems to me that
I see light, that I hear noise and that I feel heat. That cannot be false' (Descartes 1969:
175). And later: 'What, then, I who seem to perceive this piece of wax so distinctly, do
I not know myself, not only with much more truth and certainty, but also with much
more distinctness and clearness? . . . And further, if the [notion or] perception of wax
has seemed to me clearer and more distinct, not only after the sight or the touch, but

kind of knowledge was the *cogito*, which includes not just thoughts like *I am now thinking*, but ones like *I am thinking that water is transparent*. Descartes thought that he had this special kind of knowledge because of the special epistemic relation he bore to his thoughts while he was thinking them. Many have construed this epistemic relation as being at the very least *immediate*, in the sense of being *non-evidence-based*.[9] This immediacy is thought to extend beyond knowing *that* one is in a given intentional state—say, a state of thinking—to knowing what the content of that state is—say, a state of thinking that water is transparent.

For Descartes, the special status of such thoughts that derived from this immediate, non-evidence-based relation between subject and thought made for a kind of *transparency* of the thought reviewed to the reviewing subject, but not to others. It was this difference between a subject's access to the contents of her own intentional states and others' access to those contents that conferred an epistemic advantage on the subject in the sense of better placing her to know what the contents of those states are. But what exactly is it about this non-evidence-based relation that better places a subject in her own case? Why is it that another's better knowledge of the external factors that individuate certain contents (e.g. *water* ones) does not compromise this position?

I think that the relevant notion of epistemic directness, of being non-evidence-based, has two features, which can best be seen in the first instance in the case of observational properties, where they have a natural home. Consider properties other than mental ones where the notion of direct epistemic access is generally thought to apply. I know that the table visually present before me is brown, and that it is rectangular, and this knowledge is plausibly understood as being direct. One explanation of how I can know directly that the table is an instance of this particular shape property, or of this particular colour property, is that the instance is presented to me *as* an instance of that property through my sense of sight. I perceive the instance *as* an instance of that property; so no evidence is needed to come to know that it is an instance of that property.

also after many other causes have rendered it quite manifest to me, with how much more [evidence] and distinctness must it be said that I now know myself, since all the reasons which contribute to the knowledge of wax, or any other body whatever, are yet better proofs of the nature of my mind!' (ibid. 178).

[9] See Alston 1971; Heil 1988, 1992; Burge 1985*b*, 1988; Davidson 1984, 1987, 1988; and Wright 1989. Some, like Wright, emphasize the non-evidence-based character of such knowledge; others, like Heil, emphasize the non-empirically evidence-based character of such knowledge. For present purposes it does not matter which construal of epistemic directness is at issue, since both cause problems for externalism.

This is not true of other properties. Water, for example, is an instance of H_2O, but this instance is not manifested to me as an instance of that property through any of my senses. In short, certain properties seem to be ones to which we have direct epistemic access because they are observational: whether objects are instances of them can be determined just by unaided observation of those objects. This is not to say that one can know which observational property is being manifested to oneself on any one occasion just by being presented with an instance of it. One must be capable of recognizing another instance of that property as of that property when presented with it on another occasion, and this requires that one have mastery of the concept of the relevant property. This means that the notion of direct epistemic access is intentional: for one to have direct epistemic access to a colour property—say, brown—it is not sufficient that one sees an instance of that property: one must see it *as* an instance of that property.

Turn now to sensation properties, such as the property, *pain*. These also seem to be ones to which we have direct epistemic access, in the sense that we typically know non-evidentially that we are in states that are instances of such properties. The general conception of direct epistemic access appears to apply here too: when subjects are in pain, their pains are manifested to them *as* instances of the property, *pain*.

However, on the face of it, intentional properties are not like this. One difference, to which I shall return, is that they seem to contain no phenomenal element whatsoever, unlike cases of sensation and perception of primary and secondary qualities. And even in the case of sensation properties, where one would expect the analogy to work better than in the case of intentional ones, the analogy with observational properties is imperfect, for two reasons. The first is that one's access to sensation properties does not appear to be through any medium of sense. The second, much more important one is that observational properties are such that their possession by an object is importantly connected with their effects on normal perceivers. This is true both for the primary qualities, such as that of being rectangular, where the connection between an object's being an instance of the property and how things look to normal observers in optimal conditions is thought to be a posteriori and contingent, and for the secondary ones, like that of being brown, where the connection between these and the best opinion of normal observers under optimal conditions is thought to be a priori, and further, thought by some to determine the nature of the property itself.[10] However, the sensation properties of which my pains are instances, although directly

---

[10] See e.g. Wright 1987, 1989, 1992.

accessible to me, are not in general directly accessible in the observational way. For I, and only I, am the subject of my sensation states. Others may know what type of sensation state I am in through observation of its effects in actions of mine, and so, for that matter might I. But I *can* know them in ways that others generally do not.

Despite this, two features of observational properties characterize their epistemic directness in a way that I think is appropriate, within limits, to the characterization of mental properties in certain cases of self-knowledge (i.e. the *cogito*-like ones). The first feature is that observational properties are *epistemically basic* or fundamental to knowledge of objects that instance them. The point is not that grasp of the observational properties of objects necessarily constitutes knowledge of their true nature. Rather, it is that observational properties are those by which objects that instance them are typically known in the first instance. Knowing an object through instances of certain properties, and not others, favours certain ones epistemically.

The second, crucial feature of observational properties is that they *are* in general as they appear when instances of them are presented to normal perceivers in normal circumstances. Again, this is not a point about the nature of the objects that instance the properties, but about the nature of the properties themselves. The nature of water may be such as to have the chemical constitution H_2O, but this is compatible with water's instancing certain observational properties that are as they appear to normal subjects in normal circumstances.

Both of these features apply to mental properties, with the limitation that each person is alone the subject of her own intentional and sensation states, so that each person is the only subject to whom instances of her sensation and intentional properties appear in an epistemically basic way. That they apply to sensation properties needs little argument, since it is generally acknowledged that (a) sensations are known by their subjects on the basis of their sensation properties, and (b) the nature of a sensation property is constituted by how instances of it feel to its subjects. However, I think that these features also apply to intentional properties. Consider the first. When one thinks of a first-order intentional state while undergoing it, from the point of view of a second-order intentional state, one's grasp of that first-order state is first and foremost a grasp of it *as* a state of a certain contentful type. The point is not that this state cannot be known by means of other properties (intentional or non-intentional); so it is not that I cannot think of this state apart from thinking of it as a state of a contentful type. It is that, when I *do* think about a first-order intentional state of mine, I typically think of it as a state of a contentful type. Given this, all that is needed for authority is that, when I think of my state in this way, that state could not but be of the particular contentful type by which I think it.

Consider now the second feature: that such properties are in general as they appear to their subjects. I think that this feature also applies to intentional properties. The reason, to be developed more fully in the next section, is that the relation between them and normal subjects is in important respects like that between observational properties and normal perceivers. Given this, and given that subjects are the only ones to whom their contentful types appear in an epistemically basic way in the *cogito*-like cases of self-knowledge, it follows that, in these cases, one's first-order state cannot but be of the particular contentful type by which one grasps it. It could only be an intentional state other than one of the type a subject takes it to be in virtue of that subject's grasping a different contentful property. But in that case one would be thinking a different thought altogether.

So the argument for first-person authority consists of three main premises:

(1) A subject S typically thinks about her own intentional states *as* states of particular contentful types (i.e. such contents are epistemically basic to S).

(2) S's intentional states are of the contentful types that they appear to be (i.e. such contents are knowable by S in an epistemically direct way).

(3) No one *other* than S can be the subject of S's intentional states, so that when S thinks about her own intentional states as states of particular intentional types, S is the only one to whom those contentful types appear in this way.

Therefore, in general (i.e. barring special cognitive failures),

(4) S is authoritative with regard to the contents of her own intentional states.[11]

---

[11] This version of the argument differs from that advanced in Macdonald 1995, where what appears here as premise (2) appears as a conclusion derived from what here are premises (1) and (3). The reason for the difference is that to construe (2) as following from (1) and (3) is to encourage the view that authoritative self-knowledge is due to the fact that, in reflection, a subject's attitudes toward her first-order states actually *determine* the extensions of those states. However, unlike Wright (1988, 1992), who holds that one's authority with respect to one's own states consists in the fact that subjects' best opinions concerning those states fix the extensions of content types, the view favoured here is that one's authority consists in the fact that one cannot in reflection misidentify the object of one's reflection, and that this is so because the nature of the thought reflected upon determines the nature of the reflecting thought. Reflection is, in one respect at least, an appropriate characterization of the special relation which subjects' second-order thoughts

A number of points need to be made about this argument and the account of direct epistemic access upon which it is based. The first is that others can have access to my states. However, their access is evidence-based.[12] It is not that they do not grasp my states, but that their grasp is in relation to my actions. Their mode of access is, as a result, irremediably evidence-based. The second is that when *I* know my states in this evidence-based way, there is no first-person authority for me. The third is that when I know my states in an epistemically direct way, my knowledge is not only incorrigible (in that it cannot be shown by others to be false) but infallible (it cannot be false). This is so simply because I grasp the thoughts I grasp. The contentful type by which I grasp a first-order intentional state guarantees (but does not *make* it the case) that it is the state that it is. One cannot have a thought of a certain contentful type and misidentify it. Since to grasp a thought is to grasp its content, to grasp it *as* a thought of a different type would be to think a different thought altogether. In cases such as these, there is evidently no possibility of a contrast between what a subject is inclined to think, on the one hand, and what is actually the case, on the other—no possibility that one might think that one thinks a thought of a given contentful type and yet it fail to be the case that one thinks a thought of that contentful type.

How is this reconcilable with externalism? Externalism tells us that the contents of our thoughts are individuation-dependent on factors in the environment. So it is possible that, on a given occasion, unbeknownst to me, I may be thinking a *twater* thought rather than a *water* thought. But if this is so, how can I have authoritative knowledge about the contents of my first-order thoughts?

I can have such knowledge because externalism is not a thesis about individual cases. If, on a single occasion, I am (unbeknownst to me) presented with twater in an environment which has regularly presented me with water, then my *water* thought will be false. However, it will still be a *water* rather than a *twater* thought, since stability in the environment with which I interact is an externalist requirement for concept formation. So, even when my first-order thought is false because I am being presented with twater rather than water, my second-order thought that I am thinking a *water* thought will be both correct and

bear to their first-order ones. In physical reflection—say, in a mirror—under certain ideal conditions, the object cannot be misrepresented. So the object is as it appears to be. But the reflection does not determine the object to be what it is. Similarly, in mental reflection, the nature of the thought reflected upon determines the nature of the reflection. If this is right, then (2) should appear as an independent premiss in the argument.

[12] By this I do not mean inference-based. See Alston 1971 and Burge 1996.

authoritative. Indeed, only if externalism is not a thesis about individual cases can I possibly have first-order thoughts that are *mistaken* with regard to substance concepts such as the concept *water*. But I do have such thoughts. And authority is not impugned.

Look now at the case in which my environment *does* regularly present me with twater, not water. In that case, my first-order thought will actually be a *twater* thought. But in that case, my second-order thought about that first-order thought will actually be a thought about a *twater* thought. So, once again, authority is not impugned.

The result is that the common-sense intuition that we have authoritative knowledge about our own intentional states is preserved *irrespective* of the truth of our first-order thoughts. Not only does externalism fail to threaten it, but it actually looks as if the truth of externalism is required for the preservation of the intuition.

Does this authority extend to knowing whether two token thoughts had at different times are thoughts of the same type? Not on the account given here. For this account is restricted to knowledge of states that I am currently consciously undergoing and considering *while* I am undergoing them. That is to say, it is restricted to *cogito*-like cases. And my knowledge that two token thoughts, had at different times, are thoughts of the same (or different) type(s), in involving memory, does not count as a *cogito*-like case. Further, since memory is involved, error is possible. So it may not be that knowledge of this kind is in fact authoritative.

II STAGE TWO: DEVELOPING THE ACCOUNT

The argument just given for first-person authority trades crucially on there being certain clear analogies between intentional properties, which are thought while being thought about by the same subject, and observational properties. Without this, the account of direct epistemic access which forms the basis of the distinctive authority which subjects have with regard to certain of their own intentional states founders. The critical feature that observational properties possess, and whose possession by first-order intentional ones is capable of explaining a subject's entitlement to self-knowledge, is that they *are* in general as they appear to normal subjects in optimal circumstances. But note again that this feature, and the role it plays in the account of direct epistemic access, does not establish, and so is insufficient for, the *distinctive* authority that subjects have over others with regard to knowledge of their own intentional states; so it does not explain the asymmetry between first- and third-person knowledge of a subject's intentional states. What establishes *that* is that subjects are the *only* ones to whom their intentional states appear in the epistemically direct way. I shall say more about this peculiar role that subjects play with regard to their own states in the closing paragraphs of this section. For now I put it to one side in order to develop the crucial component of the strategy, an account of observational properties that is both applicable to and explanatory of the epistemic relation which subjects bear to their own states when consciously entertaining or thinking them while thinking about them.

The feature of observational properties to be accounted for and exploited in the account of direct epistemic access is that they are in general as they appear to normal subjects in normal circumstances. It has seemed to many that the way in which this feature works to explain direct epistemic access in the observational case is very different from the way in which it works in cases of self-knowledge.[13] One reason that has been given is that the relation between first- and second-order intentional states in the paradigmatic, *cogito*-like cases of authoritative self-knowledge is not, as it is in the paradigmatic case of observation, perception, a causal one.[14] Another is that, unlike the case of perception, where there is a state of perceptual *experience* which mediates between objects of perception and beliefs/judgements about them, cases of self-knowledge are not mediated by experiential states.[15]

Consider the first claim. Is it true that in the *cogito*-like cases, the relation between first- and second-order, or reflective, thoughts is non-causal? Both Tyler Burge (1996) and Sydney Shoemaker (1994) have claimed so, albeit for different reasons.

Burge's reason has to do with the way he thinks *cogito*-like cases ought to be construed. In his opinion, the proper way to view them is as cases where one's first-order thought is literally contained within, or is a constituent of, one's second-order thought, which is contextually self-verifying for the reason that in thinking the reflective thought, one *makes* that thought true. One makes it true because, in thinking the reflective thought, one brings into being the first-order thought upon which one is reflecting. The relation between first- and second-order thought is non-causal, at least in part because there are not here two separate acts of thinking: there is no first-order thought, considered as a state distinct from the second-order, reflective one, to serve as one of the relata of the causal relation.

Now it may be that, understood in this way, it is inappropriate to view *cogito*-like cases of authoritative self-knowledge as explicable

---

[13] See e.g. Boghossian 1989; Burge 1996; Shoemaker 1994; Peacocke 1992, 1996; and McDowell 1994.   [14] See e.g. Shoemaker 1994 and Burge 1996.
[15] See e.g. Peacocke 1992 and Ch. 3 above.

along the lines of the observational model. But it does not follow that the observational model is inapplicable to all cases of authoritative self-knowledge. For one thing, Burge himself (1996) considers his *cogito*-like cases as forming a very small subclass of the class of cases of self-knowledge which he intends his account of epistemic entitlement to cover, and this class will almost certainly contain cases where it is appropriate to view a subject's first- and second-order states as distinct and causally related. I am thinking here not only of cases of memory, where one can be said to 'redeploy' (Peacocke 1996) contents of an earlier experience, but also of the kinds of cases mentioned at the outset in connection with Moran's distinction between descriptive-theoretical and prescriptive roles of critical reasoning, where an intentional state is consciously present and one reflects upon it (as one does in wondering what one is presently thinking).

So, even if the observational model is inapplicable to *cogito*-like cases as Burge construes them, this would not in itself invalidate it for all cases of self-knowledge where the question of a subject's epistemic entitlement may arise. It is a moot point whether at least some of these cases are *cogito*-like ones. But there is a further question here as to whether Burge's own construal of the *cogito*-like cases is the only, or the best, way of construing them. He understands such cases to be contextually self-verifying because in them one's first-order thought is literally a constituent of one's second-order thought. However, this feature of such cases could be explained differently. It may be that a necessary condition of thinking a reflective thought with a given content is that that content refers to a first-order thought content, and that a necessary condition for this is that the contents of the two thoughts are the same. If so, then although it would be true that thinking such a second-order thought suffices for its being true, and that thinking it makes it true, this would not be because there is no first-order thought distinct from the reflective one to which it is causally related.[16]

---

[16] One might object here that our second-order, or reflective, mental states seem not to be independent of the states that they reflect upon, in that our self-monitoring seems intimately connected with the identity of what is monitored, changing and reconfiguring it as well as representing it. If so, then it would seem that the relation between first- and second-order intentional states in cases of self-knowledge is not like that between objects of perception in normal observation, and the quasi-observational account is wrong. My view is that there may be cases of self-knowledge that are like this, but not all such cases are, and that Moran's (1994) distinction between theoretical-descriptive and prescriptive bases for psychological ascriptions highlights this fact. The construal of the *cogito*-like cases offered in this paragraph is one which treats the first-order intentional states as independent of the second-order, reflective ones: states that form the theoretical-descriptive base for psychological ascriptions. In being independent of the second-order states, these states are like normal objects of observation.

In short, then, I fail to see why the fact that not all cases of authoritative self-knowledge may be ones where it is plausible to speak of a causal relation between reflective thought and thought reviewed prohibits altogether the applicability of an observational model in an account of authoritative self-knowledge. Further, I think it plausible that some of these other cases may be *cogito*-like, even if they do not conform to Burge's construal of *cogito*-like cases. Finally, though, even the cases of contextually self-verifying thoughts seem to me to be capable of being construed in a way that is compatible with the claim that there is a causal relation between reflective thought and thought reviewed. If one's interest in accounting for subjects' distinctive entitlement to self-knowledge is, as Burge's is, motivated in part by the desire to provide a uniform general account of all such cases, then this would recommend a construal of the *cogito*-like cases that brings them more into line with others in recognizing the presence of a causal element and a first-order state distinct from the reflective one.

In recognizing this, however, another problem with the observational model arises. The presence of a causal element suggests that we should be able to conceive of rational subjects in whom the quasi-perceptual faculty has broken down, and that in such cases subjects would think thoughts, have pains, and hear sounds, but not know that they are thinking, feeling, and hearing. But it is not clear that we can make sense of this.[17]

However, commitment to the observational model does not require that we can. One reason for thinking that we cannot trades on an ambiguity in 'know', in 'know that they are thinking, feeling, and hearing'. It is true that, in the sense in which to know that one is in pain, or hearing sounds, just is to be aware, or conscious, of them, we cannot make sense of having pains, or hearing sounds, and not knowing that we are feeling or hearing. But this sense does not introduce a distinction between a first-order and a second-order state: here to be in pain just is to be aware, or conscious, of it. So the fact that we cannot make sense of subjects being in pain and not knowing that they are in pain does not threaten the quasi-perceptual model at issue, where there are two items involved in self-knowledge: a first-order state upon which one is reflecting and a second-order, reflective state.[18]

---

[17] Akeel Bilgrami (Ch. 7 below) makes much of this point.

[18] Shoemaker (1994) makes this particularly clear in his discussion of self-blindness. Self-blindness with regard to pain, he argues, is not about being in a certain sensation state—say, a state of pain—and not feeling it: 'It must not be supposed that these creatures do not *feel* their pains. Pain is a feeling, and what they are self-blind to are, precisely, their feelings of pain' (1994: 274). Shoemaker proceeds to argue that self-blindness

Moreover, in the sense relevant to the argument for authoritative self-knowledge based on the observational model, where two items are involved, a first-order state and a second-order, reflective state, the model is not committed to the claim that one can make sense of subjects thinking thoughts, having pains, or hearing sounds, but not knowing that they are thinking, feeling, and hearing. What it *is* committed to is that subjects in whom the quasi-perceptual faculty has broken down would not know *through quasi-perception* that they are thinking, feeling, and hearing. Such subjects would be, in Shoemaker's (1994) terms, 'self-blind': they would be in mental states that they are undergoing but to which they are introspectively blind, just as a person who is blind-sighted sees things that she is unaware of seeing and so is having perceptual experiences of which she is introspectively unaware. Shoemaker claims that such a possibility is required by certain perceptual models of introspective self-knowledge, given that such models must presume the independence of, and so the contingency of the relation between first-order state and second-order, reflective state. This in turn is imposed by the requirement that such states be causally related. Crucial to both sorts of case is the possibility that the subject be able to conceive of those facts or phenomena to which she is blind, so that she is capable of learning of those facts or phenomena by means other than perception or introspection. What matters is that she is incapable of learning about them *perceptually*, through her perceptual experiences in the visual case, and *introspectively*, through her awareness of her first-order mental states in the case of self-knowledge.

Shoemaker himself does not think that subjects in whom the quasi-perceptual faculty has broken down would not know that they are thinking, feeling, or hearing. However, he does think it impossible for subjects to be self-blind with respect to either their sensations or their intentional states, and he thinks that this is sufficient to discredit observational models of self-knowledge. Since his reasons for thinking this cut to the very heart of observational models of self-knowledge, they need to be considered.

Shoemaker mounts two different, but compatible lines of argument against observational models of self-knowledge: one for the sensations and another for intentional states. With regard to the former, he argues that in order to make sense of a subject being self-blind to them, one must suppose that she is self-blind to a whole host of other mental states, ones which would make intelligible, say, pain behaviour, such as that

with respect to sensations is impossible, not because it would require one to be in pain and not feel it, but because it would require one to be in pain, with its characteristic phenomenological feel, without being introspectively aware of it.

one finds the sensation unpleasant, and so has a desire for this reason to be rid of the pain. But a state of pain that played only the causal role that pain plays with regard to behaviour without playing the total causal role usually associated with pain—namely, the role it plays in causing beliefs and desires which in turn cause and make intelligible pain behaviour—simply would not be pain.

The case regarding sensations is less central to the issues that are of concern here than that regarding intentional states. Still, it is worth remarking on it at least to the following extent. Subjects in whom the quasi-perceptual faculty has broken down—that is, subjects who are self-blind—are meant to be otherwise cognitively normal. However, there are many creatures, human beings included, who are otherwise cognitively normal and who seem clearly capable of feeling, or hearing sounds, without knowing that they are feeling or hearing. Dogs, cats, chickens, and human infants count as such. Are we to suppose that such creatures do not feel or hear? Evidently so, since, as Shoemaker says,

Part of the causal role of pain consists in its being caused by certain kinds of things—bodily damage of various sorts—and its causing behaviors, such as winces, grimaces, and moans, that can be involuntary and do not have to be seen as motivated or 'rationalized' by beliefs and desires. Certainly a state could play this role without its subject having introspective awareness of it. And such a state would be, if not bad in and of itself, at least indicative of something bad, namely bodily damage. This it would share with pain. But it seems obvious that a state that played this causal role, but did not play any more of the standard causal role of pain than this, would not be pain. Indeed, it would not be a mental state at all. (1994: 274)

However, this response begs the question against one who thinks that the relation between first-order states of feeling and hearing and second-order, reflective states is in fact contingent. That person will insist, plausibly on the face of it, that creatures who are incapable of forming beliefs and desires on the basis of their sensations may none the less undergo them. Nor will it do to respond that human infants are in fact capable of knowing that they are feeling and hearing because they are capable of becoming human adults, and human adults are capable of such knowledge. The fact that human infants are capable of becoming human adults does not make them human adults, and so does not imbue them with the capabilities of such beings.

So Shoemaker's case against a quasi-perceptual model *vis-à-vis* sensations is not decisive. But as I have said, the main target here is not the claim that a quasi-perceptual model will not work for sensations, but that it will not work for intentional states. What is the case for this?

Shoemaker's claim here is that self-blindness with regard to one's own intentional states is also impossible. His reason is that, in being in such states, and in having normal intelligence, conceptual capacity, and rationality, one *automatically* has second-order beliefs: 'if one has an available first-order belief, *and* has a certain degree of rationality, intelligence and conceptual capacity (here including having the concept of belief and the concept of oneself), then automatically one has the corresponding second-order belief' (1994: 288). A rational agent—that is to say, an agent who has normal intelligence, rationality, and conceptual capacity—will behave in ways that give the best possible evidence that she is self-aware, and so not self-blind. Such a person will be self-aware in that she has *normal awareness* of her own intentional states, where this sometimes involves, but *does not require*, reasoning sequentially from one premiss to another by a series of steps.

... in order to explain the behavior we take as showing that people have certain higher-order beliefs, beliefs about their first-order beliefs, we do not need to attribute to them anything beyond what is needed in order to give them first-order beliefs plus normal intelligence, rationality, and conceptual capacity. ... in supposing that a creature is rational, what one is supposing is that it is such that its being in certain states tends to result in effects, behavior or other internal states, that are rationalized by those states. Sometimes this requires actually going through a process of reasoning in which one gets from one proposition to another by a series of steps, and where special reasoning skills are involved. But usually it does not require this. I see an apple and I reach for it. It is rational for me to do so, and this can be shown by presenting an argument, a bit of practical reasoning that is available to me, in terms of my desires and my beliefs about the nutritional and other properties of apples. But I needn't actually go through any process of sequential reasoning in order for the beliefs and desires in question to explain and make rational my reaching for the apple. And no more does the rational agent need to go through a process of sequential reasoning in order for her first-order belief that P, plus her other first-order beliefs and desires, to explain and rationalize the behavior that manifests the second-order belief that she believes that P. (Shoemaker 1994: 284–5)

As this passage makes clear, Shoemaker's view is that being self-aware requires no more than being in states of belief and desire that tend to cause and rationalize other intentional states and behaviour.

But what kind of self-awareness is this? The crucial phrase in the quoted passage is 'rationalize the behavior'. Shoemaker's self-aware person is one whose beliefs and desires rationalize her behaviour, not from her own perspective, but from the perspective of *others*. It is true that she is typically *capable* of reasoning sequentially, and so of rationalizing her behaviour from her own point of view, but such reasoning and rationalizing is not required for self-awareness. So self-awareness is something subjects can possess, not by virtue of exercising a first-person perspective on their own states, but simply by behaving in such a way as to be subjects of *others'* rationalizing strategies. But then I think that Shoemaker's use of the term 'self-aware' to mean 'introspectively self-aware' is misplaced: subjects whose rationalizing behaviour counts as such only from the perspective of others do not provide the best possible evidence for being introspectively aware of their own beliefs and desires. Conscious, yes, but introspectively conscious, no. Further, any conception of self-awareness stronger than this—say, in requiring sequential reasoning—would require reflecting on one's reasons *as reasons*, and so require a more robust account of introspective self-knowledge than Shoemaker is prepared to endorse.

Shoemaker's argument is effectively that one's first-order states do not in general provide *grounds* or *reasons* for one's having second-order beliefs. As he puts it, 'believing that one believes that P can be just believing that P plus having a certain level of rationality, intelligence and so on' (1994: 289). This view, which Peacocke (Ch. 3 above) calls the 'no reasons' view, is often contrasted with a view of self-knowledge which takes such knowledge to be based on a kind of inner observation. Shoemaker's argument is that self-blindness in the case of intentional states is impossible, but not, as in the case of sensations, because it is impossible that a subject should be in first-order intentional states and have beliefs about such states based on grounds *other* than introspective ones (say, behaviour, or the subject's awareness of her own neurophysiological states). Rather, it is impossible because self-knowledge of one's own intentional states is not based on grounds or reasons of any kind. So the reason why self-blindness is impossible in this case is that the connection between having first-order beliefs and being able to self-ascribe them is too *direct* for there to be either some kind of inner awareness of or blindness to one's first-order states. Such knowledge is *baseless*.

It would not be inappropriate to respond to Shoemaker's argument here by pointing out that, as he has constructed the case of self-blindness, one might know of one's own first-order intentional states not by means of introspection, but by other perceptual means such as behaviour and/or awareness of one's neurophysiological states. And these means would seem to provide one with grounds or reasons for thinking that one is in certain first-order intentional states, albeit less direct grounds than one might have if one were to know of one's first-order states by inner awareness of them. Of course, *if* Shoemaker is right in thinking that such second-order knowledge is not acquired on the basis of any grounds or reasons, then this kind of response is irrelevant. But the question is whether he *is* right, and it would be question-begging to reject the possibility of self-blindness on this basis.

More importantly, however, even supposing that he is right with regard to certain cases of self-knowledge, why should we think that all cases of self-knowledge are of this kind? I think that Shoemaker's reasons for thinking that they are turn out, on examination, to trade on an ambiguity in the term 'rationality' and its near cousin, 'self-aware'.

It has been said that it is essential to belief possession, and to the concept of belief, that beliefs are subject to rationalistic constraints. Thus to have a belief that *p*, for some propositional content *p*, is (amongst other things) to be disposed to assert that *p*, to engage in reasonings using the content that *p*, and to be prepared to revise the belief that *p* in the light of conflicting evidence.

In one, very minimal sense of the term 'self-aware', to be self-aware is simply to employ one's beliefs in rational behaviour, to have one's first-order beliefs cause one's other intentional states and behaviour in ways that can be rationalized. It is in this sense that one can attribute to children, who may not yet be capable of critically evaluating their reasonings to see whether, for example, they conform to *modus ponens*, self-awareness of their own states. It seems clear that this is the sense of self-awareness that Shoemaker has in mind when he claims that a subject who is self-aware is rational. Suppose he is right in thinking that engaging in a process of sequential reasoning to rationalize one's own behaviour is not required for rationality in general, and so is not required for self-awareness (in his sense of the term). Still, it does not establish what Shoemaker thinks it does with regard to the observational model, for two reasons.

First, the applicability of the observational model to introspective self-knowledge does not require that it fit every case of such knowledge. Nor is it plausible to think that it should. The concern here is with a certain class of intentional states: namely, those that one is currently, consciously thinking about while thinking them. It is these states concerning which the observational model seems most appropriate. But these are not the states with which Shoemaker is primarily concerned, if at all. So even if his claims regarding self-awareness and rationality are correct with respect to beliefs about one's beliefs in cases where one is *not* currently, consciously having them while considering them, nothing of interest would follow about the applicability of the observational model in cases where one *is* currently, consciously having such states while considering them.

But second, and more importantly, it may be that one can only engage in rational *deliberation* and *reflective reasoning*, reasoning about one's reasoning, if one is capable of thinking certain kinds of thoughts, thoughts of the form *I am thinking that I am thinking that p*, and so of being self-aware in a much stronger sense than Shoemaker is prepared to countenance. The reason is that, in order to deliberate, or to reason reflectively, one needs to be able to *examine* one's reasons, and to consider them *as reasons* for behaving one way or another, or for accepting or rejecting or revising one's other attitudes. To do this evidently requires being able to view them *as objects* of reflection or deliberation. As Burge puts the point,

To be capable of critical reasoning, and to be subject to certain rational norms necessarily associated with such reasoning, some mental acts and states must be *knowledgeably* reviewable. . . . Critical reasoning is reasoning that involves an ability to recognize and effectively employ reasonable criticism or support for reasons and reasoning. It is reasoning guided by an appreciation, use, and assessment of reasons and reasoning as such. (1996: 98)

Burge considers it essential to the ability to reason critically that one be capable of thinking *cogito*-like thoughts, and he associates this ability with being rational in some sense of 'rational'. This sense of 'rational' is clearly stronger than what Shoemaker has in mind. Now it may be that one can be rational without being a critical reasoner (although it is less clear whether one can be rational without being *capable* of being a critical reasoner). So it may be that one can be rational in Shoemaker's weaker sense without being rational in the stronger sense associated with the ability to reason critically (as Burge construes it). However, if, as seems clear, it is possible to be rational in this stronger sense, then it is also possible to be self-aware in a sense stronger than that associated with Shoemaker's conception of rationality. It is to be capable of reflective reasoning, of reasoning about one's reasoning, where the so-called objects of such reasoning are one's own first-order intentional states. And if, as Burge argues, this requires the ability to think *cogito*-like thoughts, thoughts about what one is currently, consciously thinking, where one is both thinking and thinking about a propositional content, then not all self-knowledge can be construed in the way that Shoemaker construes it.

Shoemaker in fact recognizes this, but points out that his conception is the one that is in fact met by most people most of the time, and that the notion of rationality that involves engaging in critical reasoning is an ideal that most of us regularly fail to meet. However, that an ideal regularly fails to be met does not thereby make it *unapproachable*, and this is all that is necessary for the ability to engage in critical reasoning to be serviceable as a requirement on rationality in general. Further, that there is this stronger sense of rationality opens up conceptual space for an account of introspective self-knowledge for a certain class of cases, the *cogito*-like ones, which is broadly observational. This should be of interest to anyone whose concern with self-knowledge is a concern with *authoritative* self-knowledge. The *cogito*-like cases are central, not peripheral, to the issues here, precisely because they count as paradigmatic ones of authoritative self-knowledge. And the observational model is of use in helping to make intelligible these cases of self-knowledge precisely because it promises to deliver an explanation of the special epistemic right, or entitlement, that subjects have with regard to knowledge of the contents of certain of their own intentional states in just these cases.

However, the presence of a causal element in the observational model is not the only, nor the most serious, obstacle to basing an account of authoritative self-knowledge on such a model. What really seems to bother those who firmly reject this model is the thought that, to make it work, one would need to suppose that there is, in cases of self-knowledge, an analogue of *perceptual experience*, a phenomenal awareness of one's intentional states, which mediates between the 'object' of reflective awareness (the first-order intentional state) and the state of reflective awareness itself. Peacocke, for example, rejects observational models on the grounds that in perception there is a state of perceptual experience which is partly non-conceptual and whose non-conceptual component figures in the possession conditions for observational concepts, thereby mediating between beliefs and judgements that employ such concepts and the objects that they are judgements about. On his view, because there is no such analogous non-conceptual component in cases of self-knowledge, observational models (specifically perceptual ones) are not applicable to such cases.[19]

The complaint here is that observational models won't work because, whereas in observation there are three items—object, perceptual experience, and belief/judgement which experience grounds in the sense of providing 'primitively compelling grounds' (causes which are also reasons) for judgements about the perceptible properties of objects in subjects' environments—in self-knowledge there are only two items—'object' (first-order intentional state) and belief/judgement about that state.

Whether this complaint really bites, however, depends, first, on how one views the observational model as operating in perception itself, independently of the issue of its applicability to cases of self-knowledge, and second, on how it is meant to extend to cases of self-knowledge. The thesis argued for in the previous section was that certain features of

---

[19] See e.g. Ch. 3 above.

observational properties characterize their epistemic directness in a way that is applicable to mental properties in certain cases of self-knowledge. The question is: what items do these features relate to in the observational case, and can these features be said to be applicable in an analogous way to cases of self-knowledge? That there are (if there are) three items in the former case and only two in the latter is not in itself decisive against the observational model if, in the perceptual case, the features of epistemic basicness and epistemic directness relate only two of those three items. Alternatively, if there are only two items involved in the perceptual case—if, for example, there is no state of non-conceptual perceptual experience that mediates between conceptualized contents that figure in beliefs and the objects that they are about—then again, for a different reason, the objection is misplaced.

This suggests two rather different ways in which to develop the observational model for the purpose of extending it to cases of self-knowledge. One way would be to hold that in perception itself there is no state of perceptual experience which is even partly non-conceptual. In effect, this would be to deny that in perception there are three items. A version of this view has recently been advanced by John McDowell (1994), who has argued that a satisfactory naturalistic theory of mind can succeed only if the 'space' of reasons extends outward, into perception itself, so that there is no epistemic 'gap', so to speak, between mind and world. For McDowell, there is reality, and there are states of mind which, in perceptual experience of the world, deploy concepts that act both as passive receptors of information from the world (are 'passively drawn into play in experience') and as active in playing a role in judgement and, more generally, in critical reasoning. Whatever the merits or demerits of this view, the perceptual model with which it works, in dealing with two items rather than three, is structurally similar to that of self-knowledge. Might this model provide a basis for an account of authoritative self-knowledge that deploys the features of direct epistemic access, namely, epistemic basicness and epistemic directness?

McDowell claims that his view has no need for a notion such as that of direct epistemic access. This is because, on his view, the 'space' of reasons extends into the world itself: 'The idea of conceptually structured operations of receptivity puts us in a position to speak of experience as openness to the layout of reality. Experience enables the layout of reality itself to exert a rational influence on what a subject thinks' (1994: 26). What he seems to mean by this is that rational connections hold, not only between intentional and other states of mind, but between them and the world beyond the mind, and this because 'there is no ontological gap between the sort of thing one can mean, or think, and the sort of thing that is the case. When one thinks truly, what one thinks *is* the case . . . so there is no gap between thought and the world' (1994: 27). Although it is not entirely clear what exactly McDowell's thesis is here, it seems to be that in so far as the world, in being thinkable, is a conceptualized world, it exerts a rational influence on experience and judgements. The existence of rational connections between mind and world sets McDowell's perceptual model apart from the standard conception of an observational model. If it were to work—if there really is no ontological gap between thought and the world—there would be no need for the kind of observational model envisaged here, no explanatory work for the features associated with direct epistemic access to do. For if there is no 'boundary' between thought and world—if they make direct contact—then, analogously, so do first- and second-order thoughts in cases of self-knowledge. Nor would there be any need for an additional component in the argument for first-person authority to forge rational connections between thought reviewed and reflective thought. Since rational as well as causal connections are built into the perceptual model itself, its application to cases of self-knowledge seems to be a relatively straightforward matter.

However, I am not convinced that the kind of account of the relation between mind and world that McDowell envisages does work, hence that there is no need for an observational model that deploys features associated with direct epistemic access. This is because I cannot see how McDowell can make intelligible the idea that there is 'friction' between mind and world, which he recognizes to be critical to fending off the charge of idealism, *without* supposing there to be an 'ontological gap' between mind and world, and so without supposing there to be a boundary between the space of reasons and the world. So long as there is this gap, there is a need to bridge it; and the features associated with direct epistemic access are meant to do just that.

My point is not that McDowell's two-item perceptual model cannot be put to use in mounting an argument for first-person authority based on what I conceive of as an observational model. I think it can. But then one would have to abandon McDowell's position on the relation between thought and the world. But since this claim is itself problematic, abandoning it, while retaining the model, is a promising strategy for extending the observational model to cases of self-knowledge.

However, this strategy will not be viewed as a way of carrying the observational model forward by those who think that there *is* in perception a state of perceptual experience which is partly non-conceptual and which mediates between objects of perception and beliefs and judgements which perceptual experience grounds. Such a model of perception has recently been elaborated upon and defended by Peacocke (1992). Peacocke is concerned with a much larger project of providing a theory of concepts as epistemic capacities. One aspect of this is to provide non-circular necessary and sufficient conditions for the possession of concepts of various sorts, observational (perceptual) concepts being a central case. His claim is that such accounts will not be circular if mention of the concept whose possession condition is in question does not occur within the scope of psychological attributions to the possessor. So, for example, this is his account of the possession conditions for the concept *red*:

The concept *red* is that concept C to possess which a thinker must meet these conditions:
1.   He must be disposed to believe a content that consists of a singular perceptual-demonstrative mode of presentation *m* in predicational combination with C when the perceptual experience that makes *m* available presents its object in a 'red' region of the subject's visual field and does so in conditions he takes to be normal, and when in addition he takes his perceptual mechanisms to be working properly. The thinker must also be disposed to form the belief for the reason that the object is so presented.
2.   The thinker must be disposed to believe a content consisting of any singular mode of presentation *k* not meeting all the conditions on *m* in (1) when he takes its object to have the primary quality ground (if any) of the disposition of objects to cause experiences of the sort mentioned in (1). (Peacocke 1992: 7–8)

Peacocke notes that similar non-circular possession conditions can be formulated for concepts in terms acceptable to those who reject sensation properties (and so reject states with non-conceptual perceptual content). However, his view is that there are such states, that these provide 'primitively compelling' grounds for beliefs and judgements employing observational concepts about the perceptible properties of objects in perceivers' environments, and that these grounds are not only causes, but reasons for which subjects judge and act as they do.[20] The view is in fact much richer and more sophisticated than I can do justice to here. But two points are noteworthy. First, for Peacocke perceptual experiences have two layers of non-conceptual content, the second of which is proto-propositional, and both of which require mention in possession conditions for observational concepts such as *red*. Proto-propositional components include individuals, properties, and relations,

[20] A primitively compelling ground for the possession of a given concept C is a ground (1) that the subject finds compelling, but (2) not because she has inferred it from other principles and/or premises, and (3) whose correctness the subject need not take as answerable to anything else in order to possess C. See Peacocke 1992: 6.

and are necessary to capture subjects' perceptual experiences of such relations as SQUARE, CURVED, SYMMETRICAL ABOUT, PARALLEL TO, and so on. Second, although perceptual experiences have a non-conceptual component which figures in the possession conditions for observational concepts such as *red*, typically for a thinker who does possess such a concept, that concept will enter into her perceptual experiences:

> If we take an observational concept we do in fact possess, then certainly we will have difficulty in successfully imagining an experience in which the observational property is perceived but not conceptualized as falling under that observational concept. This is not surprising. For those who possess an observational concept, it enters the representational content of their experiences, and derivatively, of their imaginings. (1992: 81)

Suppose it is true that perceptual experiences have a non-conceptual component which mediates between concepts employed in beliefs and judgements about objects of perception and the objects themselves. Would this make the observational model envisaged here inapplicable to cases of self-knowledge on the assumption that there is no analogous mediating experiential state in such cases?

That depends partly on whether the features of the observational model that are meant to apply to cases of self-knowledge hold in the perceptual case between all three items. But it is implausible to suppose that the features associated with direct epistemic access do so. On Peacocke's model, perceptual experience both mediates between perceptual belief and objects of perception and provides primitively compelling grounds for judgements about the perceptible properties of objects in subjects' environments. Given this, the plausible line to take is that the features associated with direct epistemic access hold in the first instance between only two of the three items involved in perception, the perceptual experience and the beliefs and judgements which that experience grounds.

This removes one obstacle to extending the observational model to cases of self-knowledge, the response to it being that although there are indeed three items in perception and two in self-knowledge, the epistemic features in play in perception of observational properties that are relevant to the applicability of the observational model to cases of self-knowledge hold between only two of the three. This makes the cases of perception and self-knowledge structurally analogous. And this is so irrespective of the fact that since the so-called object of perception drops out as irrelevant in cases of self-knowledge, judgements in these cases are about the very first-order states to which the reflective states bear relations of epistemic directness. Nor is the difference between the two cases here as great as it may seem to be at first. For, in cases of hallucination, there is no object of perception about which to judge; and in reflective thinking, thoughts are directed beyond one's thoughts, toward the world, and often ground judgements about it.

But now there is another objection to consider. Peacocke's model is one in which, prior to concept possession, only the non-conceptual component of perceptual experience is one to which a subject is related. Further, it is this, and not any conceptual component that may subsequently enter into perceptual experience, that provides subjects with primitively compelling grounds for forming beliefs and judgements employing perceptual concepts about the perceptible properties of objects in their environment. Given this, the objection is that the features of direct epistemic access apply, if at all, to the non-conceptual component of such experiences, but that there is no such component in cases of self-knowledge, so the observational model cannot be extended to such cases.

I think that the right way to respond to this is as follows. It may be that, prior to concept possession, the perceptual experiences to which subjects are related contain no conceptual component, and further, that such experiences provide primitively compelling grounds for forming beliefs containing perceptual concepts. However, the cases of interest here are not those of subjects who lack observational concepts, but rather those of subjects who, in having self-knowledge, are in full possession of these and many other concepts, notably the concept of belief. These cases are ones where subjects' perceptual experiences will generally speaking contain observational concepts. Further, in them it is plausible to say that conceptual and non-conceptual components are inseparable from the perspective of the subject. That there may be perceptual experiences in which only non-conceptual components come into play does not establish that, in experiences in which both non-conceptual and conceptual components figure, they are separable. But if so, then the difference between the perceptual case and that of self-knowledge is a difference of degree rather than kind. For if the conceptual and non-conceptual components of perceptual experience are inseparable in experience for subjects who possess perceptual concepts, then subjects cannot be said to have direct epistemic access to one *rather than* another component of perceptual experience. (This marks a difference between Peacocke's notion of primitively compelling grounds and the notion of direct epistemic access, since the latter, on the account sketched earlier, is intentional, whereas the former is not.)

There is a further point to be made here. Peacocke supposes perceptual experience to contain a non-conceptual component. But what about the perceptual beliefs which those experiences ground? Do they too contain such a component? If so, what about beliefs about those beliefs? And if not, why not? On what basis are we to judge the point at which non-conceptual components no longer enter into the contents of intentional states? It seems unlikely that this can be determined on entirely a priori grounds. But then the applicability of the observational model to cases of self-knowledge cannot be ruled out on a priori grounds either.

Is there any need to appeal to the features of direct epistemic access in the kind of perceptual model that Peacocke employs? I have suggested one difference between Peacocke's notion of primitively compelling grounds and the notion of direct epistemic access in play in the observational model envisaged here: the latter is intentional, whereas the former is not. For one to have direct epistemic access to a colour property—say, brown—it is not sufficient that one sees an instance of that property: one must see it *as* an instance of that property. This difference might be exploited in accounting for a thesis which Peacocke takes to be central to his view and to his account of our entitlement to self-knowledge: namely, that the non-conceptual content of perceptual experiences can yield 'not merely reasons but good reasons' for beliefs formed on the basis of them. It has been said that Peacocke's defence of this thesis falls short of what is needed, since it appeals to reasons *for which* a subject forms a belief, whereas what is needed is a *subject's* reasons. Reasons for which a subject forms a belief may exist even when the subject has no reasons. Reasons are goal-oriented, and they need to be so oriented from the perspective of the subject herself.[21]

This opens up explanatory space for the notion of direct epistemic access to do some useful work. It may be that the non-conceptual component of perceptual experience provides primitively compelling grounds for forming beliefs employing perceptual concepts. But these may be too primitive to provide reasons, in the sense of a subject's reasons, as well as causes. Conceptualized perceptual content may be what is required, and this is where the notion of direct epistemic access might do some real explanatory work.

What I have attempted to make plausible here is the idea that the *source* of subjects' authority with regard to certain of their first-order states is other than the role that first-person judgements or self-ascriptions play in critical reasoning. If the argument goes through, the source lies in the epistemic relation which subjects bear to the contents of their

[21] See McDowell 1994: pt. 2.

first-order states, and the features of contentful properties. But the observational model upon which the argument is based can do no more than explain how it is possible that subjects should have direct epistemic access to such properties; it cannot account for the peculiarly authoritative status that subjects have with regard to their own intentional states.

As I have indicated, the additional factor necessary to account for first-person authority is that, in cases of self-knowledge, the subject is the *only* one to whom her first-order intentional states appear directly. On this matter I have little to add to what Burge (1996) himself has argued. In cases of self-knowledge, that subjects are the only ones to whom their contentful states appear gives them a *single*, unified perspective on those contents. Given that the content of the first-order state is the *same* content as that reviewed by the subject of the second-order state, and given that the perspectives of the subject as subject of the first-order state and as subject of the second-order state are *unified*, they cannot in general 'come apart': the thought by which a subject grasps a first-order state when thinking about it refers at the same time to it. This is not to say, however, that it is the *determinant* of it. It is to say that one thinks the thoughts one thinks one thinks.[22]

REFERENCES

Alston, W. (1971), 'Varieties of Privileged Access', *American Philosophical Quarterly*, 8: 223–41.

Boghossian, P. (1989), 'Content and Self-Knowledge', *Philosophical Topics*, 17: 5–26.

Burge, T. (1979), 'Individualism and the Mental', in P. French, T. Uehling, and H. Wettstein (eds.), *Midwest Studies in Philosophy* (Minneapolis: University of Minnesota Press), iv. 73–122.

—— (1985a), 'Authoritative Self-Knowledge and Perceptual Individualism', in R. Grimm and D. Merrill (eds.), *Contents of Thought* (Tucson, Ariz.: University of Arizona Press), 86–98.

—— (1985b), 'Cartesian Error and the Objectivity of Perception', in R. Grimm and D. Merrill (eds.), *Contents of Thought* (Tucson, Ariz.: University of Arizona Press), 62–76.

—— (1988), 'Individualism and Self-Knowledge', *Journal of Philosophy*, 85: 649–63.

[22] Versions of this essay were read at Rutgers University and Temple University, and at a conference on Self-Knowledge in St Andrews, Scotland. I have benefited greatly from comments by those who attended these readings, especially Tyler Burge, Brian McLaughlin, Colin McGinn, Jerry Fodor, Brian Loar, and Tom Baldwin. I am also indebted to Graham Macdonald, Eve Garrard, and Graham Bird, for discussions about and advice on the issues raised here.

Burge, T. (1996), 'Our Entitlement to Self-Knowledge', *Proceedings of the Aristotelian Society*, 96: 91–116.

Davidson, D. (1984), 'First Person Authority', *Dialectica*, 38: 101–11.

—— (1987), 'Knowing One's Own Mind', *Proceedings and Addresses of the American Philosophical Association*, 60: 441–58.

—— (1988), 'Reply to Burge', *Journal of Philosophy*, 85: 664–5.

Descartes, R. (1969), *Meditations*, in M. Wilson (ed.), *The Essential Descartes* (New York, New American Library, Inc.).

Heil, J. (1988), 'Privileged Access', *Mind*, 97: 238–51.

—— (1992), *The Nature of True Minds* (Cambridge: Cambridge University Press).

Macdonald, C. (1995), 'Externalism and First-Person Authority', *Synthese*, 104: 99–122.

McDowell, J. (1994), *Mind and World* (Cambridge, Mass.: Harvard University Press).

Moran, R. (1994), 'Interpretation Theory and the First Person', *Philosophical Quarterly*, 44: 154–73.

Peacocke, C. (1992), *A Study of Concepts* (Cambridge, Mass.: MIT Press).

—— (1996), 'Entitlement, Self-Knowledge and Conceptual Redeployment', *Proceedings of the Aristotelian Society*, 96: 117–58.

Shoemaker, S. (1994), 'Self-Knowledge and Inner Sense', *Philosophy and Phenomenological Research*, 54: 249–314.

Wright, C. (1987), 'Further Reflections on the Sorites Paradox', *Philosophical Topics*, 15: 277–90.

—— (1988), 'Moral Values, Projection and Secondary Qualities', *Proceedings of the Aristotelian Society*, suppl. vol. 62: 1–26.

—— (1989), 'Wittgenstein's Later Philosophy of Mind: Sensation, Privacy, and Intention', *Journal of Philosophy*, 86: 622–34.

—— (1992), *Truth and Objectivity* (Cambridge, Mass.: Harvard University Press).

6

Self-Knowledge: Special Access versus Artefact of Grammar—A Dichotomy Rejected

ELIZABETH FRICKER

———◆———

I FIRST PERSON ACCESS: THE MINIMAL PHENOMENON, AND TWO KINDS OF VINDICATING EXPLANATION OF IT

Human persons have a special capacity for self-knowledge: for a certain range of states of herself, a person is able to gain knowledge in a way which is available only to herself. The existence of this special way of knowing about oneself is shown in the fact that, when someone knows something about herself in this way, her knowledge is neither prompted by, nor rests on, the evidence which others' knowledge of her states must rest on. Such knowledge is not consciously inferred from other beliefs, but is immediate. Our theorizing about knowledge, and about the nature of the mental, must account for these facts.

The states to which a person has this *first-person access* include a range of mental states: pains and sensations, contentful sensory experiences, occurrent thoughts, intentions, and beliefs, desires, and other propositional attitudes. But first-person accessibility is not a distinguishing mark of the mental. There are other broadly 'mental' characteristics, such as character traits, which are not subject to first-person access. And one also has first-person access, through proprioception, to the position and state of one's own body—that one's legs are crossed, that one is standing upright, that one is too hot, and so forth.[1] So if the mental is

[1] See Evans 1982: ch. 7. That some bodily states are also first-person accessible serves, by providing a clear counter-example, to rebut the thesis that the very idea of a real phenomenon of non-inferential 'special access' to a state independent of that access is incoherent. The anti-special-access theorist will respond that in the case of bodily states their subject's special access to them through proprioception is contingent; and that it is the conception of a type of state for which special access is necessary, yet which is

to be picked out in terms of first-person accessibility, this will have to be through the more refined thesis that a core range of mental states can be picked out as those whose first-person accessibility is *necessary*. But the supposed necessity of first-person accessibility is not a datum; it is rather something to be argued over in the philosophical debate about the nature of mental states.[2] (The contrasting accounts of first-person access discussed in sections V–VII below vary on this matter.) Mental self-knowledge, however, has been the focus of most of the philosophical debate, and here I too will focus on self-knowledge of this range of 'avowable' mental states.

I announced our capacity for self-knowledge through first-person access as a fact, a phenomenon to be accounted for. I hold it such, since I take the epistemologist's task to be to provide explanatory understanding of how it is that we have knowledge, in the central cases in which we ordinarily take ourselves to do so, rather than to provide potentially revisionary accounts of the conditions for knowledge. Sceptical approaches to the phenomenon of our propensity non-inferentially to self-ascribe mental states—approaches which regard it as open to question whether the resulting judgements are knowledge—are thus not considered here. In section II I explain how the task of accounting for self-knowledge falls into two parts: explaining how it is that our self-ascriptive beliefs are reliably true and explaining what the critical features are in virtue of which they are epistemically entitled, apt to be knowledge. (Reliable truth is surely a necessary condition for knowledge; but whether it is sufficient, and if not, what further features of self-ascriptions make them knowledgeable, is open to debate.[3]) I regard it as beyond question both that our non-inferential self-ascriptive beliefs are reliably true, and that

independent of that access, which is incoherent. In section V. 2 I sketch an account—the Weak Special Access Functionalist Theory—which exhibits both features, and so refutes this claim. What would be strange is the (Cartesian) idea of states independent of a route of access which can be known of *only* via that route. (See sects. VI and VII.) But our mental states are not such: others can know that I enjoy a certain mental state, where their knowledge does not depend on my own avowal of it (see sect. VII); and in self-deceptive cases I may learn that I have a certain unconscious belief or desire through self-interpretative inference. Perhaps in the case of sensations and experiences first-person access cannot be lacking; but I may also, like others, have the third-person evidence at my disposal.

[2] I am grateful to Stoneham 1995 for making me aware of the significance of this issue.

[3] Scepticism about self-knowledge might be focused on entitlement, or might question whether our non-inferential self-ascriptive beliefs are even reliably true. (See Gopnik 1993 and Stich 1983: 231 ff.) Questioning this presupposes that the way in which first-level mental states are individuated is independent of their first-person accessibility: as we shall see below, both an 'Artefact of Grammar' account of first-person access and what I call the 'Weak Special Access Functionalist Theory' deny this.

they are apt to be knowledge. But it will make for clarity if we begin by seeing what are the more unquestionable data which make up the minimal phenomenon regarding our topic.

The minimal phenomenon relating to first-person access consists in certain features of the 'language-game' surrounding persons' assertions self-ascribing mental states of the core range in question (henceforth 'Self-Ascriptions'). It is often said that Self-Ascriptions are both 'authoritative' and 'non-inferential' or 'groundless'.[4] These notions need explication. On one way of explicating them, they summarize features of everyday epistemic practice in regard to Self-Ascriptions: namely: Self-Ascriptions are 'authoritative' in the sense that they are ordinarily *treated as* being such; they are accepted as very strong evidence for the person's being in the self-ascribed state, a prima-facie indication of it which is defeated only by strong counter-evidence. Call this property of Self-Ascriptions their being *language-game (LG-) authoritative*. Self-Ascriptions are also 'groundless' in one sense:[5] namely, that in everyday social intercourse they are treated as such; they are taken neither to need nor to admit of defence, and no explanation of *how* the self-ascriber knows what she claims to know is demanded or expected from her. Call this their being *language-game (LG-) basic*. To say that Self-Ascriptions are 'authoritative' and 'non-inferential', when what this means is that they are LG-authoritative and LG-basic is, therefore, merely to summarize standard social epistemic practice in relation to them.[6] We must equally acknowledge that Self-Ascriptions are psychologically non-inferred. These three features of Self-Ascriptions constitute the minimal phenomenon, one which philosophers and, equally, psychologists of whatever stripe must recognize as phenomena in need of explanation.

---

[4] See Davidson 1984, Wright 1989*a*: 630 and Ch. 1 above. Strawson (1959: ch. 3) says more guardedly that self-ascriptions are made 'not on the basis of observation'. Wittgenstein (1953: e.g. §377), observes that they are not based on any 'criteria'.

[5] Wright (Ch. 1) glosses 'groundless' in this way explicitly.

[6] The LG-authoritativeness of Self-Ascriptions is not a *distinguishing* feature, since there is a defeasible presumption of correctness of a person's testimony for a wide range of subject-matters, including their testimony about their own mental states, but much more besides. (See Fricker 1995.) To say that a Self-Ascription is a *criterion* for the self-ascribed state points to a distinctive feature; but this is not a datum, but part of a controversial theory. (See below, this section and sects. VI and VII.) Suppose one were to say that the only permissible defeaters are other aspects of that person's behaviour or psychology. This would be distinctive, but is implausible: features of context, past or present, and/or general psychological knowledge can defeat a Self-Ascription. Their LG-basicness (which includes the fact that the question 'How do you know?' is generally regarded as inapt) does, however, seem distinctive. So maybe it is the *combination* of LG-authoritativeness with LG-basicness which is rightly regarded as the distinctive feature of self-ascriptions. Alternative senses of 'non-inferential' which are not data will be examined in sect. III.

Self-Ascriptions are LG-authoritative and LG-basic: that is to say, we normally take another's Self-Ascriptions as indicating that she is in the self-ascribed state; we treat them as reliably true. I have put aside sceptical approaches which regard this as questionable. Having done so, the explanations of our tripartite minimal phenomenon to be considered will be confined to *vindicating* explanations: ones which indeed exhibit Self-Ascriptions as reliably true, thus vindicating as truth-conducive our everyday epistemic practice of treating them as such. My main project in this chapter is to introduce and examine two contrasting kinds of vindicating explanation of the minimal phenomenon.

When someone claims that another person is in a certain mental state, her claim is treated neither as authoritative nor as basic. 'How do you know that?', we may ask; and we may be sceptical about her claim, while not doubting her sincerity. So the LG-authoritativeness and LG-basicness of Self-Ascriptions of mental states suffices to mark them off from other-ascriptions. Thus to recognize these marks of Self-Ascriptions, along with their psychological non-inferredness and reliable truth, is already to recognize a phenomenon of first-person access of a kind.[7]

But the idea of first-person access may be understood in a more substantial way. On the more substantial view, the 'grammatical' features of LG-authoritativeness and LG-basicness reflect, and are vindicated by, an underlying contingent phenomenon of *Special Access*. A person's first-level mental states and second-level judgements and beliefs about them are distinct states, and the second kind reliably track the first kind in virtue of the person's possession of a special route of cognitive access, one which yields reliably true judgements and (sincere) verbal reports on them. On this account, the epistemic practice of taking Self-Ascriptions of mental states as a presumptive indication that the self-ascriber is in that state, without demanding any explanation of how it is that the self-ascriber knows what she claims to know, is a good (i.e. truth-conducive) practice, because it reflects the prior, contingent fact that people have a reliable non-inferential means of access to their own states. And people are moved to make these self-attributions through the exercise of that access link; this is their aetiology, the explanation of how they come to be made.

This idea of Special Access as a real phenomenon of reliable tracking underlying the language-game surrounding Self-Ascriptions (i.e. everyday epistemic practice in response to them), far from being a datum, is

---

[7] Gilbert Ryle heroically argued that our basis for self-knowledge is different only in degree, not in kind, from others' knowledge of us. He could not comfortably accept that Self-Ascriptions are LG-basic, or that they are psychologically non-inferred (Ryle 1949: ch. 6).

a controversial theory of what underlies the 'grammatical' phenomena. I call all theories which hold the everyday epistemic practice of LG-authoritativness and LG-basicness to reflect a prior phenomenon of reliable access *Special Access theories*.

Forming beliefs in accordance with LG-basicness and LG-author-itativeness consists in accepting another's Self-Ascriptions as correct, without demanding that she defend her claim in any way (doing so, that is, unless there is strong defeating evidence). Assuming that this epistemic practice is sound (i.e. forming beliefs thus tends to yield true beliefs about others' mental states), how could it be so if *not* because soundness is ensured by an underlying phenomenon of special access—reliable tracking of a person's first-level mental states by her judgements and sincere assertions about them? An alternative possibility is that this epistemic practice does not correlate with an *independent* phenom-enon of reliable tracking, but instead enters into the individuation con-ditions of the range of first-level mental states in question in a fashion which ensures the reliability of Self-Ascriptions of them. The sort of view considered in this chapter holds, specifically, that Self-Ascriptions come out mainly true because a person's Self-Ascribing of a mental state is a 'criterion' for her being in it. That is to say, it is a constitutive principle that, in the assignment of mental states to another, her Self-Ascriptions be taken as correct—sincere and expressing a belief which is true—unless considerations of coherence in the broader interpretation of her defeat this presumption.[8] On this sort of view, the reliability of Self-Ascriptions is not—or so it is claimed[9]—the upshot of a real phenomenon of Special Access, but is built into the individuation conditions of the mental states in question, these latter being fixed by the conventions of use, or 'grammar', of the words for them. Reliability is not an empir-ical fact prior to grammar which underlies and vindicates it; instead, the grammar of mental concepts is prior to, and creates, the reliability of Self-Ascriptions. I call theories of this kind *Artefact of Grammar the-ories* of first-person access.

---

[8] It is a feature of this sort of theory that the metaphysics of mental states, their indi-viduation conditions, is held to be consequent upon the epistemic (or pseudo-epistemic) norms for ascribing them to another person. These latter norms concerning what evid-ence warrants an assertion or judgement that a concept applies are taken to be the basic rules governing it which constitute its identity, and so fix its reference. Of course there is a logical space for explanations of the reliability of self-ascriptive judgements which trace this to the individuation conditions of the states in question, but do not link this to a criterialist account of meaning. See e.g. Burge 1988 and Stoneham 1995: ch. 1. Each maintains that self-ascriptive beliefs of some class are guaranteed true, because the second-level state includes the first-level state, but do not see this as resulting from conventions for 'use' of linguistic expressions.

[9] But see sects. V. 2 and VII below.

Special Access theories and Artefact of Grammar theories are alternative vindicating explanations of the minimal phenomenon.[10] They give
alternative explanations of the reliability of our psychologically non-
inferred self-ascriptions of mental states. Strictly, they have different
explananda: a real phenomenon of Special Access explains, in the first
instance, the reliability of self-ascriptive judgements, while an Artefact
of Grammar theory explains, in the first instance, the reliability of
Self-Ascriptions. But Self-Ascriptions are expressions of judgement in
a sincere speaker, and one way or another we can be confident that
this condition of sincerity will generally be fulfilled. (I shall not probe
the status of this fact.) Thus I shall assume that both theories can,
with appropriate ancillary premisses, explain the reliability of both self-
ascriptive judgements and Self-Ascriptions. I shall use 'self-ascriptions'
to cover all self-ascriptive judgements, beliefs, and assertions.

My main project here is to examine the leading options for theories
of these two kinds. The following summarizes the main theses I shall
put forward.

The idea that Special Access versus Artefact of Grammar explanations
of the reliability of self-ascriptions poses a dichotomous choice for us
is present in Davidson 1984. Bilgrami's (Ch. 7 below) contrast between
a 'constitutive account' and a 'perceptual' account of self-knowledge is
similar. Wright makes the contrast explicitly (see 1989a: 631–2), and
it is equally present in his chapter 1 above.[11] I shall argue that this
supposed dichotomous contrast is a false one, in several respects.

Davidson dismisses the idea of 'special access' accounts of first-
person access, and it seems that he equates the idea of Special Access
with a Cartesian conception of the nature of the mental and our self-
knowledge of it.[12] The first main thesis I am concerned to establish is

[10] Vindicating the minimal phenomenon is not the same thing as explaining its existence. It is characteristic of the Wittgensteinian outlook associated with an Artefact of
Grammar theory to hold that 'grammar', being 'bedrock', does not admit of explanation.
A Special Access theory might explain the development of the epistemic practice of
treating Self-Ascriptions as LG-authoritative and LG-basic in this way: it grew up as it
was discovered that accepting people's Self-Ascriptions as correct yielded theories
of them which meshed with, and added fine grain to, psychological interpretations of
others made on the basis of other evidence only. Even if not historically true, this story
might be a good myth.

[11] Davidson (1984) talks of 'privileged access' and of a 'special way of knowing'. 'Artefact
of grammar' is my own coinage, but picks up an idea clearly present in both Wright
and Bilgrami. I follow Wright in seeing the primary task in relation to self-knowledge
to be that of explaining the minimal phenomenon. (Explaining why self-ascriptive
beliefs are entitled is a second, separate task. See sect. II.)

[12] Davidson (1984) certainly equates 'special access' with the Cartesian conception,
and in a context which makes it clear that he is thinking of such a theory as being the
only option for a realist, rather than a conventionalist-constitutivist, explanation of the

that Cartesianism is not the only option for a Special Access theory. I take the core idea of Special Access to be that of causally mediated reliable tracking by self-ascriptive beliefs of ontologically distinct first-level mental states which they are about. A Cartesian conception of mental states takes them to be states whose essence is exhausted by their appearance to consciousness, essentially private items (EPIs[13]) whose nature is known through an essentially private acquaintance. This private acquaintance is often described as a form of 'inner perception'. We shall see that the bare idea of Special Access as reliable tracking can be divorced both from the conception of mental states as EPIs and from the idea of 'inner perception' as our means of gaining knowledge of them. Specifically, functionalist accounts of the individuation conditions of mental states naturally lend themselves to Special Access in our pared-down sense. For our present purposes, functionalist accounts of mental states fall into two broad kinds: those in which the individuation conditions of first-level mental states and second-level beliefs about them are such that they are conceptually independent of each other; and those in which they are not so. I observe that conceptual dependence in individuation is consistent with ontological distinctness. Only the second is needed for there to be a real phenomenon of reliable tracking. So we have, respectively, the Strong Special Access Functionalist Theory of first-person access and the Weak Special Access Functionalist Theory of it. These two functionalist theories are Special Access theories in which the individuation conditions of mental states are such that they are far from being EPIs, and there need be nothing like 'inner perception'—indeed no distinctive phenomenology at all—in the functionalist picture of how self-ascriptive judgements and beliefs reliably track first-level states.

Within Artefact of Grammar (AOG) theories I distinguish two possibilities: 'Pure' and 'Impure' AOG theories. In both the Impure AOG Theory and the Weak Special Access Functionalist Theory we find exemplified my second main thesis: that the supposed contrast between 'grammar' and empirical regularity as incompatible rival explanations

---

grammatical data. (I regard Davidson's own explanation of LG-authoritativeness as an upshot of the nature of interpretation as a species of Artefact of Grammar account.) Wright (1989*a*) offers two options for a 'substantial epistemology' of self-knowledge: inference or observation. He rejects inference as implausible, equates 'observation' with unsustainable Cartesianism, and then suggests what I am calling an Artefact of Grammar theory as the only remaining option. Here, I think, separation of the issue of the nature of the underlying facts from that of what confers justifiedness is needed (see sect. II), to avoid overlooking further options. Specifically, if brutely causal reliable tracking is the underlying situation, nothing grounds self-ascriptive beliefs; but the explanation of reliability is a 'special access' one (see sect. V. 1).

[13] I here use Edward Craig's neat acronym (Craig 1982: 561).

of the reliability of self-ascriptions is a false one. In both these theories constitutive principles governing the individuation of mental states conspire inextricably with underlying empirical regularities to coalesce our actual mental concepts, and produce reliability of self-ascriptions of them.[14]

Grammar can mask the underlying facts of empirical regularity. We shall see that in the Weak Special Access Functionalist Theory the way in which mental states are individuated has this consequence: necessarily, any subject of mental states is reliable in her self-ascriptive judgements. But the necessity in question is ensured by what is in effect a definitional stop in the individuation of mental states. This definitional stop masks an underlying contingent fact of reliable tracking, Special Access. This finding is important. One finds implicit or explicit in the literature this argument: It is a necessary truth about subjects of mental states that they are reliable reporters of their own mental states; this is part of what it is to be such a subject. *Therefore* the reliability of self-ascriptions does not constitute or reveal any kind of cognitive achievement on their part, since it is just a definitional truth about what it is to be a subject of mental states. My analysis shows the fallaciousness of this inference.

I also investigate what an AOG theory must be like. A *Pure Artefact of Grammar theory* is one according to which the reliability of Self-Ascriptions is ensured and explained entirely by grammar, with independent

---

[14] Does this mean that 'special access' and 'artefact of grammar' are not, after all, mutually exclusive labels for theories, since in the intermediate theories mentioned, empirical regularity and concept-fixing grammatical convention are both involved in generating the reliability of our self-ascriptions of them? For terminological convenience I define them so that the two labels none the less remain mutually exclusive. 'Special access' as defined requires not just that empirical regularity play a role in explaining the reliability of self-ascriptions, but that first-level mental states and beliefs about them be ontologically distinct states, the first kind causing the second kind. I restrict the label 'Artefact of Grammar' to theories which deny this. So defined, the two types of theory are guaranteed mutually exclusive. But the dichotomy as originally envisaged does not survive our investigation. (See sects. V. 2, VII, and VIII.) Notice that I do not claim what would be false: that AOG and Special Access between them exhaust the possibilities for explanations of the reliability of self-ascriptions. AOG theories of the kind discussed here are one alternative to tracking explanations of reliability of self-ascriptions. They are worth considering in detail, since they have some currency, and naturally flow from one well-known, though controversial, school in the theory of meaning and content. But there are other alternatives to tracking explanations: e.g. Burge's account of reflexive judgements such as 'I (hereby) think that writing requires concentration' (Burge 1988: 658). Burge argues plausibly that such judgements are self-verifying; but his theory differs from the sort of AOG theory considered here, because the fact that being in the second-level state guarantees being in the first-level state is not explained as a consequence of content-fixing epistemic norms, 'criteria', for ascribing such states.

empirical regularities playing no role. My third main result is to show that there is no coherent account of mental concepts which sustains this view. I first show that the only sort of putative mental state concept which would ensure this would be a certain sort of *one-criterion concept*: the sole criterion for a person's being in the Self-Ascribed state is that she is disposed to Self-Ascribe it. I then show that there can be no such concepts. The kind of clause which purportedly specifies this sort of concept is viciously circular. This fundamental defect has two manifestations: first, a clause of this kind fails to individuate a distinct concept at all; second, supposed 'self-ascriptions' of it cannot be seen as genuine exercises in judgement, self-applications of a concept, by the supposed self-ascriber. The clause is circular in a way which means that no content has been provided for the supposed judgement. The idea of a Pure AOG account of the reliability of Self-Ascriptions is thus ruled out, and an Impure AOG theory is the only kind left in contention.

Those who advocate, or discuss, what I am calling AOG theories, associate with them the idea that there is 'no cognitive achievement' involved in self-knowledge, and suggest that perhaps self-knowledge has 'no substantial epistemology'.[15] In section IV I consider what precise theses these phrases might express. (We will see that there are importantly different ideas to be distinguished here.) In section V I examine the varieties of possible Special Access accounts of the phenomenon of first-person access. In section VI I examine and reject the Pure AOG Theory. Finally in section VII I consider the Impure AOG Theory, and compare it with the Weak Special Access Theory. I find that the difference between them lies only in their view of the ontological status of mental states, and as part of this whether first-level mental states cause self-ascriptions of them.

But before this main business a few more preliminaries are needed. These concern the nature of the philosophical task in relation to self-knowledge (sect. II) and what is and is not a pre-theoretical datum for it (sect. III). Although I may betray some leanings, I here attempt neither to decide what is the correct account of first-person access, nor to give an account of how it is that self-ascriptive beliefs are apt to be knowledge. Establishing the theses listed above is already more than enough work for one essay. Doing so, I hope, effects a clear articulation of the issues from which argument for a particular account of their resolution may take off.

---

[15] See Wright 1989a: 631; Boghossian 1989: sect. 3; and Bilgrami, Ch. 7 below.

II THE PHILOSOPHICAL TASK OF ACCOUNTING FOR SELF-KNOWLEDGE

If the fact of LG-authoritative, LG-basic, and psychologically non-inferred Self-Ascriptions of mental states which express knowledge is our datum, what is our project? The philosophical task in relation to self-knowledge is to account for its existence. Explaining how our first-personal knowledge arises poses a task in the philosophy of mind and epistemology that is for two reasons especially challenging.

The task, as I see it, separates into two sub-tasks. I hold that the application of epistemically normative concepts like 'is justified' and 'is knowledge' in some domain of belief supervenes on the non-epistemically normative facts about how beliefs in that domain are formed, etc.[16] Given this assumption of supervenience, it must be possible to describe the nature of first-person access—the manner in which our self-ascriptive beliefs[17] are normally generated, and how they relate to the first-level mental states which they are about—without using any epistemically evaluative terms. Call these the *epistemologically neutral facts* about how first-level states and second-level beliefs about them are related. The epistemic status of self-ascriptive beliefs will supervene on these epistemologically neutral facts. So our task of accounting for the fact of self-knowledge separates into two sub-tasks: first, get straight what the epistemologically neutral facts are; second, provide a theory of how it is that features of these neutral facts constitute self-ascriptive beliefs' being *justified*, apt to be knowledge.[18] My main project here—examining

[16] This is a substantial assumption. Its defence is not a topic for this chapter. It is a presupposition, explicit or implicit, of the mainstream in modern epistemology, and it is difficult to see what epistemology would look like (how much of it would be left!) without it. (See Sosa 1991: essays 9 and 10.) For a contrary view see Williamson 1995. Suppose that beliefs could not be beliefs—i.e. states with objective informational content—unless they were generally apt to be knowledge. I think this conjecture is very plausible. But it is consistent with supervenience and the associated analytic division of the philosopher's task suggested here.

[17] The data of LG-authoritativeness and LG-basicness pertain to someone's *linguistic expression* of her beliefs about herself. I regard it as a fact that these linguistic acts are expressions of knowledgeable belief, and take our topic to be explaining the existence and knowledgeable character of these beliefs. A radical Wittgensteinian position denies that there is self-knowledge in this sense. See Wittgenstein 1953: §§244 ff.

[18] Despite the familiar difficulties it must answer, I favour a theoretical articulation in epistemology on which a property of beliefs—justifiedness, or entitlement—is characterized, and is the central notion of the theory, which is such that: justifiedness and truth are jointly necessary for knowledge, and, apart from some puzzle cases, are sufficient for it, but where justifiedness falls short of guaranteeing truth in every case (and is thus a distinct concept from that of knowledge itself). (See Fricker (forthcoming).) Are self-ascriptive beliefs generated through first-person access always true? I shall not explore this difficult question. But it seems that at least in the case of beliefs and desires, the

Special Access and Artefact of Grammar explanations of the reliability of Self-Ascriptions—is part of the first task: getting straight about the epistemologically neutral facts, from which our account of justifiedness must take off.[19]

The central questions about the epistemologically neutral facts are these: Are first-level states and second-level beliefs about them conceptually independent, or is a person's being in a certain mental state constitutively linked to her being disposed to judge herself to be in it? If conceptually linked, are they none the less distinct states? If they are distinct states, then is a self-ascriptive belief normally caused by the state which is self-ascribed? If so, what is the character of this causal mechanism: is a characteristic phenomenology involved, and does its presence have an essential explanatory role in the account of how such beliefs are caused? The answer given to the first two questions determines whether a Special Access or Artefact of Grammar explanation of the reliability of self-ascriptions is offered. The answer to the last question further determines what kind of Special Access theory is offered. This last matter is crucial for what sort of account of justifiedness for self-ascriptive beliefs can be given.

Providing a philosophical explanation of self-knowledge is a challenging task, first, because the nature of the epistemologically neutral facts is itself highly problematic. The normative epistemological question of what confers justifiedness on self-ascriptive beliefs is a debatable upshot of theory. But so, equally, as we saw in section I, is the issue of how the minimal phenomenon is explained. In the first debate the controversy is part of epistemology proper. In the second it is about the nature of mental concepts and the states they are concepts of. Since, as we have seen, a first crucial question for the explanation of the reliability of

phenomenon of positive self-deception exists. So for these mental states there could perhaps be justified beliefs which are not true, hence not knowledge.

[19] The phenomenon of LG-authoritativeness which we have accepted as a *datum* is that Self-Ascriptions are normally accepted as true without challenge. This fact has no normative smack about it. To say that Self-Ascriptions are a *criterion* of the person's being in the Self-Ascribed state would do so: a criterion *warrants* belief in what it is a criterion for. But that Self-Ascriptions are a criterion for the state in question is, as we saw above, part of a tendentious explanation of the minimal phenomenon, not a neutral description of it. It is true that if we offer an Artefact of Grammar explanation of the reliability of Self-Ascriptions, the thesis that Self-Ascription of a state is a criterion for a person's being in that state answers the question about whether and how one's belief about another's mental state formed on the basis of such criterial warrant is justified. But notice that saying that Self-Ascriptions are criteria in this way does absolutely nothing to explain how *the Self-Ascriber* knows herself to be in the state she Self-Ascribes. Indeed, as we shall see in sect. VI, the central difficulty with a criterial account is that it is hard to see how the Self-Ascriber can even be making a genuine judgement, let alone gaining knowledge thereby.

Self-Ascriptions is whether the relation between first-level states and second-level beliefs about them is criterial (concept-fixing) or *purely causal*—that is, causal and not criterial. (We shall see in sect. V. 2 that it can be both).

Our second sub-task (explaining what makes self-ascriptive beliefs justified), as I conceive it, takes its shape from the assumption of supervenience, together with the requirement that our normative epistemology provide a *unified* theory of knowledge and (as a component of this) epistemic justifiedness: we must be able to see knowledge as a single thing instanced in many different cases. (See Peacocke 1986: ch. 9.) Within this framework the properly epistemology-theoretic part of an account of self-knowledge requires the provision of a general account of how justifiedness (or 'entitlement' or 'warrant') accrues to beliefs of whatever kind; and the application of this to the case of self-ascriptive beliefs, showing how it is that they are justified, apt to be knowledge.

It is especially challenging to provide an account of self-knowledge, secondly, because there are acute difficulties faced by the theory of epistemic justifiedness about how non-inferential knowledge, of which self-knowledge is a case if anything is, can be explained as justified, hence apt to be knowledge.[20] Adherence to the unity constraint exacerbates this difficulty: the problem is to find an account of what makes non-inferential beliefs justified which lets in perception and self-knowledge, yet rules out various counter-examples, which intuition rules decisively, do not constitute knowledge, but which are difficult to discriminate from the cases of perception and self-knowledge.[21]

So a philosophical explanation of self-knowledge will be the product of two interlocking parts: an account of the epistemologically neutral facts and a general theory of epistemic justifiedness. We can get a feel for how the parts interlock by looking at two examples. A reliabilist account of knowledge would allow self-ascriptive beliefs to be knowledge so long as they are related to the first-level states which are their subject-matter in such a way as reliably to be true. If, on the other hand, justification is held to be necessary for knowledge, and an 'internalist' conception of this is held, then some sort of ground for self-ascriptive beliefs is required—either other beliefs or a non-belief ground such as a conscious experience or sensation co-present with and distinct from the self-ascriptive belief, which provides a rational basis for it. (This requires that the contents or character of the grounded and grounding states be appropriately related.) Whether there is a distinct conscious

---

[20] See, however, the distinction drawn in sect. III between a belief's being non-inferential and its being groundless.

[21] Pure reliabilism falls on this count. See Bonjour 1985: ch. 3; Haack 1993: ch. 7.

state of this kind is one question; whether such a state plays an essential role in making self-ascriptive beliefs knowledge is another. But since we have taken it as beyond question that self-ascriptive beliefs are knowledge, our normative epistemology had better not require such grounds for knowledge, unless our description of the epistemologically neutral facts in this case includes them.

This last remark highlights the usefulness of explicitly separating the two halves of our task. Philosophers confronting the question of self-knowledge generally address it already equipped with some explicit views, or at least intuitions, about the requirements for knowledge. But this may lead to attempts, unconscious or otherwise, to gerrymander the description of the neutral facts, so as to square with the already accepted epistemology. But it is normative theory, rather than the facts, that can be finessed to suit the other partner in the formula

Facts of case + general epistemological theory → first-person beliefs constitute knowledge.

Moreover, it makes for analytic clarity first to examine the full range of likely scenarios for the neutral facts, and only then to think about which of these would, in conjunction with a plausible normative epistemology, yield the result that self-ascriptive beliefs are apt to be knowledge. Failure to separate the two sub-tasks can lead an author to overlook empirical possibilities which would not in her view support the thesis that self-ascriptive beliefs are knowledge. For instance, the articulation of the possibilities in Boghossian 1989 overlooks what I call the brutely causal scenario (see sect. V. 1), for this reason, I conjecture.

I have claimed that while it is an *explanandum* that self-ascriptive beliefs generally constitute knowledge, precisely *how* it is that they do so, in virtue of what features, is not a given, but something for which we must try to construct a good explanatory theory. It follows that whether self-ascriptive beliefs possess various epistemologically loaded properties is not a given, but a matter to be argued over in our epistemological theorizing about self-knowledge. In the next section I investigate a little further this question of what matters are facts given to our enquiry into self-knowledge, and what matters are established only as the upshot of that enquiry. Beyond this I shall say no more here about the second of the two sub-tasks I have distinguished: the account of how exactly justifiedness accrues to self-ascriptive beliefs. I shall not offer a specific account of how justifiedness accrues to them.[22]

---

[22] In fact, I think that both perceptual beliefs and self-ascriptive beliefs are justificationally non-inferential (not based on other beliefs), and that their status as knowledgeable can be explained without sacrificing this view of their character. This view of perception will be defended in Fricker, forthcoming.

Nor will I defend a specific account of the epistemologically neutral facts. What I will do (in sects. IV–VII) is to address some fundamental questions about the nature of those facts. Specifically, I will examine the supposed contrast, introduced in section I, between Special Access and Artefact of Grammar explanations of the reliability of Self-Ascriptions, and argue for the theses already previewed at the end of section I.

III MATTERS OF FACT AND MATTERS FOR THEORY

We have found that the uncontroversial facts concerning first-person access are that Self-Ascriptions are LG-authoritative and LG-basic, and are psychologically non-inferred. And we saw that Special Access theories and Artefact of Grammar theories provide rival kinds of vindicating explanation of this minimal phenomenon. It is time to be more precise about what psychological non-inferredness amounts to. The property of Self-Ascriptions (and equally of judgements and beliefs self-ascribing mental states) intended here is a fact available to introspection for each of us: that self-ascriptions of mental states made through first-person access are not formed by any conscious process of inference from other beliefs.[23] It is worth noting that various other properties are not entailed by this *psychological non-inferredness*.

First, psychological non-inferredness is consistent with there being a conscious state—an experience, a sensation, or a conscious thought—distinct from the second-order self-ascriptive judgement or belief, which is prior to or co-present with it. (There may be a difference in the aetiology of self-ascriptions of sensations and experiences and some self-ascriptions of attitudes in this respect.) That we enjoy sensations, experiences, etc. is an undeniable platitude and fact of our mental life. The issue here concerns their precise relations to second-level beliefs about them. Are they more than dispositions to form such beliefs? And where such a belief is formed, is the first-level state really distinct from it?[24]

---

[23] Does it beg our main question to rely on introspection for our data here? We have taken it as beyond question that our beliefs about *what* mental states we are in are generally knowledge. But there is no reason to think that we have any special access to the aetiology of those states, or the causal relations between them. So our datum is only that self-ascriptive beliefs are not *consciously* inferred or derived from other beliefs (accessibility to self-report being a diagnostic feature of consciousness of a process).

[24] These are delicate issues in phenomenology and conceptual analysis which I cannot debate here. For the record, my own answer to both these questions is Yes. An urgent task for one who believes in conscious states distinct from, and prompting, second-level beliefs about them is to provide a conception of them on which they are not EPIs—since that Cartesian conception is shown to be incoherent by Wittgenstein's argument against 'private language'. I think this can be done. The trick is to think of conscious

Second, that self-ascriptive judgements and beliefs are psychologically non-inferred is a datum because it is neutral as to their normative epistemic status. Say that a belief is *non-inferential* if it does not depend for its justifiedness on support from other beliefs. And say a belief is *groundless* (i.e. groundlessly justified) if it depends for its justifiedness neither on other beliefs nor on any non-belief ground (e.g. a conscious perceptual experience). That self-ascriptive judgements and beliefs are non-inferential is a (non-self-evident) thesis in the theory of epistemic justification, not apt to be established through introspection; likewise the thesis that they are groundless. Moreover, the introspective datum of psychological non-inferredness does not compel a particular account of what makes self-ascriptive beliefs justified, but leaves open a number of options. Specifically, it does not compel the view that if justified, they must be groundlessly, or at least non-inferentially, so.

First, if there are indeed cases where there is a first-level conscious state distinct from the second-level judgement about it, there is room in such cases for a theory which holds that this state is a *ground* for the self-ascriptive judgement. This is simultaneously a phenomenological, a causal, and an epistemically normative claim: a *ground* of someone's judgement or belief is another conscious state of hers with an appropriately related content or character, which is part of the sustaining cause of that belief, and whose being so is essential to that belief's being justified. An experience, or a sensation, is—or so such a view would maintain—capable of furnishing a non-belief ground for a belief.[25]

Second, self-ascriptions' being psychologically non-inferred does not entail that they are non-inferential: not dependent for their justifiedness on support from other beliefs. No epistemological 'ought' follows from this 'is' alone. And even given the further premiss that they are, somehow, knowledge, no specific theory of how they qualify as such is compelled. Their psychological non-inferredness is consistent with their satisfying the requirements for inferential justifiedness: grounding beliefs may play a sustaining causal role, even though there is no conscious inference from them.

So their psychological non-inferredness leaves the epistemology of self-ascriptive judgements and beliefs undetermined. The fact that Self-Ascriptions (linguistic expressions of belief) are LG-basic similarly fails to compel a particular epistemological account of how self-ascriptive beliefs are justified. Again, it does not imply that if justified, they are

states as states which present a characteristic appearance in consciousness, rather than as states whose essence is exhausted by that appearance. See sects. VI and VII below.

[25] For such a view see Peacocke, Ch. 3, sect. II, above. See previous footnote on the urgent task for such a view.

so groundlessly, or at least non-inferentially. LG-basicness of expressions
of beliefs of a certain type would entail those beliefs being groundless
given this assumption: that everyday standards in requiring defence for
beliefs of a certain type are the sole arbiter of the justificatory status
of beliefs of that type. ('Type' here is at least partly a matter of type of
content.) I shall not explore fully here what sort of view about the relation between everyday epistemic practice, belief content, and epistemic
justifiedness would support this assumption. A full discussion is needed
of how we should theorize the property of epistemic justifiedness of beliefs.
But I shall say enough to show how LG-basicness need not be a mark
of non-inferentialness, *a fortiori* not one of groundlessness (or 'epistemic
basicness', as it is often called).

Suppose we were to think of justified*ness* (a property of beliefs) in
terms of justifica*tion* (an activity of believers), and so think of a ground
for belief as some other fact known by the believer which she can cite
in defence of her belief. Then we would equate groundlessness of a type
of belief with its neither needing nor admitting of being defended
by its subject. Suppose we equate the latter in turn with beliefs of that
type not ordinarily being taken to need defence. Given these two theory-
shaping equations, LG-basicness entails groundlessness. But we need not
make either of these equations. Instead we may think of justifiedness as
a relatively stable structural property of a person's belief system, a matter
of the appropriate sustaining relations obtaining between beliefs (and
perhaps other contentful states such as experiences) of hers with aptly
related contents. Conceiving justifiedness in this manner, we are no longer
forced to think of a belief's being justified as consisting in or requiring
that its subject be able to produce a 'justification' of it, a verbal defence.[26]
And even if our favoured account of justifiedness includes this 'driving
licence' requirement ('can produce a defence on demand'), we can yet
dissent from the second equation above: the sort of defence we hold to
be normatively required will not necessarily be just the sort, if any, which
everyday epistemic practice expects. In short, in our normative epistemological theorizing we are not compelled to regard LG-basic beliefs as
groundless: the two notions are by no means identical, and there is a
potential gap in their extensions.

In practice there are at least two theories deserving serious consideration, of what makes self-ascriptive judgements justified, on which their
status as LG-basic and psychologically non-inferred contrasts with their
normative epistemic status. First, any genuinely coherentist theory of

---

[26] Compare Robert Audi's useful distinction between dialectical versus structural conceptions of the regress of justification (Audi 1993: ch. 4, sect. 1). For a fuller account
of the notion of epistemic justifiedness I favour see Fricker, forthcoming.

epistemic justification must (on pain of allowing a foundational epistemic 'given' to creep in) hold that self-ascriptive judgements are, despite their psychologically non-inferred character, inferential: they are apt to be knowledge only when backed by the top-down endorsement provided by a background belief in their reliability. Such pure coherentism is counter-intuitive and revisionary, and is subject to severe internal difficulties. But it has some strong 'internalist' intuitions about links between justifiedness and rationality of belief at least apparently on its side, and certainly deserves to be taken seriously.[27]

Second, the theory mentioned above, that some self-ascriptive judgements are justified partly in virtue of having a non-belief ground, such as an experience or sensation enjoyed by the self-ascriber, merits careful exploration.

It is often claimed that some types of mental state—pains and other sensations, and perhaps also conscious experiences—are *transparent* to their subject. That is, when someone with the necessary conceptual resources has, say, a pain in her foot, she cannot fail, if she attends, to know this fact; and she cannot ever mistakenly believe that she has one when she does not. Is transparency, along with LG-basicness, LG-authority, and psychological non-inferredness, a datum? If there is a datum here, it is again only a grammatical one: namely, that our concepts of these states are such that we will never accept that someone has a mistaken belief about whether she is in pain, etc. On this view of the 'grammar', faced with a case in which someone declares pain, though showing no visible distress, we will always conclude either that she is insincere or that, despite appearances, she is in pain, or that she has lost her grip on the word 'pain'. What is not a datum is the explanation of this grammar in terms of an underlying fact of infallible access to a state transparently given to consciousness.

We have seen in this section that while it is a pre-theoretical datum that self-ascriptive judgements are both psychologically non-inferred and LG-basic, their normative epistemic status is not a datum, nor is it determined by these two properties. It remains an open question to be established through argument in normative epistemology. (We have taken it as beyond question *that* they are knowledge. But this does not tell us how, in virtue of what features, they are so.) Equally, that some self-ascriptive beliefs coexist with or are caused by a co-present, but distinct, conscious state which might serve as a ground for the belief is not immediately ruled out by their LG-basic and psychologically non-inferred character. This is a matter whose determination involves

---

[27] See Bonjour 1985 for, and Boghossian 1989, Sosa 1991: essay 7 against.

careful conceptual-cum-phenomenological investigation and, crucially, philosophical argument as to whether such a conception can be set out which does not conflict with the upshot of Wittgenstein's argument against a 'private language'.

IV 'NO COGNITIVE ACHIEVEMENT' AND 'NO SUBSTANTIVE EPISTEMOLOGY'?

What might it mean to say that there is 'no substantial epistemology' (NSE) of self-knowledge? I can think of three different things that might be meant.[28]

> (NSE 1)   From the subject's own standpoint, her self-ascriptive judgements have no distinctive phenomenological or justificatory aetiology. They are the upshot of doxastic inclinations which she from time to time just finds herself with, and to which she a-rationally accedes. Thus there is no 'way in which she comes to know' that is visible from her first-level standpoint, and, from that standpoint, no justificatory or explanatory story to tell herself or others.

(Of course, if she is a sophisticate, an epistemologist, she may have a meta-level story to tell about why these inclinations to believe with which she just finds herself yield knowledge—the sort of epistemological account mentioned in (NSE 3).)

> (NSE 2)   There is in fact no true causal-explanatory-cum-justificatory story to be told, of a 'substantial' kind: there is no empirical phenomenon of a special route of cognitive access possessed by persons to their own mental states, hence no account to be given of how it works, its character, or of how it renders self-ascriptive judgements apt to be knowledge.

(NSE 2) will be so just if an AOG theory of the reliableness of self-ascriptions is held. Note that (NSE 1) could be true while (NSE 2) is false. This is the situation given a brutely causal account of the relation between first-level mental states and self-ascriptions of them. By a *brutely causal* account, I mean one according to which (i) first-level states and

---

[28] I believe the senses distinguished here cover all those intended by Boghossian (1989) and Wright (1989*a*).

self-ascriptions of them are conceptually independent; (ii) first-level states cause self-ascriptions of them; and (iii) this causal process involves no characteristic phenomenology, such as might provide a first-level justifying ground available within the subject's own standpoint.

(NSE 3) There is no explanatory-vindicatory epistemological account of any kind to be given, by the philosopher of mind cum normative epistemologist, of how it is that self-ascriptive judgements are reliable, and apt to be knowledge.

(NSE 2)'s being true would of course not make (NSE 3) true. That a pure AOG theory holds would mean, rather, that the philosopher's explanation of how it is that self-ascriptive beliefs are reliable, and count as knowledge, would not be the sort of thing mentioned in (NSE 2), but of another kind. But could (NSE 3) possibly be true? There is, perhaps, one scenario in which it is true: that envisaged in the final section of Wright's chapter (1 above). On that conception of what epistemology can and should be, there is no explanatory-vindicatory task to be undertaken, at most a descriptive one. Holding (NSE 3) would be one consequence of holding to the completely general 'anti-explanatory mantra' in philosophy which Wright canvasses as a radical, but discernible, possibility.

What of the idea that there is 'no cognitive achievement' (NCA) involved in self-knowledge? I can think of two things that might be denied by this claim.

(NCA 1) It is not the case that veridical self-knowledge is an 'achievement' in that it is the upshot of something which the person can do, or try to do, an effort of some kind which she may make, in order to achieve it.

Under this heading are included making an inference, making an observation, making a judgement which is based on an experience whose content is attended to; or just attending carefully, concentrating, focusing one's attention. In contrast, there is no 'achievement' in this first sense when I simply find myself with a belief, or yield to an inclination to believe something which overcomes me.

(NCA 2) It is not the case that a person's first-level mental states and her judgements self-ascribing them are ontologically distinct states, and that the second reliably track the first.

It is obvious that (NCA 1) holds just if (NSE 1) does; and equally that (NCA 2) holds just if (NSE 2) does. We have noticed already that (NSE 1) is consistent with not-(NSE 2): it can be that a person's self-ascriptive judgements track states independent of them, although these judgements have no subjective aetiology or grounds. But that is to say that (NCA 1) is consistent with not-(NCA 2): the 'cognitive achievement' of a tracking ability may exist without there being anything the person does or can do by way of trying to 'get it right'. The tracking mechanism involved is a brutely causal one (one lacking any subjective phenomenology which could provide a ground for the prompted belief).

The converse also holds. (NSE 2) and (NCA 2) (i.e. no reliable tracking) hold given an AOG theory. But they can coexist with not-(NSE 1) and not-(NCA 1). That is to say, it is consistent with an AOG theory that there is something I may or must *do* in order to, say, judge correctly whether I am in pain or not. Although an AOG theorist holds that a person's non-inferred judgements about her first-level mental states are criterial for their nature, it is consistent with this that there is something the person can and may do, subjectively speaking, in reaching her judgements. Maybe she can focus her attention on her sensations, consider carefully what they are like, in reaching her judgement. And the AOG theorist can hold that it is just a person's *careful and attentive* judgements about the nature of her sensations which are criterial for their own truth. Careless judgements could be wrong, since, and to the extent that, they might yield a different verdict from careful ones. Thus there is one sense of 'cognitive achievement' whereby self-ascriptive judgements might involve this, even if a person's own best judgements are constitutive of truth about their subject-matter.

Usually, however, the idea that there is something a person does, a way in which she knows, is thought of as a further element strengthening a Special Access account. The minimal element of a Special Access account is that there is a tracking ability: reliable causation of self-ascriptive judgements by distinct first-level states. This may be brutely causal. Adding that there is something the person does, or a 'way in which' she knows, makes the epistemology more 'substantial'—her belief has a ground of some kind—and makes for a stronger form of Special Access theory. (See sect. V.)

In any case the *central* notion of 'cognitive achievement' is surely that of a genuine tracking ability, denied in (NCA 2). There is no cognitive achievement involved in self-knowledge, in this sense, if an AOG theory holds; and there is such a cognitive achievement if some form of Special Access theory holds. We shall return to the interesting intermediate case, the Impure AOG theory, in section VII.

V TYPES OF SPECIAL ACCESS THEORY

We saw in section I that writers who lean towards an AOG theory tend to assume that the Special Access alternative to it can be nothing less than the full-blown Cartesian picture of the nature of mental states and our self-knowledge of them: a person has introspective access, through something like inner perception, to states whose essence is wholly given in consciousness, and which thus have at most causal, not constitutive, links with the outer. Such states are essentially private items, EPIs. But if 'special access' is understood in our core, pared-down sense, as reliable tracking, then there are other kinds of Special Access theory which discard this unattractive Cartesian baggage.

The Cartesian conception combines all these features:

(i)   that mental states are EPIs;
(ii) that first-level mental states and second-level self-ascriptive judgements are ontologically and conceptually independent, the second tracking the first;
(iii) that the tracking is effected through a causal process involving a subjective phenomenology;
(iv) that this proces is a kind of inner perception by the person of her own conscious states.

Below I shall show that while (i)–(iv) are combined in the Cartesian picture, they can be separated. Specifically, I shall describe two accounts of mental states entirely different from (i), but each of which yields (ii): non-Cartesian Special Access theories. ((i) implies (ii), but *not* vice versa.) I shall also suggest, tentatively—but without attempting to provide adequate defence here—that (iii) can also be maintained without a commitment to (i). In any case, (iii) should certainly be distinguished from (iv). If this conjecture is right, then this attractive option is available: a non-Cartesian Special Access theory, which also allows for a non-belief conscious state which can serve as a ground for a self-ascriptive judgement. If this is a viable option, then non-Cartesian Special Access theories do not have to portray the tracking process as brutely causal, a view which can seem too thin to sustain the justifiedness of self-ascriptive judgements.

1   *Non-Cartesian Special Access Theories*

The reliable tracking of Special Access, as I understand it here, is a causal notion: first-level mental states are 'tracked' by second-level beliefs about them in virtue of some mechanism through which the former cause the latter.[29] We shall see in detail in section V. 2 that the ontological distinctness between two states which is a pre-condition of their being causally related is consistent with there being conceptual connections between them. Accounts of mental states which have this combination give a *Weak Special Access* account of self-knowledge. I examine such theories in section V. 2. But I shall first look at the simpler situation given by theories on which first-level mental states and second-level beliefs about them are both ontologically distinct and conceptually unconnected: *Strong Special Access* theories.

Any account of first-person access according to which the individuation conditions of first-level mental states and of second-level beliefs and judgements about them are such that they are both conceptually and ontologically independent is a Strong Special Access theory. The fact of first-person access, on such a theory, consists in the fact that a person's mental states are, contingently, wont to give rise to judgements by her self-ascribing them, and not to any inaccurate self-ascriptive judgements. When I am in a given first-level mental state S, it is contingently (and happily!) the case that this tends, given suitable cueing, to cause in me the belief that I am in S.[30]

The Cartesian conception of mental states as EPIs—states of which I am infallibly aware, yet which are distinct from the self-ascriptive judgements which they incline me to make—is a Strong Special Access theory. But so is a theory which says that what mental states really are is states of the brain, and that certain of these brain-states give rise, in a reliable fashion, to other brain-states which, in their mental aspect, are self-ascriptions of the first. More interestingly (since type physicalism is subject to well-known objections), so is one sort of functionalist theory.

Functionalism, understood broadly, and as a thesis about our ordinary mental concepts, is the theory that our common-sense mental state types are individuated by characteristic causal roles associated with each such type. (Since they are held to fix our lay concepts, these causal roles must be at least tacitly known by lay folk.) The roles specify conditions, perhaps only in terms of tendencies, regarding how mental states relate

[29] This is a restriction of the normal sense of 'tracking', which includes also nomological, non-causal linkage. But the restriction is apt for our current interests. The contrast between AOG and Special Access theories lies precisely in the fact that, in Special Access, first- and second-level states are ontologically distinct in the way which is necessary for causal relation. If we defined 'tracking' just as lawlike correlation, this would not discriminate between Special Access and AOG theories, since the latter equally yield this. But, on the other hand, to stipulate that, for tracking, the tracked and the tracking states must not be conceptually linked, would be to make a needlessly strong restriction, one which rules out the Weak Special Access Theory (see sect. V. 2).

[30] See Putnam 1975 for a suggestive probing of this view, in terms of a machine which incorporates such a routine.

causally to each other, to perceptual inputs, and to behavioural outputs. Under this umbrella conception there is room for theories which vary on details.[31]

The mental states of any actual person will stand in an unthinkable multitude of actual and potential causal relations to that person's other actual and potential mental states, her possible perceptions, and her potential behaviours. Think of these, for any particular mental state enjoyed by that person, as an immense set of counterfactuals true of that state of hers. Now a specific functionalist theory specifies certain of these counterfactuals concerning that state as being essential to its identity: as jointly constitutive of its being the *type* of state it is (say, a belief that Naples is beautiful, or a taste of pineapple). The rest of its dispositional causal connections are contingent. (Functionalism is thus consistent with each individual's psychological idiosyncrasy: idiosyncrasy coexists with persons' sharing mental state types, because the *constitutive* aspects of causal role are shared.) So there is a logical space for a functionalism which takes certain of a mental state's links from perception to other mental states, and jointly with them towards action, as constitutive of its identity; but *excludes from this constitutive role the state's disposition to give rise to self-ascriptions of itself*. In a functionalist theory of this kind, whether or not first-level mental states give rise to any self-ascriptive judgements is a contingent matter. The existence of first-person access is explained as consisting in a form of Special Access, and it is contingent that a subject of mental states enjoys first-person access to them.

This sort of functionalist theory can thus allow, as intuition surely has it, that animals and very young children lacking the conceptual resources to self-ascribe mental states none the less enjoy first-level states such as pain, fear, beliefs, and desires. This is a strong point in favour of this form of functionalist theory over one which regards the tendency to produce self-ascriptions of themselves as essential to the identities of a range of first-level mental states.

---

[31] I do not see why some of these roles should not be both causal and normative, expressing the normative interrelations between the contents of those mental states which have content. There is no need to insist that rationality can be captured wholly by such laws, fixed in advance—only that some components of the rational interconnections of contentful states can be so specified. It can also be acknowledged that the normative link is essential to the type of understanding which the explanations we give by means of them provide. I am therefore not convinced that the core idea of functionalism, that mental states have characteristic roles which are for one thing causal, and acknowledgement of the centrality to the intentional of the constitutive ideal of rationality are necessarily in tension as McDowell (1985) maintains. Whether or not it is classified as 'functionalism', a theory which associates such normative-cum-causal roles with attitudes systematically, according to the components of their contents, lends itself to the argument given here, and can generate a non-Cartesian Special Access account of self-knowledge.

From what has been specified so far, however, it could yet be necessary that, *in a subject who possesses the conceptual resources to make self-ascriptive judgements*, those judgements will in various circumstances be made by her, and when made, will generally be correct. For the relation between first-level mental states and second-level judgements about them to be wholly contingent, it must be neither part of the constitutive role of the first-level state that it tends to produce accurate self-ascriptions of itself, nor part of the constitutive role of the second-level state, the self-ascriptive judgement, that it is in certain conditions caused by the first-level state, and is caused only by that state. Where there is this sort of constitutive dependence of the second-level state on its relation to the first-level state, but not vice versa, it is contingent that the subject has the capacity to make self-ascriptive judgements, but is a necessary truth that any self-ascriptive judgements made are correct.

This necessary truth holds because of a definitional stop in the individuation of second-level mental states (see sect. V. 2). Notice that it remains contingent that a person A's mental states of type M only give rise to *utterances* of the form 'I am in $\mathcal{M}$', where $\mathcal{M}$ is a name for the type M in A's language; and that such *utterances* are only given rise to by A's being in a state of type M.

If there are—as is often held—mental states such that it is part of our concept of them to regard them as transparent (see end of sect. III), then this sort of constitutive dependence will hold for judgements and beliefs self-ascribing them. A judgement can be the judgement that I have a pain in my foot, say, only if it is non-inferredly prompted by my having such and, in normal circumstances, not non-inferredly prompted by any other condition. A judgement with a different aetiology could not have that content; were I to claim that 'my foot hurts' when this is not so, I must either be lying or have lost my grip on the meaning of some of the words I utter—or so the defenders of transparency aver.

But the supposed grammatical datum of transparency holds at most for some kinds of mental states. Any type of state for which both positive and negative self-deception is a conceptual possibility lacks the relations to beliefs about itself of *evidentness* and *infallibility*, which compose transparency. And this is surely so for propositional attitudes. Thus a functionalist theory according to which the individuation conditions of second-level mental states involve no constitutive tie to the first-level ones they are about is worth considering.

Where both first-level states and self-ascriptions of them are individuated independently of any link to each other, the relation between them is purely causal. We have Special Access in the sense of reliable tracking, with no conceptual connection. This is the *Strong Special Access*

Functionalist Theory of first-person access. On this sort of theory of the essential nature of mental states it is contingent that they are first-person accessible. That is, it is contingent that a subject of mental states is equipped to make self-ascriptive judgements at all, and equally contingent that any self-ascriptive judgements and beliefs she makes are generally correct.[32]

In type physicalism and Strong Special Access Functionalism we have two examples of Strong Special Access theories which are not Cartesian—do not conceive mental states as EPIs. Physical states of the brain, though none too easily observed, are not essentially private. And functionalism portrays the mental as having essential links with the outer: with a person's actions and her surrounding circumstances of perception, the facts we use as evidence in ascribing mental states to another. We are thus now in a position to deny Davidson's claim that any 'special access' account of self-knowledge is hopeless, since it leads into the insuperable epistemological problems about other minds (to which we may add: and other yet worse difficulties revealed by Wittgenstein's private language argument) of Cartesianism.[33] We also see that 'special access', conceived minimally as reliable tracking, can exist without the tracking relation involving 'inner perception' or awareness. For all we have said, the relation between first-level states and second-level judgements about them associated with the Strong Special Access Functionalist Theory could be a brutely causal one. In that case we have a cognitive achievement in the sense denied in (NCA 2), but (NCA 1) holds. In terms of features (i)–(iv) of the Cartesian conception, we have (ii) without any of (i), (iii), and (iv).

What is wrong with Strong Special Access Functionalism? It is only as plausible as functionalism itself, of course, and there are many difficulties to be overcome for any functionalist account of mental states.[34] None the less the best version of functionalism remains the best account of our mental state concepts that we have, in my view. But in connection with the problem of self-knowledge there is another specific problem. In section II we identified the second part of the task of giving an account of self-knowledge as that of explaining how self-ascriptive beliefs are justified, apt to be knowledge. If the manner in which functionally individuated mental states give rise to self-ascriptions of themselves is by a

---

[32] In sect. I we noted that an account of the identity conditions of mental states on which first-person accessibility is contingent, and only such an account, renders coherent scepticism about whether self-ascriptive judgements are indeed reliable indicators of the self-ascribed state. This becomes an empirical question.

[33] Davidson 1984: 104.

[34] See Stich 1983: ch. 2; McDowell 1985; Hornsby 1986.

brutely causal process, this can seem too thin to provide a basis for the latter to be justified. Perhaps this is one reason why 'special access' has been identified with the 'inner perception' idea. But there is no intrinsic connection between the notion of reliable tracking and that of a grounding phenomenology in the tracking process. As suggested in section I, even if it does have a problem explaining justifiedness, this is not a reason to overlook the brutely causal scenario within the logical space of possibilities; analytic clarity is served by surveying all of them. And it is our account of justifiedness which must be adapted to the facts (on pain of scepticism), not vice versa.

A pure reliabilist conception of justifiedness would indeed certify a reliable, brutely causal tracking process as yielding knowledge. So too would a coherentist theory, which provides an 'internalist' justification for brutely caused self-ascriptive beliefs in the form of a top-down endorsing background belief in their reliability. The trouble is that there are difficulties with both these epistemological theories. (See sect. III.)

But it is not clear that a Special Access Functionalist theory (Weak or Strong) has to be a brutely causal one. I conjecture—although the matter is too large, and difficult, to be investigated here—that a Special Access Functionalist theory can allow that it is part of the essence of certain of its functionally defined states that they have a subjective character which is distinct from the self-ascriptive beliefs to which they give rise, and which plays a role in the causal explanation of how this occurs. This is not objectionable Cartesianism; nor does it amount to the re-introduction of EPIs, if the conscious aspect of a state is thought of as precisely that: the appearance in consciousness of a state which has, essentially, connections with the outer of the functionalist kind (see sect. III). If this conception can be made good, it would allow for a Special Access theory which also satisfies 'internalist' epistemological intuitions which require that justified belief has a ground.

Whether or not this conjecture can be made good, we can certainly say that the idea of a state with a conscious aspect—a qualitative character, or a conscious entertaining of a content, which is distinct from any self-ascription of it, and which provides a ground for the self-ascription —is to be distanced from the idea of 'inner perception'. I cannot here enter into discussion of all the components of a genuine perceptual relation which are not present in this case. Suffice it to say that the idea of a distinct state which prompts and grounds a judgement in no way entails the idea of a scanning apparatus for discerning that state.[35]

---

[35] See Shoemaker 1994 for a good discussion.

2 A Weak Special Access Theory

On the Strong Special Access Functionalist Theory, first-level states and judgements self-ascribing them are *ontologically independent*—they are 'distinct existences', the first of which causes the second. They are also *conceptually independent*: what makes each state be of its kind does not involve any particular relation to the other state.

But Davidson has shown us that ontological independence and causal relation (which entails the first) can coexist with conceptual dependence. The first is a property of particulars: states, events, objects; the second is a property of pairs of descriptions of them. And two distinct events or states may be picked out by descriptions which, explicitly or implicitly, imply that they are related in a certain way. My sunburn is a condition of my skin distinct from the excess exposure to the sun which caused it; but in so describing it, I imply that it had that type of cause.[36] Davidson's point is crucial in showing how any sort of functionalist account of mental states is possible. The essence of functionalism is that it characterizes mental states as states ontologically independent of behaviour and causing it, but individuated in part via the fact of that causal relation. Mental states have *constitutive* dispositional causal links to each other and to behaviour.[37]

As regards self-knowledge, Davidson's point shows how Special Access—a real phenomenon of reliable tracking—may characterize the relation between first-level states and judgements self-ascribing them, while there is also a constitutive 'grammatical' link between these states, when they are described as the mental states they are. As we saw in section V. 1, this constitutive link may be part of the individuation of either one, or both, of such a pair. We have conceptual dependence in one direction in a functionalist account of mental states according to which the disposition to give rise to self-ascriptions of itself *is*—in contrast to the Strong Special Access Functionalist Theory—part of the constitutive role of a first-level mental state. And we have it in the other direction in the sort of theory already briefly examined in section V. 1, in which it is constitutive of the identity of a self-ascriptive judgement that it be caused by the state it concerns. These are *Weak Special Access*

---

[36] See Davidson 1986: 451–2.

[37] This is, on one conception of how the meaning of theoretical terms is fixed, the general situation with theoretical states and properties *vis-à-vis* each other and observation. This is why functionalism is aptly called the 'theory-theory' of mental states. See Lewis's (1983) classic statement and Stich 1983: ch. 2 for a good account, and some criticisms.

Functionalist theories.[38] They give an account of first-person access which combines Special Access with a 'grammatical' link between first- and second-level states. They are one type of the 'mixed' intermediate theories promised at the end of section I, in which grammar and empirical regularity combine in explaining the reliability of self-ascriptions.[39]

Whichever direction of constitutive link holds, it amounts to a definitional stop in the individuation of the type of state in question: a particular state counts as an instance of that type only if it stands in the required causal relation. This definitional stop creates a necessary truth. We saw in section V. 1 that when the second-level state must, to have its content, be caused by the first-level state it is about, it is necessary that any self-ascriptive judgements made by a subject of mental states are generally correct. Now consider the converse case, where it is part of the constitutive role of first-level states that they give rise to accurate self-ascriptions. There is indeed an empirical phenomenon of reliable tracking here. But it is obscured by the definitional stop.

Call the set of functional roles specified by this sort of Weak Special Access theory the *F-roles*. And say the *F*-roles* are the roles which result if the condition of giving rise to accurate self-ascriptions is removed from the F-roles. The definitional stop built into this sort of Weak Special Access Functionalism means that, according to it, the following is an a priori necessary truth:

> (N)   If a creature is a subject of mental states, then she has a general
> ability to make veridical non-inferred self-ascriptions of them.

But the definitional stop masks the fact that what it takes for a creature to satisfy the antecedent of this supposed a priori truth (i.e. have states with the F-roles) is that she have a reliable tracking capacity, resulting in accurate self-ascriptions,[40] for states of hers which have the F*-roles. So it is a mistake to infer from the (supposed) obtaining of the a priori truth that there is no 'cognitive achievement' involved in self-knowledge. When this is understood in the sense of reliable tracking

---

[38] Of course, a specific functionalist theory may be Strong Special Access with respect to some states and Weak Special Access with respect to others. I ignore this refinement here.

[39] Specifically, grammar ensures that if a creature is a subject of mental states, then she has a capacity for reliable self-ascription of them. Underlying empirical regularities make it the case that a creature satisfies the antecedent of that conditional, and provide a positive account of the tracking ability in question.

[40] Of course what this comes to also needs functional unpacking. On a plausibly rich account of the constitutive role of self-ascriptive beliefs, fulfilment of the specified condition will not be trivial. Being caused by what they are about may be part of that role, but certainly does not exhaust it.

(as denied in (NCA 2)), this does not follow. Genuine cognitive achievement can coexist with a conceptual connection between first- and second-level state which makes the reliability of self-ascriptive judgements an a priori necessary truth.[41]

If functionalism is the correct account of our ordinary mental state concepts, then the a priori truth (N) is just one of a host of such truths, each one generated from an aspect of the constitutive functional roles in question.[42] And the point just made can also be generalized: that the existence of these a priori truths about how mental states are interrelated should not blind one to the contingency of the facts which underlie the applicability to a creature of mental state concepts. What exactly is the underlying contingency?

On one view, call it the *Realization Account*. For a person A to be the subject of a set of (functionally specified) mental states, these states must be realized by states of her describable in some other vocabulary (e.g. that of neurophysiology) relative to their description in which it is contingent that they stand in the causal relations specified in the functionalist theory. (And perhaps, under which descriptions they instantiate exceptionless causal laws.) On the Realization Account the underlying contingency is that A indeed has such a repertoire of independently individuated states which are organized, dispositionally causally interrelated, in the fashion that the functional characterizations of mental state types given in the favoured functionalist theory specifies.

But there is another view possible—call it the *No-Realization Account*—according to which the required underlying contingency which must hold for the functionally specified mental concepts to apply to

---

[41] Thus I disagree with the supposition made by Bilgrami (Ch. 7 below) that a 'constitutive thesis' according to which it is necessary that any believer has knowledge of her own beliefs is inconsistent with there being a 'cognitive achievement' of reliable tracking involved in self-knowledge. (See e.g. Bilgrami's final sentence expressing this supposition.) Bilgrami thinks they are incompatible because, he says, any causal mechanism must be susceptible to breakdown, and so could not sustain an exceptionless link between first- and second-level states. No. Even if Bilgrami is right that, constitutively, any first-level belief must be the object of a correct second-level belief (as our first kind of Weak Special Access Functionalist theory has it), in the case of breakdown in the normal causal role of a first-level state the definitional stop in the individuation of first-level beliefs would come in here, to preserve the exceptionlessness of the constitutive link—as I have just shown. Peacocke (1996: sect. 2) notes how 'non-contingency' in the relation between first- and second-level states can coexist with a causal relation between them. See also Ch. 3, sect. II, above.

[42] Generalizing further, this is an instance of the general situation regarding what it takes for the terms of a theory of some putative domain to have reference, on the Ramsey–Lewis view (Lewis 1983). For a set of terms defined by their role in a theory thus: $\exists\, T_1, \exists\, T_2 \ldots \exists\, T_n\, (R(T_1, T_2 \ldots T_n))$, it is a priori that if $T_1 \ldots T_n$ exist, then they stand in R to each other. (To be plausible, this view needs some qualification: $T_1 \ldots T_n$ satisfy *most* of the conditions in R.)

a person is no more than this: that the way in which A's perceptual circumstances and behavioural output relate is such that the imposition of a description of her in such mental terms works, yields a good explanatory theory of her. That is, it provides good explanations of her behaviour seen as action and an intelligible story about her mental life, both in accordance with the constitutive functional connections. I shall not attempt here to adjudicate on which of these views is right. But I shall make one remark. Call *Realism* about mental states the thesis that they are states ontologically independent of behaviour, and standing in causal relations to it and to each other. My remark is that being a Realist without holding the Realization Account need not commit one to any 'spooky' Cartesian sort of dualism. This tendentious claim needs extensive argument which I cannot provide here.[43] The issue which the claim is about is urgent, since the Realization Account, seen as a view of what folk psychology is committed to, threatens to have the unattractive and counter-intuitive consequence that to establish whether or not ordinary people really do enjoy mental states, we must wait upon on as yet unmade advances in neurophysiology.

Within Weak Special Access Functionalism there is a further distinction to be made. A theory may hold with respect to some type of mental state M, that for a state m to be an instance of M, it must give rise, when the person attends to the matter, to a veridical self-ascriptive belief. But the link may be only a weaker generic one: that Ms are states such that normally or mostly an M gives rise to self-ascription of itself. This would allow for a limited number of Ms which qualify as Ms in virtue of their fulfilment of the other aspects of the characteristic M-role, despite not giving rise to a self-ascription; but the person is an enjoyer of M-type states at all only in the circumstance that most of her M-states give rise to self-ascriptions of themselves. I mention this latter possibility because it seems plausible that this is the case with beliefs, desires, and other attitudes for which we think self-deception is a—strictly limited—conceptual and empirical possibility.

There are further refinements to be explored within the range of possible functionalist accounts of mental states, which yield accounts of the relation between first-level states and self-ascriptions of them which vary on interesting and important details. But I shall not explore the possibilities further here. The point of this section has been the limited but important ground-laying one, of showing how the basic idea of 'special access' as reliable tracking can be separated from the Cartesian conception which has given 'special access' accounts of first-person

---

[43] For some of the needed argument see Hornsby 1993, Rudder-Baker 1993.

access a bad name. I have shown both that 'special access' understood as reliable tracking can exist without mental states having the sort of individuation conditions associated with Cartesianism, without their being EPIs; and that it can exist without there being a phenomenon of conscious awareness distinct from second-level judgement, something which affords a 'way in which' the subject knows, associated with self-knowledge. Strong Special Access Functionalism illustrated both these points. However, I conjectured that it should be possible to maintain the idea of a state with a qualitative 'feel' or conscious content, distinct from the judgement it prompts, while disentangling this from the idea that such a state is an EPI. This requires seeing its conscious character as one aspect, or appearance, of a state with further essential characteristics. In any case, I claimed, it is certainly wrong to identify the idea of a distinct conscious state of which its subject is aware, and which provides a ground for her second-level self-ascriptive belief, with the idea of 'inner perception.'

In Weak Special Access Functionalism we saw also that causal connection and a real phenomenon of reliable tracking, a genuine 'cognitive achievement', can coexist with a constitutive connection between first-level states and judgements self-ascribing them. In a Strong Special Access theory it is contingent that a person has first-person access to her own mental states. But in one sort of Weak Special Access theory the way in which mental states are individuated makes their first-person accessibility a necessary truth. This necessity masks a genuine cognitive achievement of reliable tracking, and an underlying contingency in what it takes for a person to be a subject of mental states at all. Two alternative conceptions of what this is were canvassed: the Realization Account and the No-Realization Account. (We will return to these in section VII.)

In sections VI and VII I will consider the options for AOG theories. I first consider the 'Pure' AOG Theory. We will see that there cannot be a concept of the kind it requires. There thus being no coherent Pure AOG option to take, I consider the only viable form of AOG theory, an 'impure' one. We will see that its sole—but crucial—difference from the Weak Special Access Functionalist Theory concerns the ontological status of mental states.

VI THE PURE ARTEFACT OF GRAMMAR THEORY

Special Access theories see the socio-epistemic fact that Self-Ascriptions are treated as authoritative and basic as reflecting an underlying contingent fact of reliable tracking. Subjects have a means of knowing about their own mental states through which they make correct judgements about them, and many of these are expressed in accurate self-ascriptive reports. So the truth-in-the-main of Self-Ascriptions is ensured because they are the upshot of a reliable tracking process. The reliability of this process is a contingent empirical phenomenon, independent of the fact that Self-Ascriptions are ordinarily accepted as authoritative and basic.

By contrast, an AOG theory sees the 'grammatical' data of LG-basicness and LG-authoritativeness of Self-Ascriptions as 'bedrock'. These everyday epistemic practices in relation to Self-Ascriptions are not answerable to independently constituted facts about how first- and second-level mental states are related, but create the facts about the subject-matter in question, our first-level mental states. Thus the truth-in-the-main of Self-Ascriptions is, on the AOG Theory, an artefact of the grammar of mental state concepts, not the upshot of a contingent fact of reliable tracking.

As remarked in section I, while both theories offer a vindication of the practice of treating Self-Ascriptions as authoritative and basic by exhibiting them as generally true, they have, in the first instance, different *explananda*. Special Access theories in the first instance explain why self-ascriptive judgements are generally correct, by giving an account of how they are generated by the first-level states they are about. By contrast, AOG theories will, in the first instance, explain why self-ascriptive *assertions* are generally correct. That is, an AOG theory will in the first instance vindicate as truth-conducive the epistemic practice of accepting Self-Ascriptions as correct without challenging them.

In this section I examine the prospects for a Pure AOG theory. I first state more precisely the general idea of such a theory. Then I consider what a concept of a type of mental state would have to be like to instantiate this general idea. I show that there cannot be a mental state concept of the required type; the general idea cannot be instantiated.

Section VII looks at the remaining option for AOG theories: an Impure AOG theory. I begin by drawing a moral about the nature of our actual mental state concepts. The negative result shown in section VI entails that all mental state concepts which exhibit the phenomenon of authoritative non-inferred self-ascription must be multi-criterial in this sense: the evidence of a sincere self-ascriptive utterance may be authoritative, but cannot be incorrigible. An account of mental concepts which holds this—holds, that is, that a person's sincere self-ascriptive utterances are a criterion, but a defeasible one, of her being in the putatively self-ascribed state—constitutes, I argue, an Impure AOG theory: that is, a theory according to which grammar and underlying empirical regularity play a *joint* role in explaining the reliability of Self-Ascriptions.

1   *The Idea of a Pure AOG Theory*

To examine closely the idea of an AOG theory, we need now to be a little more precise about the everyday epistemic practice of treating Self-Ascriptions as authoritative and basic which is to be vindicated. (That is, the AOG Theory is to exhibit that practice as guaranteed truth-conducive in virtue of what the criteria are for ascribing the concepts in question.)

Consider a sentence 'I am in $\mathcal{M}$', which is apt to express a person's belief that she herself is in M. Now standard epistemic practice is not, of course, to treat *all* utterances of the sentence 'I am in $\mathcal{M}$' as authoritative and basic. It is only those which are taken to be expressive of a belief of the utterer that she is in M which will be so treated—that is, only those which are taken to be *sincere assertions*. So the principle of LG-authoritativeness and LG-basicness which guides epistemic practice regarding a concept of a type of mental state M expressed in a language L by an expression $\mathcal{M}$ is:

> Accept as correct, without challenge, all utterances of 'I am in $\mathcal{M}$' which are identified as *sincere* self-ascriptive *assertions* made in L.

Since this is the principle which guides everyday epistemic practice with regard to the range of mental state concepts we are concerned with, it is a practice conforming to *this* principle which an AOG theory must exhibit as truth-conducive just in virtue of principles which fix the identities of the relevant concepts. (It is characteristic of the AOG approach to think of these as conventions governing the use of linguistic expressions for those concepts.) The practice will be truth-conducive, of course, just if sincere self-ascriptive assertions made by uttering 'I am in $\mathcal{M}$' are always true. So this is the precise result which an AOG account of the reliability of Self-Ascriptions of M must exhibit as fall-out from what it holds to be concept-fixing conventions of use governing $\mathcal{M}$. Bearing this in mind, we may now formulate more precisely the general idea of a Pure AOG theory of the reliability of Self-Ascriptions, having glossed these last as sincere self-ascriptive assertions.

The general idea of a Pure AOG theory   A Pure AOG theory (of the reliable truth of sincere self-ascriptive assertions) is one in which the truth of sincere self-ascriptive assertions is wholly explained by the 'grammar' of the concepts in question, with no role for empirical regularities in this explanation. More fully: A Pure AOG theory of the truth of sincere assertions self-ascribing a type of mental state M denoted by a concept *M* expressed in a language L by an expression $\mathcal{M}$, is one which holds the following:

(i)   The identity of the mental state concept M expressed by an expression $\mathcal{M}$ is fixed by conventions relating to the 'use', in a broad sense, of $\mathcal{M}$. (This will include the fact that utterances of 'I am in $\mathcal{M}$' which are identified as sincere assertions will be treated as authoritative and basic.)

(ii) The manner in which the concept is thus fixed suffices to ensure that whenever a person sincerely self-ascribes M, by uttering 'I am in $\mathcal{M}$', that person is in the mental state of type M which she thereby self-ascribes. Moreover,

(iii) The underlying explanation of how this is so adverts only to the conventions governing the use of $\mathcal{M}$, with no role for empirical regularities.[44]

(We can now say a bit more about why it is that an AOG theory in the first instance explains the truth of sincere self-ascriptive assertions, and thus *derivatively* that of self-ascriptive judgements. It is certain principles governing the 'use' of $\mathcal{M}$ which an AOG theory sees as conventions which fix the identity of M. So an AOG theory, in the first instance, offers an account of how a self-ascriptive assertion effected by uttering 'I am in $\mathcal{M}$' and the first-level state of being in M are related: namely, that they are 'grammatically' related in such a way as to ensure that such Self-Ascriptions are generally true.)

What a mental state concept would have to be like to instantiate this general idea   What would a concept M of a type of mental state M have to be like, for a Pure AOG theory of the truth of sincere assertions self-ascribing M to hold? Can there be a concept of this kind at all? If so, are there any mental concepts for which this kind of account is plausible?

Now, I suggest that, for empirical regularities to play no role at all in explaining why sincere assertions self-ascribing M are true, M would have to be a *one-criterion concept* of a certain kind. What it is for a person A to be in M would have to be fixed entirely by this one content-fixing rule for ascribing M to a person:

One Criterion Concept (OCC): M is to be ascribed to A just when A makes (what is judged to be) a sincere assertion self-ascribing M.

---

[44] (iii) is not redundant. (ii) does not ensure it, as our discussion of the Weak Special Access Functionalist Theory in sect. V. 2 shows. We saw that (ii) holds for that theory, in virtue of a definitional stop in the individuation of mental states. But since in the Weak Special Access Theory first-level states and Self-Ascriptions of them are distinct existences, there is also a positive explanation to be given of how it is that the first give rise to the second: an account of a process of reliable tracking. This explains how it is that someone satisfies the conditions required to be a subject of the functionally defined states in question.

A concept whose content is exhaustively fixed by this rule of ascription instantiates the Pure AOG Theory: if the *only fix* on what it is for A to be in M is that she is in M just when she sincerely self-ascribes M, then there is no chance of her sincere self-ascription being wrong; its correctness is guaranteed by the one criterion of application which fixes the concept. Nor is any underlying regularity in the circumstances surrounding her self-ascriptive utterances playing a role in ensuring this. I shall show first what is wrong with this supposed type of concept, and then that there is no other viable type of concept which instantiates the general idea of a Pure AOG theory.

2 The Incoherence of a One-Criterion Concept of the OCC Type

Can there be a concept of the kind supposedly specified by OCC? In general there is no problem about one-criterion concepts: consider, for instance, $(\forall X)$ (X is an uncle just if X is a brother of a parent). But where the unique criterion of a supposed concept applying to a person is her own disposition sincerely to assert or judge that it applies to her, there is an unsuperable problem.

There is one fundamental problem, which manifests itself in two ways. First, the supposed content-fixing rule OCC for a supposed one-criterion concept M fails to individuate a specific concept. It specifies that M applies to A just when A applies it to herself (a sincere assertion being the linguistic expression of a judgement). But as a definition this is circular. Telling us that we should ascribe M to A just when she self-ascribes it does not tell us *which* concept M is.[45]

A clause which said instead: Ascribe M to A when she makes a certain kind of noise (e.g. utters 'I am in 𝓜') would not be circular. But this alternative is not a way out for the AOG theorist. It does not work, first, because a concept fixed by such a clause is not apt to vindicate the precise practice which is to be vindicated: that of accepting as correct just that subclass of utterances of 'I am in 𝓜' which are identified as sincere assertions self-ascribing M. (And there will be no non-intentional way of picking out just this subset.)

Second, and more fundamentally, to switch to such a clause would be simply to acknowledge defeat as regards the other aspect of the fundamental problem with a supposed one-criterion concept: that where there is no other, potentially defeating criterion for A being in M, apart

---

[45] This insuperable defect in OCC can be seen immediately in terms of Peacocke's framework for giving an account of concepts (Peacocke 1992: ch. 1): OCC does not conform to the A(C) form, and cannot be recast to do so.

from her own (supposed) sincere assertion that she is so, this supposed judgement has no content.

OCC is not individuating, because it does not state what A's own mastery of M consists in, but instead uses ineliminably the idea of A's self-applications of M. But because the supposedly concept-fixing clause OCC thus uses the idea of A's self-applications of the concept, no coherent account can be given of what a supposed self-application of M consists in.

OCC (remember that OCC is not merely an epistemic rule, but purports by itself to fix the identity of the self-ascribed concept M) has it that what *makes it true* that A is in state M is that she sincerely asserts herself to be so. But this leaves no genuine content for that assertion, and associated judgement, to possess. There is nothing to constitute A being in M other than her asserting that she is in M. So does she assert that she asserts that she asserts that . . . ? The attempt to specify *what* A asserts regresses viciously.

A corollary is that, if there were a concept for which the sole criterion for applying it to another person is that she makes an utterance with a certain form, her doing so could not be seen as an application of a concept, an exercise of judgement forming a belief about herself with a determinate content.

The argument just given might be objected to thus. The clause OCC entails that a sincere Self-Ascription is logically sufficient and necessary for its own truth; but this does not commit one to saying that the Self-Ascription is that which makes itself true, is self-verifying. One may instead stick firmly to a redundancy conception of truth, and rehearse a homophonic truth-condition.[46] Even if this objection is sustained, the conclusive point against OCC can still be made: that there is no fix on what it is for A to be in M other than her making what appears to be a sincere assertion self-ascribing it. But this means that when A, apparently sincerely, applies the expression ℳ to herself, no distinction has been provided between applications which are correct and others which are incorrect. There being no line on what it is for the expression ℳ to apply to A, other than that she self-applies it, no sense has been provided for the thought that she might go wrong in a self-application of ℳ. But if nothing would constitute her getting it wrong, then nothing constitutes her getting it right either; and the supposition that she is

---

[46] I am inclined to think that this *is* the correct response to demands for a non-homophonic specification of what the truth of some judgeable content consists in, for a content which passes the other tests suggested here: a non-circular, individuating specification of it in Peacocke's A(C) form can be given; and (hence) there is an account of what possession consists in which is substantial, and provides a seems right/is right distinction. But the response should not be used as a way of evading any requirements for genuineness of a supposed concept.

deploying a genuine concept in self-applying 𝓜 is revealed as spurious.[47] Her self-applications of 𝓜 cannot be seen as exercises of judgement. In being too infallible about her own states, A loses any content for her own would-be infallible judgements to be about.

To summarize our findings: the fundamental problem with OCC is that it specifies what it is for a concept to apply to a person as consisting in the fact of her applying it.[48] This means, first, that as an attempt to pin down a specific concept it is non-individuating, because circular, and second that there is nothing for the supposed self-applications to consist in, no genuine content for those supposed self-ascriptive judgements. This shows up in the fact that there is nothing which A's mastery or lack of it of an expression for the supposed concept consists in.

3 No Other Viable Type of Concept Instantiates the Pure AOG Theory

I now return to defend my claim that there is no other type of concept which is viable, and which instantiates the general idea of a Pure AOG theory. I shall show that once we depart from this one-criterion model, even though it may still come out true, in virtue of a definitional stop in what constitutes understanding of 𝓜, that all sincere self-applications of 𝓜 made *with understanding* are correct, none the less, once there is some other fix on what it is for A to be in M, there is a contingent underlying regularity in her self-applications of 𝓜 at work. (Thus, while clause (ii) in the definition of a Pure AOG theory may still hold, clause (iii) does not.)

We saw that the epistemic practice to be vindicated by an AOG theory is that of accepting as correct all those utterances of 'I am in 𝓜' which are identified as sincere self-ascriptive assertions. (A concept fixed by a clause like OCC would of course vindicate this practice *if* A's self-applications of 𝓜 could be viewed as judgements. But we have seen that they cannot be.)

Consider the question of how this subset of all utterances of 'I am in 𝓜' may be identified. Now, there are sometimes clues that a person is insincere, or that her utterance is not serious (is meant as a joke, etc.), which are not dependent on the content of her utterance: they defeat sincerity or seriousness directly, as it were, rather than via their defeat of the supposition that A is in the state she apparently self-ascribes. But,

---

[47] See Wittgenstein 1953: §§201, 258.
[48] A variant of OCC uses instead 'A *is disposed to* apply M'. This makes no difference to the arguments against OCC given here. The variant principle does not give a *criterion* for applying M: that is, a usable epistemic rule for its application.

given that an utterance is sincere and serious (offered as an assertion, an expression of belief), we may raise the question as to whether the presumed correctness of a sincere assertoric utterance by A of 'I am in $\mathcal{M}$' may be defeated. We saw above that the problem with the supposed one-criterion concept model OCC is that it cannot be. And we saw, because it cannot be, that there is nothing which constitutes A's getting it right; the supposed exercise of judgement in relation to herself is no such thing.

In OCC there is no other fix on what it is for A to be in M which could *defeat* the presumption that her sincere self-application of '$\mathcal{M}$' is correct. Now, I suggest, it is this feature of the OCC model which both means that there is nothing which A's getting it right consists in, and so makes the idea that A's self-applications of $\mathcal{M}$ are genuine exercises of judgement spurious, and is also what would—if the OCC model were viable—ensure that empirical regularity has no role in the explanation of how it is that A's self-applications of $\mathcal{M}$ are correct.

That is, I claim, first, that to modify the simple model OCC enough to ensure that A's self-applications of '$\mathcal{M}$' can be seen as genuine applications of a concept, we must introduce other criteria for A's being in M which could defeat the presumption that a sincere serious self-application by A of '$\mathcal{M}$' is correct, and in so doing may defeat the supposition that she understands '$\mathcal{M}$'. Second, I claim that once we introduce such other potentially defeating criteria, we have departed from the Pure AOG Theory: empirical regularity now plays a role in explaining how it is that A's sincere assertoric utterances of 'I am in $\mathcal{M}$' are correct. I will defend the second claim first, and then return to the first claim.

The minimal departure from the one-criterion model OCC which introduces the possibility that the evidence of a sincere assertoric utterance of 'I am in $\mathcal{M}$' may be defeated is:

> Multi-Criterion Concept (MCC): M is to be ascribed to A when A makes (what is judged to be) a sincere assertoric utterance self-ascribing M, so long as this prima-facie basis for ascription of M to A is not *defeated* by any circumstance from a range of possible defeating criteria. (It is the link between sincere self-ascriptive utterance and truth whose defeasibility is here specified; not that of the imputation of sincerity or assertoricness. We may hold that defeat of a sincere assertion entails lack of understanding.)

What are possible defeating criteria need not be capable of being exhaustively specified in advance, and defeat may be an essentially holistic matter, part of the overall interpretation of a person. What is essential is that there be enough grip on what would defeat the evidence of a sincere assertoric self-ascriptive utterance for it to be a contingent empirical matter how often a person's sincere self-ascriptive utterances are thus defeated. (In section VII I give a sketch of many of our actual mental state concepts which portrays them as of this kind.)

Now, given that this is so, it is indeed contingent how often defeating criteria turn up. But if defeaters of a person A's sincere self-ascriptive assertoric utterances turned up very often, it would not be true that these were reliable indicators of A's being in the state she appeared thereby to self-ascribe. And so, for instance, if $\mathcal{M}$ is the expression for a concept governed by a rule like MCC, that a person A's sincere assertoric utterances self-applying $\mathcal{M}$ are reliable is a contingent matter: it turns on the contingency that her sincere self-applications of $\mathcal{M}$ are at most infrequently defeated. The concept-fixing conventions governing $\mathcal{M}$ do not suffice to ensure this, and so they do not suffice to ensure reliability.

Of course, if A's sincere self-applications of $\mathcal{M}$ were defeated too often, this supposed MCC-type concept would lose its viability: the rationale for taking someone's sincere self-ascriptive utterance as indicating that she is in the self-ascribed state is undermined if it is very frequently later defeated. Thus (here I leap to a quick conclusion on a matter which deserves far fuller investigation), any multi-criterion concept has empirical presuppositions of its viability: that the various criteria do indeed hang together, point the same way, most of the time.

So we have seen that a concept expressed by $\mathcal{M}$ whose meaning is fixed by conventions of use capturable in a clause like MCC depends for its viability on an underlying contingency: the contingency that the evidence of a sincere self-application of $\mathcal{M}$ is at most rarely defeated (though it is crucial that it is, in contrast with the model OCC, open to defeat). Its viability is not ensured by convention alone; rather, these conventions of use are built upon a prior fact of certain regularities— concordance between a person's self-applications of an expression for a concept and the other criteria for her being in the state which is its referent. By the same token, it is contingent that her sincere assertoric self-applications of $\mathcal{M}$ are reliably true.

It may yet be the case that it is ensured, by definitional stop, that her sincere self-applications of $\mathcal{M}$ made *with understanding* are always correct. A multi-criterial concept of the sort captured in MCC may yet be one for which the grammatical datum of transparency is maintained: that is, any defeat of the correctness of a sincere assertoric self-application of $\mathcal{M}$ is *ipso facto* treated as showing lack of understanding of the expression $\mathcal{M}$. (See the discussion of transparency at the end of sect. III.) Where a multi-criterial concept of the MCC kind is also one for which transparency is maintained, clause (ii) of the definition of a Pure

AOG theory still holds. But clause (iii) fails to do so: there is an underlying regularity, that most of a person's sincere self-applications of 𝓜
are undefeated, which is necessary for her to qualify as understanding
the expression 𝓜. This regularity is not an artefact of the 'grammar'
of the concept, but is a fact prior to it, which it is built upon. (The
position is similar to that of the Weak Special Access Theory examined
in sect. V. 2: we saw in that case that the necessary truth that self-ascriptive judgements are reliable holds in virtue of a definitional stop, which
conceals an underlying contingent fact of reliable tracking.)

I conclude that once defeasibility of sincere self-applications of an
expression 𝓜 for a concept is introduced, as in MCC, the reliable truth
of sincere self-ascriptive assertions is not wholly explained by the conventions of linguistic use governing 𝓜: we do not have a Pure AOG
theory of their reliability. It may still be a necessary truth that if A understands 𝓜, then her sincere self-applications of it are all correct; but that
she satisfies the antecedent of this conditional involves a concordance
between her self-applications of 𝓜 and the other criteria bearing on
whether she is in M.

I now return to the defence of my first claim: that A's self-applications
of an expression 𝓜 can be seen as genuine applications of a concept
only if the evidence of a sincere assertoric self-application by her of 𝓜
is defeasible. I argued that OCC is deficient, both because it fails to
individuate a specific concept, and because there is nothing which A's
mastery of 𝓜 consists in. But, it might be suggested, the first problem
is dealt with by a variant of OCC of this kind:

> (MCC*) A's making a sincere self-application of 𝓜 is a sufficient
> condition to ascribe M to her—it cannot be defeated; but there are
> other sufficient conditions as well.

Notice first that this proposal is *not* just the proposal that we have
a type of state which is transparent to its subject—one such that she
cannot falsely believe that she is in it. As we saw above, transparency
is perfectly compatible with defeasibility of the evidence of a sincere
self-application of the *expression* for a concept; transparency entails that
any defeat of truth is taken as a defeat of linguistic competence—we
take it that any error is 'purely verbal', a substantively false belief not
being possible. Now it may be that adding other sufficient conditions
suffices to make MCC*, unlike OCC, potentially able to individuate
a specific concept. I shall not pursue this question, since I think that
there are other problems with MCC*. First, it is not clear how MCC*
could be a stable sort of concept. For if there are other conditions which

provide positive evidence of A's being in M, by the same token, their absence must be evidence against her being in M. So, if A sincerely self-applies 𝓜 in their absence, this absence must constitute defeating evidence against the correctness of her self-application, perhaps by throwing doubt on whether she understands 𝓜. It is hard to see how a stipulative fiat which insulated the out-of-line self-ascriptive utterance from this sort of evidential defeat could be stable. (Incidentally, these remarks show the doubtfulness of the distinction between criteria and mere symptoms which an AOG theory must invoke.) Secondly, and conclusively, moving from OCC to MCC* is not yet enough to enable us to see A's self-applications of 𝓜 as genuine self-applications of a concept. For this, there must be a possibility of a sincere application by her of 𝓜 to herself being incorrect: otherwise, to repeat my earlier argument, there is, by the same token, nothing which constitutes her getting it right. To this claim it might be objected: But A's mastery of 𝓜 is established by her grip on the other sufficient conditions for ascribing it—which she shows her grasp of, in her applications of 𝓜 to others. Her credentials as understanding 𝓜 thus established by her use of 𝓜 in other-ascription, any self-application of 𝓜 by her is an indefeasible criterion of her being in M. This idea does not work, however. 𝓜 is to be an expression for a concept of a mental state—that is, a concept such that one who grasps it is able to apply it, one and the same concept, both to herself and to others. So its self-applications and its applications to others must be unified, responsive to the same set of considerations. But this means both that others, in their decisions as to whether A is in M, must see the evidence of a self-application by A of 𝓜 as potentially defeasible through the absence of the other presumptively sufficient conditions, as suggested above; and equally, that A herself must see her own self-applications of 𝓜 as so defeasible. If she does not, there is no reason to take her to be applying the *same* concept in, on the one hand, her ascriptions to others of 𝓜, and on the other, her ascriptions to herself. I conclude that MCC* does not provide a variant on OCC which specifies a viable concept while retaining the feature that the evidence of a sincere self-ascriptive utterance is indefeasible. This being so, the least departure from OCC which gives a viable concept is MCC. But we have seen that MCC, because it incorporates defeasibility of the evidence of a sincere self-ascriptive utterance, gives only an Impure AOG theory of the reliability of sincere self-ascriptive assertions. The idea of a Pure AOG theory—the idea that the reliability of self-ascriptive assertions is explained entirely by the conventions of linguistic usage which fix our mental concepts—is a non-starter.

4   A Moral: All Mental Concepts which Admit of Non-Inferred Self-Ascription are Multi-Criterial

The argument given above against the possibility of a concept whose conventions of use are captured by a clause like OCC is *not* a version of Wittgenstein's well-known argument against the possibility of a private language. That argument, and the one just given, use some common materials, but have different targets. Thus someone not convinced of the soundness of Wittgenstein's argument, and a steadfast believer in private objects, has no reason thereby to reject the argument just given. The Cartesian conception of the mental, as states whose essence consists wholly in their phenomenal quality as apparent to introspective awareness, has it that a person is somehow infallible and potentially omniscient about the states in this essentially private inner realm, despite their being ontologically and conceptually independent of the infallible self-ascriptive judgements to which they give rise. This conception, and its particular Special Access account of self-knowledge, is the target of Wittgenstein's argument. Wittgenstein shows it to collapse, because the notion of a genuinely independent state of affairs about which the subject is infallible cannot be sustained.[49] The present argument shows that the case is no better if the supposed infallibility of Self-Ascriptions is thought of as ensured through grammar, rather than through the transparent nature of an independent subject-matter.

The two different arguments are thus complementary. For expositional convenience I fudged a little above on precisely what the epistemic practice is, which either a Special Access or an AOG theory is to vindicate. A Pure AOG theory as represented by OCC, were it coherent, is tailored to vindicate this epistemic practice: accepting as correct, without challenge, and *indefeasibly*, all sincere[50] self-ascriptive utterances. If OCC were viable, it would ensure through 'grammar' alone that all sincere self-ascriptive utterances were true, since their being true is logically guaranteed simply by their being made. In fact, our actual practice of LG-authoritativeness is not this, but rather that of accepting sincere self-ascriptive utterances as *defeasibly* authoritative. It is the Impure AOG Theory captured by MCC, which will be considered in section VII, which is tailored to vindicate precisely this epistemic

---

[49] See Wittgenstein 1953: §§243 ff. and Wright 1989a for an extended exploration. Notice that it is quite incidental that a private linguist's verdict 'Ah, here is another S!' is thought of as silent. Suppose she makes her would-be judgements out loud, and is overheard by others; this might then be the unique criterion for a concept of *theirs* of a state of *hers*, which they on that basis ascribe to her; but this does not help at all in making her utterances into the deployment of a genuine concept *by her*.

[50] An utterance's being sincere entails that it is assertoric.

practice.[51] Now there are, broadly speaking, two alternative theories which, if viable, would vindicate precisely this epistemic practice of *indefeasible* acceptance of sincere self-ascriptive utterances. They are the Pure AOG Theory and a Cartesian Special Access theory. The argument above against the coherence of a one-criterion concept of the kind supposedly specified in OCC knocks out the first of these options. Wittgenstein's anti-private language argument knocks out the second. The two arguments conjoined entail that a practice of indefeasible acceptance as correct of all sincere self-applications of some expression for a mental concept 𝓜 cannot be vindicated: as we have seen, were there some 𝓜 governed by a practice of this kind, its self-applications by a person could not be viewed as genuine applications to herself of a concept, exercises of judgement.

Wittgenstein's uncomfortableness about 'avowals', and his suggestions of a non-cognitive expressivist account of them, surely stem from his awareness of the force of the present argument, in addition to his own.[52] However, I shall suggest below that he need not have been so uncomfortable about assertions self-ascribing our actual mental state concepts. The conclusion which is forced, if indeed both Wittgenstein's argument and the present one are sound, is not that there can be no account of self-ascriptive assertions which exhibits them as genuine exercises of judgement, but that *there can be such only for mental state concepts which have multiple criteria or sources of evidence for their ascription*—evidence, moreover, which can defeat the evidence of a sincere self-ascriptive utterance. We need to recognize that all viable mental state concepts, and all of ours, are multi-criterion ones.

It is worth emphasizing once more that the notion of a one-criterion mental state concept must not be confused with that of a concept of a type of mental state which is transparent to its subject. To say that a mental state of type M is transparent is to say this: if and only if A has a concept M of M, is A disposed to self-ascribe M just when she instantiates M. In this principle possession of the concept is the residual, fixed by its relation to the other two conditions. When, and only when, M is a multi-criterial state concept, so that there is a potential gap between A's being in M and her being disposed to make assertions apt in her language to self-ascribe M, is there is a substantial empirically ascertainable condition for A's possessing that concept.[53]

---

[51] Though they vary on details, Special Access theories will most likely generate truth-in-the-main, rather than invariable truth, of sincere assertoric self-ascriptive utterances, and will be tailored to vindicate the practice of treating them as authoritative but defeasible.

[52] See Wittgenstein 1953: §§244 ff.; Wright, Ch. 1, sect. IV above.

[53] Am I here conflating possessing a concept with being master of a linguistic expression for it? Yes, but not in this case fallaciously. There is no grip to be had on possession of the concept in this case unless it is tied to the systematic use of some expression.

We have seen that a Pure AOG theory of the reliability of sincere self-ascriptive assertions cannot be given. A one-criterion concept of the kind putatively specified by OCC would instantiate it, but we saw that OCC does not represent a viable form of concept. We saw that to obtain a clause for a concept which admits of genuinely judgemental non-inferred self-application, we must move to one which incorporates defeasibility of the evidence of a sincere self-ascriptive utterance, such as MCC. But, we saw, once defeasibility is introduced, we no longer have a Pure AOG theory. In my last section I explore further the nature of this 'Impure' AOG theory, comparing it with the Weak Special Access Theory.

VII   THE IMPURE ARTEFACT OF GRAMMAR THEORY

1   *The Multi-Criterial Character of our Actual Mental State Concepts*

I propose that all our actual mental state concepts which exhibit the phenomenon of LG-authoritative non-inferential self-ascription are multi-criterial ones, in the following sense: for each such concept, sincere utterances self-ascribing it, while they are LG-authoritative, are not incorrigible: the concept is such that there can be other evidence which defeats the evidence of a sincere self-ascriptive utterance. This is so because all our mental state concepts are of a type of state which has, constitutively, dispositional links to other mental states and, directly or indirectly (via its links to other states), with observable conditions—the circumstances of perception, intentional action, and non-intentional behaviour. For a central range of mental-state concepts, those concepts are of states which characteristically produce *both* accurate non-inferred Self-Ascriptions and a range of other linguistic and non-linguistic action. These latter links provide the basis for the evidence of a sincere self-ascriptive utterance to be overridden.

This defeasibility of sincere self-ascriptive utterances is most obviously and uncontroversially the case for our concepts of propositional attitudes: the role of beliefs and desires in jointly rationalizing action is a primary fix on them, so strong that it allows for self-deception (both positive and negative) as a conceptual possibility. Equally, I suggest, our concept of pain is of a state which produces accurate non-inferred self-ascription; but, no less essentially, a syndrome of physical and mental distress behaviour and avoidance behaviour—criteria which could show a person claiming to be 'in pain' to be insincere or to have lost her grip on the word 'pain'.[54] The defeasibility of sincere self-ascriptive utterances is less obviously true for sensations, imaginings, and conscious experiences. But, I suggest, even for these concepts careful investigation will show that they have constitutive links to other mental states and 'criteria' other than what their subject is disposed to say about their character—non-verbal discriminatory and reactive dispositions, for instance. Thus, in general, we can say: the evidence provided by someone's sincere self-ascriptive utterances is defeated if accepting it as correct assigns to her a mental state which is in acute conflict with the rest of a well-entrenched interpretative theory of her—an assignment of mental states and description of her behaviour as intentional action. Conflict consists in violation of any of the constitutive links just mentioned. This general thesis about our mental state concepts cannot be defended fully here. But, if the argument of the last section is correct, that the evidence provided by a sincere utterance apparently self-ascribing a mental state be open to defeat by other criteria is a necessary condition for the putative self-ascription to be a genuine judgement, the exercise of a concept. The upshot of the private language argument, when combined with the argument of section VI, is not just that an inner state stands in need of an outward criterion: there had better be crite*ria*—more than one;[55] or, if only one, that one had better not be the person's sincere utterance apparently self-ascribing it. If this is so, then it is not an accident, but a condition of their being genuine concepts at all, that our concepts of non-inferredly self-ascribable mental states are all multi-criterial ones. Non-inferred self-ascriptive utterances can be authoritative, but can never be incorrigible.

I think multi-criteriality is also sufficient for sincere self-ascriptive utterances to express genuine judgements. (So an Impure AOG theory is viable.) Where there are criteria for a person's being (or not being) in a state M other than her sincere utterance self-ascribing M, there is a further fact which these self-ascriptions of M are answerable to, and a seems right/is right distinction for them is provided. This is all that is required, for there to be a substantial condition which someone must satisfy, to count as being a master of M, in its use in self-ascription. This condition has two aspects. First, if a person's own self-ascriptive

---

[54] A reminder: defeasibility is consistent with transparency. But where transparency is maintained, as seems plausible for pains, deciding that a sincere self-ascriptive utterance is incorrect entails deciding that the person uttering it lacks mastery of the term in question. By contrast, we do not maintain transparency for beliefs and desires. Thus we may determine that someone incorrectly judges herself to have a certain desire, or honestly denies herself to have one which her behaviour shows her to have—that is, we are not bound to take the falsity of her defeated sincere self-ascriptive utterance to be attributable to 'merely verbal error'. [55] See Wittgenstein 1953: §580.

utterances get too far out of line with the other criteria, we will say she has lost her grip on the concept. (For evident mental states, this will happen as soon as a self-ascriptive utterance is regarded as sincere but false.) Second, for it to be the genuine, public concept which she is deploying in her self-ascriptive judgements, *she herself* must recognize the defeating force of other criteria. Thus, for instance, it is a condition of someone's deploying the concept of desire in a self-ascriptive judgement that she recognize the force of the consideration that, say, 'You can't really want to give up smoking, because if you did, you'd try to do something about it.' This is what makes it the case that someone deploys the very same concept of, say, desire, both in non-inferred self-ascription and in ascriptions to others. (This is how the functionalist 'theory-theory''s account of what it is to grasp mental concepts is consistent with the phenomenon of LG-authoritative non-inferred self-ascription: there is no problem about how the very same concept is deployed both in self-ascription and in ascription to others, once defeasibility of self-ascription by other aspects of the characteristic role is acknowledged—both by others and by the self-ascriber herself.)

2   The Impure AOG Theory and the Weak Special Access Functionalist Theory

If all mental concepts exhibiting LG-authoritative non-inferred self-ascription must have a multi-criterial character in the sense just explained, what scope does this allow for AOG theories? We are left with MCC —the idea that it is a constitutive principle that, in the ascription of mental states to another, self-ascriptive utterances are endowed with a default status as correct, this being overridden only where there is defeating counter-evidence in the form of conflict with the otherwise-best interpretation of her.[56]

I call this view the 'Impure AOG Theory'. It is 'impure' because, as we saw in section VI, on this theory the reliability of Self-Ascriptions is not explained by concept-fixing conventions of 'use' alone. Nor is it simply a matter of contingent empirical regularity, as it was on the Strong Special Access Theory. On the Impure AOG Theory, concept-fixing linguistic convention and empirical contingency play an intertwined and *inextricable* joint role in accounting for the reliability of Self-Ascriptions. Grammar contributes to the explanation of reliability, because the fact that a self-ascriptive utterance has default status as correct is (according to this theory) a 'bedrock' fact of grammar; it is part of what fixes

---

[56] I take this to be the sort of view advocated in Wright 1989*a*, 1989*b*. Wright's view has further subtleties not discussed here.

our concept of the mental state in question. But, as we saw in section VI, for any multi-criterial mental state concept, its viability depends on the contingency that the criteria hang together. Specifically, the reliability of self-ascriptive utterances is not ensured by its being constitutive that they are taken as true unless defeated; this yields their reliability only when conjoined with the empirical contingency that they are not often defeated. Just how frequent defeat could be, in regard to a certain individual, consistently with her still being regarded as a subject of mental concepts of the kind in question at all, we need not decide here. But *if the claim is upheld that the default-true status of self-ascriptive utterances is constitutive*, she could not be so regarded if we stopped taking her self-ascriptive utterances as (defeasibly) authoritative.[57] And clearly, if self-ascriptive utterances and other criteria came apart too far and too often, it would be untenable to maintain this attitude. The individual in question simply would not be interpretable by means of these mental state concepts—we could not provide a coherent, explanatory theory of her behaviour as intentional action by means of them.

We can conclude that, on the Impure AOG Theory, the reliability of self-ascriptive utterances, where it holds, is an inextricable joint product of the grammatical fact that they have default status as correct, together with the empirical contingency that defeat is relatively rare. However, this contingency—that the 'criterion' provided by a self-ascriptive utterance generally hangs together with other criteria for the state in question—is not a contingent truth about those who anyway enjoy the type of states in question, but rather an empirical presupposition of the applicability to a creature of mental state concepts of which the Impure AOG Theory gives the correct account. It remains true that for a mental state which is regarded as transparent—that is, for which we treat any defeat of the truth of a sincere self-ascriptive utterance 'I am in $\mathcal{M}$' as showing that the self-ascriber does not understand $\mathcal{M}$ —the correctness of all sincere utterances of 'I am in $\mathcal{M}$' made *with full understanding* is maintained by definitional stop. But that a person counts as understanding the expression depends upon the underlying contingency that her sincere self-ascriptive utterances of 'I am in $\mathcal{M}$' are rarely defeated. There is an underlying regularity at work here, making the 'grammar' of this concept viable.

So the Impure AOG Theory shares with the Weak Special Access Theory this feature: on the account of mental concepts it offers, it is

---

[57] This thought perhaps underlies Wright's suggestion that what distinguishes the authority of self-ascriptions is that it is inalienable. (See Ch. 1 above.) Wright (1989a) explicitly notes the 'deep contingencies' which an Impure AOG presupposes, for viability of that language-game.

an a priori necessary truth, ensured by principles fixing these concepts, that if any creature is a subject of mental states of this kind at all, then her non-inferred self-ascriptive assertions are reliably correct. But, as with the Weak Special Access Theory, this necessary truth masks an underlying contingency which must hold for a creature to qualify as a possessor of such mental states—according to the Weak Special Access Theory, that the creature have states with the causal roles characteristic of these mental states; according to the Impure AOG Theory, that, in the behaviour of the creature in question, her self-ascriptive utterances hang together with the other criteria for these states.

Noting this common feature of the Impure AOG Theory and the Weak Special Access Theory, we may ask how different they really are. Whether they are really so at all depends on how we fill in further details about the Impure AOG Theory. Consider the question of whether there is, on the Impure AOG Theory, a 'cognitive achievement' involved in self-knowledge. Clearly, there is no reason why there should not be an achievement in the sense denied in (NCA 1): it could be that it is only Self-Ascriptions made when the subject is apparently properly attentive, considers the matter carefully, whose default-truth is a constitutive principle.

But is there a cognitive achievement in the sense denied in (NCA 2), a real phenomenon of reliable tracking of first-level states by second-level assertions and judgements? This depends on what else an Impure AOG theorist is prepared to say about the mental states whose concepts, according to her, are fixed by a set of principles governing their ascription, including the default-true status of Self-Ascriptions. The underlying contingency already noted, that a creature must be such that the various criteria for ascribing mental states hang together in her case— that is, that she must be such that a good interpretative theory of her can be obtained by applying them, though an empirical presupposition of these concepts can hardly in itself be called a cognitive achievement on her part.

I suggested above that, to have any plausibility as an account of our actual mental state concepts, the Impure AOG Theory must hold that the observable 'criteria' which may defeat a self-ascriptive utterance have that status in virtue of constitutive links possessed by mental states to each other and to perception and action. In this respect, then, the Impure AOG Theory takes a similar view of mental concepts to functionalism. The crucial matter, as I see it, is whether the Impure AOG theorist is prepared to allow with the functionalist that the states ascribed in accordance with these principles are ontologically distinct existences which stand in causal relations to perceptual input, each other, and intentional action and other behaviour. If this is allowed, then the reliability of self-ascriptive assertions and judgements can indeed be seen as the upshot of a real phenomenon of reliable tracking of one distinct set of states by another. But, the reader will immediately appreciate, if the independent reality and causal efficacy of mental states is admitted, the Impure AOG Theory becomes simply identical with the Weak Special Access Functionalist Theory.

If there are distinct theoretical options here, then, they are distinguished precisely by their stand on the question of Realism: whether mental states are ontologically independent states which stand in causal relations to each other and to behaviour. To maintain distinctness, let us restrict the 'AOG' label to theories which are not in this sense Realist about mental states.

Although my primary concern here has been to lay out and compare the options, rather than to adjudicate which is best, we have seen that the supposed Pure AOG Theory is not a viable option; and numerous difficulties—most crushingly, that exposed by Wittgenstein's argument against private language—show that a Cartesian conception of mental states, with the account of special access it generates, is untenable. So an Impure AOG theory, or one or other functionalist Special Access theory, are the remaining options we have identified worthy of consideration. Which is preferable? I cannot offer a full defence of a theory, but I shall make a couple of remarks.

If Realism about mental states entailed a requirement of realization in states of some other kind, probably states of the brain, then this would be one reason to fight shy of realism. But I suggested in section V that it need not be seen as doing so. Meanwhile, any AOG theory suffers from a major weakness. Precisely because it does not hold mental states to be causes of each other and of action, including self-ascriptive assertions and judgements, an AOG theory has nothing to say about *why* a person is moved to make the Self-Ascriptions she makes. In particular, it is debarred from allowing the obvious kind of causal explanation of why a person is moved to make a Self-Ascription—namely, because she is in the Self-Ascribed state. (Of course, further conditions must be added for a complete explanation—that she is somehow prompted to consider the question.) Generalizing this difficulty, we may say: a theory which holds that mental states are ascribable to a person just if she is such that a good interpretative theory of her can be given by ascribing them, but denies that the states ascribed are causally explanatory of behaviour, has nothing to say about *why* it is that a person's perceptual-behavioural nexus is such that she can be so described. That it is so is, from the standpoint of such a theory, an amazing and unexplained anomaly.

Some writers suppose a contrast between two mutually exclusive kinds of explanation of the minimal phenomenon of first-person access (that is, of non-inferred, LG-authoritative, LG-basic Self-Ascriptions): in terms of 'grammar' and in terms of an empirical phenomenon of 'special access'. I have argued that this contrast is a false one. There is not just one Special Access theory, but a number of possibilities: not just Cartesianism, but also functionalist accounts of the nature of mental states, and of self-knowledge of them. These latter are Special Access theories which have non-Cartesian conceptions of the individuation conditions of mental states, and in which there need be nothing like 'inner perception' involved in self-knowledge of them. The idea of Special Access has been wrongly discredited by a false association with Cartesianism.

I also examined the idea of a Pure Artefact of Grammar theory, and found there was no coherent account of mental concepts which yields it. I concluded that all viable mental state concepts which admit of non-inferred Self-Ascription must be multi-criterial ones.

By restricting the label 'Artefact of Grammar' to theories which deny that mental states are ontologically distinct states which are causes of behaviour, I maintained exclusiveness between our two types of theory. But in both the Impure Artefact of Grammar Theory and the Weak Special Access Functionalist Theory empirical regularity and grammar play a joint role in explaining the reliability of Self-Ascriptions. Thus the contrast originally envisaged is, in this and in its equation of Special Access with Cartesianism, a false one.[58]

REFERENCES

Audi, Robert (1993), *The Structure of Justification* (Cambridge: Cambridge University Press).

Boghossian, Paul (1989), 'Content and Self-Knowledge', *Philosophical Topics*, 17/1: 5–26.

[58] My thanks are due to the British Academy for a Research Leave Award held in 1995. This chapter draws on work done during its tenure. I am extremely grateful to Chris Peacocke, Tom Stoneham, and Tim Williamson for very helpful discussion and comments on an earlier draft. I read earlier versions of the paper in Oriel College Oxford, and in the philosophy departments of the University of Colorado at Boulder, the University of Pittsburgh, and New York University. Comments from my audiences improved the essay greatly. I am especially indebted to comments from Ned Block, Paul Boghossian, Robert Brandom, Bill Brewer, John Campbell, Kit Fein, Jerry Fodor, Dale Jamieson, Barry Loewer, John McDowell, Colin McGinn, and Rowland Stout. Crispin Wright's writings on this topic had a formative influence on my approach to it.

Bonjour, Lawrence (1985), *The Structure of Empirical Knowledge* (Cambridge, Mass.: Harvard University Press).

Burge, Tyler (1988), 'Individualism and Self-Knowledge', *Journal of Philosophy*, 85: 649–63.

Craig, Edward (1982), 'Meaning, Use and Privacy', *Mind*, 91: 541–64.

Davidson, Donald (1984), 'First Person Authority', *Dialectica*, 38: 101–11.

—— (1987), 'Knowing One's Own Mind', *Proceedings and Addresses of the American Philosophical Association*, 60: 441–58.

Evans, Gareth (1982), *The Varieties of Reference* (Oxford: Clarendon Press).

Fricker, Elizabeth (1995), 'Telling and Trusting: Reductionism and Anti-Reductionism in the Epistemology of Testimony', *Mind*, 104, no. 414: 393–411.

—— (in preparation), *Epistemic Justification: Perception and Testimony*.

—— (forthcoming) 'Locating Epistemic Justification'.

Gopnik, Alison (1993), 'How We Know Our Minds: The Illusion of First-Person Knowledge of Intentionality', *Behavioral and Brain Sciences*, 16: 1–14.

Haack, Susan (1993), *Evidence and Inquiry* (Oxford: Blackwell).

Hornsby, Jennifer (1986), 'Physicalist Thinking and Conceptions of Behaviour', in J. McDowell and P. Pettit (eds.), *Subject, Thought and Context* (Oxford: Oxford University Press), 95–116.

—— (1993), 'Agency and Causal Explanation', in J. Heil and A. Mele (eds.), *Mental Causation* (Oxford: Clarendon Press), 161–88.

Lewis, David (1983), 'How To Define Theoretical Terms', in his *Philosophical Papers*, i (Oxford: Oxford University Press), 78–96.

McDowell, John (1985), 'Functionalism and Anomalous Monism', in E. LePore and B. McLaughlin (eds.), *Actions and Events: Perspectives on the Philosophy of Donald Davidson* (Oxford: Blackwell), 387–98.

Peacocke, Christopher (1986), *Thoughts*, Aristotelian Society Monograph (Oxford: Blackwell).

—— (1992), *A Study of Concepts* (Cambridge, Mass.: MIT Press).

—— (1996), 'Entitlement, Self-Knowledge and Conceptual Redeployment', *Proceedings of the Aristotelian Society*, 96: 117–58.

Putnam, Hilary (1975), 'Minds and Machines', in his *Mind, Language and Reality: Philosophical Papers*, ii (Cambridge: Cambridge University Press), 362–85.

Rudder-Baker, Lynne (1993), 'Metaphysics and Mental Causation', in J. Heil and A. Mele (eds.), *Mental Causation* (Oxford: Clarendon Press), 75–96.

Ryle, Gilbert (1949), *The Concept of Mind* (London: Hutchinson).

Shoemaker, Sydney (1994), 'Self-Knowledge and Inner Sense', *Philosophy and Phenomenological Research*, 54: 249–314.

Sosa, Ernest (1991), *Knowledge in Perspective* (Cambridge: Cambridge University Press).

Stich, Stephen (1983), *From Folk Psychology to Cognitive Science* (Cambridge, Mass.: Bradford Books, MIT Press).

Stoneham, Tom (1995), 'On Knowing What I Am Thinking' (Ph.D. dissertation, London University).

Strawson, Peter (1959), *Individuals: An Essay in Descriptive Metaphysics* (London: Methuen).

Williamson, Timothy (1995), 'Is Knowing a State of Mind?', *Mind*, 104, no. 415: 533–66.

Wittgenstein, Ludwig (1953), *Philosophical Investigations*, trans. G. E. M. Anscombe (Oxford: Blackwell).

Wright, Crispin (1989a), 'Wittgenstein's Later Philosophy of Mind: Sensation, Privacy and Intention', *Journal of Philosophy*, 86/11: 622–34.

—— (1989b), 'Wittgenstein's Rule-Following Considerations and the Central Problem of Theoretical Linguistics', in Alexander George (ed.), *Reflections on Chomsky* (Oxford: Blackwell), 233–64.

7

Self-Knowledge and Resentment[1]

AKEEL BILGRAMI

———•———

I

My title mimics the title of an essay by Strawson[2] which has abidingly changed the shape and direction of philosophical discussions of freedom of the will. Instructed by that essay, I will try in this chapter to add a particular context and an explanatory twist to another, only seemingly distant, Strawsonian theme: the special character of self-knowledge of our mental states, in particular, our *intentional* states.

It is a familiar point that the special character of self-knowledge was set on a new path by Descartes,[3] a path that is not much trodden these days, but all the same constantly and anxiously visible as a thing to avoid on the maps on which other paths are plotted. As it is read today, it has three broad features: first, it makes self-knowledge or self-awareness play a definitional and therefore *constitutive* role in the very idea of a mental state; second, it makes self-knowledge *infallible*; and third, it makes self-knowledge a form of infallible (inner) *perception* of one's mental states.

[1] A more primitive version of this essay has been circulating for nine years, and a very abbreviated version of it appeared as an appendix to my book *Belief and Meaning* (Oxford: Blackwell, 1992). I have read it at various conferences and colloquia, and cannot list here the names of the many philosophers in audiences to whom I owe a debt for intellectual criticism and commentary. But I am especially indebted to some who have been particularly helpful in their comments while I was revising it for the present publication They are Garrett Deckel, Elizabeth Fricker, Isaac Levi, Brian McLaughlin, John McDowell, Carol Rovane, Stephen White, and Crispin Wright.

[2] P. F. Strawson, 'Freedom and Resentment', *Proceedings of the British Academy* (1962), repr. in *Freedom and Resentment and Other Essays* (London: Methuen, 1974), 1–25.

[3] R. Descartes, *Meditations on First Philosophy*, in *The Philosophical Works of Descartes*, i, ed. E. S. Haldane and G. R. T. Ross (Cambridge: Cambridge University Press, 1911), 131–200.

The second of these features—infallibility—is almost universally discarded in contemporary discussions. Without it (or even perhaps with it) the two remaining features are hard to reconcile. Without it, the inner perception of one's mental states takes on too much the character of perception of the external world, and then it's hard to see how one can think of it as also having a constitutive or definitional role, since perception does not seem to play that role with the external world. In fact, it is precisely because so much of our knowledge of the external world is perceptual that we think of that world as having a certain independence, as being what it is whether or not we have perceptions of it, and whether or not we have the capacity to perceive it. The idea that our intentional states are not in the same way independent of our capacities for self-knowledge is what defines the idea of the constitutive role of self-knowledge, defines the idea that it is constitutive of the intentional states it is knowledge of. Thus, though there may be all sorts of things that would make inner perception of one's own states of mind special and different from the perception of outer objects and facts, it is hard to see that anything is left of what we would count as a perceptual model for self-knowledge if what is special about self-knowledge is that it has a definitional and constitutive role for the mental states it is knowledge of. On the other hand, if it does not have *either* infallibility *or* a constitutive role, then whatever it is that makes for the special character of self-knowledge will not be all that special.

It is not because of these internal difficulties, but out of a more zealous ideology, that Gilbert Ryle[4] abandoned all three features of the Cartesian picture, and notoriously proposed (or is taken to have proposed) that self-knowledge is a matter of inference from one's behaviour. Though sometimes self-knowledge is undoubtedly gained this way (see section IV for more on this and other cognitive ways of gaining it), the idea that this should be erected into a doctrine about the nature of self-knowledge has widely and wisely been cast off since Ryle's time. So the most interesting doctrinal issue on the subject of self-knowledge remains closely tied to the Cartesian elements, even as we are anxious to avoid the particular complexion these elements have in Descartes' own full and integrated picture of them. *The issue is this*: given the intolerable tension between the perceptual model and the constitutive ideal, only one of them can serve in our account of self-knowledge. So which one should it be? And how shall we think of it in a non-Cartesian setting?

The inner-perceptual paradigm would be too obviously inappropriate for self-knowledge of intentionality if it was demanded of it that

---

[4] G. Ryle, *The Concept of Mind* (London: Hutchinson, 1949).

it should always preserve an analogue to the idea of some minimal cognition—however direct and non-inferential—on the part of an agent which, in external perception, is captured by such expressions of hers as 'I saw', 'I looked', or, most generally, 'I checked' (which seems better because it allows us to include knowledge of such things as the position of our limbs). Though analogues such as, say, 'I remembered' might well apply sometimes, there are any number of cases of self-knowledge of intentionality where no such analogues are apt or forthcoming. So, here again, one should guard against taking exceptional cases and erecting them into a (perceptual) paradigm for self-knowledge.

However, there is a limitingly spare version of the inner-perceptual account, which was perhaps first hinted at in Armstrong's early work,[5] and which makes explanatory appeal to only a *causal* mechanism that takes one from an intentional state—say, a belief that p—to a belief that one has the belief that p. It does not put a great deal of weight on any kind of cognitive activity (analogues to 'checking', 'seeing', etc.), and therefore one does not feel particularly motivated to call it a *cognitive* mechanism. This account nevertheless insists on a certain minimal assimilation with the perceptual account, so as to retain the contrast, not just with the inferential, but more importantly, with the constitutive account of self-knowledge. The insistence here is that since it is a causal mechanism that is doing the central explanatory work, even if unaccompanied by cognitive trappings, there will be a certain independence of the embedded intentional states from the self-beliefs, an independence of the kind that leads one to say that, even if one were the sort of creature who has the capacity for higher-order beliefs, there is *no* sense in which if one has the belief that p, one must (as if by a rule) believe that one believes that p, and vice versa.[6] Since it is a causal mechanism, it is the kind of thing which, however reliable, *could* break down—just as our perceptual mechanisms could fail us on occasion—and so there would be *no* relevant sense in which one could think of there being this sort of necessary tie between the embedded belief and the higher-order belief. (I will use the expression 'embedded belief' for those first-order beliefs that are picked out by the embedded clauses of a statement reporting a second-order belief.) Even though our perceptions are fairly reliable, we are not even remotely tempted to say that if there is a fact

[5] D. M. Armstrong, *A Materialist Theory of Mind* (London: Routledge & Kegan Paul, 1968).

[6] I am taking for granted that this biconditional to which the constitutive theorist is committed is something that does not require her to say that animals do not have beliefs (assuming, surely correctly, that they do not have higher-order beliefs). She may rather want to restrict her constitutive thesis to creatures who have the concept of belief, which animals do not. I discuss a relevant point in n. 26.

or object present in the external environment, then we must (as if by a rule) form the perceptual belief that it is there, or vice versa. Similarly, this causal-mechanistic account of self-knowledge claims that there ought to be no such temptation to embrace a biconditional of this sort when we substitute 'higher-order' and 'embedded beliefs' for 'perceptual beliefs' and 'facts in the external world', respectively.

This intended proximity to the perceptual account, therefore, cannot be breezily dismissed by saying the following: the insistence on a merely causal mechanism is *too* spare to be controversial. That is, it cannot be dismissed by saying that *even* a constitutive account must countenance the existence of *some* underlying connecting mechanism which would allow us to see the first-order intentional state and the higher-order one as *different* states. This point would do nothing to erase the deep difference between the two accounts as explanatory positions. For part of the constitutive theorist's brief is that whatever role the underlying mechanism plays, it cannot play the sort of explanatory role which would disallow one from saying the following: that there is *a sense* in which there can be *no* breakdown in the connection that is expressed by saying that if someone believes that p, then he believes that he believes that p, and vice versa. What makes her a constitutive theorist is precisely such a claim, and what makes an Armstrong-like position approximate the perceptual account, despite its sparer appeal to a purely causal mechanism, is minimally, but also precisely, a denial of such a claim. What I called a breezy dismissal fails, then, because it does not respect the fact that, for a constitutive theorist, a concession to underlying mechanisms in the states which realize intentional states of first and second order in self-knowledge cannot be to ordinary sorts of causal mechanism, but rather to relations of cause that are necessarily embedded in some part–whole relational system, which would echo in the functional characterization of underlying physical realizations the impossibility of breakdown in the connection between 'I believe that I believe that p' and 'I believe that p'.

Because in the perceptual view, however spare, the causal mechanism is central to its explanation in a way that is just plain missing in the constitutive view, its justification of the idea of first-person authority, its account of the special character of self-knowledge, can at best be a reliabilist and inductivist account: the causal mechanism is in fact reliable (even more reliable than our perceptual mechanisms); in the past we have tended to give the right answers to questions about what we believe (even more often than to questions about what is in the perceptible world external to us), and so on. For the constitutive theorist who also wants to account for the special character of self-knowledge, these remarks are poignantly insufficient.

In what follows I will try and give an argument, or at any rate underlying considerations of support, for the constitutive position.

I have not so far done much to characterize this position in positive terms, only in negative terms of *contrast* with the cognitive[7] and causal-explanatory features of the perceptual account. I think that something like this negative thesis forms the core of what Crispin Wright[8] has been saying about self-knowledge of intentional states in a series of recent papers, and I also think it was Wittgenstein's[9] position, though, of course, no person can say that with complete confidence. Wright goes beyond this core when he develops the position in terms of an analogy between intentional states and secondary qualities, in terms of what in some of his formulations reads like a refined version of anti-realism about certain forms of sentences ascribing mentality, and finally in terms of contrast with self-knowledge about pains and sensations generally. That entire surround of the core seems to me to invite controversy, and what I shall argue for will make no explicit commitment to anything but the core of his view. Not that I think the core cannot be developed along positive lines by saying what sorts of things underlie and make possible the denial of the perceptual account, and thereby give point and rationale to the constitutive account. (See below for precisely such a development.) But the development will not be along any of the controversial lines to be found in Wright.

I will try and give grounds that support a constitutive view. Those grounds will establish that there is *a* clear sense in which, unlike the case of ordinary perception, there can be no exceptions to the claim that if someone believes that he believes that *p*, then he believes that *p*, and vice versa. What sense is that?

II

That question will not get an answer until section III, because here I must abruptly switch to a discussion of my other theme of Strawson's

---

[7] It should be obvious, but in case it is not, I should point out that when I deny that there is a cognitive element of this kind in ordinary cases of self-knowledge, I am not denying that self-beliefs are cognitive states in the sense that they are truth-value-bearing. I am only denying that in the ordinary case these truth-value-bearing states have been achieved via cognition.

[8] C. Wright, 'Wittgenstein's Rule-Following Considerations and the Central Project of Theoretical Linguistics', in A. George (ed.), *Reflections on Chomsky* (Oxford: Blackwell, 1989), 233–64. Also *idem*, 'Wittgenstein's Later Philosophy of Mind', in K. Puhl (ed.), *Meaning Scepticism* (Berlin: de Gruyter, 1991), 126–47.

[9] L. Wittgenstein, *Philosophical Investigations*, trans. G. E. M. Auscombe (Oxford: Blackwell, 1953).

account of responsibility and free will. Perhaps the transition would be less abrupt if I pointed out that some of what I have said so far is an elaboration of part of what many philosophers have described as an asymmetry between first- and third-person angles on mental states. But the asymmetry has a special character. It is not merely that there is a thoroughgoing asymmetry that afflicts the epistemology of mind (we seem to know other minds on the basis of, or at any rate by perceiving, their behaviour but not—usually—our own minds); the asymmetry has a special non-Cartesian character (we seem to know other minds on the basis of behaviour, but we don't usually seem to know our own minds either on the basis of behaviour or on the basis of inner perception).

Strawson[10] in a famous discussion of the subject remarked that this special kind of non-Cartesian asymmetry was an essential feature of the very idea of creatures with minds, the very idea of what he, introducing a term of art, called 'persons'. But he nowhere elaborated what it is about persons that accounted for the special asymmetry. I will try to do that briefly by situating Strawson's remark in the seemingly unconnected wider context of his own subsequent discussion of responsibility and freedom of the will. My elaboration is intended to consolidate the negatively drawn constitutive thesis above, thereby making it more than a mere assertion of what is needed. So far, the constitutive thesis has the effect of saying just this: since self-knowledge does not, except at the margins, seem either inferential or perceptual, and since there are no other paradigms for knowledge (at any rate, none that are relevant to self-knowledge), let us propose that self-knowledge is unique in being neither. The elaboration I have in mind, therefore, whether it amounts to an argument or not, is intended to make the constitutive thesis less purely stipulative.[11]

---

[10] P. F. Strawson, *Individuals* (London: Methuen, 1959).

[11] In trying to make the thesis less stipulative, I am claiming that it is not enough to stop at saying that, in the ordinary case, one has self-knowledge neither by perception nor inference. But, in making it less stipulative, is one 'explaining' how one has self-knowledge rather than simply saying that one has it? I don't know, since it is not clear what is meant by 'explaining' in this context. If self-knowledge is constitutive and not perceptual, it is clear that it is not going to have the kind of explanation that perceptual knowledge does. But does it have to have some other 'explanation'? Again, one does not know, and for the same reason. The elaboration and grounding that I offer which make the constitutive thesis less stipulative are certainly not trying to 'justify' self-knowledge in anything like the sense that the reliabilist justifies various kinds of knowledge. Am I, then trying to justify 'self-knowledge' in some other sense? I must repeat that I don't know, and don't particularly care. Words like 'explain' and 'justify' ring loud, jarring bells in the heads of devout Wittgensteinians. In what follows I will not be watchful of their sensitivities. Since I have explicitly distanced my own efforts from these other sorts of explanations and justifications, I will not hesitate to use these terms to describe what I am doing, and will simply hope that the reader is not misled by them.

Strawson's revolutionary strategy on the subject of freedom was, in part, a response to a crippling problem that arose for traditional ways of thinking about the compatibility, on the one hand, of responsibility (which he rightly understood in terms of all the practices surrounding ascriptions of responsibility in assigning punishment and reward for harmful and worthy actions) with, on the other hand, the doctrine of determinism. A long-standing dispute between compatibilists and incompatibilists on this problem centred on whether or not the fact of universal causation (and thus the fact that human actions are subject to causal determination) is a threat to the idea that our practices of punishment for what we consider harmful actions are ever justifiable, and therefore whether we are ever rightly held to be free and responsible. It fell to the compatibilists to establish the claim that though some causes do indeed threaten the aptness of our practices surrounding the ascription of responsibility, others do not, so the threat is not from the mere fact of causation but from the specially coercive nature of *some* causes.

Strawson first points out—rightly, I say—that the traditional compatibilist strategy (of Hume,[12] for example) of finding something differential directly in the *nature of the causes* of human action, such that one can distinguish between the free and unfree among such actions, in a way that would justify our practices regarding assignment of punishment and blame for harmful actions, is a bankrupt strategy. The reason for this is simply that there is no answer to the following insistent question of a demanding incompatibilist: *what about* these causes, rather than those other causes, justifies punishment when the actions they cause are considered harmful? Of two actions that are injurious, if one is caused by what we identify as a coercive cause and another by a non-coercive cause, the question is why, in the face of a general causal determinism, one should be punished, the other not. For the traditional incompatibilist, who thinks that determinism can leave no room for justified punishment, this is an urgent question, because from her determinist point of view there is nothing in what are identified as non-coercive causes which by itself makes evident that something like punishment is just for the sorts of harmful actions that we tend to punish. For her, nothing that we can find by just staring at the causes justifies this distinction between causes. The so-called non-coercive causes do not wear

All I can assume is that the elaboration and grounding I give for the constitutive thesis should not worry any but the most tediously dogmatic quietist.

[12] D. Hume, *A Treatise of Human Nature*, II. iii. 1 and 2 (Oxford: Oxford University Press, 1978). Hume more or less set the orthodoxy for the compatibilist position since his time.

the relevance of their non-coerciveness on their sleeves in a way that justifies our practices surrounding the assignment of responsibility.

On the contrary, our distinction between these causes, it seems, itself rests on decisions we make on the basis of normative considerations that we bring to them, rather than in the nature of the causes themselves. So, in the light of this, Strawson proposes a reversal of the direction from which we should approach the question of freedom and our practices regarding responsibility. He proposes that the compatibilist simply give up on the idea that freedom of the will is a metaphysical idea, an idea that gets its substance and point from a metaphysical basis in a specially non-coercive and innocuous conception of causality. Rather, the idea of such a conception of causality is itself derivative of, is itself a fall-out from, normative considerations that justify our practices surrounding responsibility and freedom. Strawson suggests that what is primary is our own evaluative reaction, our reactive attitudes of evaluation of people (including ourselves) and their (our) actions, reactive attitudes such as criticism, resentment, indignation, moral approbation (self-criticism, guilt and remorse, and pride), and that it is *these* which underlie and justify both the general ascribability of responsibility and freedom to our actions and the practices of punishment surrounding them, as well as justify the ascribability of non-coerciveness to the causes which bring about such actions. Only this normative turn can deflect the insistent demand of the traditional incompatibilist that I mentioned above.

In case all this talk of *reversing* the direction of explanation sounds too strong, perhaps the point should be put more cautiously. It is not so much that the relevance of a non-coercive causality is playing no explanatory role in our understanding of responsibility and its practices, but rather that there is no understanding of the idea of non-coercive causality that *leaves out* our normative responses to actions caused non-coercively. There is no understanding it in strictly metaphysical and non-normative terms, as traditional discussions have assumed.

There is a natural philosophical tendency to say at this point that both the reactive attitudes and the practices surrounding assignment of responsibility are appropriate when some non-normative properties of subjects are in place, such as, for example, that they are capable of self-knowledge, and that their actions which prompt the reactive attitudes are self-known.[13] But the nagging Strawsonian requirement on behalf of the demanding incompatibilist, at least as I interpret Strawson, is waiting

---

[13] See Jay Wallace, *Freedom and the Moral Sentiments* (Cambridge, Mass.: Harvard University Press, 1994). Wallace stresses various capacities for self-control, but the stress is on a non-normative grounding for the reactive attitudes as well as for the practices surrounding assignment of responsibility that express them.

to be posed here again. *What about* these non-normative properties justifies manifestly normative responses such as criticism, punishment, and the reactive attitudes they express? This proposed stopping-point, as much as Hume's idea of a non-coercive cause, is in danger of giving rise to a naturalistic fallacy.[14]

To say that is not to deny that self-knowledge is a necessary condition for the implementation of practices surrounding assignment of responsibility and the reactive attitudes they express. In fact, it clearly is a necessary condition, a point that will be crucial a little later. However, if Strawson's framework is right, the point remains that its being a necessary condition does nothing to elevate it from a subsidiary position. In other words, if he is right, it is quite wrong to think that self-knowledge can be one among a set of non-normatively characterized conditions that will together provide a justification of the evaluative practices which define our notion of responsibility. Hence, its status as necessary condition does not turn on some non-normative, analytic-metaphysical notion of 'appropriateness', which has it that it is in that sense 'inappropriate' to blame and punish un-self-knowing agents and actions. Rather, the 'inappropriateness' is more fully normative. Self-knowledge is necessary for responsibility *for no other reason* (and this is what shows it to have what I call a 'subsidiary position') than that our *evaluative* justifications of the practices of assigning punishment and blame seem to be apt only when self-knowledge is present.

This last point is of the utmost importance. There is simply *no quicker certification* that self-knowledge can provide for our notion of responsibility.

The urge to say that it is part of a quicker, more direct justification for *another* notion of responsibility, one that is *not* defined by our evaluative practices (some metaphysical notion of free will) does not help

---

[14] I must make clear that this demand is never made explicitly by the traditional incompatibilist, who has his eye more on showing that either we should deny the universal sway of causality and see human action as beyond its sway ('contra-causal', as they said) or we should grant complete victory to the determinist. But, as I read Strawson, in his dialectic, the incompatibilist has his eye rather on showing that any appeal to something non-normative will give rise to the naturalistic fallacy, and thereby force the compatibilist, in order to win, to change the subject, by saying that the notion of freedom and responsibility is itself a normative one. That is, in part, victory for the incompatibilist. On a related point, I should say that although I have made out that Strawson is interpreting the incompatibilist to be this interesting sort of opponent of the naturalistic fallacy in this area, Strawson himself might in the end be describable as a naturalist of a certain kind, but not the kind who thinks that our practices surrounding assignment of responsibility can be justified without appeal to such normative things as reactive attitudes. However, as we shall see below, on the question of how we should justify reactive attitudes in the face of determinism, he tends to just lay down that that is the sort of creature we are, which might be seen by some as a naturalistic stopping-point.

at all in elevating it from what I called its 'subsidiary' position as a necessary condition. For we must ask what interest there is in such a stipulated notion of responsibility which bears no relation to our practices at all. I think that there cannot be any answer to this question which does not point to *some* normative significance that that revised notion of responsibility has for us. But then, if it has some normative significance other than that it is related to practices of blame and punishment, it will *still* be bootless to justify it by pointing to a non-normative property such as self-knowledge. This seems to me to be the gist of Strawson's redirection of this subject.

Having found a normative basis for responsibility, I think Strawson's own tendency is *not* to probe further than the reactive attitudes as a way of grounding responsibility. He is usually content to say: this is how we are, we cannot imagine ourselves without these attitudes. As he might say, to imagine these away is to change the subject from philosophical anthropology (a 'descriptive metaphysics' of the 'person') to some other subject than the person. But, arguably, this tendency also entails resting at a premature stopping-point. For it is surely possible to wonder whether we should be harbouring these reactive attitudes in the face of determinism. Why, it might be thought, should we not adopt an extended version of the position, more and more common in psychiatry and surrounding disciplines, that we should increasingly replace blame and punishment with psychotherapy and medication, and do so to the limit of its possibility, and try to replace even our reactive attitudes. Strawson is, of course, quite right to say that it is unimaginable that we should *entirely* do so, for that would be to give up on agency. But what this limit of imagination shows is only that there can be no grounding of these practices and attitudes from the outside. One cannot go to more and more general grounds in justification. But it allows that there may be *internal* justifications for why we should resist the ideological tendency in the psychiatrists' conception: that is, justifications internal to our values. Why we should value agency is a question that can be answered, not from a position that is outside considerations of agency, but from within it, from values *thicker and more specific*, as it were, than the value of agency itself.

I haven't the space to discuss the question of these further values here, where my point is merely to say what the right dialectic for thinking about freedom and responsibility (and eventually self-knowledge) is, once we accept Strawson's fundamental insight.[15] The right dialectic does not

---

[15] For a full and satisfying discussion of this, see Stephen White, 'Self-Deception and Responsibility for the Self', in B. McLaughlin and R. Rorty (eds.), *Perspectives on Self-Deception* (Berkeley: University of California Press, 1988), 450–86.

rest with Strawson's stopping-point, the reactive attitudes, but grounds these too internally in further and thicker values. There is no getting outside the realm of values; nor is there a primitive resting-point within values. This point should be structurally familiar from anti-foundationalist coherentism in domains other than the study of value. So, though one may still say with Strawson that to cease to think of ourselves as creatures who react to ourselves and to one another with criticism and resentment is to change the subject of philosophical anthropology, we need not say it in the reassuringly complacent voice of a mid-century Oxford notable who means simply 'This is how we are!' Rather, we can say that if this is how we are, this is itself because of certain values and goals which we embrace and pursue; so it is our *values* which define the subject of philosophical anthropology, and not some transcendental truth or descriptive metaphysics about the nature of 'persons'. I am stressing this slight departure from Strawson because I want to claim that it converts self-knowledge itself into a normative notion, an idea I want to exploit in the next two sections.

III

Returning, then, to the question of self-knowledge, one may begin with what is pretty generally agreed upon: the denial of the infallibility of self-belief. To acknowledge failures of self-knowledge is to acknowledge a variety of phenomena, most interestingly self-deception, but also, for instance, certain kinds of quotidian lapses of memory, to correct which requires cognitive activity to dredge up a belief that one can safely say someone has.[16]

An intuitive starting-point for any effort to establish that self-knowledge is constitutive of intentional states might be to say this: despite the acknowledgement of fallibility—say, for example, of self-deception—there is nevertheless a residual sense in which the conditional—if someone believes that she believes that p, then she believes that p—is true. This sense is not the sense of a generalization that allows of exceptions, but rather of a generalization to which self-deception, even when it exists, is not really an exception. Intuitively, then, there is a kind of intentional state that we necessarily have, if we believe that we have it, even when we are self-deceived. I will refer to this as the 'intuitive starting-point' of my argument for the constitutive thesis. It is just a non-Cartesian

---

[16] As opposed to lack of memory of such things as what I did at 5 p.m. twenty years ago, where there is no reason to believe that there is any belief to be dredged up by attentive recall.

version of our intuition of first-person authority. I call it 'intuitive' only because I take it that we all have some residual intuition about first-person authority despite the widespread abandonment of Cartesian doctrine. What that intuition amounts to exactly, and whether we can justify it and justify this starting-point, will be recurring subjects (see particularly the end of this section and the first half of sect. V).

What the intuition in the starting-point implies is that when someone believes that she believes that p, but is self-deceived, she *has* a belief of this kind (the belief that p), *as well* as a belief that is inconsistent with it, even sometimes a straightforward negation of it.[17] (The point, of course, is not restricted to beliefs about *beliefs*. It is true of beliefs about intentional states, generally.) To take a canonically crude example, suppose someone avows or believes that he believes that his father is a fine person, worthy of his respect and so on, and suppose also that his behaviour betrays a consistently hostile, contemptuous attitude toward his father. The intuition is that we should *not* say that his second-order belief is false. We should say instead that it is true, and that therefore he has the first-order belief that makes it true, but that he also has another first-order belief that is inconsistent with it, a belief that his father is not worthy of respect, and so on. It is the latter which captures his self-deception under these circumstances, not the falsity of the second-order belief. This ensures that the relevant cases of self-deception do not threaten the conditional about self-knowledge which expresses our intuition about first-person authority. (And the fact that it is something like self-deception which is being accommodated in the intuition ensures that the intuition itself cannot be seen as part of any Cartesian doctrine.) Of course, such cases of self-deception threaten the conditional going in the *other* direction, the conditional that if someone believes that p, then he believes that he believes that p. This is because the belief inconsistent with the avowed belief is presumably not known by its possessor, assuming him not to be a logical idiot who knowingly believes the simplest inconsistencies.[18] I will return to the conditional in this direction later in this section, and show that this threat to it does nothing to threaten a properly formulated constitutive thesis.

Starting with our intuition, we can then go on to say that there is, intuitively speaking, a *kind of* belief (or intentional state, generally) about

---

[17] Of course, of this belief which is inconsistent with the embedded belief, the conditional in the other direction does not hold: i.e. the conditional 'If someone has a belief, then she has a belief that she has that belief' does not hold. I return to the matter of this conditional in the other direction shortly.

[18] I will ignore here the subtler point that often in self-deception there is a sort of half-knowledge of the very intentional states that one is self-deceived about. It is enough here to say that there is no full, explicit knowledge.

which our second-order judgements cannot be wrong, in the sense that whenever we make a second-order judgement about a belief, we have that belief. A better way of putting the point is that the conditional, in the embedded clause of its antecedent, picks out a certain kind of intentional state, which stands in contrast with the intentional states that are inconsistent with it in each relevant case[19] of self-deception. The expression 'a kind of intentional state' is awkward here, but I use it because I want to ask: *what* kind of intentional state is it? What kind of intentional state is picked out by the emphasized expression in the next sentence? If I believe that *I believe (or desire or intend, etc.) that* p, then I believe (or desire or intend, etc.) that *p*. What must be said in any illuminating answer to this question will help us say a little bit more about what makes for the constitutiveness of self-knowledge for intentional states.

It is, at first blush, tempting to say that the kind of intentional state it is (as opposed to the one that is inconsistent with it when one is self-deceived), is just a *conscious* state. But that isn't very promising, because for many philosophers the idea of a conscious state is to be analysed in terms of being the object of a second-order state, and that does not get us any further than where we started. And if we reject this analysis of a conscious state for some other analysis of it—say, a more phenomenological analysis—then it is doubtful that the description 'conscious' always correctly characterizes the kind of intentional state we are interested in. How, then, shall we characterize the kind of state it is, if the characterization 'conscious' is not satisfactory?

It is here that the excursus about agency impresses with its relevance. The proposal I have been working up to is this: the kind of intentional state that is picked out by the embedded clause in a higher-order belief ascription is one which potentially (along with other such intentional states) leads to actions or conclusions that can be the objects of (internally) justifiable reactive attitudes: that is, actions which are, in the modified Strawsonian picture of responsibility just sketched, free and responsible actions. The point becomes vivid if we compare this kind of intentional state with those that are inconsistent with it in the relevant cases of self-deception. These latter states are precisely not ones which, when they lead to actions (or conclusions), lead to actions which are the objects of (internally) justifiable reactive attitudes, blame and punishment, etc.

[19] I have been saying, and will continue to say, *'relevant* cases of self-deception' in this context because self-deception need not always take the form of one believing not-*p* or a belief inconsistent with *p* when one believes that one believes that *p*. It may also take the form of believing that one does not believe that *p*, when one believes that *p*.

Someone may wish to deny this last point (and therefore the proposal) on the grounds that we do in fact blame self-deceived agents, and do generally take ourselves to be justified in doing so, in a way that we do not (usually) blame those deceived by others.[20] This observation needs careful handling. Since the plausibility of my proposal depends on it, I shall spend some time showing that our blame of self-deceived agents does not affect its plausibility.

We need to remind ourselves of the fact that, in the end, self-knowledge of the kind I am claiming to be constitutive is grounded in evaluative responses and a system of internal evaluative justification. That we should ultimately even support the reactive attitudes which ground self-knowledge internally by further appeal to our values brings out well that the notion of self-knowledge is itself a value commitment. Putting it somewhat barbarously, to the extent that it is our *values* which internally justify the justifiers of self-knowledge, self-knowledge is itself a form of commitment. The modification of Strawson which I made before applying the Strawsonian framework to self-knowledge clearly leads to this conclusion. Over and above the constitutive thesis, then, I am also saying that, in a quite literal sense, if I have an intentional state, I am *committed* to believing that I have it. If this claim sounds a bit much, it should seem less so when we think that philosophers have argued for the existence of far more abstract commitments, such as that we are committed to being consistent, committed even to believing the logical consequences of our beliefs.[21] Much needs to be said about the nature of this commitment that I cannot say here. It needs to be shown that we are committed to self-knowledge, even though there are many excusing conditions to this commitment when the costs are too high to pursue them, which is often (e.g. just think of the time and money required by a New York psychoanalyst). But the commitment to self-knowledge, unlike, say, my commitment to knowing a lot about Indian history, is primary, with these conditions coming in secondarily as exactly what they are

[20] I am not of course denying that we sometimes blame people who are deceived by others. We sometimes think that people ought to have been more vigilant about deceiver. But once the explanation for blame of self-knowledge I give in the text becomes clear, it will be obvious that this sort of occasional blame of those who are other-deceived is on a quite different basis.

[21] For pioneering work on the notion of commitment in the very concept of intentionality, see I. Levi, *Enterprise of Knowledge* (Cambridge, Mass.: MIT Press, 1980). Though I am in serious disagreement with Levi about a number of details regarding what commitments are entailed in having intentional states, my remarks in section V on the normative reading of 'preparedness' come round to something very like his general (and novel) idea on the subject of intentional states. See also R. Brandon, *Making it Explicit* (Cambridge, Mass.: Harvard University Press, 1994), for the place of commitment in intentionality.

properly called, *excusing* conditions for a commitment *already in place*. My desire to know Indian history or, for that matter, my desire to know the intentional states of others around me, even if it is intense and even if I believe I *ought* to pursue these matters, are simply not commitments in this sense. I pursue these interests as and when I want and need to, without there being any philosophical ground on which I must say that, when I do not pursue them, my reasons for not doing so count as excusing conditions for a commitment to know these things which is already in primary place. 'Do it, unless the costs are high' and 'If you want and need to, do it' are forms of imperative which have different places and roles in our moral-psychological economies.

But putting such refinements aside, the point of making the claim that self-knowledge is a commitment was to show why the fact that we do by our lights justifiably blame the self-deceived subject does not spoil my other claim, the claim implied by my proposal, that the beliefs that are inconsistent with the embedded, higher-order beliefs in cases of self-deception fall outside the scope of responsible agency. This other claim remains true despite the fact that we blame the self-deceived agent, because in that case our blame is not of his actions or conclusions issuing from those beliefs that are inconsistent with the embedded beliefs, but is rather blame for having beliefs which are *not* the object of higher-order beliefs: that is, for failing to live up to his *commitment* to self-knowledge. I therefore conclude that if we give a fine-grained enough description of what is going on when we blame the self-deceived person, it becomes clear that what we are justifiably blaming him for is not knowing (himself, his thoughts and motives) better, rather than for anything he does or concludes. So the fact that we blame him cannot be taken to be a counter-instance to my proposal connecting self-knowledge of one's intentional states with reactive attitudes such as criticism and blame, and therefore with responsible agency. For the proposal claims that wherever there is scope for internally justifiable reactive attitudes to a person's (potential) actions and conclusions, the necessary condition of self-knowledge of the (potential) actions, conclusions, and the intentional states that rationalize them must be met. And in cases of self-deception there is no justifiable reactive attitude to the self-deceived agent's (potential) actions and conclusions, only to the fact of there not being the requisite self-knowledge.

(There is an obvious complication here. I have claimed two seemingly inconsistent things: first, if X is justifiably blamed for something, this presupposes that X knows what he is blamed for; and second, that we may justifiably blame X when he is self-deceived for not knowing his own thoughts. This might seem to imply that if X is to be blamed for a particular case of self-deception, he must know that he does not know some thought of his, about which he is self-deceived. But that cannot be right, of course. Blame for self-deception provides an exception to the first claim. Why? Because in this case it is blame for a lack of a specific case of knowledge, so knowledge of the lack of knowledge cannot be presupposed in the blaming. It is incoherent to say that someone knows that he does not know some particular truth. He could not know that without knowing the particular truth. Of course, one can know in a *general* way that there is something in a region of one's thoughts that one does not know. That sort of thing sometimes propels us to go to analysts or in other ways to cognitively enquire about our own submerged or suppressed thoughts. But of any *particular* thought of ours, we could not coherently be said to know that we do not know it. When it comes to justifiable blame for self-deception, therefore, the requirement laid down in the first claim above lapses as a requirement. So there is no inconsistency in my claims.)

Let me return to the central theme of the constitutive thesis about self-knowledge. I have characterized the kind of intentional state that is embedded in higher-order beliefs which are true despite the fact of self-deception, not in terms of them being conscious, but in terms of responsible agency. Once we see this, all we have to do is to keep in mind the sort of analysis of responsible agency I gave in the last section; we are then in a position to make the main claim of this section. We are in a position to state the condition under which the *entire* biconditional we have targeted to be the constitutive thesis is true and relevant to self-knowledge: that is, we are in a position to say that under the condition of responsible agency (understood as in the last section), if someone believes that he has some intentional state, then he has it, and if someone has an intentional state, then he believes that he has it.

It should be obvious how it puts us in a position to say this. Take first the conditional that if someone has an intentional state, then he believes that he has it. Suppose that the qualifying condition for this conditional —the qualifying condition of responsible agency—is met; that is, suppose that it is the kind of intentional state that potentially leads to actions (or conclusions) that can be the objects of internally justifiable reactive attitudes. For the sake of simplicity, suppose that he has *actually* acted (or concluded), and that we or he himself can have internally justifiable reactive attitudes regarding that action. Then, given what we have established in the last section—namely, that self-knowledge is a necessary condition of responsible agency—he must know that he has that intentional state: not merely know that he has acted or concluded something, but also know the intentional states which cause and explain (rationalize) the action or conclusion; for we may assume (familiarly) that there is no correctly describing the self-known action except in terms of the intentional states that explain (rationalize) it. Thus, once we qualify the conditional with the condition of responsible agency, even the example of self-deception we considered earlier cannot be a threat to it, which it certainly would be—as we admitted earlier—if we had not qualified it. If we hadn't qualified it, the conditional would certainly be false, since it is quite false to think that we have knowledge of all the intentional states we have. In fact, much more than the fact of self-deception would threaten the unqualified conditional. It would also be threatened by the plain fact that even when we do not motivatedly block out our intentional states, we are to some extent simply too deep for ourselves, as it were, and are just not aware of many of our intentional states. But with the qualification in place, the conditional is protected from the threat of these facts, which now become irrelevant to it, since they all place the potential actions (and conclusions) outside the scope of responsible agency.

Take now the conditional going in the opposite direction: if someone believes that he has a certain intentional state, then he has it. The point of the conditional in this direction is to claim that (under conditions of responsible agency) avowals and second-order beliefs can not fail to be true and can not fail to amount to self-knowledge. Why is this so? Suppose once again that the condition of responsible agency is fulfilled, and yet again, for simplicity's sake, that we have an agent who has *actually* acted or concluded something on the basis of the intentional state in question, and, since he is responsible, it is an action or conclusion that we or he can have justifiable reactive attitudes towards. Now suppose that he judges (avows) that he has that intentional state, thereby expressing his second-order belief. Or suppose, more simply and directly, that he has the second-order belief. Again, under these conditions of responsible agency, he cannot fail to have knowledge of that intentional state, cannot be deluded about it; hence the second-order belief must be true. So the conditional holds.

Somebody might protest that this last is just trivially so, because we are assuming in the way we set things up in the last paragraph that he *has* the (first-order) intentional state in question; hence it cannot be news that the avowal or second-order belief which is mentioned in the conditional amounts to self-knowledge. The protest is misguided. After all, one can judge that there is a dagger before one and fail to have knowledge that there is a dagger before one, *even when there is a dagger before one*. Standard analyses of knowledge require more for knowledge than that a dagger be there when one judges that it is there. So too one must demand that there be more in our understanding of self-knowledge than that the first-order intentional states that make second-order beliefs true exist. The fact is that self-knowledge, if I am wrong and the causal-perceptualist-reliabilist account is right, would be something like the perceptual knowledge of daggers. And if perceptual knowledge requires something more than the presence of daggers when daggers are judged to be present, self-knowledge too requires more than the presence of first-order intentional states when second-order judgements are made about them. It requires some analogue to the condition of the *right sort of* causal link between daggers and judgers. Now just because I am denying the causal-perceptualist account of self-knowledge does not mean that I am saying that nothing more than the first-order intentional state is required for the second-order belief about it to amount to knowledge. On the other hand, because I *am* denying the causal-perceptualist account, the further thing required, for me, is not any condition requiring the right sort of causal link. Some quite different kind of further thing is required. And my proposal has been that the further requirement is that the condition of responsible agency must be fulfilled; that is, the actual or potential actions or conclusions must be responsible in the sense required. It is this condition of responsibility being fulfilled (and not merely the existence of the first-order intentional state) which presupposes that there is self-knowledge. This shows that, if the causal-perceptualist thesis is wrong, then the mere existence of the first-order intentional state (*without* the truth of my argument) would be powerless to establish that the truth of the second-order belief amounts to self-knowledge. Without my argument in place, even if the conditional in this direction is true because there is in fact the first-order intentional state which would make the avowal and second-order belief true, the conditional would be of no interest in a thesis about self-knowledge. In other words, the conditional in this direction would need *either* the support of the idea that the condition of responsibility is fulfilled *or* the support of an idea of the right sort of causal link (*or* some other further thing) before the second-order belief cited in the conditional could be said to amount to self-knowledge. And, of course, in *my* argument, the *first* of these disjuncts is giving the support. Thus the conditional in this direction is *not* established as relevant to self-knowledge trivially on the mere basis of the existence of the first-order intentional state, as was being protested.

Though I will not spell it out in detail here, this response to the protest can also be seen as providing the basis of a repudiation of a quite different position from the protester's—that of the extreme Wittgensteinian quietist on the subject of self-knowledge, who says, 'We don't need to bother to say anything to justify or even to ground the idea of self-knowledge; we just have it.' The quietist precisely needs to have something to say to the sort of philosopher, who, by the way, is not a sceptic (whom the quietist may rightly refuse to answer) but a philosopher who asks the following sort of good question: what *is it* to have self-knowledge? Or, more elaborately: for the reasons just traversed, to have self-knowledge cannot be just to have a first-order intentional state and a second-order belief that one has it. So what else is needed? This is not a sceptical question, because no impossible Cartesian demand of indubitability is being made of any candidate answer. All that is being demanded is *some* answer, rather than lazy indifference to a good question. Both the causal-perceptualist account and the sort of account I am giving, in their very different ways, offer something by way of an answer to this sort of philosopher, which the quietist does not. (And, of course, it is the brief of this essay that the causal-perceptualist offers quite the wrong answer.)

The entire *bi*conditional has now been established, under a certain condition of responsible agency. I still need to show why the biconditional, so established, demonstrates that the causal-perceptualist account of self-knowledge is both wrong and unnecessary. I will show this when I respond to the two objections below. But first let me quickly repeat that the most generally statable condition under which the targeted biconditional about self-knowledge of intentional states is true is that an agent's potential actions and conclusions be the appropriate objects of internally justifiable reactive attitudes. The idea that the targeted biconditional is true under this condition is not surprising—indeed, was already implicit in the idea that self-knowledge of one's intentional states is a necessary condition for the practices surrounding assignment of responsibility and for the reactive attitudes which justify them. However—and this is absolutely crucial—if one keeps in mind the point I made about the *subsidiary* nature of the necessary condition, then the following seemingly natural thought is completely wrong: if self-knowledge is a *necessary condition* for justifiable reactive attitudes, then it should be accounted for *independently* of any mention of the reactive attitudes (as a perceptual and non-constitutive account might seek to do). This is because, as I said, there is no way to understand the attributions of higher-order beliefs in self-knowledge without understanding that they take as their embedded objects the kind of intentional states which are essentially caught up with the reactive attitudes, whether those of others or self-reactive attitudes. We have seen that these embedded objects cannot be satisfactorily characterized as 'conscious' states. And the temptation to think that they can be characterized more generally as one understands *all* intentional states (i.e. understand them generally in terms of having a role in the explanation of action) must be resisted. It must be resisted because in that case we will have *lost our contrast* between these first-order states which are embedded in higher-order beliefs and those states which are inconsistent with them in the relevant cases of self-deception. For the latter too *do* explain our actions; the point is that they *lack* the connection with the reactive attitudes that the embedded intentional states have. We simply do not, with internal justification, have reactive attitudes to the actions and conclusions that issue from the states that are inconsistent with the embedded states in the relevant cases of self-deception. It is only the embedded states which have this connection with the reactive attitudes. And the idea that self-knowledge (which is carried in the second-order states in which they are embedded) is itself a necessary condition for responsible agency does nothing to remove this essential *conceptual* connection that these embedded states have with the reactive attitudes and with responsible agency.

I have argued that we have no better argument—at any rate, no more general argument—for the entire biconditional than that it ultimately, and most deeply, rests on our very notion of agency and freedom, properly understood. At the beginning of the chapter, I said that I would show that there is *a* sense in which there can be no breakdown or exceptions in the connection (or, to put it differently, that there is *a* sense in which there is a rule-like quality to the connection) between an intentional state and a self-belief about it. The conditions of responsible agency under which the biconditional holds provide *the* sense I had in mind. Putting it in full dress, the following claim can be stated as conveying a kind of rule, rather than as a generalization that allows for exceptions: *If an intentional state is potentially linked by practical or theoretical reasoning to actions or conclusions that can be the internally justifiable objects of the reactive attitudes, then for each such state, its possessor believes that she has it, and has it if she believes that she has it.*

This, I claim, has some right to be thought of as a constitutive thesis about self-knowledge of intentional states. And since this biconditional, so conceived, is, as I have argued, compatible with there being self-deception, etc., the constitutive thesis holds in a non-Cartesian setting of a frankly acknowledged fallibility.

Let me now turn to the task of making entirely explicit why the claims of this section amount to a constitutive thesis about self-knowledge. In section I, I sketched the constitutive thesis by contrast with the causal-perceptual account of self-knowledge. That the claims of this section amount to a constitutive thesis can thus be made explicit by responding to two objections which would seem to grant the claims of this section but which nevertheless favour the causal-perceptualist account of self-knowledge. The reasons for dismissing the objections will thus also make entirely explicit why the proposal of this section amounts to a refutation of the causal-perceptualist account.

First, it may be thought that all that my claims in this section show is that there is a conceptual setting for self-knowledge of our intentional states in considerations of agency, but not that self-knowledge is not in every case a product of a causal mechanism that connects an intentional state with the belief that one has it. Why may we not grant that self-knowledge has conceptual links with agency, yet also insist on it being a product of such a mechanism? What is it about the conceptual links that spoils the idea that there is such a causal, reliabilist, and sparely perceptual account of self-knowledge? The answer to this question is as follows. Any causal-perceptualist account worth its name (taking perception of the external world as a paradigm, even if we drop the demand that it should involve analogues to cognitive activity such as 'looking', etc.) must allow that there can be a breakdown in the causal-perceptual mechanism, however reliable it is. But, as I have argued, there is *no* possibility of a breakdown in the connection between intentional states and beliefs about them (so long as the agency condition is fulfilled) in the way that there is between external objects and our perceptual experiences and beliefs about them. Now there is a temptation to think that to the extent that I have granted exceptions *at all*—that is, to the extent that I have allowed that there is self-deception, etc.—I *have* allowed for breakdowns akin to those that occur in causal mechanisms; so why am I insisting on the incompatibility between my constitutive thesis and the causal-perceptualist account? The temptation is based on the simplest of confusions. My constitutive thesis, even though it allows for self-deception and fallibility, does not (*given conditions of responsible agency*) allow for breakdowns in the connection between the first-order and second-order beliefs mentioned in the biconditional; and the crucial condition in the parentheses above is something that falls outside the scope of anything that is relevant to the operations of a causal mechanism. *The operations (and breakdowns) of causal mechanisms are blind to normative considerations of responsible agency.* This point is of the utmost importance to my claim that the constitutive thesis is true, to the claim that the biconditional, as I have argued for it via considerations of responsibility, amounts to a thesis that self-knowledge is constitutive of intentional states, and is not to be thought of along causal-perceptualist lines. Causal mechanisms of the kind that are involved in perception simply do not operate and break down with an eye to whether such normatively characterized conditions of responsible agency have obtained. That is why there is a failure of fit between the claim that, given conditions of responsible agency, there is a connection between first-order intentional states and second-order beliefs about them and the claim that there is a causal mechanism connecting first-order intentional states and second-order beliefs about them. To say there is such a failure of fit is just to underscore that there cannot be a breakdown of the former connection, while there can be one of the latter sort of connection.

Given what I have said so far, this is a relatively weak claim, even though it does amount to the constitutive thesis that I promised. It is not so much that I have shown that there *cannot* be any such causal mechanism. Rather, what I have shown is that even if we can imagine possible worlds in which there is a breakdown of the causal mechanism, there is nevertheless self-knowledge and responsible agency. The point is that although it is an accident that there is no causal mechanism operative where there is self-knowledge and responsible agency, it is not an accident that whenever there is responsible agency, there is self-knowledge.

(Moreover, my denial of a causal-perceptualist account of self-knowledge does not mean that there are *no* causal relations at all involved in self-knowledge. In fact, my brief earlier remark in section I, granting the possibility of a causal-functional *part–whole* framework, is proof that I am happy to grant that there are causal relations present. They just do not amount to a causal-perceptualist *account* of self-knowledge, which is all that the constitutive thesis needs to establish. The point is that even if there are such causal relations involved in self-knowledge, they, unlike the case of perceptual knowledge, operate outside the scope of anything the subject does by way of cognition—analogues to 'seeing', etc.—to acquire knowledge, for she usually does nothing. And, more important, these causal relations do not amount to a mechanism of the ordinary causal variety which would explain self-knowledge in a way that a causal mechanism explains perceptual knowledge of the external world, since, as I have said, the kind of breakdown one could at least grant as possible in causal mechanisms—however reliable they may be —has no echo in an allowance of exceptions to the biconditional about self-knowledge under conditions of agency.)

Second, it may be objected that I have shown that anyone who has states of mind that are involved in responsible agency must have self-knowledge of them, but that since to count as a responsible agent means nothing other than being interpretable as one, and someone won't be interpretable as one if she lacks self-knowledge, this shows that we must have a prior, independent grip on her self-knowledge. And the spare causal-perceptualist account is there precisely to explain how we do have that independent grip. Thus the constitutive thesis, which is defined by contrast with the causal-perceptualist account, is false. The answer to this objection was implicit in my earlier discussions of the way in which self-knowledge is a necessary condition for responsible agency. I argued that its being a necessary condition does not elevate it from its 'subsidiary' status, i.e., it does *not* mean that we could think of it as independent of what it is a necessary condition for. That was part of the point of interpreting Strawson as claiming that his opponent is committing something akin to the naturalistic fallacy, if he thinks he can justify the practices surrounding assignment of responsibility by appeal to non-normatively characterized considerations. I won't rehearse that argument here. But it is worth pointing out that those who demand of my constitutive thesis about self-knowledge that it cannot be genuinely constitutive unless the considerations which conceptually account for self-knowledge (in my case, considerations of responsible agency) do their accounting *without* appealing to self-knowledge as a necessary condition for those considerations themselves to hold, are demanding something very strong indeed. An analogy may be useful here in bringing out why the demand in this objection is too strong. An analogous objection might make the following sort of demand. For someone to be counted as a linguistic agent is no more than for her to be interpretable as meaning various things, and she will not be interpretable as meaning various things unless we interpret her as having various complicated sets of interrelated beliefs and desires; so we insist that there must be a grip that we have on her complicated sets of interrelated beliefs and desires which is prior to, and independent of, interpreting her meanings, and which makes no appeal to her linguistic agency. This demand is quite extraordinarily strong.[22] The conceptual links that someone may take to hold between meanings and complicated sets of interrelated beliefs and desires, and the conceptual links that I take to hold between responsible agency and self-knowledge, need answer to no such strong demands. And if the demand need not be met, there is no place for the causal-perceptualist account to step in, so the constitutive thesis remains unthreatened.

With these objections answered, and with the causal-perceptualist account repudiated, the constitutive thesis (which I have defined in terms of contrast with the causal-perceptualist account) is in place.

---

[22] I use the words 'complicated sets of interrelated beliefs and desires' with deliberate intent. They are intended to stave off the response that since non-linguistic creatures might be said to have beliefs and desires, there is an independent grip (independent of meaning) to be had of beliefs and desires. There should be no temptation to make this irrelevant response if the beliefs and desires are described at the outset as being of a sort that we know non-linguistic creatures not to have.

I began this entire line of thought toward the constitutive thesis with what I claimed was an intuitive starting-point: namely, that there is a sense in which if someone believes that she believes (or desires or intends) something, then she is always right, adding that this was so even in cases of self-deception, because self-deception under such circumstances would show only that I also had a belief inconsistent with *p*, not that I did not believe that *p*. However, I gave no argument for this starting-point. This was because my interest in it was not intrinsic, but merely a step to raise a certain question about the nature of a certain kind of embedded intentional state. I simply tried to characterize what kind of belief or intentional state that conditional picked out in the embedded clause of its antecedent. And having done that, I formulated a general condition (citing responsible agency) under which that conditional itself, as well as the conditional in the opposite direction (in short, a certain familiar biconditional), were necessarily true. This, I argued, would suffice to establish a constitutive thesis about self-knowledge which I had proposed in contrast to a causal-perceptualist account of self-knowledge. However, a demanding reader might not be fully satisfied with this line of argument, on the ground that the intuitive starting-point was simply plonked down without comment. This unease cannot amount to a scepticism about the constitutive thesis, since the thesis does not depend on the truth of the starting-point. The starting-point could be false but the constitutive thesis true, because the conditional in the starting-point is unqualified, whereas the corresponding conditional in the constitutive thesis is weaker and qualified (the whole biconditional in the constitutive thesis is qualified) by the condition of responsible agency. All the same, the unease should be addressed; so let me make a stab at a justificatory comment on the starting-point. (There is much more on the starting-point in section V.)

I think that there are obvious arguments for this starting-point, not least that one would not know what role second-order beliefs could have in our psychological economy if they did not emerge in actions that indicated the existence of their embedded beliefs—or if not in actions, then in a *preparedness* to act on the beliefs (or desires) that are embedded. Of course, one could *say* that one believed (or desired) that *p*, and not be prepared to act on it. That would be because one was insincere or because one was just sounding off, not 'really saying', as it were. But the point here is one about *believing* that one has the belief or desire, not just saying that one has it. So if one were genuinely to express this second-order belief in one's avowal, then the avowal, it would be assumed, would not be insincere or a mere sounding off. It would have to reflect, therefore, that whether one actually did so or not, one was at least *prepared* to deploy the belief (or desire) that *p* in one's thinking, both in reaching other theoretical propositional conclusions on the basis of it and in coming to act on the basis of it (and other intentional states). In other words, an absence of the disposition to act on the belief (or desire) that *p*, or to come to any conclusions on the basis of it, may lead one to be sceptical as to whether to attribute to the agent the second-order belief, or whether to attribute to his mouthing of an avowal any sincerity. But it would not lead one to attribute a false sincere avowal or a false second-order belief. If this is right, then what it shows is that whether we do or do not have the disposition to act on the belief that *p*, that matter would by itself also be enough to decide on whether there is or is not the *second*-order belief as well, or whether or not the avowal is sincere or not. They stand or fall together.[23] So there is no reason to deny my intuitive starting-point that one's second-order beliefs cannot fail to be true, even if there is self-deception. If we are correct in attributing a second-order belief or sincere avowal in the first place, then the belief avowed must also exist, thus making the avowal and the second-order belief true.

The point is in fact much stronger. Indeed, the intuition that our second-order beliefs are always true holds in more cases than I just envisaged. That is to say, a second-order belief is properly attributable more often than I just envisaged. The conditions under which such beliefs are properly attributable are very weak, and because this is so, the stronger point that second-order beliefs are true in even more cases is established. I have said above that they are attributable when one is prepared to act on the basis of the first-order beliefs which they are about. And the idea of being *prepared* to act on one's first-order intentional states is an idea that holds even if one *lacks the disposition* to so act. All that is needed is that one should be prepared to accept criticism for lacking the disposition, and be prepared to make efforts to cultivate the disposition, even—if necessary—by therapy. This fact about avowals and second-order beliefs reveals a very fundamental feature of the nature of intentionality (first-order intentionality) itself; it reveals all the real depth of the normativity of intentional states. This very natural intuition concerning avowals implies about first-order intentional states that we can fully possess an intentional state as a commitment, as a normative stance or stances, even when we do not have any disposition to act on it. Or, to put it symmetrically, this point about the radically

---

[23] This discussion assumes for the moment that intentional states are to be thought of as dispositional states, an assumption that I will reject later on. But the rejection of the assumption will do nothing to spoil the point about the second-order states and first-order states standing and falling together.

normative nature of intentionality is of a piece with the very weak conditions under which sincere avowals and second-order beliefs are properly attributable.

In any case, even without this stronger point, I think it should be clear that the intuition that second-order beliefs are true even when there is self-deception is quite justified. So there should be no lingering unease with my argument for the constitutive thesis for which that intuition was a starting-point.

IV

My case for the constitutive thesis situated it and the special character of self-knowledge in considerations of agency, in particular in a Strawsonian account of responsibility. What makes self-knowledge special on this picture is that, unlike other kinds of knowledge which are based on cognition of various kinds, what is known (intentional states) lacks a certain independence from the ability to know it; intentional states lack the independence, for example, that items in the external world have from our cognitive abilities for perception. Our cognitive abilities for perception thus do not constitute facts and objects in the external world in the way that our capacity for self-knowledge constitutes our very idea of intentionality.[24] And my claim and argument have been that our agency is essential to seeing self-knowledge in this constitutive way. However, there is a potential source of embarrassment.

As I said, I have claimed that it is because these considerations of agency are so intrinsically and conceptually linked to self-knowledge that cognition is besides the point in giving an account of the nature of self-knowledge. But from the very beginning I also conceded to Ryle, and to other quite non-Rylean philosophers too, that very often self-knowledge is indeed achieved by cognition. So what is going on here? With the relevance of Strawson's framework to self-knowledge fully in place, we can now say something about why it is that the plain fact that there are clear cases of cognitive exercises by which we often do acquire self-knowledge is *not* an embarrassment to the constitutive thesis, as I have elaborated it.

Psychoanalysis is of course only the most institutional and interesting of cognitive forms of self-enquiry; more everyday forms, as when we find ourselves asking 'What was I thinking?', 'Do I really feel

---

[24] For an importantly relevant qualification see n. 6. See also n. 26 for more on the subject of the qualification.

angry with him?', 'Where did I put my keys?' (asked in circumstances where attention and memory would dredge up an image—say, of walking into a room and placing keys on a table), are also modes of cognitive self-enquiry which are often exercised, and exercised fruitfully. What my modified Strawsonian framework allows me to say of *all* these exceptions to the constitutive thesis is that they are forms of *cognitive therapy*,[25] which we undertake in order *to live up to the commitment to self-knowledge* when we have failed to live up to it. (In section II, during the discussion of our blame of self-deceived subjects, I explained why the modification and extension of Strawson has the effect of making self-knowledge a commitment.)

Freud saw the acquisition of certain kinds of psychoanalytically achieved self-knowledge as therapy, and it is obvious why he did so. But I think that the less obvious idea of therapy that is relevant to self-knowledge is much more general than the obvious notion of therapy which *he* had in mind, which was to remove the neuroses and anxiety that often accompany specific cases of lack of self-knowledge. The normative framework which I have briefly sketched in my appeal to, and extension of, Strawson's picture gives us the right to say that since the commitment to self-knowledge is much more general and in a sense much more fundamental than the desire to alleviate the neuroses sometimes engendered by certain kinds of lack of self-knowledge, the notion of cognitive therapy I am invoking is much more general than Freud's framework allowed, general enough to see these other more routine and quotidian exercises I mentioned as *also* falling under the notion of cognitive therapy. To meet our commitment to rid ourselves of certain neuroses no doubt requires the elaborate and interesting cognitive acquisitions of self-knowledge of motives and beliefs that the process of psychoanalysis partly consists in. To live up to the very much more general commitment to self-knowledge requires not merely the psychoanalytic cognitive acquisitions, but also the much less interesting sorts of everyday cognitive enquiries I have listed. That these cognitive enquiries are less interesting, and that they are not related to curing neuroses, should not distract us from seeing that they too are forms of therapy. They too are efforts to live up to a certain commitment when we have failed to do so.

This way of describing what goes on in cognitive cases of self-knowledge depends centrally on the idea, established earlier in the chapter, that we are committed to knowing the intentional states we have. But

---

[25] I realize that the term 'cognitive therapy' has a life of its own in the diverse spread of available psychoanalytic theories, but here I use it strictly to mean a therapy that involves cognition, nothing more specific.

notice that the idea that self-knowledge is itself to be thought of as a commitment is a claim that stands *over and above* the constitutive thesis about self-knowledge.

Thus, in the picture of self-knowledge I have been sketching there are three elements: (1) a commitment of the sort I have just mentioned; (2) a separate claim, which I have called the 'constitutive thesis' (formulated in the biconditional that holds under conditions of agency), a thesis which, in the context of (1)—that is, in the context of the idea of self-knowledge being a commitment—says that we ordinarily *live up* to this commitment, *not* (normally) by exercising some cognitive capacity or due to the operation of a causal mechanism, *but simply to the extent that we think and act as free and responsible agents*. The constitutive claim thus being a claim about the nature of *livings-up-to* the commitment to self-knowledge; and finally, (3), forms of *both* everyday and institutionalized cognitive therapy that we often undertake when we do not so live up to the commitment in the way that the constitutive thesis claims, in order to live up to it. The cases mentioned in (3) are the exceptional cases of cognitive self-knowledge.

The idea that cognitive acquisitions of self-knowledge are exceptional and peripheral *despite their frequency* can now be characterized without embarrassment. The notion of 'exceptional and peripheral' here is not captured by the fact that these are *rare* exceptions to the constitutive thesis, for they are *not* rare. They are peripheral in the sense that these cognitive exercises do not provide the paradigm for self-knowledge; the paradigm for self-knowledge is rather that it is a form of commitment which we live up to simply by having intentional states that are essentially linked with our agency. In other words, they are peripheral in the sense that, however frequent, the cognitive exercises are nevertheless to be understood as *merely* picking up a very specific sort of slack: they are forms of cognitive therapy that help us to live up to this commitment when we have failed to do so—that is, when our intentional states have fallen outside the conditions of responsible agency.

With the cognitive exceptions accounted for without any embarrassment to the constitutive thesis, I conclude that a minimal claim to the special character of self-knowledge has been established by the constitutive thesis, and move on now to further, stronger claims about the relation between agency, intentionality, and self-knowledge.

V

Agency and responsibility, I have argued, are central to locating the special character of self-knowledge. The condition citing responsible agency was essential to the biconditional of section III which captured the special constitutive character of self-knowledge. But a question arises as to whether in making these claims I was arguing for the view that agency is sufficient for self-knowledge of our intentional states, or, more strongly, that it was both sufficient and necessary. Could someone grant all that I have been saying so far, but see it as amounting only to a sufficiency claim? Could they grant what I have been saying so far and say that there would be self-knowledge of intentional states even if we were not agents? If the answer to this last question is 'Yes', then that is significant, because the causal-perceptualist account would step in and account for such self-knowledge. The question is a difficult and fundamental one, and must be approached with some indirection, since an answer to it turns on whether or not our concept of intentional states itself requires agency as a necessary condition.

To do so, let me ask you to imagine, even if the effort defeats you (for it is the question of the defeat upon which the point turns), *a wholly passive subject*, an extreme version of Oblomov, the eponymous hero of Goncharov's novel. Such a subject will lack what Kant calls the perspective of agency or freedom, or what might properly be called the first-person point of view if that phrase had not been ruined by all that Nagelian hysteria about the mental life of bats. Our Oblomov will lack the agent's point of view—let us say because he takes himself to be an object. He takes an exclusively third-person perspective on himself, and so for him the future is just like the past; he has no thought that he can make a difference to it. In a word, this subject does not act; he does not even think if that means that he thinks actively, for it is an actor or agent that he precisely is not. So if he has thoughts, they happen to him.

But now, *if* we allow that what happen to him or assail him are indeed *thoughts*, it may seem that he exemplifies many of the things that seem to exhibit self-knowledge. It may be possible to say, for instance, that his thoughts are rational. For instance, he might have the following three thoughts assail him: 'All men are mortal', 'Socrates is a man', 'Socrates is mortal'; and so on for other such trios of thoughts. But, if the picture of self-knowledge I have been arguing for is right, we are not even slightly tempted to say that he has self-knowledge. Perhaps we would be more tempted to say that he has self-knowledge if he had the following four thoughts assail him in the following order: 'All men are mortal', 'Socrates is a man', 'It is not the case that Socrates is mortal', 'Socrates is mortal'. And so on for other such quartets of thoughts. Remember, however, that if we are allowing this passive subject to have thoughts, we can still at best say only that he *exemplified* irrationality

until the fourth thought, and then with the fourth thought, he *exemplified* rationality (assuming, of course, that the third thought is missing
by the fourth and final stage). There is on my picture, therefore, still
no reason to think that he has self-knowledge. Why not? Because *ex
hypothesi* he did not arrive at the fourth thought as a result of any
active thinking or critical reaction to the third thought. That is, he did
not do it as a result of any reactive attitudes to his own thinking and
his own conclusion. (I am assuming here, as throughout, that criticism
of theoretical irrationality is a special, possibility-limiting instance of a
reactive attitude.) In fact, he did not *bring* the first three thoughts together
in a way that could have made him go on to have a reactive attitude
to the third thought, since he *does* no thinking or bringing together,
being a passive subject. For this very reason, even if the following two
thoughts were said to assail him, we would still not be tempted, on
my picture, to attribute self-knowledge: 'Socrates is mortal', 'I believe
that Socrates is mortal'. And so on for other such duos of thoughts.
Actually, that is of course a facetious exaggeration. The right thing to
say is that, *on my picture*, it is a complete mystery what role there could
be for the second in these duos of thoughts to play in a totally passive
subject like Oblomov.

Now it is possible that we might want to say (in a question-begging
sort of way, since it does not really amount to an argument) that if a
subject exemplifies irrationality and then rationality, as in the quartet
of thoughts mentioned above, and for all the myriad other similar, even
more complex transitions that he undergoes, then there is no reason to
think that the subject is any less active than any of us.[26] And then the

---

[26] It is important to emphasize that he is as active as any of *us* are. I think animals
and little children (and we sometimes) might be said to be active in making transitions
of a kind that are somewhat similar to the example in the quartet of thoughts above.
(Think of examples when children seem to believe something on the basis of evidence,
and then make a transition to another conclusion on the basis of new incoming evidence.)
But these will be essentially unlike the kinds of transitions that *only* more or less adult
human beings could, and normally would, make. In a creature capable of reactive attitudes to its own conclusions the transitions are often a result of these reactive attitudes;
i.e. the transition is not a brute change from one conclusion to another due to noticing
new evidence, but to reacting to the wrongness of the last conclusion by noticing its
inconsistency with the present one based on new evidence. (Of course, none of this need
happen in a very deliberative and phenomenologically self-conscious way.) The point is
that self-knowledge is not presupposed until the transitions are due to the exercise of
such reactive attitudes. That is why I am emphasizing that Oblomov, if he can make
all these transitions, must be active as *we* are. My claim would be that if Oblomov
made transitions as in the quartet, and we thought that this allowed us only to think
that he had the limited agency and rationality of animals and little children, then he
would lack thought and agency in the full sense that presupposes self-knowledge. For
us to be able to say that he was as active as one of us, his transitions would have to

subject would have self-knowledge if any of us do. But to say this *is just to say* that it is the rational *agency* which is making the difference, not the rationality by itself. And it is the agency that I have been stressing.

This introduces the right kind of generality for how to understand the basis of self-knowledge.

(I should add in a long aside that this last point shows that, though my overall position is in deep sympathy and agreement with Shoemaker's and Burge's recent claims that our efforts at adjusting to our norms of rationality presuppose self-knowledge, I think the relation between our closely related positions is thrown into visible relief by the Oblomov example. For, in the example, it emerges explicitly that it is the *activity* of, the *agency* involved in, making certain kinds of rational adjustments that presupposes self-knowledge. And if this is so, then we can say something *much more general* than Shoemaker[27] and Burge[28] say. We can say that it is *all* agency, not merely when I reflect on my thoughts in order to adjust them to rational norms, but *all* thought and action which is accountable that presupposes self-knowledge. What I have called the reactive attitudes generally and the sorts of considerations of rationality that Burge and Shoemaker emphasize as relevant to self-knowledge can be jointly seen, then, as part of a single integrated picture of self-knowledge. Here is how I would develop the argument for the picture. Our concepts of belief and of intentional states generally see their rationale largely in terms of explanation of actions. So a question arises about what sorts of actions a very specific kind of belief (the higher-order belief involved in self-knowledge) explains. Since it is higher-order beliefs that

include thoughts that assailed him about the inconsistency of some his thoughts and the wrongness of some of his conclusions. And the point I was making above (even though it does not amount to an argument) was that the thought experiment may well be self-defeating because if it is supposed to bring out that *all these* thoughts merely assailed him, since he was totally passive, we might well want to say that we simply cannot tell the difference between thoughts assailing him and him thinking them with full agency as any of *us* do.

[27] S. Shoemaker, 'On Knowing One's Own Mind', *Philosophical Perspectives*, 2 (1988), 183–209. In chapter 2 of my book *Belief and Meaning* (Oxford: Blackwell, 1992) I tied self-knowledge to questions of rationality in an overly elaborate discussion of the lack of self-knowledge that must account for the irrationality of the protagonist Pierre in Kripke's puzzle about belief. When I wrote that, I had not read Shoemaker's wise and convincing discussion of the relation between rationality and self-knowledge, which was already in print, and my discussion would have been much more elegant had I read it. However, even then, in the appendix to the book which was also on the subject of self-knowledge, I explicitly mentioned the point I am making here: viz. that it is necessary to situate the point about the relationship of self-knowledge to rationality in the more general relation of self-knowledge to agency. Most of the present chapter is an elaboration of that appendix.

[28] See T. Burge, 1996: 'Our Entitlement to Self-Knowledge', *Proceedings of the Aristotelian Society*, 96, 91–116.

we are concerned with, the answer is bound to be that they explain actions that are directed upon first-order intentional states. What sorts of actions could these be? Here the answer must be: actions such as *revisions* of first-order states. So could we now just say that the higher-order beliefs involved in self-knowledge come in to explain revision of belief? That cannot be right, because there is a lot of revision of belief that is, as it were, *brute* change due to new incoming evidence, and that need not involve any higher-order belief. So it can only be revision of belief that is due to criticisms we make of our own intentional states—that is to say, due to *self-reactive* attitudes. The idea that *self*-knowledge exists whenever there are *self*-reactive attitudes seems undeniably true, but not all that informative. But we can articulate the point more informatively than that, and thus add a generality and further grounding to Shoemaker's and Burge's point. *Both* self-knowledge *and* self-reactive attitudes are to be understood as something that we ascribe to subjects when their actions seem appropriate objects of justifiable reactive attitudes *generally*: that is, when they are responsible in the general sense that my Strawsonian embedding for self-knowledge requires.)

However, none of this redeems the fact that on the question of the necessity of such agency to self-knowledge I seem to have begged the main question when I said that *on my picture* of self-knowledge a subject like Oblomov, who lacks agency, lacks self-knowledge. And, as I said earlier, I also more or less begged a different question when I said that anybody who has all the instances of the various duos, trios, and, crucially, the quartets of thoughts mentioned above must be taken to be active and not passive. These two question-begging claims are closely related.

In begging the second question, it is implied that the effort to imagine such an Oblomov defeats us, that the very idea of him is incoherent. But *if I was wrong about this*, then that would have implications for the first question about Oblomov's self-knowledge. For if it were coherent that he should have thoughts—that is to say, if it were coherent that someone who had thoughts merely assail him, should genuinely be said to have *thoughts* assail him—then he could very well have self-knowledge, for there can now be no bar to the following idea: a reliable mechanism which *causes* him to have the thought that he has the thought that p assail him every time he has a thought that p assail him fully accounts for his self-knowledge. On such a conception of *thoughts*, the spare perceptual-cognitive account of *self-knowledge* of thoughts would be a perfectly feasible one. In fact, I am claiming that it is *only* on this conception of thoughts that such an account could be feasible. So, equally, it is *only* if we deny that there can coherently be thought at all in conditions of such passivity, in conditions which do not include agency, that we would be able to deny that he had self-knowledge. But to deny that Oblomov has thought is to claim the essential relevance of agency to thought. And with agency in place, this chapter's argument for the constitutive account of self-knowledge can make its claim. Thus a radical assumption about the deep relation between agency and thought itself has to be in play before one can establish that agency is *necessary* for self-knowledge, and not merely sufficient.

It is precisely this radical assumption that I *did* try to bring into play at the end of section III with the stronger and fully normative notion of intentional states revealed by the nature of second-order beliefs and avowals. Viewing them as normative in this sense makes them candidates for objects of internally justified reactive attitudes as much as an agent's actions are; therefore thoughts and intentional states are caught up directly in agency just as much as actions are. If so, Oblomov would lack thoughts and intentional states, over and above his failure to produce actions or speech.

And he would lack thoughts not just because of the usual Wittgensteinian drill about how the publicness of thoughts requires actions, which are missing in Oblomov.[29] It is, of course, true that in Wittgenstein's overall picture of mind the Oblomov of my thought-experiment does not count as a thinker at all. This disallowance of thought in the absence of any criterial link to action is just his demand for publicness. Read in this way, his position merely rules out Cartesian internalism; but it also rules out its modern kin, the physical reductionism of mental dispositions, where publicness is still missing in the ordinary sense of availability in communication and everyday behaviour. What I am claiming on behalf of this Wittgensteinian position, *when it is supplemented by the Strawsonian embedding for self-knowledge in considerations of free agency*, is a way of reading the disallowance of thought to Oblomov much more interestingly—something roughly like this.

For Wittgenstein the dispositions that amount to thinking, *real* as they may be, are *not* real in the transcendent sense that would allow Oblomov to have them. That would be too attenuated a notion of dispositions for Wittgenstein. For the transcendental *realist* about mental dispositions, the perspective of freedom, or what I call the first-person or agent's point of view (which Oblomov lacks), is *not* constitutive of mental dispositions, but merely a necessary condition for the *activation* of these dispositions which are *there anyway*, independent of the perspective of freedom. The phrase 'there anyway' captures well the kind of

---

[29] Wittgenstein, *PI* §§241 ff.

metaphysically realist position that is being denied by the transcendental idealist. Why am I invoking the Kantian categories of 'transcendental realism' and 'transcendental idealism' here? The idea is this. The phrase 'perspective of freedom' which I have been using liberally is, of course, taken from the third section of Kant's *Groundwork*.[30] Kant did not speak explicitly of mentality in the context of this issue, so far as I know, but his general transcendental idealism of the *Critique of Pure Reason*,[31] *when it is applied to the realm of the experience of the intentional*, would have presumably made him join Wittgenstein in the conviction that Oblomov altogether lacked the dispositions that amount to having thoughts. And I am suggesting that this amounts to a transcendental idealism about intentionality, because it says that without the perspective of freedom there can be no experience of intentionality, any more than there can be the objective experience of an external world without the contributions of what Kant called 'understanding'. The perspective of freedom constitutes intentionality; it is not some further thing that subjects have over and above having intentional dispositions which are then activated by this perspective. Though I will not show it here, Kant, I believe, held this view of thought. And it is a view exactly parallel to his idea, crudely put, that our concept of cause, say, constitutes our experience of an objective world, and is not something that we happen to have and apply to an objective experience that is 'there anyway' independent of our concept of causality.[32]

The first-person or agent's perspective thus constitutes our dispositions in a way that makes *our* interest in them something necessarily absent from *someone else*'s perspective on them, whence they might seem quite reducible in principle, and whence there can be no freedom of the agent involved in the prospect that these dispositions may be something that

---

[30] I. Kant, *Foundations for the Metaphysics of Morals*, trans. Lewis White Beck (Indianapolis: Bobbs–Merrill Company, Inc., 1959).

[31] I. Kant, *The Critique of Pure Reason*, trans. Norman Kemp Smith (London: Macmillan, 1929).

[32] Strictly speaking, of course, free agents cannot qualify as objects of empirical knowledge within Kant's system—precisely because they are free, and hence defy the causal determination in terms of which he defines all objects of empirical knowledge. For this reason, it might seem odd to some that I should characterize the perspective of freedom as the *epistemological* perspective of self-knowledge. But if we want to allow that agents are ever objects of self-knowledge—and here I mean *qua* agents—then the perspective of freedom must be brought in. And my point is that it must be brought in in a way that shares the basic features of Kant's framework of transcendental idealism: there is a feature of agency which is crucial to the self-knowledge of agents which they themselves must contribute, and which they cannot think of as being there independently of their own nature as self-knowing agents who engage in evaluative activities (just as subjects of experience must not think of space and time as being there independently of their own nature as things with sensibility).

he can try to control or modify in the light of his normative stances. Of course, others, taking a third-person perspective on him, may try to control his dispositions too; but in doing so, they will necessarily, treat him as an object, and think of his mental life from an angle that makes it in principle reducible. It is only if others respect an angle that *he* has on his own dispositions that they will acknowledge that *from that point of view* (his, not theirs) there is an aspect of his mental life which is not dispositional but fully and genuinely intentional (an area of mental life which is peopled with commitments or normative stances, not dispositions) and which therefore is irreducible. It is only if they reason with him internally, by acknowledging his commitments or normative stances and appealing to *them*, that they would be respecting an angle that he alone has upon his dispositions.

This point has deep reverberations in this chapter's question about self-knowledge.

It would be a most satisfying solution to the problem of accounting for the special character of *self*-knowledge if the *very thing* that accounted for its *non*-perceptual character accounted also for the fact that *other* kinds of knowledge were indeed *perceptual*, by contrast. That would be more satisfying, for a philosopher anyway, than if the one kind of knowledge (self-knowledge) was accounted for by one sort of thing and other kinds of knowledge by another sort of thing, because philosophers want to account here not just for the difference but for the asymmetry. The appeal to Strawson (and the whole question of freedom and agency in this chapter) has been made precisely with a view to identifying such a *common* resource, a single resource for such an accounting of *both* these things at once. For though it is a central conclusion of this essay that efforts to account for the asymmetry between self-knowledge and other kinds of knowledge have to go deeper than has perhaps hitherto been noticed, its point has also been that it has to go *no* deeper than the effort of noticing that the perspective of freedom resides uniquely in our angle on our own thoughts which no one else can have on them. That simply *is* the relevant asymmetry.

In the past, philosophers have found the idea of freedom in a deterministic universe a mystery. More recently, they have found the asymmetry between our knowledge of our own thoughts and our knowledge of others and the world another kind of mystery. If I am right, these are the same mystery. And one small sign of progress in philosophy might be measured by the fact that we can sometimes reduce two mysteries to one.[33]

---

[33] This last claim and argument, and indeed all the basic claims and arguments of this chapter, are developed at much greater length in my forthcoming *Self-Knowledge and Intentionality* (Cambridge, Mass.: Harvard University Press).

8

Reason and the First Person

TYLER BURGE

———◆———

A small but persistent tradition in philosophy insists that there is a large divide between knowledge of one's thoughts and attitudes, and knowledge of one's thoughts and attitudes *as* one's own. The introduction of the *I* concept (please allow this convenient barbarism) has been characterized as a misleading, or at any rate momentous, step in need of special argument.[1] Hume complained that he could not find a self when he introspected.[2] He wondered whether 'the self' was simply an evolving

[1] By the *I* concept or (ignoring the plural *we* for now) the first-person concept, I intend an indexical concept shared by fully mature language-users by virtue of their mastery and understanding of the term 'I', or exact translations thereof. This is only a rough reference-fixing explication. I do not assume (though I think it may be true) that only language-users have the relevant full first-person concept. The main argument of the essay does not depend on any very exact understanding of what is essential to having the concept. But I assume that having what I call the full first-person concept involves having other concepts and conceptual abilities that go beyond mere egocentric awareness—for example, concepts of thought and agency and some re-identification or self-tracking abilities. I believe that autonomous use of the full first-person concept is possible only for persons, and that it applies to entities of a certain important kind—persons or selves, which I take to be by nature (in part) critical reasoners. But the argument of the essay does not depend on, or establish, this view either. Nor does it depend on distinguishing this concept from lower-level egocentric sensitivities or modes of reference (even perhaps egocentric concepts) utilized by animals that are not persons. The argument I shall give only supports the view that necessarily when critical reasoners use the full first-person concept, it fulfils certain functions. I want to start with a notion that is relatively noncommittal from a theoretical point of view and assume that it is familiar. I think it would be a mistake to get into deep issues about ontology of persons, selves, and concepts, or fine-grained issues about concept-individuation, in advance of considering the argument I will offer as applied to a recognizable element in intentional thought contents that is commonly expressed with the word 'I'. Concepts are elements in intentional thought contents. If one wants to avoid calling intentional indexical elements in intentional thought contents 'concepts', one can find a different terminology. The key assumption is that there is a structural intentional element or aspect of thought that is shared by all thoughts properly expressed using the first-person singular pronoun. I am interested in the role and epistemic status of this element or aspect.

[2] David Hume, *A Treatise of Human Nature*, I. iv. 6.

bundle of sensations and ideas, which he thought he *could* find in introspection. Lichtenberg suggested that Descartes' *cogito* is less certain, or more objectionable, than an impersonal substitute: He recommended that one substitute *a thinking that there are physical objects is occurring* for *I am thinking that there are physical objects*. He wrote:

We are acquainted only with the existence of our sensations, imaginations, and thoughts. 'Thinking is going on' (*Es denkt*) is what one should say, just as one says, 'Lightning is occurring' (*Es blitzt*). Saying '*Cogito*' is too much, as soon as one translates it as 'I am thinking'. Accepting, postulating, the *I* is a practical requirement.[3]

Some have extrapolated these suggestions to the point of holding that there is something suspect about the use of the *I* concept to indicate an individual. A few have held that it is epistemically and metaphysically appropriate to dispense with the *I* concept altogether.

Lichtenberg's epigrammatic remarks provide a text for my discussion. Let me begin by taking up his emphasis on acquaintance. Lichtenberg is surely right, as was Hume before him, in claiming that what yields a usage for the *I* concept is not an acquaintance with something. We do not seem to 'introspect' a self. A view loosely associated with Hume maintains that since we cannot introspect a self, we should not regard *I* as having a referent. I mention this view only to set it aside. It stems from empiricist dogma so crude as not to merit serious consideration. There is no reason to accord such weight to the notions of acquaintance and looking-within in arbitrating an issue about reference or self-knowledge.

One could advance a less dogmatic point along similar lines, however. Lichtenberg's and Hume's observation that we are not directly acquainted with a self might be combined with the view that we do 'introspect' our thoughts, or at any rate have more immediate access to them. Then 'postulating' an agent (to echo Lichtenberg's words)— an agent in addition to the thought itself—may seem like a significant *step* that might be doubted. The result of forgoing the *I* concept, and making do with impersonal reference to thinking's going on, may seem less subject to doubt than the *cogito* itself.

It is not clear in what sense we 'introspect' thoughts, any more than we do a self. Thoughts present no inner-perceptual resistance (as perceptions of a physical object do); they commonly have no phenomenology. Moreover, the notions of acquaintance and introspection are elusive. They can hardly be taken as firm tools for understanding these matters. Still, we do, sometimes, 'run through' thoughts. In such cases, we seem to

---

[3] G. C. Lichtenberg, *Schriften und Briefe*, ii (Carl Hanser Verlag, 1971), 412, §76.

have some occurrent grasp or understanding of them. There is, as far as I can see, no analogous occurrent grasp of a self. If one were impressed with this difference, one might sympathize with the view that the move from awareness of a current thought to the assumption of a self involves a *step* that is problematic in a way that the awareness of the thought is not.

But there is something misleading about this reasoning. It is entirely external to actual uses of *cogito*-like thoughts. For someone who has the *I* concept, there is no step from recognition of the occurrence of a thought to the conclusion that there must be a self. There is no step, inference, or postulation at all. There is no identification of a self based on awareness or based on anything. Normally one simply applies the first-person concept immediately, not in *response* to anything. Such applications fall under the rule that the referent is the author of the thought. Given that the first-person concept is applied, there is no possibility of reference failure. And if one's ascription of the thought to oneself is immediate and non-inferential in this way, there is no possibility of misattribution or misidentification of the thinker of the thought.

The claim of differential certainty based on considerations of relative closeness to introspection seems uninteresting. The epistemic issues do not concern missteps within one's cognitive economy. Moreover, the character of the rule that governs reference with the first-person concept suggests that the introspectionist or perceptual model is mistaken. Mastering the first-person concept is sufficient to guarantee that applications will be successful. This suggests that the epistemic warrant associated with applications of the concept comes with mastery of the concept—and is non-empirical. It does not derive from experiences associated with particular applications of the concept. I shall return to this point.

In so far as we are to find a philosophically interesting challenge in Lichtenberg's remarks, I think that we must associate them with issues about the point and commitments of the first-person concept. The challenge is that acquisition of the *I* concept contains some error, or at least is dispensable for cognitive purposes.

Some have held that the first-person concept carries an objectionable commitment to mental substance separable from physical entities. I think this a mistake caused by overreaction to Descartes' claims to derive dualism from mere reflection on the *cogito*. Uses of the *I* concept make no obvious commitment regarding the metaphysical nature of its referent, other than that it be an author of thoughts. Deriving metaphysical implications from this commitment would require further argument, which would have to be evaluated on its merits.

But Lichtenberg seems not to be raising a question about the nature of thinkers. He is questioning whether there are thinkers—referents of applications of the first-person concept—at all. Or at any rate, he is questioning whether belief in their existence, via judgements involving application of the first-person concept, stands on an epistemic par with knowledge of the existence of thoughts.

An issue often raised about Descartes' use of the *cogito* is whether one could refer to oneself in the first-person way if one did not have various perceptual experiences that enabled one to individuate oneself, or at least re-identify oneself over time. This question was raised sharply by Kant and has been pressed by Strawson and others in modern times. Sometimes it is inferred that one could not have purely intellectual knowledge of oneself or of one's thoughts as one's own; for self-knowledge inevitably depends on perceptual experience. But to know that certain thoughts are occurring, we seem only to have to think about the matter.

It is surely true that self-knowledge and the mastery of the first-person concept depend on perceptual experience. But it does not follow that reference with the first-person concept, or knowledge of oneself through employment of the first-person concept, rests for its justification on sense experiences. It is important here to distinguish dependence on sense experience for the mastery of concepts—ability dependence—from dependence on sense experience for fixing a reference or for being justified in or entitled to one's judgements. Perhaps understanding any concept—including logical ones—depends on having sense experiences of stable objects. But it does not follow that the reference of all concepts is fixed through sense experience.

The referent of a use of the *I* concept is *not* fixed by sensory experience. It is fixed purely by the rule: the referent is the author of the occurrence of thought containing application of the *I* concept. No perceptual ability to track that author enters into fixing the referent in any given instances.

The role of sensory experience in justification of *cogito*-like judgements is equally indirect. Although the very thinking of the thoughts depends on having had certain types of sensory experiences, one's epistemic right to accept such judgements does not rest on such experiences. The relevant judgements are not reactive. One does not find oneself in introspection and then make a judgement about what one is thinking. One does not, or need not, connect oneself with some body that one tracks through time and base one's first-person judgement about one's own thoughts on this connection. One simply makes the judgement. One's epistemic right to make it is, at least prima facie, purely intellectual. It does not rest on any warrant given by sense experiences epistemically associated with the judgement.

So the dependence of the conceptualized first-person perspective on having some third-person perspective on oneself or on other stable objects is not one that enters into the account of one's epistemic warrant for making such judgements. I think that Descartes was entirely right in his view that many first-person judgements are warranted through no more than their being understood. His being right about this in no way shows that it is coherent to conceive of someone with the *I* concept who takes only the first-person perspective. So Lichtenberg's claim that thoughts involving the first-person concept are epistemically less basic than thoughts (about thoughts) that lack that concept cannot be usefully developed by reflecting on the role of third-person perspectives in enabling us to think about ourselves.

There is, I think, a point about conceptual priority that one *can* usefully associate with Lichtenberg's remarks. They suggest the question of whether the *I* concept could be 'dispensed with'. On this line, one would employ only propositional attitude concepts impersonally attributed in Lichtenberg's format. Lichtenberg compares the thought *that thinking is going on* (*es denkt*) to the thought *that lightning is striking* (*es blitzt*). A closer grammatical equivalent in English to the German *es denkt* would be *it is thundering* (*es donnert*). What would be lost if one followed Lichtenberg in using only these conceptions?

For the sake of argument I will not take a position on whether it is possible to have the concept of propositional attitudes, or even to reason critically, yet lack the full first-person concept. (To reason critically in my sense, one must correct, suspend, change attitudes, conceived as such, on the basis of reasons acknowledged as such.) But I think that such beings would be conceptually deficient. They would lack a full conceptual perspective on themselves and their acts. I want to explain the deficiency and indicate what epistemic rights attach to self-attributions of thoughts containing the full first-person concept. I would like to do this without begging questions against Lichtenberg's position. I will develop an answer to Lichtenberg that assumes only what he is surely committed to: that reasoning occurs, and that it is a worthwhile theoretical enterprise to understanding reason and reasoning.

Given this objective, I will neglect other answers to Lichtenberg that I think obvious and sufficient in themselves. For example, I think that the idea of mental states and events without an individual *subject* is incoherent. Thinking requires an agent that thinks. For *persons* who think, the first-person concept makes possible reference to themselves from the perspective most basic to their thinking.

One can take the dependence of mental states on a subject further back ontogenetically. Consider subjects which have phenomenal or intentional states, but which by their nature lack critical reason—and hence, in my view, are not persons and are not (or lack) selves. The very existence of perceptual states or sensations—even in the absence of propositional ability—requires a subject, an individual with subjectivity or consciousness. Perceptual systems of lower animals require a subject; and it is clear that those systems have some sort of non-conceptual egocentric sensitivity. Similarly, animals that think but by their nature lack critical reason lack selves; I think that they lack a full first-person concept. Their thinking too requires an individual subject. Animals with propositional attitudes certainly have non-conceptual egocentric sensitivity; perhaps they also have some indexical concept that applies to themselves and that is an ontogenetic predecessor of the full first-person concept. All these beings' mental states require a subject, whose subjectivity is a necessary aspect of their sensations, perceptions, or propositional attitudes (cf. n. 1).

Lichtenberg's format ignores the conceptual requirement that such states and events presuppose an individual subject with a subjective perspective. Egocentric sensitivities or concepts mark this perspective. I think that these truisms are decisive. Pursuing them might carry us further into the nature of persons or selves and into the ontological and ontogenetic roots of the first-person concept.

But my project here is not primarily to determine the nature or ontology of persons or selves, or the range and variety of egocentric sensitivity and conceptualization. It is to answer Lichtenberg's epigrammatic challenge to explicate the cognitive role and epistemic status of the first-person perspective, assuming only things about reason that Lichtenberg is committed to. Thus my argument will not depend on how one views the relation between persons and animals, or between selves and mere subjects. It does not even depend on my view that only beings whose natures make them capable of critical reason can have the full first-person concept. It depends only on an argument that that concept has a certain necessary and unique role in fully understanding reasoning.

So what does Lichtenberg's format leave out?[4] One deficiency is articulated by Bernard Williams. Williams points out that Lichtenberg's formulation, 'Thinking is going on', needs 'relativization'—intuitively, to a thinker or point of view. For there is a distinction between cases in which we regard thinkings of mutually contradictory propositions

---

[4] One relatively minor intuitive deficiency is that there is no self-referentiality or self-verification in Lichtenberg's purported analogies to the *cogito*. Even laying aside issues about the first-person concept, the realization that thinking is going on is different from the realization that it is thundering. The former realization is, or will become on reflection, self-referential, and not subject to illusion or error. This difference could be admitted by Lichtenberg. He could simply understand *thinking is going on* as *thinking is in this very thought going on*.

as indicative of a violation of a law of logic and cases in which we regard them as indicative of disagreement. Similarly, there is a distinction between cases in which a thinking that p and a thinking that q indicate some normative pressure in the direction of a thinking that p and q—and cases in which there is no such pressure. The first case in each pair intuitively involves thoughts by a single thinker (at roughly the same time). The second case in each pair involves thoughts by different thinkers, or within different points of view.[5]

These points do force some sort of 'relativization'. But it is not evident from them alone what the relativization should be. Lichtenberg might still resist use of the *I* concept. He might maintain the impersonality of formulation that he began with. Derek Parfit has tried to remain true to Lichtenberg's spirit by providing a substitute for the *cogito* that makes explicit use of the notion of a point of view: *In the point of view or life to which this thought belongs, thinking is, in this very thought, going on.*[6]

I will assume that the key element in Lichtenberg's position is captured by this proposal. The key element is a claim that full understanding of reason or cognition can dispense with the first-person concept: the concept has no special epistemic status or cognitive value. It has at most merely 'practical' uses.

I think that this position is untenable. To understand fully the fundamental notions associated with reason, including the notions of reasoning, judgement, change of mind, propositional attitude, point of view, one must have and employ a first-person concept. Indeed, understanding the notion of reason itself—epistemic or practical—requires the first-person concept. I will not prejudge whether one must *have* the *I* concept in order to have these other concepts. Here I will argue that any being that had concepts of propositional attitude, reason, change of mind,

[5] Bernard Williams, *Descartes: The Project of Pure Enquiry* (Harmondsworth: Penguin, 1978), 95–100. Williams does not pursue the question whether impersonal (third-person) specifications might replace the first-person way of specifying a subject that thinks, or even whether the reference must be to an agent. Williams accuses both Lichtenberg and Descartes of failing to provide a basis for individuating minds, and claims that some reference to physical bodies is necessary. In this, he follows Strawson, *Individuals* (Garden City, NY: Doubleday, 1959), 93–100.

[6] Derek Parfit, *Reasons and Persons* (Oxford: Clarendon Press, 1984), sects. 81, 88. Parfit goes beyond Williams in developing the questions whether the 'relativization' to a mind must specify a person in unreduced terms, and whether the specification must be with the *I* concept. He suggests a negative answer to both questions. He hopes to provide a reductive explanation of what a person is by specifying various sorts of continuity among mental states and events. And he purports to express the truth of the *cogito* by dispensing with the *I* concept in favour of self-referential demonstratives. The project of giving a reductive description of what persons are is not presently at issue. But the proposal to de-personalize the *cogito* will be the subject of what follows.

and so on, but lacked an *I* concept, would be conceptually deficient in the sense that it would lack the conceptual resources to understand fully the most basic necessary and apriori knowable features of the relevant notions. The notions of reason and first-personhood are, at the deepest levels, necessarily and apriori involved in understanding one another.

Reasoning is necessarily governed by evaluative norms that provide standards that count reasoning good or bad—reasonable or unreasonable. But to understand reasons and reasoning fully, it is not enough to understand abstractly that some purported reasons are good and others are bad. For reasons necessarily not only evaluate but have force in forming, changing, confirming attitudes in accord with the reasons. All reasons that thinkers have are *reasons-to*, not merely rational appraisals. But to understand reasons and reasoning, it is also not enough that one understand that rational evaluations should be, and normally (in thinkers) are, associated with some motive or impulse to think or act in accord with the reason or rational evaluation. One must, further, have and understand this motive or impulse in one's own case, and actually apply reasons as rational evaluations to affect judgement and action—to support a judgement, change an attitude, or engage in action. In other words, fully understanding the concept of reason involves not merely mastering an evaluative system for appraising attitudes or relations between thoughts, and not merely realizing abstractly that in any reasoning such evaluations must be (somehow) associated with a motivating impulse to implement them. It requires mastering and conceptualizing the application of reasons in actual reasoning. And this requires being immediately moved by reasons in reasoning and understanding what it is to be so moved. There are thus applicational, or implementational, and motivational elements in understanding reasons.

These motivational elements are intrinsic to a broad notion of agency. I do not mean by 'motivational' to imply some interposition of desire or motive or volition. I mean that to understand reasons one must know how to use reasons, and indeed actually use them, to support or change one's own attitudes in one's own thinking practice. To understand the notion of reason, one must be susceptible to reasons. Reasons must have force for one, and one must be able to appreciate that force. Considerations seen as reasons must have some tendency to affect one's judgements and inferences according to the norms associated with the reasons. And one must recognize that this is so.

Having reasons and having some capacity to be moved by them—to think or otherwise act on account of them—are necessarily connected. The connection is not that everyone who has reasons must at every moment have some tendency to be moved by them. One can perhaps imagine schizophrenics or mystics or quietists lacking such a tendency some of the time. But to have reasons one must, I think, have had some tendency to have one's thoughts and attitudes be affected by them. Beings who have reasons must sometimes be in continuing, uncoopted control of some events, in the sense that the events are a direct guided product of the reasoner's central rational powers. Events guided by reasons issuing from a thinker's uncoopted central rational powers (from the thinker *qua* individual) are acts, as are the guiding events.

So in reasoning, no thinker can be a mere observer of reasons and their effects on reasoning. For having reason requires at some point having some tendency to be affected by reason's power in motivating reasoning. *Understanding* what a reason is, is partly understanding its motive force, as well as its evaluative norms. To understand reason and reasoning, this force must be operative in one's own case; and one must conceptualize its implementation. That is, one must be susceptible to the force and implement normative evaluations in guiding thought and other acts that fall under those evaluations; and (to understand reasoning), one must regard reasons as effective in one's judgements, inferences, and other activity. Doing so amounts to an acknowledgement of one's agency. If one conceptualizes this fully, one recognizes oneself as an agent. Here we see a point about agency that Lichtenberg missed in comparing thinking to lightning's occurring. Thinking is necessarily associated with reasoning—thinking guided by reasons—and reasoning cannot in general be a mere 'going on'. In making inferences, a being is *ipso facto* an agent.

Let me depart from the main line of argument to elaborate these remarks about agency. The relevant effects of reasons are effects on one's judgements, inferences, and other acts. In recognizing the effect of reasons on one's judgements and inferences, one cannot reasonably think of oneself as powerless. Reasons give one reason to make, change, or confirm a judgement or inference. Recognition of a contradiction in one's attitudes gives one reason to change them. Recognition that one's means will not suffice for one's end gives one reason to change one's means or end. To understand reasons, one must understand their force and application in one's reasoning. To understand their force and application one must have some tendency normally to make them effective in forming, changing, or confirming one's attitudes or inferences.

An instance of this sort of point is commonly associated with a view about moral reasons—the view that reasons that are associated with obligation or with a good must, at least in normal cases and given that the person understands the reasons, be associated with some sort of motivation. This view is shared by many who differ over the relation between reason and motivation (whether, for example, the motivation must reside in an independent desire and is a prior condition on a reason, or derives from understanding the reason itself). The point is normally applied to what are commonly called practical reasons. I think that it is embedded in the broader, less restrictive notion of reason, and applies no more to practical reasons and practical agency than to epistemic reasons and epistemic agency. The notions of agency and practice that I am explicating are broader, and I think more fundamental, than the standard notions of action and practical reason.

I return to the main line of argument. Reasons must sometimes provide immediate reason to—must sometimes be rationally applicable to affect an attitude or action—*immediately*. On pain of regress, in actual reasoning one cannot require a premise or further reason for applying reasons, for implementing rational evaluations. In reasoning, reasons must have force in a way that is obvious and straightway. The rational relevance of reasons to their first implementation within one's thought must be rationally necessary and rationally immediate.

A fully explicit understanding of reason must be capable of marking conceptually the cases in reasoning where evaluating or appraising attitudes or activity under rational norms rationally motivates *immediate* implementation of the evaluations in shaping the attitudes or activity being evaluated. One can evaluate a system of attitudes (in another person or in the abstract) as unreasonable without its being immediately rational for one to change those particular attitudes, or even immediately rational that those attitudes be changed from the perspective in which implementation has to occur. To understand reason one must distinguish conceptually from such cases those cases where particular evaluations immediately rationally require being moved to affect the attitudes or activities being evaluated in accord with the evaluations.

These distinctions are knowable apriori. We can know apriori not only the distinction between evaluation and implementation. We can also know apriori how to conceptualize and recognize instances where implementation is immediately incumbent, and understand wherein these instances are relevantly different from cases where an evaluation of attitudes does not rationally demand immediate implementation of the evaluation on the attitudes being evaluated.

Many thinkers with reasons—many animals, I think—cannot mark the distinction. They lack full understanding of reason. They have not conceptualized what is fundamentally involved in reasoning. Full understanding of reasoning requires a form of thought that marks conceptually those particular attitudes where implementation on those attitudes of a rational evaluation of those attitudes is rendered immediately rationally incumbent by the evaluation.

The first-person concept fills this function. Its association with a thought ('I think . . .', 'I judge . . .', 'I infer . . .') marks, makes explicit, the immediate rational relevance of invocation of reasons to rational application, or implementation, and motivation. It both designates the agent of thought and marks the acts and attitudes where a rational evaluation of the act or attitude immediately rationally requires using that evaluation to change or maintain the attitude. Acknowledgement of a reason for or against an act or attitude to which one attaches, or can attach, one of these forms of 'I think' makes it immediately rationally incumbent on one to give the reason weight in making the act or attitude accord with it.

Acknowledging, with the *I* concept, that an attitude or act is one's own is acknowledging that rational evaluations of it which one also acknowledges provide immediate (possibly defeasible) reason and rationally immediate motivation to shape the attitude or act in accordance with the evaluation. Unless further evaluations of the attitude must be taken into account, there need be no further intervening reasoning involved for it to be rational to have the reason affect the attitude or act. The first-person concept fixes the locus of responsibility and marks the immediate rational relevance of a rational evaluation to rational implementation on the attitude being evaluated—to epistemic or practical agency.[7]

First-person concepts, of which the singular is paradigmatic, are, I think, the only ones that fill this function. (I lay aside the plural 'we', though I think this notion deserves reflection.) Let me try to make this claim plausible by considering alternatives.

One can attribute irrationality to a judgement of the form 'It is judged that . . .'. But such an assessment makes explicit no immediate reason to change the commitment being evaluated, for the judgement is not attached to anyone who makes the judgement. The assessment marks no locus of responsibility or power associated with the judgement. One can conclude only that someone has reason to change the judgement.

Judgements in third-person form—like 'She judges that . . .' and 'Burge judges that . . .'—do identify an author of the judgement. So they do identify a locus of power, responsibility to norms of reason, and rational motive. But these forms cannot mark the immediate rational

[7] John Perry, 'The Problem of the Essential Indexical', Nous, 13 (1979), 3–21, repr. in *The Problem of the Essential Indexical* (Oxford: Oxford University Press, 1993), insightfully makes the point that attribution of beliefs involving the first-person indexical is essential to the explanation of certain actions. Perry does not connect the point to fundamental features of reason, or to the broader notion of agency, that includes mental agency, that I have highlighted.

relevance of a rational assessment to modifying or standing by the judgement. Here the notion of *immediacy* is significant. I want to clarify the role of this notion in the account.

As I have noted, reasons enjoin thinking or acting in accordance with them. And anyone who has a reason normally has some motive force for implementing it in thought or action. But there is a further point. Anyone who has a reason that evaluates any act or attitude, no matter who is actor or subject of the attitude, has some rational motive— however attenuated—to affect the act or attitude in accordance with the reason. That is, reason has the *transpersonal function* of presenting true thoughts and guiding thought to truth, regardless of individual perspective or interest. This function is valid for any rational agent. But such a function operates only through the reasoning of individuals. So an individual's assessment of some judgement as irrational carries with it some prima-facie ground not only that it be altered—but some prima-facie ground to alter it, regardless of who the source of judgement is. But when the source is not understood to be oneself, the reason to implement the evaluation cannot be *immediate*, in at least two respects.

One respect has to do with the person- or system-dependence that attaches to the having of reasons. What may be a reasonable evaluation by person (or system) A of an attitude held by a person (or system) B may not be a reasonable evaluation for B. For example, if A knows something on which the reason is based that B does not know (and has no reflective access to), then A's reasonable evaluation cannot be immediately rationally applicable for B. B would have to acquire the additional background knowledge. Similarly, if A's all-things-considered reasonable evaluation of B's attitude were based on information that B had but which was superseded by knowledge that B had but A lacked, then A's all-things-considered reasonable evaluation of B's attitude could provide no all-things-considered rational motivation for B. Again, the rational applicability of A's rational evaluation of B's attitude would not be immediate. This is a variant of Williams's point, discussed earlier. The fact that it is reasonable for A to make an inference with premisses for which A has good reasons does not immediately imply that it is reasonable for B to make the inference, since B may lack reason to believe one or more of the premisses. Since mismatches in information on which reasons can be based are always possible, no rational evaluation that is not universally self-evident, however reasonable, has rationally immediate application, with consequences for immediate implementation, across persons or across points of view. As long as the attitude is not taken to be one's own, there is always the possibility of a gap, and filling that gap involves a rational step.

The second respect in which rational evaluations of attitudes not understood to be one's own are necessarily non-immediate in their implementation has to do with means. When the subject of the evaluated attitude is not understood to be oneself, one can propose to affect the attitude in accordance with the evaluation only non-immediately, by some *means*. One can propose to do so only by force or persuasion. One's power over, and responsibility for, the attitude (or activity) are not direct. So the question of how one is to bring about any alteration must inevitably arise. One cannot simply alter the thought immediately, with no intervening practical premises.

In one's own case, these questions do not normally arise. One may ask what element in one's point of view to modify in the face of reasons that count against a thought or an attitude. But, except in special cases, the rational relevance of reasons to implementation is direct, and does not pass through premises about means.

The special cases are cases in which an attitude is psychologically immovable in the ordinary way, or those in which one sees one's own attitudes as objects, rather than as parts of one's critically rational point of view. One may then have to reason about one's attitudes as if they were those of another person, perhaps even using methods of manipulation on oneself. But then there must be other attitudes and thoughts over which one has immediate power. If there were no such attitudes and thoughts, one would not be a reasoner at all.

So third-person attributions do not mark the immediate rational relevance of rational evaluation to implementation of the evaluation. Even when a third-person attribution is to oneself, the relevance is not rationally immediate. For one could fail to know that the third-person attribution applied to oneself. I could fail to know that I am Burge. And although I do know, the *rational* relevance of reasons to their affecting my attitudes is not conceptually immediate. It must pass through the assumption that I am Burge.

Even third-person attributions that draw on the epistemology of first-person authority do not mark the immediate relevance of reasons to reasoning. For example, the Lichtenberg-like formulation—'in the point of view or life to which this thought belongs, it is being judged, in this very thought, that . . .'—does not do so. Such a specification constitutes no acknowledgement of proprietary power over, or responsibility for, the thought, much less a locus of power and responsibility. There is nothing in the content of 'this very thought' that ensures that it is one's own and makes for immediacy of rational evaluation to rational implementation. We tend to presume that *all and only* thoughts referred to that way, and that can be known non-inferentially, *are* one's own.

But there is no rational necessity that this be so. Even if there were, understanding the necessity would require that one make explicit that such thoughts are necessarily one's own. And doing this would require use of the first-person concept. So any presumption of immediacy associated with such conceptualizations relies on an implicit premiss identifying the thoughts as one's own. Lacking such a premiss, the rational relevance of reasons to implementation is not immediate.

Similarly, specifications of oneself like 'the thinker of this very thought judges that . . .' or 'the agent of the point of view that contains this very thought thinks that . . .' do not do so. They do specify a locus of power. But they do not acknowledge proprietary power over, and responsibility for, the thought. They are simply objectively descriptive of the thought's owner. Such specifications express a point of view on oneself from the outside.

The relevance of third-person self-descriptions, and of the Lichtenbergean description of a 'point of view', to implementation of rational evaluations is not rationally immediate. They depend on connection to the first-person conception. The premiss that one is the relevant thinker—or that one is the author of the relevant point of view—is necessary for making the description immediately rationally relevant to connecting reasons to their application in reasoning.

Only the acknowledgement of authorship or ownership for thoughts or attitudes makes conceptually explicit the immediate rational connection between rational assessment of those thoughts and the affecting of the attitudes according to the norms of the assessment. Any way of thinking of oneself, or of one's point of view, that does not carry this acknowledgement conceptualizes associated attributed attitudes as objects of thought, but not necessarily and immediately ones to reason with in accordance with the evaluations.

Recognition that a thought is one's own—taking up the subjectivity and proprietary ownership expressed in the first-person concept—is the only basis for conceptually expressing having a rationally immediate and necessary reason to tend a point of view, to make the reasons effective on the attitudes they evaluate. Attributions of attitudes in first-person form instantiate recognition of ownership and power of agency, and of the rationally immediate motive force and implementational encumbency of reasons. Rational activity presupposes a distinctive rational role for the first-person singular concept.

Much of the content of science and mathematics includes no first-person elements. Scientific writing leaves out such elements on principle. Such omission acknowledges the transpersonal function of reason. It also acknowledges the fact that theory and evidence in these disciplines are perspective-independent, in the sense that anyone could have made the same observations or come to the same theory. But the application of reasons within such theorizing—indeed, the very notion of reason—nevertheless presupposes the first-person concept. Understanding reason and the objective point of view of science and mathematics is inseparable from taking on and acknowledging explicitly a first-person way of thinking.

The reason why this is so is that reason has an essential relation to reasoning, to the *practice* of being moved by reasons. The practice of reason, not just the form and content of reasons, is inseparable from the nature of reason. Having reason and having a reason are essentially associated with some impetus to think or otherwise act in accordance with reason. Understanding reason requires being inclined to be affected or motivated by reasons—to form, change, or confirm beliefs or other attitudes in accordance with them—when those reasons apply to one's own attitudes. So understanding reason entails some optimism and commitment regarding the possibility and effect of reason in one's thinking. Here Lichtenberg was on to something deep in the last remark of the passage we began with: 'Accepting, postulating, the *I* is a practical requirement.' Despite the misleading point about postulation, and despite the fact that Lichtenberg was wrongly thinking of a practical requirement as in some opposition to epistemic or theoretical requirements, the linkage of the first-person concept with practice is on to a fundamental point.

Let me summarize the main line of argument. To fully understand basic features of the concept of reason, it is not enough to understand the concept in the abstract. It is not enough to understand the evaluation of attitudes or thoughts as being reasonable or unreasonable. And it is not enough to understand, in the abstract, that reasons enjoin and normally motivate thinking or acting in accordance with the normative standards that they set. Fully understanding the concept of reason also requires engaging in reasoning, and understanding basic features of such reasoning. Engaging in reasoning requires implementing reasons or rational evaluations immediately on the attitudes to which the reasons or rational evaluations apply—being moved to think in accordance with one's reasons. Understanding basic features of such reasoning requires understanding such implementation. Fully conceptualizing and understanding such implementation requires an ability to mark conceptually, in actual particular instances, the attitudes or acts for which it is rationally immediate that one's all-things-considered reason or rational evaluation of the attitude or act enjoins shaping it in accord with the reason or rational evaluation. Such understanding requires being able to distinguish those attitudes from attitudes in which one's all-things-considered evaluation of the attitude indicates (as always) that the attitude should be shaped in accordance with the evaluation, but in which this indication does not presume to be all-things-considered in the point of view from which the implementation must be carried out. That is the implementational relevance is not rationally immediate: it is subject to further possible rational considerations that bear on the rational appropriateness of its implementation. The first-person concept marks the former set of attitudes. Its use marks those attitudes where the individual's rational evaluation of them carries a rationally immediate incumbency to shape the attitude in accord with the evaluation. Acknowledging them as one's own is acknowledging such responsibility. The first-person concept is the only concept that fills this function in the actual practice of reasoning. So fully understanding the concept of reason, and engaging in reasoning in the most reflective and articulated way, require having the *I* concept and being able to apply it for this purpose.

I have summarized this argument in a way that brings out that it does not beg the question against Lichtenberg. It assumes only that Lichtenberg is committed to understanding reason and reasoning. The argument shows that the first-person concept is indispensable to a full understanding of reason, including theoretical reason. Given the understanding of agency expressed earlier, and given the fact that thinking presupposes reasoning, the argument yields a corollary—thinking presupposes agency. Each of these points is incompatible with the view I have associated with Lichtenberg.

The argument also undermines the view that the first-person concept is of *merely* practical significance. As I noted, Lichtenberg holds that accepting the first-person concept is a 'practical requirement'. The context suggests that practical requirements are to be distinguished from more 'substantive' requirements that might be relevant to knowledge or reality. But the first-person concept is essential to understanding reasoning of any sort—theoretical or practical. The understanding involved in marking conceptually, through the first-person concept, individual cases where rational evaluation of attitudes rationally requires immediate implementation of the evaluation on the evaluated attitudes is no less theoretical than practical. In fact, a sharp distinction between the theoretical and the practical makes no sense at this level of reflection. Any reasoning necessarily involves agency. Fully understanding all reason and all reasoning requires the first-person concept. So the first-person concept is as relevant to metaphysics and scientific reasoning as it is to 'merely practical' matters.

Thus the role of the first-person concept in understanding reason cannot be taken as 'merely practical' in a way that would undermine the natural idea that uses of the concept *refer*. I have in effect provided an argument, as if one were needed, that such uses do refer: True accounts of subject-matters of theoretical importance are committed to referents for their irreducible singular terms. True accounts of the nature of reasoning are theoretically important and are irreducibly committed to uses of the first-person concept. Uses of the first-person concept constitute uses of a singular term. So in being committed to such accounts, we are committed to referents for uses of the first-person concept.

It is not my purpose to rebut attempts to show that the first-person concept is non-singular, or attempts to challenge the standard view of referential commitment just sketched. I know of no interesting, clear-headed challenges of these sorts to the ordinary view that uses of the first-person concept refer. To this extent, Descartes and common sense are confirmed.[8] My main purpose, however, has not been to argue reference, but to establish the role of the first-person concept in understanding reason and reasoning.

The first-person concept plays a central role in apriori understanding of reason, agency, and ourselves. I want to say a little about the place I have given understanding in this account. I have not argued that to reason, in the weak sense of making good inferences, one must *have* the first-person concept. I think that animals engage in rudimentary thinking, which (given that it *is* thinking) constitutively occurs in normal cases according to norms of reason. Inferential thinking is caused or guided by reasons, and is explained by their being reasons. But animals lack the first-person concept that interests me. They have some sensitivity to their own points of view, but I think that they lack the conceptualized self-attributions necessary to employ a full-blown first-person concept.

I have not even argued that engaging in *critical* reasoning—the sort that evaluates attitudes as reasonable or unreasonable, and that shapes attitudes according to such evaluations—requires, by necessity, having a first-person concept. I have not argued this because I think the relevant issues need further clarification. In our actual social development, it is of course true that one acquires the first-person concept before or during the development of critical reasoning. The hard issue is whether

---

[8] As I noted earlier, I do not think that Cartesian dualism can be inferred from applications of the first-person concept. But I do think that the concept's cognitive role is relevant to metaphysics and epistemology. The argument just sketched helps show why it is mistaken to embrace the strange idea that Lichtenberg's remarks have sometimes inspired—that thinking is best seen (perhaps best seen for 'metaphysical' purposes) as going on without a thinker, or that the first-person concept never literally has a reference. Note that the earlier argument that thinking requires agency also tends to undermine this view, in so far as it is especially hard to conceive of agency without an agent. It is not an accident that Lichtenberg's formulations gravitate to locutions that do not attribute agency. In so far as the first-person concept is necessary to a full understanding of any sort of reason, including theoretical reason, there is no room to see its implications as dispensable or merely practical.

this order is necessary and knowable by apriori reflection. On the other hand, we can certainly imagine critical reasoning proceeding without explicit *linguistic* expression of a first-person point of view. Whether it is necessary and knowable by apriori reflection that the first-person point of view be *implicitly* conceptualized whenever critical reasoning occurs is the delicate matter that I have left open.

So I have allowed, for the sake of the present argument, that a critical reasoner might lack the full first-person concept. Such a reasoner would conceptualize reasons and attitudes as such, and would be sensitive to cases where attitudes had to be shaped immediately by reasons. But the reasoner could not mark those cases conceptually in the implementation of reasoning.

Critical reasoning is the sort of reasoning that we associate with the nobility of being a person, with science, mathematics, art, practical reasoning, and with rational enquiry of all kinds. So supposing for the sake of argument that such reasoning does not require having the first-person concept, what philosophical significance is there in the argument that one cannot *understand* reason (*a fortiori* critical reason) without that concept?[9]

I want to highlight two types of significance. One stems from the sort of understanding that is involved. The understanding is apriori, and can be derived from reflection on fundamental aspects of the nature and functions of reason. I maintain that every step of the argument which established the role of the first-person concept in fully understanding reason is apriori.

Such understanding can be derived from reflection—on concepts and on actual reasoning. And it is not part of some esoteric theorizing about reason. It normally arises from the most elementary cognitive development in a social setting.[10] Uses of the first-person concept in claiming acts or attitudes as one's own are normal acknowledgements of authorship and responsibility in critical reasoning. They are part of a full expression of what it is to be reasonable. A being that reasoned but lacked a first-person concept would not have conceptualized or rationally expressed a *fundamental* function of reason. Being able to conceptualize, for implementation in reasoning, the cases where there is a rational demand and motivation immediately to shape evaluated attitudes in accordance with the evaluation is placing under conceptual control one

---

[9] I owe this question to Barry Stroud.

[10] Thus, although it is a delicate question whether critical reasoners metaphysically *must* have the first-person concept, it is certainly normal for critical reasoners to have it; and the concept enters into ordinary understanding of those critical activities that mark their nobility.

of the most basic functions of critical reasoning. Use of the first-person concept is a conceptual expression of one of the central functions of reason.

As a consequence, use of the concept is underwritten by reason. We are entitled to first-person concepts in judgements partly because they are necessary to the fully articulated exercise (as well as understanding) of reason. The first-person concept earns its place in the general non-empirical entitlement to self-attributions of thoughts partly through its constitutive association with a particular fundamental feature of critical reasoning.

Thus I believe that I have provided a rational 'deduction', in Kant's sense, of the first-person concept. I have shown that we have a right to use the concept, a right that is grounded in reason. The steps of this exposition of right are warranted apriori. Moreover, the points that I have made about the dependence of our understanding of reason on practice—actual applications—and on understanding practice suggest a sense in which our apriori understanding of the concept of reason, and of the first-person concept, is not purely 'analytic', in the sense of being grounded in abstract conceptual analysis.[11] Fully understanding the concept of reason requires understanding reasoning. Understanding reasoning requires use and understanding of the first-person concept. The relevant use and understanding resides in conceptualizing an awareness of the rationally immediate applicability of rational evaluations to affecting attitudes *in the actual practice of reason*. Such awareness must be an understanding of actual applications of reasoning. It cannot be obtained from conceptual analysis alone. So the 'deduction' is synthetic by any measure.

---

[11] I reject any conception of analyticity that claims truth independent of the way 'the world' (or a subject-matter) is. The notion of analyticity that applies simply to truths of logic plus definitions seems to me harmless if one does not build bad theory into one's understanding of logic or definitions. I am not hostile on principle to the third notion of analyticity—the one associated with analysis of concepts. But I am agnostic about how fruitful or important the notion is. There may be broader and narrower conceptions of such analysis. On the narrower, traditional conception, analysis must take the form of decomposition. On a broader conception, analysis might include any constitutive account of the nature of a concept partly or purely in terms of its relations to others. I am doubtful that there is any clear historical basis for calling truths that are the products of analysis in the broader sense 'analytic'. Conceptual truths that 'go beyond'—or depend on conceptual relations beyond—the putative components of a concept are, I think, traditionally counted synthetic. On the interpretation in terms of the narrower notion of analysis, I think that the conception of analyticity has nowhere near the importance accorded to it by Leibniz or even by Kant. I presume that analyses of either sort, like the truths of logic, are true not only in virtue of the nature of concepts, but in virtue of (presumably necessary) features of the world. Cf. my 'Philosophy of Language and Mind: 1950–1990', *Philosophical Review*, 101 (1992), esp. 3–11.

The second type of significance bears on the role of the first-person concept in conceptualizing rational agency. Part of being a fully rational agent is, in Kant's phrase, to act under an idea or concept of that agency. A being that lacked the first-person concept could be sensitive to the norms of reason, and might (I am conceding for the sake of argument) even sensitively shape its attitudes according to a *conception* of good and bad reasons and reasoning. But the agent would lack full conceptualization of what it is doing.

More specifically, it could not conceptualize cases in which reasons had immediate rational relevance to implementation of the reasons on the acts or attitudes that they bear on. It could not fully conceptualize its agency and acknowledge its responsibility to rational norms. It would not be 'acting under the idea' of its responsibility or agency. In so far as *full* intellectual (or any other) responsibility requires the capacity to understand the way norms govern agency and the capacity to acknowledge the responsibility, a being that lacked the first-person concept would not be fully responsible intellectually. It would not have a fully realized rational agency. Conceptualized self-consciousness seems a necessary condition for fully responsible agency. Using the first-person concept is necessary to being a fully realized person.

* * *

I want to step back now and consider briefly how this discussion of the role of the first-person concept in reasoning bears on self-knowledge and knowledge of other minds. This is a subject that needs fuller development on another occasion. But a brief sketch may place in a sharper light the preceding discussion.

Elsewhere I have maintained that self-knowledge has a special epistemic status by virtue of its role in critical reasoning. I argued that the nature of critical reasoning requires that some self-knowledge, that which is essential to rational review, must be epistemically different from observation of objects. I maintained that our epistemic entitlement to relevant self-attributions derives, in one sense, from the essential role of such judgements in critical reasoning.[12] The relevant self-knowledge is non-inferential and intellectually grounded. Whatever the details of this account, it is natural to think of self-knowledge as independent of perception of objects for its epistemic warrant.

How does self-knowledge differ from knowledge of other minds? A natural answer contrasts the intellectually grounded character of the relevant self-knowledge with the observationally based character of

---

[12] See my 'Our Entitlement to Self-Knowledge', *Proceedings of the Aristotelian Society*, 96 (1996), 91–116.

knowledge of other minds. The relevant self-knowledge is epistemically warranted by an immediate intellectual entitlement, one sanctioned by reason and present in a being with the right conceptual equipment as a consequence of his simply thinking normally. By contrast, according to this natural answer, knowledge of other minds is indirect in that it requires an empirical inference from the perceived behaviour of another being—or else it is drawn from complex criteria applied to observed behaviour. In any event, its epistemic warrant rests on perception of behaviour.

It may be that self-knowledge requires as a psychological condition that one have or have had knowledge of other minds. It might even be (though I doubt it) that it is impossible in some more metaphysical sense to know one's own mind without knowing another mind, or the existence of another mind. But, runs this natural reasoning, self-knowledge has an immediacy and non-empirical intellectual epistemic warrant that is not shared by knowledge of others' minds. Its warrant derives from intellection, whereas knowledge of other minds rests on sense-perceptual observation.

I think that the situation is more complicated. Both self-knowledge and knowledge of other minds can, of course, be inferential or perceptually grounded. But in my view both self-knowledge and knowledge of other minds can be epistemically immediate and epistemically grounded in intellectual, non-empirical entitlements. The fundamental epistemic differences between self-knowledge and knowledge of other minds are more subtle. I do not have the space to elaborate and defend my view that knowledge of other minds can be non-inferential and can rest on an intellectual, non-perceptual entitlement. But I will sketch the main line of reasoning.[13]

This sketch is necessary to motivate the point of this concluding section. The point will be this: The role of the first-person concept in reasoning illuminates a common source, as well as a key difference between self-knowledge and knowledge of other minds.

I think that we can have a non-empirical, apriori epistemic entitlement to knowledge of other minds through our intellectually grounded entitlement to accept our seeming understanding of speech as genuine understanding. We have an apriori entitlement to prima-facie reliance on our seeming understanding of an apparent utterance of content as genuine understanding.

A justification or entitlement is apriori if neither sense experiences

---

[13] Much of the reasoning that immediately follows is layed out in my 'Content Preservation', *Philosophical Review*, 102 (1993), 457–88.

nor sense-perceptual beliefs are referred to or relied upon to contribute to the justificational force particular to that justification or entitlement. So, roughly, *justifications or entitlements* are apriori if their force derives from intellection, understanding, or the nature of other cognitive or practical capacities. *Knowledge* is apriori if it is grounded in an apriori justification or entitlement that suffices to make the knowledge knowledge. This conception of apriority allows that one can know apriori of the existence of particulars—for example, particular mental events—if one's justification or entitlement is intellectual, not sense-perceptual. For example, I think that one knows apriori, in this sense, *cogito*-like thoughts. The argument I will sketch supports the view that one can know with apriori (defeasible) entitlement of the existence of other minds.[14]

Let me emphasize that the issues here have to do with the nature of the epistemic warrant, not the mechanism that makes the knowledge possible. Of course, we need perception to hear or see words. So we need perception to understand speech emanating from another mind. That is *how* we do it. This *is* a difference between knowledge of other minds and knowledge of one's own. For one normally does not need perception to know one's own thoughts. But these points concern the mechanism of knowledge acquisition, not, in my view, the nature of our epistemic warrant—justification or entitlement. I believe that our epistemic entitlement to our understanding of content need not have, and sometimes lacks, a perceptually based element.

We can apprehend the presentation of propositional content in speech by simply understanding it, by thinking the content and understanding it as being presented. This understanding depends causally and psychologically on perception. But that dependence need not be justificational.[15]

---

[14] This conception of apriority is discussed at greater length in ibid. I hope to show elsewhere that the conception is a traditional one, rooted in Kant, despite the fact that apriority was traditionally not associated with defeasibility, and was often not applied to knowledge of events in time (even sometimes the *cogito*). (Kant refused to apply his conception in any of these ways, but I think that this was the upshot of ancillary doctrine, not a direct consequence of his conception of apriority.) I think users of the conception did not always see possible consequences of its use, or were blocked from accepting such consequences by other doctrines. Earlier in the essay I spoke of apriori reflection. Reflection or understanding is apriori if it rests on an apriori justification or entitlement.

[15] When the understanding is not purely intellectual, it may involve perceptual elements. For example, if to understand what someone is saying in pointing to some observed object, I have to see the object, or have some perceptual or imaginative image of how they are thinking of an object, then the understanding is not purely intellectual. One's general prima-facie entitlement to rely on seeming understanding of apparent utterances of content is always apriori. But instantiation of this entitlement to (seeming) understanding of a particular (apparent) utterance of content is apriori only if the understanding in the particular instance is intellectual. I take it that although such perceptually infected *de re* cases are very widespread, they are not ubiquitous. Utterances in pure mathematics and

The epistemic entitlement has its force in abstraction from the background dependence on perception. Perception of words, of utterance events, commonly plays an enabling role but not a justificatory role, in our understanding and, indeed, acceptance of intelligible, expressed contents.

I see the matter on partial analogy with the way in which traditional rationalists saw the role of diagrams or symbols in enabling one to apprehend and see the truth of geometrical or mathematical contents.[16] The fact that perceiving something (symbols or utterances) is psychologically necessary to understanding the content is fully compatible with the epistemic warrant's deriving from understanding and being non-empirical, in the sense that the justificational force of the warrant does not derive from perception. In the mathematical case, one's warrant for believing the content derives from genuine understanding of the content alone. In the interlocution case, one's warrant for presuming that one understands derives from one's seeming understanding of an apparent *instantiation*, or *token occurrence*, of content.[17]

Understanding content requires (in normal cases) understanding the attitudinal (e.g. assertive) mode of the content. And understanding attitudinal mode is further inseparable from understanding instantiations, or token occurrences, of content. One's entitlement to rely on one's seeming understanding is fundamentally an entitlement to rely on seeming understanding of instantiations. This is, other things being equal, an intellectual or apriori, defeasible entitlement. Its probity or justificational force as a rational starting-point derives not from experience, but from conceptual understanding. In my view, where perception of physical events functions to provide access to an instantiation (utterance) of content with its attitudinal mode, not to provide information about objects, perception is no more an element in the justification of the understanding (and of beliefs based on the understanding) than memory is an element in the justification of deductive

some empirical generalizations provide examples. What interests me is the very possibility of apriori prima-facie entitlements to believe in the existence of other minds.

[16] In 'Interlocution, Perception, and Memory', *Philosophical Studies*, 86 (1997), 21–47, I discuss this analogy, and its partialness, in some detail.

[17] For the sake of my argument about knowledge of other minds, I do not need the claim, which I defend in 'Content Preservation' and will allude to later, that we have an apriori prima-facie default entitlement to *accept as true* (particular) seemingly understood apparent *assertions*. All I need for present purposes is that one has an apriori prima-facie entitlement to accept one's seeming understanding of an apparent *utterance*, as genuine understanding of a genuine utterance. Such seeming understanding is to include seeming understanding of the content and mode of use of the utterance (for example, understanding the instantiated content as asserted). One needs seeming understandings of the form: 'It is asserted that *p*.' More qualifications to this argument are needed in a full statement.

reasoning.[18] The role of perception is to make understanding possible. But the seeming understanding carries justificational force in itself, in abstraction from its genetic reliance on perception.

So seeming understanding provides an apriori prima-facie entitlement to presume genuine understanding of an instantiation of content. But the presumption of the existence of an instantiation (for example, an assertive utterance) of content in explicit propositional form provides an apriori prima-facie entitlement to presume that the event has a rational source. For instantiation of content can be known apriori to be constitutively dependent on a system of rational practices for belief formation and content formation.

There are many difficult issues about the points just made. I will have to leave them in undeveloped form for present purposes. So seeming to understand an instantiation of content, together with its mode, gives one apriori prima-facie ground to presume that it ultimately has a rational source. That is enough to give one apriori prima-facie ground to presume the existence of a rational agent or mind. It seems to me that if the presumption is undefeated and veridical, one will have knowledge of the existence of a mind on the basis of seeming understanding of what is prima facie intelligible.

This presumption need not be the product of an inference, any more than there need be an inference to the existence of oneself in the thinking of *cogito*-like thoughts. Anyone with the requisite conceptual equipment (concepts of thoughts, and first- and third-person pronouns) will be apriori entitled to the presumption of a rational agent both from first-person thinking of one's thoughts and from understanding of thoughts articulated by others. Indeed, anyone unable to immediately associate an instantiated propositional content with the existence of a rational source—a rational author, agent, or locus of power—would be conceptually deficient in something like the way that someone confined to Lichtenberg's formulations would be conceptually deficient. For a reflective understanding of propositional instantiation of content entails understanding that rational norms associated with uses of content apply to agents, loci of rational power. In the first-person case, one indicates rational agency with the *I* concept. As I have argued in the main part of this essay, application of that concept marks acknowledgement of intellectual responsibility and agency. Since this acknowledgement expresses a fundamental function of reasoning, we are rationally entitled

---

[18] Cf. 'Content Preservation', 476–84. The points in the next paragraph are also argued for in that article. All of these points require more development and support than I have given them.

to the application of the concept. What sort of epistemic entitlement do we have for attribution of authorship to *others* when we understand their utterances?

I have argued that when one seemingly understands an utterance in interlocution, one is apriori prima-facie entitled to a belief in the existence of a *rational source*—some agent capable of producing utterances with propositional content and attitudinal force, and responsible for acting under rational norms. For one to be entitled to presume that such a source is *another* agent, one with *another* mind, one must be entitled to presume that it is not oneself. So knowledge of other minds is distinguished from self-knowledge not by being necessarily inferential or by being necessarily grounded in perception, but by being in some known contrast with acknowledgement of an understood instantiation of content as one's own.[19]

The key feature of the first-person concept is that it marks acknowledgement of the immediate relevance of reasons to intellectual practice. In understanding utterances in interlocution, one lacks ground for this acknowledgement. I think that to be critically rational, one must have, and be apriori entitled to, a capacity for a fallible sensitivity as to whether an act associated with a seemingly understood instantiation of content is one's own.

One is also apriori prima-facie entitled to rely on particular applications of this capacity. To be critically rational, one must have, in normal cases, sufficient awareness as to when and whether one is the agent of propositional acts to distinguish instances in which one is committed under rational norms governing thoughts with the relevant attitudinal modality from instances in which one is not. This sensitivity is necessary for the ability to apply reasons straightway. Indeed, it is, as we have seen, a constitutive part of reasoning and understanding reason. So entitlement to it is apriori. If norms of critical reason that indicate how one ought to reason (or otherwise act reasonably) are to apply to one's mental states, one must have, and be rationally entitled to, awareness of instances where they apply and where they do not. This is to say that one must have some apriori entitled awareness for one's *not* being the agent of relevant instantiations of content, and for one's thereby

---

[19] I do not claim that one develops this other-attribution only *after* one makes self-attributions. The issues here concern the relation between the entitlements. My point does not even entail any priority of entitlement to take agency as one's own over entitlement to take agency as coming from another.

I have moved freely from talk about prima-facie epistemic entitlement to talk about knowledge. I think that entitlement or warrant is the main philosophical issue in a philosophical account of the relevant knowledge. But there are separate issues about knowledge that a full account should address.

not being rationally committed under rational norms governing the relevant agency.

To know the author of an instantiation of content to be oneself or another, one needs to apply concepts in accordance with the sensitivities discussed above. As indicated before, to be fully responsible to the relevant norms, one needs to be able to act under the idea of the norms. One needs to be able to know and acknowledge one's responsibility. Thus conceptualization of the sensitivities is necessary for being fully responsible to the norms of critical rationality.

These remarks apply to any utterances in interlocution that fall under rational norms—to assertions, to suppositions, to promises, perhaps even to story-tellings. Any understood utterance might be such that one is apriori entitled not to see oneself as its responsible author, relative to whatever rational norms are relevant. Ability to apply the rational norms entails an awareness of differences between reception and initiation. This sort of awareness is fundamental to being a rational agent. Given that one has first- and third-person concepts and the concept of agency, and given that one understands—and is entitled to understand —some particular content instantiations which one is aware of as not being one's own, one's entitlement to this awareness gives one apriori prima-facie entitlement to presume that there is a rational agent other than oneself.[20] One's entitlement to believe in other minds can depend for its justificational force on intellectual understanding of instantiations of intentional content—intellectual 'experience'—rather than sense-perceptual experience.

Let me illustrate these ideas for the case of understanding assertions in interlocution. Suppose that we are apriori prima facie entitled to rely on seeming understanding of events as presentations-as-true, more particularly as assertions (cf. note 17). Of course, one's understanding is compatible with one's not accepting what is asserted. Unless one accepts an assertion, one is not rationally committed to there being rational support for the assertion, much less rationally committed to defend it. This conceptual space between understanding and acceptance of an actual assertion is one to which a rational agent must be sensitive—and be apriori entitled to be sensitive—if he is to be subject to rational norms governing acceptance. So to be subject to such norms, one must be apriori entitled to a sensitivity that differentiates merely understanding assertions from making assertions. But this is equivalent to a sensitivity to whether the source of an assertion is another or oneself.

[20] I should say that I think that entitlement to an awareness of the type of rational commitments one has obtains in cases other than interlocution—in inference, perception, memory, and so on.

To articulate another side of this same point: a critically rational being must be able to—and be apriori entitled to—discriminate the sorts of rational warrant that are relevant to acceptance of understood propositional content. In the case of one's own judgements, one must be able to advert to grounds, accessible to one, that would provide some justification. Or else one must (as in perceptual judgements) have access to some mark of one's entitlement (for example, one's experience). But the norms of reason governing *interlocution* allow that one be rational in one's acceptance of an assertion and lack independent epistemic warrant for the proposition accepted. One is not rationally responsible for defence of one's beliefs in the same way as one is for defence of one's autonomous beliefs. One must rely on rational entitlements or justifications (in others) that one lacks. One's acceptance presumes justifications, or entitlements, that one may not oneself have. To be subject to the epistemic norms governing interlocution, one must have and be apriori entitled to awareness of this dependence. This awareness yields apriori entitlement to presume that the agent of an assertion is not oneself.

So one is apriori entitled to awareness of whether or not a commitment associated with a putative assertion is one's own. For to be subject to epistemic norms one must be able to discriminate cases in which one is committed to rational support of the commitment from cases in which one is not. To be rational one must have, and be apriori entitled to, some sense for one's *not* accepting actual assertions. Where one's seeming understanding of an apparent assertion is accompanied by an awareness that one is not the agent of the assertion, one has an apriori prima-facie ground for presuming that there is another mind, another rational agent.

These entitlements to an understanding of the type of rational commitments that our intellectual activities fall under underwrite a non-inferential ability to discern one's authorship or non-authorship of intellectual (or practical) acts or commitments. We need not *infer* that a rational source of interlocution is another mind. We believe it through understanding an assertion in the third-person attributive way. If one has the requisite conceptual equipment to make explicit third-person attributions of propositional content, one can know immediately in understanding an utterance its being a sign of another person, just as in using the first-person concept in *cogito*-like thoughts, one knows non-inferentially a thought as one's own.

Thus, at the base of rational practice is an awareness of the source of rational agency. We are entitled to a non-inferential belief that there is another agent through the very understanding of utterances in interlocution. Third-person attributions have a source in a rationally required and rationally entitled ability to distinguish, at least in normal cases, our own acts and commitments from acts and commitments that are not our own.

We can be mistaken. Something that appears to have a rational source or to be endowed with mind can be random. Something that appears to come from another mind might have its well-spring in our own unconscious. But infallibility is too much to hope for. Our apriori entitlements in these matters are inevitably defeasible.

What Lichtenberg missed is the role of the first-person concept both in designating a source of rational agency and in acknowledging subjection to epistemic norms and power to act under them. The reverse side of this ability to acknowledge the commitments of one's rational agency is an ability to acknowledge sources of commitments other than one's own. One can sometimes do this non-inferentially, on the basis of intellectual understanding of utterances of content. When this is so, one's ability to recognize and understand other minds is not epistemically grounded in sense experience. It is grounded in understanding content in interlocution, and in an entitlement, underwritten by apriori requirements of rational agency, to recognize one's liabilities and entitlements as a rational agent.[21]

[21] An earlier version of the main part of this essay was given as the fourth of six Locke Lectures at Oxford in 1993 and as the second of two Whitehead Lectures at Harvard in 1994. I have benefited from audience comments on those occasions. I have subsequently benefited from discussions when drafts of the whole paper were given at St Andrews, Berkeley, and New York University, where Tom Nagel presented valuable comments.

9

What the Externalist Can Know A Priori

PAUL A. BOGHOSSIAN

———•———

Even after much discussion, it remains controversial whether an externalism about mental content is compatible with a traditional doctrine of privileged self-knowledge.[1] By an externalism about mental content, I mean the view that what concepts our thoughts involve may depend not only on facts that are internal to us, but on facts about our environment. It is worth emphasizing, if only because it is still occasionally misperceived, that this thesis is supposed to apply at the level of sense and not merely at that of reference: what *concepts* we think in terms of—and not just what they happen to pick out—is said by the externalist to depend upon environmental facts. By a traditional doctrine of privileged self-knowledge, I mean the view that we are able to know, without the benefit of empirical investigation, what our thoughts are in our own case. Suppose I entertain a thought that I would express with the sentence 'Water is wet'. According to the traditional doctrine, I can know without empirical investigation (a) that I am entertaining a thought, (b) that it has a particular conceptual content, and (c) that its content is that water is wet.

Let us call someone who combines an externalist view of mental content with a doctrine of privileged self-knowledge a *compatibilist*. In this essay, I will present a *reductio* of compatibilism; in particular, I intend to argue that, if compatibilism were true, we would be in a position

[1] This paper was presented to a meeting of the Aristotelian Society, held in the Senior Common Room, Birkbeck College, London, on Monday, 24 February 1997 at 8.15 p.m. It was originally published in the *Proceedings of the Aristotelian Society*, August 1996. Earlier versions of the argument of this essay were presented to my seminar on 'Self-Knowledge' at Princeton in the Spring of 1991, to my seminar on 'Mental Content' at the University of Michigan in the Spring of 1992, and to the plenary session of the Conference on Self-Knowledge at the University of St Andrews in August of 1995. I am grateful to those audiences for helpful comments and reactions. I am especially grateful to Anthony Brueckner and Stephen Schiffer for detailed comments on a previous draft and to John Gibbons and Christopher Peacocke for numerous helpful conversations on the general topic.

to know certain facts about the world a priori, facts that no one can reasonably believe are knowable a priori. Whether this should be taken to cast doubt on externalism or on privileged self-knowledge is not an issue I will attempt to settle here. Anti-compatibilist arguments with this general form have been attempted in the past, but I believe that those earlier efforts have misstated the case that needs to be made.[2] Before we get into the details, however, it will be useful to outline certain semantical preliminaries.

I SEMANTICAL PRELIMINARIES

In the case of a general term—for instance, 'water'—I recognize a three-fold distinction between its extension, its referent, and its meaning. A term's extension is just the set of actual things to which it correctly applies. In the case of 'water', it is all the bits of water existing anywhere in the universe. Since we know that those bits of water are just aggregates of H_2O molecules, we may also say that the extension of 'water' consists in the set of all aggregates of H_2O molecules that exist anywhere (including those aggregates that we may never encounter).

By a term's referent, I mean the property that it denotes. In the case of 'water' it will be natural to say that its referent is the property of being water. It is possible to wonder whether it would be equally correct to say that it is the property of being H_2O. That depends on whether the property of being water may be identified with the property of being H_2O, an example of an interesting question in the theory of properties, but not one that I need to settle for present purposes. What is important here is to be able to distinguish between a term's extension and its referent, so that we are able to say that a term may express a property that nothing actually has. I think of a sentence's *truth-condition* as the proposition it expresses; and I think of the proposition it expresses as composed out of the referents denoted by its terms. Thus, the truth-condition of the sentence 'Water is wet' is the proposition made up out of the property of being water and the property of being wet which says that anything that has the one has the other.

I distinguish between the property that the term 'water' denotes and its *meaning*. The terms 'water' and 'H_2O' may have the same referent,

---

[2] See e.g. Michael McKinsey, 'Anti-Individualism and Privileged Access', *Analysis*, 51 (1991), 9–16, and the effective response by Anthony Brueckner, 'What an Anti-Individualist Knows A Priori', *Analysis*, 52 (1992), 111–18. This style of anti-compatibilist argument is to be distinguished from the 'traveling case' arguments discussed in my 'Content and Self-Knowledge', *Philosophical Topics*, 17 (1989), 5–26.

but they do not have the same meaning. What do I mean by the meaning of a term? I wish to be as neutral about this as possible, and not to presuppose any particular view. I will let the reader decide to what extent I have succeeded in my neutrality.

Finally, I identify a word's meaning with the concept it expresses, so I take the meaning of the sentence 'Water is wet' to give the content of the belief that a literal assertoric use of the sentence would express. I use quotes to name words and underlining to name the concept those words express: thus, water is the concept expressed by 'water'. Now for the argument.

II EXTERNALISM AND TWIN EARTH

Abstractly speaking, externalism is easily enough defined. It is simply the view that facts external to a thinker's skin are relevant to the individuation of (certain of) his mental contents. So stated, externalism does not commit one to any specific form of dependence of mental contents on external facts, just to some form of dependence or other.

However, philosophers who embrace externalism don't do so because they regard it as a self-evident truth. They embrace it, rather, because their intuitive responses to a certain kind of thought experiment—Putnamian Twin Earth fantasies—appear to leave them little choice.[3] And that sort of thought experiment motivates externalism only by motivating a specific form of dependence of mental contents on external facts. In particular, it underwrites the claim that, in the case of an atomic, natural kind concept C, the substance actually picked out by C enters into the individuation of C. To put the claim another way: the substances with which a person actually interacts help determine what atomic, natural kind concepts, if any, that person has.[4]

To see this, let us remind ourselves how the Putnam thought experiment is supposed to work. Whereas Oscar, an ordinary English speaker, lives on Earth, his molecular and functional duplicate, Toscar, lives on Twin Earth, a planet just like Earth except that the liquid that fills its

[3] Here I will be restricting myself to externalist theses that are motivated by Putnamian Twin Earth experiments concerning natural kind concepts. In particular, I want to put aside for present purposes externalist theses that are motivated by the influential Burge-style thought experiments involving deference to the usage of linguistic communities. I believe that an argument parallel to the one given here can be mounted for those sorts of externalism as well, but will not argue for this now.

[4] By the schema 'x individuates y', I just mean that if the value of x had been different, the value of y would have been different too. By itself, this doesn't tell us anything about what the value of y is for any particular value of x. More on this below.

lakes and oceans, while indistinguishable from Earthly water in all ordinary circumstances, is not H_2O but some other substance with a different chemical composition—call it XYZ. Going by whatever criteria are relevant to such matters, water and twin water are distinct kinds of substance, even though a chemically ignorant person would be unable to tell them apart. Now, widespread intuition appears to have it that, whereas Oscar's tokens of 'water' apply exclusively to H_2O, Toscar's tokens of 'water' apply exclusively to XYZ. Widespread intuition appears to have it, in other words, that Oscar's and Toscar's 'water' tokens have distinct extensions. If this intuition is sustained, then that implies either that their 'water' concepts are not individuated individualistically, or that they are not individuated in terms of their referents. For Oscar and Toscar are molecular and functional duplicates of each other: they are alike in all internal respects (up to intentional description). Yet the referents of their concepts differ. Hence, either those concepts don't determine what they refer to in some context-independent way (they are not individuated in terms of their referents), or they do determine what they refer to, so are not individuated individualistically.

It is worth emphasizing that a Twin Earth experiment by itself does not get you all the way to an externalism about concepts; it only gets you as far as this disjunction. It is possible to respond to the experiment, and to the intuitions it generates, by opting for the individualistic disjunct and abandoning the idea that concepts are individuated in terms of their referents. That is the response favoured by so-called narrow content theorists. To get an argument for concept externalism, you need not only Twin Earth intuitions; you also need to insist that any notion of mental content deserving of the name has to be individuated in terms of its truth-conditions, has to determine the conditions for its truth or satisfaction in some context-independent way. Given this further assumption, there is then no option but to say that Earthly and Twin Earthly tokens of 'water' express distinct concepts—<u>water</u> in the case of the former and, let us say, <u>twater</u> in the case of the latter.

Let us make explicit, then, the various presuppositions involved in using the Twin Earth thought experiment as a basis for concept externalism. First, and least controversially, water and twater have to be thought of as distinct substances, distinct natural kinds; otherwise, it won't be true that Oscar's word 'water' and Toscar's word 'water' have distinct extensions and referents. Second, the word 'water'—whether on Earth or on Twin Earth—must be thought of as aiming to express a natural kind concept; otherwise, the fact that water and twater are distinct natural kinds will not be semantically relevant. Third, Oscar and Toscar have to be thought of as chemically indifferent, as having no views about the chemical composition of the liquid kinds around them; otherwise, they won't end up as functional duplicates of each other in the way that the experiment requires. Fourth, the concepts expressed by the Earthly and Twin Earthly tokens of 'water' have to be thought of as atomic concepts, not compound concepts that are compositionally built up out of other concepts in well-defined ways. For example, the experiment presupposes that <u>water</u> can't be thought of as capable of being defined as <u>a tasteless, odourless liquid that flows in the rivers and faucets</u>. For if it were a compositional concept of that sort, its extension would be determined by the extension of its ingredient parts. Hence, a conclusion to the effect that <u>water</u> and <u>twater</u> have different extensions would have to proceed differently than it does in Putnam's original experiment, by showing that one of the *ingredients* of water—the concept expressed by 'liquid', for example—has a different extension from that expressed by its Twin Earth counterpart. Finally, as I have recently noted, concepts must be thought of as individuated in terms of their referents.

III THE ARGUMENT

Now, let us suppose that Oscar—our prototypical Twin Earth subject—is a compatibilist. I claim that Oscar is in a position to argue, purely a priori, as follows:

(1) If I have the concept <u>water</u>, then water exists.

(2) I have the concept <u>water</u>.

Therefore,

(3) Water exists.

Since the conclusion is clearly not knowable a priori, one of the premisses in Oscar's evidently valid reasoning had better be either false or not knowable a priori. The question is: can Oscar, *qua* compatibilist, safely count on one or the other claim? I shall argue that he cannot, that he is committed to both premisses (1) and (2) and to their being knowable a priori. If I am right, then the compatibilist is committed to the manifestly absurd conclusion that we can know a priori that water exists.

Now, the a priori knowability of premiss (2) just *is* the view that I have called the doctrine of privileged self-knowledge, so we don't have to spend any time debating its dispensability for compatibilism. The only real question concerns premiss (1), to an extended discussion of which I now turn.

IV PERHAPS WATER IS NOT REQUIRED FOR <u>WATER</u>

Two possible objections need to be considered. On the one hand, an opponent might wish to reject the first premiss out of hand, on the grounds that it isn't necessary, on an externalist view, that water exist for someone to have the concept <u>water</u>. On the other, he might wish to argue that, although it is true that water is required for <u>water</u> on an externalist view, that fact is not knowable a priori. Which, if any, of these two alternative strategies is available to the compatibilist? Let us begin with a discussion of the first.

How might Oscar have acquired the concept <u>water</u> without actually interacting with some water, according to a Twin Earth externalist? He couldn't have acquired it merely by virtue of its internal functional role, for his duplicate shares that functional role, yet is said not to have the concept <u>water</u>. And he couldn't have acquired it by theorizing that the liquid around him is H_2O, for it is stipulated that Oscar is no chemist, and has no specific views about the microstructure of water.

An externalist could claim that Oscar might have acquired <u>water</u> from other speakers who have the concept. This suggestion harbours a number of difficulties which limitations of space prevent me from discussing here.[5] Even if it were ultimately sustained, however, its impact on the argument I'm pursuing would be minimal—it would simply force us to slightly complicate the absurd conclusion that I have claimed the compatibilist is in a position to derive a priori. Instead of (3), we would now have the equally unpalatable disjunction:

(3′) Either water exists, or other speakers who have the concept <u>water</u> exist.[6]

For now, however, I propose to set aside this complication and say, simply, that if Twin Earth externalism is true, then contact with water is required for possession of the concept <u>water</u>.

---

[5] Part of what I have in mind here is that not all speakers could reason in this way, for some of them must have acquired the concept without any help from others. But it would be a needless distraction to go into this now.

[6] It is interesting to note that here I am in agreement with Tyler Burge, if not on the apriority of the disjunction, then at least on its truth, as far as externalism is concerned. 'What seems incredible is to suppose that [Oscar], in his relative ignorance and indifference about the nature of water, holds beliefs whose contents involve the notion, even though neither water nor communal cohorts exist' Burge, 'Other Bodies', in A. Woodfield (ed.), *Thought and Object* (Oxford: Oxford University Press, 1982), 116.

V WATER IS REQUIRED FOR <u>WATER</u>, BUT THAT FACT IS NOT A PRIORI

The most important challenge to the line of argument I'm pursuing derives not from opposition to the truth of this claim, but from opposition to its alleged apriority. This opposition can be stated in a number of related ways; I shall present the strongest version I can think of.

According to the externalist, we know that water is required for possession of the concept <u>water</u> because we know, roughly, that 'water' is one of those words on which a Twin Earth experiment can be run. But doesn't our knowledge that a given word is Twin Earth-eligible rest on empirical information? Compatibilists are very fond of saying that it does;[7] however, it is rare to find their reasons explicitly spelled out. Where exactly do empirical elements intrude into the Twin Earth experiment? Let us look at this in some detail. What conditions does a word have to meet if it is to be Twin Earth-eligible?

As we have seen, it has to be a word that expresses an atomic concept. It also has to aim to name a natural kind. Furthermore, the user of the word must be indifferent about the essence of the kind that his word aims to name; he must be chemically indifferent.

But aren't all these conditions available a priori to the user of the word? More to the point, wouldn't a compatibilist have to hold that they are?

The answer is perfectly straightforward, it seems to me, in the case of the latter two conditions. Whether or not a person has beliefs about the microstructure of the kinds around him, and whether or not he intends one of his words to name one of those kinds, are matters that not only seem intuitively a priori, but that a believer in privileged access would have to hold are a priori. Notice that we are not asking whether the word actually names a natural kind, but only whether its user intends it to do so. And according to the doctrine of privileged access, the contents of one's intentions and beliefs are available to one a priori.

It might be thought, however, that the question about atomicity is somewhat more delicate. For is it so clear that facts about compositionality are a priori? Haven't we, as philosophers, often been in the unhappy position of assuming that a concept was compositional, investing a lot of effort in seeking its definition, only to conclude that it has none, that it must be deemed atomic after all?

It is important not to conflate apriority with ease. A fact may be a priori, but very difficult to uncover, as the example of any number of

---

[7] Tyler Burge has urged this in conversation; for a statement in print, see Brueckner, 'What an Anti-Individualist Knows A Priori'.

mathematical or logical theorems might illustrate. We need not claim that facts about atomicity are easy, only that they are not empirical. And in fact it is hard to see how they could be otherwise. What sense can we make of the idea that knowledge of whether a concept is internally structured might depend on empirical information about the external world?

So far, then, we have not come across a Twin Earth-eligibility criterion that could plausibly be claimed not to be available a priori. We are now about to consider another criterion, however, which, if it really were a criterion, would definitely make Twin Earth-eligibility an empirical matter. The criterion is this: in addition to *aiming* to express a natural kind, a word must *actually* name a natural kind, if it is to be Twin Earth-eligible. One cannot run a Twin Earth thought experiment on a word that aims, but fails, to name a kind.[8]

In support of this claim someone might offer the following. Putnam's original experiment is carried out on a term—'water'—in full knowledge that it does refer to a kind: namely, H_2O. That knowledge plays a central role in the experiment. Twin Earth by itself doesn't speak to what we should say about a term that doesn't name a natural kind. So, for all that Twin Earth overtly commits us to, actually naming a natural kind is a condition on Twin Earth-eligibility, and that is certainly not a condition that is available a priori. True, Twin Earth teaches us that water is required for the word 'water' to express the concept <u>water</u>, such an objector would concede; but we only learn this because we know— empirically—that water is the kind actually named by 'water'. Hence, Twin Earth-eligibility is not a priori.

Now, I think that this objection, as stated, isn't correct; buried within it, however, is another objection that is considerably more challenging. The reason this particular objection doesn't succeed is that it is quite clear that we *can* run a Twin Earth experiment on a word that doesn't actually name a natural kind. Suppose we had such a word, W, on Earth. Then, to get a successful Twin Earth experiment, all you need to do is describe a Twin situation in which, although the users of the word type W are functional and molecular duplicates of their counterparts on Earth, W does name a kind in the Twin situation. Provided intuition still has it that the extension of Earthly tokens of W are different from the extension of the Twin tokens of W—which of course they will be, since the extension of the former will be empty and the extension of the latter won't be—the experiment will succeed.

---

[8] I am grateful to my colleague John Gibbons for helping me see the need to confront this objection and the general line of argument that it opens up.

Now, however, the objector would appear to be in a position to pose a more difficult challenge. For if this is in fact right, and we can run Twin Earth experiments even on terms that fail to refer, then how do we know a priori that water is required for 'water' to express <u>water</u>? We can't infer that claim merely from the fact that 'water' is Twin Earth-eligible, for we have established that even empty terms are Twin Earth-eligible. Maybe <u>water</u> is the concept that 'water' expresses when it fails to name a natural kind, when there is no water for it to name. If we can be said to know that water is required for <u>water</u>, we know that only by virtue of our knowledge that 'water' does name a natural kind: namely, water. And that, of course, is something that we could only have come to know empirically. Hence, our knowledge that water is required for <u>water</u> is not a priori.

Here, finally, we come across the most important challenge to the line of argument I've been pursuing. It will be interesting to uncover the reason why it doesn't ultimately protect compatibilism from the charge of absurdity.

VI THE EMPTY CASE

I want to approach a response to this objection somewhat indirectly, by focusing on the following question: what should a Twin Earth externalist say about the case where a word aiming to name a natural kind fails to do so? Two sorts of scenario might lead to such an outcome. On the one hand, a word like 'water' may fail to name a natural kind because the liquids to which it is competently applied don't form a natural kind, but rather a heterogeneous motley. On the other hand, a term may fail to name a kind because there fails to be anything at all out there—motley or otherwise—to which it could correctly be said to apply. Here I want to concentrate on the second more extreme sort of case, because it throws the issues of interest into sharper relief.

So let us imagine a planet just like ours on which, although it very much seems to its inhabitants that there is a clear, tasteless, colourless liquid flowing in their rivers and taps and to which they confidently take themselves to be applying the word 'water', these appearances are systematically false, and constitute a sort of pervasive collective mirage. In point of actual fact, the lakes, rivers, and taps on this particular Twin Earth run bone-dry. All this may seem very far-fetched, and no doubt it is. However, the scenario described is not substantially different—except in point of pervasiveness—from what has actually turned out to be true in the case of such terms as 'phlogiston' and 'caloric'; and, anyway, the point isn't to describe a genuine possibility. Rather, it is to enquire how a particular semantical theory proposes to treat cases of reference failure, and whether it is committed to treating such cases in a particular way. What *concept*, if any, should a Twin Earth externalist say would be expressed by tokens of the word 'water' on this Dry Earth?

Some may think the answer to be obvious. Since externalism is the view that the concept expressed by a word is individuated in part by the referent of that word, then it follows, does it not, that if the word has no referent, it expresses no concept?

This reasoning would be far too hasty. It confuses the claim that a concept is individuated in terms of its referent with the claim that the existence of the concept depends on the existence of a referent. To put matters in terms of a familiar technical vocabulary, it confuses externalist individuation with object dependence. All that Twin Earth externalism is committed to, strictly speaking, is the claim that, if the referent of a given word were different, the concept it would then express would be different, too. And that is consistent with the claim that the word would express a concept in a case where it fails to refer, provided that the concept it would there express is different from any it would express in a case where it does refer. To say it again, externalist individuation, in the sense in which Twin Earth externalism is committed to it, is just the view that if two words differ in their referents, then they also differ in the concepts they express; strictly speaking, that is consistent with a word's expressing some concept or other even when it fails to have a referent.

But what concept should we say 'water' expresses under the conditions described, in which there fails to be any natural kind for it to refer to? We may consider options under two main headings: compound and atomic.

We could try saying that under the envisioned dry conditions, 'water' expresses a suitable compound concept made up in the familiar way out of other available concepts. Which compound concept? Most plausibly, I suppose, something like: the clear, tasteless, colourless liquid that flows in the taps and the rivers around here and. . . . It won't matter much for the purposes of this argument how precisely this proposal is fleshed out. On any such view, the word 'water' will contribute a complex property to the proposition expressed by whole sentences involving it, one which, as a matter of contingent fact, nothing in that environment possesses.

Intuitively, this seems to me to be a plausible view of the matter. When I think of a group of people just like us, applying the word 'water' confidently to something that appears to them to be a clear, colourless, tasteless liquid in their environment, when in fact there is no such liquid in their environment, I feel tempted by the sort of error theory of their linguistic behaviour that the present proposal delivers. It seems plausible to me to say that what these people mean by the word 'water' is this clear, colourless, tasteless liquid etc., which, however and unfortunately, is not to be found in their environment.

The problem is that it is very difficult to see how such a view could be available to the Twin Earth externalist. Remember, the Twin Earth externalist is committed, for reasons detailed earlier, to holding that 'water' expresses an *atomic* concept under conditions where it has a non-empty extension, whether that extension be H_2O or XYZ or whatever. That is one of the presuppositions of the Twin Earth experiment. But, then, how can the very same word, with the very same functional role, express an atomic concept under one set of external conditions and a compound, decompositional concept under another set of external conditions? A concept's compositionality is exclusively a function of its internal 'syntax', and can't be contingent upon external circumstances in the way that the present proposal would require.

Let me forestall a possible misunderstanding of this point. My argument here is not that, if the compatibilist were to embrace the compound notion, that would undermine his commitment to privileged access. For although it is true that embracing the compound option for 'water' on Dry Earth, while being committed to its atomicity on Earth, would have the effect of making facts about compositionality come out a posteriori, that would not flout any doctrine of privileged access that I have defined.

Nor is my argument here that the compound option is unacceptable because it runs into conflict with the independently plausible claim that facts about compositionality are a priori, although, as I noted above, that is something I believe, and would be prepared to defend.

In fact, my argument here is not epistemic at all, but rather metaphysical. The compound option requires the externalist to say that one and the same word, with one and the same functional role, may express an atomic concept under one set of external circumstances and a compound decompositional concept under another set of external circumstances. But it is hard to see how the *compositionality* of a concept could be a function of its external circumstances in this way. Compositionality, as I understand it, can only be a function of the internal syntax of a concept; it can't supervene on external circumstances in the way that the compound proposal would require. (This is especially clear on a 'language of thought' picture of mental representation, but is independent of it.)

How do things look with the other main class of available options, that according to which the empty tokens of 'water' express an atomic concept? On this branch, too, we need to answer the question: which atomic concept will that be, according to the Twin Earth externalist?

The externalist will know quite a lot about which concepts it cannot be: in particular, he will know that it cannot be identical with any of the concepts that are expressed by non-empty tokens of 'water'. To suppose otherwise would contradict his overriding commitment to individuating a concept in terms of its referent. But can he tell us, in line with his overriding commitment, what concept *is* expressed by the empty tokens of 'water'?

Unfortunately, there would appear to be a compelling argument showing that the externalist will not be able to say what atomic concept is expressed by the non-referring tokens of 'water', because by his own lights there can't be such a concept. Let me explain.

We have seen that one of the assumptions that is needed to transform a Twin Earth experiment into an argument for externalism is the assumption that concepts have context-independent conditions of satisfaction, or, in the case of thought contents, context-independent conditions of truth. So let us ask this: what are the satisfaction conditions for 'water' on Dry Earth; to what sorts of liquid does it apply? By assumption, of course, the actual extension of 'water' is empty on Dry Earth, so there is no liquid in its actual environment to which it applies. But the question I am asking is consistent with the word's actual extension being empty, and consistent even with its extension being empty in all worlds. What I want to know is: what proposition—what truth-condition—is expressed by sentences of the form 'Water is wet', for example, as uttered on Dry Earth? What is it that gets said? Never mind if such sentences are ruled false in the actual world, or even in all worlds.

On the line we are currently investigating, the answer has to be that there is no fact of the mater what truth-condition is expressed by sentences involving 'water' on Dry Earth, for there is no fact of the matter what property is denoted by those tokens of 'water'. Since there is no natural kind at the end of the relevant causal chain leading up to uses of 'water' on Dry Earth, there is no fact of the matter what the referent of 'water' is, and so no fact of the matter what proposition is expressed by sentences involving it.

But on an externalist view, this admission is fatal to the claim that there is a concept there in the first place, for an externalism about concepts is fuelled in part by the conviction that thought contents must possess context-invariant conditions of satisfaction or, as appropriate, of truth. If, in a given context, there is no fact of the matter what the referent of a given concept is, then to that extent there is also no fact of the matter what the concept is.

We have looked at two possible tacks that an externalist might take regarding empty tokens of 'water', and we have found them both to be irremediably problematic. Letting the empty tokens express a compound concept, while having the virtue of supplying the word with a property to refer to, runs directly into conflict with the externalist's commitment to the atomicity of 'water'. Evading this problem by letting the word express an atomic concept, on the other hand, runs into direct conflict with the externalist's commitment to the idea that concepts must possess determinate, context-independent conditions of satisfaction.

What, then, is the externalist to say about the empty case? The answer would appear to be that he has to say just what the proponent of object dependence said he should say all along—namely, that the empty tokens simply don't express a determinate concept. That turns out to be the right thing to say not because Twin Earth externalism is conceptually equivalent to object dependence, but because Twin Earth externalism, in conjunction with its other commitments, entails object dependence.

VII THE ARGUMENT COMPLETED

If this is right, then the compatibilist is in a position to conclude— via purely a priori reasoning—that if a term expresses a concept in the first place, it must have a non-empty extension. Moreover, privileged access assures him that he will be able to tell a priori whether or not a given term does express a concept, and indeed, if it does, which one. In particular, our friend Oscar will be able to tell non-empirically that his term 'water' expresses a concept, and in particular that it expresses the concept water. Putting these two bits of information together, he is in a position to conclude, a priori, that water must have existed at some time. And that, we are all agreed, is not something he ought to be able to do.[9]

[9] To generate our problem for the compatibilist, we have had to assume that when Oscar reasons as we have described, his a priori warrant for the premises of his argument transmits, across the a priori known entailment, to the entailed conclusion. Recently, some philosophers have taken to questioning whether this principle is correct. Aren't these cases, they have asked, where although A is known a priori, and although A is known a priori to entail B, nevertheless B is not known a priori. See e.g. the interesting contribution of Martin Davies, Ch. 11 below. I have to say that I would be very surprised if there turned out to be any such cases that survived scrutiny. However, defending this claim in full generality is something that deserves separate treatment, and will have to be left for another occasion. Here, I will settle for discussing one such case that has been suggested to me (by Stephen Schiffer). Consider the following inference:

If I have toothache, then teeth exist.

I have toothache.

Therefore,

Teeth exist.

I have defined 'a priori knowledge' as 'knowledge that is obtained without empirical investigation'. Relative to this (admittedly vague and informal) characterization, don't the premisses of this argument come out a priori? Can't I know that I have toothache without empirical investigation? Also, that if I have toothache, then I have teeth? However, the conclusion of this argument is clearly not a priori. Therefore, there must be something wrong with the transmission of warrant principle that we have been assuming.

My perhaps predictable reply is that it is not at all clear that the premisses of the toothache argument are a priori, relative to the intended notion of 'a priori'. That we are in pain, and even that we are in a particular kind of phenomenologically classifiable pain (a 'toothachey' pain)—these matters seem clearly a priori. But there is no intuitive reason to believe, it seems to me, that we can know a priori that we have toothache, if that is supposed to mean, as it evidently does in the objection under consideration, that we have an ache *in a tooth*. Imagine a toothless person insisting that he has toothache; would we have to defer to his alleged a priori access to that fact?

10

Externalism, Twin Earth, and Self-Knowledge

BRIAN P. MCLAUGHLIN AND MICHAEL TYE

————◆◆————

INTRODUCTION: OUR MAIN QUESTION

Externalist theories of thought content imply that the contents of certain thoughts fail to supervene on intrinsic physical properties of thinkers. They thus imply that it is possible for two individuals to be exactly alike in respect of their intrinsic physical properties while differing in respect of the contents of at least certain of their thoughts. The well-known Twin Earth thought experiments of Hilary Putnam (1975) and Tyler Burge (1979) support content-externalist theses, because they support theses to the effect that certain thought contents are individuated, at least in part, by environmental or socio-environmental factors. Since variation in such factors can make for variations in thought contents without variation in the intrinsic physical properties of the thinker, it follows that the contents of the thinker's thoughts fail to supervene on the thinker's intrinsic physical properties. In large part, because of the intuitive force of Twin Earth thought experiments, many philosophers today endorse some version of content externalism; and in the wake of these thought experiments, naturalistic theories of content have been developed that imply externalist theses about at least certain thought contents.[1]

The claim that some thought contents are individuated, in part, by environmental or socio-environmental factors has prompted a concern in some quarters, one based on considerations about our knowledge of

---

[1] See e.g. Dretske 1980 and 1988; Fodor 1987; Millikan 1984; and Papineau 1987. We will not discuss the externalist consequences of these theories since, first, they do not purport to be stating *conceptually* true externalist theses, but at most metaphysically necessary externalist theses, and, second, the externalist theses they state are not supportable by Twin Earth thought experiments. We will be concerned exclusively with externalist theses that have been taken by externalists to be conceptual truths supported by Twin Earth thought experiments alone. We are thus concerned exclusively with a family of externalist theses that might be called 'Twin Earth externalist theses'.

our thoughts. It is claimed that we have a kind of 'privileged access' to what we are thinking; and the concern is that content externalism comes into conflict with this fact.[2]

The first question that should be raised is what, exactly, is meant by the claim that we have such privileged access. It is common ground that we can normally know what we are currently thinking in a way different from the way we can know what others are thinking. Is there, however, a privileged access thesis that receives sufficient intuitive support to at least motivate the incompatibilists' concern?

Consider the following thesis:

> *Privileged access thesis*: It is conceptually necessary that if we are able to exercise our actual normal capacity to have beliefs about our occurrent thoughts, then if we are able to occurrently think that *p*, we are able to know that we are thinking that *p* without our knowledge being justificatorily based on empirical investigation of our environment.[3]

We believe this thesis has considerable intuitive support. Moreover, there is a prima-facie tension between it and (Twin Earth) externalism. According to externalism, whether one is occurrently thinking that *p* will, in at least some cases, depend on environmental factors. This suffices to raise a concern about whether privileged access is compatible with externalism. Before addressing the incompatibilists' concern, however, let us first make some preliminary explanatory remarks about the privileged access thesis.

The thesis invokes the notion of occurrently thinking that *p*. Occurrently thinking that *p* is a kind of conscious thought episode, a kind of mental event; it is not a belief. Beliefs are dispositional states. Dispositional states have manifestations. Beliefs are typically manifested in behaviour (both non-verbal as well as verbal). And they are also manifestable in conscious thought—at least in the case of self-conscious beings such as ourselves. Thought episodes of occurrently thinking that *p* are,

---

[2] See e.g. Boghossian 1989, 1992, and Ch. 9 above; McKinsey 1991 and 1994; and Brown 1995.

[3] To avoid prolixity, we will hereafter typically drop the qualification 'given that we are able to exercise our actual normal capacity to have beliefs about our occurrent thoughts'. It should be kept in mind, however, that it is possible for us to be able to occurrently think that *p*, yet be unable to have the sort of knowledge in question because we lack our actual normal capacity to have beliefs about our occurrent thoughts (say, due to severe impairments in short-term memory), or because while we possess that capacity, we are somehow blocked from exercising it at the time in question (by, say, a radical dissociation from our occurrent thoughts as might be supposed to happen sometimes in certain extreme cases of multiple personality disorder).

arguably, the characteristic manifestation of believing that *p* in conscious thought.[4]

Now asserting that *p* is arguably the characteristic manifestation of believing that *p* in speech. This idea, coupled with the idea that occurrently thinking that *p* is the characteristic manifestation of believing that *p* in conscious thought, might lead one to characterize occurrently thinking that *p* as silently asserting that *p* to oneself. One can occurrently think that *p* by silently asserting *p* to oneself. However, occurrently thinking that *p* is not always a matter of silently asserting that *p* to oneself; indeed, it does not even typically involve silently asserting that *p* to oneself. Asserting that *p*, whether out loud or silently to oneself, arguably involves communicative intentions. But occurrently thinking that *p* need involve no such intentions. This is, of course, by no means to deny that public language-users such as ourselves can occurrently think that *p* in their public language. An English speaker can, of course, occurrently think that *p* in English. Indeed, that is arguably the typical way that a monolingual English speaker occurrently thinks that *p*.

The privileged access thesis concerns, then, only conscious thought episodes of thinking that *p*, mental events which are thinkings that *p*. The thesis is silent about believing that *p*, hoping that *p*, intending that *p*, and the like. Thus, the privileged access thesis is silent about whether we have privileged access to what kind of propositional attitudes we have towards *p*.[5] The thesis is also silent about whether we have privileged access to mental states that have been traditionally regarded as not contentful at all—for example, the feeling of pain.[6] We embrace privileged access to sensations; but privileged access to sensations will not be a topic of discussion here.

The beliefs that count as knowledge of one's occurrent thoughts are, of course, second-order beliefs. An example is believing that one is now

---

[4] See McLaughlin 1988.

[5] While occurrently thinking that *p* is the characteristic manifestation of the belief that *p* in conscious thought, we leave open whether it is always a manifestation of the belief that *p*. Perhaps occurrently thinking that *p* can be a manifestation of an intense desire that *p* be true (as might be held to occur in wishful thinking). We also leave open whether one can insincerely say that *p* silently to oneself, yet not realize one is insincere (as might be held to occur sometimes in self-deception), and thus not be expressing a belief. We thus take no definite stand on the question of whether one can occurrently think that *p*, yet not believe that *p*. Still, we are inclined to believe that this is possible. We note too that from the fact that one believes that *p* and that one can occurrently think that *p*, it does not follow that were one to reflect on whether *p*, one would occurrently think that *p*. For the act of reflection might eradicate the belief, or one might be dissociated from the belief at the time, or the belief might be suppressed, or repressed. For further discussion, see McLaughlin 1988.

[6] For a discussion of whether pain and other feelings really do lack content, see Tye 1995.

thinking that water is a liquid. It is important to note that the pronoun 'one' here should be understood as Hector Casteñedas's (1975) 'one*'. 'One*' is his useful linguistic device for indicating that the thinker is exercising the first-person indexical concept. Whenever we write 'One is thinking that one . . .', the second occurrence of 'one' should be read as 'one*'; likewise for other pronouns that immediately follow 'thinking that'. The second-order beliefs in question are thus so-called *de se* beliefs.

Tyler Burge (1988) has offered a well-known example of self-knowledge involving a self-referential thought, one that is partly about itself. His example is that of believing that one is now thinking, with this very thought, that water is a liquid. In this case, the second-order belief that counts as knowledge is itself expressed by an occurrent second-order thought. In Burge's example, the occurrent thought that manifests the second-order belief that *one is thinking, with the very thought in question, that water is a liquid* is, of course, the occurrent thought *that one is thinking, with the very thought in question, that water is a liquid*. According to Burge, when one has this occurrent thought, one is, in part, thinking that water is a liquid. Thus, there are two occurrent thoughts: the one that expresses the content of the second-order belief that counts as knowledge, and the one that is contained as a component of that occurrent thought. Here is another example of a second-order belief that is itself manifested by an occurrent thought: believing that one is now thinking about water.[7] This example is simpler than Burge's, since it arguably does not involve one's occurrent thought containing another occurrent thought as a constituent.[8]

Burge calls thoughts that manifest second-order beliefs about what one is occurrently thinking '*cogito* thoughts'. *Cogito* thoughts are especially interesting second-order occurrent thoughts. They are, however,

---

[7] We use 'about' here in the ordinary, non-technical sense in which one can think about things that not only do not exist, but which one believes do not exist, in the sense that we can think about Santa Claus or unicorns or phlogiston. Thus, believing that one is now thinking about unicorns counts as a case of self-knowledge; and so does one's belief that one is now thinking that there are no unicorns.

[8] Here we want to clear up one sort of misunderstanding of Burge's example that we have encountered in discussions with others. Suppose that one occurrently thinks that one is now thinking, with this very thought, that if it rains, one will not go to the picnic. Is Burge committed to the view that *in* occurrently thinking that thought one is, thereby, in part, occurrently thinking that it will rain? If he were, then his proposal should certainly be rejected. But he is not so committed. He is committed only to the claim that in thinking that thought one is, in part, *entertaining* the thought that it will rain tomorrow. One can entertain the thought that it will rain tomorrow, even when one is convinced that it will not rain tomorrow.

not typical occurrent thoughts. One has such thoughts only in self-reflective moments. It is important to note, then, that the kind of self-knowledge alluded to in the privileged access thesis is by no means restricted to beliefs that are manifested by *cogito* thoughts. The kind of self-knowledge in question includes cases in which one is occurrently thinking that p, one knows that one is thinking that p, but one's belief that one is thinking that p is not *itself* manifested by any occurrent thought. Thus, one might know, for instance, that one is now thinking that water is a liquid, on occasions in which one's only occurrent thought is that water is a liquid. The kind of beliefs that count as self-knowledge thus need not themselves be manifested by occurrent thoughts.

We will call the kind of knowledge alluded to in the thesis 'a priori knowledge'. The reason is that the knowledge in question is not justificatorily based—either directly or indirectly—on empirical investigation of the environment. Thus, subtleties aside, the thesis of privileged access is that if one is able to occurrently think that p, then one is able to know a priori—in this special very broad sense of 'a priori'—that one is thinking that p.

We will say more later about the privileged access thesis. We hope that we have said enough to make the thesis appealing. We certainly find it so. Indeed, we find it sufficiently compelling that if Twin Earth externalism is indeed incompatible with it, we would regard that as a grave matter indeed. If Twin Earth externalism is incompatible with this privileged access thesis, that is a powerfully compelling reason for rejecting Twin Earth externalism. Indeed, were we ourselves to come to think that the incompatibilist view is right, we would reject Twin Earth externalism. We believe, however, that no one has made a compelling case for incompatibilism.

Our concern, then, is specifically whether privileged access is incompatible with any version of externalism that is supported by Twin Earth thought experiments *alone*. We find *both* privileged access and such versions of content externalism sufficiently compelling that we regard the burden of proof to be on the incompatibilist. Given the plausibility of both doctrines, what reason is there to think they are incompatible?

In this essay, we will examine one of the leading lines of argument for incompatibilism in the literature. The line of argument attempts to show that the conjunction of externalist theses and privileged access implies that we can have a priori knowledge of truths that in fact we patently cannot have a priori knowledge of (even in our very broad sense of 'a priori'). This line of argument, we will try to show, invariably rests on false assumptions about what externalist theses are supported by Twin

Earth thought experiments *alone* and/or about the intended scope of the privileged access thesis.[9]

I MCKINSEY'S RECIPE

Michael McKinsey (1991) has described a recipe for making a case that externalist theses are incompatible with privileged access. Suppose a version of externalism implies that certain thought contents are individuated, at least in part, by environmental factors. Let *that p* be a thought content of the type in question. McKinsey's recipe for trying to show that the version of externalism is incompatible with privileged access is essentially the following: find some E such that (1) E cannot be known a priori—even in our very broad sense of 'a priori'—yet (2) the version of externalism implies that it is a conceptual truth that if one is thinking that p, then E. According to McKinsey, if such an E can be found, it can be successfully argued that *either* one cannot know a priori that one is currently thinking that p *or* it is not a conceptual truth that if one is thinking that p, then E, from which it may be inferred that the version of externalism is incompatible with privileged access. Given this incompatibility, one would either have to reject the version of externalism in question or reject the claim that we have privileged access to *that p* thought contents, or reject both.

McKinsey's recipe is, we believe, a perfectly fine one.[10] For if it is a conceptual truth that if one is thinking that p, then E, then it is a priori knowable that if one is thinking that p, then E. (We assume here that all conceptual truths are knowable a priori.) Moreover, if this is a priori knowable, and one can also know a priori that one is now thinking that p, then it is surely safe to conclude that one can know a priori that E. But, by hypothesis, one cannot know a priori that E. The crucial issue is whether any externalist thesis supportable by Twin Earth thought experiments will serve as an ingredient for McKinsey's recipe. We will argue in due course that none will.

[9] The line of argument we will discuss is one of the *two* leading lines for argument for incompatibilism. The second line of argument appeals to so-called travelling cases (or 'slow switching cases'). In McLaughlin and Tye, forthcoming, we argue that this second line of incompatibilist argument fails as well.

[10] Martin Davies (Ch. 11 below) addresses the issue of whether McKinsey-type arguments can be used to refute Twin Earth externalism. He argues that they cannot. He challenges the validity of arguments of the form in question. According to Davies, knowing a priori that p and knowing a priori that if p then o does not always entitle us to conclude that o can be known a priori. We lack the space to discuss his interesting proposals. Suffice it to note that we hold that one is so entitled in the cases at issue.

As we will see in section II, there are content-externalist theses that imply that if one is thinking that p, then E—where E is not knowable a priori. However, as will become apparent, *no one*—neither externalists nor internalists—understands the privileged access thesis in a way that implies we have a priori knowledge of the sorts of thought contents in question.

We will proceed as follows. In section II, we will consider some non-Twin Earth versions of content externalism that have been held and that are incompatible with the claim that we have privileged access to the thought contents in question. This will lead to our making some further clarificatory remarks in section III about the privileged access thesis. In section IV we will consider a version of externalism that Colin McGinn maintains is supported by Putnam's Twin Earth thought experiment, and defend it against a McKinsey-type argument. In section V we will consider a Putnam-type Twin Earth thought experiment proposed by Burge (1982) that we believe shows that McGinn's principle is too strong. In section VI we will consider a McKinsey-style incompatibilist argument due to Boghossian. In section VII we will consider another version of externalism that Burge argues is supported by his own Twin Earth thought experiment, and defend it against a McKinsey-type argument. Finally, in section VIII, we will examine an *ad hominem* charge that has been levelled against Burge: namely, that he holds views that are inconsistent with the privileged access thesis he espouses. We will argue that this charge is mistaken.

II   OBJECT-DEPENDENT AND KIND-DEPENDENT THOUGHTS[11]

As is well known, it has been claimed that some thought contents are singular propositions, propositions that contain concrete individuals as constituents. Thoughts that have singular propositions as their contents form a subclass of what are sometimes called 'object-dependent thoughts'.[12] If there are indeed such thought contents, then they are, of course, individuated in part by environmental factors: the existence of the concrete individual(s) in question. Thus, such thought contents will not supervene on intrinsic physical properties of thinkers.

McKinsey's recipe can be employed to show that we lack privileged access to such thought contents. If p is a singular proposition, and if

---

[11] The literature on the general topics discussed in this section is truly vast. Suffice it to note that the notion of a singular proposition is due to Russell; see e.g. Russell 1954. For an especially insightful discussion of singular thoughts, see Evans 1982.

[12] The term 'object-dependent thought' is, we believe, due to Evans 1982.

thinking that p has the singular proposition, p, as its content, then one cannot know a priori that the content of one's thought is p. To see this, consider the singular proposition that Cicero is an orator, a proposition that contains Cicero himself as a constituent. Suppose that this singular proposition could be the content of a thought. It is a conceptual truth that if there is a singular proposition that Cicero is an orator, then Cicero exists.[13] Thus, it is a conceptual truth that having a thought with the singular proposition that Cicero is an orator as its content requires the existence of Cicero. But, of course, one cannot know a priori that Cicero exists. Hence, one cannot know a priori that there is a singular proposition that Cicero is an orator. So, one cannot know a priori that one is having a thought with that singular proposition as its content. It is obvious how to generalize this example.

To our knowledge, no one holds that we have privileged access to such thought contents of object-dependent thoughts. Indeed, to our knowledge, no one holds that we have privileged access even to whether we are having an object-dependent thought; for, given that there are such thoughts, there are also cognitively illusory object-dependent thoughts, so to speak; that is to say, one can be under the cognitive illusion that one is having an object-dependent thought.[14] Think of a young child's thought on Christmas Eve that Santa Claus is coming.

None the less, *were* someone to maintain the wildly implausible thesis that we have privileged access to whether our thought is genuinely object-dependent, we could, as we have just seen, use McKinsey's recipe to show that he or she is mistaken. We have here, then, a version of externalism that is incompatible with the claim that we have privileged access to such thought content. This incompatibility will come as a surprise to no one. The privileged access thesis that enjoys wide acceptance is understood in such a way that it does not imply that we have privileged access to the singular propositions associated with singular thoughts—but of this, more in section III.

It is well known that once one postulates kinds, there will be a related notion of kind-dependent thoughts. Since *water* = H_2O, the singular proposition that water is wet = the singular proposition that H_2O is wet. As we will now see, the privileged access thesis does not imply or presuppose that we have privileged access to the singular contents of such kind-dependent thoughts. Indeed, there can be illusory kind-dependent thoughts. The thought that phlogiston caused the fire would be an example: a thinker of the thought might be under the cognitive illusion that it is a kind-dependent thought.

---

[13] Here we use 'existence' atemporally.   [14] Cf. Evans 1982.

III   MORE ON THE PRIVILEGED ACCESS THESIS

Subtleties aside, the privileged access thesis states that if one is able to occurrently think that *p*, then one is one able to know a priori that one is thinking that *p*. Occurrent thoughts, like anything that can be type-individuated, can be so individuated in no end of ways. They can be typed by their physical realizations; they can be typed by the conceptual roles of their constituent concepts and their constituent structure; and, if they have associated singular propositions (with either concrete individuals or universals as constituents), they can be typed by their associated singular propositions. The general point here is the utterly trivial one that individual states can be typed by any properties they possess. It is important to see that the privileged access thesis is concerned with occurrent thoughts typed in as *fine-grained* a way as is necessary for the purposes of *any* rationalizing explanation. Whether typing occurrent thoughts by their contents will suffice for typing them in a way fine-grained enough for such purposes will depend on what sorts of contents are in question.

As is well known, there are nowadays many distinct notions of content that are subjects of philosophical discussion. Not all will serve to individuate thoughts in a way that captures their role in rationalizing explanations. Consider the notion according to which contents are sets of possible worlds. On this notion, the content that $2 + 2 = 4$ equals the content that *bachelors are unmarried*. Now the state-type thinking that $2 + 2 = 4$ plays a different role in rationalizing explanations from the state-type thinking that *bachelors are unmarried*. Thus, if the contents of the occurrent thoughts are taken to be sets of possible worlds, then occurrent thoughts cannot be type-individuated for the purposes of rationalizing explanations by their contents alone. It will not be true that no two occurrent thought types can have exactly the same content.

Similarly, if there is a sense in which singular propositions can be thought contents, then typing occurrent thoughts by their contents (in this sense of content) will not suffice for typing them in a way sufficiently fine-grained for every sort of rationalizing explanation. Consider propositions that contain kinds as constituents. Since water $= H_2O$, any thought associated with a singular proposition that contains the kind water as a constituent is trivially associated with a singular proposition that contains H_2O as a constituent: namely, the one that contains water as a constituent. None the less, as Saul Kripke pointed out, while one can know a priori that water = water, one cannot know a priori that water $= H_2O$.[15] So, if a thought can have as its content a

---

[15] See Kripke 1972.

singular proposition that contains the kind in question as a constituent, then typing the thought by its content will not enable us to type it in a way sufficiently fine-grained for all rationalizing explanations.

Indeed, the mental state type *thinking that water is wet* can play a different role in rationalizing explanation from the role played by the mental state type *thinking that H_2O is wet*. They are distinct mental state types. One can be in a state of the first type without being in a state of the second type. This is because while water = H_2O, the concept of water is distinct from the concept of H_2O. These distinct concepts afford us two different ways of thinking of a single kind of stuff. Thus, thinking of something as water is different from thinking of it as H_2O. While the concept of water and the concept of H_2O are necessarily co-extensive, that fact cannot be known a priori; so it cannot be known a priori that water = H_2O.

The issue of fine-grained individuation is, of course, of crucial importance for the present discussion. For the privileged access thesis concerns a priori knowledge—knowledge that is not justificatorily based on empirical investigation. The beliefs that count as such knowledge are typed in an appropriately fined-grained way. The that-clauses we use to ascribe such beliefs are hyperintensional: substitution of necessarily co-designating terms (e.g. 'water' and 'H_2O') can fail to preserve truth.

It is fairly common for philosophers who maintain that thoughts have singular propositions as their contents to maintain two-factor theories of thought types.[16] On this view, it is not true that no two thought types can have exactly the same content. What is true, on this view, is, rather, that no two thought types can have exactly the same content and the same mode of presentation of that content. Some philosophers, however, maintain that singular propositions are not thought contents, but are, rather, components of thought contents. They embrace a two-factor theory of *content*, with singular propositions as (sometimes) one of the two factors and a mode of presentation as the other.[17] On this view, it *is* true that no two thought types can have exactly the same content. Thought types can thus be individuated by their contents. However, propositions, and thus singular propositions, are not themselves thought contents, but rather one of two components that comprise thought contents.

The difference between two-factor theories of thought types and two-factor theories of content strikes us superficial—indeed, as verbal. Which view to adopt seems a matter of deciding how one wants to use

---

[16] Fodor 1987; McLaughlin 1991 and 1993.
[17] For discussion of various theories of this sort, see McGinn 1982.

the word 'content'. If by 'content' one means whatever information that-clauses provide that suffices for the purposes of even the most demanding rationalizing explanation, then one will opt for a two-factor theory of content. If, on the other hand, by 'content' one means truth-conditions or propositions (on certain conceptions of these, e.g. the possible worlds conception), then one will opt for a two-factor theory of thought types, and deny that thought types can be individuated by their contents in a sufficiently fine-grained way.[18]

The privileged access thesis is neutral between a two-factor theory of content and a two-factor theory of thought types. The thesis is just that one can always know a priori that one is occurrently thinking that *p* (*that* water is wet, *that* snow is white, etc.)—provided, of course, that one can form beliefs about one's occurrent thoughts in the normal way. There is no implication that one can know a priori that one's thought that *p* has a singular content or that it has a content into which a singular proposition enters as a component. No doubt that point is obvious. Perhaps it is too obvious to bear repeating. We have underscored it only because of its importance. Were an incompatibilist to insist that privileged access should be understood in such a way as to imply that we have privileged access to whether our occurrent thoughts have associated singular propositions, then the proper response would be to reject the absurdly strong privileged access thesis.

IV McGINN'S EXTERNALISM[19]

Consider an externalist thesis that McGinn (1989: 35–6 and 47–8) claims to draw from Putnam's Twin Earth thought experiment. It deserves our attention since it is, we believe, the strongest externalist thesis that any proponent of externalism has claimed to be supported by Putnam-type Twin Earth thought experiments. The thesis is this:

> (M) If the concept of *X* is an atomic, natural kind concept, then it is metaphysically impossible to possess it unless one has causally interacted with instances of *X*.

McGinn takes this to be a conceptual truth, knowable a priori on the basis of Putnam-type Twin Earth thought experiments.[20]

---

[18] For further discussion of these issues, see McLaughlin 1991 and 1993.

[19] We are concerned in this section with what McGinn (1989) calls 'strong externalism', not with his thesis of 'weak externalism'.

[20] As we will argue later, it seems to us that the thesis in question cannot be supported by Putnam-type Twin Earth thought experiments *alone*. We should note that McGinn has informed us that he now thinks that as well.

We should note, however, that McGinn explicitly rejects a certain stronger thesis: namely, that if the concept of X is a natural kind concept, then it is metaphysically impossible to possess it unless one has causally interacted with instances of X. (Even though water is H_2O, the concept of water, according to McGinn, is distinct from the concept of H_2O. We take the same view: one can have the concept of water without having the concept of H_2O.) The concept of H_2O is a natural kind concept, but it is not atomic. An atomic concept lacks any conceptual constituents. The concept of H_2O is molecular, since it has constituents, among which are the concept of hydrogen and the concept of oxygen.[21] The concept of H_2O is constructed out of other concepts. McGinn maintains that it is not required for someone to have the concept of H_2O that the person have causally interacted with any instances of H_2O. He says:

consider the concept H_2O: this is a natural kind concept in the intended sense, but it is surely possible for someone to grasp it in the absence of water, i.e., H_2O; all that is necessary is a grasp of the concepts that make up this concept. . . . complex natural kind concepts [can be] grasped derivatively upon the grasp of their constituent parts. Grasp of these conceptual parts may yet require the presence of instances of their extensions, but it does not follow that the complex concept can be grasped only in the presence of its extension. I take it this point is pretty obvious. (1989: 35)

McGinn is surely right. Scientists theorize about the possibility of chemical compounds that have never actually existed; similarly, biologists theorize about the possibility of species that have never existed. Moreover, new chemical compounds and new species (of e.g. plants) are sometimes intentionally created for the first time in the laboratory. Prior to their creation, the concepts of such species and such molecules lacked any extension.[22]

While McGinn rejects the stronger thesis in question for the reason noted above, he nevertheless embraces, as we said, the weaker thesis (M). He tells us that 'if [a natural kind] concept is primitive [i.e. atomic], then it cannot be possessed derivatively upon the possession of its constituent concepts, and will therefore be subject to twin earth cases: this is the situation with water, cat, and the like' (1989: 35). Given that McGinn holds that the concept of water is a primitive or atomic natural kind concept, his externalist thesis commits him to the view that one cannot think that water is wet unless one has causally interacted with instances of water.

---

[21] Cf. Fodor 1987.   [22] Cf. Burge 1982: 120.

Given this commitment, it might be thought that McGinn's (*M*) can be refuted by a McKinsey-type argument. For, surely, one cannot know a priori that water exists.[23] Thus, someone might argue as follows that McGinn's (*M*) is incompatible with privileged access:

(p1) It is a conceptual truth that if one is thinking that water is a liquid, then one has the concept of water. Since this is a conceptual truth, it is a priori knowable that if one is thinking that water is a liquid, then one has the concept of water.

(p2) It is a conceptual truth that the concept of water is an atomic, natural kind concept. (Hence, it is a priori knowable that the concept of water is an atomic, natural kind concept.)

(p3) It is a conceptual truth that (and hence a priori knowable that): (*M*) if the concept of *X* is an atomic, natural kind concept, then it is metaphysically impossible to possess it unless has one causally interacted with instances of *X*.

(p4) Hence, it is a priori knowable by one that if one is thinking that water is a liquid, then one has causally interacted with instances of water. (From (p1)–(p3).)

(p5) It is not a priori knowable by one that one has causally interacted with instances of water.

Therefore,

(c) It is not a priori knowable by one that one is thinking that water is a liquid.

Conclusion (c) is incompatible with privileged access. The argument purports to derive (c) from (p3)—i.e. the claim that it is a priori knowable that (*M*)—with the help of only conceptually necessary truths. Thus, if the argument is sound, then (p3), the claim that it is a priori knowable that (*M*), itself analytically implies (c). It follows that the claim that it is a priori knowable that (*M*) is incompatible with privileged access. McGinn's version of externalism is that it is a priori knowable (via Putnam's Twin Earth thought experiment) that (*M*). Hence, McGinn's externalism is incompatible with privileged access.

The pattern of reasoning in the above incompatibility argument is correct. However, the argument is, we believe, unsound. McGinn has nowhere asserted (p2), the claim that it is a *conceptual* truth that the concept of water is an atomic, natural kind concept. Given that he holds that such concepts cannot lack an extension, he obviously should reject

---

[23] Warfield 1995 discusses the application of a McKinsey-type argument to McGinn's specific brand of externalism, and responds to the argument by embracing the view that we can know a priori that water exists. As we indicated, we reject the view.

the claim that it is a conceptual truth that the concept of water is an atomic, natural kind concept. Without premiss (p2), the incompatibility argument does not go through.

Would it be *ad hoc* for McGinn to reject the claim that we can know a priori whether a concept is an atomic, natural kind concept? Should he not instead reject the claim that atomic, natural kind concepts cannot lack an extension, and thus, instead, reject (*M*)? We think it can often be known a priori that a concept is not atomic. We think it is an open question, however, whether it can always be known a priori whether a concept is atomic. The issue seems to us a difficult one.[24] But in any case, as McGinn uses the notion of a natural kind concept, one certainly cannot always, or even typically, know a priori that a concept is a natural kind concept. For as he uses the notion, the concept of *X* is a natural kind concept if and only if *X* is a natural kind. And one typically cannot know a priori that some *X* is a natural kind. In particular, while water is a natural kind, we cannot know a priori that it is. It is a very familiar point that it is *epistemically* possible that water might have turned out to be like air, or like jade. We could conceivably discover, for example, that there actually is no single sort of substance to which the concept of water applies. Very unlikely, of course, but certainly epistemically possible. Indeed, as we will see in the following section, it seems epistemically possible that the concept of water could turn out to be like the concept of phlogiston. It seems epistemically possible for us to obtain (misleading) evidence that there neither is nor ever has been any water, that our entire community has long been under a grand illusion.[25] That would not show that we lack the concept *water*. (Indeed, for it to be epistemically possible for us to obtain such evidence, we would have to *have* the concept *water*.) If, in a highly sceptical frame of mind, one were now to think to oneself, 'There neither is nor ever has been any water,' one would certainly not be making a *conceptual* mistake.

We thus maintain that the conjunction of (*M*) and McGinn's claim that the concept of water is an atomic, natural kind concept is compatible with the claim that one can know a priori that one is thinking that water is a liquid. For that conjunctive claim does not commit him to the view that one can know a priori that the concept of water is an

[24] Boghossian (Ch. 9 above) commits himself to the strong thesis that we can always know a priori whether a concept is atomic. We will remain agnostic on that complex issue.
[25] This sort of case first appears in Burge 1982: 116. We will return to it below in the discussions of Burge 1982, Brown 1995, and Boghossian, Ch. 9 above.

atomic, natural kind concept. He can and should reject the claim that we can know a priori that the concept of water is a natural kind concept; for we patently cannot know a priori that water is a kind, or even that it exists. Indeed, anyone who embraces (M) should reject the claim that we can know a priori when a concept is an atomic, natural kind concept: we could not, since such concepts, by hypothesis, cannot lack an extension.

Parallel points hold for the earlier case of object-dependent thoughts. Such thoughts are individuated in part by external factors: namely, by the existence of the relevant object or individual. Thus, suppose that the thought that Cicero is an orator is an object-dependent thought, because the concept of Cicero is in fact a singular concept of an actual individual: namely, Cicero. Then, in any possible world, w, someone can think that Cicero is an orator in w only if Cicero exists in w. For the thought that Cicero is an orator will contain as a component of its content the singular proposition that Cicero is an orator, a proposition that contains Cicero himself as a constituent. Obviously, one cannot know a priori that Cicero exists; it is epistemically possible that Cicero is a fictional character. Does it follow that one cannot know a priori that one is thinking that Cicero is an orator? In a word, 'No'. What the theory of object-dependent thoughts implies is that *if* Cicero actually exists, then in any possible world, w, one can think that Cicero is an orator in w only if Cicero exists in w. Since one cannot know a priori that Cicero actually exists, one cannot know a priori that there is some actual individual, Cicero, such that one's singular concept is a concept of that individual. If one's thought that Cicero is an orator is an object-dependent thought, that is an a posteriori fact about it. One can know a priori that one is thinking that Cicero is an orator. What one cannot know a priori is that one's thought that Cicero is an orator is a singular thought. The externalist doctrine that there are object-dependent thoughts is thus compatible with privileged access. For, as we noted, the privileged access thesis does not imply that we can know a priori whether our thought is a singular thought, a thought with a singular proposition as a component of its rationalizing content.

We conclude, then, that the above line of argument fails to show that McGinn's (M) is incompatible with privileged access. And, as we noted, (M) is the strongest thesis any *externalist* has claimed is supported by Putnam-type Twin Earth thought experiments.[26]

---

[26] We will, however, return to the issue of whether (M) is compatible with privileged access when we discuss a line of argument due to Boghossian (Ch. 9 above).

V IS (M) TOO STRONG?

While we hold that (M) is compatible with privileged access, the thesis seems to us too strong to be supportable by Putnam-type Twin Earth thought experiments alone. A Putnam-type Twin Earth case proposed by Tyler Burge (1982) seems to us to show this.

Burge (1982) argues that it is possible to have water thoughts (thoughts involving the exercise of the concept of water) without the existence of water. Burge describes a kind of case that Boghossian (Ch. 9 above) aptly dubs a 'Dry Earth' case. Burge tells us:

it is logically possible for an individual to have beliefs involving the concept of water (aluminum, and so on), even though there exists no water. An individual or community might (logically speaking) have been wrong in thinking that there was such a thing as water. It is epistemically possible—it might have turned out—that contrary to an individual's beliefs, water did not exist. (1982: 114)[27]

Burge asks us to imagine a world in which an individual, Adam, is a member of community that is under 'a communal illusion' (1982: 116) that there is a certain liquid with such-and-such phenomenal properties (the phenomenal properties of water) that fills their oceans and lakes, flows in their rivers and streams, that often falls from the sky, that can freeze solid or be heated into a gaseous state, and so on, and so forth. Burge goes on to tell us that the experts in Adam's community theorize that the (illusory) liquid, which they and Adam intend to call 'water', is H_2O. That requires, of course, that they have the concept of H_2O. But, as we noted earlier, the concept of H_2O is a molecular concept that it is possible to possess even if there is no H_2O, and thus no water. In the situation in question, some members of the community have causally interacted with hydrogen and with oxygen; however, the rare hydrogen and oxygen atoms in the area have never been sufficiently close enough to bond to form the molecule H_2O. Burge plausibly claims that in such a situation, Adam counts as having the concept of water.

Is Adam's concept atomic? While Burge does not address this question, absolutely nothing in his scenario suggests otherwise. The notion

[27] It should be noted that since we hold that the metaphysically possible worlds = the logically possible worlds, we regard it as logically impossible for an individual to have beliefs involving the concept of water in a world without water, *if* this is metaphysically impossible. Some logical impossibilities (e.g. that water is not H_2O) are such that we cannot know a priori that they are logical impossibilities. (It is logically impossible that *p*, in this sense, if and only if *p* fails to hold in *any* possible world. For a discussion of this general point, see Hill and McLaughlin, forthcoming.) However, as we will see below, Burge makes a compelling case that it is metaphysically possible for an individual to have the concept of water in a world without water.

of an atomic concept makes clearest sense on a language of thought view.[28] On the language of thought view of concepts, a concept is a mentalese symbol that a thinker is disposed to use in certain ways in thoughts. The concept is atomic if and only if the relevant mentalese word is syntactically atomic.[29] Burge's scenario is perfectly compatible with Adam's concept being atomic in this syntactic sense. Moreover, while this is the standard understanding of an atomic concept,[30] one could, if one wished, add the further requirement that the word not be *definable* in terms of other mentalese words. For that condition too is met in Burge's Dry Earth scenario. Not even the experts in Adam's community take the concept of water to be a priori equivalent to the concept of H_2O. They do not define 'water' as H_2O. They just hypothesize, on the evidence, that water = H_2O.

We take this Burge Dry Earth case to show that Putnam's Twin Earth thought experiment fails to support McGinn's thesis (*M*). We are inclined to think, however, that a Putnam Twin Earth thought experiment supports an externalist thesis like the following:

(M+) If the concept of X is an atomic natural kind concept, then one cannot possess it unless one has either causally interacted with instances of X or one has causally interacted with instances of the kinds that make up the kind X.

It is important to keep in mind that while the concept of water may well be atomic, the kind water itself is made up of other kinds (the kinds hydrogen and oxygen).[31]

Notice that in the Dry Earth world in question, people other than Adam exist. Does having water thoughts require the existence of other people? Surely not. As Burge (1982: 116) correctly notes, one might causally interact with water and, as a result, form the concept of water, even if there were no other people. Just imagine Adam alone in a world, but causally interacting with water and forming beliefs about it.

We see, then, that it is possible for Adam to have the concept of water even if there are no other people in Adam's world. And it is possible

[28] It is worth noting that it is sometimes maintained that a syntactic notion of conceptual constituency can be accommodated within connectionist architectures employing distributed representations, without those architectures implementing a language of thought (see Smolensky 1995). For an argument that no such architecture has yet been proposed, see McLaughlin 1997 (which is a response to Smolensky 1995).

[29] On this view, the mentalese orthographic type the relevant word falls under is not an essential feature of a concept. This language of thought view of concepts does *not* require that there be a single mentalese language. See McLaughlin 1991.

[30] See e.g. McLaughlin 1987; Fodor 1987; Fodor and McLaughlin 1990; and McLaughlin 1997.

[31] For a discussion of kinds making up other kinds, see Forrest 1986.

for Adam to have the concept of water even if there is no water in Adam's world. But is it possible for Adam to have water thoughts without *either* water *or* other people existing?[32] It seems to us that the answer is 'Yes'. A variation on Burge's Dry Earth example can be used to argue this; we think the example stands or falls with his original Dry Earth example presented in the second paragraph of this section. Let the Dry Earth example be just as Burge describes it, with these exceptions: Adam exists alone in his world, but manages to develop a theory of chemistry on his own, and eventually comes to the conclusion that the (illusory) liquid is H_2O. (While Adam has causally interacted with hydrogen and with oxygen, he has not causally interacted with H_2O.) We maintain that Adam has the concept of water. Yet Adam is in a world without either water or other people. We take this example to show that Twin Earth thought experiments are consistent with the view that one can possess the concept of water in a world without water or other people.

In our example, Adam possesses the concept of H_2O. Suppose, however, that Adam lacks the concept of H_2O, and indeed has no opinion about the chemical structure of what he intends to apply his word 'water' to, being entirely ignorant of chemical theory. And suppose further that there are no other people in his world. In *that case, given* the empirical fact that water is really a natural kind, we share Burge's attitude that it 'seems incredible . . . to suppose that Adam, in his relative ignorance and indifference about the nature of water, holds beliefs whose contents involve the notion, even though neither water nor communal cohorts exist' (1982: 116). Given that water is really a natural kind, given that Adam is ignorant of the nature of water, given his lack of any causal interaction with water, and given the fact that he is not a member of any linguistic community with a word that means water (since there are no other people), there seems to be nothing that would *make* Adam's concept the concept of water. In this scenario, it seems to us reasonable to conclude that Adam lacks the concept of water.

VI   BOGHOSSIAN'S DRY EARTH ARGUMENT

Boghossian asks us to

suppose that Oscar—our prototypical Twin Earth subject—is a compatibilist. I claim that Oscar is in a position to argue, purely a priori, as follows:

---

[32] This question has been pressed by Brown (1995), and is raised by Boghossian (p. 276 above), though he does not press the issue. We discuss Boghossian, Ch. 9, and Brown 1995 below.

(1) If I have the concept *water*, then water exists.

(2) I have the concept *water*.

Therefore,

(3) Water exists.

Since the conclusion is clearly not knowable a priori, one of the premises in Oscar's evidently valid reasoning had better be either false or not knowable a priori. The question is: can Oscar, *qua* compatibilist, safely count on one or the other claim? I shall argue that he cannot, that he is committed to both premises (1) and (2) and to their being knowable a priori. If I am right, then the compatibilist is committed to the manifestly absurd conclusion that we can know a priori that water exists. (p. 275 above)

This is, of course, an application of McKinsey's recipe.[33]

The first question to ask, then, is what doctrine the externalist is alleged to hold. Boghossian tells us that he has in mind specifically the view that the 'Putnamian Twin Earth fantasies' underwrite

the claim that, in the case of an atomic, natural kind concept C, the substance actually picked out by C enters into the individuation of C. To put the claim another way: the substances with which a person actually interacts help determine what atomic, natural kind concepts, if any, that person has. (p. 273 above)

It appears, then, that Boghossian is concerned with McGinn's principle (M). We have argued that (M) is too strong to be supportable by Twin Earth thought experiments alone. However, we have also argued that (M) is compatible with privileged access. For that reason, we must address Boghossian's incompatibilist argument. But there is a further reason. As will become clear, if his incompatibilist argument against (M) succeeds, it will succeed against the weaker thesis (M+) as well. And we maintain that (M+) *is* supportable by Putnam-type Twin Earth experiments. For simplicity, we will follow Boghossian in framing the issue in terms of (M); and we will speak of (M)-externalists, as a shorthand for proponents of (M).

In section IV, we said that proponents of (M) can, and should, maintain that we cannot know a priori that if we have the concept of water,

---

[33] Boghossian cites McKinsey 1991, after saying 'Anti-compatibilist arguments with this general form have been attempted in the past, but I believe that those earlier efforts have misstated the case that needs to be made' (p. 272 above). And he accurately cites Brueckner 1992 as an 'effective response' to McKinsey 1991. As we will see in due course, Brown 1995 offers a version of the same McKinsey form of argument, but does not fall prey to the response in Brueckner 1992. It will become apparent, however, that Boghossian's argument differs from McKinsey's and Brown's in an important respect: he offers a novel defence of the claim that compatibilists are committed to the first premiss of the argument—'If I have the concept of water, then water exists'—being a priori. We examine his novel defence below.

then water exists. For we cannot know a priori whether water is a natural kind. Boghossian anticipates this compatibilist response to the McKinsey line of argument. He claims that it 'doesn't ultimately protect compatibilism from the charge of absurdity' (p. 279 above). We believe that Boghossian fails to substantiate this charge, and thus fails to show that (M) is incompatible with privileged access. But before examining the considerations he offers in support of his incompatibilist claim, we want first to pave the way for a fluid discussion by presenting some of his terminology, and by quickly conceding some assumptions he makes.

Boghossian invokes the notion of a term or concept that *aims* to name a natural kind. By aiming to name a natural kind, he means purporting to name a natural kind; so a concept can aim to name a natural kind even when there is no natural kind such that the concept aims to name it.[34] Moreover, Boghossian holds that one can always know a priori whether one's concept aims to denote a natural kind *and* whether it is an atomic concept. For the sake of argument, we will grant this twofold assumption. Finally, we will take it as given (albeit not a priori) that our concept of water is an atomic concept that denotes a natural kind.

As we noted, Boghossian argues that the compatibilist response mentioned above to McKinsey-type arguments 'doesn't ultimately protect compatibilism from the charge of absurdity'. He tries to establish this by arguing that (M)-externalists are committed to the thesis that 'if a term expresses [an atomic concept that aims to name a natural kind], it must have a non-empty extension' (p. 283 above). After having purported to establish that claim, he says that a compatibilist

will be able to tell non-empirically that his term 'water' expresses [an atomic concept that aims to name a natural kind], and in particular that it expresses the concept *water*. Putting these two bits of information together, he is in a position to conclude, a priori, that water must have existed at some time. And that, we are all agreed, is not something he ought to be able to do. (p. 283 above)

We deny that (M)-externalists are committed to the thesis that 'if a term expresses [an atomic concept that aims to name a natural kind], then it must have a non-empty extension.' We maintain that (M)-externalists can consistently hold that such a term can fail to name anything at all.

Let us see, then, how Boghossian argues for the claim we are denying. He presents a Burge-type Dry Earth scenario. He asks us to

[34] This notion requires explication. Can a concept at one time aim to denote a natural kind, but then fail to so aim at later time? Did the concepts of air, of earth, and of fire once aim to name natural kinds, but no longer do? Did the concept of phlogiston once aim to name a natural kind, though not any longer? We will not pursue these questions here. For a discussion of these questions in connection with this notion of a term/concept that purports (but fails) to name a natural kind, see Bach 1987: ch. 13.

imagine a planet just like ours on which, although it very much seems to its inhabitants that there is a clear, tasteless, colourless liquid flowing in their rivers and taps and to which they confidently take themselves to be applying the word 'water', these appearances are systematically false, and constitute a sort of pervasive collective mirage. In point of actual fact, the lakes, rivers, and taps on this particular Twin Earth run bone-dry. All this may seem very far-fetched, and no doubt it is. However, the scenario described is not substantially different—except in point of pervasiveness—from what has actually turned out to be true in the case of such terms as 'phlogiston' and 'caloric'; and, anyway, the point isn't to describe a genuine possibility. Rather, it is to enquire how a particular semantical theory proposes to treat cases of reference failure, and whether it is committed to treating such cases in a particular way. (pp. 279–80 above)

(M)-externalists are, to be sure, committed to the view that *if* water is a natural kind, then the Dry Earthers are not expressing the concept of water. It is important to see that they are committed *only* to this conditional claim. For a proponent of (M) can maintain that we cannot know a priori that we are not Dry Earthers. It is instructive to compare (M), once again, with the thesis that *if* Cicero exists, then occupants of a world in which he fails to exist cannot have the concept of Cicero. A proponent of this thesis can hold that we can know a priori that we have the concept of Cicero, even though we cannot know a priori whether Cicero exists. Likewise, a proponent of (M) can hold that we can know a priori that we have the concept of water, even though we cannot know a priori whether water exists.

Immediately after the remarks quoted above, Boghossian asks: 'What *concept*, if any, should a Twin Earth externalist say would be expressed by tokens of the word "water" on this Dry Earth?' (ibid.) This question involves a mistaken presupposition: namely, that there is an answer to it to which *all* (M)-externalists are committed. They *are* committed to a specific possession condition for atomic natural kind concepts: namely, that the possessor of the concept have causally interacted with instances of the kind in question. But proponents of (M) are *not* committed to any view about the specific possession conditions for atomic concepts that aim, but fail, to name natural kinds. While Dry Earthers have a concept that aims to name a natural kind, their concept is not a natural kind concept in the intended sense of (M), since, by hypothesis, it fails to name a natural kind. Thus, (M) is silent about the case in question.

Still, (M)-externalists can, and we believe should, allow that an atomic concept that aims to name a natural kind can fail to name a kind, either natural or motley. Suppose some Dry Earther, Toscar, is an *intrinsic physical duplicate* (and thus a functional duplicate) of an

Earthling, Oscar, who possesses the concept of water.[35] It is consistent with (M), and in no way contrary to the spirit of (M), that Toscar has a concept that has exactly the same (narrow) conceptual role as Oscar's concept of water. Atomic concepts have conceptual roles. Proponents of (M) can allow that whether an atomic concept *aims* to name a natural kind supervenes on its conceptual role. That is contrary *neither* to the letter *nor* to the spirit of (M). Proponents of (M) claim only that *what* atomic, natural kind concept, if any, one possesses is not determined by conceptual role, since it depends on causal relations with the environment. Given that the conceptual role of a concept determines whether it aims to name a natural kind, by hypothesis, Toscar's atomic concept aims to name a natural kind. Moreover, we can suppose that Toscar's atomic concept is associated with the same reference-fixing description as is Oscar's concept of water. The difference in the case of Toscar is that nothing answers to the reference-fixing description; and, further, in Toscar's case, unlike Oscar's, 'there is no natural kind at the end of the relevant causal chain leading up to [his] uses of "water"' (p. 282 above). Indeed, in unfortunate Toscar's case, there is not even a motley kind at the end of the relevant causal chains. His concept fails to denote any kind at all, natural or motley.[36]

(M)-externalists can maintain all of the above about Toscar *without* being committed to the view that atomic concepts that aim to name natural kinds have *two* sorts of contents, narrow and wide.[37] To avoid commitment to narrow contents, they can claim that the possession conditions for atomic concepts that aim to name a natural kind (whether or not they succeed) are, in part, external conditions. That would not commit them to *specific* possession conditions for atomic concepts that purport to name natural kinds. Proponents of (M) can differ, for instance, over which environmental factors are relevant to *what* concept

---

[35] This Earthly Oscar is *not* Boghossian's compatibilist Oscar who believes that water = H$_2$O; he is the more familiar Oscar of Twin Earth thought experiments, the Oscar who lacks any knowledge of chemistry.

[36] While Boghossian nowhere mentions the direct theory of reference, it is tempting to think that he may have *mistakenly* assumed that proponents of (M) are committed to such a theory for atomic, natural kind concepts. According to a direct reference theory, the reference of a term or concept *exhausts* its content. Proponents of (M) *are* committed to the Kripke–Putnam model of natural kind terms and concepts; but, as Michael Devitt has repeatedly pointed out (see e.g. Devitt 1983), that model does *not* presuppose a direct reference theory. Proponents of (M) can, and we believe should, flatly reject a direct reference theory for atomic, natural kind concepts. (Moreover, if any proponents of (M) opt for such a theory (thereby eschewing a two-factor theory of content), then they should adopt a two-factor theory of atomic concept types that aim to denote natural kinds, one that appeals to conceptual roles as one of the two individuating factors. (See our discussion in section III.))

[37] Thesis (M) is, however, *consistent* with the view that there is narrow content.

is possessed in the cases in question, and over the contribution of conceptual role. So proponents of (*M*) can differ over what concept Toscar expresses with his word 'water'.

Still, for the sake of illustration, it is useful to have a concrete proposal on the table. Suppose, then, that the concept of water has conceptual role *CR*. Since Toscar's concept has the same conceptual role as Oscar's concept (which is, of course, the concept of water), Toscar's concept has role *CR*. Here, then, is a proposal available to proponents of (*M*). What concept is Toscar actually expressing when he uses 'water'? He is expressing the concept one possesses if and only if one has an atomic concept with conceptual role *CR*, but nothing satisfies the reference-fixing description associated with it, and there is no kind, natural or motley, at the end of the relevant causal chains leading to one's use of it.[38]

Of course, if Boghossian wants a description of Toscar's concept that has the form 'the form *F*', then a new term must be coined; for, by (empirical) assumption, we are not Dry Earthers, and so the concept Toscar is expressing is not the concept of water. Consider the situation of XYZ-Twin Earth. As Burge pointed out in that case, 'In translating into English occurrences of "water" in the mouths of Twin-Earthians, we would do best to coin a new non-scientific word (say "twater")' (1982: 100). Having coined the term 'twater', we can say: XYZ-Twin Earthers have the concept *twater*. While Burge (1982: 116) did not explicitly make this point about translation in connection with his Dry Earth case, the same is true of that case. To translate, we would need to coin a new term, say 'dwater'. Having coined the term, we can say that Toscar has the concept *dwater*—the concept whose possession condition we stated above.

After raising his question—'What *concept*, if any, should a Twin Earth externalist say would be expressed by tokens of the word "water" on this Dry Earth?' (p. 280 above)—Boghossian answers his question as follows:

Unfortunately, there would appear to be a compelling argument showing that the externalist will not be able to say what atomic concept is expressed by the non-referring tokens of 'water', because by his own lights there can't be such a concept. Let me explain. (p. 282 above)

Since we have just denied that proponents of (*M*) must say that Toscar lacks a concept, let us look at Boghossian's explanation in detail.
He first tells us:

We have seen that one of the assumptions that is needed to transform a Twin Earth experiment into an argument for externalism is the assumption that

---

[38] Other proposals are available. We offer this one just for simple illustration.

concepts have context-independent conditions of satisfaction, or, in the case of thought contents, context-independent conditions of truth. (p. 282 above)

By saying that, on the externalist view, concepts have context-independent conditions of satisfaction, he means that externalism implies that natural kind concepts are entirely non-indexical; and, similarly for the relevant thoughts. This is, of course, correct.

Boghossian immediately goes on to say:

So let us ask this: what are the satisfaction conditions for 'water' on Dry Earth; to what sorts of liquid does it apply? By assumption, of course, the actual extension of 'water' is empty on Dry Earth, so there is no liquid in its actual environment to which it applies. But the question I am asking is consistent with the word's actual extension being empty, and consistent even with its extension being empty in all worlds. What I want to know is: what proposition—what truth-condition —is expressed by sentences of the form 'Water is wet', for example, as uttered on Dry Earth? What is it that gets said? Never mind if such sentences are ruled false in the actual world, or even in all worlds.

On the line we are currently investigating, the answer has to be that there is no fact of the matter what truth-condition is expressed by sentences involving 'water' on Dry Earth, for there is no fact of the matter what property is denoted by those tokens of 'water'. Since there is no natural kind at the end of the relevant causal chain leading up to uses of 'water' on Dry Earth, there is no fact of the matter what the referent of 'water' is, and so no fact of the matter what proposition is expressed by sentences involving it.

But on an externalist view, this admission is fatal to the claim that there is a concept there in the first place, for an externalism about concepts is fuelled in part by the conviction that thought contents must possess context-invariant conditions of satisfaction or, as appropriate, of truth. If, in a given context, there is no fact of the matter what the referent of a given concept is, then to that extent there is also no fact of the matter what the concept is. (pp. 282–3 above)

This, then, is the complete text of Boghossian's explanation. We deny that (M)-externalists are committed to saying that there is no fact of the matter what the referent of Toscar's concept is. The (M)-externalist will say that it is a determinate fact that Toscar's concept fails to refer to anything. Moreover, (M)-externalists can hold that there is a fact of the matter as to what Toscar's concept is: he has the concept *dwater*— a concept whose possession conditions we stated earlier.

Consider, then, the questions Boghossian raises in the above quotation: (1) 'What are the satisfaction conditions for "water" on Dry Earth . . . ?' (2) 'What I want to know is: what proposition—what truth-condition—is expressed by sentences of the form "Water is wet", for example, as uttered on Dry Earth? What is it that gets said?' To see what Boghossian takes the force of these questions to be, it is instructive to look at what he claims truth-conditions and propositions are. He tells us:

I think of a sentence's *truth-condition* as the proposition it expresses; and I think of the proposition it expresses as composed out of the referents denoted by its terms. Thus, the truth-condition of the sentence 'Water is wet' is the proposition made up out of the property of being water and the property of being wet which says that anything that has the one has the other. (p. 272 above)

If Boghossian is employing a pleonastic conception of properties in this passage, then the (M)-externalist will happily grant that Toscar's word 'water' refers to a property, since it expresses a concept. For saying that the term 'water' in Toscar's mouth denotes a pleonastic property just amounts to saying that it expresses a concept.[39] On this conception of properties, Toscar will be able to use a *T*-sentence of his Dry English to express the truth-conditions for his sentence 'Water is wet', and to use an *R*-sentence of his Dry English to say what 'water' purports to refer to. Boghossian's questions, then, just raise the issue of how we are to translate 'water' from Dry English to English.[40]

If, however, as seems more likely, Boghossian is employing a robust (metaphysical) conception of properties in the above passage, then the (M)-externalist will say that Toscar's term 'water' fails to denote a robust property, and that 'Water is wet' in his mouth fails to have a truth-condition in the robust sense in question. But the (M)-externalist will insist that it does not follow from this that Toscar fails to express a concept by his term 'water'; for an atomic concept can be non-denoting.[41] (M)-externalists will take the Dry Earth case to demonstrate this very point. Moreover, the (M)-externalist will deny that Toscar fails to assert anything when he utters 'Water is wet'. For the (M)-externalist will emphatically reject the thesis that Toscar's utterance must express a proposition that contains a robust property as a constituent in order for Toscar's utterance to have a truth-condition. The sentence he utters will have disquotational truth-conditions, and that will suffice for Toscar's being able to use the sentence to assert something.

It is instructive to consider what Boghossian thinks may be the correct answers to his questions. He says:

[39] See Schiffer 1989.

[40] According to (M)-externalists, the meanings of T-sentences and R-sentences will not supervene on the conceptual roles of the concepts expressed by terms in the sentences, if any of those concepts aim to denote natural kinds. But, as we have noted, (M)-externalists can hold that the meanings will supervene in such cases on the conceptual roles (plus constituent structure) together with relevant environmental conditions.

[41] Of course, nominalists maintain that *no* concepts denote robust properties, since there are no such properties.

But what concept should we say 'water' expresses under the conditions described, in which there fails to be any natural kind for it to refer to?

We could try saying that under the envisioned dry conditions, 'water' expresses a suitable compound concept made up in the familiar way out of other available concepts. Which compound concept? Most plausibly, I suppose, something like: *the clear, tasteless, colourless liquid that flows in the taps and the rivers around here and . . .* It won't matter much for the purposes of this argument how precisely this proposal is fleshed out . . .

Intuitively, this seems to me to be a plausible view of the matter. When I think of a group of people just like us, applying the word 'water' confidently to something that appears to them to be a clear, colourless, tasteless liquid in their environment, when in fact there is no such liquid in their environment, I feel tempted by the sort of error theory of their linguistic behaviour that the present proposal delivers. It seems plausible to me to say that what these people mean by the word 'water' is this clear, colourless, tasteless liquid etc., which, however and unfortunately, is not to be found in their environment. (pp. 280–1 above)

Notice that the description that Boghossian is tempted to take as expressing the meaning of their word 'water' is one that externalists would maintain is a *reference-fixing* description, rather than a definition. Boghossian is tempted to treat it as definitional, rather than reference-fixing. He is thus tempted to treat Toscar as using his word 'water' to express an indexical, descriptive concept, and thus not as using it to express an atomic context-invariant concept.

As Boghossian himself holds (see pp. 281–2 above), Oscar's concept is atomic if and only if Toscar's is. Indeed, Oscar's concept is an indexical descriptive concept if and only if Toscar's is.[42] Since, by hypothesis, Oscar has the concept of water, Boghossian's temptation should lead him to claim that the concept of water is an indexical, descriptive concept, and so to the view that it is not an atomic, context-invariant concept.

Boghossian says at one point:

In the case of 'water' it will be natural to say that its referent is the property of being water. It is possible to wonder whether it would be equally correct to say that it is the property of being H_2O. That depends on whether the property of being water may be identified with the property of being H_2O, an example of an interesting question in the theory of properties, but not one that I need to settle for present purposes. (p. 272 above)

[42] On Burge's brand of externalism (to be discussed below), the non-indexical descriptive content of an indexical, descriptive concept can fail to supervene on what is in the head, even if no natural kind concepts are constituents of it. But proponents of (M) need not hold that. And, in any case, that is not being challenged above. For perhaps physical twins are such that the one has an indexical descriptive concept if and only if the other does, even *if* the non-indexical descriptive *contents* of their descriptive concepts might differ due to socio-environmental factors.

If Boghossian succumbs to his temptation, he will take a stand on this issue. For suppose that the concept of water is the indexical, descriptive concept described earlier. Then, it is false that water = H_2O. For, at best, H_2O merely happens to be the clear, tasteless, colourless, liquid that flows in the taps and the rivers . . . around here. Something else might have been water. XYZ might have been water.

Boghossian's position seems to be that there are no *atomic*, context-invariant natural kind concepts. He appears to be tempted by a cluster theory of reference for kind terms and concepts.[43] Putnamian Twin Earth externalists presuppose the Kripke–Putnam model of natural kind terms and concepts, a model according to which there are atomic, context-invariant natural kind terms and concepts.[44] Boghossian seems to hold that this comes into conflict with the thesis that we have privileged access to our atomic, context-invariant natural kind concepts. But earlier we noted that proponents of (M) will distinguish two claims:

(1) We can know a priori that we have the concept of water, even if the concept of water is an atomic, natural kind concept.

(2) We can know a priori that the concept of water is an atomic natural kind concept.

(M)-externalists embrace (1), but they can and should reject (2); for we cannot know a priori that the concept of water is in fact a natural kind concept; that is, that it in fact denotes a natural kind. Indeed, we cannot know a priori whether it denotes anything at all. Boghossian, we contend, has not shown that this is an untenable position. He has not reduced the compatibilist position 'to absurdity'.[45]

We want to close by noting that whether the cluster theory that tempts Boghossian is superior to the Kripke–Putnam model of natural kind terms depends on broad considerations of theoretical simplicity and overall coherence. It is well beyond the scope of this essay to adjudicate this dispute. Suffice it to note that (M)-externalists can respond to Boghossian by maintaining that such considerations favour the Kripke–Putnam model over a cluster theory.

---

[43] Recall that Boghossian tells us: 'I think of a sentence's *truth-condition* as the proposition it expresses; and I think of the proposition it expresses as composed out of the referents denoted by its terms' (p. 272 above). Unfortunately, he does not say how he proposes to treat non-referring singular terms (terms that purport singularity of reference but fail to refer) and non-referring general terms. Would he treat the terms in questions as descriptions and take the sentences to be false, since nothing answers to the descriptions?

[44] Burge need not presuppose that semantic model in his Twin Earth thought experiments, however. See section VII.

[45] As we said, (M)-externalists will hold that the issues Boghossian raises are issues of translation.

VII   BURGE'S EXTERNALISM

The version of externalism that is alleged to follow from Burge's *own* (1979) Twin Earth thought experiment is more general than any version alleged to follow from Putnam's Twin Earth thought experiment. Burge says:

The [Putnam] Twin-Earth thought-experiment may work only for certain propositional attitudes. Certainly its clearest applications are to those whose contents involve non-theoretical natural kind notions. But the arguments of 'Individualism and the Mental' [Burge 1979] suggest that virtually no propositional attitudes are described [as] irreducibly non-individualistic, no purely individualistic account of these notions can possibly be adequate. (p. 117)

We will, however, place one restriction on relevant concepts: namely, that they be *deferential*—that is, that they be concepts such that their possessor is disposed to defer about their application in at least certain circumstances.[46]

Burge's (1979) well-known thought experiment involving the concept of arthritis can be used to argue that the contents of thoughts that involve the exercise of a deferential concept are essentially open to social intrusion. Rather than presenting that thought experiment, however, we will illustrate a Burge-type Twin Earth thought experiment using an example we think is a little simpler than his arthritis example, and that highlights how his thought experiment is different from Putnamian ones. Our example can be used to try to argue that thoughts involving the exercise of deferential concepts fail to supervene on *intrinsic* physical properties of thinkers.[47] Suppose that when Tom, a student in one's introductory logic class, is asked to define validity and soundness, he responds 'An argument is sound if and only if, were all its premises true, its conclusion would be; and an argument is valid if and only if it is sound, and all of its premises are true.' If Tom is expressing his belief correctly, then he has made a conceptual mistake: he has confused validity and soundness; and thus his belief is false. Were we to correct him, he would, we shall suppose, defer and accept the correction. Now we can imagine a possible world that contains an intrinsic physical twin of Tom who is a member of a community that speaks a language just

---

[46] This notion is Brian Loar's (1990). We should note that Burge has not confirmed to us that he believes that the restriction to deferential concepts is necessary. Whether it is, is a question beyond the scope of this chapter, and one whose answer will not affect anything we say below.

[47] Burge's (1979) arthritis example is not intended to be restricted to showing failure of supervenience on *intrinsic* physical properties.

like English, except for the fact that in that language, Twin English, 'validity' is used as we use 'soundness', and 'soundness' is used as we use 'validity' (and any other differences that logically follow from this). Twin Tom would express a true belief if he answered the Twin Earth teacher by saying, 'An argument is sound if and only if, were all its premises true, its conclusion would be; and an argument is valid if and only if it is sound, and all of its premises are true.' For what he would be saying, translating into English, is that an argument is valid if and only if, were all its premises true, its conclusion would be; and an argument is sound if and only if it is valid, and all of its premises are true. Thus, while Tom has a false belief involving a conceptual mistake, Twin Tom, by contrast, has a true belief. Yet Tom and Twin Tom are intrinsic physical twins.[48]

Burge's Twin Earth thought experiments arguably support the following thesis:

> (O) If a thinker is a member of a linguistic community, then if the thinker exercises a deferential concept in thinking that p, then the content of the thought is individuated partly by social-environmental factors.

The social-environmental factors will include the relevant linguistic conventions of the community in question. Since two intrinsic physical twins can be members of different linguistic communities with relevantly different conventions, or one twin can be a member of a linguistic community and the other not, the following is implied by (O):

> (O*) If a thinker exercises a deferential concept in thinking that p, then the content of the thinker's thinking that p fails to supervene on intrinsic physical features of the thinker.

Neither of these externalist theses appears to be incompatible with privileged access for McKinsey-type reasons. For even if one can know a priori that one is exercising a deferential concept in thinking that p, one cannot know a priori whether one is a member of a linguistic community.

---

[48] We should note that some philosophers accept Putnam-type Twin Earth thought experiments while rejecting Burge-type Twin Earth thought experiments, and conversely. We find both sorts of thought experiments fairly compelling, but it is not our aim here to defend either sort. Our main aim is to make a case that no combination of either sort of Twin Earth thought experiments supports an externalist thesis that is incompatible with privileged access.

VIII   THE BROWN–MCKINSEY CHARGE OF INCONSISTENCY

Both McKinsey (1991) and, later, Jessica Brown (1995) charge that Burge is committed to a version of externalism that implies for certain *p*s, that if one is thinking that *p*, then *E*—where *E* cannot be known a priori. This charge is made as part of an *ad hominem* argument against Burge. For Burge explicitly endorses a privileged access thesis.[49] Thus, it is argued that he holds two incompatible theses.

As has been correctly pointed out by Brueckner (1992), McKinsey offers no textual evidence for this charge of inconsistency. Brueckner (1992) also correctly notes that Burge (1982) explicitly *denies* that the existence of water is required for possession of the concept of water. Moreover, we argued earlier that he is not committed to the view that the existence of water or other people is required for possession of the concept of water.

Brown (1995), however, offers textual evidence for her charge of inconsistency. Moreover, as we will see, her charge does *not* essentially rest on the (mistaken) assumption that Burge is committed to the view that one cannot have the concept of water unless water or other people exist. We will first present her case and then argue that she fails, none the less, to show that Burge holds an inconsistent position.

Brown cites a passage from Burge's discussion of his Dry Earth case; a passage that we quoted in section V: 'it seems incredible . . . to suppose that Adam, in his relative ignorance and indifference about the nature of water, holds beliefs whose contents involve the notion, even though neither water nor communal cohorts exist' (1982: 116). Appealing to this passage, Brown (1995) maintains that Burge is committed to the following thesis:

> (Q)   Necessarily, if *x* has a thought involving the concept of a natural kind *k* and *x* is agnostic about the application conditions of the concept of *k*, then either *x* is in an environment which contains *k*, or *x* is part of a community with the concept *k*. (p. 152)

---

[49] See his 1988. Burge does not explicitly commit himself to our specific version of privileged access; but that won't matter for present purposes. His discussion of privileged access is confined to the special case in which one thinks that one is thinking, with the very thought in question, that *p*. Our notion extends to that case and others. Thus, we believe that our privileged access thesis implies any privileged access thesis Burge is committed to endorsing. As will become apparent, we maintain that Brown fails to show that Burge holds views incompatible with the privileged access thesis we have stated.

While this goes beyond what is actually in the passage, Burge makes it clear elsewhere that he intends the water example to generalize to any concept that is in fact a concept of a natural kind. Moreover, Brown is explicit that the phrase 'the concept of a natural kind k' is being used to mean 'the concept of k, where k is a natural kind'; so a natural kind concept must actually denote a natural kind. It is clear that Burge is employing that notion of a natural kind concept. Further, by Adam's agnosticism about the application conditions for the concept of k, we take Brown to mean that Adam is agnostic about the hidden (chemical) nature of the (illusory) stuff he intends to call 'water'. (We take it that Adam accepts an appropriate disquotational R-sentence in his language for his term.) Given these qualifications, we believe that Burge is indeed committed to (Q).

Now Brown does not attempt to argue that (Q) itself commits Burge to denying privileged access. She correctly notes that one cannot know a priori that the concept of k is a natural kind concept, since one cannot know a priori that k is a natural kind. She correctly points out that the concept of water could have turned out to be like the concept of jade. However, she maintains that, in addition to Burge's being committed to (Q), he is also committed to a second thesis, (R), which, in conjunction with (Q), commits him to denying privileged access. The second thesis is this:

> (R) necessarily, if x has a thought involving a non-natural kind concept, c, and x is agnostic about the application conditions of c, then x is part of a community which has the concept c.

We contend that Brown is mistaken in attributing (R) to Burge, and thus that she fails to substantiate her charge of inconsistency. We take (R) to be false; and we see no evidence that Burge believes it. But of this, more shortly. Let us first see how Brown argues that holding (R) commits Burge to an inconsistent position.

Brown correctly maintains that this second thesis, (R), in conjunction with the first thesis, (Q), implies the following thesis:

> (S) Necessarily, if x has a thought involving a concept c, and x is agnostic about the application conditions of c, then either x is in an environment which contains instances of c and c is a natural kind concept, or x is part of a community which has the concept c, whether or not c is a natural kind concept.
> (1995: 155)

If (S) can indeed be known a priori, then privileged access is false. For the following claims are inconsistent:

(A)   It is knowable a priori by one that one is having a thought involving the concept of *c*.

(B)   It is knowable a priori by one that one is agnostic about the application conditions of *c*.

(C)   It is not knowable a priori by one that one is in an environment which either contains instances of *c* and *c* is a natural kind concept, or one is part of a community which has the concept *c*, whether or not *c* is a natural kind concept.

Claims (A) and (B) follow from the thesis of privileged access. So (S) is incompatible with privileged access. We thus have, in (S), a version of externalism that cannot be squared with privileged access. If Burge is really committed to (S), then he cannot consistently maintain privileged access. Brown concludes: 'Burge's position is inconsistent . . . Burgian anti-individualism and the Principle of Privileged Access are incompatible' (1995: 155).

As we said, we acknowledge that Burge is committed to (Q). But Brown has succeeded in showing that he is also committed to (S) only if she has succeeded in showing that he is committed to (R). (For her argument that he is so committed appeals to the fact that (Q) and (R) imply (S).) And, as we noted, we deny that he is committed to (R).

Consider, once again,

(R)   Necessarily, if *x* has a thought involving a non-natural kind concept, *c*, and *x* is agnostic about the application conditions of *c*, then *x* is part of a community which has the concept *c*.

Why does Brown believe that Burge is committed to (R)? We will quote her at length:

Burge's argument for the claim that [Adam, who, you will recall, is ignorant of the nature of water] could not have a water thought unless water or other speakers exist, seems applicable to thoughts involving non-natural kind concepts. Imagine that [Adam] is agnostic about the application of the word 'sofa'. For example, he may apply it firmly and correctly to what we call 'sofas', but be unsure about whether it also applies to broad single seat armchairs. According to Burge, if [Adam] is part of an English speaking community then, despite his agnosticism, he has thoughts involving the concept sofa. But if, counterfactually, [Adam] had been part of a community in which 'sofa' is applied both to what we call 'sofas' and to broad single seat armchairs, then [Adam] would have had chofa thoughts, where the concept of a chofa applies both to what we call 'sofas' and to broad single seat armchairs. Now imagine that there are no other speakers in [Adam's] environment. How could [Adam] have propositional attitudes involving the concept of sofa? Since sofa is not a natural kind concept, [Adam's] natural environment cannot help him to acquire the concept.

There are no other speakers. Nothing seems to show that his attitudes involve the concept of sofa as opposed to chofa. (1995: 153–4)

On the basis of this reasoning, she concludes that Burge is committed to (R).

We agree with Brown that, in the scenario she describes, 'nothing seems to show that [Adam's] attitudes involve the concept of sofa as opposed to chofa'. Indeed, there seems to be nothing that makes it the case that Adam's attitudes involve the concept *sofa*, and nothing that makes it the case that his attitudes involve the concept *chofa*. It seems that Adam lacks both concepts. But in inferring (R), Brown seems to be tacitly assuming that there is no concept that Adam expresses using his word 'sofa'. We see no justification whatsoever for that assumption. Why can't an individual have a *non*-natural kind concept and be agnostic about the necessary and sufficient conditions for its application without being a member of a linguistic community? Brown does not say.

Notice that were it true that one cannot have a non-natural kind concept, be agnostic about the necessary and sufficient conditions for its application, yet not be a member of any linguistic community, then one could refute the view that one is alone in the world just by determining that one is agnostic about the necessary and sufficient conditions for a concept that one recognizes is not a natural kind concept. Suppose, for example, having taken oneself to have just learned the concept of a priori knowledge, a concept one recognizes not to be a natural kind concept, one wonders what, exactly, the necessary and sufficient conditions are for its application. Could one, from these considerations alone, without assuming one has actually learned the concept, conclude that other people exist? There seems no reason to think so. But if (R) were true, one could. So much the worse for (R).

Notice, moreover, that in the scenario Brown describes, Adam has a concept that he applies to things which are in fact sofas, and that he is unsure whether to apply to things which are in fact broad single-seat armchairs. She tells us that the concept is not a natural kind concept, and that he is not a member of any linguistic community. Indeed, she tells us that Adam applies the term expressing his concept 'firmly and correctly to what we call "sofas"' (1995: 153), even though he is 'unsure whether ["sofa"] applies to broad single seat armchairs'. Thus, it is part of the description of the case that Adam has certain non-natural kind concepts despite the fact that he is not a member of any linguistic community. It follows, then, that the case could not possibly support (R). For the case, which seems perfectly coherent, is itself a counter-example to (R).

In conclusion, McKinsey's recipe is perfectly fine. It is just that no externalist thesis actually supported by Twin Earth thought experiments can serve as an ingredient.[50]

REFERENCES

Back, Kent (1987), *Thought and Reference* (Oxford: Oxford University Press).
Boghossian, Paul A. (1989), 'Content and Self-Knowledge', *Philosophical Topics*, 17: 5–26.
—— (1992), 'Externalism and Inference', *Philosophical Issues*, 2: 11–28.
Brown, Jessica (1995), 'The Incompatibility of Anti-Individualism and Privileged Access', *Analysis*, 53/3: 149–56.
Brueckner, Anthony (1992), 'What an Anti-Individualist Knows A Priori', *Analysis*, 52: 111–18.
—— (1994), 'Knowledge of Content and Knowledge of the External World', *Philosophical Review*, 103: 327–43.
Burge, Tyler (1978), 'Belief and Synonymy', *Journal of Philosophy*, 75: 119–38.
—— (1979), 'Individualism and the Mental', *Midwest Studies in Philosophy*, 4: 73–121.
—— (1982), 'Other Bodies', in A. Woodfield (ed.), *Thought and Object: Essays on Intentionality* (Oxford: Oxford University Press), 97–120.
—— (1988), 'Individualism and Self-Knowledge', *Journal of Philosophy*, 85: 649–63.
—— (1996), 'Our Entitlement to Self-Knowledge', *Proceedings of the Aristotelian Society*, 96: 91–116.
Casteñeda, Hector (1975), *Thinking and Doing* (Dordrecht: Reidel).
Chisholm, Roderick (1977), *Theory of Knowledge*, 2nd edn. (Englewood Cliffs, NJ: Prentice-Hall).
Church, Alonzo (1954), 'Intentional Isomorphism and Identity of Belief', *Philosophical Studies*, 5: 65–73.
Devitt, M. (1983), 'Realism and Semantics', *Nous*, 17: 669–81.
Dretske, Fred (1980), *Knowledge and the Flow of Information* (Cambridge, Mass.: MIT/Bradford).
—— (1988), *Explaining Behavior: Reasons in A World of Causes* (Cambridge, Mass.: MIT/Bradford).
Evans, Gareth (1982), *The Varieties of Reference* (Oxford: Clarendon Press).

[50] Parts of this paper were read at London University, Oxford University, the University of St Andrews, the University of Bielefeld, and in Bled, Slovenia. We wish to thank Ansgar Beckermann, Paul Boghossian, Christian Nimtz, Michael Pietioforte, Chris Peacocke, Katice Saporiti, Barry Smith, Tom Stoneham, Jerry Vision, and Crispin Wright for their comments. We also wish to thank Kent Bach, David Benfield, Carl Gillett, Brian Loar, Cynthia Macdonald, and Colin McGinn for helpful discussions over the years about whether externalism and privileged access are compatible. Finally, we owe special thanks to Barry Loewer and Fritz (Ted) Warfield.

Fodor, Jerry (1987), *Psychosemantics* (Cambridge, Mass.: MIT/Bradford).

—— and McLaughlin, Brian P. (1990), 'Connectionism and the Problem of Systematicity: Why Smolensky's Solution does not Work', *Cognition*, 35: 185–204.

Forrest, P. (1986), 'Ways Worlds Could Be', *Australasian Journal of Philosophy*, 67: 15–24.

Hill, Christopher, and McLaughlin, Brian P. (forthcoming), 'There are Fewer Things in Reality than are Dreamt of in Chalmers's Philosophy', *Philosophy and Phenomenological Research*.

Kripke, S. (1972), 'Naming and Necessity', in G. Harman and D. Davidson (eds.), *The Semantics of Natural Language* (Dordrecht: Reidel), 253–355.

Loar, Brian (1990), 'Personal References', in E. Villanueva (ed.), *Information, Semantics and Epistemology* (Oxford: Blackwell), 117–33.

Mates, Benson (1952), 'Synonymity', in Leonard Linsky (ed.), *Semantics and the Philosophy of Language* (Urbana: University of Illinois Press), 111–36.

McGinn, Colin (1982), 'The Structure of Content', in A Woodfield (ed.), *Thought and Object: Essays on Intentionality* (Oxford: Oxford University Press), 207–58.

—— (1989), *Mental Content* (Oxford: Blackwell).

McKinsey, Michael (1991), 'Anti-Individualism and Privileged Access', *Analysis*, 51: 9–16.

—— (1994), 'Accepting the Consequences of Anti-Individualism', *Analysis*, 54: 124–8.

McLaughlin, Brian P. (1987), 'Tye on Connectionism', *Spindel Conference on Connectionism, Southern Journal of Philosophy*, 26: 185–93.

—— (1988), 'Exploring the Possibility of Self-Deception in Belief', in Brian P. McLaughlin and Amelie Rorty (eds.), *Perspectives on Self-Deception* (Berkeley: University of California Press), 29–62.

—— (1991), 'Dretske on Naturalizing Content', in Brian P. McLaughlin (ed.), *Dretske and his Critics* (Oxford: Blackwell, 1991), 157–79.

—— (1993), 'On Punctate Content and on Conceptual Role', *Philosophy and Phenomenological Research*, 53: 653–60.

—— (1997), 'Classical Constituents in Smolensky's ICS Architecture', in M. L. Dalla Chiara *et al.* (eds.), *Structure and Norms in Science* (Dordrecht: Kluwer), 331–43.

—— and Tye, Michael (forthcoming), 'Is Content-Externalism Compatible with Privileged Access?'.

Millikan, Ruth (1984), *Language, Thought and Other Biological Categories* (Cambridge, Mass.: MIT/Bradford).

Papineau, David (1987), *Reality and Representation* (Oxford: Blackwell).

Putnam, Hilary (1975), 'The Meaning of "Meaning"', in Keith Gunderson (ed.), *Language, Mind and Knowledge*, Minnesota Studies in the Philosophy of Science, vii (Minneapolis: University of Minnesota Press); repr. in Putnam, *Philosophical Papers*, ii (Cambridge: Cambridge University Press), 139–52.

Russell, B. (1954), *The Analysis of Matter* (New York: Dover).

Schiffer, S. (1989), *Remnants of Meaning* (Cambridge, Mass.: MIT/Bradford).

Shoemaker, Sidney (1988), 'On Knowing One's Own Mind', *Philosophical Perspectives*, 2: 183–209.

Smolensky, P. (1995), 'Reply: Constituent Structure and Explanation in an Integrated Connectionist/Symbolic Cognitive Architecture', in C. Macdonald and G. Macdonald (eds.), *Connectionism: Debates on Psychological Explanation* (Oxford: Blackwell), 223–90.

Tye, Michael (1995), *Ten Problems of Consciousness* (Cambridge, Mass.: MIT/Bradford).

Warfield, Ted. A. (1995), 'Privileged Access and Externalism' (Ph.D. dissertation, Rutgers University).

II

Externalism, Architecturalism, and Epistemic Warrant*

MARTIN DAVIES

───────◆◆───────

This chapter addresses a problem about epistemic warrant. The problem is posed by philosophical arguments for externalism about the contents of thoughts, and similarly by philosophical arguments for architecturalism about thinking, when these arguments are put together with a thesis of first-person authority. In each case, first-personal knowledge about our thoughts plus the kind of knowledge that is provided by a philosophical argument seem, together, to open an unacceptably 'non-empirical' route to knowledge of empirical facts. Furthermore, this unwelcome prospect of transferring a 'non-empirical' warrant from premises about our own mental states and about philosophical theory to a conclusion about external environment or internal architecture seems to depend upon little more than the possibility of knowledge by inference. (The

* An early version of this paper was given as an Invited Paper at the Eastern Division Meeting of the American Philosophical Association in December 1994; Joseph Owens commented, and Kirk Ludwig chaired the session. Essentially the same version was presented at the conference held at St Andrews in August 1995, on which this volume is based; Diana Raffman commented. The present version differs from that presented at the conference—the version on which Raffman's comments (this volume) are based—in two main ways. There is a more thorough discussion of externalism in the lengthy section I, and there is some indication of the direction that future work might take in the brief section V.

I am grateful to the many colleagues and friends who have made comments and suggestions, or raised objections, including especially Bill Brewer, Jessica Brown, Graeme Forbes, Jay Garfield, Richard Holton, Frank Jackson, Wolfgang Künne, Rae Langton, David Lewis, Kirk Ludwig, Joseph Owens, Christopher Peacocke, Diana Raffman, Nigel Shardlow, Daniel Stoljar, Tom Stoneham, and Mark Textor. Many of the points which they made will need to be addressed more adequately in future work.

Discussions at the Graduiertenkolleg Kognitionswissenschaft in Hamburg helped me to clarify the issues, and the paper was completed while I was a Visiting Fellow in the Research School of Social Sciences, Australian National University. I am grateful to both institutions.

use of the scare-quoted term 'non-empirical' is explained a couple of paragraphs further on.)

INTRODUCING THE PROBLEM

For the purposes of this introduction to the problem, *externalism* about some mental property is the thesis that whether a person (or other physical being) has that property depends, not only on conditions inside the person's skin, but also on the person's environment and the way that the person is embedded in that environment. *Architecturalism* about some mental property is the thesis that whether a person (or other physical being) has that property depends, not only on the person's (actual and counterfactual) patterns of behaviour, but also on the person's internal cognitive architecture.

In each thesis, the dependence in question is supposed to be not causal but conceptual. It is the kind of dependence that can be revealed by philosophical theory, deploying arguments of a broadly a priori character. If the business of conceptual analysis is to develop the best elaborations and precisifications of the concepts that we actually use, then the methodology of externalist and architecturalist arguments will be conceptual analysis applied to the concept of having the mental property in question. (For a recent defence of conceptual analysis and an account of its role in metaphysics, see Jackson 1994, 1998.)

The problem about epistemic warrant arises when externalism or architecturalism is put together with a thesis of *first-person authority*. For present purposes, a thesis of first-person authority about some mental property says that we have a distinctively first-personal and specially authoritative way of knowing that we ourselves have that property, when we do have it, without needing to conduct any detailed empirical investigation either of the environment and our relation to it or of our internal cognitive architecture. (We are not concerned here with differences that might be drawn between a thesis of first-person authority and a thesis of privileged access. Indeed, the privileged access thesis stated by Brian McLaughlin and Michael Tye (p. 286 above) could serve, with little modification, as a precisification of the idea of first-person authority that is in play.)

We shall be considering a number of arguments of the following form (MC):

    (1)   I have mental property M.
    (2)   If I have mental property M, then I meet condition C.

Therefore:

(3) I meet condition C.

These arguments are potentially problematic to the extent that premiss (1) is something that can be known with first-person authority, while premiss (2) is something that can be known by way of a philosophical argument for the general thesis:

($\forall x$) (If x has mental property M, then x meets condition C).

The scare-quoted term 'non-empirical' (used in the first paragraph) is intended to cover both the kind of epistemic warrant that attaches to first-personal judgements about mental properties and the kind that attaches to the consequences of philosophical theory. The term is non-optimal in a number of ways, and perhaps 'non-investigative' would be less misleading; but let it stand. The rough idea is that both kinds of knowledge can be had without rising from the armchair. Given this use of the term, knowledge of premiss (1) and of premiss (2) is 'non-empirical'; and it is obvious a priori that the conclusion (3) follows from those two premisses. So, the transparently valid argument from (1) and (2) to (3) seems to offer a route to knowledge of (3), and with a warrant that is still 'non-empirical'. But, in the particular arguments that we shall be considering, it is intuitively implausible that the conclusion (3) is something that can be known in a 'non-empirical' (non-investigative, armchair) way. Rather, knowledge of (3) would seem to require detailed empirical investigation of the world (whether outside the skin or inside the skull). This is the problem about epistemic warrant that is posed by externalist or by architecturalist arguments, when those arguments are put together with a thesis of first-person authority. Is there any principled way of blocking the transfer of the 'non-empirical' warrant for (1) and (2) across the a priori known entailment to (3)?

This way of setting out the problem—at least as it concerns externalism about the content of thoughts—owes a good deal to Michael McKinsey (1991). (McKinsey uses the term 'a priori' where I use 'non-empirical'. McLaughlin and Tye (Chapter 10, this volume) provide a detailed discussion of what they call 'McKinsey's recipe'. See also Boghossian, Chapter 9, this volume.) McKinsey uses the problem to argue that externalism is incompatible with privileged access. If externalist philosophical theory delivers a 'non-empirical' warrant for premiss (2), and the conclusion (3) cannot be known 'non-empirically', then privileged access does not extend to premiss (1).

Critics of McKinsey's argument often claim that, to the extent that the conclusion (3) is not something that could be known 'non-empirically', premiss (2) cannot be known 'non-empirically' either, even given the correctness of externalism. (See Brueckner 1992 for this kind of response.) Like these critics, I want to maintain that externalism is compatible with first-person authority (privileged access). But, unlike these critics, I am not confident that it will always be possible to defuse a threatening McKinsey-style argument by claiming either that the conclusion (3) is so thin as to be knowable 'non-empirically' or else that knowledge of premiss (2) depends on detailed empirical investigation of the world.

It is because I envisage a kind of worst-case scenario, in which this more usual line of compatibilist response is not available, that I focus on the question of whether there is a principled way to block the transfer of the 'non-empirical' warrant from premisses to conclusion. Further motivation for this particular focus is then provided by the problem that is posed by architecturalist arguments (though it is, of course, perfectly possible to be an externalist about the content of thoughts without believing that there are any good architecturalist arguments that have a broadly a priori character).

Epistemic Warrant and Knowledge by Inference

Expressing the problem in terms of transfer of epistemic warrant might be misleading, for it might suggest that our project is to devise a cunning restriction on a general rule which otherwise permits properties of epistemic warrant to be transmitted across a priori known entailments.

In fact, there is no such general rule of transfer, for there are many properties of epistemic warrant which cannot be transferred across known entailments. The most obvious example is the property of being a kind of epistemic warrant that is non-inferential. But disjunctive properties of epistemic warrant would also raise questions about any general rule of transfer. Suppose that each of two properties, F and G, of epistemic warrants can be transferred across known entailments, in the sense that if all the premisses have warrants with the property, then the conclusion also has a warrant with that property. And suppose that some of the premisses of an argument have epistemic warrants with property F, while the other premisses have epistemic warrants with property G. Then each of the premisses has a warrant with the disjunctive property F or G; but there is no reason to suppose that the epistemic warrant for the conclusion has either property F or property G (since not all the premisses have warrants with property F, and not all the premisses have warrants with property G). So there is no reason to suppose that the disjunctive property, F or G, of warrants can be transferred.

Consider an example. Perhaps, if all the premisses of an inference are known a priori then the conclusion can be known a priori. And perhaps, if all the premisses of a sufficiently obvious inference are known with first-person authority, then the conclusion can be known with first-person authority. But it would not follow from those suppositions about transfer of warrant that if one of two premisses is known with first-person authority, and so is known either a priori or with first-person authority, and the other premiss is known a priori, and so is also known either a priori or with first-person authority, then the conclusion is known either a priori or with first-person authority.

This example might, for a moment, encourage the thought that we already have a solution to our epistemological problem in the fact that 'non-empirical' warrants are supposed to include both the a priori and the first-personal. But, in fact, considering the prospects for general rules of transfer of warrant is not the best way to see what the nature of the problem is. It is more helpful to consider that 'non-empirical' is a negative notion. For the arguments that we shall consider, I do not need to engage in any detailed empirical investigation of the world (outside or within) in order to know premiss (1); I just need to introspect (in a suitably neutral use of that term). Nor do I need to engage in any detailed empirical investigation in order to know premiss (2); I just need to follow through a philosophical argument. I do not need to conduct any empirical investigation to draw the conclusion (3) from the premisses (1) and (2); the validity of the instance of *modus ponens* is obvious. So, unless there is some restriction on the possibility of knowledge by inference, by drawing that conclusion I gain knowledge of (3)—and still without any detailed empirical investigation.

The problem posed by the arguments that we shall be considering is that they seem to call for some restriction on knowledge by inference.

Knowledge by Inference and Deductive Closure

We can distinguish between questions about knowledge by inference and questions about the closure of knowledge under known entailment. A question about closure would be whether I can know premiss (1) and know premiss (2) but fail to know, or be in a position to know, the conclusion (3). Our question about knowledge by inference is whether I can know premiss (1) and know premiss (2), but fail to be in a position *thereby* to know the conclusion (3).

Expressing the two questions in this way makes it clear that, in principle, there could be some restriction on knowledge by inference without there being any failure of closure. Knowing the premisses (1) and

(2), one might be in a position to know the conclusion (3), but not to know it by way of knowing those premises. It might even be that anyone who knew those premises would also know the conclusion, even though knowledge of the conclusion could not be arrived at by inference from those premises.

Of course, if knowledge is not closed under known entailment—in the sense that someone could know certain premises without being in a position to know a conclusion which she knows to be entailed by those premises—then *a fortiori* someone could know those premises without thereby being in a position to know the conclusion; so there must be some restriction on the scope of knowledge by inference.

It appears, then, that while any failure of closure requires some restriction on knowledge by inference, it might be possible to restrict knowledge by inference without breaching closure. But it would be reasonable to suppose that, in the context of the arguments that we shall be considering, the strategy that we just mentioned for securing a restriction on knowledge by inference without denying closure may not be a plausible one. So we should assume (pending detailed discussion) that restricting knowledge by inference will involve denying closure. I shall briefly mention, at the end of the chapter (in the second part of section V), how the epistemic situation can be redescribed in such a way as to honour the closure principle, by invoking the idea of context shifting (DeRose 1995; Lewis 1996).

Outline

In section I, I explain in some detail how the epistemological problem is posed by arguments for externalism about the content of thoughts. In section II, I turn, much more briefly, to the apparently parallel problem posed by architecturalist arguments. In section III, we begin our journey towards a solution by considering some arguments that are superficially of the right form to be anti-sceptical arguments, but which cannot be used for anti-sceptical purposes. This leads to a principle for limiting the transfer of epistemic warrant across even a priori known entailments. However, this first limitation principle does not itself provide a solution to the problems that arise from externalist and architecturalist arguments. In section IV, I introduce a second limitation principle on transfer of epistemic warrant—a principle that does close off the unwelcome prospect of a 'non-empirical' route to knowledge of empirical facts. The final section indicates some possible directions for future work.

I EXTERNALISM

I have said that externalism about a mental property, M, is the thesis that whether a person (or other physical being) has M depends, not only on conditions inside the person's skin, but also on the person's environment and the way in which the person is embedded in that environment. It may be helpful, now, to distinguish between two kinds of externalist thesis: *constitutive externalism* and *modal externalism*.

1 Constitutive and Modal Theses

Constitutive externalism and its opposite, constitutive individualism, are theses about the kind of philosophical account that can be given of what it is for an individual to have a certain property. Constitutive individualism (as it concerns mental property M) says that the fundamental philosophical account of what it is for an individual to have M does not need to advert to the individual's environment (whether physical or social), but only to what goes on within the spatial and temporal boundaries of the individual. Constitutive externalism says that the fundamental philosophical account of what it is for an individual to have M does need to advert to the individual's physical or social environment. (We shall not be concerned with social externalist theses (Burge 1979) here.)

Modal externalism and its opposite, modal individualism, are theses about the existence or otherwise of Twin Earth examples. A Twin Earth example for a property exhibits a person (or other physical being) in an environment and a duplicate person (or other physical being) in a second environment, such that the first person has the property in question, and the second person does not, despite being the same as the first person from the skin inwards. A modal externalist thesis (concerning mental property M) says that there are Twin Earth examples for M. Modal externalist theses differ in modal strength along various dimensions, according as the two environments are allowed to be two parts of the actual world, or two parts of some single possible world, or parts of different possible worlds one of which is the actual world, or parts of two possible worlds neither of which need be actual. A modal individualist thesis, being the opposite of a modal externalist thesis, denies the existence of Twin Earth examples for M. Modal individualist theses are local supervenience claims varying, once again, in modal strength.

It would not be quite correct to say that constitutive individualism, as defined, entails modal individualism. The reason is that an individual may have properties (impure intrinsic properties) whose specification does not advert to anything outside the skin of that individual, yet which are not shared by duplicates. Cases in point, for an individual a, would include the property of being identical with a and the property of having a's brain as a proper part. Even if a and b are duplicates, a has, but b lacks, the property of being identical with a and the property of having a's brain as a proper part. So, it is a straightforward matter to provide Twin Earth examples for these properties—and without even needing to have the second environment different from the first. These cases do not involve mental properties; but it is clear that there are mental properties which can, prima facie, be specified without talking about anything outside the individual's skin, but which would not be preserved across duplicates.[1]

It is a good question whether what is really at issue in debates about externalism and individualism is best characterized in terms of properties that can be specified without adverting to the environment or in terms of properties that are preserved across duplicates. But for present purposes, I shall simplify the discussion by treating constitutive individualism (concerning mental property M) as saying that the fundamental philosophical account of what it is for an individual to have M does not need to advert to the individual's physical or social environment, but only to properties of the individual that are shared by duplicates. (That is, we simplify by ignoring impure intrinsic properties.) With this simplification, it becomes trivial that constitutive individualism entails modal individualism, of whatever modal strength: supervenience holds, and Twin Earth examples do not exist.

Likewise, modal externalist theses (of whatever modal strength) entail constitutive externalism. If there is a Twin Earth example for mental property M, and if that example works by placing the duplicates in different environments (and does not trade on differences in impure intrinsic properties), then the fundamental philosophical account of what it is for an individual to have M must advert to the individual's environment. However, the converse entailment is not guaranteed to hold: a property that is canonically specified in externalist terms might yet be preserved across duplicates. Frank Jackson and Philip Pettit (1993: 271) give the example of dispositional properties. An account of the property of being soluble in water will surely advert to conditions external to any individual thing (such as a sugar cube) that has that property. But still, if this sugar cube, c, is water-soluble, then any duplicate sugar

---

[1] This paragraph corrects a claim made in earlier work about the relationship between constitutive and modal individualism (Davies 1991*b*, 1992*b*, 1993, 1996). I am grateful to Richard Holton and Rae Langton for discussion of this issue. For the distinction between pure and impure properties, see Langton 1993; Langton and Lewis, 1998; Humberstone 1996; Khamara 1988.

cube, *d*, is also water-soluble, even if *d* is located in an environment devoid of water. (Perhaps we need to restrict attention to nomologically possible environments; but this complication does not matter for present illustrative purposes.)

Someone might conceive of cognitive abilities, like the ability to have thoughts of one or another type, as analogous to solubility. Having the ability to think about water (to think water thoughts) would be conceived of as a constitutively, but not modally, externalist property of thinkers. Having the ability to think about perceptually presented sugar cubes might be conceived of in the same way—as a property shared by duplicates. On this conception, it would be allowed that one thinker, *a*, might deploy this ability when presented with sugar cube *c*, and so think about *c*, while a duplicate thinker, *b*, thought instead about sugar cube *d*. So, the mental property of thinking about sugar cube *c*, in particular, would be both constitutively and modally externalist; while the mental property of being able to think about sugar cubes would be constitutively, but not modally, externalist.

Someone favouring this conception of cognitive abilities might take a further step. Perhaps *a* thinks, 'That sugar cube is old,' thereby thinking a thought that is true just in case *c* is old, while *b* thinks, 'That sugar cube is old,' thereby thinking a thought that is true just in case *d* is old. Perhaps *a*'s thought is true, while *b*'s thought is false: they think different particular thoughts. But still, it might be said, they think thoughts of the same type (the 'That sugar cube is old' type), and the mental property of thinking a thought of that type is shared by duplicates, even though it is a constitutively externalist property.

Once that step has been taken, it may be extremely tempting to describe the situation in the following way. Thinking, concerning sugar cube *c*, that that sugar cube is old is really a composite matter. There is a genuinely mental component, which is the deployment of a cognitive ability; and there is an environmental relational component, which is the presence, near the thinker, of sugar cube *c*. The thinkers, *a* and *b*, are just the same in respect of the genuinely mental aspect of their thinking; they differ only in that *a* is environmentally related to *c* in the way that *b* is related to *d*. So we might just as well say that *a* and *b* think thoughts with the same *content*, even though they think *about* different sugar cubes. So far as the content (properly so-called) of the thoughts goes, modal externalism has not been shown to be correct. A Twin Earth example might demonstrate modal externalism for the aboutness of the thoughts; but this is not of very much interest if aboutness is a matter of environmental relational properties that are wholly extrinsic to the content of the thoughts. So it might be said. (This use of the term 'aboutness' to contrast with 'content' should be distinguished from the use in which aboutness is more or less the same as intentionality.)

If the situation is described in this way, then it becomes difficult to see how the form of argument (MC):

(1) I have mental property M.
(2) If I have mental property M, then I meet condition C.
Therefore:
(3) I meet condition C,

could lead to the kind of epistemic problem that we have described. Premiss (1) is supposed to be known with first-person authority; but first-person authority plausibly extends only to the content, not to the (environmental relational) aboutness, of thoughts. On the other hand, premiss (2) is supposed to follow from a general (and not merely contingent) thesis:

$$(\forall x) \text{ (If } x \text{ has mental property M, then } x \text{ meets condition C)}$$

that would support modal externalism. (If an individual x does not meet (environmental) condition C, then x does not have mental property M, even if x is a duplicate of me.) But modal externalism seems (so far) to apply to the aboutness properties, not to the content properties, of thoughts.

We need to have some idea of a range of externalist examples in which, on the one hand, the externalism concerns the content of thoughts— content that is within the range of first-person authority—and yet, on the other hand, the externalism is modal as well as constitutive. But before we turn to some of the varieties of externalist examples (section 3 below), we must deal with one further question. How is the externalist supposed to argue for premiss (2)?

2   *Arguing for Premiss (2)*

This question is potentially puzzling when asked against the background of the distinction between constitutive and modal externalist theses. Although there is no guarantee that every constitutive externalist thesis entails modal externalism, still, it might be possible to argue for premiss (2) via a constitutive modal thesis in a specific case. But the problem here is that a thesis about the fundamental philosophical account of the mental property of having thoughts with certain contents would seem to depend on a detailed theory of intentionality. So, in the absence of any agreed theory of intentionality, it is little wonder that actual externalist arguments typically make use of Twin Earth examples; even if they are aimed, ultimately, at a constitutive externalist conclusion, they go via modal externalism.

But, if premiss (2) is the target, then arguments from Twin Earth examples have a disadvantage, in that they do not make it clear exactly what the commitments of externalism are. They are liable to underestimate the environmental requirements for having a thought with a certain content. An individual x has mental property M in possible world w_1. The environmental differences between w_1 and an alternative possible world, w_2, are supposed to be enough to secure that y in w_2, though a duplicate of x in w_1, differs from x in respect of property M. Typically, the aim is not merely to show that y lacks M in w_2, but also to exhibit y as having some determinate different mental property M′ in w_2. Now, in order that the Twin Earth example should carry conviction even while there is no agreed theory of intentionality, it is likely to involve inter-world differences that go well beyond what is strictly speaking required according to whatever theory of intentionality turns out to be correct. In particular, the description of possible world w_2 may well pile on respect after respect in which w_2 differs from w_1, in order to provide a plausibly sufficient condition for y to have M′ rather than M. But then, when we come to read off something of the form:

$$(\forall x) \text{ (If } x \text{ has mental property M, then } x \text{ meets condition C)}$$

from the example, all that we can fill in for 'condition C'—a necessary condition for having M—is the negation of a perhaps quite lengthy conjunction of features of y's environment in w_2.

We can make some progress with this problem, and offer the prospect of a more substantial necessary condition in premiss (2), if we note that there is no need for a Twin Earth example to do any more than make it plausible that y lacks M in w_2. To the extent that the sufficient condition for lacking M is thinner than that for having M′, it will yield, under negation, a thicker substitution for 'condition C'. Or, if we consider again arguments that proceed via constitutive externalist theses, we can note that, in order to argue for premiss (2), we do not, in fact, require a complete theory of intentionality. We need only spell out necessary conditions, not sufficient conditions, for a thinker to have a thought with a certain content.

Even with these points noted, however, someone might urge that, to the extent that philosophical theory uncovers externalist necessary conditions for having thoughts with certain contents, these conditions will be so thin that there will be nothing counter-intuitive about the prospect of being able to know, from the armchair, that we meet them. To this I offer two partial replies. The first is (to repeat a point made earlier) that, since I want to defend both externalism and first-person authority, and since we are as yet some distance from agreeing whether certain conditions are necessary for a thinker to have thoughts with this or that content, I would prefer to be prepared for a worst-case scenario. The second partial reply consists in sketching some externalist examples.

3 Varieties of Externalist Examples

Let us return to the contrast between content and aboutness and the need for some modal externalist examples that decisively concern content. At the beginning of 'Other Bodies', Tyler Burge comments on a case that is similar to our example of thinkers *a* and *b* and the sugar cubes, but involves a single thinker, Alfred, thinking about two apples (1982: 97):

> We may say that Alfred has the *same* belief-content in both situations. It is just that he would be making contextually different applications of that content to different entities. His belief is true of apple 1 and false of apple 2. The *nature* of his mental state is the same. He simply bears different relations to his environment. . . .
>
> This deflationary interpretation seems to me to be correct.

So Burge, like our imagined theorist who started out from the analogy with solubility, does not regard Twin Earth examples that work by replacing an object that is thought about (apple 1 or sugar cube *c*) with a different object (apple 2 or sugar cube *d*) as demonstrating externalism about content.

In Burge's writings, there are at least three other kinds of Twin Earth example. There are examples that are intended to illustrate social externalism, such as the 'arthritis' and 'sofa' examples (Burge 1979). There are examples that are intended to illustrate externalism about the content of perceptual experiences, such as the example of the shadows and the cracks (Burge 1986). And there are examples that are intended to illustrate externalism about natural kind concepts (particularly as those concepts are exercised by thinkers who lack relevant scientific knowledge), such as the 'water'/'twater' example (Burge 1982; Putnam 1975). The first kind of example is not strictly relevant to our present purposes, since we are setting aside the question of social externalism. The second kind is potentially problematic, because it concerns the non-conceptual content of experiences. Although it is possible to provide convincing Twin Earth examples of this type (in my view: Davies 1991*b*, 1992*b*, 1996), the examples involve imagined systems or creatures of great simplicity (Davies 1993), and this simplicity counts against the idea of concept deployment. The third kind of Twin Earth example, involving natural kind concepts, is certainly relevant. But despite the fact that this is often taken to be externalism's most favoured case, it introduces a number of difficult and complex issues.

Externalism and natural kind concepts   Davies and Humberstone (1980) pointed out, in effect, that much of what Putnam (1975) said about the natural kind term 'water' would be consistent with the term's having the same sense as a definite description: 'the chemical kind to which that liquid belongs which actually falls from clouds, flows in rivers, is drinkable, colourless, odourless' (1980: 18). But if thoughts that are expressed and reported by using the word 'water' are really thoughts in which some such definite description concept is deployed, then the contrast between content and aboutness can be invoked once again. The fact that the chemical kind H_2O fits the description is arguably a matter that is quite extrinsic to the content of the thought. (This conclusion does not depend on our ignoring the presence of the 'actually' in the description. See also Evans 1979, 1982: 50.)

It is vital, then, that natural kind concepts, if they are to figure in externalist examples that genuinely concern content, should not be definite description concepts. Let us suppose that this is so, and move on to ask what might be the environmental relational necessary conditions for a thinker to have thoughts in which, say, the natural kind concept *water* is deployed. Burge says (1982: 114):

We want to say that it is logically possible for an individual to have beliefs involving the concept of water . . . even though there is no water . . . of which the individual holds these beliefs . . .

I think we also want to say something stronger: it is logically possible for an individual to have beliefs involving the concept of water . . . even though there exists no water.

So, on Burge's account, no encounters between a thinker and any samples of water are required for the thinker to think, say, that water is wet; indeed, no water need exist in the thinker's world at all. The concept would remain available to a thinker—even a thinker who showed 'relative ignorance and indifference about the nature of water' —because we (other members of the thinker's community) 'would still have our chemical analyses' (Burge 1982: 116).

The only entailment to which Burge is explicitly committed is this (1982: 117): 'In some instances, an individual's having certain *de dicto* attitudes entails the existence of entities other than himself and his attitude contents.' This raises the question of whether externalism can generate good anti-sceptical arguments of the (MC) form—a question that will not be addressed directly here (though it is implicit in what is said here that it cannot). But we can ask whether any more specific entailments might be forthcoming.

On Burge's own account, where social externalism is in play, it might well seem that:

> ($\forall x$) (If x has thoughts involving the concept of water, then either there is water in x's environment, or else there are other members of x's community).

If social externalism is set aside, then we might even have:

> ($\forall x$) (If x has thoughts involving the concept of water, then there is water in x's environment).

Jessica Brown considers the following 'entailment between mind and world' (1995a: 152):

Q: Necessarily, if x has a thought involving the concept of a natural kind K and x is agnostic about the application conditions of the concept of K, then either x is in an environment which contains K, or x is part of a community with the concept of K.

She argues that this is something to which Burge is committed. So, if Burge's philosophical theory is correct, then Q is something that could be known 'non-empirically'. Furthermore, it is plausible to suppose that a thinker can know 'non-empirically' that he is agnostic about the application conditions of a natural kind concept: he might know, for example, that he knows nothing about the chemical analysis of water. But Brown suggests that this entailment still cannot readily be used in an argument of the (MC) form so as to create an epistemological problem, since—at least by Burge's lights—'a subject could be mistaken about whether a concept is a natural kind concept and still have that concept' (1995a: 154).

We might try taking the matter further by considering, alongside Q, a corresponding entailment concerning non-natural kind concepts (ibid.):

R: Necessarily, if x has a thought involving a non-natural kind concept, C, and x is agnostic about the application conditions of C, then x is part of a community that has the concept C,

with a view to constructing an argument of the (MC) form with conclusion:

> Either I am in an environment that contains instances of water, and *water* is a natural kind concept, or I am part of a community which

has the concept *water* (whether or not *water* is a natural kind concept).

But Brown herself (1995*b*) raises a difficulty for this strategy: namely, that the application conditions of a non-natural kind concept may leave it indeterminate whether the concept applies in certain cases. Someone could have complete understanding of such a concept and still be unsure about whether the concept applied to one or another object. As a result, it is not easy to maintain that a thinker can know, just by reflection, that he is agnostic about the application conditions of a non-natural kind concept (Brown 1995*b*: 215–16; see also McLaughlin and Tye, p. 317 above).

The overall situation concerning externalism and natural kind concepts is unclear. Suppose that we grant, for a moment, the claim that a subject could be mistaken about whether a concept is a natural kind concept and still have that concept. Then, one point to note is that this seems to be consistent with the idea that a subject who is not mistaken in judging that the concept *water* is a natural kind concept has knowledge of that fact—and perhaps even 'non-empirical' knowledge. But, second, we might question whether a subject could be mistaken about whether a concept is a natural kind concept. If social externalism is set aside, then this claim might look less plausible. Many issues would need to be settled before we could be confident about what is the right thing to say. But there seems to be at least the prospect of a 'non-empirically' knowable entailment along the lines of:

> $(\forall x)$ (If x has thoughts involving the concept of water, then there is water in x's environment);

or even:

> $(\forall x)$ (If x has thoughts involving the concept of water, then x has had such-and-such encounters with water).

And such an entailment could be used to construct an argument of the (MC) form. So we had better be prepared.

Externalism and object-dependent thoughts   There are two rather different kinds of case in which someone might draw a contrast between content and aboutness. Consider first a thought that involves a definite description concept, a thought of the form 'The F is H'. Perhaps c is the F; so the thought is about c. Perhaps d might have been the F; in that case the thought would have been about d. But, it might be said, the content of the thought would be the same in either case.

Consider second a thought that involves a perceptual demonstrative concept (or mode of presentation), a thought of the form 'That G is H'. If c is the perceptually presented G, then the thought is about c. If d had been the perceptually presented G, then the thought would have been about d. But, it might be said, the content of the thought would be the same in either case.

There is a conception of the content of a thought, familiar from the work of Gareth Evans (1982) and John McDowell (e.g. 1984, 1986), according to which the first kind of case does, but the second kind of case does not, allow a contrast between content and aboutness to be drawn in the way described. On this conception, thought is essentially representational, and the content of a thought specifies how the world would have to be for the thought to be correct. Furthermore, the thinker, in having the thought, knows how the world would have to be for the thought to be correct. As McDowell puts it, (1986: 140): 'The underlying idea is that to entertain a proposition one must know how one's thinking represents things as being.'

In the first kind of case, if we abstract away from the question of which object is the F, there is still a condition for the correctness of the thought: namely, that there should be a unique object which is F, and that whichever object is (uniquely) F should be H. Furthermore, this condition for correctness is a condition that the thinker grasps just by having the thought. In the second kind of case, however, the situation is very different. If we abstract away from the question of which object is being perceived, and thereby being thought about, then we abstract away from the question of which object needs to be H in order for the thought to be correct. There is, of course, a condition for correctness that we, as theorists, can frame. There should be a unique object that is G and that is being perceived (and perhaps attended to) by the thinker, and this object should be H. But this is not a condition that the thinker grasps just by having the thought. For the thinker is not thinking about himself, or about perception (or attention); the thinker is just thinking that that G is H.

On this conception we cannot separate content from aboutness, in the second kind of case. The content of the perceptual demonstrative thought is dependent on the object that the thought is about. If the object were different, then the content would be different; if there were no object, then there would be no content (no way that the world is represented in thought as being). It is part of this conception that, in order to have a thought that is object-dependent in this way, the thinker must, in some sense, know which object is in question. (This is what Evans calls 'Russell's Principle' (1982: 65).) This does not mean, of course, that in order to think, concerning a perceptually presented man, 'That man is tired', I need to know whether the man before me is Frank or Ernest. Indeed, just what is required, in order to meet the 'know which' requirement, is not easy to specify. As Evans himself says (1982: 89), 'The difficulty with Russell's Principle has always been to explain what it means.' But however exactly it is cashed out, the 'know which' requirement does, it seems to me, have a consequence that is of considerable importance for the purposes of this essay. Given that requirement, and the more general idea that 'one must know how one's thinking represents things as being', it would be unmotivated to insist that, in the case of object-dependent thoughts, first-person authority extends only to some (not fully representational) aspect of content that abstracts away from the object that is being thought about.

Someone who favours this conception of content has to disagree with Burge over the 'deflationary interpretation' of putative Twin Earth examples that involve perceptual demonstrative thoughts. On this conception, my thought, 'That man is tired', can be the basis for an argument of the (MC) form (cf. McLaughlin and Tye, p. 292 above).

Externalism and indexical thoughts   Much of what we have said about perceptual demonstrative thoughts goes also for indexical thoughts. When someone thinks, 'The treasure is buried here,' or thinks while lying in bed in the dark, 'There's a bottle of whisky there' (Evans's example (1982: 161)), the content of the thought is place-dependent. A duplicate subject located at a different place would think a thought with a different content. To acknowledge this is not to blind ourselves to the similarity between the thoughts entertained by the two subjects. The two thoughts, with their different contents, are intuitively of the same type; and it is a requirement on any theory of these matters that it should give a proper account of that common type.

As before, it seems plausible to say that first-person authority extends to the content of such an indexical thought. Given Russell's principle, it would be unmotivated to claim that the thinker's first-personal knowledge extends only to the type of the thought, and not to which place is in question. And we can easily construct a Twin Earth example, by having a thinker x located at a place p_1 and a duplicate thinker y located at place p_2. But it is not clear that we can use these resources to develop an epistemologically problematic argument of the (MC) form. Suppose that I am located at p_1. I may think that the treasure is buried here, and may know with first-person authority that I think that the treasure is buried here. Furthermore, I may know as a piece of philosophical theory that, in order to think a 'here' thought about a place, a thinker needs to be located at that place. But I cannot know 'non-empirically' that, in order to think that the treasure is buried here, I need to be located at p_1 and not at p_2, say. For I cannot know 'non-empirically' that p_1 is here. So the only conclusion that looks to be available from an argument of the (MC) form is that I am located here; and there is nothing problematic about the idea that I might know that 'non-empirically'.

However, we need to consider the fact that being able to think about a particular place is not a trivial matter (Evans 1982: 161):

We are prepared to suppose that there is a determinate thought here—that the subject has a definite place in mind—because we know that subjects do have a capacity to select one position in egocentric space, and to maintain a stable dispositional connection with it. . . . If the subject . . . does know which place his thought concerns . . . this will be manifestable only in manifestations of that stable dispositional connection.

What this suggests is that someone who is unable, for a while, either to maintain a stable dispositional connection with a position or to keep track of his movement through space is likewise unable, for that while, to have (determinate) indexical thoughts about places.

Evans himself presents an example that we can adapt (1982: 201):

A person might lie in bed in hospital thinking repeatedly 'How hot it was here yesterday'—supposing himself to be stationary in the dark. But his bed might be very well oiled, and be pulled by strings, so that every time he has what he takes to be the same thought, he is in fact thinking of a different place, and having a different thought.

As Evans describes the case, this thinker has several instantaneous thoughts about different places. But we can imagine that the person thinks, slowly, carefully, not wanting to knock anything over in the dark, 'There's a bottle of whisky just here.' Suppose that, during the time that it takes him to compose this putative thought, he moves several yards. Then it seems that we could reasonably deny that the subject manages any determinate thought at all—deny that the subject has a definite place in mind.

It might have been expected that while the mental property of thinking a 'here' thought about a particular place, p_1, would be both constitutively and modally externalist, only a thesis of constitutive externalism would hold for the property of thinking a thought of the 'here' type. But these last reflections suggest that we might be able to construct a Twin Earth example for that property. In one possible world there is x, stationary in bed in the dark, thinking, 'There's a bottle of whisky just here'—a thought that is correct if there is indeed a bottle of whisky located at a particular position just next to the bed. In the alternative possible world there is *y*, moving silently along darkened corridors, and failing to think any 'here' thought at all.

We seem to have the resources for an epistemologically problematic argument of the (MC) form; and they are resources that are available even to someone who adopts a 'deflationary interpretation' of Twin Earth examples that rely on object-dependent or place-dependent thoughts.

We have been considering three kinds of externalist example that concern the contents of thoughts: examples of thoughts involving natural kind concepts, of object-dependent thoughts, and of indexical thoughts and thought types. None of these cases is uncontroversial. But perhaps the discussion in this subsection has been sufficient to suggest that the prospect of an epistemological problem posed by arguments of the (MC) form is not wholly illusory.

4 Externalist Entailments and the Problem of Epistemic Warrant

The arguments of the (MC) form that concern us here make use (at premiss (2)) of entailments issuing from externalist philosophical theory. These externalist entailments, in their generalized versions, are of the form:

ExtEnt: $(\forall x)$ (If *x* believes that *p*, then $E(x)$),

Where '$E(x)$' is some statement about *x*'s environmental embedding. An example of the relevant form, involving a natural kind concept, would be:

$(\forall x)$ (If *x* believes that water is wet, then *x* has had such-and-such encounters with water).

Other examples, involving object-dependent thoughts or indexical thoughts, could be provided.

We assume that the methodology of philosophical theory is broadly a priori in character, and that the aim of philosophical theory is conceptual analysis: that is, the development of the best elaborations and precisifications of the concepts that we actually use. Thus, externalist philosophical theory aims, *inter alia*, at elaboration and precisification of the concept of believing, for example, that water is wet—the concept that we actually use in our judgements to the effect that we ourselves, or that others, believe that water is wet.

The potentially problematic arguments are of the form Ext(MC):

Ext(1): I believe that *p*.
Ext(2): If I believe that *p*, then E(me).
Therefore:
Ext(3): E(me).

I do not need to engage in any detailed empirical investigation of my environment to know premiss Ext(1); for example, to know that I believe that water is wet. Nor do I need to conduct any such investigation in order to know the conditional premiss Ext(2): for example, to know that if I believe that water is wet, then I have had such-and-such encounters with water. And the conclusion Ext(3) obviously follows from these two premisses. Yet it is implausible that I can know, without empirical investigation (from the armchair), the conclusion Ext(3): for example, can know 'non-empirically' that I have had such-and-such encounters with water. This is our epistemological problem, as it is posed by philosophical arguments for externalism about the contents of thoughts when these are put together with a thesis of first-person authority about the contents of thoughts.

Although we assume that philosophical theory is broadly a priori, there is no need for us to be purists about this. There may be some empirical, a posteriori assumptions in externalist theories. Suppose we consider the conditional made up of the conjunction of these assumptions as antecedent and the conclusion Ext(3) as consequent. Then the epistemological problem remains if it is implausible that this conditional can be known in a 'non-empirical' way.

If externalism is to allow for first-person authority, then we need some principled limitation on the transfer of epistemic warrant from Ext(1) and Ext(2) to Ext(3). We need to specify some restriction on knowledge by inference.

We might call our problem the *consequence problem* for first-person authority, given externalism. It should be distinguished from a different problem, which we can call the *achievement problem* for first-person authority, given externalism. How can I achieve a specially authoritative kind of knowledge about my own mental states, given that my being in those mental states depends on my environmental relational properties? For I am not specially authoritative about those properties.

5 The Achievement Problem for First-Person Authority

Approaches to this problem typically make use of the fact that the content of my second-order beliefs—my belief that I believe that water is wet, for example—is dependent on the environment in just the same way as the content of my first-order beliefs—my belief that water is wet.

Knowledge is an achievement, so there will be conditions that must be met if my second-order belief is to amount to knowledge. But there is no special problem in the fact that the content of the first-order belief is partly externalistically determined. My second-order belief, like my first-order belief, involves the natural kind concept *water*. So, in order for me to have that second-order belief at all, I need to have certain environmental relational properties; and if I do stand in those relations to my environment, then I meet the externalist conditions for having the first-order thought.

Consider, for example, a reliabilist account of knowledge, and suppose, for a moment, that we think in a language of thought. Then we can imagine the transition from the first-order belief to the second-order belief to be subserved by a causal mechanism that takes a language of thought sentence, S, as input, and produces a sentence, O^S, as output, where O is a language of thought sentential operator meaning 'I believe that——'. Because the externalist conditions that must be met if a language of thought sentence, S, is to have the content that water is wet are the same as those that must be met if O^S is to have the content that I believe that water is wet, this mechanism reliably produces true second-order beliefs. So, given reliabilism, those second-order beliefs count as knowledge. (Somewhat similarly, externalism is no impediment to the self-verifying character of the thought 'I think, with this very thought, that water is wet'. See Burge 1988.)

Alvin Goldman (1993) considers this mechanical kind of account of first-personal knowledge of mental states, and complains (p. 22) that 'it would leave the process of mental-state classification a complete mystery'. The complaint here is not an epistemological one. Rather, the worry is that the subpersonal-level story about a mechanism operating on sentences of the language of thought does not tell us how to conceive of these transitions at the personal level. To deal with this worry, Goldman adds to the account 'a plausible-looking hypothesis': namely, that 'mental states are states having a phenomenology' (p. 24).

This is a potentially problematic move to the extent that it suggests a particular account of first-personal knowledge of mental states. On this account, first-personal knowledge rests on evidence that is constituted by the presentation of mental states as something like sensations or images (or else by the presentation of mental states via intermediaries that are like sensations or images). Such an account, with sensation-like or image-like states presented to the subject as objects standing in need of interpretation, is disastrous for the idea of first-person authority.

It is arguable that we do have to allow that there is something that it is like to have the (conscious, occurrent) belief that water is wet, and that this fact may, in at least some cases, figure in a personal-level explanation of how a subject comes to be in a position to make the second-order judgement that he or she believes that water is wet. We might express the point by saying that there is a phenomenology of (conscious) thought. But it would then be important to separate the idea of phenomenology or phenomenal consciousness from the idea of sensational (non-representational) properties of mental states.

It will be helpful to have before us an example of an account of first-personal knowledge about beliefs that is clearly pitched at the personal level (rather than the level of subpersonal mechanisms), but that does not appeal to sensational, or image-like, presentations of conscious thoughts. Within the framework developed by Christopher Peacocke (1992), first-personal knowledge of beliefs is a fairly immediate product of mastery of the concept of belief. Peacocke's proposal is that part of what is required for mastery of the concept of belief (part of the 'possession condition' for the concept of belief) is precisely that, whenever the subject has the (conscious) belief that p, he or she should find 'primitively compelling' the first-person thought 'I believe that p'; and, furthermore, should find it compelling because he or she has that first-order belief. The resulting judgements constitute knowledge, Peacocke suggests, because there is a general principle linking possession conditions and knowledge (1992: 157):

Take any mental state of the thinker [here, believing that p] that a possession condition for a concept [here, the possession condition for the concept of belief] says is sufficient for the thinker finding primitively compelling a given content [here, the content: I believe that p] containing the concept. Then when the thinker judges that content and for the reason that he is in that state, his judgement constitutes knowledge.

To put it very roughly, the idea here is that if a thinker makes just the judgement that is required in order to meet the conditions for the most basic mastery of a concept, then that judgement should (provided that there is nothing abnormal going on) yield knowledge.

There are, of course, many more questions that can be raised about the nature of our entitlement to self-knowledge (see Burge 1996; Peacocke 1996). But it seems reasonable to assume—as McLaughlin and Tye (this volume) also argue compellingly—that externalism about the content of thoughts does not pose any insuperable achievement problem for first-person authority. And, of course, it is the presumed solubility of the achievement problem for first-person authority, given externalism, that makes the consequence problem pressing.

II ARCHITECTURALISM

We have spent some considerable time setting up the epistemological problem that is posed by philosophical arguments for externalism when these are put together with a thesis of first-person authority. We now turn, much more briefly, to the apparently parallel problem that is posed by architecturalist arguments.

1 *Architecturalist Entailments*

We have said that architecturalism about some mental property, M, is the thesis that whether a person (or other physical being) has M depends, not only on the person's (actual and counterfactual) patterns of behaviour, but also on the person's internal cognitive architecture. It may be helpful, now, to consider two examples of architecturalist arguments.

In earlier work (Davies 1991*a*, 1992*a*), I have offered an argument with a broadly a priori character in support of the language of thought hypothesis. That argument comes in two main stages. First, a certain kind of causal systematicity of inferential transitions is argued to be an a priori requirement for being a thinking subject. Second, it is argued that this kind of causal systematicity requires some syntactic articulation in the states that are the inputs to those inferential transitions. In short, the principal claim is that certain internal architectural conditions of systematicity and syntax—of rules and representations—are a priori requirements for being a thinking subject.

Whatever the merits of this argument concerning the language of thought, it is structurally analogous to a more familiar argument offered by Ramsey, Stich, and Garon (1990). Their principal claim is that the folk-psychological scheme is committed to a thesis of propositional modularity, to the effect that 'propositional attitudes are *functionally discrete, semantically interpretable*, states that play a *causal role* in the production of other attitudes, and ultimately in the production of behaviour' (1990: 504).

In each of these two cases, the aim of the argument is to establish, by more or less a priori means, an entailment of the form:

ArchEnt: $(\forall x)$ (If x has beliefs, then $A(x)$),

where '$A(x)$' is some statement about x's internal cognitive architecture. Ramsey, Stich, and Garon's instantiation of the form, for example, would be:

($\forall x$) (If x has beliefs, then x's internal cognitive architecture exhibits propositional modularity).

The instantiation of the form to which my own earlier work leads would be:

($\forall x$) (If x has beliefs, then x's internal cognitive architecture is a language of thought architecture).

In each case, the consequent ('$A(x)$') is a highly non-trivial claim that far outruns anything that is guaranteed by facts about x's patterns of behaviour. Whether this claim is true of any particular physical being cannot be settled without substantial empirical investigation.

2 Architecturalist Entailments and Eliminativism

An architecturalist entailment imposes a necessary condition for a physical being to be a thinking, believing subject, and so presents the possibility of an eliminativist *modus tollens*. Given any physical being whose behaviour prima facie warrants the attribution to it of beliefs and other attitudes, in accordance with the intentional stance (Dennett 1987), it is a genuine epistemic possibility that the being does not meet the imposed condition on internal cognitive architecture. So a quite general question that architecturalist entailments raise is whether it is philosophically acceptable that an a priori argument should open up the epistemic possibility that we ourselves might not be thinking, believing subjects.

Suppose, for a moment, that we were to find ourselves in a disobliging world. Suppose, that is, that developments in the scientific investigation of the mind—whether in cognitive psychology or in neuroscience—were to show that the purportedly necessary conditions for us to have beliefs were not, in fact, met. Then we would have a number of theoretical options. One option would be to conclude that the substantive pieces of philosophical theory deployed in the architecturalist argument in question are wrong: that they do not provide a good elaboration and precisification of our current conception of thinking, believing subjects. Another option—the opposite extreme—would be to abandon wholesale our folk-psychological practice of describing, interpreting, and explaining people's behaviour as made up of actions performed for reasons based upon beliefs, wants, hopes, fears, and the rest.

When just these two theoretical options are in view, the thought that the second option is not genuinely available to us—that our engagement in ordinary folk-psychological practice is philosophically non-negotiable

—may provide a powerful source of resistance against all architecturalist arguments. But, in fact, it is not really clear how one could argue from the non-negotiability of our engagement in folk-psychological practice to the incorrectness of all architecturalist analyses of the concept of being a thinking, believing subject.

One problem with the putative line of argument is that it seems to overlook the possibility that we might maintain the practice even though many of the claims made in folk-psychological descriptions, interpretations, and explanations were false. A second problem is that the competing piece of conceptual analysis that is suggested by this line of argument is itself arguably out of line with our intuitive judgements about which physical beings have beliefs. What the blanket rejection of all architecturalist arguments suggests is that an analysis of the concept of a thinking, believing subject should impose no necessary conditions at all on internal cognitive architecture and, indeed, no necessary conditions that go beyond behaviour. This entails a form of behaviourism— not analytical behaviourism, to be sure, but a doctrine that we can call *supervenient behaviourism*. If two physical beings are behavioural (or, perhaps better, trajectorial) duplicates in actual and nearby counterfactual situations, then either both have beliefs, or else neither does. But this doctrine is revealed as being out of line with our intuitions when we consider imaginary examples of beings that produce the right behaviour by way of unusual internal architectures, such as the string-searching machine of Block (1981) or the Martian marionette of Peacocke (1983). The string-searching machine, which stores a finite but massive collection of interpretable sequences of behaviour, can *ex hypothesi* meet any behavioural requirements for thinking. But, as Block remarks in a later paper (1990: 252), 'it has the intelligence of a jukebox'.

In between the two options of, on the one hand, rejecting architecturalist arguments and, on the other hand, abandoning our folk-psychological practice, there lies the possibility of conceptual negotiation. Suppose that the philosophical theory deployed in a particular architecturalist argument does correctly elaborate and precisify our current conception, and that the argument does correctly uncover the commitments of that conception. Suppose, too, that those internal architectural commitments are not met in the real world. Then it follows that we ourselves do not fall under (the best elaboration and precisification of) our current concept of a physical being with beliefs. But we may still be able rationally to sustain the greater part of our folk-psychological practice if we negotiate our way to a new, revised conception of what it is to be a thinking, believing subject. The details of the negotiations would depend on the particular discoveries that might be made in cognitive psychology and neuroscience—and also, of course, on the philosophical theories that connect those discoveries with our current conception of folk-psychological phenomena.

From this suggestion, a certain picture of philosophical theorizing itself emerges. The picture involves three phases. First, there is relatively pure a priori conceptual analysis. Then, there is the empirical discovery that we live in a disobliging world. Finally, there is the phase of conceptual negotiation, in which philosophical theory has to be much more answerable to the details of how the world turns out to be.

We have been considering the question of whether it is philosophically acceptable that an a priori argument should render it epistemically possible that we ourselves do not have beliefs—that we do not fall under our own current conception of thinking, believing subjects. The provisional answer that we have reached is that this is acceptable—that it is no objection to an architecturalist argument that it presents the possibility of an eliminativist *modus tollens*.

However, it might be replied that there is something unsatisfactory in this discussion of the non-negotiability of folk-psychological practice. My strategy has been to suggest that, if it is to be guaranteed that those who engage in the practice really are thinking, believing subjects, then what is required is a counter-intuitive doctrine of supervenient behaviourism. But, it might be said, there is something that can be known, at least in the case of the first person singular, which goes beyond behaviour, yet has nothing to do with internal cognitive architecture. So, it would be possible to reject architecturalism without commitment to supervenient behaviourism by saying that an analysis of the concept of a thinking, believing subject should impose no necessary conditions that go beyond behaviour plus whatever can be known to be true by introspection.

This reply will not protect the status of all those who engage in folk-psychological practice, since it is restricted to the first-person singular. But, even setting aside that point, we can note that the reply is liable to seem question begging. For, according to architecturalism, in a disobliging world I would not be a being with beliefs; so I could not know myself, whether by introspection or any other way, to be a being with beliefs.

The reply may be dialectically inadequate, because question begging; but it is difficult not to sense that the appeal to first-personal knowledge points to a problem with architecturalist arguments. The claim of this chapter is that the real problem for architecturalism is parallel to the consequence problem for externalism, given first-person authority.

3 Architecturalist Entailments and First-Person Authority

The arguments of the (MC) form that concern us here make use (at premiss (2)) of architecturalist entailments of the form:

ArchEnt: $(\forall x)$ (If x has beliefs, then $A(x)$),

where '$A(x)$' is some statement about x's internal cognitive architecture. The specific form of the problematic arguments is Arch(MC):

Arch(1): I have beliefs.
Arch(2): If I have beliefs, then $A($me$)$.
Therefore:
Arch(3): $A($me$)$.

I do not need to engage in any detailed empirical investigation of my internal cognitive architecture to know premiss Arch(1); I know with first-person authority that I have many beliefs, such as the belief that water is wet. Nor do I need to engage in empirical research in order to know premiss Arch(2); according to architecturalism, it is a piece of conceptual analysis. It is obvious that the conclusion Arch(3) follows from these two premisses. Yet, even supposing that the conclusion is true, it is massively implausible that its truth can be known from the armchair. Questions about internal cognitive architecture cannot be settled without major programmes of empirical research. A thoroughgoing defence of architecturalist arguments requires some principled limitation on the transfer of epistemic warrant from Arch(1) and Arch(2) to Arch(3).

We have now described the epistemological problem that is posed by philosophical arguments for externalism, or for architecturalism, when these arguments are put together with a thesis of first-person authority. What is needed, if we are to provide a solution to this problem, is some principled limitation on knowledge by inference. The remainder of this chapter sketches some initial, tentative, and provisional steps in the direction of such a solution.

III SCAFFOLDING AND SCEPTICISM

We can begin our journey towards a limitation principle on knowledge by inference by recalling an example from Wittgenstein, *On Certainty* (hereafter *OC*) (1969).

1 *Justification and Comfortable Certainty*

At OC, §§208–11, we find this:

208. I have a telephone conversation with New York. My friend tells me that his young trees have buds of such and such a kind. I am now convinced that his tree is . . . Am I also convinced that the earth exists?
209. The existence of the earth is rather part of the whole picture which forms the starting-point of belief for me.
210. Does my telephone call to New York strengthen my conviction that the earth exists?
   Much seems to be fixed, and it is removed from the traffic. It is so to speak shunted onto an unused siding.
211. Now it gives our way of looking at things, and our researches, their form. Perhaps it was once disputed. But perhaps, for unthinkable ages, it has belonged to the *scaffolding* of our thoughts. . . .

The argument that we need to consider here is Tree:

> Tree(1): My friend in New York has a . . . tree in his garden.
> Tree(2): If my friend in New York has a . . . tree in his garden, then the Earth exists.
> Therefore:
> Tree(3): The Earth exists.

It is not obvious that Wittgenstein is arguing for a failure of closure of knowledge under known entailment. Rather, it seems that he allows that there is no harm in saying that I do know that the Earth exists. But the mistake would be to think that, in order to know Tree(3), I need a justification. Thus:

357. One might say: ' "I know" expresses *comfortable* certainty, not the certainty that is still struggling.'
358. Now I would like to regard this certainty, not as something akin to hastiness or superficiality, but as a form of life. . . .
359. But that means I want to conceive it as something that lies beyond being justified; as it were, as something animal.

Someone might respond at this point that we often find ourselves with things that we do not need. So, even if I do not need a justification for Tree(3), still the argument from Tree(1) and Tree(2) to Tree(3) does furnish a kind of justification. In order to rebut that suggestion, we can consider what Wittgenstein says in a related case:

188. It strikes me as if someone who doubts the existence of the earth at that time [150 years ago] is impugning the nature of all historical evidence. . . .

An argument to which this remark could be applied would be Tree':

Tree′(1): There was a . . . tree growing in such-and-such a garden
150 years ago.

Tree′(2): If there was a . . . tree growing in such-and-such a garden
150 years ago, then the Earth existed at that time.

Therefore:

Tree′(3): The Earth existed 150 years ago.

Wittgenstein's thought seems to be that if Tree′(3) were subject to doubt, then we could not take what would ordinarily be reckoned as historical evidence for Tree′(1) to be evidence. So, the argument from Tree′(1) and Tree′(2) to Tree′(3) can scarcely furnish a justification for Tree′(3).

What we have from Wittgenstein, then, is a form of argument that proceeds from some workaday proposition, via a readily known entailment, to a proposition that belongs to 'the scaffolding of our thoughts'. The idea to which the examples tend is that justification (or epistemic warrant) cannot be transferred from the workaday proposition via the known entailment to the scaffolding proposition. Thus, in the original example (Tree), I do have a justification for believing:

Tree(1): My friend in New York has a . . . tree in his garden.

—a justification that is furnished by what my friend has told me about the buds and so on in our telephone conversation. And I can readily know:

Tree(2): If my friend in New York has a . . . tree in his garden,
then the Earth exists.

But that does not result in my having a justification for believing the conclusion:

Tree(3): The Earth exists.

Nor, according to Wittgenstein, do I need any such justification.

2 Scepticism and Cognitive Achievement

In his 1985 British Academy lecture 'Facts and Certainty', Crispin Wright suggests that, in general, reasonable or justified belief is transmitted over known entailment, but that this is not so when the entailed proposition falls outside the domain of what he calls *cognitive achievement* (1985: 470). This is not necessarily a matter of denying that knowledge is closed under known entailment. We can say that we do know the negation of the sceptical hypothesis, provided that we allow knowledge to include both justified belief and comfortable certainty. The issue is, rather, one about transfer of justification or epistemic warrant.

What our brief discussion of *On Certainty* suggests is that justification or warrant cannot be transferred to the entailed proposition because that proposition is already operating as a kind of presupposition of the justificatory, or epistemic, project. It is 'giving our researches their shape' and underpinning the relevant evidential relations.

Wright explicitly considers the issue of a limitation on transfer of epistemic warrant in the context of a sceptical response to Moore's (1959) anti-sceptical argument for the existence of the external world:

> Moore(1):   This is a hand before me.
> Moore(2):   If this is a hand before me, then there is an external world.
> Therefore:
> Moore(3):   There is an external world.

The sceptic begins by allowing that we can, indeed, know Moore(2). But still, we cannot arrive at knowledge of Moore(3) by inference from Moore(1) in the case where that latter piece of knowledge is warranted by sensory experience. For the sensory experience supports Moore(1) only in the context of our prior commitment to Moore(3). As Wittgenstein himself might have said (in the style of OC, §188): 'It strikes me as if someone who doubts the existence of the external world is impugning the nature of all sensory evidence.' Or, as Wright puts it (1985: 437):

Once the hypothesis is seriously entertained that it is as likely as not, for all I know, that there is no material world as ordinarily conceived, my experience will lose all tendency to corroborate the particular propositions about the material world which I normally take to be certain.

Wright goes on to point out (p. 458) that, taken not merely as a rejoinder to Moore's anti-sceptical argument, but as a purported sceptical argument in its own right, the force of the challenge would depend on the assumption that we need to have some evidential or inferential warrant for our commitment to Moore(3). That assumption is, of course, just what Wittgenstein denies. The scaffolding proposition, Moore(3), falls outside the domain of cognitive achievement; we accept it without reason or warrant. Then, within the framework of the scaffolding provided by Moore(3), we have the evidential support for the propositions that do need it—workaday propositions such as Moore(1).

3   A Limitation Principle

What I want to take from this brief discussion of Wittgenstein and Wright is a rough first shot at a principle for limiting the transfer of epistemic warrant (or limiting the scope of knowledge by inference) from premisse(s) A to conclusion B.

> First Limitation Principle: Epistemic warrant cannot be transferred from A to B, even given an a priori known entailment from A to B, if the truth of B is a pre-condition of our warrant for A counting as a warrant.

Given the discussion from which this principle has emerged, we should expect that it can be used in discussions of scepticism in rather the same way that the denial of the closure of knowledge under known entailment is used by Robert Nozick (1981).

As is very well known, the denial of closure permits a strategy for neutralizing the admission that we do not know the negation of some sceptical hypothesis. Thus, consider some workaday proposition, such as the proposition that I am working in an office in Oxford; some sceptical hypothesis, such as the hypothesis that I am a brain in a vat on Alpha Centauri; and the following argument, Scep:

Scep(1): I am working in an office in Oxford.
Scep(2): If I am working in an office in Oxford, then I am not a brain in a vat on Alpha Centauri.
Therefore:
Scep(3): I am not a brain in a vat on Alpha Centauri.

I can surely know Scep(2). If knowledge is closed under known entailment, then the admission that I do not know Scep(3) involves the admission that I do not know Scep(1). But denying closure opens up the possibility of claiming that I can and do know Scep(1) and a host of other workaday propositions, even though I do not know Scep(3)—and, indeed, do not know the negation of any radical sceptical hypothesis. (I cannot, of course, know Scep(1) with first-person authority; my knowledge of Scep(1) is based on empirical evidence furnished by the senses.)

We can now use the First Limitation Principle to explain why I cannot know Scep(3) by inference, even though I do know Scep(1) and I know (near enough to a priori) Scep(2): that is, I know that Scep(1) entails Scep(3). The application of the limitation principle is triggered if the truth of Scep(3) is a pre-condition of my warrant for Scep(1) counting as a warrant. And the basic idea—in line with what Wright said about Moore's argument—is that, if I seriously entertain the brain-in-a-vat hypothesis as something that might, for all I know, be true, then I can scarcely count my sensory experience as supporting my belief that I am working in an office in Oxford.

It would be entirely reasonable for someone to complain that the First Limitation Principle, as presently formulated, is imprecise and is almost certainly open to counter-examples. A legitimate focus for dissatisfaction is the notion of a pre-condition; and if this is glossed simply as a necessary condition, then plausible counter-examples are easily constructed. Thus, for example, consider the simple inference from the premiss:

> I have a warrant for p

to the conclusion:

> I have a warrant for something.

It is plausible that if I know this premiss, then I can gain knowledge of the conclusion by inference. But, of course, the truth of the conclusion is a necessary condition for my warrant for the premiss counting as a warrant; so application of the principle would be triggered, and transfer of warrant from premiss to conclusion would be blocked.

In order to improve on the present formulation of the First Limitation Principle, the first step would be to provide a more explicit account of the relevant notion of a pre-condition, so as to make clear that not all necessary conditions are pre-conditions. But I shall not start on that here, since the First Limitation Principle cannot, in any case, be used to deal with the problems of epistemic warrant that are posed by externalist and architecturalist arguments when these are put together with a thesis of first-person authority. (See below, at the end of the first part of section IV, for some suggestions as to how the notion of a pre-condition might be refined.)

In the case of externalist arguments, for example, it is difficult even to make sense of the idea that if I seriously entertain the notion that perhaps I have not had such-and-such encounters with water, then that undermines my taking as evidence what I usually take to be evidence in support of my belief that I believe that water is wet. The epistemological problems posed by arguments of the forms Ext(MC) and Arch(MC) turn on first-personal knowledge of premiss (1), and first-personal knowledge does not seem to rest on any special kind of evidence. If we are to deal with these problems, then some other restriction on knowledge by inference is required.

IV   A SECOND LIMITATION PRINCIPLE AND FIRST-PERSON AUTHORITY

The motivation that we have offered on behalf of the First Limitation Principle may seem to involve a particular picture of what our epistemic situation would be if we were brains in vats on Alpha Centauri. That picture has it, in part, that if I really were a brain in a vat on Alpha Centauri, then I would be able to frame the proposition that I am working in an office in Oxford—just as I can frame it now—but my sensory experience would no longer constitute any warrant for that belief. But this aspect of the picture of our other-worldly epistemic situation is something that many philosophers—certainly many externalist philosophers, and most notably Hilary Putnam (1981)—would reject. According to the alternative view that these philosophers would defend, the truth of the brain-in-a-vat hypothesis would actually undermine my ability to believe the proposition—indeed, even my ability to frame the hypothesis—that I am working in an office in Oxford.

1   A Second Limitation Principle

We may suppose that these philosophers would want to block the transfer of epistemic warrant from premises to conclusion in the argument Scep:

Scep(1):   I am working in an office in Oxford.
Scep(2):   If I am working in an office in Oxford, then I am not a brain in a vat on Alpha Centauri.
Therefore:
Scep(3):   I am not a brain in a vat on Alpha Centauri.

(Even someone who thinks that Scep(3) can be established by way of a transcendental argument is unlikely to think that knowledge of Scep(3) can be attained simply by inference from Scep(1) and Scep(2).) But, on their view, the truth of Scep(3) is not so much a pre-condition of our warrant for Scep(1) counting as a warrant as it is a pre-condition of Scep(1) even being a potential candidate for epistemic warrant. The truth of Scep(3) is a pre-condition of Scep(1) being believed or even entertained as a hypothesis. So we can obtain a limitation principle that will block the transfer of warrant from premises to conclusion in Scep if we simply plug this in as the triggering condition (in place of the condition that the truth of B is a pre-condition of our warrant for A counting as a warrant). Thus we arrive at a rough first shot at a second principle for limiting the transfer of epistemic warrant (or limiting the scope of knowledge by inference) from premiss(es) A to conclusion B.

> Second Limitation Principle: Epistemic warrant cannot be transferred from A to B, even given an a priori known entailment from A to B, if the truth of B is a pre-condition of the knower even being able to believe the proposition A.

It would be fair to comment that the motivation that we have provided for the Second Limitation Principle has been somewhat oblique.
We have simply transposed the First Limitation Principle so as to
achieve the same blocking effect, while taking account of the more
radical view of the cognitive and epistemic consequences of being a brain
in a vat. So the route to the Second Limitation Principle is bound to
appear opportunistic and even *ad hoc*.

The intuitive idea behind both limitation principles is something like
this. In any given epistemic project, some propositions will have a presuppositional status. Suppose that the focus of the project P is the proposition A, and that the investigation is carried out using method N.
Then within P it is presupposed, for example, that A is a hypothesis
that can be coherently entertained (can be believed, doubted, confirmed,
disconfirmed); and it is also presupposed that N is a method that can
yield knowledge, at least with respect to A. Suppose that B is some
proposition that has this presuppositional status in project P. Then P
cannot itself yield knowledge that B; nor can P play an essential role
in yielding knowledge that B.

The First Limitation Principle can be regarded as an attempt at codi-
fying this idea as it relates to the presupposition about the method: our
warrant for A counting as a warrant stands in for the investigative method
being such as to yield knowledge. The Second Limitation Principle likewise attempts to codify the idea as it relates to the presupposition about
the hypothesis: the knower being able to believe the proposition A stands
in for the hypothesis being such as can be entertained coherently. If in
the principles we gloss the notion of a pre-condition as a necessary
condition, then this amounts to saying that if B has presuppositional
status in P and B is sufficient for C, then C also has presuppositional
status in P.

Just as, with this gloss on the notion of a pre-condition, it is easy to
construct counter-examples to the First Limitation Principle, so too there
are counter-examples to the Second Limitation Principle (when the same
gloss is used). Consider, for example, the simple inference from the
premiss:

> I believe that water is wet

to the conclusion:

> Someone is able to believe something.

It is not obvious that we should want to block the possibility of knowledge by inference here. But the truth of the conclusion is a necessary

condition for my being able to believe the premiss; so application of the Second Limitation Principle would be triggered.

We need to tighten up the Second Limitation Principle (and the First Limitation Principle, too) by introducing a more constrained notion of a pre-condition. Rather than allowing all necessary conditions to count as pre-conditions, we shall, perhaps, reckon as pre-conditions only those necessary conditions that can be shown to be such by way of theoretical considerations that have particular salience. Salient considerations might include elements of a theory about which methods are knowledge-yielding (a theory about epistemology) and elements of a theory about which hypotheses are coherently entertainable (a theory about the contents of thoughts). Furthermore, if proposition B has presuppositional status in epistemic project P, and C can be shown to follow from B by using considerations that are already being deployed in project P, then perhaps that is enough to confer presuppositional status on C as well.

We cannot now pursue the question of whether refinements like these will yield a version of the Second Limitation Principle that is not open to obvious counter-examples, or whether some quite different line of improvement will need to be considered. Instead, we turn to confirming that the principle does indeed deal with the problems of epistemic warrant that are posed by externalist and architecturalist arguments when these are put together with a thesis of first-person authority.

2 Externalist Arguments and First-Person Authority

The epistemological problem posed by externalist arguments is that when they are combined with a thesis of first-person authority, they seem to offer me an unacceptably 'non-empirical' route to knowledge of substantive empirical facts about the world outside my skin.

The Second Limitation Principle deals with the problem by blocking the transfer of epistemic warrant from premisses to conclusion in arguments of the form Ext(MC):

> Ext(1): I believe that p.
> Ext(2): If I believe that p, then E(me).
> Therefore:
> Ext(3): E(me).

The philosophical theory that issues in the externalist entailment, for example.

> $(\forall x)$ (If x believes that water is wet, then x has had such-and-such encounters with water)

and thus provides the epistemic warrant for:

> If I believe that water is wet, then I have had such-and-such encounters with water

also has the consequence that I need to have had those encounters even to believe that I believe that water is wet. For that second-order belief is also a belief involving the concept *water*. So, if the externalist philosophical theory is correct, then, according to the Second Limitation Principle, epistemic warrant cannot be transferred from Ext(1) to Ext(3), even given the a priori known entailment in Ext(2). I cannot come to know the conclusion Ext(3) by inference from the premisses Ext(1) and Ext(2).

3   Architecturalist Arguments and First-Person Authority

The epistemological problem posed by architecturalist arguments is that when they are combined with a thesis of first-person authority, they seem to offer me an unacceptably 'non-empirical' route to knowledge of substantive empirical facts about the world inside my skull. As would be expected given the apparent parallel between the two cases, the Second Limitation Principle deals with this problem by blocking the transfer of epistemic warrant from premisses to conclusion in arguments of the form Arch(MC):

> Arch(1):   I have beliefs.
> Arch(2):   If I have beliefs, then A(me).
> Therefore:
> Arch(3): A(me).

The philosophical theory that issues in the architecturalist entailment, for example:

> ($\forall x$) (If x has beliefs, then x's internal cognitive architecture is a language of thought architecture)

also has the consequence that my cognitive architecture must be a language of thought architecture if I am even to believe that I have beliefs. This architecturalist philosophical theory might be wrong, of course. But if it is right, then it triggers application of the Second Limitation Principle, and epistemic warrant cannot be transferred from Arch(1) to Arch(3), even given the a priori known entailment in Arch(2). Given the Second Limitation Principle, the piece of philosophical theory that gives rise to the epistemological problem also provides for its solution. So, given that principle, it would be wrong to press the epistemological problem as an objection against architecturalist arguments.

V TO BE CONTINUED . . .

If we accept the Second Limitation Principle, then we can avoid the epistemological problem that is otherwise posed by philosophical arguments for externalism about the contents of thoughts, and by philosophical arguments for architecturalism about thinking, when those arguments are put together with a thesis of first-person authority. But we can scarcely be content with the present situation.

1 *Improving the Principle*

The Second Limitation Principle allows us to block the unacceptably 'non-empirical' route to knowledge of empirical facts. But we have provided little enough motivation for the principle, and we have acknowledged that, as presently formulated (and with the notion of a pre-condition glossed as a necessary condition), the principle is open to counter-examples.

On the other hand, we can give the principle some plausibility in terms of the idea of presuppositions in an epistemic project. And we have been able to make some suggestions as to how the principle might be improved. The question that remains, of course, is whether, as the principle is tightened up, it can continue to do the work for which it was introduced. It might turn out, for example, that despite the apparent parallel between the externalist and architecturalist cases an improved version of the Second Limitation Principle will deal with one problem and not with the other. These are issues for future work.

2 *Closure and Context Shifting*

The limitation principles block the transfer of epistemic warrant, and thereby limit the scope of knowledge by inference. And, as I mentioned near the outset, it is reasonable to suppose (even though this does not strictly follow) that the limitation principles generate failures of the closure of knowledge under known entailment. In a recent discussion of the way that Fred Dretske (1970) uses the denial of closure in a response to sceptical arguments (cf. Nozick 1981), David Lewis says (1996: 564):

What Dretske says is close to right, but not quite. Knowledge *is* closed under implication. Knowing that I have hands *does* imply knowing that I'm not handless and deceived. Implication preserves truth—that is, it preserves truth in any given, fixed context. But if we switch contexts midway, all bets are off. . . . [I]n the sceptical argument the context switched midway, and the semantic value of the context-dependent word 'know' switched with it.

Lewis's definition of knowledge is this (p. 551): 'Subject *S knows* proposition *P* iff . . . *S*'s evidence eliminates every possibility in which not-*P*.' But, as he explains, the definition 'requires a *sotto voce* proviso' (p. 554): '*S knows* that *P* iff *S*'s evidence eliminates every possibility in which not-*P*—Psst!—except for those possibilities that we're properly ignoring.' The key idea here is that in any given context certain possibilities are properly ignored. Thus (p. 564):

> The premise 'I know that I have hands' was true in its everyday context, where the possibility of deceiving demons was properly ignored. The mention of that very possibility switched the context midway. The conclusion 'I know that I am not handless and deceived' was false in *its* context, because that was a context in which the possibility of deceiving demons was being mentioned, hence was not being ignored, hence was not being properly ignored. . . . If we evaluate the conclusion for truth not with respect to the context in which it was uttered, but instead with respect to the different context in which the premise was uttered, then truth is preserved.

This is not the place to explore the question of whether Lewis is right to maintain closure and Dretske is wrong to deny it. But some interest attaches to the way in which the limitation principles on transfer of epistemic warrant (or knowledge by inference) could be transposed into the context-shifting framework as constraints on which possibilities can be properly ignored (or on which possibilities remain as relevant alternatives).

Under the transposition, the Second Limitation Principle (as presently formulated) becomes a pair of constraints on which possibilities are relevant in a context.[2]

> First Constraint: If you know that A (in context C), then (in C) all possibilities in which you are unable even to believe A are irrelevant alternatives.

> Second Constraint: If you attend to the question whether B (in context D), then (in D) at least some not-B possibilities are relevant alternatives.

If the truth of B is a necessary condition for the knower even being able to believe the proposition A, then all not-B possibilities are irrelevant alternatives in context C, although at least some not-B possibilities are relevant alternatives in context D. So, given these two constraints, the condition that triggers application of the Second Limitation Principle enforces a shift of context.

---

[2] I am grateful to David Lewis for discussion of these issues and for formulating the two constraints. That is not to say, of course, that he himself is committed to them.

Since A entails B, any not-B possibility is a not-A possibility. So, if someone's evidence eliminates all the relevant not-A possibilities, then it eliminates all the relevant not-B possibilities. But since more not-B possibilities are relevant in context D than in context C, it may happen that someone's evidence eliminates all the not-A possibilities that are relevant in C, but does not eliminate all the not-B possibilities that are relevant in D. In this way we get the appearance of a limitation on knowledge by inference.

Lewis suggests (p. 554): 'Say that we *presuppose* proposition Q iff we ignore all possibilities in which not-Q.' Then we can restate the way in which, according to the two constraints, the context shifts between premiss A and conclusion B. When A is in question, we presuppose B, since B is a necessary condition for the knower even being able to believe A (First Constraint). But when B is itself in question, we cannot presuppose B, for that would trivialize the claim to know B (Second Constraint).

Here we see plainly that constraints on which possibilities are relevant in a context, like the corresponding limitation principles on knowledge by inference, can be motivated by ideas about presuppositions in epistemic projects. But further exploration of these ideas and comparison of the relative merits of the two approaches—denying closure and context shifting—must wait for another occasion.

REFERENCES

Block, N. (1981), 'Psychologism and Behaviorism', *Philosophical Review*, 90: 5–43.

—— (1990), 'The Computer Model of the Mind', in D. N. Osherson and E. E. Smith (eds.), *An Invitation to Cognitive Science*, vol. iii: *Thinking* (Cambridge, Mass.: MIT Press), 247–89.

Brown, J. (1995*a*), 'The Incompatibility of Anti-Individualism and Privileged Access', *Analysis*, 55: 149–56.

—— (1995*b*), 'Thought, the Environment and Privileged Access' (D.Phil. diss. University of Oxford).

Brueckner, A. (1992), 'What an Anti-Individualist Knows *A Priori*', *Analysis*, 52: 111–18.

Burge, T. (1979), 'Individualism and the Mental', in P. A. French, T. E. Uehling, and H. K. Wettstein (eds.), *Midwest Studies in Philosophy*, vol. iv: *Studies in Metaphysics* (Minneapolis: University of Minnesota Press), 73–121.

—— (1982), 'Other Bodies', in A. Woodfield (ed.), *Thought and Object* (Oxford: Oxford University Press), 97–120.

—— (1986), 'Cartesian Error and the Objectivity of Perception', in P. Pettit and J. McDowell (eds.), *Subject, Thought, and Context* (Oxford: Oxford University Press), 117–36.

Burge, T. (1988), 'Individualism and Self-Knowledge', *Journal of Philosophy*, 85: 649–63.

—— (1996), 'Our Entitlement to Self-Knowledge', *Proceedings of the Aristotelian Society*, 96: 91–116.

Davies, M. (1991*a*), 'Concepts, Connectionism, and the Language of Thought', in W. Ramsey, S. Stich, and D. Rumelhart (eds.), *Philosophy and Connectionist Theory* (Hillsdale, NJ: Lawrence Erlbaum Associates), 229–57.

—— (1991*b*), 'Individualism and Perceptual Content', *Mind*, 100: 461–84.

—— (1992*a*), 'Aunty's Own Argument for the Language of Thought', in J. Ezquerro and J. M. Larrazabal (eds.), *Cognition, Semantics and Philosophy: Proceedings of the First International Colloquium on Cognitive Science* (Dordrecht: Kluwer Academic Publishers), 235–71.

—— (1992*b*), 'Perceptual Content and Local Supervenience', *Proceedings of the Aristotelian Society*, 92: 21–45.

—— (1993), 'Aims and Claims of Externalist Arguments', in E. Villanueva (ed.), *Philosophical Issues*, vol. iv: *Naturalism and Normativity* (Atascadero, Calif.: Ridgeview Publishing Company), 227–49.

—— (1996), 'Externalism and Experience', in A. Clark, J. Ezquerro, and J. M. Larrazabal (eds.), *Philosophy and Cognitive Science: Categories, Consciousness and Reasoning* (Dordrecht: Kluwer Academic Publishers), 1–33; repr. in N. Block, O. Flanagan, and G. Güzeldere (eds.), *The Nature of Consciousness: Philosophical Debates* (Cambridge, Mass.: MIT Press, 1997), 309–28.

—— and Humberstone, L. (1980), 'Two Notions of Necessity', *Philosophical Studies*, 38: 1–30.

Dennett, D. C. (1987), *The Intentional Stance* (Cambridge, Mass.: MIT Press).

DeRose, K. (1995), 'Solving the Skeptical Problem', *Philosophical Review*, 104: 1–52.

Dretske, F. (1970), 'Epistemic Operators', *Journal of Philosophy*, 67: 107–22.

Evans, G. (1979), 'Reference and Contingency', *Monist*, 62: 161–89; repr. in *Collected Papers* (Oxford: Oxford University Press, 1985), 178–213.

—— (1982), *The Varieties of Reference* (Oxford: Oxford University Press).

Goldman, A. I. (1993), 'The Psychology of Folk Psychology', *Behavioral and Brain Sciences*, 16: 15–28.

Humberstone, I. L. (1996), 'Intrinsic/Extrinsic', *Synthese*, 108: 205–67.

Jackson, F. (1994), 'Armchair Metaphysics', in M. Michael and J. O'Leary-Hawthorne (eds.), *Philosophy in Mind: The Place of Philosophy in the Study of Mind* (Dordrecht: Kluwer Academic Publishers), 23–42.

—— (1998), *From Metaphysics to Ethics* (Oxford: Oxford University Press).

—— and Pettit, P. (1993), 'Some Content is Narrow', in J. Heil and A. Mele (eds.), *Mental Causation* (Oxford: Oxford University Press), 259–82.

Khamara, E. J. (1988), 'Indiscernibles and the Absolute Theory of Space and Time', *Studia Leibnitiana*, 20: 140–59.

Langton, R. (1993), 'Stich on Intentionality and Naturalism', in K. Neander and I. Ravenscroft (eds.), *Prospects for Intentionality: Working Papers in Philosophy*, 3 (Canberra: Research School of Social Sciences, Australian National University), 115–20.

—— and Lewis, D. (1998), 'Defining "Intrinsic"', *Philosophy and Phenomenological Research*, 58 (1998).

Lewis, D. (1996), 'Elusive Knowledge', *Australasian Journal of Philosophy*, 74: 549–67.

McDowell, J. (1984), 'De Re Senses', *Philosophical Quarterly*, 34: 283–94.

—— (1986), 'Singular Thought and the Extent of Inner Space', in P. Pettit and J. McDowell (eds.), *Subject, Thought, and Context* (Oxford: Oxford University Press), 137–68.

McKinsey, M. (1991), 'Anti-Individualism and Privileged Access', *Analysis*, 51: 9–16.

Moore, G. E. (1959), 'Proof of an External World', in *Philosophical Papers* (London: Allen and Unwin), 127–50.

Nozick, R. (1981), *Philosophical Explanations* (Oxford: Oxford University Press).

Peacocke, C. (1983), *Sense and Content* (Oxford: Oxford University Press).

—— (1992), *A Study of Concepts* (Cambridge, Mass.: MIT Press).

—— (1996), 'Entitlement, Self-Knowledge and Conceptual Redeployment', *Proceedings of the Aristotelian Society*, 96: 117–58.

Putnam, H. (1975), 'The Meaning of "Meaning"', in *Mind, Language and Reality* (Cambridge: Cambridge University Press), 215–71.

—— (1981), *Reason, Truth and History* (Cambridge: Cambridge University Press).

Ramsey, W., Stich, S., and Garon, J. (1990), 'Connectionism, Eliminativism and the Future of Folk Psychology', in J. E. Tomberlin (ed.), *Philosophical Perspectives*, vol. iv: *Action Theory and Philosophy of Mind* (Atascadero, Calif.: Ridgeview Publishing Company), 499–533.

Wittgenstein, L. (1969), *On Certainty* (Oxford: Basil Blackwell).

Wright, C. (1985), 'Facts and Certainty', *Proceedings of the British Academy*, 71: 429–72.

I 2

First-Person Authority and the Internal Reality of Beliefs

DIANA RAFFMAN

———•◆•———

At issue in Davies's chapter (11) are two arguments which seem to show that substantive empirical facts can be known in a 'non-empirical' way. Davies attributes this dubious result to an overly liberal policy on the transfer of epistemic warrant across a priori known entailments. Accordingly, he proposes a principled restriction—his Second Limitation Principle—on such transfers. Though the latter principle seems to me *ad hoc*, I will not target it here; in other words, I shall grant for the sake of argument that 'epistemic warrant cannot be transferred from A to B, even given an a priori known entailment from A to B, if the truth of B is a pre-condition of the knower even being able to believe the proposition A' (p. 353). Instead, I will show that appeal to the latter principle is superfluous in the present context. The epistemic anomaly that worries Davies, and a number of others, has a cure more straightforward than any limitation on the transfer of warrant. Indeed, I suspect it admits of several straightforward treatments, but I shall focus on just one of these here.

The difficulty with the two arguments at issue—or rather, with Davies's interpretation of them—can be formulated as a trilemma: in each case, either (i) I do not enjoy first-person authority with respect to premiss (1), or (ii) I do not know premiss (2) a priori, or (iii) the argument equivocates. Let me flesh out the details. I shall begin with the Architecturalist Argument and then take up the Externalist variant.

The Architecturalist Argument, recall, runs like this:

(1) I have beliefs (e.g. I believe that *p*).
(2) If I have beliefs, then *A*(me).
(3) *A*(me).

where '*A*(me)' is some statement about my internal cognitive architecture. As Davies explains, the argument appears to show that I have a non-empirical way of knowing something substantive about the causal order within my skin (see p. 356). How so? Well, I have a non-empirical way of knowing that I believe that *p*, and I have (or at least can have) a priori knowledge of the entailment from my believing that *p* to my having a certain internal cognitive architecture, and so it seems to follow that I have a similarly non-empirical way of knowing that I have that architecture.

Before we go further I should point out that there are those who will object to Davies's use of the term 'non-empirical' as applied to our first-person way of knowing our beliefs. As I understand it, most current theories of epistemic justification, even where they regard the warrant for first-person beliefs as non-inferential in nature, still regard it as empirical. In the present context, however, this objection is a red herring, for at least two reasons. First, what Davies intends, I take it, is just that my knowledge of my own beliefs is not *inferred from evidence*—or anyway not inferred by *me personally* from evidence available to *me personally*. (He could allow, following some recent psychological theories, that such knowledge is the product of 'inferences' by some 'subpersonal components' of me.) Second, it is at least prima facie plausible to suppose that, whatever exactly their nature may be, 'empirical' or not, our warrants for premisses (1) and (2) are importantly different in kind from our warrant for (3). And Davies's concern is that the Architecturalist and Externalist Arguments appear to show otherwise; that is, they appear to show that (3) enjoys the same warrant as—indeed, inherits its warrant by inference from—(1) and (2). That is the worry on which our attention should focus.

To return now to the Architecturalist Argument, the trouble with Davies's reasoning here is that my self-knowledge cannot do double duty in the way he envisions: specifically, my knowledge that I have beliefs cannot be both knowledge in respect of which I am authoritative and knowledge from which I can infer a priori that I have a certain internal cognitive architecture. Why not? Think of it this way. It must be the case that whatever I know authoritatively about my beliefs is compatible, *as far as I can know*, with the ontology of so-called instrumentalist views according to which propositional attitude ascriptions are mere heuristic devices for explaining and predicting behaviour.[1] These views

---

[1] See e.g. Daniel Dennett, 'Three Kinds of Intentional Psychology' and 'Reflections: Instrumentalism Reconsidered', in his *The Intentional Stance* (Cambridge, Mass.: MIT Press, 1987), 43–82. Though rather more debatable, the claim that our authoritative self-knowledge is, for all we can know, compatible even with (e.g.) a 'syntactic' theory

unite in endorsing the truth of belief ascriptions while denying what I'll call the *internal reality* of beliefs: they deny the existence of any underlying features of the brain (or its functional equivalent) with which beliefs could be identified. My present point is that my authoritative self-knowledge is not knowledge that I have beliefs in any sense of 'having beliefs' that would conflict with these instrumentalist views. Simply put: I have no introspective knowledge of the internal reality of my beliefs. This much is, I take it, self-evident—since otherwise I could know by introspection that the instrumentalist theories were false.

What this means for the Architecturalist Argument is that, from what I know authoritatively, I can infer nothing a priori about my internal cognitive architecture. Intuitively speaking, my authoritative self-knowledge tells me nothing about what's inside my head; for instance, it fails to rule out an instrumentalist theory, and if an instrumentalist theory proves correct, then I may have no internal cognitive architecture at all. Consequently, unless the antecedent of premiss (2) is assigned a 'realistic' interpretation radically different from the 'authoritative' interpretation of premiss (1)—that is, unless the argument equivocates —I cannot know a priori that if I have beliefs then I have a certain internal architecture.[2] The 'architecturalist' should simply deny that premiss (2) is known a priori. What I can know a priori, if anything at all, is that if I have beliefs then I have a certain internal cognitive architecture *where 'I have beliefs' is understood realistically in a manner incompatible both with first-person authority and with an instrumentalist*

of the mind, or with the connectionist models discussed by Ramsey, Stich, and Garon, may be true as well. (See Stephen Stich, *From Folk Psychology to Cognitive Science: The Case Against Belief* (Cambridge, Mass.: MIT Press, 1983), and W. Ramsey, S. Stich, and J. Garon, 'Connectionism, Eliminativism, and the Future of Folk Psychology', in John Greenwood (ed.), *The Future of Folk Psychology* (Cambridge: Cambridge University Press, 1991), 93–119.) However, my brief against Davies does not require this stronger claim. All it requires is that our authoritative self-knowledge be compatible with at least some theories that deny the 'internal reality' of beliefs. See above for discussion.

  [2] It is worth pointing out that Ramsey *et al.*, 'Connectionism, Eliminativism, and the Future of Folk Psychology', cited by Davies, clearly would interpret the antecedent of (2) realistically in the sense here at issue. Specifically, they would express premiss (2) as the proposition that if folk psychology is true, then our internal cognitive architecture is compatible with the thesis of propositional modularity (p. 111). For these authors, to claim that folk psychology is true is to claim *inter alia* that the ontology of folk psychology is internally real: that is, that there are some internal features or other of the underlying architecture—ultimately features of the brain—with which 'the propositional attitudes of commonsense psychology can plausibly be identified' (ibid. 116). Thus, on their view, one who endorses the truth of folk psychology assumes an ontological commitment. Indeed, only on the supposition of such a commitment does anything follow (if it follows at all) about the propositional modularity of the internal architecture. Again, so-called instrumentalist theories of belief, according to which belief ascriptions are heuristic devices for explaining and predicting behaviour, carry no architectural implications.

theory of belief. Call such a realistic interpretation of 'I have beliefs' an ontologically 'fat' interpretation, as opposed to the ontologically 'thin' interpretation in respect of which my self-knowledge is authoritative.

Note that I am not *simply* denying the a priori status of premiss (2), or *simply* denying that we can have authoritative knowledge of our internal architecture.[3] Rather, I am denying that we can have authoritative knowledge of the internal reality of our beliefs; that is, I am denying that we can know authoritatively whether there are states of the brain with which our beliefs can be identified. (Indeed, we don't even know authoritatively whether we have brains; *pace* the wishful thinking of some eliminative materialists,[4] I cannot know by introspection that I have a brain; in order to know that, I must learn some science or open my head and take a look.) And if we cannot know authoritatively whether our beliefs are internally real, then we have no authoritative knowledge from which we could infer a priori a conclusion about our internal cognitive architecture. (Perhaps it goes without saying that our authoritative self-knowledge may entail some ontologically *thin* architectural conclusions a priori; but of course those are then not substantive empirical conclusions of the sort that worry Davies.)

So much for the Architecturalist Argument. Let us turn now to its Externalist cousin:

(1) I believe that p.
(2) If I believe that p, then E(me).
(3) E(me).

where 'E(me)' is some statement about my environmental situation. Now it seems to me that the externalist is committed to a line analogous to the one I levelled against Davies in connection with the Architecturalist Argument. The externalist should insist that my authoritative self-knowledge is, as far as I can know, compatible with an instrumentalist theory of the propositional attitudes. The brand of instrumentalism at issue here, however, concerns not the internal reality of my beliefs but rather the reality of my environmental situation, as one might put it. Such an instrumentalism is perhaps best understood in terms of Davidson's example of Swampman:[5] the instrumentalist will say that I have beliefs even if I am Swampman, that is, even if I am not environmentally situated in the way required by the externalist, so long as the

---

[3] Here I respond to a criticism by Davies (in conversation).

[4] Paul Churchland, for a prime example; see his 'Qualia, Reduction, and the Direct Introspection of Brain States', *Journal of Philosophy*, 82 (1985), 8–28.

[5] See Donald Davidson, 'Knowing One's Own Mind', *Proceedings and Addresses of the American Philosophical Association*, 60 (1987), 441–58.

ascription of beliefs serves to explain and predict my behaviour. (To be sure, the instrumentalist may grant that in order for those ascriptions to succeed, my ascribers must regard me *as if* I am environmentally situated in the relevant ways; but he need not require that I *be* so situated.) The point is that whatever I know authoritatively must *as far as I can know* be compatible with the possibility that I am Swampman. (I cannot know by introspection that I am not Swampman, after all.) Hence the externalist should simply deny that, on the basis of knowing authoritatively that I have beliefs, I can infer anything a priori about my environmental situation. I can infer a substantive conclusion a priori only if I know that I have beliefs in a sense that is, minimally, incompatible with my being Swampman.

The argument just mooted, like the parallel one I aimed at the Architecturalist Argument, turns on the question whether, and in what sense(s), I can know that I have beliefs. It does not touch upon the question, central to the externalist project, whether and in what sense(s) I can know *which* beliefs I have. I am not certain what Tyler Burge, for one, would say about my argument. However, if I'm right, we needn't worry over that question here, since Burge offers his own reasons to deny a priori status to (2)—reasons having to do with the individuation of beliefs. And that is all we need to block any unwanted transfer of epistemic warrant from (1) and (2) to (3) in the Externalist Argument. Let us briefly examine his reasoning.

Burge characterizes first-person authority in this way:[6]

When one knows that one is thinking that *p*, one is . . . thinking that *p* in the very event of thinking knowledgeably that one is thinking it. (p. 654) . . . Such knowledge consists in a reflexive judgment which involves thinking a first-order thought that the judgment itself is about. The reflexive judgment simply inherits the content of the first-order thought. (p. 656) . . . The source of our strong epistemic right, our justification, in our basic self-knowledge is not that we know a lot about each thought we know we have. It is not that we can explicate its nature and enabling conditions. It is that we are in the position of thinking those thoughts in the second-order, self-verifying way. (p. 660)

Shortly thereafter, Burge appears to pull the rug out from the idea that premiss (2) of the Externalist Argument can be known a priori—at least where its antecedent expresses something known authoritatively:

The tendency to blur the distinction between a priori knowledge . . . and authoritative self-knowledge [invites the mistake of] exaggerating the implications of authoritative self-knowledge for impersonal knowledge of necessary truths.

[6] Tyler Burge, 'Individualism and Self-Knowledge', *Journal of Philosophy*, 85 (1988), 649–63.

One clearly does not have first-person authority about whether one of one's thoughts is to be explicated or individuated in such and such a way. Nor is there any apparent reason to assume that, in general, one must be able to explicate one's thoughts correctly in order to know that one is thinking them . . . *One should not assimilate 'knowing what one's thoughts are' in the sense of basic self-knowledge to 'knowing what one's thoughts are' in the sense of being able to explicate them correctly in order to know that one is thinking them.* (ibid. 662; emphasis added)

In light of these remarks it seems reasonable to suppose that Burge would say the following about (Davies's construal of) the Externalist Argument: in so far as I can know a priori that if I believe that *p* then I am causally situated in my environment in such-and-such a way, then my self-knowledge is a case of ' "knowing what one's thoughts are" in the sense of being able to explicate them correctly in order to know what they are'.[7] And the latter kind of knowledge is not authoritative; it is not ' "knowing what one's thoughts are" in the sense of basic self-knowledge'. In other words, I can know the entailment in premiss (2) a priori only if my knowledge of my belief is or involves knowledge of its individuation conditions; and my knowledge of its individuation conditions is not authoritative knowledge. Therefore, if my self-knowledge *is* authoritative, as Davies's story requires, then I can infer nothing a priori about my environmental situation.

Interestingly, Burge warns against an equivocation closely allied to the one I have emphasized here:

The view that anti-individualism is incompatible with authoritative self-knowledge is easily engendered by forgetting the essentially first-person character of self-knowledge. We switch back and forth between thinking our thoughts and thinking about ourselves from the point of view of another person who knows more about our environment than we do. . . . As one thinks a thought reflexively, it is an object of reference and knowledge, but simultaneously a constituent of one's point of view. The essential role that the first-person singular plays in the epistemic status of authoritative self-knowledge differentiates this knowledge not only from empirical knowledge, but also from most a priori knowledge, the justification of which does not depend on the first-person point of view in the same way.[8]

---

[7] In fact, there is much in Burge's work to suggest that he would deny a priori status to (2) on any reading. (See e.g. 'Individualism and the Mental', *Midwest Studies in Philosophy*, 4 (1979), 73–121; 'Other Bodies', in A. Woodfield (ed.), *Thought and Object: Essays on Intentionality* (Oxford: Oxford University Press, 1982), 97–120; and 'Individualism and Self-Knowledge'. See also Anthony Brueckner, 'What an Anti-Individualist Knows A Priori', *Analysis*, 52 (1992), 111–18, for helpful discussion.) To that extent, what I say above is generous to those who would follow Davies's lead in the present context.

[8] Burge, 'Individualism and Self-Knowledge', 661–2.

Burge's point seems to be that only from 'third-person knowledge' of our beliefs can we infer anything a priori about our environmental situation. Knowledge of our beliefs 'from a first-person point of view'—namely, authoritative self-knowledge—sustains no such a priori inferences.

At bottom, the problem with Davies's interpretations of the Architecturalist and Externalist Arguments is that substantive empirical content does not arise *ex nihilo*. In particular, it seems plausible to suppose that if the consequent of premiss (2) in each case is a substantive empirical proposition, *and* the relationship of antecedent to consequent in (2) is one of a priori entailment, then that antecedent too must express a substantive empirical proposition. Intuitively speaking, if an entailment is known a priori, then its antecedent must contain at least as much substantive empirical content as its consequent. But in that case the antecedent does not express something we can know authoritatively. If our self-knowledge is authoritative, then it is not substantive empirical knowledge—at least, not substantive empirical knowledge of the sort that worries Davies.[9]

[9] I am grateful to William Taschek, George Pappas, Jonathan Vogel, and Deborah Tollefsen for helpful discussion.

13

The Simple Theory of Colour and the Transparency of Sense Experience

JIM EDWARDS

—————•—————

INTRODUCTION

John McDowell has claimed that perceptual experiences are passively structured by concepts—experiences of colours by colour concepts, for example.[1] Assuming this is so, the question arises: is the conceptual structuring of a sensory state transparent to its possessor, provided she is sufficiently attentive? That is the question with which we shall be concerned. To construct a test case, I shall deploy two other philosophical theories, one controversial, the other orthodox. The controversial theory is John Campbell's Simple Theory of Colour.[2] The orthodox theory is the external fixing of the semantic values of words which are intended to track properties of objects.

I want to draw a consequence of holding all three theories—McDowell's theory that sense experience is passively structured by concepts, Campbell's Simple Theory of Colour, and an externalist theory of the determination of the semantic values of colour words—for the transparency of colour perception. To that end I shall construct a science fiction example and apply the three theories to it. We shall find that the result is philosophically incoherent. It does not follow that the three theories are mutually incoherent when applied in normal circumstances, since the incoherence arises from the peculiarity of the science fiction example. But there is, I shall argue, a corollary to be drawn about normal circumstances—namely, that ordinary experience of colour is *not*

---

[1] John McDowell, *Mind and World* (Cambridge, Mass., and London: Harvard University Press, 1994), esp. lectures 2 and 3.

[2] John Campbell, 'A Simple View of Colour', in J. Haldane and C. Wright (eds.), *Reality, Representation and Projection* (Oxford: Oxford University Press, 1993), 257–68.

transparent even to an attentive possessor of that experience—assuming that the three theories are co-tenable in normal circumstances.

Some might think that externalism combined with McDowell's theory implies that the concept structuring an experience is not transparent to its possessor, leaving the Simple Theory of Colour with no real role to play in the argument. However, I take the view that externalism applied to predicates applies only to predicates which are intended to *track* properties of objects. Externalism is a thesis about the *semantic value*, not about the sense, of a such a predicate. There are other accounts of colours—response-dependent or projective accounts—in which colour predicates are not intended to track properties. Hence, the Simple Theory will be needed to ensure that the correct uses of colour words are indeed intended to track properties of objects, so that externalism is applicable.

In what follows I shall first outline the relevant features of the three theories, then construct my example, then apply the three theories to the example and bring out their mutual incoherence in that setting, then discuss how the incoherence is to be resolved, and finally draw a consequence for the transparency of colour experience in normal circumstances.

THE THREE THEORIES

I shall briefly outline the three theories under separate heads.

The Passive Structuring of Experience

John McDowell has argued that sensory states are structured by the passive operation of sensory concepts. 'Passive' here means that the structuring by such concepts is not the result of any conscious act, not the conscious application of a concept to a yet-to-be conceptualized state of consciousness. Rather, a sensory state first appears in consciousness, so to speak, already conceptually structured, as an appearance that *p*. What concept passively so structures Jill's experience in which an object looks green to her? Obviously the concept of looking green.

McDowell claims that experience is conceptually structured, because by being so structured experience can *warrant* judgements; whereas experience not so structured could only *cause* judgements, not warrant them. We can turn this around: only if an experience warrants a judgement do we have reason to claim that it is conceptually structured.

We now need to go beyond McDowell's text. Although Jill's experience may warrant various judgements given appropriate collateral information, there is one judgement that her experience *canonically* warrants —'canonically warrants' meaning that the experience warrants this judgement independently of collateral information. Jill's experience of an object passively structured by the concept of looking green will canonically warrant the following judgement concerning the object:

It is green if conditions are standard and I am normal,

where the truth of this judgement is independent of whether conditions are in fact standard and Jill is in fact normal. It is a feature of the concept which structures Jill's experience, the concept of looking green and its embedded concept of greenness, that such experiences canonically warrant such judgements. A warrant for a judgement is a state of information which makes it *likely*—at least, relative to the conditions in which such warrants are actually obtained—that the judgement so warranted is *true*. In the case of canonical warrants which do not rely upon collateral information, the link between warrant and truth is direct and a priori.

The Simple Theory of Colour

Let us suppose that colour properties are as described in the so-called Simple Theory of Colour. The Simple Theory makes two particular claims about colours:

(a) The colours of objects are the intrinsic causal grounds in coloured objects which cause those objects to look the colours they do to normal observers in standard conditions. Greenness, for instance, is the categorical ground of the disposition of an object to look green to normal observers in standard conditions.

(b) A colour property, like greenness, is exactly as it is represented as being in the relevant kind of experience.

Thus, according to the Simple Theory, the property of greenness is not a disposition to look green to normal observers in standard conditions; nor is the property of greenness the microphysical ground of such a disposition, a ground whose character is not apparent to observers, because it does not match the phenomenology of the experience of looking green. Rather, according to the Simple Theory, the property of greenness is the categorical ground of the disposition which objects have to look green to normal observers in standard conditions, and this property is as it appears to be.

Suppose the Simple Theory is in fact true. Now let us feed it into McDowell's theory. Jill's experiences of colours will be passively structured by concepts which *accord with* the Simple Theory. That is to say, such features of colours which the Simple Theory holds to be *observable* features of colours will be incorporated in the concepts which passively structure Jill's experiences of colours. For example, if the concept structuring an experience of Jill's in which something looks green accords with the Simple Theory, then the experience will present greenness as a *categorical* property of the object in question, and as a property which such experiences, when veridical, *track*. The Simple Theory itself claims further that the property of greenness in standard conditions with a normal subject *causes* the experience of greenness. But since Hume, it has been controversial to claim that causal agency is observable, rather than being theoretically postulated. If causality is not observed, then the concept of causation cannot passively structure perceptual experience. So, to be cautious, I shall not suppose that it is built into the experience that tracking is a *causal* relation. But I shall suppose that it is part of the content of such experiences that they *track*, *ceteris paribus*, the property of greenness. I shall suppose this because the experience presents greenness as a categorical property of the object, and because the experience presents itself as a warrant to assert that, *ceteris paribus*, the object possesses this categorical property of greenness.

Externalism

Externalist accounts of reference-fixing assign semantic values to those predicates which are intended to track properties of objects. We are supposing that Jill intends her use of 'green' to track a property of objects. Externalism identifies the semantic value of 'green' as *whatever* property of objects normally causes the experiences which canonically warrant her applications of the word 'green' to those objects in standard conditions—where 'normally causes' and 'standard' are whatever are actually normal and actually standard for Jill's language community.[3]

---

[3] Cynthia Macdonald in 'Self-Knowledge and the "Inner Eye"', *Philosophical Explorations* 1 (2) (1998), 81–104, gives a biological account of reference-fixing, which might appear to clash with the causal account which I have given. In Macdonald's account, briefly, colours are those properties of objects which it is the *function* of colour experiences to track. But the upshot will be the same, since, as Macdonald remarks, functions need underlying mechanisms. Colours are the grounds of the powers of objects to cause colour experiences when those experiences function as they biologically ought to do. On a biological account it is analytic that the experiences of normal observers in standard conditions function as they ought to do. The interesting cases of so-called normal

The semantic value of the predicate is that property whose presence or absence determines the truth-values of judgements employing 'green'.[4]

Having the three theories before us, consider the *sense* and the *semantic value* of the predicate 'green'. I take it that an experience in which an object looks green, by being a canonical warrant for a judgement employing 'green', contributes to the *sense* of the predicate 'green'. Such an experience presents the object in question as possessing a certain property, the property of greenness. The sense of the word 'green' is therefore the concept of being green, and it is part of the sense that correct applications of 'green' are intended to track this property. This property is, according to the Simple Theory, a categorical property of objects which causes the experiences which canonically warrant judgements employing 'green'. By externalism, therefore, the property of greenness is the *semantic value* of the predicate 'green'—the property uses of 'green' are intended to track. Happily, then, the sense of the predicate 'green' *matches* its semantic value in that the following holds:

(1)   Necessarily, if an object possesses the property presented in those experiences which determine the sense of the predicate 'green'—that is, the property which correct applications of that predicate are intended to track—then it possesses the property which is the semantic value of the predicate 'green'.

If (1) were not satisfied by the predicate 'green', then there would be a possible world and an object in it which possessed the property presented by the sense of 'green', hence it would satisfy the predicate, but that object does not possess the property which is the semantic value of the predicate, hence it does not satisfy the predicate—which is impossible, no object in any possible world can both satisfy and not satisfy a predicate. (1) is satisfied by the predicate 'green' because the property presented in the experiences is the very same property as the semantic value, and because property identities are necessary, like any identity.

---

misperception which Macdonald cites—cases in which a slow change of colour in fixed conditions of illumination is misperceived as being a case of sameness of colour with changing conditions of illumination—will be ruled out as involving *non*-standard conditions of observation, since the colour experiences are here not functioning as they biologically ought to—they are not tracking the properties for which those experiences were selected. In this way the biological story will bear interestingly upon the specification of standard conditions and normal observers, but the outcome will be as externalism requires: colours are the properties which cause colour experiences in whatever are normal observers in whatever are standard conditions.

[4] Or we might take the semantic value of 'green' to be not the property greenness, but the extension of the predicate, or its value range. It makes no difference for the argument of this chapter.

THE EXAMPLE

Suppose we travel to a world—or to part of our world, if you like—where apparently the colours of things have all been systematically inverted. When we emerge from our spaceship, the world around seems to be stocked with familiar objects, except that what we would otherwise have taken to be healthy grass looks red, not green, whilst what we would otherwise have taken to be poppy flowers look green, not red, etc. The conditions for viewing seem standard, and we are not aware of any change in ourselves. However, further investigation solves the mystery. The conditions of viewing are not standard: this world is subject to the influence of invisible Z-rays, whose effect is to make red things look green to normal observers in otherwise standard conditions, and green things look red, and so on through a systematic permutation of the colours. The plant which forms the lawn is in fact green, as we confirm by taking samples home and viewing them by daylight, and the flowers in the border are similarly revealed to be red poppies, and so on. So now we have an explanation of why colours are *apparently* inverted in Z-land: they are *not* inverted in Z-land, but conditions there are nonstandard such that the colours appear to be inverted.

Now suppose we add an isolated tribe of people living in Z-land. Their visual systems are anatomically and cognitively normal. The evidence for this is that, when shipped back to our neck of the woods, Z-landers are puzzled by the sight of things, as we were when we arrived in Z-land; but they have no difficulty learning our colour vocabulary and declaring the grass around them in our neck of the woods to be green and poppies red. However, in their own tongue, Z-talk, they have what appears to be a colour vocabulary of their own. So as not to beg questions, let us say Z-talk has a colour* vocabulary and expresses colour* concepts. But of course, their colour* concepts take the conditions prevailing in Z-land to be their standard conditions. Let us suppose that, in Z-talk, normally sighted people viewing grass in Z-standard conditions declare it to be 'green*', and poppies to be 'red*'. *Ex hypothesi*, normal Z-landers are normally sighted by our anatomical standards. And, *ex hypothesi*, what they take to be standard conditions are not what we take to be standard conditions—their standard conditions produce a systematic permutation of the colours things look to us to be from the colours they are, as our daylight produces a systematic permutation of the colours* things look to them to be from the colours* they are.

Grass in the conditions prevailing in Z-land looks red to us, and poppy flowers look green, but how do they look to Z-landers? Some readers might be inclined to suppose that because the grass is green and poppies are red in Z-land, then grass will look green and poppies will look red to Z-landers, because Z-landers are habituated to their, to us, non-standard conditions of viewing. The real case of spectacles which produce spatial inversion might be cited in support of this view. The familiar and true story goes that subjects were asked to wear spectacles which made things around them appear, as they reported, upside-down. They then blundered around for a while trying to navigate their way employing a sense of sight which made things appear upside-down. But then after a while they adjusted. They no longer reported that things looked upside-down, and they no longer had difficulty moving relative to the objects around them on the basis of sight. Famously, when they finally took the spectacles off, things then looked upside-down again, and they again had difficulty navigating by sight, until with time they adjusted once again, and were restored seemingly to their original phenomenology of visual and locomotor abilities. So the suggestion is that Z-landers have had a lifetime to adjust to their, to us, strange habitat —to adjust by getting the phenomenological contents of their colour experiences into line with the colour properties of the objects seen, as the spectacle-wearers made an adjustment which brought the phenomenological contents of their spatial experiences into line with the spatial dispositions of things around them. Hence we can identify colour and colour* concepts, and identify the properties of redness* and greenness* with the properties of redness and greenness respectively, it might seem.

Still supposing that the case of inverting spectacles is analogous, if one of us moved to Z-land, then initially grass would look red and poppy flowers green, but after a while the phenomenology of our experiences would switch into line with that of a native Z-lander, and grass would look green to us and poppy flowers red even in Z-light. This is a change we would notice. We would be led to say: 'When I first arrived grass looked red and poppy flowers green, but now I find grass looks green again and poppy flowers red, just as they did back home.' In short, according to this view, the traveller who tarries too long will adjust to Z-light. On returning home, grass will initially look red and poppy flowers green, until the returned traveller adjusts again to the Z-free conditions of home, when grass at home will again look green and poppy flowers red.

However, the two cases are crucially disanalogous. The case of the inverting spectacles is different, because donning the spectacles creates a co-ordination problem between sight and movement. Hence the initial blundering around—adjustment is achieved when the senses are again co-ordinated. And this is what gives sense to the reported change in visual phenomenology when the spectacles are finally removed, because the senses have to be again co-ordinated, and once again the subject reports a normal phenomenology when co-ordination has been re-established. In contrast, Z-land does not present a co-ordination problem to a new arrival, and our neck of the woods does not present a co-ordination problem to a newly arrived Z-lander. True, things look the 'wrong' colours (or colours*) to a new arrival. But there is no reason why a naïve and incurious traveller should expect things to be the same colours (or colours*) there as back home. There is no call to make an adjustment, no problem of co-ordinating one sensory mode with another. The traveller who settles in the new country need not adjust, beyond becoming familiar and so no longer surprised that things are, seemingly, odd colours (or colours*) there compared to back home. The traveller may retain a clear memory of how the meadows looked when the poppies were in bloom back home, so different from how the meadows hereabouts look, and the traveller need not be surprised when she returns and finds the meadows at home just as she remembered them. No processes of adjustment and readjustment are called for. The real case of inverting spectacles gives no support for the view that the phenomenology of a Z-lander's experience is different from the corresponding experience of a newly arrived traveller, and no support for the view that the phenomenology of the traveller's experiences will switch if she stays long enough.

There is a strong philosophical intuition that the phenomenology of sensory experiences is supervenient upon physiology and neurology. We and Z-landers are physiologically and neurologically identical from the bodily surface inwards. So, since the grass of Z-land looks red to us on arrival in Z-land, it looks red to them, and since the poppy flowers look green to us on arrival in Z-land, they look green to them, the philosophical intuition implies. Further, there is no reason to postulate switching if the traveller tarries. If grass looks red to a native Z-lander, as it does to a newly arrived traveller, then there is no reason to suppose that there will be any switch in the phenomenology of the traveller's experiences should they tarry in Z-land. Their phenomenologies match from day one. And similarly, of course, for the traveller's perceptions of poppies, etc.[5]

---

[5] Standard Twin Earth switching stories also respect the philosophical intuition. In those stories Jill on Earth sees her friend Oscar drinking water, but when she is, unbeknownst to herself, transported to Twin Earth, she sees Toscar drinking twater. After a while the contents and the semantic values of her thoughts switch from Oscar to Toscar and from water to twater. But in such standard cases the visual experience of seeing Toscar drink water is phenomenologically *indistinguishable* from the visual experience of seeing Toscar drink twater. So there is a phenomenological type which both kinds of visual experience fall under, such that more detailed specifications of the various tokens of this single type, specifications under which one token may differ from another (e.g.

So far, we have reason to suppose that the grass looks red to the native Z-lander, as it does to the traveller, and the poppy flowers look green to Z-lander and traveller alike, and no reason to suppose otherwise.[6]

APPLYING THE THREE THEORIES TO THE EXAMPLE

I have described the example without recourse to the three theories. Let us now apply the three theories to the perceptions of Z-landers in their Z-land home. So far, we have it that grass in the standard conditions prevailing in Z-land looks red to them, and poppy flowers look green to them. Applying the first theory, we suppose that the visual experiences of Z-landers when looking at grass are passively structured by the following concept:

> (2)   Looking red.

Such a conceptually structured experience canonically warrants the judgement:

> (3)   It is green* if I am normal and the conditions of viewing are standard.

We now ask: what is the *sense* of the predicate 'green*' in this judgement, and what is its *semantic value*?

To determine the *sense* for a Z-land thinker of the predicate 'green*' in judgements of type (3), we need to remember that such judgements are canonically warranted by experiences of type (2), that those experiences are—or so we are assuming—phenomenologically identical to

---

Toscar for Oscar, twater for water) do not record *noticeable* differences between the various tokens. It is this more general typology which is supervenient upon physiology and neurology from the bodily surface inward. Thus the standard Twin Earth switching cases respect the philosophical intuition. The philosophical intuition requires of the standard cases a continuity of phenomenology despite a switch of semantic value, and of my example a switch in phenomenology despite a continuity of the colour properties of things.

[6] Actually, it seems to me unqualifiedly plausible that things look the same colours to a Z-lander as they do to a traveller. So why the qualification 'So far'? The qualification is needed because, as we shall soon see, when we apply the three theories to the example, the result is incoherent, and something has to give. Assuming for the purposes of this chapter that the three theories do apply to us in our situation, I shall recommend that we abandon the claim that the visual experiences of Z-landers are passively structured by concepts relating them to colours. But then, since a traveller's experiences are passively structured by colour concepts and a Z-lander's experiences are not, things do not look the same so far as colours are concerned to traveller and Z-lander, after all. Hence I am only claiming at this stage that we have not yet been shown reason to abandon the philosophically plausible claim that things look the same colours to Z-lander and traveller alike.

the experiences of a traveller to Z-land, and that to the traveller the grass of Z-land looks *red*. Thus the traveller's experience is passively structured by the concept of redness; so the Z-lander's experiences of type (2) are passively structured by the concept of redness too. But these experiences, being the canonical warrants for judgements of type (3), give the sense of those judgements. Hence the sense of the predicate 'green*' for Z-landers is the concept of redness. The Simple Theory then tells us that redness is a categorical property which such experiences are intended to track. Hence the *sense* of the word 'green*' is that its correct use tracks the property of *redness*. To get the *semantic value* of 'green*', we apply our third theory. The example decrees that the grass of Z-land is in fact green. Hence the third theory, the external fixing of semantic value, tells us that the property of *greenness* is the semantic value of the predicate 'green*' in judgements of type (3).

We thus have a mismatch between the sense of the word 'green*' for a Z-lander, call her 'Zoe', and its semantic value. The analogue of (1) above fails for 'green*':

(4)   Necessarily, if an object possesses the property presented in those experiences which determine the sense of the predicate 'green*'—that is, the property which correct applications of that predicate are intended to track—then it possesses the property which is the semantic value of the predicate 'green*'.

Its sense represents the object to which the word is applied as having the property of being red, whilst the semantic value of the word is the property of being green, and these are contrary properties, possessed by no object in any possible world.

Such a mismatch does not pose a mere *sceptical* problem. It is not merely that the *sense* of Jill's judgement expressed by (3)—a judgement that the object is, *ceteris paribus*, red—renders (3) *false*, because the object is in fact green and not red. We also have it that the judgement expressed by (3) is *true*, because the object referred to possesses that property, greenness, which is the *semantic value* of the predicate 'green'. Thus the mismatch between the sense and the semantic value of 'green*' is mutually destructive. Applications of the predicate 'green*' by Zoe do not have satisfaction conditions; at best they correlate more or less closely with the objects in question being green.

Exactly parallel moves could have been made if we had considered instead Jill's perceptions of the poppy flowers of Z-land and her utterances employing 'red*'. Poppy flowers look green, so the conceptually structured content of her visual experiences presents the poppies as being green. These experiences canonically warrant the assertion:

(5) Poppy flowers are red*, if I am normal, and conditions are standard.

Hence the *sense* of '*x* is red*' is that *x* is green. But the Simple Theory of Colour applied to the conditions prevailing in Z-land and the external fixing of semantic values make the property of being red the *semantic value* of 'red*'. Again, we have a mutually destructive mismatch between the sense of 'red*' and its semantic value.[7]

---

[7] A. D. Smith, in 'Of Primary and Secondary Qualities', *Philosophical Review*, 99 (1990), 221–54, offers a more direct example in which, assuming the Simple Theory, experiences of colours do not phenomenologically present the colour properties which normally cause experiences of that type. Smith uses his example as an argument against the Simple Theory. But Smith's example, if it worked, could be exploited in a similar way to my example.

Smith supposes, as the Simple Theory does, that colours are the intrinsic properties which are the grounds of the dispositions of objects to cause colour experiences in normal humans in standard conditions, and that those properties are as they appear to be in those experiences. He then argues that if colours were such intrinsic properties, it would be possible for there to be a creature who perceived colours by the sense of touch. The supposition would be that the phenomenology of this creature's tactile experience when touching a green object, for example, presents the object as possessing the property of greenness, the very same property as is presented in visual experience. The claim is not merely that the tactile experience presents the object as having some *other* property merely caused by the greenness of the object. However, contrary to this supposition, Smith takes it as obvious that the phenomenology of any tactile experience caused by a colour would be different phenomenologically from our visual experiences of colour. In my terms, any tactile experience caused by a green object would be structured by some concept which presents the object as having some property *other* than a colour, some property which could be perceived by touch. Hence, supposing colour properties are as they look to us to be, Smith concludes that tactile experiences caused by colours do not phenomenologically present colour properties. As with my example, taking 'It is green*' to express a judgement canonically warranted by such tactile experiences, the sense bestowed upon 'green*' by the tactile experiences fails to match its externally determined semantic value—because it is not a priori that an object which possesses the property which is presented in the phenomenology of the tactile experience possesses also the property of greenness.

However, this example can be resisted. Firstly, it is not obvious that experiences which are phenomenologically distinct cannot present the very same property. Prima facie, a tactile experience in which an object feels round presents the very same property, roundness, as a visual experience in which something looks round. Secondly, a determined opponent could claim that such tactile experiences, if they are genuinely experiences of colours, are phenomenologically like our visual experiences of colours. The only sense the opponent will admit to making of the thought experiment is to suppose that feeling colours is phenomenologically like seeing them. It's like having little torches in the tips of your fingers, so that you can 'see' with your fingers the surfaces you are touching. So the concepts which structure the experiences do, after all, pick out colour properties. The discussion thus ends in an impasse.

By contrast, in my own thought experiment there is no doubt about the phenomenological nature of the experiences of Z-landers when looking at grass, and which properties they present the grass as possessing. So there is no doubt about what sense those experiences bestow upon 'green*', and no doubt that the semantic value of 'green*', as determined by externalism, is inverted.

Ned Block, in his 'Inverted Earth', *Philosophical Perspectives*, 4 (1990), 53–80,

I set out to apply the three philosophical theories to the example. The Simple Theory of Colour decreed that the greenness of the grass in Z-land is the categorical property which causes the grass of Z-land to look red. The externalist theory of reference-fixing then decreed that this property of greenness is the semantic value of 'green*' employed by Zoe. McDowell's theory of the passive structuring of experience by concepts decreed that the concept of redness passively structures Zoe's experiences of grass in Z-land, and hence—here going beyond McDowell's text—that the sense of 'green*' for Zoe is a conception of redness. But this result is incoherent, being a violation of a necessary condition—(4) above—relating sense to semantic value. (Similarly, of course for poppies and 'red*'.)

In developing this incoherence, two of the theories, the Simple Theory of Colour and an externalist theory of reference-fixing, were essentially involved. Instead of the Simple Theory, we might have favoured an extension-determining view of the concepts which passively structure colour experiences. Then the concepts which structure colour experiences would take the experiences of normal observers in standard conditions to determine their extensions, but *not* to do so by *tracking* properties in the objects which ground the powers of objects to cause such experiences.[8] Since greenness does not then purport to be a property which those experiences track, no externalist fixing of the semantic value of 'green*' in terms of the normal causes of the relevant experiences is called for. Hence externalism could not generate a mismatch for Zoe between the sense of 'green*' as fixed by the canonical warrants for judgements employing 'green*' and the semantic value of the predicate —because greenness is not a property purportedly tracked by such experiences. It is consistent both that the grass of Z-land is green, where the extension of the concept of greenness is determined by our responses in the conditions prevailing at home, and that the grass of Z-land is green*, where the extension of the concept of greenness* is determined by experientially different responses in the different conditions prevalent in Z-land.

However, the development of the incoherence only superficially involved McDowell's theory of the passive structuring of experiences

develops an example in which the property presented in a colour experience, which he calls the 'qualitative content' of the experience, differs from the externally determined semantic value of the experience, which he calls the 'intentional content' of the experience. But Block does not see that the resulting mismatch—between the content of a warrant for a judgement of colour and its semantic value—renders the position unstable.

[8] See esp. Crispin Wright, 'Moral Values, Projection and Secondary Qualities', *Proceedings of the Aristotelian Society*, suppl. vol. 62 (1988), 1–26.

by concepts. In the example, grass in Z-land looks red to Zoe. It is a commonplace, and therefore a datum which any theory of colour must respect, that such an experience canonically warrants a judgement of the grass that it is red if the observer is normal and the conditions are standard. The sense of the word 'green*' for Zoe is therefore the concept of redness. McDowell's theory claims that a necessary condition of such an experience being such a warrant is that the experience be passively structured by the concept of redness. Be that as it may, any theory of colour must acknowledge the link between the experience and the sense it bestows upon 'green*' by being a canonical warrant. So developing the incoherence has not drawn upon any feature specific to McDowell's theory. But we shall now see that, whilst McDowell's theory was not essential to the development of the incoherence—in contrast to the Simple Theory of Colour and an externalist theory of reference-fixing—it does provide a way of resolving the incoherence by denying a crucial feature of the example.

RESOLVING THE INCOHERENCE

We could resolve the incoherence either by denying the Simple Theory of Colour or by denying the externalist fixing of reference, since both were essential to developing the incoherence. But here I shall not question either. Instead, we can resolve the incoherence by applying more of McDowell's theory.

McDowell distinguishes human sense experiences from the sensitivity of brutes. Brutes are sensitive to colours, in that they respond to them and are in some sense conscious of them. But, in McDowell's picture, the visual consciousness of brutes does not make colours available to them as 'inner' objects of contemplation. Hence a brute's states of consciousness are not passively structured by concepts—since the application of a concept is necessarily something that can be recognized. Hence too their states of consciousness are not warrants for judgements—since a warrant to judge is necessarily something the potential judge can know she possesses. Brutes are not makers of rational judgements. In McDowell's terminology, brutes do not have experiences: McDowell reserves the term 'experience' for a conscious state which is apt to warrant a judgement— because it is available to its owner as an object of contemplation and is conceptually structured.

Although Zoe is a rational animal in the Aristotelian sense, unfortunately due to her circumstances we have been unable to assign matching senses and semantic values to her terms 'green*' and 'red*'.

So her employment of these terms does not express judgements about colour, but only the illusion of judgements. Further, she cannot *make*, even to herself, so to speak, judgements about colour. For judgements are essentially apt for truth or falsity. Hence, given that the judgements in question are intended to track categorical properties, they require semantic values as well as senses to be apt for truth-values. These semantic values are fixed externally by what in her circumstances are normal causes of the experiences canonically warranting the judgements, and hence a retreat from public senses and semantic values to private senses and semantic values will not help Zoe—the mismatch will recur over her private thoughts about grass and poppy flowers. Zoe can neither publicly express nor privately entertain propositions about colours.

It follows that the states of consciousness excited in Zoe by colours are not warrants for making judgements about colours. For it is impossible for a subject to possess a warrant which she cannot recognize as such, and Zoe cannot recognize it as such because she cannot entertain the proposition which it warrants. So we arrive at the conclusion that Zoe's sensibility is not after all passively structured by colour concepts. Of course, since she is otherwise a rational agent, she utters 'green*' and 'red*' in ways which systematically correlate with objects being green and red respectively, and she takes herself to be expressing propositions thereby, and propositions which are warranted by features of her experiences of those objects, moreover. But there are no such features of her experiences, and she does not entertain propositions about colours.

It follows that (4) above is not violated, and the incoherence is resolved. Zoe's encounters with coloured objects in Z-land no longer present a counter-example to:

(4) Necessarily, if an object possesses the property presented in those experiences which determine the sense of the predicate 'green*'—that is, the property which correct applications of that predicate are intended to track—then it possesses the property which is the semantic value of the predicate 'green*',

because she does not have experiences of colours.

By so resolving the incoherence, the description of my example needs modifying. I concluded my exposition of the example by claiming that we had reason to suppose that grass in Z-land looks red to Jill the traveller and to Zoe the native alike, and that poppy flowers look green to both, and no reason to suppose otherwise. But now we do have reason to suppose otherwise. Jill has experience passively structured by concepts of greenness and redness, whereas Zoe does not.

Furthermore, we shall have to discount the strong philosophical intuition that if Zoe and Jill are physiological and neurological twins, then their sensory states are phenomenologically identical—since Jill has colour experiences, but Zoe does not. Whether a person has experiences which are conceptually structured and can be recognized as warrants for judgements, or has mere sensory states, depends upon their external circumstances.[9]

THE TRANSPARENCY OF COLOUR EXPERIENCE

McDowell claims that our experiences of colours are passively structured by concepts of colours. Clearly, he means by 'passive' that such structuring is not subject to voluntary control—the experiences enter consciousness, so to speak, structured. Are our experiences so structured transparent to us? That is, given that Jill has an experience which is passively structured by a concept C, might she wrongly take it to be an experience passively structured by some other concept D? I take it that it makes no sense to ask whether an experience was *correctly* structured by C, given that it was structured by C. An experience passively structured by some other concept D would have been a different experience from the experience passively structured by the concept C. So the question is not whether Jill can misclassify a given experience which might be structured by C or by D. The question is whether Jill might *misidentify* her current experience—might take it to be an experience passively structured by D when in fact it is an experience passively structured by C.

Setting aside the relatively trivial fact that she can misidentify her own experience if she is insufficiently attentive, perhaps because she was quite confident that it would be a D, I shall argue that the three theories—the passive conceptual structuring of experience, the Simple Theory of Colour, and the external fixing of semantic values—together imply that Jill might fail to identify her colour experiences in an altogether deeper way.

The Simple Theory of Colour carries with it certain empirical presuppositions arising from its claim that the categorical causal grounds of

---

[9] Having abandoned the strong philosophical intuition, why not go the whole hog and claim that the grass of Z-land looks green to Zoe and the poppy flowers red? Thereby the senses and semantic values of 'green*' and 'red*' would match, and the incoherence would not arise, and would not require resolution by downgrading Zoe's rationality. Well, you pay your money, and you take your choice. I prefer to retain the strong philosophical intuition and to avoid the incoherence by abandoning the Simple Theory of Colour. But the purpose of this chapter is to shop around. You discover the value of your preferred option by comparing prices.

the powers of objects to produce colour experiences are, given standard conditions and normal perceivers, properties which are as they appear to be in those experiences. We should not expect the causal powers of colours to be brute, and we would expect the theory of perception to *explain* those powers by showing how they emerge from or are reducible to some mechanism, so that at a deeper level of explanation colour properties would be revealed to have hidden natures. So an adherent to the Simple Theory should claim that whilst colour properties are as they appear, she expects there to be more to them than meets the eye. Hence, the claim that colours are categorical properties which play a causal role has to meet whatever requirements arise from our theory of causation by categorical properties in general, when applied to the process of perception in particular.

The presuppositions of the Simple Theory might be falsified by further empirical enquiry and the Simple Theory rejected. One way in which those presuppositions might not be met is as follows. Suppose experiences in which objects look green are found to be caused, *ceteris paribus*, by a categorical property of objects, and similarly, experiences in which objects look red are caused by another such property. But suppose our best and deepest theory of how colour experiences are caused distinguishes colours from the properties causing those experiences, does not treat colours as categorical properties of objects which colour experiences track, and does not treat colours as properties which are emergent from, or reducible to, the properties which cause colour experiences, but instead treats colours in some response-dependent or projective way. The criteria of identity for properties are not well understood, but I take it that we cannot currently rule out as a bald epistemic possibility that theory might develop as described. My claim is not that I can describe in detail how such a position might be reached. My claim is only that we do not have the resources to rule out the epistemic possibility of future empirical enquiry reaching such a position. The epistemic possibility which we cannot rule out comes to this: colour experiences do indeed track categorical properties of objects, but no *colour properties presented in those experiences* are themselves categorical properties which the experiences track.[10]

However, suppose that in fact the Simple Theory is true. Then Jill's experiences of colours will be passively structured by concepts which

---

[10] An adherent to the Simple Theory might retreat to an anodyne interpretation of that theory which claims only that in *some* sense colours are 'properties' which in *some* sense 'cause' experiences, but these are not senses of 'property' and 'cause' employed in, or answerable to, our best supported and explanatorily deepest theories of perception. But then the Simple Theory would have lost its distinctive bite and interest.

accord with the Simple Theory and which inherit some of the empirical presuppositions of that theory—in particular, the presupposition that colours are categorical properties which colour experiences, *ceteris paribus*, track.

None the less, Jill herself cannot rule out the epistemic possibility described in the last paragraph but one: namely, that her colour experiences do indeed track categorical properties of objects, but no colour properties presented in those experiences are themselves the categorical properties which the experiences track. Consider how this epistemic possibility looks from Jill's point of view: it is one in which her colour experiences do *not*, after all, track the very categorical properties which are seemingly presented by the concepts which passively structure her experiences.

Considering the matter from Jill's point of view, if the epistemic possibility were to turn out to be the case, would her colour experiences after all have been presenting colours as categorical properties of objects which those experiences track? It is easy to see that they would not. Her colour experiences, by being conceptually structured, warrant judgements. For example, an experience in which something looks green warrants the judgement which she would express by:

(6)   It is green if I am normal and conditions are standard.

If conditions were standard and Jill were normal, and if her experience were structured by a concept which presented greenness as a categorical property of the object which experiences of this kind track, then (6) would be both true and false. The sense, as determined by the role of the experience as canonical warrant for (6), would present greenness as a categorical property of the object, but the possibility that Jill is contemplating is one in which the object does not possess such a property, and so (6) would be false. But externalism does provide a property, a different property, as the semantic value of 'green', and this property the object in question has, so (6) is true. The sense of 'green' in (6) would thus not match its semantic value. We have again a mutually destructive mismatch between sense and semantic value. Hence the alleged conceptual structure of her experience, in which something looked green, would prevent the experience from warranting (6). But it is a datum which any theory of colour must respect that an experience in which something looks green warrants a judgement of the form (6). Hence the experience cannot be so conceptually structured. Thus, the epistemic possibility which Jill cannot rule out is one in which her colour experiences would *not* after all be structured by concepts which present colours as being categorical properties of objects which, *ceteris paribus*, those experiences track.

We are assuming that the Simple Theory is in fact true, and that Jill's experiences of colours are structured accordingly. We have seen that she cannot rule out the epistemic possibility that they are not so structured— because the empirical presuppositions of the Simple Theory may fail in the manner described. So although she may recognize that her experiences are structured in accordance with the Simple Theory, she cannot be certain that they are so structured, that she has not misidentified them. Thus the passive conceptual structuring of Jill's colour experiences is not transparent to her.[11]

Does the argument generalize to other concepts structuring experience which carry with them empirical presuppositions? Some claim that their visual experience when looking at a glass of water is characterized by the concept of water, so that being water is an observable property, in contrast to claiming that the experience is characterized merely by the concepts of being liquid, colourless, etc.[12] It is a priori that water is the abundant natural kind which is, in its pure form, a colourless, odourless, tasteless liquid. Thus we presuppose that the majority of samples so identified do form a unitary natural kind. Whether they do or not is clearly an a posteriori matter. Hence our concept of water embodies an empirical presupposition. If that presupposition is not satisfied, because there is no single natural kind which the majority of samples of water fall under, then there is no water, as there is no caloric and no phlogiston.

However, the discovery that the samples of liquid found in nature which, when distilled, are colourless, etc. do not form a natural kind would not lead us to think there was anything amiss with the *sense* of the word 'water'. This is because the sense of a natural kind term like 'water' attempts to select its semantic value *by description*, as it were. *Whatever* chemical property actually identifies the natural kind of the majority of such samples will be the semantic value of 'water'. Since the sense does not present any *specific* property, there is no possibility of the actual semantic value of 'water' provided by Nature failing to match the property presented by the sense of 'water'. The worst that can happen is that 'water' has no semantic value, because the samples which

---

[11] As we saw above, there are other conceptions of colours available which do not generate the possibility of a mismatch. If the Simple Theory turns out a posteriori to be false, Jill's experiences might, unbeknownst to herself at the time, have been passively structured by a response-dependent conception of colours.

[12] Gregory McCulloch makes such a claim in *The Mind and its World* (London: Routledge, 1995), ch. 8.

fit the description do not form a kind. But no worry is generated about the *sense* of the word 'water'.

This contrasts with the sense of the word 'green' if it accords with the Simple Theory. Like 'water', the sense of 'green' carries an empirical presupposition about the experiences which warrant its application —that they track a property which therefore is the semantic value of 'green'. But the sense of 'green' presents that semantic value *by acquaintance*, as it were. It is this combination which generates, for all we know, the possibility of a mutually destructive mismatch between putative sense and alleged semantic value of the predicate 'green', and therefore prevents the passive conceptual structuring of Jill's colour experiences being transparent to her.[13]

[13] I would like to thank in particular Bob Hale, Cynthia Macdonald, Scott Meikle, Alex Miller, Pat Shaw, Crispin Wright, and Nick Zangwill for helpful comments on earlier drafts.

14

On Knowing One's Own Language[1]

BARRY C. SMITH

————•————

We rely on language to know the minds of others, but does language have a role to play in knowing our own minds? To suppose it does is to look for a connection between mastery of a language and the epistemic relation we bear to our inner lives. What could such a connection consist in? To explore this, I shall examine strategies for explaining self-knowledge in terms of the use we make of language to express and report our mental states. Success in these strategies will depend on the view we take of speakers' understanding of the words they use to speak their minds. The key is to avoid circularity in the account of how they know what they mean; for if knowing what one is saying in speaking a language provides a means of knowing one's own mind, it cannot simply be a part of it. I shall look at ways in which we might proceed here, and examine whether the strategy can make room for a genuinely first-person point of view. But first let me try to motivate the problem of self-knowledge.

I THE PROBLEM OF SELF-KNOWLEDGE

It is hard at first to see what the problem of self-knowledge is supposed to be. As thinkers, we take ourselves to have immediate knowledge of

[1] The writing of this paper was made possible by a College Research Grant from Birkbeck College, University of London, and a visiting position in the Department of Philosophy at the University of California at Berkeley. Thanks are due to a number of people with whom I have had invaluable discussions about the material presented here. My thanks, in particular, go to Paul Boghossian, Marcia Cavell, Donald Davidson, Ariela Lazar, John McDowell, and Crispin Wright. I am indebted to Jim Higginbotham for a very rewarding discussion before the conference and his replies to my paper at the conference and in this volume. I am grateful to Michael Morris for a written comment. And most of all, to Maria Muller-Smith go my love and thanks for astute readings of drafts, insightful advice, and strong support.

our thoughts and feelings and to know our minds intimately and in a way that no one else can know them, all of which can easily incline us towards a conception of the mind as a repository for inner thoughts, a sphere whose contents are inspected privately. But however intuitive this picture seems from our own point of view, we conceive the mind quite differently when thinking about others. In taking up the third-person perspective, we are convinced that we know a lot about other people's minds. Not, to be sure, in the way we know our own; but we are convinced that others' behaviour can teach us a good deal about what they are thinking, what they want, and what they are up to. We see others' minds at work in their acts and utterances, and have little difficulty in describing their activity as displaying their preferences, showing their feelings, and revealing their motives. Were the workings of people's minds not on show in this way, we would be unable to recognize them as persons.

It would appear, then, that common sense presents us with conflicting views on the nature of mental life, depending on whether we are thinking of the accessibility of minds to others or of their accessibility to themselves. We are left in the curious position of believing that whereas the minds of others can be displayed in observable behaviour, the contents of our own minds are a matter for private consumption. Clearly, this is nothing more than a comforting illusion. For we are just as likely as anyone else to reveal aspects of our mental lives publicly.

The problem arises when we try to square this objective and outward aspect of the mental with the special way in which we know our own minds from the first-person perspective. How can states whose natures belong partly in the public sphere be so readily available to us from the first-person point of view? I take this to be the key problem raised by self-knowledge.

As subjects, we are inclined to think of such states as being automatically available to us, part of our inner lives. But this merely makes the philosophical difficulties more acute. How can the facts of mental life be part of the inner world of a subject if they are also objective facts knowable by others on the basis of outwardly observable behaviour?

The problem we confront here partly stems from a lingering attachment to the intuitive picture of the inner with which we began. That picture took our states of mind to be inner in a wholly private and subjective sense. But the mental states that make up our inner lives can be known by others. We need a new conception that does not remove the mental from other people's scrutinizing gaze. After all, it is not privacy that makes for an inner life. It is the fact that we have unmediated knowledge of our mental states. Each of us is familiar with the details of inner life through the thoughts and feelings that are immediately known to us. Others do not have this unmediated knowledge of our minds, although they will know their own minds in this way. So it is not the privacy of the object known, but the exclusive means of knowing it, that makes room for the inner world. We credit minded creatures with an inner life, or point of view, only if they have the capacity to know their own minds in this way. The inner and public aspects of the mental are connected.

Still, the way we know and the way others know what we are thinking differ markedly. We know our own minds, when we do, in a direct and authoritative manner. We do not have to observe our own behaviour or consult the opinion of others to find out what we think and feel. We just know. We can offer no grounds for what we take ourselves to be thinking; nor are we expected to. Others do not ask us for justification, because they regard us as authorities on matters of our own psychology. We just assume that we know our own minds, and it makes little sense, in general, for us to doubt this. Hence, far from undermining our claim to knowledge, the absence of grounds, in the case of claims about our current psychological states, gives us an authority that our ascriptions of psychological states to others, and their ascriptions to us, simply lack. In this way, first-person authority is the hallmark of self-knowledge, and provides the most telling asymmetry between first- and third-person knowledge of someone's mind. The problem is to find a way to do justice to the special authoritative character of self-knowledge, while respecting the publicly determinable character of the psychological states known. This is the problem of self-knowledge.

The problem tends to get overlooked if, like Descartes, we focus on sceptical questions. For we cannot doubt that we have knowledge of our own minds. Taking this for granted, it appears to be knowledge of other minds and of the external world which we need to account for. However, the ease of acquiring self-knowledge, compared to the efforts it takes to figure out what others are thinking, should not mislead us as to the nature of that knowledge or the ease, or otherwise, of explaining it. Just assuring myself that I know *that* I am thinking does nothing to illuminate how I know *what* I am thinking, or to settle questions about the relation of self-knowledge to knowledge of other minds or to the world. So we must ask: How is it possible to know what we are thinking?, where this is not a sceptical question requiring an answer that will assure us that such knowledge really is possible. That is scarcely coherent. Rather, we are asking for an explanation: How do we know what we are thinking, given that we usually do?

Traditional epistemologies of mind are of little help, since they often end up at odds with elements of common sense we are keen to preserve. Cartesians, for example, conceive the domain of the mental as a private realm whose layout is fully transparent to its subject but inaccessible to others. Mental states are constituted by how things appear to the subject and are answerable to nothing else. This appears to ensure the subject knowledge of what he is thinking, but it puts at risk his knowledge of other minds and access to the world. Moreover, it utterly distorts the nature of self-knowledge. For we are neither infallible nor incorrigible judges of our own intentional states. Our actual epistemic predicament is at once less certain and more difficult to explain. When we believe, desire, or intend something, we usually know that we do. But this is not always the case. And since what we believe, desire, or intend is open to determination by others on the basis of our behaviour, our states of mind must be accessible from perspectives other than our own. It is this knowledge that others can have of us which makes lapses in our self-knowledge intelligible. For their knowledge of our minds need not be arrived at via the views we have of what we are thinking. Our behaviour can reveal a good deal more about our outlook and attitudes than we suppose. And this is likely to be the case even at times when, for whatever reason, we are blind to our own intentions. Thus people, if they are sufficiently insightful, may draw our attention to aspects of our psychology about which we are deceived or un-self-knowing. They may convince us that our intentions are less than honourable, and we may feel the shame of motives late revealed. In this way other people's perceptions can provide a valuable source of self-knowledge: an insight lost on the Cartesian.

However, it would be wrong to conclude with the behaviourist that knowledge of mind is based solely on what is publicly observable. I usually know what I am thinking without consulting the evidence available to others. And it is this more familiar way of knowing our own minds that we need to account for. The behaviourist is simply at a loss to explain how a person can form correct opinions about her states of mind when she doesn't rely on behavioural observations to do so. Having nothing more to go on than what is publicly observable, the behaviourist is incapable of recognizing the peculiar immediacy of our self-knowledge. At best, he will see the advantage that subjects enjoy in reporting their mental states as a function of the enhanced opportunities they have to witness their own activities and infer conclusions about their mental lives. But we need make no such inferences to secure first-personal advantage. We are peculiarly qualified to pronounce on our own states of mind, and we do this without reference to our outwardly observable activities.

The difficulty is to explain how this is possible when knowledge of our mental states is not a matter of each of us having privileged access to some private realm. To its credit, behaviourism recognizes the public aspect of mental states, but it loses sight of the inner, and with it the subject's point of view.

It should now be clear why neither Cartesian nor behaviourist conceptions of mind can explain self-knowledge. Each fails to recognize that it is in the nature of mental states—particularly intentional states like belief, desire, and intention—to be known both first-personally and third-personally. Both the Cartesian and the behaviourist, in their different ways, recommend a conception according to which the facts of mental life are exhausted from a single perspective. Cartesians assume that mental states are always and only available from the first-person point of view, while behaviourists suppose that they are exclusively available third-personally. Each stresses an important aspect of the mind at the cost of neglecting a feature stressed by the other. The behaviourist is right to point out that we often know the minds of others on the basis of observing what they say and do, but is wrong to suppose that self-knowledge is continuous with knowledge of other minds. The Cartesian is right to stress that we can be directly aware of what we are thinking, but wrong to suppose that this is a matter of acquaintance with a private inner item. The special unmediated knowledge we have of our own minds furnishes us with an inner life, but this does not preclude others from knowing the states of mind we are in. Other people's inner lives are not always hidden from us, nor ours from them.[2] Nevertheless, each individual is uniquely placed to judge what he, or she, wants, intends, or believes. And we need to know what puts one in such a position. What makes one groundlessly authoritative about attitudes that are accessible from perspectives other than one's own?

II THE NATURE OF SELF-KNOWLEDGE

Initially it might appear that the public side to mental life threatens the possibility of self-knowledge. But on the contrary, publicity ensures that self-knowledge lays claim to a genuine subject-matter, the external

---

[2] Wittgenstein's remarks here are useful reminders of how we should guard against faulty conceptions of the inner: 'One can say "He is hiding his feelings". But that means that it is not a priori that they are always hidden. Or: there are two statements contradicting one another: one is that feelings are essentially hidden; the other that someone is hiding his feelings from me' (1992: 35e).

dimension ensuring that whether a subject is in a given mental state is
an objective, or, at any rate, intersubjective, matter answerable to more
than just the subject's opinions. Thus, the states that are available to
us as part of our inner world can be credited with an objective reality
over and above our immediate impressions of them. What is puzzling is
just how one's immediate impressions can provide one with knowledge
of objective empirical facts—one's being in certain publicly determinable
states of mind. Why should the immediate, groundless psychological
claims we make about ourselves be largely correct? Having groundless
authority about what is objectively the case is what makes this variety
of knowledge so puzzling. How are we to explain it?

Our mental states are not the sorts of things to which we are guaranteed access: *being in a mental state* is one thing; *knowing which
mental states one is in* is another. Something is required of us to close
this epistemic gap. Yet, our thoughts and feelings are so familiar to us
that it is hard to consider our knowledge of them as amounting to a
genuine cognitive accomplishment. We tend to think our thoughts are
available to us in the very act of thinking them. This is because no gap
opens up, *from the first-person point of view*, between being in a mental
state and knowing one is. The thinker will be unaware of the potential
for a gap until others draw his attention to it, or he appreciates such
a gap in them. Whether one is in a mental state or not is not a matter
exclusively settled by how things appear to the person in that state. As
we have noted, the existence of an independent third-person perspective
secures a certain objectivity for claims about a person's psychology. It
is from these other-person perspectives that one can establish the distinction between *how things seem* to a person psychologically and *how
things are*: the distinction necessary to guarantee the objectivity, or, at
any rate, intersubjectivity, of a subject's claims. Appreciating this requires
that one recognize that one's inner world is part of the world of others.
Without this, 'no distinction between "seems right" and "is right" opens
up from the subject's point of view' (McDowell 1991: 160).

What we need to do now is to connect up these two distinctions: the
distinction between *being in a mental state* and *knowing that one is*
and the distinction between *how things seem to a thinker*, psychologically, and *how they are*. Obviously, being in a psychological state will
correspond to how things are, but we have yet to understand why, and
under what conditions, knowing what psychological state we are in will
correspond to how things seem to us. Why does how things seem to
us amount to knowing what psychological states we are in?

In the psychological domain we cannot separate the nature of mental states from their epistemology. Our fix on how things are with a
thinker—the external check on his impressions—is determined by the

psychological states we would be properly justified in attributing to him on the basis of what he says and does, against a vast background of previously ascribed psychological states that make sense of his behaviour to date. Thus, publicity is guaranteed in our conception of these objective states of affairs. As Davidson puts it, states like belief and desire

> are just those states whose contents can be discovered in well-known ways. If other people or creatures are in states not discoverable by these methods, it can be, not because the methods fail us, but because these states are not correctly called states of mind—they are not beliefs, desires, wishes or intentions. (Davidson 1989: 160)

What we now need to discover is whether, and if so, how, a subject's unsupported views about what he currently believes, wants, or intends can count amongst these well-known ways. Why should a subject's merely *thinking* that he is in a certain mental state be a reliable guide to his *actual* mental state? More is needed than his merely supposing that he has these beliefs, desires, or intentions, to make his suppositions true. The third-personal grounds for ascription provide an independent basis for evaluation. So, we can say that a subject counts as knowing his own mind provided he comes up with ascriptions of attitudes to himself which others would be prepared to ascribe to him given all the available evidence and in accordance with the correct standards for mental attribution. In this way, claims to self-knowledge, although not based on behavioural evidence, will still be answerable to it. For if a subject cannot be correctly said to believe, desire, or intend something according to well-known methods of ascription, his merely claiming that he does will establish nothing.[3] We can count a subject's current impression of what he is thinking as one amongst other well-known ways of discovering his present state of mind just so long as this way of knowing can be harmonized with the other methods of discovery. This provides an important publicity constraint on any adequate account of self-knowledge. It means that the problem of self-knowledge and the problem of other minds arise with respect to the same state of a thinker's mind. We must solve them simultaneously to produce a complete, satisfying epistemology of the mental.

The difficulty is to see why, of the two ways of discovering what someone is thinking, the first-personal means is authoritative even though

---

[3] Hence more is needed than the suggestion by Rorty (1981) that it is just a courtesy of the interpreter to grant subjects authority for what they say about their own states of mind. We do not slacken all the standards we exercise in assessing what people tell us just because, in this case, the subject-matter concerns their states of mind. They are authoritative, but the authority can be defeasible on cognitive grounds, and not merely lack of courtesy.

someone's first-personal claims about what he is thinking are ultimately answerable for their truth to third-personal claims about which attitudes it would be correct to ascribe to him. This points to a certain strain between first-person authority and the objectivity of self-knowledge. The more subjective a thinker's judgement, the less it concerns anything other than how things seem to the subject. And in such cases, it is easy to see why the thinker should be an authority about this. By contrast, when there is an objective fact of the matter about which the subject can be right or wrong, it is hard to see why, without having any grounds for his judgements, he should be, in Crispin Wright's words, effortlessly authoritative about the facts.

There is a prima-facie tension between first-person authority and objectivity. Objectivity requires that there be room for a distinction between how things seem to the subject and how they are, between whether a judgement seems right or is right. While having first-person authority is based on there being no appreciable difference between how things seem and how they are. I am authoritative just in case, typically, whatever seems right to me is right. First-person authority requires us to close the gap between having beliefs and having opinions about them, while objectivity insists on leaving room for a gap between them. However, first-person authority is not really incompatible with the objectivity of self-knowledge. There is room for a distinction between how things seem to the subject and how things are, even if they coincide, because the existence of perspectives other than the subject's own provide us with an independent means of knowing how things are with him. We use these to confirm, or challenge, the subject's self-assessments. Meanwhile, the fact that how things seem to a subject, psychologically, is usually how they are, means that he retains authority about his current psychological states. What remains to be explained is why being in a mental state, and thinking that one is, should so regularly coincide. Why should one's groundlessly authoritative conviction that one is in a particular mental state be a good guide to the independently confirmable fact of the matter?

The problem of self-knowledge has become a little clearer. We asked what closes the epistemic gap between being in a mental state and knowing that one is. The answer we gave has two parts: (i) without any grounds subjects simply take themselves to be in particular mental states; and (ii) whenever they take themselves to be in particular mental states, they are usually right. Therefore, any solution to the problem will have to address two issues. What equips thinkers to make psychological judgements about themselves, and why do these judgements mostly relate thinkers to their inner lives? A solution to the problem depends on finding satisfactory answers to these key questions:

(1) What is it for things to seem a certain way to a person, psychologically?
(2) Why is it that how things seem, psychologically, usually provides knowledge of how they are?

We need an answer to (1) to make room for the subjective point of view of a thinker, and an answer to (2) to make good the thinker's claim to objective knowledge of his own mental states. No treatment of self-knowledge will be satisfactory unless it addresses both of these requirements. For only then can we reconcile the inner and outer aspects of mind: how things subjectively seem to us and how they objectively are.

III MODELS OF SELF-KNOWLEDGE

What makes objective psychological facts about ourselves subjectively available to us? This question presents no difficulties for the Cartesian, for whom there is only what is subjectively available to us; or, as Cartesians would have it, what is subjectively available always coincides with the facts. The motivations for this view are clear, but deeply flawed. As we have seen, no gap opens up from the subject's point of view between what is, and what seems to be, going on in the subject's mind. And since, for the Cartesian with regard to the mental, the subject is incorrigible—his view of what is going through his mind is the only view there is—no gap can open up *at all* between how things seem to the subject and how they are. The assumption is that the mental landscape is so well lit that there are no parts of it he cannot see. This makes him an infallible judge of his own mind; and infallibility (more than) guarantees first-person authority. There is no gap to close between what we believe and our opinions about this, so we need no justification for our view of what we are thinking. And since there is no justification for the sceptic to call into question, this makes self-attributions immune to sceptical doubt and the firmest foundation for all knowledge.

However, this is a Pyrrhic victory over the sceptic, since it is at the cost of surrendering the objectivity of what we judge. If there is only how things seem to us, then whatever seems right, is right, and as Wittgenstein tells us, this just means we cannot speak of right here. The Cartesian looks as if he is setting out to answer question (2) by telling us that how things seem will always coincide with how they are in the mind; but in denying the publicity requirement—the possibility of another knowing what states of mind we are in—he cannot secure any objectivity for our self-ascriptions.

It is also worth nothing that Cartesianism gives us no help with (1). It simply takes for granted the subjective point of view, with occasional hints about the mind's eye perceiving its own inner items. It is not hard to see why the perceptual model seems attractive. Perception can give us immediate knowledge of objective states of affairs (on at least some views), so the 'inner' perception model may still appeal as an explanation of how we know our own minds even though we have rejected Cartesianism. The rejection of the Cartesian picture obliges us to acknowledge that what is inwardly perceived is not a private inner item. Others can have knowledge of it too.

What are the prospects for such an inner perception model of self-knowledge? How might it provide answers to (1) and (2) above? With respect to (2), to secure the claim to knowledge of an objective psychological state of affairs, it is necessary to show that the states whose contents are presented to us directly, through their perceptible features, are the very same states we would be apt to ascribe on third-personal grounds, without reference to those features. Only then can we be sure that what is inwardly observable by the subject is not solely inner and private, but discoverable by others in well-known ways. While in relation to (1), the thought is that since others lack direct *perceptual* access to the contents of my mind, they cannot be presented with my states in the way I am, and will lack the authority with which I judge what I am thinking—hence the asymmetry between the first- and third-person perspectives.

There is no disguising the fact that the non-Cartesian dimensions to the mental make trouble for the inner perception model. We do not have exclusive access to our intentional states, so there must be more to the mental than meets the mind's eye. And since we are not infallible judges of our inner lives, inner vision, like outer vision, may be less than twenty-twenty. Given these limitations, can it be guaranteed that what we perceive inwardly are the same states that are individuated third-personally, non-perceptually? To turn the trick, what we inwardly observe has to be something that spans the first- and third-person divide, something that can be individuated on purely third-personal grounds. But although we have immediate perceptual access to our states, we do not have such access to their individuating conditions. This creates a problem, because public and external factors can enter into the identification of the states which people ascribe to us. In ascribing particular thoughts to a thinker, people observe not only the thinker's behaviour but his connections to things in his environment. According to externalists about content, these factors play an essential role in individuating many of our mental states. But if the contents of many of our thoughts are determined in part by our causal or socially mediated relations to the people, places, or things in our vicinity, there will be public aspects of our thinking more easily appreciated by those who can see exactly how we are placed in relation to these objects. So how do we retain first-person authority? Whatever *is* directly apprehended in inner perception may fail to discriminate between environmentally distinct states with internally *similar* perceptible properties.[4]

Externalism is thought to present a special problem for first-person authority, but in fact it is just part of the general problem of self-knowledge outlined above. It adds a further refinement to the question of how we are to reconcile the inner with the public aspects of the mind.[5] But is it compatible with the inner perception model of self-knowledge? The only way we can know what externally individuated states of mind we are in is by perceiving the contents of those states. So now we need a detailed account of how the externally individuated contents of our states are perceptually presented to the mind, and, as yet, we do not have one. The trouble is that the evidential bases on which other people ascribe attitudes to us are only contingently connected to these immediately apprehensible features of our thoughts. No explanation is offered of the coincidence in properties here. Why should there be two quite different ways of being presented with the *content* of a mental state? It remains wholly unexplained why the content of a state should exhibit perceptible features *and* bear connections to the subject's publicly displayed behaviour. This appears more like a re-description of the problem than a solution to it.

There are other difficulties too. Intentional states can occur without registering their presence in the mind. We know this because there can be good grounds for ascribing states to someone who shows no inner recognition of them. Hence the properties by which we consciously apprehend mental states (or our conscious apprehension of them) cannot be

---

[4] Notice that failure to discriminate between thoughts will not prevent it being the case, on each occasion, that we are in inner perceptual contact with the particular thought actually tokened, *whatever thought that is*. This may not satisfy those who had hoped for a more substantive account of first-person authority.

[5] Notice that no advantage is gained by being an individualist about the mental. Those who suppose that it is scientific psychology that individuates our internal states still need to provide an account of how a person knows what internal states he is in without a theory, while those who favour a purely phenomenological account of individualism have still to explain how such states can have any objective content. The debate between externalists and individualists is simply orthogonal to the issue of self-knowledge.

essential to those states. Why, then, should we suppose that the directly apprehensible properties of mental states are good guides to their true natures? And, if we can be mistaken about the states we are in, not being infallible, then how things appear to us, psychologically, can fail to show us how things are. The inner appearances and the mental states can come apart. The inwardly perceptible features of our states will not always coincide with the mental states they purport to reveal. Does this mean that intentional properties can appear to be before the mind without an appropriate intentional state being present? Or does it mean that inner states can take on different appearances, as if there were tricks of the light? Can we misperceive the contents of the thought we are thinking? A more likely explanation is that we can *misjudge* our current states of mind, as when we misjudge a mood, or a feeling. This would make it the element of judgement, not perception, that we should concentrate on. The inner appearances do not always play a verifying role, nor do they explain our mistaken views of our own psychology. Inner perception may have some claim to cast light on the epistemological asymmetry between first- and third-person knowledge, but it has some way to go to explain how there can be a common object of knowledge.[6]

Whether or not these problems can be ironed out, the most telling objection to the inner perception model is the absence of any phenomenal or perceptual quality to accompany many of the beliefs and intentions over which we have first-person authority. In many cases there is simply no perceptible item before the mind from which we can read off our current thoughts or motives. In the case of intentions, as Moran (1988) points out, discovering what one intends is more akin to making up one's mind than reading off the properties of a perceptually salient inner item. And what distinctive perceptual experience corresponds to the intention to read more contemporary fiction or to go to bed earlier? For many of our psychological states, there is simply no experiential item, but only the judgements we make about them. There may be nothing at which to direct my inner gaze—whatever that means—and yet I can be firmly of the opinion that I want to go to Scotland. I have no grounds for the judgement that this is what I want; *a fortiori*, I have no perceptual grounds for taking that to be what I want. In coming to have knowledge of our own minds, we arrive at opinions, without inference or evidence, about what we are thinking, and we are usually right. To explain this, we need a radically different approach based on a non-perceptual epistemology.

What are the options here? Why are we so effortlessly authoritative about our present states of mind? An answer, oft repeated, is that it

---

[6] For attempts to deal with these and other objections see Macdonald, Ch. 5 above.

is a fact about us that when we are in first-order mental states with a certain content, this reliably causes the tokening of second-order states whose contents are about, or contain, the content of the first-order states. Thus the capacity for self-knowledge is thought to consist in the presence of a reliable connection between first-order and higher-order mental states. But where a gap exists, like the one pointed out above, between *being in a mental state* and *knowing that one is*, it is hard to see why *being in a another state* (albeit reliably caused by the first, and related to it in content) amounts to knowing the first state one is in. How does *being* in the second-order state enable us to *know* its content? Accounts of the reliable causal connection between second- and first-order states are simply silent on the crucial epistemic gap. So I shall not pursue the reliabilist option any further.[7]

Some may be tempted to say that we know our thoughts and feelings by *introspection*. This is undoubtedly true, if by 'introspection' we mean no more than having direct knowledge of what we think and feel. But this takes us no further forward. On the other hand, if we mean by 'introspection' some special and privileged relation between a thinker and his thoughts, what is this relation? It cannot be perceptual. But we have nothing more to go on. Talk of introspection appears to be no more than a place-holder for some, as yet, unspecified account.

Another popular answer is that consciousness explains self-knowledge. A subject knows what mental states he is in when he is *conscious of* them. Once again, if we mean by 'being conscious of' no more than 'having immediate knowledge of' or 'having access to', we are no further forward. On the other hand, if consciousness plays a more substantive role, we are owed an explanation of how it enables a thinker to know *which* states of mind he is in. How do momentary episodes in conscious experience constitute knowledge of beliefs and intentions which sustain rational connections to other attitudes and to actions. Conscious experiences *per se* are too transitory to provide what is needed here. No such ephemeral items could *by themselves* sustain the rational connections to behaviour, and further mental states, necessary to individuate the content of thought. Only the exercise of conceptual judgement could do this. Even in the case of our knowledge of our own

---

[7] Tyler Burge (1988) has proposed a non-causal way of relating first- and second-order thoughts in the case of self-verifying claims of the form 'I am thinking the thought that water is wet'. In such cases the external factors that determine the embedded content contribute to determining the content of the reflective thought. In this case, just being able to think these thoughts ensures comprehension of what one is thinking, and the tokening of the thought one is thinking about. However, not all cases of self-knowledge take this form.

conscious experiences, it is not merely their being conscious that gives
us knowledge, but our having the classificatory competence to identify
and discriminate them. No one denies that Wittgenstein's private linguist is conscious. What is at issue is whether he has the wherewithal
to set up and maintain objective standards for judgements regarding
his own experiences.

None of the foregoing epistemologies successfully reconciles the
immediate availability of thoughts to a thinker with the public and external dimension of thought. Observational epistemologies force us to look
either inside for some special subjective item or outside at patterns in
our behaviour. But mental states should be conceived as neither inwardly
nor outwardly perceived items. Perception cannot locate states with both
an inner and an outer dimension properly. We need a fundamentally
different epistemology for our psychological states. And I want now to
consider whether the alternative epistemology should be based on our
use of language to identify and discriminate our psychological states.

IV   THE LINGUISTIC STRATEGY

A language-based epistemology of mind will have to offer a solution
to the problem of self-knowledge outlined above. It must explain what
equips someone to make groundless but authoritative judgements
about himself, as well as explain what makes his judgements mostly
correct. Remember that these judgements will be correct when how the
subject takes things to be is how they are. This is a matter of a
thinker's being in particular mental states, an objective matter of his
meeting the third-personally accessible conditions for being ascribed such
states. In this way, publicity is guaranteed. Any mental states we know
ourselves to be in must be knowable (not necessarily known) by others.
So any satisfactory solution must accommodate the fact that the same
mental states will be accessible from the first- and the third-person points
of view. I will also have to preserve the asymmetry due to first-person
authority.

Now if language has a key role to play in how others know what
we are thinking, and the same states of mind are accessible from both
perspectives, could it have a similar role to play in how we know our
own minds?

The linguistic strategy has a lot to recommend it. Meanings, like mental states, have a first- and a third-person epistemology. There are also
externalist elements to linguistic meaning. (Putnam's celebrated argument
that meanings are not in the head was the first defence of externalism.)

In so far as we convey meaning to others, the words by which we make our thoughts available to them are words which express those thoughts for us. Hence the same thing can be apprehended from the first- and the third-person point of view, although there is also the question of authority. You may have to work out what my words mean, whereas I do not. The meaning of my words is immediately available to me. But this is not to deny the public nature of meaning. I cannot make my words mean whatever I want them to; nor do mere subjective impressions of meaning constitute knowledge of meaning. Whether or not I use words as others do, the publicity requirement ensures that all I can mean by my words is all I can be known to mean. There is still asymmetry, because I have *immediate* knowledge of what I mean. Clearly, there are interesting parallels between the linguistic and the mental, but more is needed if we are to use language to explain self-knowledge.

Language can enter the picture in different ways, and there are stronger or weaker positions on the connection between knowing one's language and knowing one's own mind, depending on whether one's knowledge of language is considered to be constitutive of, necessary, or merely sufficient for knowing one's mind. The choice here depends on one's view of the precise relations between thought and language. At one end of the spectrum is the view that language is the vehicle for thought. This is a view held by John McDowell, amongst others. He tells us that 'acquiring a first language is, not learning a behavioural outlet for antecedent states of mind, but becoming *minded* in ways that language is anyway able to express'. For McDowell, this is because 'our ability to have dealings with content can be, not a mere natural endowment . . . but an achievement, which an individual attains by acquiring membership of a linguistic community' (1987: 74). On this view, language is essential for thought, and knowledge of language plays a constitutive role in knowing one's mental states. I know what I am thinking by understanding the words that furnish me with thought.

An attractive feature of this view is that it avoids making our ordinary knowledge of what we are thinking too reflective. Finding the words to express thoughts is what it is to think, and our immediate comprehension of our words gives us immediate knowledge of what we are thinking. If understanding is present in the act of saying something, we shall seldom need to make second-order judgements to know about the intentional states we are in. Our comprehending use of the meaning and form of language makes conceptually structured thought possible. We know our beliefs through what we are prepared to assert. (Of course, this is the case only if understanding embraces knowledge of the force of our utterances, as it does for McDowell.) I recognize the content of what I am saying because I understand the words I speak.[8] But what is it for words to have the meanings they have for us? We need an answer to this question if linguistic understanding is to serve in the explanation of self-knowledge. What equips a speaker to take his words to have the meanings they do? Notice also that, in order to secure first-person authority, it will have to be shown that we know what our words mean in a way that differs from how others know this.[9] Having authoritative knowledge of meaning gives us authoritative knowledge of the thoughts we express. Reflection can serve up judgements about what we think (doubt, hope for, fear, or intend), though we will have an immediate and correct view of what we are thinking just so long as we understand what we are saying. An account of self-knowledge becomes an account of how I know what I mean by the words that express my thoughts.

Notice that such a strong position commits us to denying thought to animals and pre-linguistic infants: a highly controversial claim which requires detailed empirical as well as philosophical investigation. However, nothing so strong is required for one to exploit the linguistic strategy. For, whether or not thoughts are essentially linguistic, we often find out what we think by saying it. Language can help us to formulate our thoughts more precisely. And the greater our linguistic competence, the greater the clarity with which we realize what we really think. On this view, although it is not necessary, knowledge of language is sufficient on these occasions for knowing what one is thinking. It provides one means among others of knowing one's mind. I shall return to this view below.

There is another way that language can enter the picture. This is the view that language provides the folk-psychological concepts of belief,

---

[8] It may be objected that we do not always have to speak our thoughts aloud. (These days many people feel they do!) Nevertheless, most of us are all too familiar with the restless interior monologue.

[9] I suspect McDowell would baulk at this, though it is worth noting that the idea finds some endorsement in Wittgenstein: 'My own relation to my words is wholly different from other people's' (1953, iix: 192e). As he says, 'I do not listen to them and thereby learn something about myself' (1992: 9e). 'If I listened to the words of my mouth, I might say that someone else was speaking out of my mouth' (1953, iix: 192e)—a clear indication of why linguistic understanding cannot consist solely in a perceptual capacity, as McDowell sometimes appears to think. (Note that this would reintroduce a perceptual epistemology of mind. We would no longer have *inner* perception of the content of mental states, but we would be able to perceive the contents of mental states, our own and others', by perceiving the linguistic meanings of utterances that expressed them.) We need to focus instead on the states of linguistic knowledge at work in both the perception and the production of speech.

desire, and intention, with which we taxonomize our psychological states. The vocabulary of the attitudes, together with a potentially infinite repertoire of declarative sentences, embedded by constructions like 'X believes that', 'X intends that', 'X desires that', provide us with the means to identify and discriminate the thoughts of a rational agent.[10] And since the nature of mental states is bound up with our well-known means of discovering them, the same indispensable taxonomy is at work, so the story goes, in finely individuating our own thoughts. The story, in its most subtle and systematic form, is given to us by Donald Davidson. To see the full force of it, we have to begin with our knowledge of other minds.

All we see of other people is their behaviour; yet we often know what they are thinking. We arrive at knowledge of their minds by interpreting their behaviour, and we do this by making sense of their activities in rational terms. In order to see someone as a rational agent, we must be able to see his behaviour as action, and we do this by describing bits of behaviour in intentional terms. This brings in its wake attributions to the agent of beliefs and desires that would rationalize his actions. We cite as his reasons for acting, particular beliefs and desires that it would be reasonable for him to have, given what we describe him as doing, and given what else he thinks and wants, as judged against the other psychological ascriptions we would be prepared to make of him. Each attribution is tested by how well it fits into a larger scheme of interpretation of what he says and does elsewhere. This will be a coherent, holistic pattern of ascription of attitudes and meanings that makes the best overall sense of the agent's actions and utterances. Only when an agent's behaviour can sustain these intentional descriptions and attributions can he be said to have beliefs, desires, and intentions. The intentional descriptions are our means of individuating his mental states, but they also play a constitutive role in identifying the nature of mental states. For Davidson, particular events in a person's physical history are, at the same time, events in his mental life. But an event is mental only as described. It is only when an otherwise physically describable event, or state, can be given an intentional description that it can be said to be

---

[10] Again, there are weaker and stronger readings of this position. On the weaker version, language may not be necessary for thought, but it is necessary for *thought about thought*. So, while the objects of self-knowledge may not be linguistic, language and our knowledge of it will still play an essential role in the epistemology of mind. The stronger reading maintains that to have thoughts—in particular, beliefs—one must have the concept of belief, thus be able to think about thoughts. And since language is necessary for thought about thought, it is therefore necessary for thought, though not constitutive of it. Once again, this denies thought to language-less creatures.

a mental state at all. And since we rely on the language of belief–desire psychology to individuate mental states finely enough for the rational explanation of behaviour, so the taxonomy of folk-psychological terms will have a role to play in fixing the identity of mental states. According to this view, it is necessary to deploy the intentional vocabulary of psychology to know one's own mind. But so far, we have no explanation of a subject's ability to ascribe attitudes to himself; far less have we any explanation of why these groundless self-ascriptions should carry the authority they are standardly granted.

Davidson's is an essentially third-personal view of meaning and mind: the mental and the meaningful are constituted by the intentional categories we impose on behaviour to make sense of ourselves and others in rational terms. All there is to a thinker's mind is all that can be discovered through the method of interpretation.[11] A theory of interpretation is a device to show how we can provide a systematic justification for the ascription of belief, desire, intention, meaning, and action to a person who exhibits a suitably wide range of behaviours. To be correct, any claims a thinker makes about himself must be justifiable in terms of an overall interpretation of his behaviour.

Notice that it is not Davidson's intention to deny that thinkers have a point of view of their own. He accepts the asymmetry between first- and other-person ascriptions of mental states and the existence of first-person authority, which he understands as the presumption of correctness which attaches to first-person attributions. It is just that, ideally, attributions from the first- and third-person perspectives should converge. The phenomenon of convergence is reflected in the practice of reporting beliefs and other attitudes. When I say, 'I believe (desire, hope, fear) that the guests will be on time', this is true if and only if the corresponding statement, 'He believes (desires, hopes, fears) that the guests will be on time' is true, when said by you about me. There is an agreement in truth-conditions, but there is an asymmetry in how the truth of each claim is arrived at. The problem, of course, is how to reconcile the *truth-conditional symmetry* and the *epistemological asymmetry* between self- and other-ascriptions to a person of a given mental state.[12] Because of the agreement here, we know that settling the truth-values of third-person claims will settle the truth-values of the corresponding first-person claims. But that is not how subjects arrive at the truth of their

---

[11] 'What a fully informed interpreter could learn about what a speaker means is all there is to learn; the same goes for what the speaker believes' (Davidson 1986a: 315).
[12] I owe this way of putting the problem to Marcia Cavell.

self-ascriptions. On the contrary, when we attribute attitudes to people on the basis of what they say and do, we expect them to know these attitudes, and are surprised if they do not. We often take first-person pronouncements as confirmation of our views about what they are thinking; what people say about themselves chimes in with the views we had arrived at by previous knowledge of their speech and action. In this way, when we ascribe attitudes to people, we try to figure out *their view* of the situation. For unless the beliefs and desires we ascribe to them are the states that shape *their* outlook on the world and give *them* reasons to act, we shall not be really understanding their behaviour. Thus, it is the aim of any accurate interpretation to respect the subject's point of view. We want to ascribe to people the attitudes they really have and could confirm by what they say about themselves first-personally.[13]

This may go some way to assuaging a worry about our self-ascriptions having to be too strictly accountable to the judgements which others would be prepared to ascribe to us third-personally. Still, there remains the question, for Davidson, of how the person himself knows what he is thinking. We know the minds of others by interpreting their behaviour. But we hardly ever need to study ourselves to come up with views about what we are thinking. The key question for Davidson is:

(I)   How do we know our own minds given that we do not interpret ourselves?

V   LINGUISTIC MODELS OF SELF-KNOWLEDGE

The predicament is by now familiar. We seem to come up with claims about our own minds which are not based on evidence or inference, but which carry greater authority than the claims which others make about us. What is more, if one is in a position to report authoritatively on what is on one's mind, one is usually right. What is the source of the authority these statements carry? And what explanation can be given of their frequent convergence with the psychological states that others are apt to ascribe to us third-personally?

The most deflationary anwer that can be given is that offered by Richard Rorty (1981), who supposes that it is a convention of our

---

[13] Notice that a subject's being in a mental state is not enough to ensure that it contributes to his point of view. Merely to take it on someone else's word—that is, on good third-person grounds—that I have certain intentions or motives will not count either. The subjective outlook from which a person views the world is structured by states of mind about which he is authoritative. This determines the extent to which he is self-knowing.

language that we respect what people say about their own minds. This makes the authority granted to the speaker's self-pronouncements merely a courtesy of the interpreter, not a fact about the speaker's standing with respect to his own psychology. Notice that deferring to speakers in this way ensures the truth-conditional symmetry between first- and third-person ascriptions. Granting truth to the former, we thereby settle the truth of the latter. However, this does not guarantee first-person ascriptions any real subject-matter, or explain their convergence with third-person ascriptions of the same state arrived at independently. Nor will it allow room for us to criticize someone's self-assessments on cognitive grounds. The problem of self-knowledge requires us to reconcile first-person authority with objectivity. But this is not a candidate solution, since it ensures authority by surrendering objectivity. The intersubjective agreement about these claims is simply fabricated.

But if we respect the genuine authority of subjects' views of their current mental states, and we acknowledge the fact that whenever they have such views they are usually right, we need a better account of what gives them access to their inner lives.

But what do subjects have such access to? Whatever it is, it must be the same thing that we can have access to by interpreting them. And in interpretation, 'the objects to which we relate people in order to describe their attitudes need not in any sense be *psychological* objects; objects to be grasped, known or entertained by the person whose attitudes are described' (Davidson 1987: 62). Instead, the objects to which we relate people to keep track of their thoughts are the sentences of our language, sentences which function semantically as the complements of that-clauses in propositional attitude reports. This gives us knowledge of other people's mental lives without any perceptual, or other, access to what they are thinking. But what gives the subject knowledge of his own mental life?

For Davidson, someone's being in a mental state is a matter of him being in a physical state that can be described in intentional terms. Such states are inner in the sense of being identical with particular physical states of the agent. But this will not help the person in those states to know *which* intentional states he is in. A state is individuated as the mental state it is by its intentional description. And while interpreters can know which states of mind an agent is in, because interpretation licenses particular intentional descriptions of him, this does not help the agent himself to know which intentional descriptions his states satisfy. To suppose it did, would be like his trying to read a label on his forehead without a mirror. The Davidsonian agent finds himself in this predicament, because the idea of direct access to the mind 'from the inside' has been abandoned. The agent has no direct cognitive contact with his inner states, no privileged access to an inner realm. What Davidson is urging on us is a radical shift in our conception of states of mind:

The central idea I wish to attack is that these are entities the mind can 'entertain', 'grasp', 'have before it', or be 'acquainted' with . . . Of course people have beliefs, wishes, doubts, and so forth; but to allow this is not to suggest that beliefs, wishes, and doubts are entities before the mind, or that being in such states requires there to be corresponding mental objects. (Davidson 1987: 61–2)

In similar Wittgensteinian spirit, Crispin Wright suggests that there is no inner epistemology of intentional states: 'knowing of one's own beliefs, desires and intentions is not really a matter of "access to"—being in cognitive touch with—a state of affairs at all' (Wright 1989a: 631–2).

Having dispensed with the inner realm, it is easy to appreciate why both these thinkers should conceive of language as what relates us to our mental lives. But how does this help us to know our own minds? All that has to be explained, according to Davidson and Wright, is the first-person authority that speakers have in reporting their own mental states. First-person authority distinguishes the way we know our minds from the way others know them. But this is not some form of contact with our mental states. It is simply an asymmetry between first- and other-person psychological ascriptions of a state to a thinker, in that the former carry a presumption of correctness which the latter do not. Davidson tells us that the problem of self-knowledge can be raised 'either in the modality of language or of epistemology', and goes on to say: 'I assume therefore that if first person authority in speech can be explained, we will have done much, if not all, of what needs to be done to characterise and account for the epistemological facts' (Davidson 1984b: 102). However, the role which language plays in Davidson's strategy is stronger than these remarks suggest. We are also told that 'the only access to the fine structure and individuation of beliefs is through the sentences speakers and interpreters of speakers use to express and describe beliefs' (Davidson 1986a: 315). A thinker's self-ascriptions can be justified by the interpreting descriptions which others give of his behaviour. For Davidson, what needs to be explained is why, without the aid of these justifying descriptions, a thinker can come up with psychological self-ascriptions which are usually correct. A full account will have to address questions (1) and (2) above. So, as well as explaining their typical correctness, we will need to know what equips speakers to make these effortless self-ascriptions. A necessary part of this will be accounting for the speaker's understanding of the words used to make ascriptions.

Wright envisages a similarly strong connection between language and self-knowledge: 'Intentional states are *avowable*: they are subject to groundless, authoritative self-ascription, and it belongs to their essence that they are so' (Wright 1989a: 629). At first sight, he seems to be committed to the claim that linguistically expressed self-knowledge is necessary even to have such intentional states. This seems too strong. But perhaps all Wright is committed to saying is that creatures with language, who can usually express their opinions linguistically, will be able to express the opinions they usually have about their states when they are in them. Creatures without language would probably lack the kind of intentional states of which we normally have authoritative knowledge. In the normal case, the avowals that subjects produce are largely correct. Normally, how things are in our minds is how we avow them to be. If this is the usual state of affairs, perhaps we need no special account of how we achieve self-knowledge. Special explanations will be necessary only when the subject is self-deceived, or for some other reason is unable to avow his beliefs, desires, or intentions. The default position is that our avowals will be true, and that our ability to avow them is what it is for us to be in those states. This is Wright's deflationary suggestion. No explanation is needed of how we close the epistemic gap between being in a mental state and knowing that we are. On this approach, the status of the judgements which subjects make about their mental states plays an important role in framing the truth about the states of mind they are in. The psychological facts of the matter are not independent of the judgements we make about them. As Wright puts it:

the authority standardly granted to a subject's own beliefs, or expressed avowals about his intentional states is a constitutive principle: something that is not a by-product of the nature of those states, and an associated epistemologically privileged relation in which the subject stands to them, but enters primitively into what a subject believes, hopes and intends. (Wright 1989a: 631–2)

The judgements which a subject makes are not always correct—so it is not the case that whatever seems right to him is right—but truth is the default assumption. These judgements can only be overturned when the interpretations we can give of someone's behaviour, which leave out or reject the subject's self-pronouncements, give better service in interpreting his linguistic and other behaviour than interpretations which respect them. For Wright, the judgements a subject makes about what he believes, desires, or intends, when made under cognitively ideal conditions, determine the truth of those claims. In this way, such judgements do not track independently constituted states of affairs; rather, they enter into the constitution of such states. In Wright's words, they are extension-determining, not extension-reflecting judgements (1989b).

This is an attractive strategy, but it shows some strain. For instance, there is no scope on this account for the idea that what subjects say about themselves can confirm, or be confirmed by, how we had understood them up until now. Similarly, we often take what people say about themselves to ring true, given what we know about them. But people's self-ascriptions cannot be given independent confirmation by what others are prepared to ascribe to them, because the facts about which mental states subjects are in is not something settled independently of their opinions about this. There are no independent facts by which to assess a subject's opinions about himself. Which ascriptions it is correct for us to make of a subject, and which of his self-ascriptions are correct, are arrived at all at once, by providing the most internally coherent system of attitude attributions that will make best sense of the subject's behaviour and try to respect the authority of his self-pronouncements. So it would be inaccurate on this picture to say that someone lacks self-knowledge because his view of himself is at odds with what we know about him. Strictly speaking, there is no sense in which someone's self-ascriptions are compatible, or incompatible, with the facts. A subject's opinions have an impact on determining the overall pattern of assignments that settle the facts about which intentional states he is in. Why he is largely right about this, on no grounds at all, is for Wright, a relatively a priori matter. It is because it is an a priori constraint on any successful interpretation of a subject that it regards truth as the default assignment for his avowals.[14] We must always strive to accommodate as much of the subject's view of himself as we can. What we are inclined to think about someone cannot confirm, because it includes as evidence, what they say about themselves.

Another puzzling feature of Wright's account arises because it is possible to have intentional states without having knowledge of them. As Wright acknowledges (1989a: 633 n.), our judgements regarding our own intentional states are only sufficient (by default) for us to be in those intentional states, not necessary. So in the case where we lack self-knowledge, the presence in us of intentional states owes nothing to our judgements about them. Why, then, should it be that in cases where I

---

[14] It is interesting to note that although Wright sees first-person authority—the default truth of status of avowals—as an a priori constraint on successful interpretation of others, he also speaks of it being 'a deep contingency' that interpretations which respect a subject's self-pronouncements give better service in making sense of him than those which overturn them. But notice that the contingency here is substantial, and therefore the case is unlike the combination of contingency and aprioricity that Kripke envisages in the case of the standard metre bar being one metre long. Here, the contingent fact is created by convention. Self-knowledge should not treated as this kind of contingent a priori knowledge unless one is attracted, like Rorty, to the idea that its products do depend on convention.

do know my own mind, my judgements help to determine, or perhaps constitute, which states I am in? Why is the presence of intentional states dependent on my judgement in one case, but not in the other?

Leaving these concerns to one side, we should note that the great virtue of this account is that it serves to explain why it is that when we think we are in a particular state we are usually right. However, I said above that any satisfactory solution to the problem of self-knowledge, as well as explaining why we are usually in the psychological states we take ourselves to be in, should explain what it is for us to take ourselves to be in any given state in the first place. Wright offers little on this, save to say that we are 'inundated day by day with opinions for which truth is the default position', and that 'we are each of us ceaselessly but—on the proposed conception—*subcognitively* moved to opinions concerning out own intentional states which will give good service to others in their attempt to understand us' (1989*a*: 632, emphasis added). They spring fully formed from the subject's lips with nothing to guide them but causal forces. We produce them without forethought. But even if there is no story of why subjects produce the particular judgements they do, we can still ask how they understand these self-ascriptions? If a subject finds himself merely subcognitively compelled to produce sounds from time to time, which it transpires are true by default, and thereby fix the truth of claims about his first-order states, this will not allow room for a genuinely first-person point of view.

To understand our self-opinions is to know what we mean by our avowals. This must amount to more than just mouthing something subcognitively produced. We need some account of our first-personal comprehension of what we are saying. But where in Wright's approach are the resources for this? The materials are to be found in work by Wright (1989*b*) in which he examined the appealing idea that meanings are secondary qualities and share the same epistemology. Here too, our opinions, under cognitively ideal conditions for judgement, determine the truth of claims about what our words mean, or where they are to be applied. However, the details of this account make ineliminable reference to the intentions of speakers, and their judgements of meaning, and this introduces a threat of circularity into the linguistic strategy's attempt to explain self-knowledge. Perhaps, it could be said that we do not know the intentions with which we use our words. But this would deprive us of the effortlessly authoritative knowledge we have of the meanings of our words. This does not close off the options for this strategy, but more is needed.

Let us turn, at last, to Davidson's approach. It is a clear instance of the linguistic strategy. The account of first-person authority is an account of an asymmetry between speaker and interpreter, derived from the general conditions for interpreting a person's speech and actions. To know what a person believes, one must know which sentences he holds true. We can identify his attitude towards a sentence even though we do not know what the sentence means. We know that someone will take a sentence, say S, to be true because of what S means in his language, and what he believes to be the case. So, if we know what the sentence means, we know what he believes to be the case. While, if we know what he believes, we know what the sentence held true means. Instead, we have to try to solve for two unknowns simultaneously: this is the programme of radical interpretation. Davidson points out, however, that in the general scheme of interpretation, when it is the case that a speaker holds S true, and knows what S means, it is only the speaker who is in an immediate position to know what she believes. For the interpreter to find out what the speaker believes, he will have to interpret S. But this is unnecessary for the speaker, who already knows what she means by S. And because speakers know what they mean, they will have one less hurdle to go through in moving from holding sentences true to knowing what they believe. This puts them in a better position to know their own minds. In this way, Davidson explains the asymmetry of first-person authority by means of a linguistic asymmetry between speakers and interpreters. Speakers have to be interpreted by others, but they do not have to interpret themselves. They quite literally speak their minds, and in understanding what they say, they immediately know what they think.

But how well does this explain *first-person authority*? It certainly points to an asymmetry, but the linguistic asymmetry it is based upon appears to remain unexplained. Is Davidson resting an explicable asymmetry on one that is inexplicable? Not quite. The linguistic asymmetry is based on the difference between answers given to the questions:

(a) How do we know what others mean by their words?
(b) How do we know what we mean by our words?

The answer to (a) is that we know by interpreting them. In answer to (b), the key point is that we know what we mean without interpretation. Speakers do not, and could not coherently, interpret themselves. But the question we must now ask parallels (I) above:

(II) How do speakers know what they mean, given that they do not interpret themselves?

The answer to this question is important, since it will explain what puts them in a better position than their interpreters to know their own minds.

In answer to (II), Davidson tells us that speakers could not fail to know what they mean by their words. They must be credited with knowing what their words mean because we cannot suppose that speakers are usually in error, or continually misapply their words, without thereby supposing that they are uninterpretable, and therefore unintelligible. In so far as someone is interpretable, he must be using his words correctly more often than not. This is why, to be competent speakers, we must typically mean what we do by our words.[15]

Does this constitute an answer to (II)? It tells us that we usually do know what we mean by our words, but not *how* we know this. It can be agreed that our words usually do mean what we take them to mean, and that they must do. But what is it for *us* to take our words to mean something in the first place? Surely, it is intelligible to ask: How do we know what our words mean, *given that we usually do*? When the corresponding question was asked about thought, it was treated as an explanatory, rather than a sceptical, question which required a substantial answer. But we see a subtle shift in Davidson's handling of the two cases. When asked how we could know our minds without interpreting ourselves, Davidson was able to say, we know our own minds because we know what we mean when we say what we think. But when we ask the corresponding question about how we know what we mean without interpreting ourselves, Davidson treats this as the sceptical question and gives a transcendental argument in response. We could not fail to know what we mean and still be speakers. But scepticism is not the issue, just as it was not the issue with respect to knowledge of our own minds. The response to the sceptic assures us that we have to know what we mean, but we can still ask: How do we know this? This is important, because what a speaker takes himself to believe is what he understands by the sentences he holds true.

Has Davidson explained how thinkers know what they are thinking without interpreting themselves? Given that there is something the speaker means when he holds a sentence true, there is something he believes. But in order to *know* what he believes, surely he has to *know* what he means. We know what this is by constructing an interpretative truth-theory for his language that assigns truth-conditions to the

---

[15] As another sign of the close affinities between Davidson's thinking and that of Wittgenstein in the later writings, consider the following passage from Wittgenstein (1992: 36e): 'The inner is hidden from us means that it is hidden from us in a sense in which it is not hidden from *him*. And it is not hidden from the owner in this sense: *he utters it* and we believe the utterance under certain conditions and there is no such thing as his making a mistake here. And this asymmetry of the game is brought out by saying that the inner is hidden from someone else.'

sentences he holds true. But how does *he* know what he means? As an account of self-knowledge, it tells us *that* the speaker knows what he believes, but not *how* he does. There is the interpretatively guaranteed fact of meaning something, or of our *words* meaning something. But what kind of knowledge does this give us of what we mean and think?

For Davidson, there *is* no more to be said here. The reason has to do with his third-personal approach to meaning and mind. Apart from special circumstances, he sees no difference between someone meaning something and his knowing what he means. Of course, it is uncontentious that these two notions should coincide. But the question is whether the former includes or deflates the latter. Davidson prefers to replace the locution 'knowing what we mean' by 'meaning what we say'. And this is part of his deflationary tactic. For we mean what we say, according to Davidson, if we can be *interpreted* as meaning this more often than not. But this, of course, is to turn from the speaker's point of view, and to concentrate on the third-personal perspective of the interpreter. Speakers, we will be told, mean what they do by their words because those words are regularly applied to the same things. But in applying them they do not act blindly. We do not just use words: we understand them. Speakers know what they mean by the sentences they hold true. This is fixed by the truth-conditions they take them to have, and it is this knowledge that is available to them without interpretation. So what does a speaker's knowledge of truth-conditions consist in?[16] Once again, there seems to be a missing level of knowledge.

It is as if no more is required of the speaker than for him to produce movements and sounds which, by the interpreter's lights, turn out to be regularly interpretable as meaning one thing rather than another. But where in this picture is there room for the immediate understanding of our words? The phenomenological experience of hearing the meaning in someone's words is undeniable. We do not first hear sounds which we then have to make sense of. Normally, uptake is immediate: we just hear what someone is saying. It is also involuntary. If someone speaks audibly in a language I understand, I have no choice but to hear their words as meaning what they do. What people say can get straight through to my mind uninvited.[17] I am not suggesting that this inner experience of comprehension should be construed as a private or wholly inner act. The meaning and understanding of a speaker's language should be publicly ascertainable. But we are missing something crucial to the

[16] This is something that Michael Dummett has repeatedly called for an account of. See Dummett 1975, 1976.
[17] The phenomenon is stressed, though for quite different reasons, by both John McDowell and Jerry Fodor.

first-person perspective of the language-user if we do not recognize a sense of comprehension beyond that of the speaker producing words the *interpreter* can find meaningful. However, the immediate comprehension of speech depends on more than just a subjective impression of meaning. It amounts to the inner recognition of public and objective facts. (This makes it the perfect place to locate our knowledge of our own minds.) The task, in trying to account for the first-person point of view of the language-user, the point of view from which he knows his own mind, is to see how the phenomenology can deliver knowledge and why it is also an epistemology of understanding.[18]

We cannot just resort to unexplained notions of understanding, or first-person knowledge of meaning, to say what it is for the speaker to mean something by his words. On the other hand, we cannot settle for such a resolutely third-personal view of what it is to possess a language, where this is mainly a matter of how one is interpreted. Davidson is not unaware of the need to say more about how the speaker understands the words he uses. However, all we are told about what the speaker means by the sentence he holds true is 'that in reporting on his understanding of a sentence, the speaker "cannot improve on" on the claim, "my utterance of the sentence 'Wagner died happy' is true if and only if Wagner died happy"' (1984b: 110). But precisely what *piece of knowledge* is expressed in the report the speaker cannot improve upon? What is expressed by an instance of the disquotational schema, and how substantial, or otherwise, is this knowledge?

Davidson will insist that there *is* more to the speaker's meaning something than his just uttering words that others regard as meaningful. In particular, he will point out that speech is an intentional activity, and that the speaker must intend to be understood in a particular way. There is a worry, here, however, if one has to know one's intentions in order to understand the words used to speak one's mind; after all, thinkers usually do know what they intend, as part of having first-person authority. Likewise, if one has to know how one intends to be interpreted, one may have to know what could be discovered by an interpreter of one's behaviour, and this amounts to knowing what an interpreter would be justified in ascribing to us on the basis of our behaviour. But how, without appeal to a theory, does the speaker know this? This threatens to make knowing what we mean a highly reflective matter of knowing how we could be interpreted. However, Davidson avoids these worries.

---

[18] I am entirely in sympathy with Jonathan Lear's (1984) insightful remarks, which I have found helpful here, and with the way he sets up the problem of meaning and understanding in the later Wittgenstein.

We are told that to have reasons, or to act on intentions, 'the speaker does not usually "form an express intention" and he does not "hold a theory" '. Further, 'intentions are not normally attended by any special feelings' (1992: 259). It is enough for the speaker to be credited with the intention of being interpreted in a certain way, and it is enough for someone to be acting 'intentionally when there is an answer to the question what his reasons in acting were', where this is a matter of the intelligible sense which the interpreter can make of his reasons. Once again, Davidson is doing a highly laudable job of trying to accommodate the first-person perspective, but he shifts in his description of that predicament to what the interpreter would ascribe or recognize. What is not being acknowledged sufficiently here is that reasons have insides as well as outsides. They are reasons the subject can appreciate from his own point of view. To suppose otherwise is to leave the Davidsonian agent in the position of Hamlet as seen by Goethe's *Wilhelm Meister*, who thinks of the prince as saying: 'I am in a play full of purpose but have none of my own'.

If the Davidsonian strategy cannot accommodate the first-person perspective of the language-understander, it will ultimately fail to make room for the first-person point of view. As a strategy, it offers us genuine insight into the connections between knowing one's mind and knowing one's language; but more is required to explain what it is to know one's language. In so far as an account can be given which preserves the first-person point of view of the language-user, and first-personal awareness of meaning, we shall be able to use the strategy illuminatingly; but in so far as these features of the language-user's predicament are missing, or neglected, the account will lack the materials to explain the first-person perspective on our minds.

To recap: the linguistic strategy is the idea that we know our states of mind by making largely correct and authoritative claims about them in a language we understand. We need an account of what equips us to produce and understand the claims we make about what we are currently thinking, and an explanation of why what we think we are currently thinking is usually a good guide to what we are thinking. In their different ways, Davidson and Wright give answers to the second question. But an account of self-knowledge is not complete until we have a satisfactory answer to the first question.

Where are we to find the resources to account for the first-person point of view of the language-user, the point of view from which he knows his own mind? I have suggested that more is needed to explain how speakers know what they mean. This involves the immediate experience of hearing, or understanding, utterances as meaningful. But how are we going to cast light on this immediate first-person awareness of meaning? We are faced with a dilemma. If we draw upon first-personal aspects of our psychology, the sort of states for which we have first-person authority, this threatens to make knowledge of what we mean depend on knowledge of our own intentional states. So the strategy of explaining knowledge of one's own mind via knowledge of one's language will be circular. On the other hand, if we prescind from any notions in the domain of personal-level mental states, we will we lack the resources to explain first-person aspects of linguistic understanding, and hence knowledge of what we are thinking.

On the second horn of the dilemma, we may suppose that some highly modular part of the brain is dedicated to handling language. Call this the language faculty. It is this faculty which is called upon to handle speech produced in the expression of judgements we make about our current states of mind. The modular view of the language faculty avoids circularity in the linguistic strategy because it amounts to one part of the mind—a subpersonal part—being put to service in understanding another. However, it is hard to see why what is competently handled by the underlying linguistic system can deliver instances of self-knowledge to the subject, and contribute to elaborating the notion of a first-person point of view. Alternatively, on the first horn, if we reach for more states of the subject at the personal level to flesh out a conception of the speaker's first-personal awareness of meaning, we risk helping ourselves to notions we are trying to explain.

So what is the nature of our knowledge of meaning? Ordinary reflection gives us few clues, except to confirm that we are effortlessly authoritative about what our words mean, whether word strings are grammatical sentences, and how words in our language are pronounced (Higginbotham 1991). What does this *first-person linguistic authority* consist in? For instance, what is the knowledge reported in the disquotational scheme? Is disquotational knowledge the best we can do to cast light on what a speaker knows?

In a way, disquotation is trivial. In using expressions to state their own meanings, we cannot fail to express a piece of linguistic knowledge. But this is only the case so long as the expressions as disquoted mean something to us. Genuine instances of disquotation merely reflect the familiar fact that, as speakers, we cannot be alienated from our own language and the meanings of our words. This is relatively trivial. But what it takes for something to be a genuine instance of the disquotation scheme is strictly non-trivial. So I agree with Akeel Bilgrami, that 'Disquotation, if it is to be at the service of an account of meaning is not a wholly trivial idea. It must be anchored in something which is not made explicit in the disquotational clause itself' (1992: 247).

What is required for something to be a genuine instance of the dis-quotational scheme for a speaker? Obviously, we need to understand the sentences featured as they are used. And since speakers do not carry knowledge of sentences around from one occasion to another—sentences, like thoughts, are ephemeral—a speaker's knowledge of meaning and grammar must be at work in delivering an understanding of a sentence, quoted on the left-hand side and used on the right. If we did not exer-cise knowledge of grammar, we could not tell which assemblies of words were sentences, or what compositional structure the sentences had. The standing linguistic knowledge we carry from one occasion to another consists in the words and means by which we produce and comprehend anything that counts for us as a meaningful utterance.

In accordance with Chomsky's notion of an I-language (Chomsky 1986), I am taking a grammar to be an internalized system of representations, or body of knowledge, whose workings are not known to the ordinary language-user, but which have an effect on his conscious recognition and production of speech. My grammar will assign structure to strings of signs or sounds which will determine the sentences or expressions I hear. I will typically hear strings as structured, and thus be able to recog-nize them as utterances of particular sentences. The sentences I hear will depend for their identity on the internal states I am in, the struc-tural assignments that the language faculty makes to sounds or signs I encounter. This is because, as Higginbotham puts it, 'the crucial pro-perties of sentences are not revealed by thinking of them as they are outwardly presented to us, namely as strings of signs, but rather by their unobservable grammatical structure' (1991: 555). Which sounds or signs are sentences for me is a matter settled entirely by my internal linguistic system. The same sounds or signs could be interpreted quite differently by others, or not count as sentences at all. 'What it is for something to be a sentence for a person is for it to be a grammatical structure that is apprehended and applied to certain perceptible objects' (ibid. 556). Only if the speaker has the linguistic competence to confer lexical mean-ing and sentence structure on the string of words quoted in any pur-ported instance of the disquotational schema will this produce a true instance of the schema. Not everyone agrees that even *this much* is needed.

Higginbotham (1989), for instance, thinks the following counts as a genuine instance:

(T1)　'All mimsy were the borogoves' is true-in-L iff all mimsy were the borogoves.

Would this count as knowing 'the first thing' about the meaning of the sentence featured in (T1)? Higginbotham says we would know its logical form, in skeletal terms, and that the categories of the words that occur in it typically play certain semantic roles in the language. When we know how the parts of the sentence are combined to form something with that skeletal form, we know its compositional structure up to the meanings of certain lexical items. What is lacking is just knowledge of the lexical axioms. But these can be provided as follows:

(L1)   'mimsy' means mimsy (*whatever that is*);
(L2)   'borogoves' means (or refers to) borogoves (*whatever they are*).

Higginbotham concludes that this is all one knows of meaning from disquotational knowledge, and he is happy to accept that disquotational knowledge of truth and reference is trivial. We could, as speakers, go in for explications of word meanings, but these may be quite unreliable guides to use, and do not (or do not wholly?) fix meaning, or reference.

By my lights, not only am I unable to know which (as opposed to which kind of) proposition is expressed by (T1), it fails to express a truth about my language, and therefore is not, as I utter it, a genuine instance of the disquotational schema. For me, whether any featured word string gives rise to a genuine instance will be a matter of whether my language faculty, together with my knowledge of word meaning, can assign the string of words semantic, syntactic, and phonetic properties that determine it as a meaningful sentence of my language, or idiolect. It will be a fact about me, whether I understand a sentence and can report my understanding in this disquotational form. Notice that the disquotational form may be a genuine instance for one speaker but not for another; and for the same speaker, two different pieces of disquotational knowledge can be reported by one and the same form when the featured string is ambiguous.

For Davidson, on the other hand, what would establish whether there is a truth of my language expressed by any putative instance of disquotation is success in interpretation. A fully formed interpreter can derive, by means of an interpretative truth-theory for my language, a T-theorem corresponding to the form of the disquotational sentence:

'Wagner died happy' is true in L iff Wagner died happy

that gives the truth-conditions of my sentence mentioned on the left-hand side. It will not necessarily be homophonic, unless the interpreter's use of those words, and my use, coincides. The theorist will give his rendering of the same piece of knowledge, available to me without the help of a theory. And on Davidson's reading of the publicity constraint, all I can mean by this sentence is all I can be known to mean as determined by the pronouncements of an interpretative truth-theory: '... what the interpreter needs to know of the semantics of the speaker's language

... is conveyed by the T-sentences entailed by a theory of truth' (1990: 319). But just what is expressed by a T-sentence? The piece of knowledge it records will express what I believe in holding true the sentence it mentions. Remember, an interpretative truth-theory is confirmed by the totality of evidence concerning the speaker's behaviour, linguistic and otherwise, and the only empirically significant notions of meaning and structure are those which supervene on that behaviour. Although it is not reducible to behaviour, 'meaning is entirely determined by observable behaviour. . . . That meanings are decipherable is not a matter of luck; public availability is a constitutive aspect of language' (1990: 314). And for Davidson:

what is open to observation is the use of sentences in context, and truth is the semantic concept we understand best. Reference and related semantic notions, like satisfaction, are, by comparison, theoretical concepts (as are the notions of singular term, predicate, sentential connective and the rest). There is no question of the correctness of these theoretical concepts beyond the question whether they yield a satisfactory account of the use of sentences. (1990: 300)

I suggest words, meanings of words, reference and satisfaction are posits we need to implement a theory of truth. They serve this purpose without needing independent confirmation or empirical basis. (1984a: 222)

Thus, the content of T-sentences will not involve the theoretical notions used, purely instrumentally, within the theory to derive T-sentences. So the content of the speaker's knowledge: what he means by the disquotational report, which can also express what he believes, will be very lean indeed. What Higginbotham, at any rate, helps us to see is that there is knowledge of grammar at work in understanding the quoted sentence. Facts about grammar that determine some aspects of meaning have to be called upon the explain what goes into my understanding. This will call upon, and provide, more than the interpreter sees from the evidence he is typically exposed to. So we can give some of the items on Davidson's list empirical confirmation in terms of the properties of the speaker's grammar. These will include meaning-affecting properties of scope and the referential dependence of nominal items within the sentence, all of which constrain my semantic interpretation of sentences.[19]

But there is more to understanding than this. As Michael Dummett stresses, language is a conscious and rational activity, and speakers are consciously aware of what is said. Certainly, language understanding

---

[19] For example, for reasons to do with purely syntactic binding principles, we cannot read the sentence 'John shaved him' as referring to the same person in both positions, whereas 'John's father shaved him' may be understood as John's shaving himself, but not his father shaving himself.

depends on the unconscious workings of my internal language system. But there is a product delivered to consciousness. The purpose of conscious experience, from a cognitive processing point of view, is that it functions to present a single interpretation of a diversity of information. For example, we cannot see both faces of a Necker's cube at once; nor do we hear two (or more) readings of an ambiguous sentence string simultaneously. We always hear one reading, and recognize that another reading is available. But we are never presented with something that encompasses both or is neutral between the two. We always hear the string as an utterance of one particular sentence rather than another, even though the string of sounds or signs may be assigned more than one reading—may be seen or heard as the utterance of one or another sentence type.[20] These events of perceptual awareness in speech processing depend counterfactually on the underlying states of the language faculty and which structural assignments were made to which strings. Had my grammar assigned another structural description to this string, I would have heard another sentence uttered. We know this because we know how recent exposure to other structures affects the internal states we can be in when hearing the next sentence. For example, reading the sentence 'Time flies like an arrow' immediately after reading the sentence 'Fruit flies like a banana' will make one immediately aware of another construal of the first sentence, and a previously unnoticed ambiguity. This depends on our linguistic system assigning different grammatical categories and sentence structure to the string we read.

What are we to make of all this in trying to explain a speaker's first-person linguistic authority, and how can we avoid the dilemma faced by the linguistic strategy?

For the case of our knowledge of grammar we simply steer between the horns of our dilemma. First-person authority about which sentences are grammatical can be secured by adopting what Higginbotham (1991) calls *representationalism*. This is the view that in language, how you represent things is how they are. How things are, grammatically, will be a matter settled by the internal states of my language faculty. Whether or not a string of words is a sentence for me, will depend on whether I, or, rather, my language faculty, can assign it a structural description that makes it well formed. If it can, I shall recognize it as a sentence. If not, I shall simply hear it as deviant. Which strings of signs or sounds count as normal or deviant will differ from speaker to speaker. There is a huge variation across speakers of what is called English. For

[20] I doubt whether sentences have tokens, although utterances and inscriptions do. These will be typed by sentences and expressions.

me, the pair, 'I am/Amn't I' is normal, whereas the (curiously?) plural form in the pair, 'I am/Aren't I' sounds odd. Many of you will have the opposite reaction. There is no standard of right and wrong here, save what is produced in accordance with our own internalized grammars. And as ambiguous strings show, the grammatical structure of sentences is not in the sounds or signs themselves, but in our perception of them. I do not have conscious knowledge of the internal facts in my linguistic system, but I am aware of the effects of this tacit knowledge on me as a conscious language-user. In language, how you represent things grammatically is how they are. Hence we are authoriative about our own grammar. However, this is not to surrender the objectivity of grammatical judgement. We need not lose sight of the distinction between how things seem and how they are, because I do not have perfect knowledge of how my internalized linguistic system represents things. I am not entirely blind to its properties, because they make a conscious impact on me delivering one rather than another parsing of a syntactic string. But other factors, such as memory and attention, influence my speech processing. So I am not infallible. What is more, linguists can construct and test hypotheses about the grammar of my idiolect. So there is an independent perspective on the facts.

But if we all speak different idiolects, how can we understand one another? The crucial consideration here is whether speakers have largely shared, or overlapping, vocabularies. Their grammars will differ, but this will be less important. As Chomsky (1986) has shown, grammars vary within strict parametric limits, since speakers are innately endowed with a Universal Grammar whose principles are common to all human languages. Universal Grammar describes the initial state of the language faculty of every speaker. Its principles are parameterized, and set locally by the environmental influence which other speakers have on the child. The people we are most in contact with, and from whom we learn our vocabulary, will have grammars that overlap with our own. And even where there is greater variation, of the sort we often encounter when communicating with non-native speakers of a language, influenced by the parameters of their mother tongue, we usually have enough to go on to know what they mean when their grammatical constructions use words that are familiar to us. Thus, I do not need to speak as they do to know what they mean, although the closer people's languages are to mine grammatically, the easier and more direct my understanding of them.

What is important is that we have largely shared knowledge of the meanings of words. However, knowledge of word meaning is not part of the underlying linguistic system, and is not, like representations of structure, entirely a matter of what is internal to me. Knowledge of word meaning is knowledge of the norms that govern our use of words. These are public norms which introduce third-personal standards to our first-personal use. It is also the case that the meanings of many of our words are fixed, as externalism suggests, by reference to entities in our environment. Yet, we have immediate authoritative knowledge of what words mean. This raises the familar issue of how to reconcile first-person authority with objectivity. And here, unlike the case of grammar, we still await a satisfying account of how this is to be done. Knowledge of word meaning belongs within the conscious rational mind. Command of word meaning, as McDowell insists, is a conscious mental ability. So these are first-personal dimensions to our understanding which remain unexplained. This leaves a lacuna in the linguistic strategy, and it is only when we have an explanation of the phenomenon of first-personal, authoritative knowledge of meaning that does not draw upon non-linguistic elements of our knowledge of our own minds that we can provide a non-circular explanation of our psychological self-knowledge. So there is work still to be done.

The first part of this task is to say how we can be effortlessly authoritative about the objective standards governing the proper use of words. This is, of course, just the issue Wittgenstein faced in the rule-following considerations, and to which he did not have a fully satisfying answer. Most of the elements of the problem of self-knowledge occur here. We use words without justification, and yet, as Wittgenstein tells us, 'To use a word without justification is not to use it without right' (1953: §289). What counts as using a word correctly is settled, for him, by shared standards of communal use. But this leaves him to ask: how can the meaning of a word seem to be all there at an instant when it is also the unfolding of use through time? (see §138), a question to which he gives no satisfactory answer.

In answering this question, McDowell would suggest that the meanings are there to be perceived on the surface of our communal practices, described in content-involving terms. These facts are available only to those who have acquired membership of this shared linguistic practice. But there is no good empirical evidence that speakers do share a common language. Nor do they need to in order to communicate successfully. Furthermore, McDowell's epistemology of language understanding mislocates elements of this understanding, such as our knowledge of syntax, on the surface of our practices where it simply cannot belong. There may be no unified linguistic object, no single locus of linguistic significance. To appreciate word meaning is to be responsive to something out there, but responses to our own assignments of structure may dictate much of what we hear said. And this points to another role for the conscious, first-personal perspective of the speaker to play. The experience of conscious comprehension is required to unify, in the first-personal realm, elements from the third and subpersonal domains which all have their impact on linguistic understanding, The form and character of the conscious products of understanding are shaped by these factors. When we ask, finally, what do we know when we know a language, the conscious experience of understanding tells us that it will not be the indeterminate or inscrutable product that the interpreter assigns to us. What is given in genuine instances of disquotational knowledge must be much richer than the interpreter's T-theorem assignments suggest, and only when we know more of this, can we call upon what we know when we know our own language to explain how we know our own minds.

REFERENCES

Bilgrami, A. (1992), 'Can Externalism be Reconciled with Self-Knowledge?', *Philosophical Topics*, 20: 233–67.

Burge, T. (1988), 'Individualism and Self-Knowledge', *Journal of Philosophy* 85: 649–63; repr. in Q. Cassam (ed.), *Self-Knowledge* (Oxford: Oxford University Press, 1994), 65–79.

Chomsky, N. (1986), *Knowledge of Language* (New York: Praeger).

Davidson, D. (1984a), *Inquiries into Truth and Interpretation* (Oxford: Oxford University Press).

—— (1984b), 'First-Person Authority', *Dialectica*, 38: 100–11.

—— (1986a), 'A Coherence Theory of Truth and Knowledge', in E. Lepore (ed.), *Truth and Interpretation* (Oxford: Blackwell), 307–19.

—— (1986b), 'A Nice Derangement of Epitaphs', in E. Lepore (ed.), *Truth and Interpretation* (Oxford: Blackwell), 433–46.

—— (1987), 'Knowing One's Own Mind', *Proceedings and Addresses of the American Philosophical Association*, 60: 441–58; repr. in Q. Cassam (ed.), *Self-Knowledge* (Oxford: Oxford University Press, 1994), 43–64.

—— (1989), 'The Myth of the Subjective', in M. Krausz (ed.), *Relativism: Interpretation and Confrontation* (Notre Dame, Ind.: Notre Dame University Press), 159–72.

—— (1990), 'The Structure and Content of Truth', *Journal of Philosophy*, 87: 279–328.

—— (1992), 'The Second Person', *Midwest Studies in Philosophy*, 17: 255–67.

Dummett, M. (1975), 'What is a Theory of Meaning?', in S. Guttenplan (ed.), *Mind and Language* (Oxford: Oxford University Press), 97–138; repr. in Dummett, *The Seas of Language* (Oxford: Clarendon Press, 1993), 1–33.

—— (1976b), 'What is a Theory of Meaning? II', in G. Evans and J. McDowell (eds.), *Truth and Meaning*, (Oxford: Oxford University Press); repr. in his *The Seas of Language* (Oxford: Clarendon Press, 1993), 34–93.

Higginbotham, J. (1989), 'Knowledge of Reference', in A. George (ed.), *Refelections on Chomsky* (Oxford: Blackwell), 153–74.

—— (1991), 'Remarks on the Metaphysics of Linguistics', *Linguistics and Philosophy*, 14: 555–66.

Lear, J. (1984), 'The Disappearing "We" ', *Proceedings of the Aristotelian Society*, suppl. vol. 58, 219–42.

McDowell, J. (1984), 'Wittgenstein on Following a Rule', *Synthese*, 58: 325–63.

—— (1987), 'In Defence of Modesty', in B. Taylor (ed.), *Michael Dummett: Contributions to Philosophy* (Dordrecht: Martinus Nijhoff Publishers), 59–80.

—— (1991), 'Intentionality and Interiority in Wittgenstein', in K. Puhl (ed.), *Meaning Scepticism* (Berlin: de Gruyter), 148–69.

Moran, R. (1988), 'Making Up Your Mind: Self-Interpretation and Self-Constitution', *Ratio*, 1: 135–51.

Rorty, R. (1981), *Philosophy and the Mirror of Nature* (Oxford: Blackwell).

Wittgenstein, L. (1953), *Philosophical Investigations*, trans. G. E. M. Anscombe (Oxford: Blackwell).

—— (1992), *Last Writings on the Philosophy of Psychology*, ii (Oxford: Blackwell).

Wright, C. (1989*a*), 'Wittgenstein's Later Philosophy of Mind: Sensation, Privacy and Intention', *Journal of Philosophy*, 78: 622–34; repr. in K. Puhl (ed.), *Meaning Scepticism* (Berlin: de Gruyter), 126–47.

—— (1989*b*), 'Wittgenstein and the Central Project in Theoretical Linguistics', in A. George (ed.), *Refelections on Chomsky* (Oxford: Blackwell), 233–64.

15

On Knowing One's Own Language

JAMES HIGGINBOTHAM

I INTRODUCTION

At the Texas Linguistic Forum of 1959 there was a panel discussion of Noam Chomsky's then novel theory of generative grammar, in the course of which Chomsky remarked by way of illustrating a general point that a certain expression of English—call it X—was not an English sentence. One of the panellists asked Chomsky how he knew that. Had he done a survey of speakers? Had he consulted a sufficiently large corpus, verifying that X and expressions like it did not occur? Chomsky replied, 'What do you mean, how do I know? I am a native speaker of the English language.'

Chomsky's reply brings forth a special case of the problem of self-knowledge, the problem of explaining the basis for our intuitive knowledge of our own language. The fact that our reflective judgements are a good source of data about our languages is one that calls for explanation within an overall theory of the properties of human languages and our cognitive relation to them. We may dismiss, as Chomsky rightly did, the credo of a social-scientific methodology that looks only to what for this or that or no reason at all actually happens to occur (and often fails to see that what is so documented can be misleading); but we cannot take the general reliability of reflective judgements as a brute fact, orthogonal to the project of exposing the structure and expressive powers of language.

In this discussion I shall mostly consider judgements about meaning; but the distinctions that I will draw, and most of the consequences of my examination, will apply equally to questions of syntactic and phonological form. The phenomenon, then, is our reflective knowledge of our own meanings, and the question what sort of phenomenon this is, and what its explanation might tell us about the role of language in our mental lives.

In this domain, I believe, it really is necessary to make some preliminary distinctions; I will make three, of which the first is threefold.

I distinguish between the meaning that an expression actually has for a speaker and what I will call the speaker's *conception* of the meaning. I intend the notion of the speaker's conception to amount to what the speaker assigns, or in Chomsky's sense cognizes, as the meaning. The speaker's conception is not something of which the speaker is generally aware; still less are speakers always capable of giving explicit accounts of their conceptions. One's conception of a meaning may diverge from the meaning in various ways: the conception may be only partial, and so fall short of fixing it; may contain redundancies, and so overdetermine it; may be mistaken, or even contradictory; and may involve the speaker's having a set of communicative intentions that, in the light of external factors, it is impossible to realize. Examples of such divergences can be given from one's own experience, including adult experience: I had heard the word many times before discerning to some degree the meaning of the British epithet 'twee'.

Both the meaning of an expression for a speaker and the speaker's conception of it are to be distinguished from the speaker's *views* about either of these matters. Competent speakers have views about meaning very early on—for example, about whether something is properly called a 'bedtime story'—and they will express them forcefully by saying, for example, that very short stories don't count. Views about one's conception of the meaning are less common, and tend to occur only when one is concentrating on one's own perhaps idiosyncratic meanings. But views about meaning or about one's own conception, consciously held and usually articulate, are distinct both from that conception and from meaning itself. Such is my first, threefold distinction.

My second distinction is between self-knowledge and entitlement to a view. One can have an entitlement that does not amount to knowledge. Into that category might go, for instance, my entitlement to an opinion about what I would do if I had a million dollars. If we are entitled to our opinions about ourselves on some basis other than that which would be required for the case of third-person attribution, then the asymmetry between the two sorts of entitlement demands explanation, even if it falls short of knowledge.

There has been considerable discussion of how to reconcile knowledge of one's own meanings with externalism. In standard versions of externalism, where meaning is allowed to vary with the physical or social environment, knowledge of meaning threatens to lapse, because some of the environmental features are unknown. The standard response to the threat consists in observing that one's belief co-varies with the facts, in such a way that in counterfactual circumstances where the facts were different, the beliefs would be different also. In counterfactual circumstances where my sentence 'Snow is white' does not mean that snow is white, I don't believe that it does, and I do believe that it means what it in fact means there.

As Barry Smith noted in his chapter (14), Davidson takes it that disquotational knowledge of meaning, exemplified by the knowledge that 'Snow is white' means that snow is white, is all that is required for first-person authority over meaning, or at any rate that we 'cannot improve' on it. I will return to this question below.

What now of entitlement that may fall short of knowledge? It is this kind of phenomenon to which Chomsky's response in Texas draws attention. One can certainly be wrong about whether something is or is not a sentence of one's language. But whether one is right or wrong, one's belief is generally arrived at without evidence, and it carries a presumption of correctness. As soon as we move away from the disquotational case, we arrive at questions about first-person authority that are not dismissible as objections to externalism by the standard invocation of co-variance of belief with counterfactual circumstance.

My third distinction is between one's view about what one means or meant on a particular occasion, or would mean on an occasion of some type, by the words that one employed there, and one's view about what one's words or the sentences in one's repertoire mean. The structure of first-person authority in the first case appears to admit what in mathematics is called reduction to the previous problem. Speech is intentional action, so the question what I meant on a particular occasion is the question what I intended to say on that occasion. But I know what I intend to say, just as I know what I intend to do, because I have knowledge of my own intentions generally.

What is special to the problem of knowledge of one's language, then, is not that we have knowledge of what we intend to say when we speak, but rather that we know, or are entitled to a presumptively correct view of, what we in fact say when we speak. I take it that a speaker 'gets her language right' in Davidson's sense if she regularly says what she intends to say, or, in another of Davidson's formulations, 'knows what she means'. Presumably, knowledge of what a sentence means is knowledge of what one would say by using it (what assertion one would make by asserting it, etc.). In this way we can at least connect the meanings of sentences with what is said, although more is needed to get at the meanings of words.

In light of the above distinctions, I see the problem of knowledge of one's own language as having two components. One is that of self-knowledge proper, the disquotational knowledge that my words 'Snow is white' mean that snow is white. The other is that of the source of my entitlement with respect to non-trivial facts about my own speech, where we are considering what words mean, and not just what I intended to say on particular occasions. This component is not explained by Davidson's defence of self-knowledge proper, or by any other of which I am aware. I consider these components in turn.

II SELF-KNOWLEDGE

Davidson's view is that it is a presumption of interpretation that a speaker knows what she means—hence first-person authority. Partly because of the weight that it appears to place on the role of the interpreter, Barry Smith is doubtful of the finality of Davidson's account. The appearance to which he objects can be mitigated by the reflection that, if Davidson's argument is cogent, we can apply it to ourselves. Knowing as I do that those who are interpreted know what they mean, I know of myself, *qua* interpreted, that I know what I mean.

The twist that I have just applied is, I believe, analogous to the twist of an argument that Davidson gave elsewhere, to the effect that we cannot but think that most of our beliefs are true. I quote the argument in full.

We do not need to be omniscient to interpret, but there is nothing absurd in the idea of an omniscient interpreter; he attributes beliefs to others, and interprets their speech on the basis of his own beliefs, just as the rest of us do. Since he does this as the rest of us do, he perforce finds as much agreement as is needed to make sense of his attributions and interpretations; and in this case, of course, what is agreed is by hypothesis true. But now it is plain why massive error about the world is simply unintelligible, for to suppose it intelligible is to suppose that there could be an interpreter (the omniscient one) who correctly interpreted someone else as being massively mistaken, and this we have shown to be impossible. (Davidson 1977: 201)

The argument may be criticized (and has been, in Stich 1984 on the ground that it merely shows that *if* omniscience can interpret us, then our beliefs are mostly true. However, since we each deem ourselves to have a coherent language, we hold there to be a complete theory in that language all of whose sentences are true. The omniscient being is just one whose language is that language, and who believes that theory. How is it conceivable that I should be uninterpretable by such a being?

Criticism of the application to oneself of the argument from interpretability to first-person authority would take the form: my first-person authority is conditional upon my being interpreted; so I can know what I mean only if I am in fact interpreted (I do not, of course, have to know that I am). But I do not see a way to scepticism here, any more than I see my way to scepticism about whether omniscience could interpret me.

I quoted above Davidson's view that we 'cannot improve' on the disquotational formulation of what one knows when one knows what one means. How thick, or thin, is disquotational knowledge? Elsewhere (Higginbotham 1988 and 1992) I have defended the view that it is pretty thin; more precisely, that to know

(1)   'Snow is white' means that snow is white

and similar things, it is only required (i) that one be a user of the language, or that piece of the language, that one is mentioning, and (ii) that one have the concept of meaning. The truth of the disquotational (1) follows from the fact that the that-clause refers to the sentence it contains, understood as if it were uttered, and the fact that a mentioned sentence must have the meaning that it has, so understood. Much is involved, of course, in being the user of a language, including, in the case of (1), the capacity to deploy the concepts that it involves, of snow and of something's being white. But there is no requirement that one have *mastered* the concepts, so that knowledge that (1) (and not merely knowledge that (1) is true) is possible for a person who does not fully understand (1), or whose conception of the meaning of 'Snow is white' is perhaps erroneous.

The view that I have articulated does not depend upon that-clauses being taken in the specific way I am inclined to take them. It may be reformulated in Fregean terminology as follows: the that-clause refers to its customary sense, and *means* (or *means for me*) has for its reference that relation between expressions and senses that yields truth when the sentence has the sense. The sentence 'Snow is white' has whatever sense it has, and so I will know (1) provided that I can deploy the senses it involves. The Fregean terminology must not conceal a departure from Frege: it is not required that, besides being able to deploy the senses, I am master of them. Allowing that departure, and in fact allowing a conception of language wherein sense may be only partially grasped, knowledge of the disquotational facts about meaning is again routine.

A recent discussion by Christopher Peacocke (1996) has made me aware that besides the capacity to use the language in which the disquotational meaning facts are stated, and possession of the concept of meaning, one must use another feature: namely, the relation between the content of the that-clause, as it occurs in (1), and the content of that same clause,

as it occurs in my expression of my self-ascription of the belief or knowledge that (1). This relation Peacocke calls *redeployment*. Redeployment
is what sustains the thesis that the sense of 'Snow is white' as it is used
in (1) is the same as its sense in the doubly oblique context of 'I know
that "Snow is white" means that snow is white'. It must be that there
is no divergence in sense, since otherwise my knowledge that (1) is true
would not, however much I might be master of the sense of 'Snow is
white', underwrite my self-ascription that I know it, and not merely that
it is true. Redeployment must be appealed to here as it is appealed to
in the case of self-ascription of belief, where the singly oblique context
is, say, that of the complement of 'I believe that Napoleon was defeated
at Waterloo', and the doubly oblique context is that of the same clause
in 'I know that I believe that Napoleon was defeated at Waterloo'.

To the line of thought I have been articulating, Richard (1992)
objects that the thin conception of disquotational facts about meaning—
allowing us to pass, for users of the language who have the concept of
meaning, from the trivial knowledge that the sentence (1) is true to knowledge of (1) itself—is too generous, especially in allowing us not only to
say things we at best dimly understand, but even to have propositional
attitudes about those things. He also suggests that standard cases of
partial understanding of a word take place against a rich background
that shows a solid grasp of hyponyms, or more general categories. In
cases of the sort first advanced by Hilary Putnam, where one knows
about the word 'beech', say, only that it names some kind of tree, the
background is substantial; as Richard puts it, the uninformed person
'can describe typical trees and presumably has a fair amount of general
tree theory under his belt' (1992: 42).

There is certainly scope for disagreement over cases. Perhaps the
requirements for disquotational knowledge of meaning, or the capacity
for having attitudes that involve concepts on which one's only handle
is that there is some word around for them that one has happened to
pick up, are stronger than merely being a user of the language in general.
The point should still stick, however, that disquotational knowledge need
not presuppose conceptual mastery.

I remarked above that the standard reconciliation of disquotational
knowledge of meaning with externalism consisted in the observation
that one's beliefs would co-vary with the counterfactual circumstances,
in such a way as to preserve the truth of the relevant sentences under
those circumstances. But this reconciliation may nevertheless be thought
to leave unexplained the peculiar status of disquotational statements such
as (2):

(2) '*x* is standing' is true of *y* if and only if *y* is standing.

We all have, or so I will suppose, thorough mastery of the concept of standing. We know, however, that there are counterfactual circumstances under which (2) would not have been true; and we know that we are not in those circumstances (whatever they are). There appears to be at least a kind of quasi-aprioricity about (2) that we have not captured.

Loar (1994) emphasizes the point that if we believe that the relation *true of* depends upon, and is at least partly constituted by, external and obviously contingent matters, then we need to explain how we can know (2) independently of knowing how these matters stand. His own account has our knowledge flowing from what he calls a 'first-person perspective' on our own language use—in this case, a particular 'mention–use perspective' that secures for us the power to deploy in words the very concepts the words for which we are mentioning. It would take us far afield to examine Loar's view here; but there is an aspect of it that I will support (although this aspect may be far from Loar's intentions).

It is a commonplace that a grasp of disquotations such as (2) is a touchstone of our grasp of the notion *true of* itself. But a capacity actually to use this notion does not follow automatically from a grasp of the disquotational schema; otherwise, a person who knew only that all instances of the schema were true would know that they would remain true under various counterfactual circumstances. The case may be compared with Saul Kripke's (1970) examples of the contingent a priori, statements of the type of 'The standard metre is one metre long'. One knows this a priori because one knows how the extension of '*x* is one metre long' is determined: namely, as *x*'s being of the length of the standard metre. The knowledge thus follows on one's ability to stipulate, or to grasp the stipulation of, the extension of the predicate; and this stipulation is sufficient to guarantee its truth. In the case of (2), however, nothing has been stipulated, and so our knowledge that it would express a truth in counterfactual settings cannot follow in this way. We have, therefore, to recognize that what Loar calls the 'immunity from external doubt' that attaches to (2) and the like reflects our participation in the linguistic practices that fix the relation '*A* is true of *x*' in any of a variety of possible circumstances, of which we certainly do not know a priori where we find ourselves.

Even with the point just advanced, I have not disputed the thesis that first-person authority plausibly flows from Davidson's considerations, or the thesis that an adequate expression of at least part of its realm is the effortless knowledge that we have of disquotational truth about meaning. Nevertheless, the defence of first-person authority does not explain my entitlement to views about my own meanings, and I turn now to this question.

III   ENTITLEMENTS

A typical example of our entitlements to linguistic knowledge, which may make more vivid the domain under consideration, is afforded by the properties of English durational modifiers, whose function it is to add information about how long some event went on. Consider two of these, the expressions 'for an hour' and 'in an hour'. They have distinct distributions in that, for example, the first is felicitous in (3) but not in (4), and the second is felicitous in (5) but not in (6):

(3)   I consumed beer for an hour.

(4)   I consumed a bottle of beer for an hour.

(5)   I consumed a bottle of beer in an hour.

(6)   I consumed beer in an hour.

Why? On a view that I have proposed elsewhere (Higginbotham 1995), the reason is that the modifier 'for an hour' takes a single event as argument, and has it simply that an hour is the measure of its time; whereas the modifier 'in an hour' requires an ordered pair of events as arguments, of which the second is the telos or *terminus ad quem* of the first, and it measures the temporal spread between the commencement of the process aiming at the telos and the onset of the telos. An act of beer consumption, that activity, is a single event, lacking a telos. Hence 'for an hour' is felicitous in (3). An act of consumption of a bottle of beer, however, constitutes a complex, ordered pair of events, of which the first is the act of consumption, and the second is the state of all the beer in the bottle being down one's throat. Hence (3) is felicitous, and (4) is not; and inversely, (5) is felicitous, but (6) is not.

The divergence between these modifiers is seen also in constructions that may be in construction only with telic predicates like 'consume a bottle of beer'. Violations of this restriction, using instead predicates of pure activity, give the perception of category mistakes. Thus one can say (7) but not (8):

(7)   It took me an hour to consume a bottle of beer.

(8)   It took me an hour to consume beer.

Facts of this kind are, of course, known effortlessly by native speakers of English, and comparable facts by native speakers of other human languages. The question is why these facts are so obvious to us, given that we use no evidence in seeing that they are true, and have no conscious knowledge of the principles that make them true.

Another example, involving some simple features of tense reference: during September, and in particular on 30 September at one minute before midnight, I can say (9):

(9)   It has been a rainy September.

Once it is October, I can no loner say this, but must say (10):

(10)   It was a rainy September.

I can also say (11), but the interpretation differs from that of (10):

(11)   It had been a rainy September.

In the case of (11), I give you to understand that it was rainy in September up to some point in September that I have so far left unspecified (thus I could commence a story with (11)). The phenomenon is quite general, in that assertions like (9) in the present perfect presuppose that the state or process mentioned overlaps the time of speech, whereas assertions with the past tense presuppose that it is prior to the time of speech (compare 'This has been an interesting discussion', 'That was an interesting discussion'); and the past perfect requires the resetting of the temporal co-ordinate to some time prior to the time of speech, which it is said that the state or process overlaps. Again, we do not, prior to theoretical reflection, have an understanding of the data with respect to assertions of (9)–(11); but the data themselves are completely obvious.

As I understand him, Barry Smith holds as I do that our first-person grasp of language is not exhausted by the realm of first-person authority seen in disquotational knowledge, and he wants to explain our entitlement to views about such examples as (7) and (8), and (9)–(11). He begins by assuming a version of Chomsky's conception: that a language is nothing but a certain internal system of representations. Since I can be out of step with my own internal system, my opinions are not authoritative; I am, however, entitled to them in so far as there isn't any reality beyond my system to which they have to answer. Smith formulates two objections, or problems, for this conception.

The first is that my entitlement depends upon some capacity for keeping track of my own subpersonal states. My words have the meanings they do, and I say what I say, because of the operation of the subpersonal system, and I know what I mean only if my views about what

I say are in step with that system. Couldn't the two come unstuck? In any case, the sense we have of knowing what we mean doesn't seem to involve keeping track of the outputs of some black box. When I speak, I am not conscious, and probably could not be conscious, of the principles that govern my judgements about the status of sentences or the stress patterns of words; nor am I aware of any machinery at all whirring away while I wait for the answer it will deliver.

The second problem is that on Chomsky's conception the normative dimension of meaning seems to be lacking altogether. Smith's response to this point is to concede that the cognitive psychology of language, the object of linguistic enquiry, indeed has no normative component. There is plenty of normativity involving language, but those aspects of language are not part of linguistics, in this sense of the term. On the other hand, where there is normativity, there is no entitlement (apart from real first-person authority). Hence, Smith concludes, entitlement to a view about it can be used as a diagnostic for whether an aspect of meaning belongs to cognitive psychology or not.

Let me put this problem, and Smith's response to it, in terms of the distinctions that I introduced above. Distinguishing between the meaning of something and one's conception of its meaning, the domain of cognitive enquiry is to extend no further than one's conception of meaning. One's views about meaning track one's conceptions, but they do not always track the meaning: the domain of entitlement is therefore restricted. If it were always possible for one's conception of the meaning to deviate from the meaning, then there would be no entitlement to knowledge of one's own language at all, contrary to fact. But there is something left over when the normative is deleted: namely, the realm within which meaning is what it is because of the way we are made— that is, because of the (for us) inevitable structure of the subpersonal system.

Smith's view is a version of what in Higginbotham 1991 I called representationalism, the view that in language, or anyway in that part of linguistics that has psychological import, things are as they are represented. There are arguments for representationalism, widely subscribed to especially by linguists: for example, the view that since I have the political right to say 'tom/ae/to' rather than 'tom/a/to', there isn't any such thing as saying a word correctly; or the observation that individual languages are commonsensically individuated on a socio-political basis. These points are of course irrelevant. Smith's argument is different. On his view, representationalism holds because we are in fact all built the same way, and language is not conventional. His reason for thinking that meaning cannot, at least in certain domains, deviate from one's conception of meaning is not one that Chomsky has ever given.

I think that Smith's point is worth pursuing. As I understand it, he aims for an analogue in the mental realm of the familiar point that our psychological knowledge is made possible by the fact that animal responses are correlated with emotional states. We can be confident that flinching is a sign of fear, because we are so built that it is. Likewise, we can be confident that sentences with two noun phrases and a verb express propositions of the form *aRb*, because we are so constructed that our languages come out that way. Smith's central idea is reminiscent also of Fodor's (1983) conception of the 'language module' as delivering structured representations to speaker-hearers, where the information that they supply falls far short even of what is commonly thought of as grammatically determined (e.g. possible relative scopes of quantifiers), and still further short of significant fragments of meaning.

I differ from Smith (and Fodor) in thinking that it is always in principle possible for one's conception of meaning to deviate from the meaning. I am also sceptical of Chomsky's internalist conception of language: that is, of restricting the domain of enquiry to elements over which, in practice at least, our conception of meaning coincides with meaning. But I agree with Smith on the problem (also discussed at length by Crispin Wright) that a simple appeal to our reliability in tracking our subpersonal states is not a satisfactory explanation of our entitlement to claims, made without evidence, to knowledge of meaning.

Wright (1986) suggests that our knowledge of meaning, I believe in the sense in which it concerns me here, derives from the fact that subjects' best opinions about their meanings, past and present, are (provisionally) extension-determining (rather than, in his terminology, extension-reflecting). The problem he discerns with the standard theory of linguistic competence is that it aims to be a psychological theory, offering our unconscious grasp of rules and rule systems in partial explanation of our linguistic behaviour and dispositions, and so appears to violate the requirement that we have knowledge of what rules we use. Wright's dilemma, then, is that either familiar talk of rules or principles of language internalized by native speakers should be understood as metaphorical merely; or else we must admit unconscious rule-following, a conception that faces the task of explaining how a rule can be blindly applied and at the same time something that the organism heeds.

I cannot here respond to Wright's objection, which has been echoed by a number of authors. But it may be worth observing that the sharp distinction between what is available, either off the bat or upon reflection, to us as guiding our behaviour and what is for ever sealed off from consciousness, so that we can no more be aware of ourselves as following the principles in question than we can be aware of the ways in which visual information gives us the boundaries of objects, has no evident role to play in the construction of linguistic theories. Even so, we do not have an explanation of our entitlement to views about our own language.

In closing, I want to suggest that part of the explanation of our entitlement is exactly inverse to Smith's, consisting not in the fact that our language just is as we represent it, or that we are simply so built that our languages must have certain fixed properties, but rather in the fact that language must be deployed critically if we are to adjust successfully to one another. In speaking and interpreting, we must often deploy not merely our subpersonal language machines, but also the second-order ability to determine whether our views about another's meaning are correct, how far our own speech coincides with another's, how it will be taken, and the like.

Consider a person who recognized, say, 'I consumed beer in an hour' as deviant when it was actually uttered, but could not give an intuitive judgement, or else gave a random intuitive judgement, about whether it actually was deviant; or who recognized when the situation arose that a certain assertion was warranted or unwarranted, but could not answer the question whether it would be warranted in a hypothetical situation. A strange and crippling pathology! In negotiating the physical world, we have not only to actually expect an object to fall when we witness circumstances C, but also to know in advance that an object will fall if the circumstances C should arise. The knowledge of laws and counterfactuals extends to language as well. Without it, we would lack many of the capacities we routinely exercise (I am on the point of saying X, but, recognizing that it might be misinterpreted, switch to Y, which more or less says the same but avoids the possibility I feared). I see much of our entitlement to our views, and the security of our intuitive judgements, as stemming from the demands that speech places upon conscious thought.

How do we actually meet these demands? And when we deliver our intuitive judgements, do we in some sense unconsciously consult our grammars, or simply imagine a setting in which certain words were uttered, and conceive our own reactions? I do not know that anything substantial is known about these questions, and anyway we must recognize that intuitive judgements can be wrong. But since we put our language to use in the complex ways we do, we are entitled to a presumption of their correctness.

REFERENCES

Davidson, Donald (1977), 'The Method of Truth in Metaphysics', in Peter A. French, Theodore E. Uehling, Jun., and Howard K. Wettstein (eds.), *Midwest Studies in Philosophy*, vol. ii: *Studies in the Philosophy of Language* (Minneapolis: University of Minnesota Press), 244–54; repr. in Davidson, *Inquiries into Truth and Interpretation* (Oxford: Clarendon Press, 1984), 199–214.

Fodor, Jerry (1983), *The Modularity of Mind* (Cambridge, Mass.: MIT Press).

Higginbotham, James (1988), 'Knowledge of Reference', in Alexander George (ed.), *Reflections on Chomsky* (Oxford: Blackwell), 153–74.

—— (1991), 'Remarks on the Metaphysics of Linguistics', *Linguistics and Philosophy*, 14 (4): 555–66.

—— (1992), 'Truth and Understanding', *Philosophical Studies*, 65: 3–16.

—— (1995), *Sense and Syntax*, Inaugural Lecture, University of Oxford (Oxford: Clarendon Press).

Kripke, Saul (1970), 'Naming and Necessity', repr. in Donald Davidson and Gilbert Harman (eds.), *Semantics of Natural Language* (Dordrecht: Reidel, 1972), 253–355.

Loar, Brian (1994), 'Self-Interpretation and Reference', in James E. Tomberlin (ed.), *Philosophical Perspectives*, vol. viii: *Logic and Language, 1994* (Atascadero, Calif.: Ridgeview Publishing Company), 51–74.

Peacocke, Christopher (1996), 'Entitlement, Self-Knowledge and Conceptual Redeployment', *Proceedings of the Aristotelian Society*, 96: 117–58.

Richard, Mark (1992), 'Semantic Competence and Disquotational Knowledge', *Philosophical Studies*, 65: 37–52.

Stich, Stephen (1985), 'Could Man Be an Irrational Animal? Some Notes on the Epistemology of Rationality', *Synthese*, 64: 115–35; repr. in Hilary Kornblith, (ed.), *Naturalizing Epistemology* (Cambridge, Mass.: MIT Press, 1987), 249–67.

Wright, Crispin (1986), 'Theories of Meaning and Speaker's Knowledge', in Wright, *Realism, Meaning, and Truth* (Oxford: Blackwell), 204–38.

INDEX